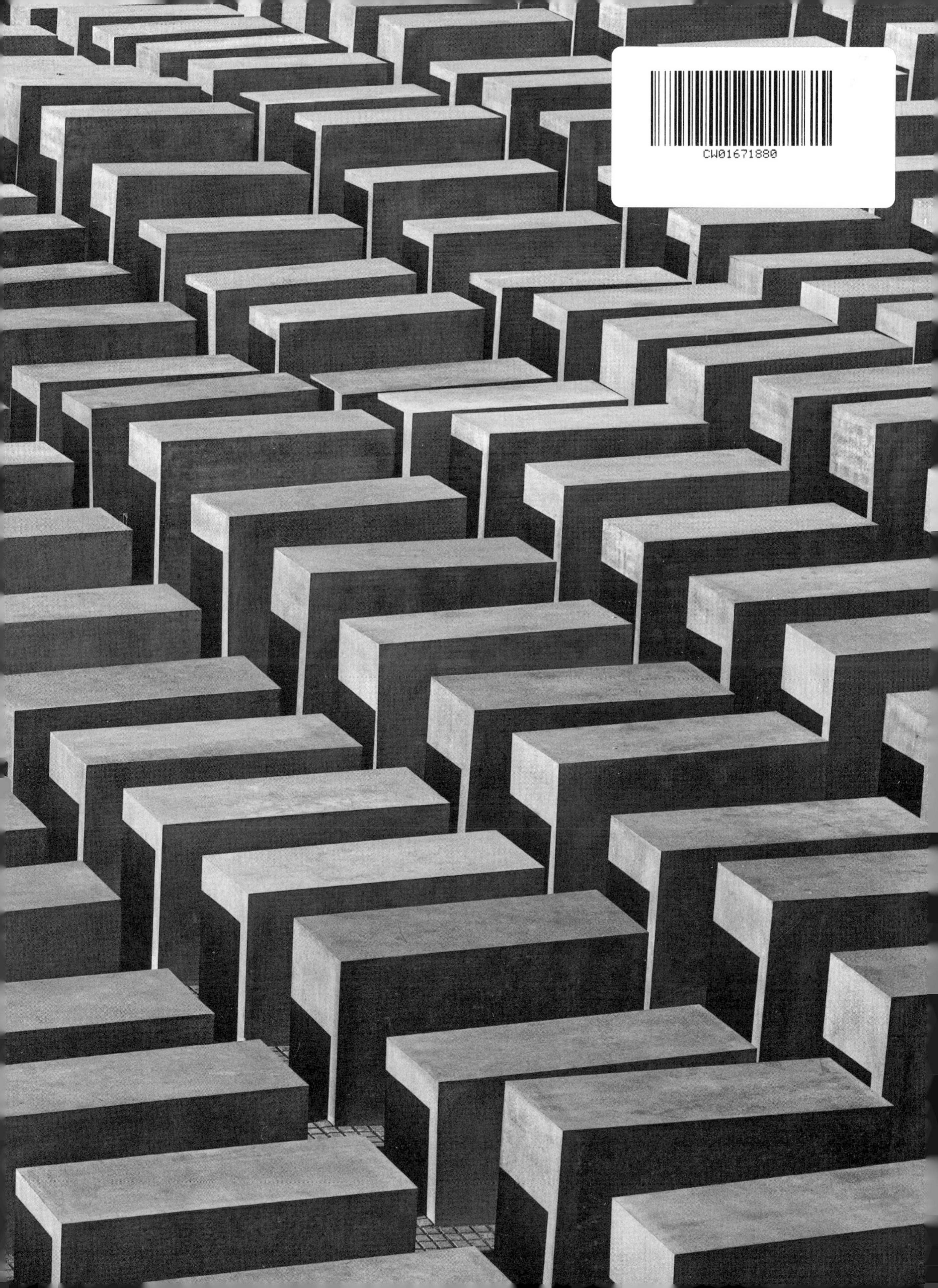

abstraction and the holocaust

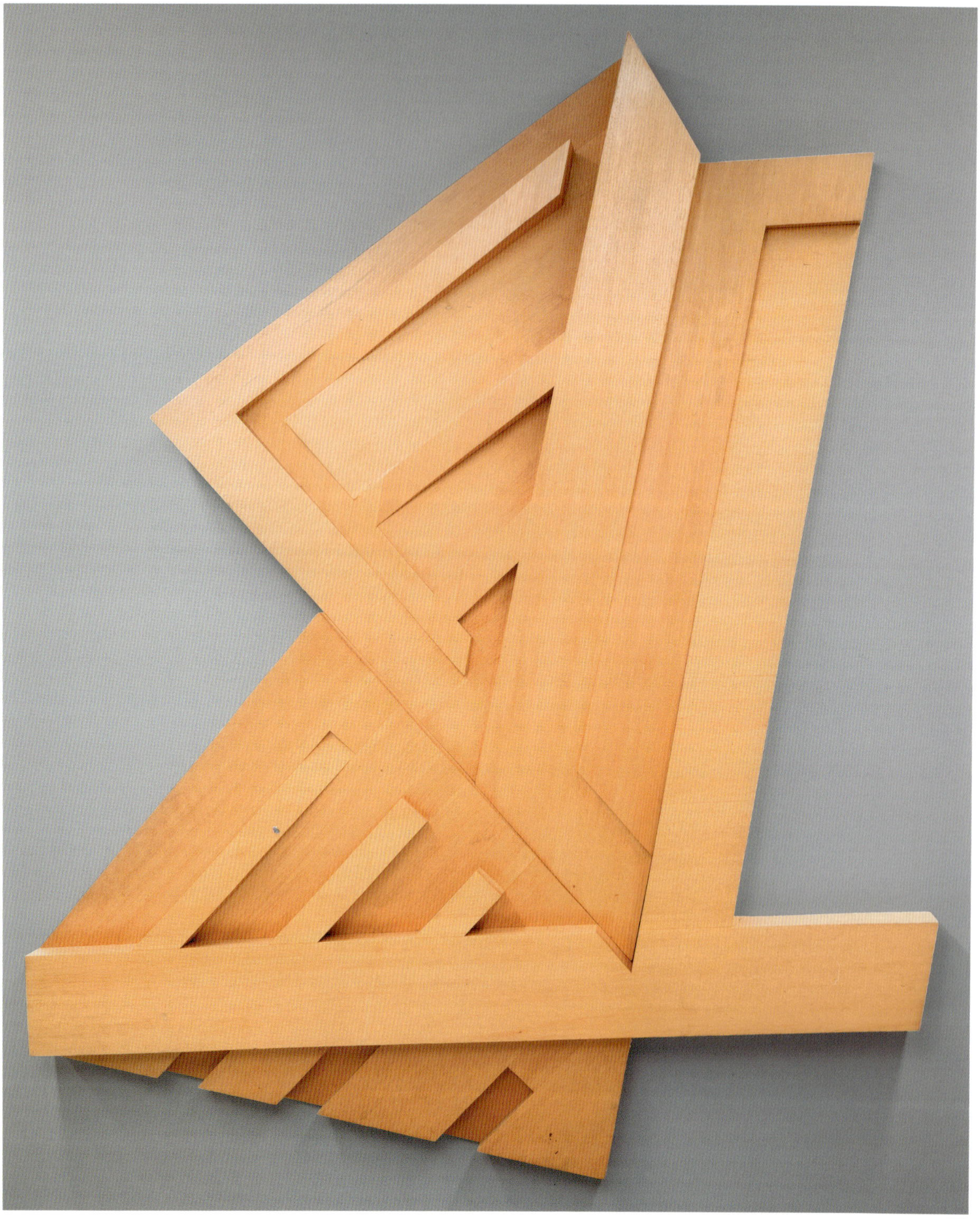

mark godfrey

abstraction and the holocaust

yale university press new haven and london

TO MY FAMILY

Printed in China

Designed by Paul Sloman

Library of Congress Cataloging-in-Publication Data

Godfrey, Mark.
Abstraction and the Holocaust / Mark Godfrey.
p. cm.
Includes bibliographical references and index.
ISBN 978-0-300-12676-1 (cl : alk. paper)
1. Holocaust, Jewish (1939–1945), and art. 2. Holocaust, Jewish (1939–1945), and architecture. 3. Art, Abstract–United States. 4. Architecture–United States–20th century. I. Title.
N72.H63G63 2007
709.04'052–DC22
2007014684

IMAGES

P. II
Frank Stella, *Nasielsk IV*, 1972, unpainted wood, 279.4 x 227.4 cm, The Art Institute of Chicago.
Copyright © ARS, NY and DACS, London 2006.

P. VI
Richard Serra, *Gravity*, 1993, © Richard Serra, photograph by Dirk Reinartz.

ENDPAPERS
Peter Eisenman, Memorial to the Murdered Jews of Europe, view from above. Courtesy Peter Eisenman Architects.

contents

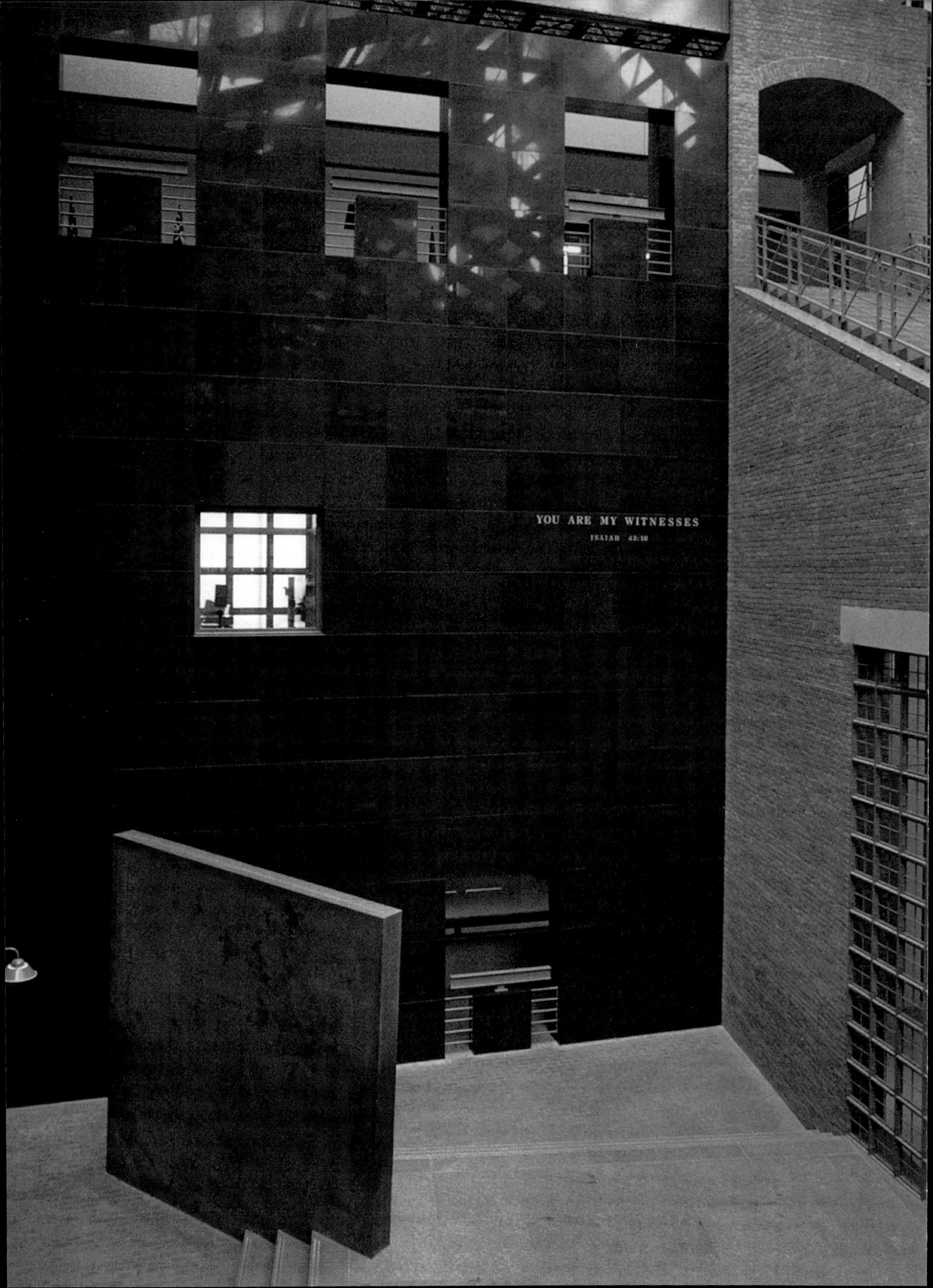
YOU ARE MY WITNESSES
ISAIAH 43:10

acknowledgements

My research for this book began in 1996 when I decided to enrol for an M.A. in the Department of History of Art at University College London on the advice of a close friend of mine, Miriam Hyman. Miriam had just completed her B.A. degree in the department, and recommended it to me, correctly guessing that I would be inspired by the art historians teaching there. Miriam followed the progress of my M.A., PhD and this book with close interest and enthusiasm. Miriam was tragically killed in London on 7 July 2005 and I wanted to begin these acknowledgements by remembering her and thanking her for her encouragement, and for setting my study on its way.

In the History of Art Department I was fortunate to work with Briony Fer, Tamar Garb, Frederic Schwartz and student colleagues including Simon Baker and Andrew Brown. All of these people helped me formulate initial ideas for this book, and have continued to be supportive. Tamar Garb gave expert advice as second supervisor of my PhD. However it is Briony Fer to whom I owe the most. Through every stage of this project, from supervising the PhD, through helping to find this publisher, from hearing me practice papers for conferences, through to reading over draft chapters for this book, Briony has been the most incredible teacher and friend, ever encouraging, always helping me to develop my own approaches to the subject. No student could hope for more support.

Since finishing my PhD, I have been based at The Slade School of Fine Art in University College London. There I have been helped by my Head of Department, John Aiken, and by my colleagues Joy Sleeman, Amna Malik and Penny Florence, particularly over the 2005–6 Academic year, when they kindly took on extra administrative roles to allow me to take up a Leverhulme Fellowship. Caroline Nicholas and Jacqueline Readwin in the Slade office have given invaluable help in the administration of grants.

Juliet Steyn, Griselda Pollock, and Sarah Wilson all gave useful and insightful feedback when the research for the book was at a relatively early point. At a crucial and slightly later stage of this project, just at the end of my PhD, and before I sent a proposal to Yale University Press, I was invited by Ann Temkin and Melissa Ho to present a version of the material on Barnett Newman at the Philadelphia Museum of Art. This was a fantastic opportunity for which I was very grateful, and I met a number of scholars who have been extremely encouraging and helpful since then: Yve-Alain Bois, Benjamin H. D. Buchloh, Lynne Cooke and Hal Foster. I have also been very grateful for the support of Norman Kleeblatt of the Jewish Museum, New York, and James Meyer, who read through the manuscript of this book, and who told me about Mel Bochner's work at *Via Tasso*.

Many of the artists and architects that I discuss have generously given their time, letting me conduct interviews and publish images of their work. I want to thank James Ingo Freed and Sol LeWitt, both of whom sadly passed away while this book was in its latter stages. I also want to thank Peter Eisenman, Susan Hiller, Ellsworth Kelly, Richard Serra, Joel Shapiro and Lawrence Weiner, and in particular, Mel Bochner and Beryl Korot, whom I visited on many occasions. My book has also been informed by conversations with artists whose work is not discussed here, but who are also concerned with history and memory: Matthew Buckingham, Tacita Dean, Thomas Demand, Omer Fast and Anri Sala, all of whom have helped me think through issues discussed in these pages.

Each chapter in the book has involved archival research and extensive work collecting images. Diane Upright helped me begin my research on Morris Louis and put me in contact with Louis's widow, Marcella Louis Brenner, who was generous with both her time and image permissions. The staff at the Barnett Newman Foundation, John P. O'Neill, Heidi Colsman-Freyberger, Sarah Henry and Brigid Herold, have all been fantastically helpful in allowing me to access files and images. Paula Pelosi, who works with Frank Stella, kindly allowed me to view unpublished images of Stella's work and of installations. Thank you also to Paul Kasmin and to Edye Weissler of Knoedler Gallery for these. At the Architectural Archives of the University of Pennsylvania I was lucky for the help of Julia Converse and William Whitaker who allowed me to look at the papers of Louis I. Kahn. Research for the Kahn chapter was also aided by meetings with Susan Solomon and Vladka Meed, one of Kahn's commissioners. Carolyn Christov-Bakargiev kindly shared her memories of organising Mel Bochner's *Via Tasso* project. While researching the commissions for the Washington D.C. Holocaust Museum, I met a number of people who were generous with their time: Nancy Rosen, Susan Morganstein and Sara Bloomfield, amongst them. Jeff Carter helped me to find important files in the museum archives. Trina McKeever at Richard Serra's studio, Eva Walters at Ellsworth Kelly's, and Susanna Singer who worked with Sol LeWitt have all been kind in supplying images. Many thanks also to Mathew Ford at Eisenman Architects and to the Timothy Taylor gallery for images in the final chapter.

This project has been financially supported in a number of ways. My PhD was funded by the British Academy, the UJIA, and the Memorial Foundation for Jewish Culture. Early research trips were partly funded by the University College London Graduate School. Most importantly, a Research Fellowship awarded by the Leverhulme Trust allowed me a year to complete the book. I am grateful for all these awards.

It has been a huge privilege to work with Gillian Malpass at Yale University Press who has given expert guidance and support throughout. Paul Sloman edited and designed the book with great sensitivity and patience as I moved images around. Thanks also to Emily Angus who helped to gather the images.

Very early versions of Frank Stella and Louis Kahn chapters in this book appeared in the student journals *Object* and *New Voices in Jewish Thought*. An early version of the Morris Louis chapter appeared in the *Jewish Quarterly* and a later one in Florence Jacobowitz and Shelley Hornstein's edited collection *Image and Remembrance: Questions of Representation and the Holocaust*. A version of the Barnett Newman chapter appeared in *October* and in Melissa Ho's edited collection *Reconsidering Barnett Newman*. My thanks to the editors of these publications.

I began these acknowledgements by saying that the book originated with my postgraduate studies at UCL, yet its roots go back much further. It was only after I had written the chapter on Newman that I recalled that it was my father, David Godfrey, who first triggered my fascination with his paintings *Adam* and *Eve* when he took me to see them at the Tate in 1986. I am truly grateful for all the time we have spent together looking at art; meanwhile my mother, Sharon Godfrey together with her parents, instilled an interest in Jewish history: the photographs from *Wooden Synagogues* reproduced in the chapter on Frank Stella come from my grandparent's copy of this book. To both my parents, and to my sister Sarah, I am indebted for all the support in so many ways towards this book.

Just after I passed my PhD, I married Ray Lewis, who had then just become, as all our friends were insistent to point out, a real Doctor. Despite the more genuine stresses of her work, Ray has listened to me as I have worried over the various ups and downs of this book. Though she has accompanied me on trips to see the art I discuss here, even when those trips were initially advertised by me to her as museum-free 'holidays', what I really owe to her has nothing to do with the content of *Abstraction and the Holocaust* and more with her love and with the distractions from writing the book. And in the last two years Noah has been the most incredible love and distraction of all.

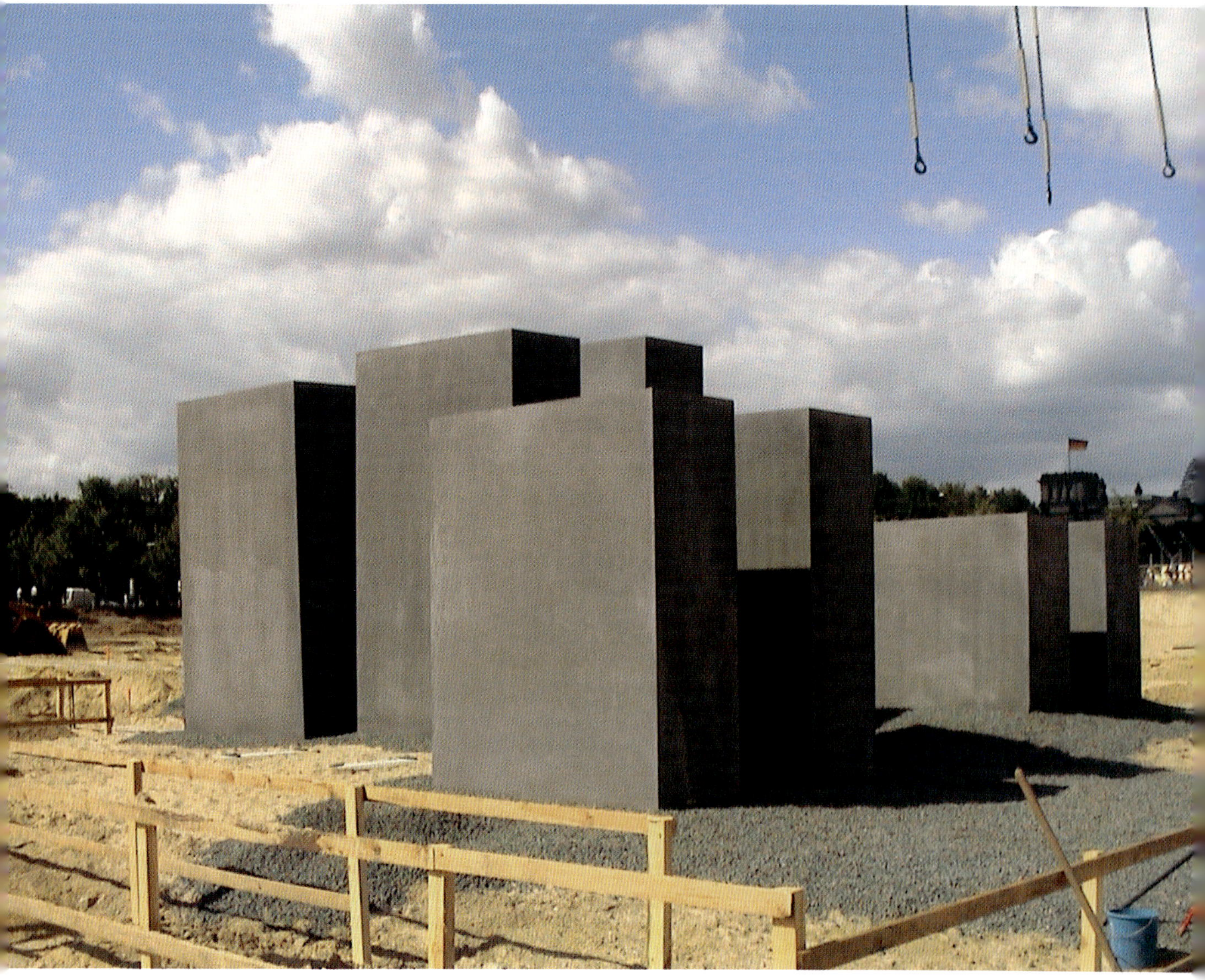

one

abstraction and the holocaust

berlin blocks

In the summer of 2002, I travelled to Kassel to see Documenta 11, which for many signalled a final nail in modernism's by now well-sealed coffin. Documentary film was privileged and abstraction – on account of its presumed incapacity to engage history – was nowhere to be seen. En route to Kassel, I passed through Berlin, visiting the city for the first time in my life. I was staying with artist friends in Mitte, and took a walk from their apartment down Unter Den Linden towards the Brandenburg Gate. A left turn would bring me to the new architecture of the Potsdamer Platz, and I could see in the distance cranes hoisting up sheets of mirrored glass to clad new office blocks. But before reaching this vertical building site I found myself on the periphery of a horizontal one, a huge space that I have since read is the size of two football pitches. It was cordoned off by a wire fence and I peered through to see what was going on. It was all pretty messy: the grass had not been cut back; there was the odd portacabin here, a small truck there. And yet something was definitely happening: I could see, against the sandy soil, groups of grey concrete rectangular blocks (fig. 1). Were these the raw materials for some kind of new building? Would they be placed one on top of another as the edifice grew in height? In some sections of the swampy field these blocks were arranged in rough grids, the regularity of their placement upset by the difference of their height. Suddenly I realised where I was standing. Without recognising it at first I had arrived next to the site of the long-debated Berlin Holocaust monument, Peter Eisenman's *Memorial to the Murdered European Jews*.

1 Peter Eisenman, *Memorial to the Murdered Jews of Europe* in progress.

Eisenman's design had first been put forward in 1997. At this point the architect was working with the artist Richard Serra, and their proposal was one of nineteen submitted to a closed competition.[1] From the account of the process given by James Young, one of the jury members, Eisenman's and Serra's stood out for its abstraction. Other proposals ranged from the figurative (a twenty-foot tall statue of the matriarch Rachel) to the textual/conceptual (a number of signposts, each with the text 'Warum'); many employed unquestioningly symbolic forms (Stars of David; broken walls), or numbers. Eisenman's and Serra's plan, however, was abstract. The number of piers had no particular referent; nor did their shape or material. The abstract structure would act on the viewer as they walked through the piers; memorial would be conceived as a mental and physical process, thought encouraged by the movement of the body through this field of space and stone, light and shadow. By the time it came to the groundbreaking, Richard Serra had dropped out, unwilling to sanction particular changes required by the commissioning body. Eisenman's firm, meanwhile, had made up a new model, and had produced photographs of it depicting visitors wandering through its space. But in Berlin, as I peered into the building site, no matter how much I tried to reconstruct the photographic representations in my imagination, what I saw was too chaotic to allow me to visualise its future as a memorial; to wonder about how it would one day work.

Two years later, a picture of the memorial appeared in the press (fig. 2). Someone, perhaps standing where I had been, had taken a rather extraordinary photograph. While I had had some difficulty recognising the memorial when standing right over it, in the image it was absolutely unmistakable. Of course, two years on, it was much more complete than it had been when I had been there, but from the photograph, it appeared as if it were finished. The piers stretch right across the diagonal plane of the photograph, filling its frame. And in the centre towards the bottom stood the architect, only his bow-tied neck and head visible. Eisenman faced a throng of journalists pushing to take his picture, hoisting microphones above the pillars to catch his every word. Looking at the newspaper I wondered: what was this photograph *of*? It was not a photograph of the site: all effort had been made to block out the surrounding buildings of Berlin. It was not a photograph made to show that the memorial had reached a particular stage of construction: the photographer had cropped the image in such a way as to cut out whatever portions of the field remained unfinished. It was not a photograph to indicate how the memorial could be used, like the photographs Eisenman's firm had made of his model: for this, it would have to have been made perhaps from where Eisenman stood, facing away from where he looked. It was not a photograph of Eisenman either: it is far too distant from him for that. Rather, this was an image of the memorial as a news story, not so much a publicity image as an image of publicity. As I prepared to introduce a book about abstraction and the Holocaust, the photograph suggested that in 2004, even before the inauguration of Eisenman's memorial, the union of the two terms that this memorial marks has itself become a media event. And this came as quite a surprise.

It is hardly surprising that the first Berlin Holocaust memorial should attract so much attention. There are so many questions raised by Eisenman's work, all of them difficult: what does it mean to memorialise Nazism's victims in the centre of Berlin? What

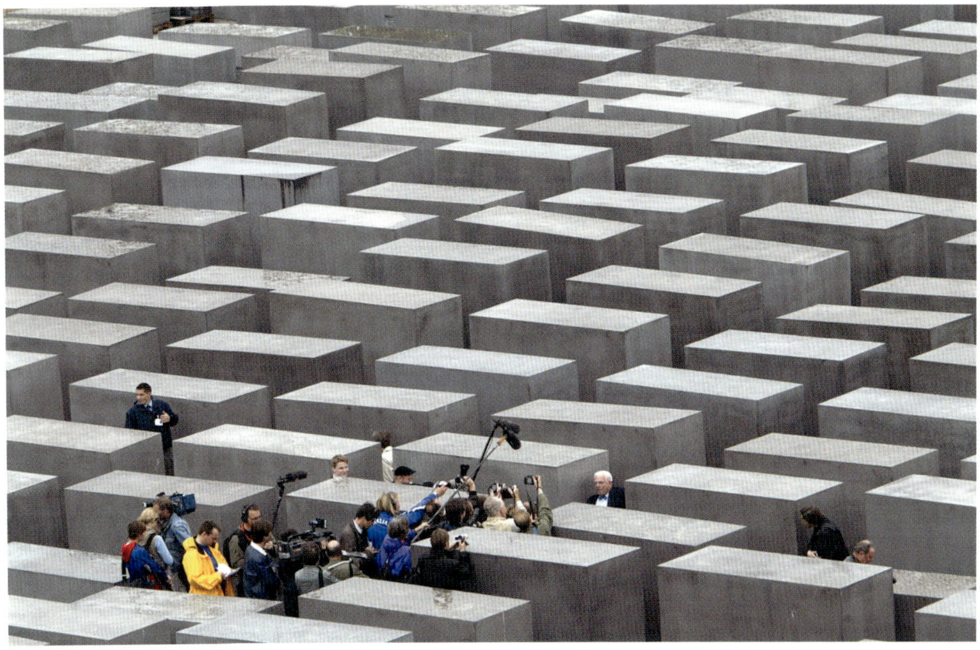

2 Peter Eisenman at the topping our ceremony of the *Memorial to the Murdered Jews of Europe*, 12 July 2004.

does it mean to take the opportunity of the reunification of Germany and the reestablishment of Berlin as its capital to do this? What, and who exactly is being remembered in this site? Why is it necessary to employ an American architect to address these questions anyway? Whilst the attention received by the memorial is entirely understandable, what is surprising for me is that abstraction and Holocaust memory had come together in such a public way; that this grid of concrete blocks, if not universally supported, was accepted by enough constituencies as a Holocaust memorial to be constructed, to make front page news. It is surprising because, previously, the linkage of the two terms had not been widely recognised. Since 1997, when I started working on this material, I have often been asked by other art historians to specify the subject of my research. I start by saying 'American abstraction', which gets a nod of recognition. As I continue 'and Holocaust memory', knowingness turns to confusion. 'Just what do the two have to do with each other?' The category 'Holocaust art' usually summons up tortured figuration (for instance, Rico Lebrun), social-realist or sentimental symbolic memorials (Nathan Rapoport), the more self-questioning but still figural painting of Anselm Kiefer or Luc Tuymans, the counter-monuments of Hans Haacke and Jochen Gerz, or the textual and photographic work of artists like Nancy Spero and Christian Boltanski. All this but certainly not abstraction. And yet in Berlin, in public, and on the front page of newspapers, abstract art and the Holocaust are joined. However, if the connection of abstraction and Holocaust memory has become as concrete and as present as Eisenman's blocks, the history of this connection remains to be articulated. I see Eisenman's memorial at the end of a fifty-year trajectory, and to date, this union has gone unrecognised.

In this book, I shall consider this fifty-year history of the relationship of abstraction and Holocaust memory, plotting this history through a number of specific case studies. It is my claim and argument that since the 1950s, American artists who were already working with abstraction have initiated groups of works in deliberate attempts to confront the memory of the Holocaust, or accepted commissions to make memorial works. I confine my study to deliberate (rather than unconscious) confrontations of Holocaust memory,[2] and to works made by Americans.[3] I will look at groups of paintings by Morris Louis (1951), Barnett Newman (1958–66), and Frank Stella (1970–74); at an architectural proposal of Louis Kahn's (1966–74), at a video installation by Beryl Korot (1974), at a site specific sculpture by Mel Bochner (1993), and at commissioned works in the United States Holocaust Memorial Museum by Richard Serra, Joel Shapiro, Sol LeWitt and Ellsworth Kelly (all 1993). Some of these works have gained attention, but most have been pretty much passed over both in the literature on the artists and in the wider literature on Holocaust representation. It is certainly true to say that until now, they have not been considered together, which is what I will be doing. I hope that by discussing them together, it will be possible to learn something new about abstraction, and to think about Holocaust representation in a new way; I am absolutely sure, however, that Holocaust representation does not tell us all we need to know about abstraction, nor abstraction about Holocaust representation. By bringing together abstraction and Holocaust memory, I by no means want to suggest that 'abstraction' is a general mode of art after Auschwitz. Nor do I mean to suggest that Holocaust representation was the main concern of the artists I discuss. Unlike the many artists who have made the Holocaust their continual subject, the ones I am concerned with here only addressed its memory in the isolated instances I examine. Generally within the artists' careers, the work I look at has an exceptional rather than exemplary status, but this very awkwardness interests me. It means that I am every bit as much interested in asking how a particular art work might engage the memory of the Holocaust as I am in asking how this very engagement participates in, or cuts against the wider concerns of the artist.

'abstraction' and 'the holocaust'

Before going much further it seems necessary to explain how I approach the two main terms at work here, 'abstraction' and 'the Holocaust'. Abstraction, first, will be considered in a very expansive way. Abstraction has recently been called 'a type of art which does not allow us to interpret it with reference to what is depicted.'[4] Abstract artists eschew depiction and figuration and sometimes, overt symbolism, but this is not to say that their work refuses signification. In front of abstract art works, the lack of a depicted image tends to heighten our awareness of materials, of compositional (or anti-compositional) structures, of the process of looking itself. Some abstract works are importantly titled, some are importantly not. Many abstract works deliberately conceal the processes by which they were made, or insistently foreground them, and for many different reasons. Clearly, the shared lack of a recognisable depicted referent does not render every abstract work similar, or if it does, then it is only in the least significant way. This would seem obvious were it not for the way that abstraction is sometimes treated as a homogenous, consistent art form, constant in its blanket refusal of meaning. The fact that, since the beginning of the twentieth century, artists have been compelled to make abstract works in different ways is the first witness to the heterogeneity of the field. And the furious debates that occur between critics, art historians and artists, often over the same abstract art works, proves the point that abstract works can generate different meanings.

But what kind of interpretation can abstract art works bear? Rather than imposing one general methodological framework on the objects of my study, I will allow the different works in my discussion to open themselves up to different interpretative enquiries. In some cases, it will be necessary to consider how an art work structures the viewer's encounter with it; to pay attention to the significance of the process of perception. In others, I will think about how a title might suggest certain meanings during this encounter. Some of the works are made for specific sites, and the relationship between the work and its architectural or institutional setting will be important. Some works I will discuss demand close attention to their materiality and their materials signify importantly; elsewhere, the materials are less important than the compositional structure of the work. In many cases, despite the resistance of many abstract artists to symbolism or iconographic suggestions, precisely these aspects have to be considered, and it may well be the case that a work of art both suggests a symbolic meaning and resists it at once. Debates around abstraction have shifted a great deal between 1951 and now, and an art work's meanings might be generated by considering how the artist responded to or contested a particular discourse about abstraction current at the time of their practice. And the context of the artist's wider work, as already suggested, also generates meaning. The significance of a form, a structure, a material or a colour might depend on its irregularity or familiarity within the rest of the artist's production, its former significance within their output.

As is already clear, my examples of abstract art works are made in many different mediums. The first three chapters treat painting, and later ones treat sculpture, and in relation to these mediums, the term 'abstraction' seems to provide few problems: no one would contest the claim that Morris Louis and Frank Stella make abstract paintings, that Richard Serra makes abstract sculptures. But what does it mean to call an architectural proposal 'abstract'? This is a question that will be confronted in the chapter on Louis Kahn, but the Eisenman/Serra proposal already mentioned suggests how the term might be appropriate, and that an architect might as well work with an artist as alone on an abstract structure. Probably more contentious is the inclusion in this study of Beryl Korot's video installation, in which images of Dachau concentration camp are broken up and played on TV monitors. How can such a work be 'abstract'? Korot's work was made at an historical moment where abstraction in painting was increasingly marginalised in the context of ambitious art, but it is my claim that the term abstraction can continue to serve in the analysis of video work, particularly in a case – such as Korot's – where editing and installation create formal structures that destroy narrative meaning. Artists, I will be arguing, can deploy strategies of abstraction as much as making work that looks obviously abstract. Abstraction, I will suggest, is not only a term to describe the appearance of an art work, and not simply a style or movement associated with a particular historical moment. Abstraction, rather, is an ongoing and urgent mode of contemporary art, and one as useful for contemporary artists who address the Holocaust as for artists working in the 1950s and 1960s – the decades conventionally hailed as the heyday of American abstract painting and sculpture.

In the introduction to his excellent book *Caught by History*, the art historian Ernst Van Alphen briefly mentions the art works I treat in my final chapter, writing that in the Washington Holocaust museum, 'formalist abstraction [Kelly, LeWitt, Serra] evokes the sublime unrepresentability of the Holocaust.'[5] Considering the title *Abstraction and the Holocaust,* many readers, I imagine, will suppose that I will be taking a line similar to this, and arguing that abstraction, as a non-representational art, is the most appropriate kind of art to respond to an event that is beyond representation. However, this is not a formulation I can accept, nor an argument I will be making. I find problematic the notion that the Holocaust is sublime or unrepresentable, but I will come to this later. The problem to address now is the way in which abstraction is conceived as a mode of art that refuses meaning; which 'evokes unrepresentability'. The more attentive one is to 'formalist abstraction', the less it seems a consistent mode, and the less it seems a mode of non-representation. Abstract art works can signify; can make meaning in so many different ways. The meanings of an abstract art work will depend on its materiality, its situation, the processes of its making, its composition, its title, its symbolic suggestions and counter-suggestions, its context in a discussion of abstraction, and in the artist's work. In other words, the way in which a work of abstract art generates meaning can be extremely complicated. Considered in this way, it might seem entirely possible that an abstract work can represent the Holocaust in complex ways, and just how this representation occurs will be my subject.

Before leaving the term 'abstraction' to move onto 'the Holocaust', I wish briefly to consider the implications of two instances where the terms have come together outside a discussion of abstract art. Opening a seminar on his film *Shoah* given at Yale University in 1990, Claude Lanzmann said 'I prefer that we avoid, if possible, generalities. Because I have spent my whole life fighting generalities and I think that *Shoah* is a fight against generalities. I prefer that we try to examine *Shoah* specifically.'[6] With these words, Lanzmann directed the discussion to analyses of particular scenes rather than the entire project of the film. Some time later, justifying his precise discussion of a fine detail of a scene, he said: 'There wouldn't be any film if for me these details were not so important. Everybody knows six million have been killed, which is an abstraction.'[7] In this context, Lanzmann was using the term 'abstraction' not to describe a mode of art, but a wider approach of thinking and representation. 'Abstraction' was that kind of approach to the Holocaust which treated it in its entirety and therefore lost sight of the details that for Lanzmann were essential to confront. Abstraction for Lanzmann was obfuscating, a block to an adequate confrontation with history.

Some years later, Zygmunt Bauman wrote an afterword to a revised edition of his book *Modernity and the Holocaust* in which the term 'abstraction' again appeared. Bauman wrote:

> Abstraction is one of the modern mind's principal powers. When applied to humans, that power means effacing the face: whatever marks remain of the face serve as badges of membership, the signs of belonging to a category and the fate meted out to the owner of the face is nothing more yet nothing less either than the treatment reserved for the *category*, of which the owner of the face is but a *specimen*. The overall effect of abstraction is that rules routinely followed in personal interaction, ethical rules most prominent among them, do not interfere where the handling of a category is concerned, including every entity classified into that category just on account of having been so classified.

With this theory of abstraction in place, Bauman went on to argue that Nazism worked by separating 'the one and only "abstract Jew" from the many "concrete Jews" known to the Germans as neighbours or workmates'. 'Only the abstract Jews could be subjected to genocide . . . For genocide to be possible, personal differences must first be obliterated and faces must be melted into the uniform mass of the abstract category.'[8]

In forging these critiques of abstraction, Lanzmann and Bauman were clearly not thinking about abstract art, but nevertheless their comments might serve to construct a criticism of the project of this book. How – following Lanzmann – can works of art that ignore the specificities of history help to memorialise that history, and do they not instead serve to obscure it? How – following Bauman – can abstract art be of consequence in the negotiation of an historical event when both this kind of art and that event are the products of the abstracting tendencies of modernity? These are tough questions but, as I hope will become clear through the course of the book, I do not think that the majority of the abstract artists whose works I examine looked at the Holocaust in the general terms that Lanzmann finds problematic; in this and so many other ways, their thought was far removed from the abstracting tendencies of Nazism. Indeed Morris Louis hoped his paintings would address the book burnings; Frank Stella, the destroyed synagogues of Poland; Beryl Korot represented the concentration camp at Dachau; Mel Bochner made a work in a former Gestapo prison in the Italian capital 'for the Jews of Rome'. The reason each artist reflected on each specific subject will become apparent in the course of each discussion.

Many of the artists discussed in this book did not attempt to address the entirety of the Holocaust in the abstract way that Lanzmann criticises, but for others, the very concept of 'the Holocaust' did not exist. By this I mean that they made work after the events of 1933–45, and after learning about these events, but before the concept 'the Holocaust' had been formed to categorise and separate some events (the murder of the European Jews) from other events in the wider history of Nazism and World War II. The formation of the concept of 'the Holocaust' was a gradual one, and it is important to register this because doing so helps to understand why some artists working in the first half of the period charted here addressed history in different ways from others working later. Before the cementing of the category, the calamity of the mid-century to which an art work might be directed could include more than what we now think of by 'the Holocaust' (for instance, it could include Hiroshima, as it did for Barnett Newman), or much less. In chapter four, I consider Louis Kahn's commission to build a memorial in New York. This commission took place right at the very moment when the category was cementing, and it shows in the letters Kahn received from the commissioning body and from other correspondents. The subject of his work was variously referred to as 'the tragedy', 'the Holocaust', 'the Nazi Holocaust' and 'the Jewish Catastrophe', each one having different implications.[9] (It is neither my purpose here to contest whether or not the separation achieved through the use of the term 'the Holocaust' has validity, nor to debate whether the destruction of the Jews was a war of its own or should only be understood in the context of wider Nazi policy: I am more simply concerned to indicate that the categorisation happened gradually, affecting artists of different times in different ways.)

Having argued that some artists addressed specific events, communities or locations, and that other artists were unable to address 'the Holocaust' because such a category did not yet exist, the question I must now answer is why I use the term 'the Holocaust' at all? This question is made even more difficult when one considers the critique of the word put forward by many scholars interested in this history, and particularly the critique forged by Giorgio Agamben in his book *Remnants of Auschwitz*. Agamben insists that he will 'never make use of this term' and provides two substantial etymological arguments for his resistance. He traces the term 'holocaustum' to a Latin translation of Leviticus: the translated Hebrew word is 'olah' and names one of the four ritual Jewish sacrifices described in the Bible. Early Christians used the term 'as a polemical weapon against the Jews' when they condemned Jewish sacrificial practices.[10] The term 'Holocaust' has thus in its history been used as a weapon of anti-Semitism, and so it is problematic to use it to name the modern murder of Jews.[11] Agamben traces another problematic history of the term. Having initially served as a translation of a Jewish animal sacrifice, 'Holocaust' (and its derivatives) in other texts came to describe the fates of Christian martyrs and Christ himself, eventually signifying 'a supreme sacrifice in the sphere of a complete devotion to sacred and secular motives.'[12] According to this etymology, 'Holocaust' implies that the European Jews in the mid-twentieth century were martyrs dying for a higher cause. Agamben utterly rejects this interpretation of the genocide of European Jews, and thus his second reason for resisting the term: it is an offensive euphemism.

Given these various arguments, why do I persist in using 'the Holocaust'? First of all, no other term seems able to cover the range of concerns addressed by the artists I am looking at. Certainly Agamben's own term, 'Auschwitz' will not do, given that none of the artists was exclusively concerned with the manner of death in that camp. Secondly, I use it simply because it was the term that – at least for artists working after the mid-1960s – was the predominant one in use in America, and the one that (as a construction with its own somewhat misleading implications) they faced when making their work. So I use the term 'the Holocaust' in full recognition of its problematic status – a status somewhat shared by the term 'abstraction'.

To sum up: just as I think 'abstraction' works differently in each case study I will be considering, so too the second term, 'the Holocaust' must be considered differently in each case, not only because some artists were addressing much more specific or indeed more wide-scale events than the term implies, but because some worked at different stages of its formation, and because some might have even resisted the implications of martyrdom that the term has been seen to suggest.

adorno and lyotard

The union of abstraction and Holocaust memory in such a public way as in the media image of Eisenman was quite a surprise because the two had neither been discussed together in the literature on abstraction, nor in the accounts on Holocaust art. But there is a powerful body of philosophical and theoretical literature that could seem to sanction the use of abstraction in a Holocaust memorial, indeed to confirm abstraction as *the* form for such a memorial. I am thinking here of the writing of Theodor Adorno, Maurice Blanchot and Jean-François Lyotard.[13] Though their writing rarely deals with the visual arts, more often taking as its subject philosophy and writing itself, and though it emerges in Germany and France rather than America, it nevertheless needs to be discussed here. At the outset, however, I should emphasise that there is a huge difference of approach between an art-historical one such as my own, which asks how specific artists have attempted to engage with the Holocaust at different moments, and a philosophical one, which considers how art should or should not respond to calamitous history. One of the reasons I want to address some of the ideas of Adorno and Lyotard now (and later, in connection with Morris Louis's paintings, Blanchot's text *The Writing of the Disaster*) is that they are central to many discussions of Holocaust representation, and it is interesting to see how their ideas can inform a discussion of abstraction. But I am also raising these figures now to fend off casual conclusions about abstraction that might be drawn from careless responses to their writing. If the ideas of Adorno or Lyotard are mistreated, they could lend support to the kind of blanket claims about abstraction and its relationship to the Holocaust that I refuse. Abstraction could seem a vague condition of art after Auschwitz; a refusal to depict what cannot or should not be represented realistically; an art of respectful silence before sublime history.

Yet these have not been the positions of these thinkers. What have Adorno and Lyotard had to say about abstraction and Holocaust memory? There are no particular texts in which Adorno joins the two, but one can look to several of his texts to see why it should seem that he might unite them, starting with Adorno's most famous comment from 1949, 'to write poetry after Auschwitz is barbaric', a sentence that appeared at the end of the essay 'Cultural Criticism and Society'.[14] Would this sentence imply that for Adorno there can be no visual art after Auschwitz either, and that any art after Auschwitz was barbaric? Perhaps. Would it imply that any attempt to depict Auschwitz is barbaric, and that abstraction, therefore, is somehow appropriate? As many writers anxious to correct misreadings of Adorno have argued, Adorno's sentence was not offering prescriptions or recommendations about the representation *of* Auschwitz. At this moment, Adorno was not concerned with whether or not Auschwitz, on account of its unprecedented horror, could or could not be represented by poetry. Nor was he yet concerned with the problem that a poem about Auschwitz wrested some aesthetic pleasure from a place of mass murder and therefore stood as a false gesture of redemption. Adorno had other concerns, and so it is pointless asking whether or not abstraction emerges as a 'non-barbaric' art form, somehow avoiding Adorno's censure.

As Michael Rothberg has argued, Adorno's comment of 1949 was concerned with the impact of Auschwitz on the possibility of any kind of poetry. Poetry relies on the premise that the individual has the freedom to express themselves. Modernity has exposed the fallacy of this premise, on account of total reification of experience, and Auschwitz is the moment of greatest exposure. Before Auschwitz, writing poetry was a naïve activity. But to continue to write poetry after Auschwitz, after this moment of exposure, is not so much naïve as wilfully false. It is to mystify social conditions; to pretend that they were otherwise. The poet would be blind to the impossibility of their practice and poetry would be a barbaric force of obfuscation, preventing the knowledge of its impossibility.[15] Likewise the artist. The very continuation of their practice would involve a misunderstanding of their position, and of the possibilities of art. But this would be the case for any kind of art, abstract or not.

If Adorno's first statement about poetry after Auschwitz does not help us to consider abstraction in its specificity – in its difference from any other kind of art, visual or not – what about his later comments? In the 1960s, Adorno produced more writing about art and Auschwitz, but under changed circumstances. Much more was known about Nazism, and with this knowledge came an imperative on mankind 'to arrange their thoughts and actions so that Auschwitz will not repeat itself, so that nothing similar will happen'.[16] But what was the proper cultural response to this demand? Certainly not the continuation of culture as if nothing had taken place. In Germany, Adorno found the memory of the Holocaust was hardly acknowledged, and culture continued as if uninterrupted. 'All post-Auschwitz culture, including its urgent critique, is garbage. In restoring itself after the things that happened without resistance in its own countryside, culture has turned entirely into the ideology it had been potentially . . .'[17] If Adorno was deeply critical of this continuation and viewed the unimpeded recovery of culture as proof of its barbarism, the alternative route – to 'say no to culture' – was only a means of 'furthering the barbarism which culture showed itself to be'.[18] A third route would be silence, but Adorno was also sceptical about this: 'Not even silence gets us out of the circle.' Bringing abstraction back into the picture, rather than abstraction being an adequate response to this situation, it could seem to risk two of these three criticisms: first, it could appear akin to lyric poetry, a bland continuation of pre-war 'culture', and second, it could appear an art of 'silence', failing to take part in the project of preventing the repetition of Auschwitz.

At times, Adorno's response to the demand to make sure 'nothing similar will happen' was to support an art of suffering. Whereas Adorno's 1949 statement was not concerned with poetry about Auschwitz, this became the concern in the essay 'Commitment' and in the section 'Meditation on Metaphysics' from *Negative Dialectics*. Adorno wrote in the first that 'I have no wish to soften the saying that to write lyric poetry after Auschwitz is barbaric'.[19] The addition of the term 'lyric', absent from the 1949 passage, opened up permission for a non-lyrical poetry – 'it is now virtually in art alone that suffering can still find its own voice'.[20] In *Negative Dialectics* he revised this to say that 'perennial suffering has as much right to expression as a tortured man has to scream; hence it may have been wrong to say that after Auschwitz you could no longer write poems'.[21] These sentences suggest Adorno approved art which expressed the suffering of the survivor (the survivor in the widest sense meaning all those who come after Auschwitz), and which refused the easy continuation of culture by keeping alive the memory of the destruction. Adorno wrote about the poetry of Celan and the drama of Beckett especially as their work not only kept alive the memory of suffering but because it refused to redeem the horror of the camps by affording aesthetic pleasure to its audience.

Perhaps then we might not think of abstraction as a silent art,[22] but as a tortured art, akin to the poetry of Celan or the drama of Beckett. Certainly many of the works I will consider refuse to offer to their viewers simple pleasures and deny redemptive narratives, but that is not to say Adorno's ideas quite translate, for these works do not represent suffering as directly as Celan or Beckett, or at least they represent it in a different way. Though the work of Celan and Beckett has been called 'imageless' in discussions of Adorno's support of it, imagelessness means something quite different when we are thinking of twentieth-century art, and the huge realm of abstraction.[23] However, one aspect of Adorno's thought does seem to describe well the operations of many of the art works I will discuss. Adorno writes in *Negative Dialectics* about a kind of thinking: 'If negative dialectics calls for the self-reflection of thinking, the tangible implication is that if thinking is to be true – if it is to be true today – it must also be a thinking against itself.'[24] This is a demand about the practice of philosophy, but it does describe the kind of thinking demanded by some abstract works, especially when their form or appearance calls for one kind of interpretative approach, and their context or title might call for another.

One of the problems of trying to think about Adorno's ideas in the context of works negotiating Holocaust memory is that for the most part, Adorno was not concerned at all with the actual representation of Auschwitz, but with art as a separate terrain. Modernist, autonomous art might resist the logic of instrumental reason that underwrites modernity and capitalism, and Auschwitz itself. With its afunctionality and resistance to instrumentality, abstraction in general could then appear as an Adornian art. However, I will be arguing that specific works attempt to address the Holocaust, and this is not an argument for Adornian autonomy. A memorial such as Eisenman's might employ a formal language developed in the autonomous sphere of art, but when such language is put to use, the autonomy of art is threatened. Such a memorial would seem to be anathema to Adorno's approach: 'To instrumentalize art is to undercut the opposition art mounts against instrumentalism.'[25]

I hope to have shown, even if briefly, that Adorno's thought, which itself developed and changed over time, cannot and should not be applied to the objects of my study in the hope that there might be anything like a neat fit. His thinking will not bear being used to support or attack abstraction, nor to describe its appropriateness or its pitfalls; but it can serve to articulate some of the challenges artists face in confronting the Holocaust.

Jean-François Lyotard confronted both the Holocaust and the problem of its representation in a different way from Adorno, but also in a different national context and at a different historical moment (the 1980s and 1990s, after the crystallisation of the concept of 'the Holocaust', after the emergence of some revisionism, and, of course, after Adorno). In *The Differend*, Lyotard considered the situation of a survivor in front of a denier. How can a survivor prove the existence of the gas chambers if they did not see them with their own eyes, as the denier requires? The only way to prove them would be to have died, but that would only serve the denier's purpose. By being ignored, the survivor is rendered a victim. Lyotard began his book with this situation but not just to treat the question of Holocaust denial; he was interested in situations where two parties in an argument will not accept the discourse of the other, and where as a consequence there can be no agreement or judgment about the existence of the event that brings them together. This is an argument about litigation and ethics (ethics must override litigation), but it has implications for representational practices. The event happened, but though the established discourses will not be able to articulate it, it must be witnessed. The 'differend' was the name Lyotard gave to the state of representation for such an event: 'The differend is the unstable state and instant of language wherein something which must be able to be put into phrases cannot yet be.'[26] 'In the differend, something 'asks' to be put into phrases, and suffers from the wrong of not being able to be put into phrases right away.'[27] It was the task of art and philosophy to find differends and witness them: 'What is at stake in a literature, in a philosophy, in a politics perhaps, is to bear witness to differends by finding idioms for them.'[28] The concept of 'the differend' therefore conveys a sense of urgency (the event must be represented) and frustration (the event has destroyed the representational tools). Auschwitz was the most powerful example of such an event, as it had destroyed the tools used to understand and measure it.

Some commentators have expressed a concern with the inconsistency of the term 'Auschwitz' in Lyotard's writing, complaining of the way it is at times a specific historical event, and at other times, an example amongst many others.[29] Another, perhaps more worrying problem associated with Lyotard's account of Auschwitz is the notion that it is beyond any representation, since all representational tools are broken by it.[30] If only this aspect of Lyotard's thought is considered, the Holocaust can be made to seem sublime, ineffable, mysterious, rendering political and historical enquiry (as well as any kind of artistic representation) useless. Such a formulation tends to deliver 'the Holocaust' into the hands of the religious right, as Slavoj Žižek has recently argued.[31] However, Lyotard's arguments suggest that representation must take place; but when it does, it should witness the very shattering of traditional representational forms. This insight is extremely interesting in terms of some of the works to be discussed here, which collectively mount a challenge to the conventional forms of history painting and the monument. Lyotard's critique of inscription is also important. In his book *Heidegger and 'the jews'*, he writes 'only that which has been inscribed can, in the current sense of the term, be forgotten'.[32] However, 'One *must*, certainly, inscribe in words, in images. One cannot escape the necessity of representing. It could be a sin to believe oneself safe and sound. But it is one thing to do it in view of saving the memory, and quite another to try to preserve the remainder, the unforgettable forgotten, in writing.'[33]

Lyotard never addressed art works that deliberately attempted to represent the Holocaust so it is hard to tell how he felt a work of art could actually 'bear witness to a differend', or how a piece of writing could save memory without inscribing, but he did write frequently about abstraction, and indeed about Barnett Newman (fig. 3). Interestingly, for Lyotard, both the art work and an event such as Auschwitz could produce similar kinds of reactions. If Auschwitz rendered us numb, not knowing how to respond to it, so too can an abstract painting of Newman's: before it, we know something has happened, but not how to voice this. 'Newman's *now* is a stranger to consciousness and cannot be composed in terms of it. Rather, it is what dismantles consciousness, what dismisses consciousness; it is what consciousness cannot formulate, and even what consciousness forgets in order to compose itself.'[34] So the abstract art work was paralleled with the event in that both were unassimilable to existing modes of encounter or interpretation; but in no way for Lyotard could the abstract work be a deliberate response to an event. In 'The Sublime and the Avant-Garde', Lyotard argued that Newman was concerned with 'the sensation of time', but that this was not the time 'laden with references and history – the usual subjects of painting'.[35] Lyotard could not countenance the possibility that abstract art works might constitute a response to history, albeit without the traditional representational and depictive devices of history painting. His 1980s essays on avant-garde visual art consistently argued that it was the task of painting to bear witness to the unrepresentable, and that this special role was necessitated by modern capitalism with its desire for realism and quick communication. This formulation is far from my own approach, which argues that the work of art attempts to represent the calamities of modernity. So, although Lyotard's description of the bankruptcy of traditional representational forms informs my own approach, the art works I look at put some pressure on his account of abstraction.

clement greenberg on auschwitz and modernism

In 1966, Lyotard's paradigmatic artist, Barnett Newman, produced a statement that in many ways echoed Adorno's paradigmatic statement of 1949. Looking back to that decade, Newman said that:

> The feelings I had at the time of the War in '41 was that the world was coming to an end. And to the extent that the world was coming to an end, the whole issue of painting, I felt, was over because it impossible to paint flowers, figures, etcetera, and so the crisis moved around the problem of what I can really paint.[36]

3 Barnett Newman, *Onement I*, 1948. Oil on canvas and oil on masking tape on canvas, 69.2 × 41.2 cm, The Museum of Modern Art, New York. Gift of Annalee Newman, 1992.

Recalling the early 1940s from the mid-60s, Newman knew much more about what had been happening in 1941 than he knew at the time, and of course what would happen after, but even if we must read these words as tempered by hindsight, Newman's statement suggests that historical calamities changed what was considered impossible and possible as art. In Adorno's terms it might have seemed to Newman barbaric to continue to paint flowers and figures as if nothing happened; in Lyotard's terms, Newman faced a differend: the event (the 'War in '41' and the 'world . . . coming to an end') required witness, but the event rendered traditional tools of witness (figurative painting) useless. Later, I will argue that in a particular series of works, Newman addressed the situation of the survivor, but for now I want to raise another question. If I am making a claim about the importance of this statement of Newman's for an account of his, and others' works, how come those writing closest to him did not situate his work at all in terms of this 'crisis'? Most New York critics, and certainly those responsible for the early reception of the other painters Morris Louis and Frank Stella, were Jewish, and might we not expect them to have been particularly sensitive to the 'world coming to an end'? In asking why these critics produced no discussions of the representation of the Holocaust, I am of course pointing to the difference between my approach and modernist criticism, the initially dominant critical approach to post-war American abstraction.[37] But I am not raising this question in order to promote my approach and claim simply that earlier critics were blind to what I have noticed. It is more complicated. I see the modernist critical project itself as a response to the situation Newman described above, but a response that necessarily forbade the discussion of historical representation in art, a response that necessarily required that abstraction be addressed in terms of form alone.

As is well known, Clement Greenberg argued that modernist arts separated themselves from each other, every one finding its own specific area of competence. For a modernist, it was appropriate to address a painting or sculpture by situating it within a developing history of its medium, but not in any way in relation to world history – historical and mnemonic representation were the preserves of writing.[38] It is less well known that Greenberg developed this theory whilst himself working day to day, from 1944 until 1957, for the New York Jewish journal *Commentary*.[39] The journal had been founded specifically in response to the news from Europe, and had been described in Elliot Cohen's opening editorial as a 'candle' lit in memory of the destruction. 'With

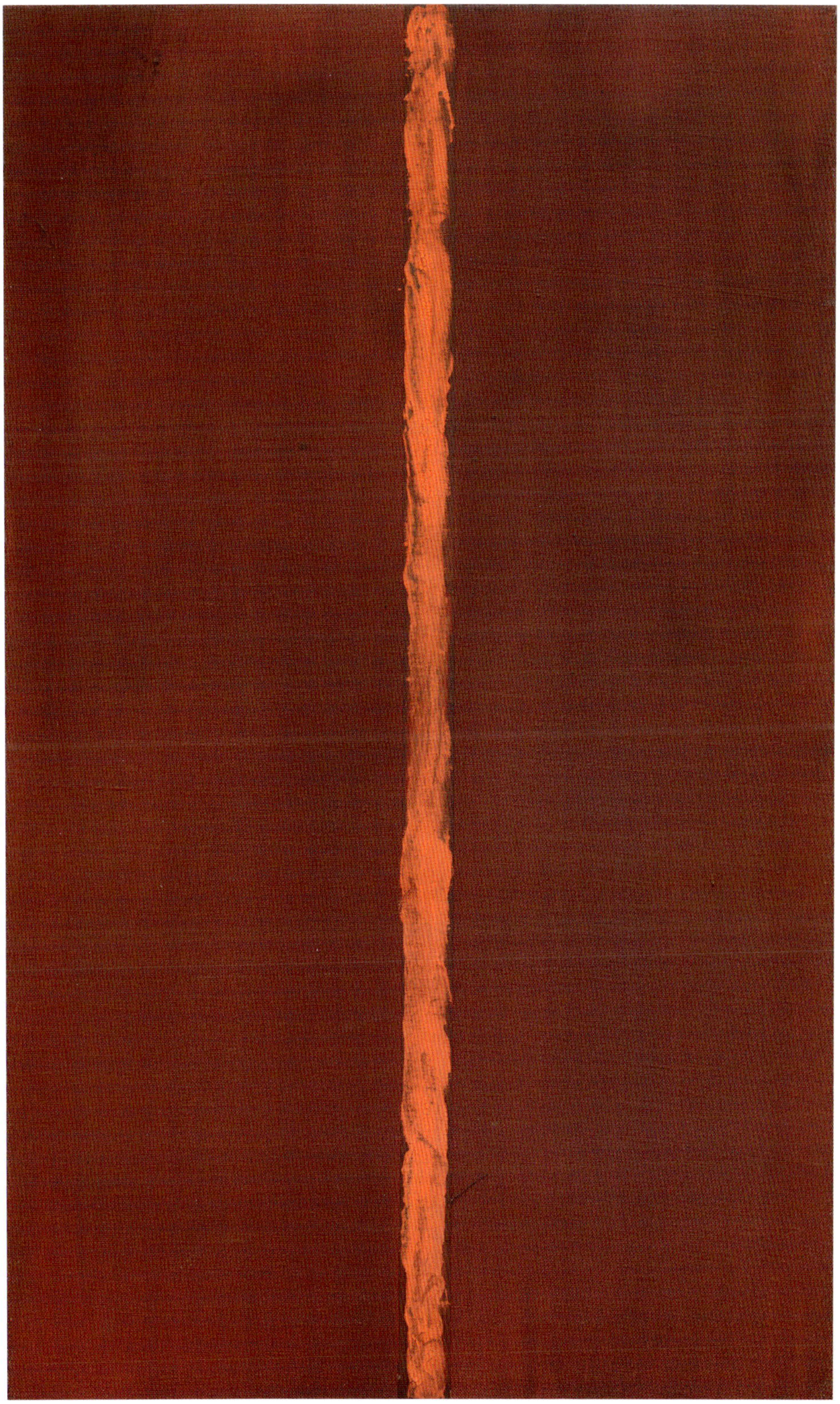

Europe devastated, there falls upon us here in the United States a far greater share of the responsibility for carrying forward, in a creative way, our common Jewish cultural and spiritual heritage.'[40] During his thirteen years as managing editor, Greenberg wrote many reviews of Jewish books, described and differentiated the Jewishness of Soutine and Chagall, and even wrote the first English translation of Paul Celan's poem 'Todesfuge', which he published in 1955.[41] His most sustained article was 'Self-Hatred and Jewish Chauvinism', published in November 1950. In this text, Greenberg confronted accusations of self-hatred, setting his ambivalent feelings about his Jewishness against the problem of a rising aggressive nationalist Jewish sensibility. Greenberg argued that, like the self-haters they derided, chauvinist Jews were unable to live at ease with their Jewishness, and he blamed both attitudes on the impact of Auschwitz on the Jewish psyche. Though he recognised that '[i]t is . . . more than time that we all began to make a real effort to digest the fact of Auschwitz psychologically', Greenberg also recognised the time was not yet right: 'If the "positive" Jews don't want to start the necessary discussion, none of us others seems to want to either. Not only is the mind unable to come to terms with the dimensions of the event and so resolve some of its oppressiveness, and not only does it prefer to remain numbed in order to spare itself the pain; as I have just said, the mind has a tendency, deep down, to look on a calamity of that order as a punishment that must have been deserved.'[42] Greenberg's involvement in the discussion of post-Holocaust Jewish subjectivity was therefore pretty sustained – these were brave questions to tackle in 1950. Considering his involvement in these issues, the question as to why he did not bring this context to bear on artists such as Newman, Mark Rothko, Morris Louis and others is increasingly perplexing.

Some critics have sensed a kind of assimilationist repression in Greenberg's writing: he was happy to write about Jewish topics in book reviews, but not to tarnish American artists (who happened to be Jews) with any reference to concerns that might affect Jews more than other Americans.[43] However, this argument seems to ignore the fact that to have explored any Jewish content in the work of abstract artists in the 1950s would have been politically dangerous (I am thinking here of the politics of the Jewish cultural world). Had any critic of the time emphasised the Jewishness of artists such as Newman, Rothko, Gottlieb and Louis, they would have risked playing into the hands of the chauvinists, who would have been delighted to 'claim' such figures as Jewish artists without due consideration of their work. In the aftermath of the war, many arguments *were* put forward about 'Jewish art', pleading for such a category, but never convincingly. They seem instead to be desperate responses to the destruction of Jewish culture and the post-war texts about the non-existence of Jewish culture.[44] One reviewer writing in March 1950 for *Commentary* dismissed a book on *Jewish Artists of the Nineteenth and Twentieth Centuries* as 'a piece of nationalist propaganda',[45] manifesting exactly the kind of chauvinism that would concern his editor, Greenberg, in the essay published later that year.[46]

Rather than argue that Greenberg underplayed the Jewishness of abstract artists for reasons of assimilation, I would like to think instead that Greenberg (and his followers) could not address the historical calamities that affected modern Jewish subjects because to have done so would have been to broach modernism. Modernism had been constructed precisely as a protective barrier; a wall against the threat of history. This argument – suggested first by Susan Noyes Platt – can be drawn from a reading against the grain of those essays in which Greenberg *did* bring modernism and Jewishness together – his three essays on Franz Kafka.

Greenberg showed that the 'middle-class orderliness, routine, prudence, [and] sedentary stability' of Kafka's characters acted as a kind of shield against a potentially oppressive history. Middle-class routines served for secular Jews the same role as Halacha had done for religious Jews, blocking off 'Gentile history'. If we consider Greenberg's comments on Kafka as somehow descriptive of his own criticism, modernism itself might act as a similar shield, as Greenberg's Halacha. There are some passages about Halacha by Greenberg that could almost serve as descriptions of modernism: 'Halacha . . . is motivated by the . . . desire for logic and order. It attempts to relate every iota, every habitual triviality to life, to the ultimate.' Halacha, and middle class values, came with some cost: 'the price Kafka pays for the safety he may feel [. . .] in this secular, unwritten and unspoken neo-Halachic system is claustrophobia'. The cost paid by modernism is attentiveness to the mnemonic capacities of modernist art; the possibilities of the historical representation in art. There are times where Greenberg seems to acknowledge this: 'Might not all art begin to appear falsifying to the Jew who looked closely enough?' Greenberg asked in the version of the Kafka essay that appeared in *Art and Culture*. 'Does not art always make one forget what is literally happening to oneself as a certain person in a certain world?'[46] Kafka's work poses this question and by doing so 'tests the limits of art'; Greenberg's modernism might be an agent of forgetting, but a consciously chosen one.

My own approach to abstraction departs in fundamental ways from Greenberg's modernist one, but the Greenbergian emphasis on the continuity of post-war with pre-war art ('Nothing could be further from the authentic art of our time than the idea of a rupture of continuity. Art is – among other things – continuity, and unthinkable without it.') is actually quite helpful for one aspect of my argument. I am wary of blanket claims about abstraction as a generalised response to Auschwitz, and no more so than because abstraction *predated* Auschwitz. The Greenbergian line (from Manet to Cézanne to Picasso, and Mondrian, and Newman) serves the extremely useful purpose of reminding us of this. Recalling these continuities, and the long history of abstraction, helps to explain why it was never the case that the artists I discuss 'chose' abstraction instead of figurative realism as a means of confronting the Holocaust; rather, abstraction was the tradition in which they worked.

the drowned and the saved

Clement Greenberg's texts were some of the first written on the work of Morris Louis and Barnett Newman; Rosalind Krauss, meanwhile, wrote one of the first accounts of the Frank Stella paintings I will discuss later, and also the most important early essays on the work of Mel Bochner, Richard Serra, Sol LeWitt and Joel Shapiro, the artists I

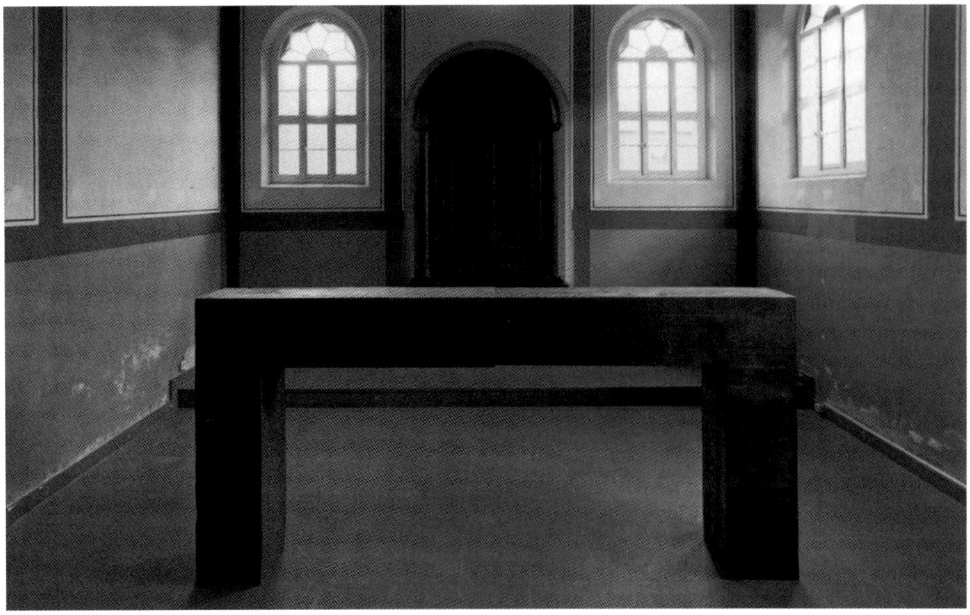

4 Richard Serra, *The Drowned and the Saved*, 1992 installed in Stommeln Synagogue. Forged weatherproof steel. Collection Erzbischöfliches Diözesanmuseum, Cologne. © Richard Serra.

look at in the later stages of my argument. Krauss also penned one of the first major essays on video art, though it did not cover Beryl Korot's work, and an important essay on Peter Eisenman. Since most of the works I discuss were made long after these essays, it is meaningless to ask why Krauss did not address them, but it is still important to state that the revisionist approaches to abstract art her work has pioneered continue to hold one aspect of Greenbergian theory intact – namely that abstraction and historical representation are incompatible. But if recent approaches to these artists have not so far located abstraction in relation to Holocaust memory (Anna Chave's feminist critique of minimalism being the exception[47]), I want to emphasise that like modernism, poststructuralism itself can be seen as responsive to the rupture of the Holocaust, and in many ways, more directly responsive. If, as I have argued, Greenbergian modernism attempts to construct a narrative of continuity to hold history at bay, poststructuralist criticism approaches art works with all the scepticism that the mid-century imposed on thought. The artist's intentionality is questioned as the source of all content; the meaning of art works are contingent upon the shifting movement of the viewer; site plays a determining role; spectatorship becomes a matter of desire; the unconscious now plays a role in visuality; horizontality and the Bataillian 'informe' are put to work against the sureties of verticality and modernist form.

If these approaches have completely shifted the way in which we think about the work of Jackson Pollock, or Richard Serra, or Ellsworth Kelly, they also have meant that those critics following Krauss who have been most interested in challenging the modernist prohibitions on 'the mnemonic dimensions of representation', and in resurrecting an art of historical representation, have done so by examining artists who abandoned abstraction. With the demise of the Greenbergian account, the stars of Morris

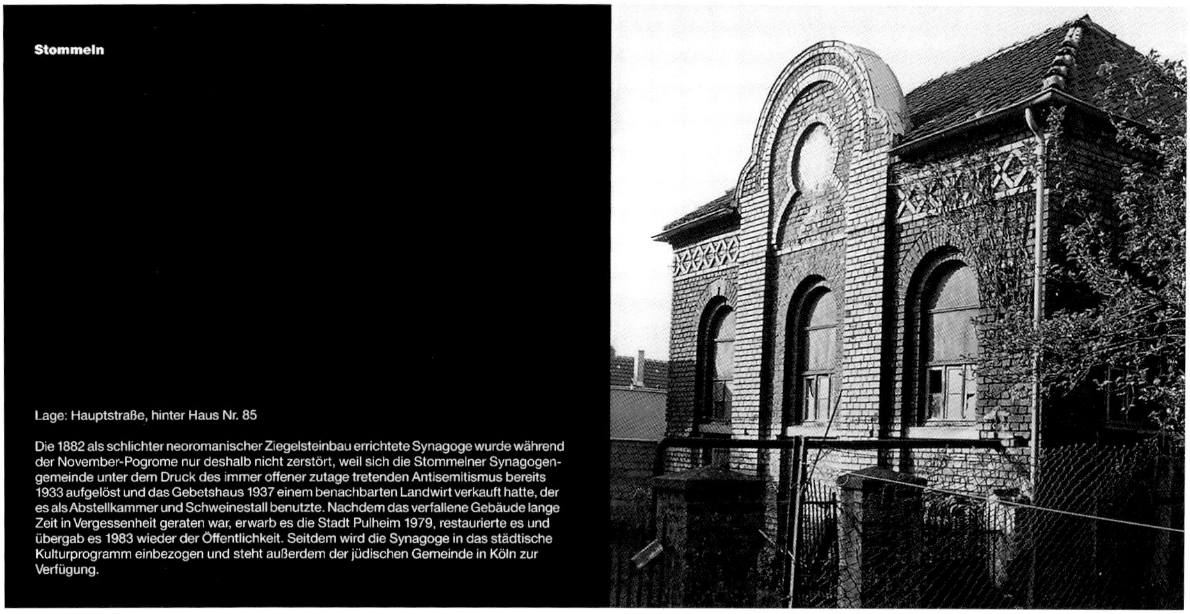

5 Richard Serra, Spread from the book published to accompany exhibition of *The Drowned and the Saved* showing Stommeln Synagogue in disuse after 1938.

Louis and Frank Stella, for instance, have waned, and attention has shifted to artists such as Nancy Spero, Martha Rosler, Hans Haacke and Allan Sekula. With their employment of photography and text, such artists are able to right the repressions of modernism.

Much of the recent work on Holocaust representation examines the work of similar artists. Like some of the theoretical literature on Holocaust representation, some of the art-historical accounts can be extremely prescriptive, judging what is and is not appropriate. By asking questions about abstract art I do not wish to validate it as a more sophisticated or respectful way of confronting historical catastrophe. (For instance, though none of the artists I discuss attempted graphically to depict the suffering of the Holocaust, nor have artists such as Hans Haacke or Christian Boltanski.) Abstraction is not being posited as a better form of engagement; instead, I am arguing that at times, it was necessary and compelling for abstract artists to engage with history without jettisoning the language of their work – just as compelling as it was for other artists who felt instead that that the only way to confront history was to reject abstraction.

In order to give a sense of the urgency of this project, I will conclude this introduction close to where I started, with an example. When Richard Serra, Peter Eisenman's original partner in the Berlin Holocaust memorial pulled out, one of the reasons that he felt able to do so was that he had already confronted the memory of the Holocaust in Germany without having to compromise his work. In 1992, Serra had accepted an invitation to make a work in Stommeln Synagogue in the Rhineland, a building which had ceased functioning as a synagogue after Kristallnacht. This was a much smaller project than the Berlin one – not only was the space much smaller, it was also a temporary work rather than a permanent memorial. But its importance to Serra should not be underplayed. For all he had worked with specific architectural spaces before, Serra had not previously placed work in such a resonant location, one which was only a venue for art on account of a violent history which had terminated its original use as a synagogue. Serra installed a work titled after Primo Levi's memoir *The Drowned and the Saved* (fig. 4), but before coming to the work itself I want to pay attention to the publication he put together to accompany the exhibition. Serra produced a small book, for which he had collected images of various synagogues in the area all affected by the 1938 pogrom (his first venture into archival photographic work; fig. 5). In the book, Serra also published a statement, and it is one of the most personal pieces of writing he has ever produced.

> It is difficult to defend yourself against retributions for an unknown. There is no preparation. To keep good faith with yourself, to understand yourself requires truthfulness, sincerity, a moral effort. Is that possible if part of your identity cannot be revealed?
>
> When I was five years old I would ask my mother: What are we, who are we, where are we from? One day she answered me: If I tell you, you must promise never to tell anyone, never. We are Jewish. Jewish people are being burnt alive for being Jewish.
>
> I was raised in fear, in deceit, in embarrassment, in denial. I was told not to admit who I was, not to admit what I was.[48]

Serra's statement is important for a number of reasons. First, it evidences the impact that the Holocaust made on those born far away from its geographical location, those who grew up after the end of the war. Second, it demonstrates the complexity of this impact: Serra was not learning what happened, but half-hearing in an atmosphere of secrecy and shame. Third, the statement indicates that the difficulty of confronting the Holocaust much later had as much to do with its immensity as with particular personal circumstances – in this case, a mother's warning to her infant. Fourth, in its very publication, the statement shows that despite its difficulty, the task of facing the memory of the Holocaust was absolutely urgent. No matter how painful the memory of this childhood encounter, there came a time when it had to be acknowledged in public.

This statement, the catalogue, and the site are all exceptionally uncharacteristic in the context of Serra's work, but the sculpture itself – considered in terms of its shape and materiality alone – was absolutely in place. *The Drowned and the Saved* is a sculpture in two parts – two rotated L shapes whose short sides stretch vertically from the floor, and whose longer sides meet each other at their ends, propping each other so each half is prevented from falling forward. The meeting of the two halves creates a bar, dividing space above it from space below. The sculpture dramatises principles of balance, weight, load and gravity. This is the syntax of Serra's sculpture, syntax in use for over twenty years before this work was made. But in this location, with this title, with such an accompanying publication, the way we might think about this sculptural language changes. Hal Foster, for instance, has considered the work in connection to its title and Levi's text: 'There are those who span the bridge, who pass over it, the saved, and those who pass under it, the drowned. These two passages, these two fates, are opposed, but they come together as the two beams come together, in support.'[49] The placement of the work was also meaningful. It formed a kind of barrier in the middle of the synagogue space, dividing one half from the other, too low to frame the architecture; just high enough to suggest a *bimah*. Many other works of Serra's become most powerful as one walks around them; this one seemed to demand one viewing position (in this respect the frontal photograph is a good representation).[50] As a viewer stood before the sculpture, they would find themselves placed in the situation of those who had one day read from the *bimah*, and they might remember others who had been in that place before. Serra's work would have alerted viewers to the space around them but also to the time that had passed since that space served as a synagogue, to the irretrievable status of the place. Solidifying Levi's language within the room, Serra's sculpture refused to let the memory of its status as a former synagogue slip away; to let the space become just any other building.

Many of the meanings that would have been available from the exhibition of *The Drowned and the Saved* within Stommeln Synagogue would have been unavailable had the sculpture been encountered elsewhere, perhaps without the viewer knowing its title, reading Serra's statement, or looking at his catalogue. The meanings I have described were delicate and very much contingent – they are propped up by site, supported by these various peripheral texts. If this could point to the difference between *The Drowned and the Saved* and Serra's other sculptures that do not usually have these textual supplements, we could also approach these delicate meanings by recalling that contingency itself has been a feature of Serra's work since the late 1960s. So many sculptures rely on balance; on the counterweight of one part to prop another up. In Stommeln, then, contingency itself gains added significance, becoming a broader force. While Serra may have had to change to some extent his way of working for the purposes of this project, so too he put the vocabulary and principles of his practice to work, and in so doing, expanded and complicated, rather than diverted or betrayed, the possibilities of his abstraction. *The Drowned and the Saved* offers an idea of how abstraction might work at a site of memory and a complex idea of how Holocaust representation might occur through abstraction. The sculpture will not tell us any stories of the Holocaust, or treat its images, but it materialises one of the themes in one of the most famous Holocaust testimonies (Levi's), and creates a resonant place for memory. It does this without forcing meaning on the viewer; instead, its meanings are balanced on delicate props. As such, it is an appropriate example of the kind of works that I will be looking at.

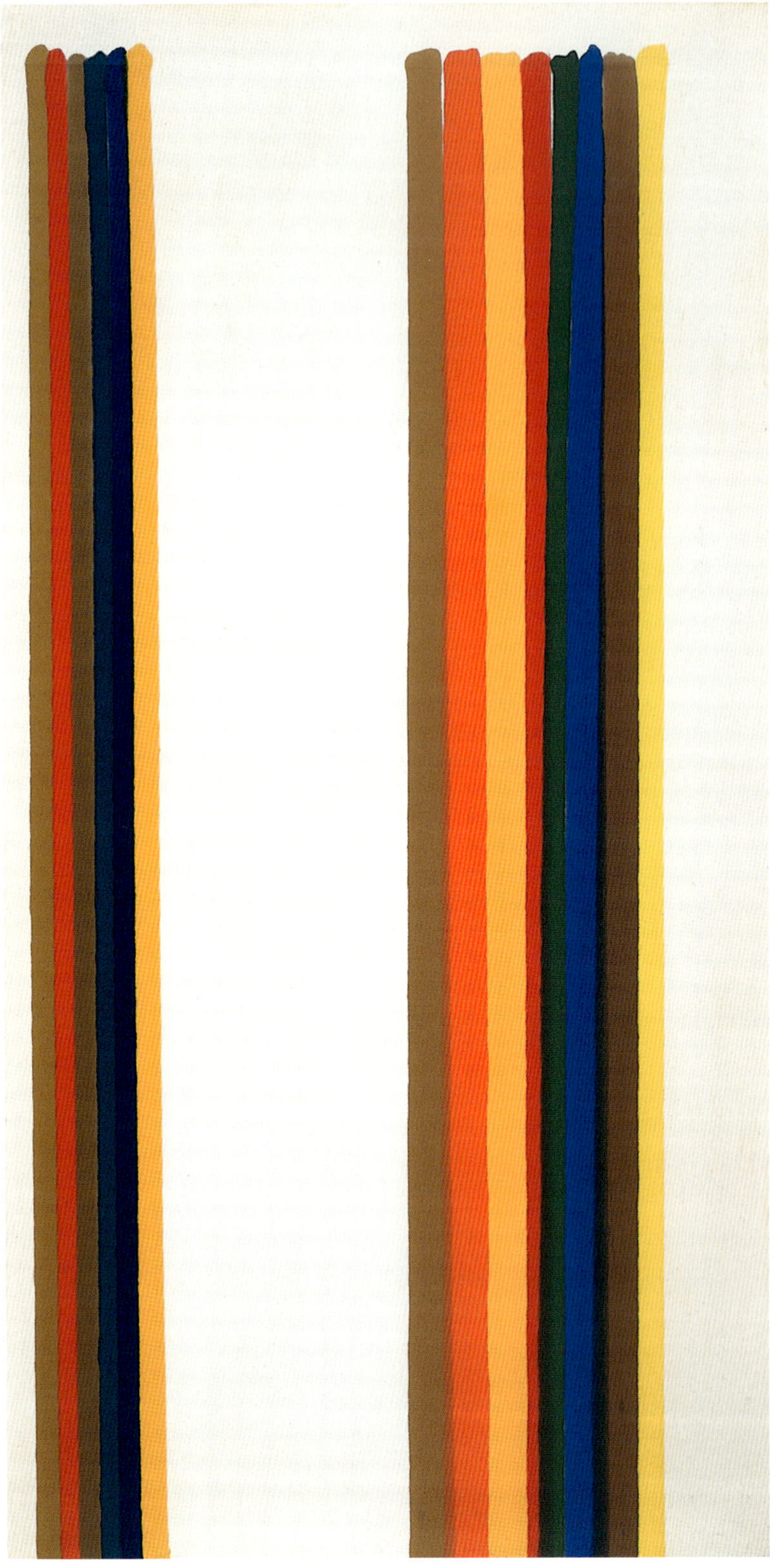

two

morris louis's *charred journal: firewritten* paintings

the modernist morris louis

6 Morris Louis, *Canopus*, 1962. Acrylic on canvas, 209.6 × 104.1 cm, Private Collection.

The proposition that an abstract painter might make work as a complex response to the Holocaust would seem to be no more unlikely than if the painter was Morris Louis. Born Maurice Bernstein in 1912 to immigrant Jews living in Baltimore, Louis, along with Kenneth Noland and Jules Olitski, is one of the artists whose association with high modernist criticism has been least questioned. Whereas the work of Jackson Pollock or Barnett Newman has been mobilised in arguments by critics of the modernist position, Louis now seems to stand for modernist orthodoxy, and as modernist criticism has been set aside, so too Louis's work has been waylaid. He is known primarily for three series of paintings made between his 'breakthrough' encounter with Helen Frankenthaler's *Mountains and Sea* in 1953, and his early death in 1962: the 'Veils' (fig. 7), the 'Unfurleds' (fig. 8), and the 'Stripes' (fig. 6).[1] Though long ago heralded as the work of 'one of America's greatest painters', these are now often housed in museum storerooms.[2]

Louis's 'mature' work was introduced by Clement Greenberg in the essay 'Louis and Noland', published in *Art International* in May 1960, and in various texts that Michael Fried published throughout the 1960s and revised for his 1971 Abrams monograph.[3] Looking at these modernist accounts helps indicate how Louis's work was first described. They also provide a useful way into my concerns. Greenberg's article marked the first time for many years that he had written on a little-known artist. It started with an analysis of the problem of 'provinciality'. Before the war, American artists had always seemed provincial when set on the world stage. New York was now producing many young artists who exhibited internationally. They appeared to escape the trap

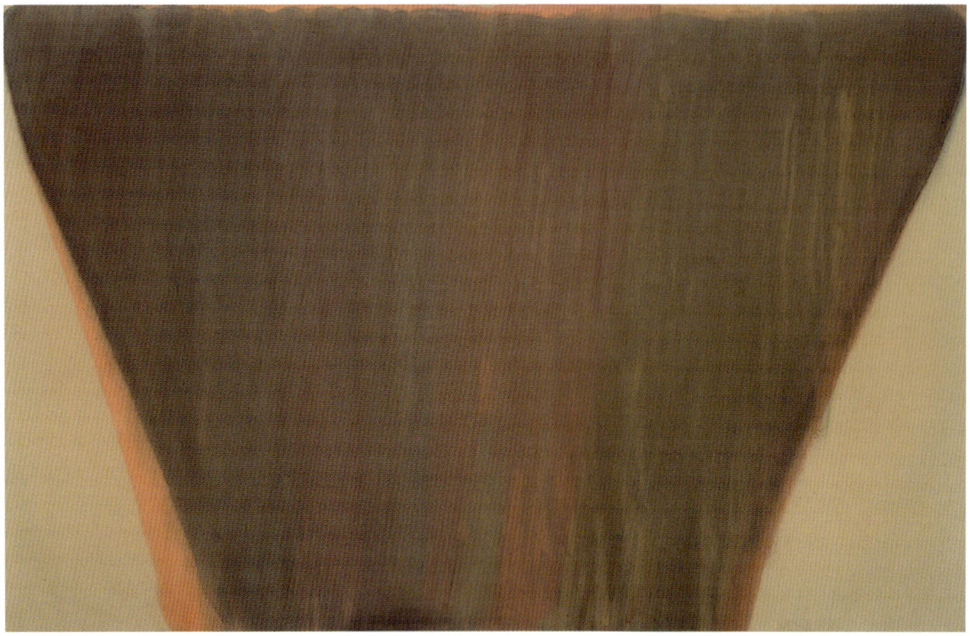

7 Morris Louis, *Plenitude*, 1958. Acrylic on canvas, 233.7 × 360.7 cm, Estate of Morris Louis.

of provinciality, but their achievement was minor. Louis and Kenneth Noland, though living in the cultural provinces (Washington D.C.), were able to distance themselves from the changing fashions of New York painting, and make non-provincial, major work.

Greenberg's account of Louis proceeded by securing the artist's modernist status. Paying little attention to the mythical narratives, social themes and symbolic vocabulary of Louis's work of the 1930s and '40s, Greenberg explained that Louis had abandoned his early style because it was cubist, and therefore 'sculptural'. Louis's 'revulsion against cubism' was an advance in modernist painting.[4] The critical terms in play in Greenberg's account were sculpture and painting: the medium of writing was not discussed, nor the possibility that a painting might figure writing. His other remarks concerned Louis's ability to make colour 'optical'. This analysis was extended in Michael Fried's account, and for Fried too, the notion of medium was crucial in explaining Louis's importance.

Fried posited that Louis's achievement was in subsuming drawing to the demands of painting. Like Greenberg, he skirted over Louis's pre-breakthrough work. The *Charred Journals*, for instance, were too influenced by Pollock and 'Pollock remains exactly that, an influence'.[5] For Fried, Louis's 'Veil' paintings, the first after his breakthrough, marked an extension of Pollock's achievement in turning drawing's tools to painting's purposes. Pollock had freed the line from the traditional role of drawing, delimiting the outlines of objects, but his interest in figuration had led to paintings such as *Out of the Web* (1949). In the 'Veils', Louis managed to overcome the figurative, shape-making role of drawing, but through his technique, he enabled a new kind of figuration to occur in the process. When canvas was stained with successive waves of acrylic paint placed on top of each other, the contours of each wave were visible through

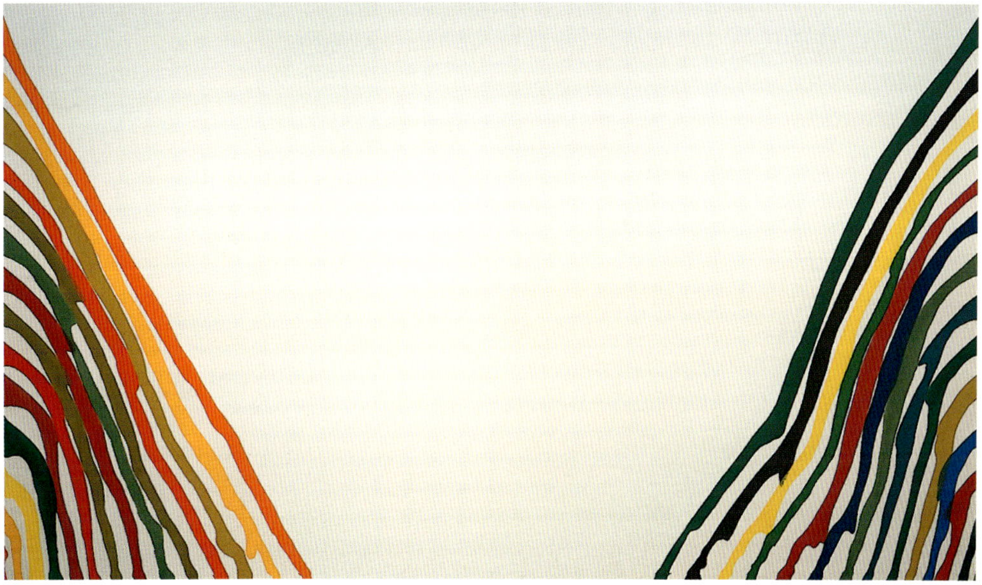

8 Morris Louis, *Beta Kappa*, 1961. Acrylic on canvas, 262.3 × 439.4 cm, National Gallery of Art, Washington. Gift of Marcella Louis Brenner, 1970.

each other as a kind of shape-forming figuration.[6] The 'Unfurled' paintings also overcame drawing: the rivulets running down the bottom corners did not mark the perimeter of shapes, but seemed '*all* perimeter'.[7] Their positioning against the central expanse of blank canvas was especially significant. Fried quoted Greenberg's comment that 'the first mark on a surface destroys its virtual flatness.'[8] Louis's lines seemed to play out the '*firstness of marking*': these paintings were about what happens when a mark is made on the surface; when the mark announces itself as figure against the ground behind.[9] Since this ground was so expansive, the untouched canvas at the centre of the 'Unfurleds' seemed to Fried like an 'infinite abyss': 'One's experience of the Unfurleds can be vertiginous.'[10]

Fried concluded his essay by thinking through the consequences of Louis's process. 'Louis's eschewal of traditional drawing amounted to the refusal to allow his hand, wrist, and arm to get into his paintings'.[11] Fried continued: 'this, I suggest, amounted to the refusal to allow himself to get into his paintings in what he felt was the wrong way'.[12] Where other artists of Louis's period sought to abandon expressionism by choosing to paint recognisable configurations (Jasper Johns) or serial configurations (Frank Stella), Fried was claiming that Louis's *process* enabled a kind of distance: the artist's hand was entirely separated from the canvas, with the brush no longer even present as a dripping stick. 'Louis's paintings, more than those of any previous painter, give the impression of coming into existence as if of their own accord, without the intervention of the artist.'[13]

I want to pick up one important aspect of Greenberg's account and two important points of Fried's to introduce the concerns of this chapter. Greenberg placed the entire account of Morris Louis in the context of a discussion about provinciality. Greenberg's anti-provincialism might have been the flip-side to his hope for a pan-national, universal art, but his way into the essay immediately foreclosed the possibility that the artists under consideration could address questions pertaining to history and to their cultural backgrounds: to do so would only cement their provinciality. Fried, meanwhile, felt that Louis's process meant that he avoided 'getting into his paintings in the wrong way'. The wrong way was the way of emotive, gestural action painting: second generation abstract expressionism or 'Tenth Street' art. The right way, enabled by Louis's process, was the way of impersonality, of the minimal 'intervention of the artist'. A third way of getting into the paintings, and a way closed off in Fried's account, would be to find a means of enabling the concerns of memory and politics – not personal or emotional concerns so much as those which address a subject of history – to play a part in the making and meanings of the work. These concerns, which for Greenberg could threaten a painting with the undesirable fate of appearing 'provincial', have little to do with the dynamics of visual space, with the 'first' mark as the first seen thing, and rather more to do with the mark as writing.

9 Morris Louis, *Charred Journal: Firewritten II*, 1951. Acrylic on canvas, 88.9 × 76.2 cm, Louisiana Museum of Modern Art, Humlebaek, Denmark. Gift of Marcella Louis Brenner / The American Federation of Arts, 1981.

In more than one place in his text, Fried discusses the empty canvas through the metaphor of the page. The empty space of the 'Unfurleds' has the 'original blankness (the blankness, one feels, of an enormous *page*).'[14] Louis's paintings, meanwhile, are 'wholly abstract embodiments or correlatives of . . . the will or impulse to draw, to make one's mark, to take possession, in characteristic ways, of a plane surface'.[15] The idea of the *page* (as opposed to canvas) would *seem* to invoke the mark on it as a mark of writing. But Fried thinks of the first mark on the 'page' as a visual mark, the mark that initiates a relationship between figure and ground, and that creates optical space. The impulse to 'take possession' of the page can thus only be the impulse to mark it with visual content. However, if the implications of the canvas *as* page were followed in the most obvious manner, the first mark on it would then be considered as a written (not drawn) mark. Then, rather than having a status as the initiators of visual content, these first marks would initiate content associated with writing. The first mark would signify the impulse to make meaning; to signify.[16]

In order to shift attention to the possibility of writing and of engaging politics and memory, I will be addressing the *Charred Journal: Firewritten* paintings. Made in 1951 before Louis's 'breakthrough', and considered 'immature' by the modernists, the series was exhibited in April 1953 at the Washington Workshop Center of the Arts, a small artist-run institution where Louis had gained a teaching position in 1952. The notions of the 'page' and of 'writing', kept separate in Fried's account, are jointly written into the titles of these works. 'Charred *Journal*' (my emphasis) speaks also of a personal sphere of interest – the diary – quite distanced from Fried's idea of 'impersonality'. As we will see, the kind of content that Louis wanted these paintings to have would have been impossible for a modernist critic to notice. But as I have indicated, Greenberg's and Fried's (non)accounts of the series had less to do with their recognising and then repressing their subject matter than with the limitations of their critical outlook. Modernist theory simply could not make sense of Louis's project in this instance, but that is not to say that the modernist approach to Louis's work is entirely redundant. Indeed I shall return to Fried's manner of viewing in due course.[17]

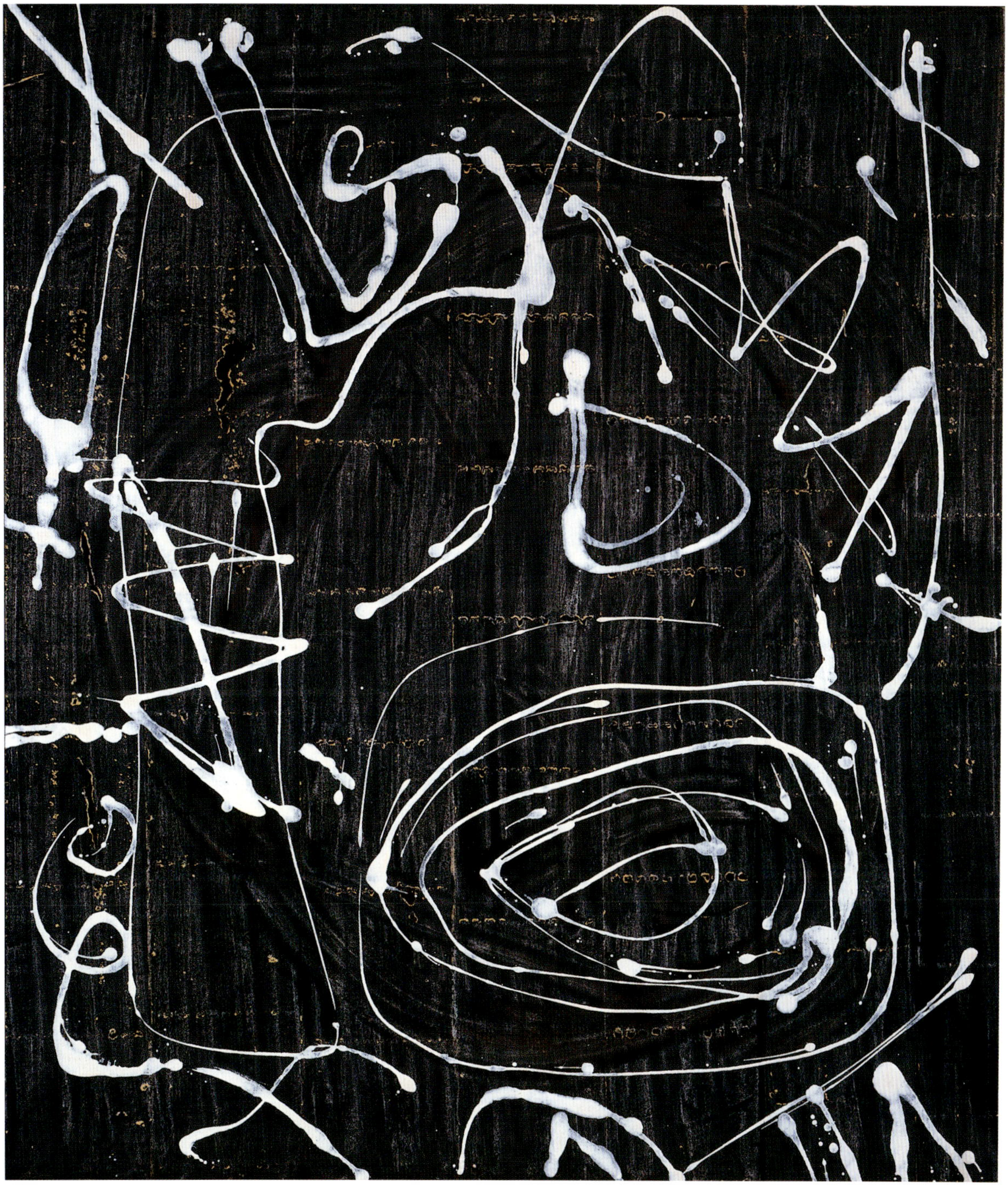

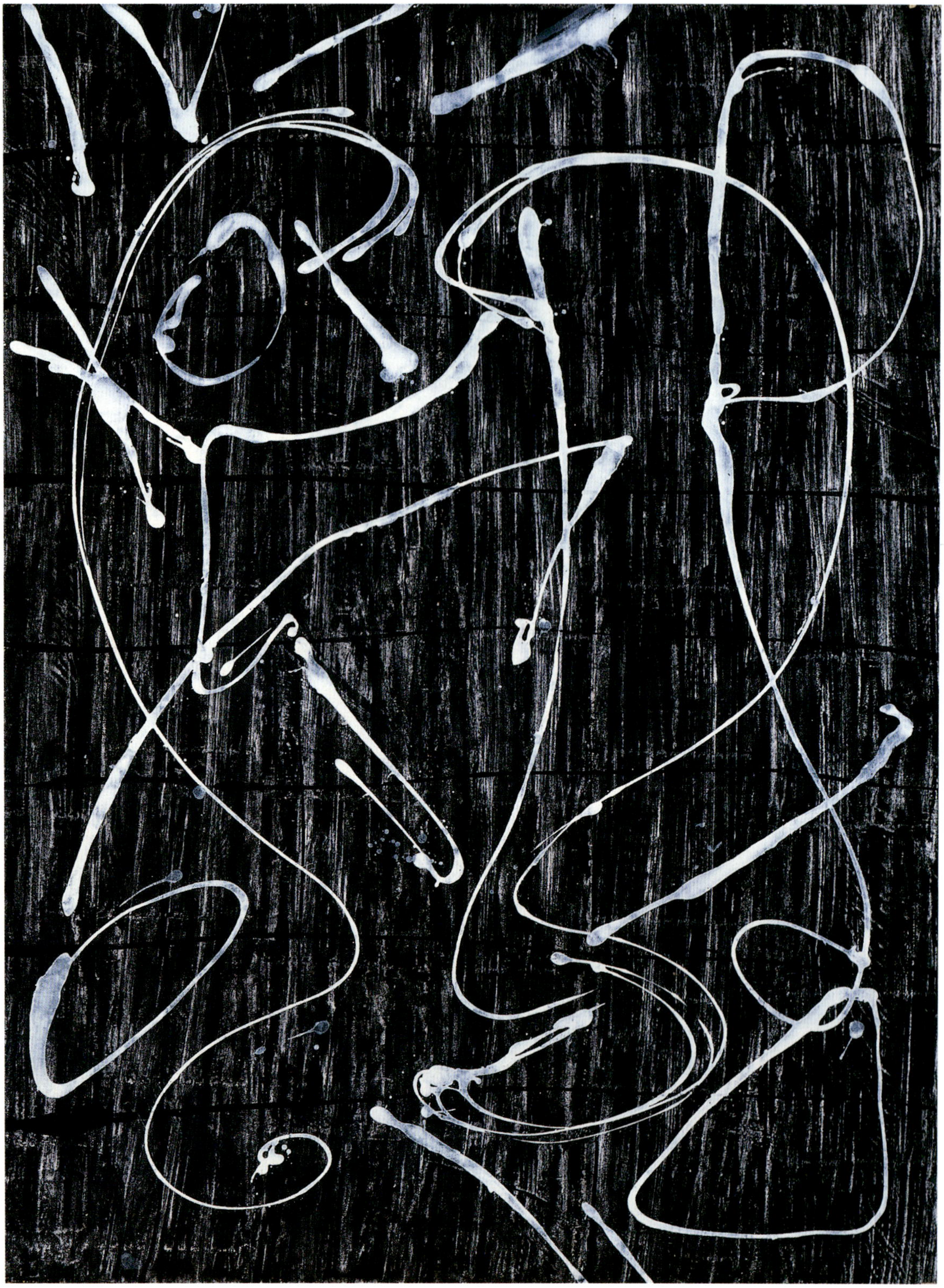

paintings and process

The *Charred Journal: Firewritten* series (figs 9–12, 17) comprises seven small canvases around thirty-five inches high and thirty inches wide, differentiated in their titles by a number or letter – these are I, II, IV, V, A and B. The seventh painting is listed in *The Complete Paintings* simply as 'Charred Journal'; I will refer to it here as 'C'. Alongside the enveloping expanses of Louis's later work, these paintings might seem frail and insubstantial. Their surfaces, however, reveal a complexity that requires sustained description. While a spectator might see the canvases as flat surfaces, to reconstruct Louis's work we have to prise the surface apart, working from the bottom layer of paint upwards.

10 Morris Louis, *Charred Journal: Firewritten IV*, 1951. Acrylic on canvas, 89.5 × 76.2 cm, Louisiana Museum of Modern Art, Humlebaek, Denmark. Gift of Marcella Louis Brenner / The American Federation of Arts, 1981.

The first strata of paint was a coloured under-layer. In his post-'breakthrough' years, Louis would work directly on raw canvas, but in 1951, he primed his surfaces. A light monochrome coat would have sufficed to seal the holes in the weave, but here, particularly when close up, a range of tones is visible. These vary between paintings: in *Charred Journal: Firewritten II*, they are yellowy brown, in *IV*, salmon pink. In *Charred Journal: Firewritten B*, they are a light sky blue. All of these pigments are pale and subtle, and all of them appear to the viewer where the next layer of paint, a black, fails to cover the surface. Once the under-layer was dry, Louis applied black acrylic with a knife or a brush, and rather than covering the entire surface, the brush marks left gaps through which the coloured under-layer can be seen. These gaps are both between strokes and between bristles, suggesting that the brush was either not loaded with paint, or was somewhat dry when it touched and moved down the canvas. The strokes are always vertical, so that the black resembles the carbon trace a candle marks on a wall. They leave the surface looking dirty rather than covered, looking patchy and chary.

The next stage of the process was the construction of grid lines. These become increasingly clear to sight as one moves back from the painting. The grid lines lie over the black layer in three paintings: *IV*, *B* and C. Here, the grids have been made by pouring a dark black in thin lines across and down the surface. The lines stretch to all four edges of the canvas, dividing the surface into unequal squares. They are deliberately wavy and their thickness wavers too. In *B*, some verticals are allowed to split, and before rejoining, they momentarily appear as double lines similar to those in Brice Marden's *Cold Mountain* drawings of 1990–92. In the other four paintings, the grid has been marked quite differently. Here, patches of the under-layer of paint stretch across or up the surface. These grids have been made by the removal, rather than the addition, of paint, and the lines' colours are the yellowy and salmon hues described before. Leon Berkowitz, who ran the Workshop, described the extraordinary procedure Louis employed. After 'pressing lengths of toilet paper into the wet paint of the background', Louis removed the paper and with it, the black paint.[18] If this gives a sense of Louis's experimentation, the painstaking nature of the procedure is exposed when we notice that in these four paintings the horizontals are not straight, but broken up between the verticals. Short lengths of paper must have been pressed individually

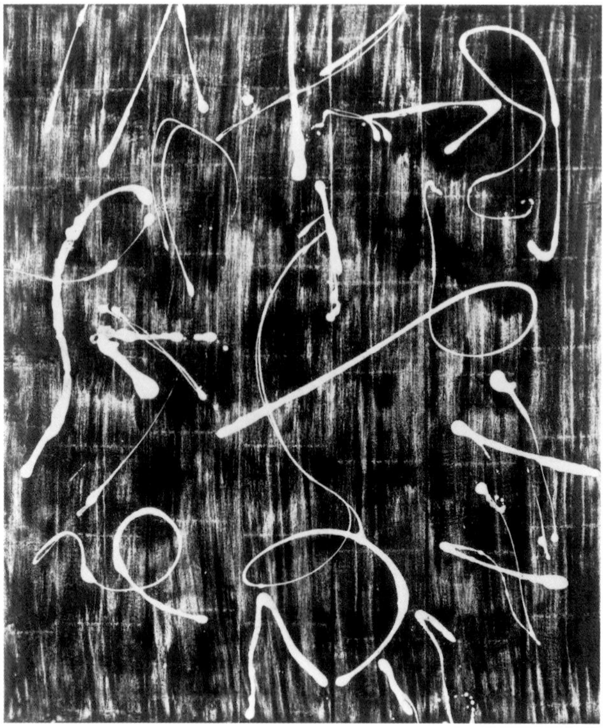

11 Morris Louis, *Charred Journal: Firewritten A*, 1951. Acrylic on canvas, 91.8 × 76.2 cm, Louisiana Museum of Modern Art, Humlebaek, Denmark. Gift of Marcella Louis Brenner / The American Federation of Arts, 1981.

between the vertical lines, carefully removed, and then placed again in between the next two verticals, still along a horizontal, but at a slightly higher or lower level. The top layer of paint is the white acrylic swerving around the surfaces. Once the black was dry, and the grids complete, the canvases would have been lifted from their easels and placed on the floor. Bending low down over the canvas, Louis then must have poured white paint, using an instrument that enabled him to control the flow without over-precision: the white lines differ in their width, suggesting that paint flowed at different speeds as he moved the pouring instrument over the surface. Louis must have been close to the paintings when he poured the white paint: there are very few instances where we see splash marks at the beginning of a strand, a necessary consequence of pouring from a distance.

In each painting, the white lines cover the surface rather than being concentrated in the centre or towards one edge. But though there are several lines across each painting, they do not dominate or crowd the surface as much as traverse it with a fairly regular density. The number of individual pours differs between paintings: in *V* and *C*, Louis poured around ten different trails of white paint across the surface; in *I* and *II*, there are at least double the number of individual pours. Compared to a Pollock painting such as *Number 26A, 1948: Black and White* (1948), in all the *Charred Journal: Firewritten* paintings the pouring is sparse. Whereas Pollock blotted out most of the underlying canvas, the black ground of these paintings is never eclipsed. The sparseness of lines also means that each line can be distinguished separately, read as a char-

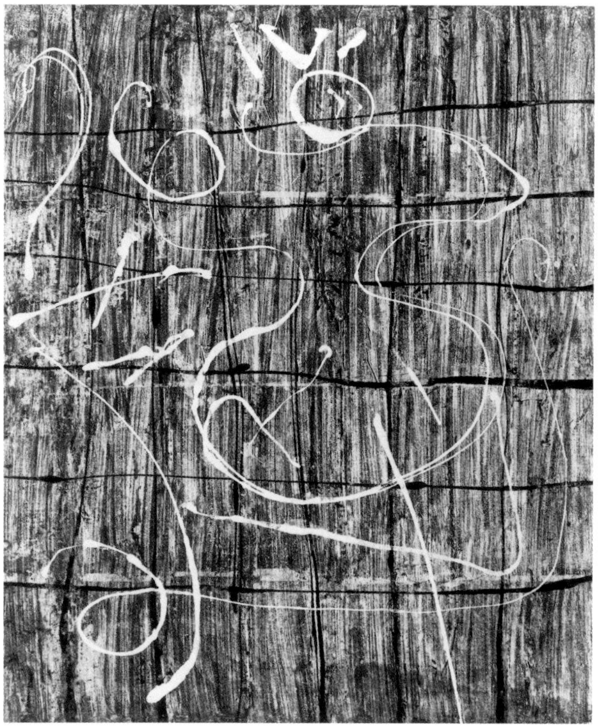

12 Morris Louis, *Charred Journal: Firewritten B*, 1951. Acrylic on canvas, 91.8 × 76.2 cm, Louisiana Museum of Modern Art, Humlebaek, Denmark. Gift of Marcella Louis Brenner / The American Federation of Arts, 1981.

acter would be. Each painting contains a variety of long lines and short lines, angular jolts and graceful curves. There are collections of lines that seem to resemble recognisable configurations – the number three (*I*), a zigzag (*II*), a triangle within a triangle (*I*), a spiral (*II*), a cross (*V*, *A*) – and collections that look like a chaotic mess. There are moments where a line is followed by another, bending with it as it copies its contours (*IV*), and moments when white lines – for instance the two longest lines in *IV* – seem to mirror each other across an invisible line of symmetry. A final feature of the white lines is revealed when really close to the surface. The white paint, though slightly raised from the surface, has a rather weak consistency, and is somewhat transparent. The black beneath it is always visible.

This kind of description provides as accurate as possible an account of appearance and process. As was clear from the account of Michael Fried's text, the issue of process has always been important in descriptions of Louis's work. In his 1968 essay 'Anti Form', Robert Morris championed artists who attempted to use materials in non-associative ways, bringing out what Morris argued was their essential physical properties. Pollock was a kind of figurehead, as he 'was able to recover process and hold on to it as part of the end of the work'.[19] Louis 'was even closer to matter in his use of the container itself to pour the fluid [and] used directly the physical, fluid properties of paint'.[20] Rather than the consummate modernist painter, Louis could momentarily be seen as an alternative precedent for the 'process' artists like Morris, Eva Hesse, and Richard Serra. If Morris's anti-form and Fried's formalism were poles apart, the two agreed on the importance of impersonality in Louis's process, an impersonality that blocks out expressionism, but which also blocks out the possibility of other kinds of meaning. They also agreed on a rather restricted understanding of process confined to the physical activity of making a painting alone, excluding from consideration the processes of thinking prior to working, and of bringing a painting to its audience.

The actual conditions of Louis's post-'breakthrough' processes have been described, but have remained obscure on account of Louis's unwillingness to accept studio visits.[21] His widow, herself restricted from entering Louis's studio, has provided accounts of his daily routine: 'He rose very early, worked every day – often seven days a week – until early afternoon when he was obliged to stop to allow the canvas to dry. He seemed never to run out of ideas, and was halted from time to time only by a non-delivery of cotton duck or paint or by a strained back. He could scarcely tolerate these interruptions and was always in a fury to get back to work.'[22] Here we have the notion of the artist in private (and bodily) consort with materials. However, another account from Marcella Louis Brenner describes Louis's working day: 'He was an avid newspaper reader. He would get up very early in the morning, come downstairs, drink very strong coffee which he made in a white coffee pot, read the paper with great understanding. He was an excellent prognosticator of political events. As a matter of fact uncomfortably so.'[23] Brenner's remarks might seem an appropriate place to begin a reconsideration of the process of painting the *Charred Journal: Firewritten* series. Rather than imagining an artist at work with materials, we are forced to think of an artist who starts his days with actual journals, whose thoughts and 'prognostications' might not end at the breakfast table, but might be brought into the studio. The story introduces the vexed and massive question of the impact of world events on the process of painting. It also helps introduce an extended notion of process: titling and exhibiting of work can also be thought of as an essential part of this extended process.

The precise circumstances of how Louis gave titles to his work are not known. Information comes in the form of memories provided in the mid-1970s over twenty-five years after the paintings were made. Leon Berkowitz recalled that while Louis painted at the Washington Workshop, Louis and Ida Berkowitz, his wife and the co-director of the Workshop, would have 'naming sessions. For several days he would free-associate, and then came those titles like *Tranquilities*, *Charred Journal: Fire Written*, and so on'.[24] Diane Upright, after interviewing the Berkowitzs in 1975, wrote that 'Ida encouraged Louis to talk about his feelings during the execution of the works.'[25] Neither story is very helpful in establishing precisely how, or at what point in the process of making the work, the title was conceived; nor is it possible to know whether the free-associative process of titling applied in the same way to different series of works made in the years Louis worked at the Workshop. In any case, it seems from existing chronologies of Louis's career that he had completed the *Charred Journal: Firewritten* series *before* he joined the Workshop in 1952.[26] This would suggest that the naming sessions that took place with Ida Berkowitz related to the titling of the paintings of 1952, and not to the *Charred Journal: Firewritten* series of 1951. The actual verbal makeup of the title suggests this further. The words 'Charred Journal: Firewritten' hardly have the whimsical, poetic feel one might expect of a title generated in a free-association session, such as is in evidence, for instance, in the titles *The Tranquilities*, *Within-Without* or *Vertical Vertigo*, all 1952 works exhibited with the *Charred Journal: Firewritten* paintings in 1953. Rather, 'Charred Journal: Firewritten' seems an awkward collection of words – a past participle and noun positioned across a colon next to another verbal adjective, 'firewritten', this an invented word, somehow a shortening of 'written by' or 'in fire'.

Both Berkowitz's and Upright's accounts, moreover, are provided from the position of modernist orthodoxy – one from a high modernist artist, another from a modernist scholar. Earlier in her text, Upright quoted William Rubin's remark that: 'As with certain other modern artists, titles were of little interest to Louis, who preferred them to numbers simply for reasons of convenience. Many of the titles of his works were suggested by friends.'[27] Rubin was responding to a mistake he perceived Joseph Masheck to have made in 1971 when Masheck over-analysed Louis's later titles in an *Artforum* review. Rubin was right in arguing that Louis had ceased titling works himself in his late years: the generic names for the 'Veils', 'Unfurleds' and 'Stripes' *had* been provided by friends. Yet the title was a problem for modernism in general, introducing the possibility of non-visual content into the meanings of the work.[28] At worst, a title could suggest to a viewer a literary meaning of a visual work.

I will be arguing that the titles of the *Charred Journal: Firewritten* paintings might have provoked viewers to make meanings in a more complex manner than the direct and literal ways that the modernist critics feared. What is important to stress now in relation to the *Charred Journal: Firewritten* series – before we come to consider what a viewer might have made of them – is that Louis did have agency in the writing of this title. Indeed, it is not only the complexity of its associative possibilities that indicates a greater degree of deliberation than is suggested in the accounts of Berkowitz and Upright, but its awkward verbal makeup.

The most important indication that the title meant a lot to Louis comes from the press account of his show. Louis's 1953 show was his first ever solo exhibition, and the first that would grant him press coverage. The paintings were the first on display at the Workshop, and the first listed in the small pamphlet that contained a brief paragraph on Louis's work written by Leon Berkowitz. Berkowitz recorded artistic influences and praised formal innovations: 'One is sometimes reminded of Miró's sureness of control, sometimes of Klee's finality of linear statement.'[29] The *Washington Post* review of the exhibition, however, sidestepped formal influences to state that the *Charred Journal: Firewritten* paintings were 'based, according to the artist, on the book burnings of the Nazis'.[30] Louis must have found time at the opening to speak to his reviewers, to supply information not found in the pamphlet, and only (as we shall explore) suggested by the paintings' titles. It was not the case that the titles were unnecessary and unfortunate supplements to the proper visual content of the work, as a critic like Rubin might contend. Rather, the title was insufficient, and had itself to be supplemented by this comment. Perhaps Louis was anxious that the significations of the paintings would be missed. Perhaps he had wanted the information to be included in the pamphlet, and was making up for its absence. Whatever the circumstances, the event constitutes another part of the process by which his work was introduced to his audience. The story requires us, as it might have required the readers of the *Washington Post*, to re-insert into the imagined idea of Louis in the studio an ongoing sense of purpose during the construction of the *Charred Journal: Firewritten* series; a desire for the paintings not just to look formally ambitious, but to have historical significance.

'reading' the *charred journal: firewritten* series

Today, the *Charred Journal* paintings are divided between the Jewish Museum in New York, and the Louisiana Museum in Denmark. The latter institution received them from Louis's widow in recognition of Danish support for Jews during the Holocaust. When they are viewed the encounter is affected by these institutional circumstances and, of course, by theories of spectatorship and interpretation that have developed since the 1950s. But what would attentive viewers have made of the paintings in 1953? The historical spectators – and it is necessary to retain a notion of their plurality and diversity – were conditioned by other circumstances to our own; no less determined, but different. Some of the meanings such spectators were able to generate were available because of historical contingencies: they might not, for instance, have been as readily available to viewers of the paintings in 1970. Some of the meanings were available to viewers with particular kinds of knowledge determined less by historical situations, and more, for instance, by ethnic background. Ascertaining whether viewers actually 'read' the paintings in the manner I will go on to describe is less important than acknowledging the availability of a multiplicity of meanings.

Nonetheless one can explore what a viewer might have expected of abstract painting shown at the Workshop in 1953. Though the institution's primary function was to offer courses such as 'Ceramics for Beginners', 'Understanding Music', and Louis's own 'Oil Painting', it was also the venue for ambitious art in Washington D.C. Familiar with the Workshop programme, and with recent advanced painting, a visitor might have expected many things of abstraction. Knowing the work of Jackson Pollock, they might have desired a surface to deliver what Greenberg had described in 1949 as 'a sumptuous variety of design and incident'.[31] Eagerly awaiting Willem De Kooning's debut Washington exhibition, which opened at the Workshop a month after Louis's closed, they might have looked forward to a 'an uncrowded canvas' with 'heavy somatic shapes'; again, Greenberg's words.[32] But in 1953, modernist theory was not yet entrenched enough for viewers to expect of abstraction *only* surface. Though Greenberg did not see the relevance of symbols for the quality of a painting, writing about an exhibition by Adolph Gottlieb in 1947, he had attended to 'the "symbols" [Gottlieb] puts into his canvases'. Though these had 'no explicit meaning', they called up 'racial memories, archetypes, archaic but constant responses'.[33] So paintings might contain symbols, but the 'racial memories' they prompted were never specific. A work might even relate to recent history. Recalling paintings such as *The Escape Ladder* from his 'Constellations' series, which were made under the shadow of Spanish fascism, Joan

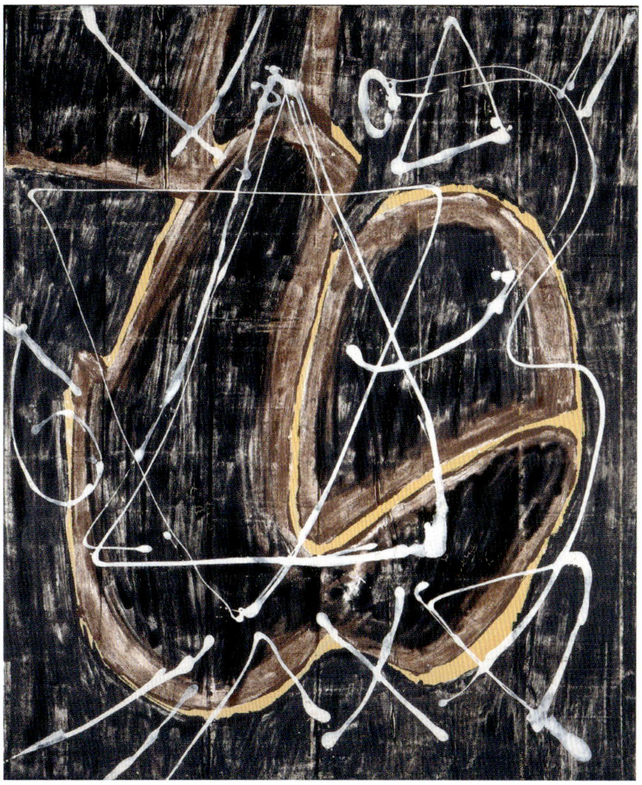

13 Morris Louis, *Untitled (Jewish Star)*, 1951. Acrylic on canvas, 86.4 × 72.4 cm, The Jewish Museum, New York.

Miró had spoken of his use of a ladder-like grid in an interview of 1949 as a form that meant 'escape'. Miró stumbled over his terms, calling the form, within three sentences, 'nostalgic', 'plastic', 'symbolic' and 'poetic'.[34] Louis had participated in the 1930s in the pro-Republican movement and had recently used Miró's metaphorical form. A 1949 painting called *The Ladder* shows such a one stretched across its surface. This brief context reveals that the symbol still had some currency within abstraction. It suggests that a spectator might have anticipated some vague symbolic referent. But the idea that an abstract painting could refer to a specific historical moment, a particular catastrophe such as the book burnings, would have been, and indeed remains, extremely problematic.

However, a painting with an explicit symbol might have been able to work in this way. Apart from the *Charred Journals*, the only other painting of 1951 that Louis allowed to survive was *Untitled (Jewish Star)* (fig. 13). Though he had shown it at the Workshop in a group exhibition some months before his solo exhibition, this painting was importantly never part of the *Charred Journal: Firewritten* series. Yet, unlike all the rest of Louis's paintings, it is constructed in exactly the same way as the *Charred Journals*, except for the presence of strokes of orange and yellow paint *above* the black acrylic as well as below it. The painting's significant difference, though, is that *its* white lines form the well-known configuration of two interlocking triangles.[35] 'Racial memories' were certainly conjured here, but unlike Gottlieb's symbols, they were specifically Jewish references. The presentation of the Star of David might very well have enabled a spectator to consider the history of persecution through the recollection of Nazi laws decreeing that the Jew wear the yellow star. In 1949, Gershom Scholem had investigated 'The Curious History of the Six Pointed Star', and, stressing its non-religious history, he recognised that its contemporary meaning grew from its having been the 'badge of shame for millions of our people'. Hitler had

> compelled them to wear it publicly on their clothing as the badge of exclusion and of eventual extermination. Under this sign they moved along the road of horror and degradation, struggle and heroism. If there is such a thing as a soil that grows meanings for symbols, this is it. Some have said: the sign under which they went to destruction and to the gas chambers deserves to be discarded for a sign that will signify life. But it is also possible to think in the opposite fashion: the sign that in our days was sanctified by suffering and torture has won its right to be the sign that will light up the road of construction and life.[36]

For Scholem the star suggested light as well as death, and it could be used as a symbol of cultural optimism as well as memorial. Perhaps this is true of the star in Louis's painting, surrounded as it is by a halo of yellow and orange. Like Jasper Johns' *Star* of 1954 (fig. 14; commissioned by a Jewish friend who had fled Nazi persecution[37]), the canvas points backwards to a traumatic history and forwards to tentative but much desired senses of optimism and unashamed pride. While doing so it suggests the multiple potentials of the symbol, rather than its redundancy. However, these readings seem of little help when we return to the starless surface of the *Charred Journals*.

What is the significance of the absence of the star in the *Charred Journal: Firewritten* paintings? Why did Louis abandon the easy symbolism of the Jewish star? Perhaps the star was 'too Jewish'. This is not necessarily to suggest that the public declaration of ethnic identity was difficult for Louis – his widow stresses he never shied away from Jewishness[38] – but it is worth remembering Greenberg's argument of 1950 about 'positive Jewishness'. Overt proclamation of Jewish identity was, Greenberg had indicated, just an inverted form of self-hatred. Alternatively, the problem of *Untitled (Jewish Star)* might have been that the star excluded the memory of other, non-Jewish victims of Nazi persecution. The absence of the star might equally reveal a hesitancy about the employment of the symbol *per se*, a hesitancy we might even detect on the surface of *Untitled (Jewish Star)*, which, it should be stated, presents its star only tentatively, in juxtaposition with indecipherable collections of white lines. The roots of this hesitancy are divided. Totalitarian reliance on the organising power of the symbol might have made any use of symbols problematic after the Holocaust. Just as, for some survivors, the German language was forever tarnished, so too symbolic language was problematised. From the perspective of art practice, any use of a symbol on a surface was increasingly difficult. Though Johns could paint *Star* as a commission the year after the exhibition of the *Charred Journal: Firewritten* paintings, this was only months before his *White Flag* (1955) strategically emptied out the symbol, posing its abstraction as a counter to its obvious 'meaning'. So the Magen David in *Untitled (Jewish Star)* might

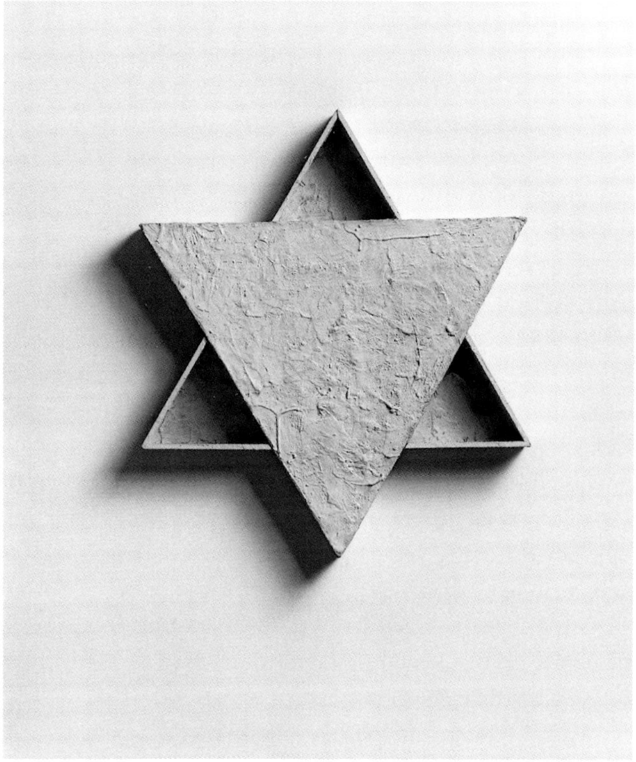

14 Jasper Johns, *Star*, 1954. Oil, beeswax, and housepaint on newspaper, canvas, and wood with tinted glass, nails, and fabric tape, 57.2 × 49.5 × 4.8 cm, The Menil Collection, Houston.

signal the swansong for the symbol that would be absent from advanced painting from then on.

These are possible answers, but I want to suggest that the absence of the star allows for the presence of interpretative indeterminacy. The *Charred Journal: Firewritten* paintings respond to the Holocaust through their very refusal of the direct symbol; through the possibilities created by the spectator's inability to establish a straightforward connection of surface – through symbol – to history. This is an argument to which I will return, but first it is necessary to describe how interpretative possibilities might have been built up during the encounter with the *Charred Journal: Firewritten* paintings.

The most obvious springboard for interpretative activity in these paintings would be the black paint. Confronted by blackness, and recognising the colour of mourning, the historical spectator might have been given cause to consider an object of mourning. The context for the *Charred Journals* was Picasso's *Guernica*, whose 'shock lies in the very fact that colour is totally absent. The black, grey and white treatment of a particular theme serves to give it great force.'[39] These last words are Louis's: they could draw us to think that he used black and white in a similar way. However, there is problem with any argument that positions blackness as a straightforward signifier of mourning here. At this precise time, black-and-white painting, rather than indicating gloom, was the *mode par excellence* of advanced artistic practice. Writing on Willem

De Kooning, Arshille Gorky, Adolph Gottlieb and Jackson Pollock in 1948, Greenberg had commented that 'by excluding the full range of colour, and concentrating on black and white and their derivatives, the most ambitious members of this generation hope to solve [. . .] the problems [of painting].'[40] In 1950, there had even been an exhibition devoted to 'Black or White: Paintings by European and American Artists' at Samuel Kootz, which included Hans Hofmann, William Baziotes, Mark Tobey and Bradley Walker Tomlin. Robert Motherwell wrote the catalogue.[41]

Nonetheless many viewers did still think of blackness in terms of mourning or destruction at this time. Robert Rauschenberg's black paintings of 1951 were received in this way. Rauschenberg later complained that 'people thought the black was about old and burned and tarred. . . . They couldn't see black as a pigment. They moved immediately into association with "burned-out", "tearing", "nihilism", and "destruction"'.[42] As Brandon Joseph has recently noted, this reception was problematic for Rauschenberg, who wanted to wrestle materials and colours from metaphoric associations, but Louis's project was different. If Rauschenberg's viewers saw burning without any prompt from his titles, even more could Louis's audiences consider the associative possibilities of black paint when faced with the name 'Charred Journals'. It is through the series' title that the black paint gains its importance: the words tempt the connection of the canvases' blackened surfaces to the idea of a burnt page, and the consequent bond between the delicate under-layer colours with that which was burnt. This metaphor might actually be grounded in resemblance, for, next to the very different black surfaces made by these various painters, Louis courted the look of a burnt page: Pollock's, Still's, Kline's, Motherwell's and even Rauschenberg's blacks might appear reflective, textured, intense, or dull; but never so much like charred paper. Through the connection of surface to the burnt page, a link (which is always necessarily frail) is established with the Nazi book burnings. Louis's spectators would have been provoked to ruminate on this event.

Of course the book burnings could not be recalled as a self-contained event, cut off from subsequent Nazi activities and their contemporary ramifications in the 1950s. Even in 1933 when the book burning had been reported in New York they had been understood as an incident with much wider significance.[43] On 11 May, the editor of the *New York Times* wrote that: 'They certainly symbolise something! Such an exhibition of the new national spirit, silly and shameful as it seems, bespeaks a mass-movement plainly touched with insanity.'[44] In a cartoon from *The Nation* published a week after the event, the incident was understood to embody the threat posed by Nazism to enlightened thought and culture everywhere (fig. 15). In the flames were books bearing the names of Heine, Mann, Einstein, Felix Mendelsohn and Jack London, as well as 'The Bible' and 'The Nation' itself. By 1953, with twenty years of historical hindsight, the symbolic significance of the book burnings would have expanded even more.

To probe what the memory of the book burnings might have meant for a spectator in 1953 we can explore two overlapping spheres. The first sphere is that of the secular Jewish intellectual, and the second, of the leftist, anti-Stalinist American. Louis and

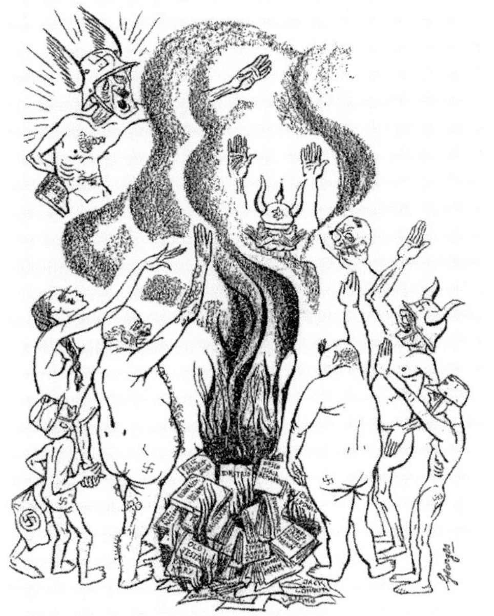

15 *The Burning of the Books*, cartoon published in *The Nation*, 17 May 1933.

some of his viewers might have been positioned within the overlap, but for a while it is helpful to unfix the spheres. For the secular Jewish intellectual, the memory of the book burnings contributed to an ongoing cultural anxiety. In the immediate post-war period, writers were busy interrogating the fuller implications of the cultural exclusion evidenced most concretely in May 1933. Immediately after the book burnings, Nazi legislation had prevented Jews from publishing in German and from using the Gothic typescript. Such laws were premised on notions that just as Jewish blood infected the Aryan body, so Jewish use infected his language. Of the many kinds of debates prompted by the Holocaust that took place in the Jewish journals after the war, one of the most fascinating revolved around the questions raised by these laws – questions of the diasporic Jew's relationship to the writing, language and literature of their host countries.

In 1953, the widespread nature of the premises that led to the book burnings was increasingly clear. Sartre's *Anti-Semite and Jew*, much discussed after its American publication in 1948, recalled those who 'declared a Jew forever incapable of understanding a line of Racine'.[45] Sartre's text highlighted the pervasiveness of cultural anti-Semitism but it was also a symptom of the problem, as his schema left no space for authentic secular Jewish culture. Commentators such as Harold Rosenberg responded with articles such as his 'Does the Jew exist?'[46] and had barely recovered from Sartre's text when later in 1949 they were forced to negotiate a local offence. The Bollingen Poetry award for that year was awarded to Ezra Pound. In the wake of the award, *Commentary* published a symposium entitled 'The Jewish Writer and the English Tradition'. Intellectuals who had once sidelined reservations about anti-Semitism in literary culture now met this threat head on. Clement Greenberg's brother Martin

Greenberg expressed the situation of the culturally excluded Jew most forcefully. 'To use a language and not to own it,' he wrote, 'to live with a literature and not to possess it – this is only to say that I am a Jew.'[47] The secular Jewish intellectual subject, already divided by the multiple allegiances to Jewishness, to America, to tradition and to progress (those rifts Clement Greenberg had described), was unable even to 'own' the language with which to communicate these rifts. Martin Greenberg's comment even suggests that in protesting Pound's award, the Jewish intellectual was compromised by the condition that the means of protest (the English language) and object of protest (literature in English) were not really felt to be the Jew's to start with. Alfred Kazin, meanwhile, questioned whether to burn Pound's book. 'No, no', he concluded. 'There have been too many books banned and burned already. We have been too long on the *index expurgatorius* to make one of our own.'[48]

So the book burnings were invoked in 1949 only to be discarded as an impossibility, a reaction to a threat that might be suited to barbaric regimes, but never to Jews. But books *were* burnt in the States at this time, not by enraged New York Jews, but by American librarians. This brings us to the second sphere. During the McCarthyite period, librarians were known to destroy books whose presence might suggest their un-American affiliation. A 1959 study on censorship records a librarian telling the researcher 'in a self-pitying way . . . "Did you ever try to burn a book. It's *very* difficult"'.[49] Though he worked right at the heart of Washington, we cannot tell if Louis knew of such events. His wife was a school principal, and perhaps encountered pressures to censor reading lists. However, in interview she indicated that though each day brought more news of old friends now hounded by the House Un-American Activities Committee, she had never known of actual book burnings in early 1950s Washington, and indeed, the examples were extremely rare.[50]

It is more likely that Louis knew of the McCarthyite reaction to contemporary artists and art critics. In 1949, for instance, Congressman George Dondero of Michigan had suggested that newspapers exercise 'proper supervision' and 'start cleaning house in the smaller compartments of their organisations' to rid themselves of art critics glorifying 'the vulgar, the distorted, and the perverted' work of artists who themselves constituted a threat to the state.[51] This 'hysteria' had drawn Peyton Boswell of *Art Digest* to invoke the book burnings. Ridiculing Dondero's claim that 'it is not my purpose to suggest that newspapers should clap censorship on their art critics', Boswell exclaimed 'Like hell Dondero doesn't want censorship! What else does he mean by "proper supervision"? In other words, do as Hitler once did with "degenerate" modern art and burned books.'[52]

Louis himself might not have shared common political ground with Boswell, but like him, he seems to have found the book burnings a compelling memory to raise at this turbulent moment. But where Boswell invokes this memory directly, Louis seems to have been more reticent. The memory of Nazi book burnings was invoked to share a critique of McCarthyism through 'private communication' with 'trustworthy and intelligent readers'.[53] These are the terms of the Chicago-based Jewish philosopher Louis Strauss, who in 1952 published *Persecution and the Art of Writing*. Also contemporary with Louis's paintings was Ray Bradbury's novel *Fahrenheit 451* (1950), which

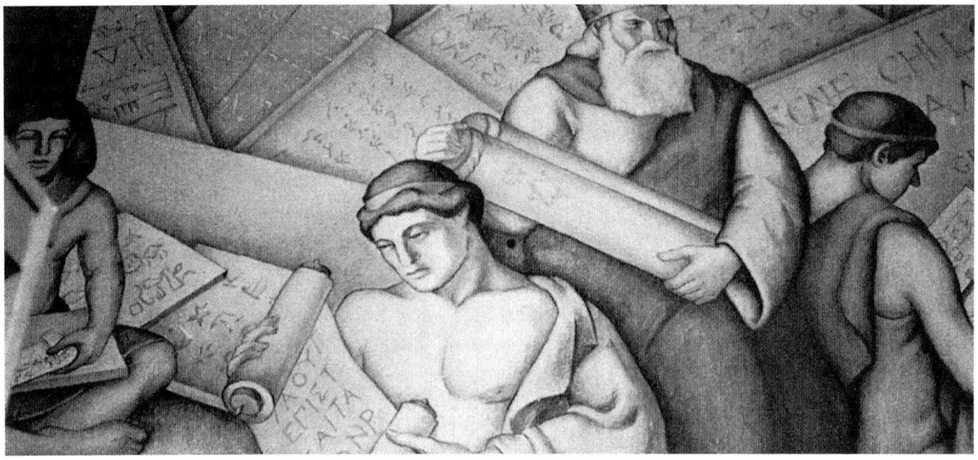

16 Maurice Bernstein (Morris Louis), Sam Swerdloff and Calvin Hisley, *The History of the Written Word*, detail of panel 1, 1934. Hampstead Hill School, Baltimore, Maryland.

described a dystopia in which firemen hunt libraries to burn. Bradbury's symbolism was an indictment of the present.

Provoked to recall the book burnings, the spectators of the *Charred Journal: Firewritten* paintings might have been reminded both of the cultural anxieties facing contemporary Jewish intellectuals, and of the more tangible threats bearing on those – including artists – whose sympathies lay on the left. For some spectators, as for Louis, both these burdens were felt at once. The acrylic paint maker Leonard Bocour was one of the only spectators who recorded memories of the paintings. He located the series' significance exactly within the overlap of these concerns. Remembering that Louis's 'whole gang was very, very left', he went on to state that Louis 'did a whole series of paintings called the *Charred Journal: Firewritten* paintings. And I have one of them. . . . It was all black and white really. And, as I say, he was aware of the world he lived in and he was certainly anti-Nazi.'[54]

Like the surface of the paintings, the experience of the encounter was never so black and white, but before turning from the black paint to the white, we should take a moment to posit another dimension of the metonymic rhetoric of the *Charred Journal: Firewritten* paintings. They might prompt memories of the human disaster, at the same time as thoughts of a cultural and political one: from the burning of the books, we move in thought to the burning of bodies. Through the ancient naming of Jews as 'the people of the book', through the knowledge that traditionally, Jewish artists could only be scribes, and through the resonance of Heine's prophetic words, 'where they burn books, they will burn people', the hand-made Jewish book is bound up with the body. Though these phrases plunder Jewish history, all the destroyed bodies of the Holocaust, Jewish and non-Jewish, seem tentatively addressed through the memory of the book burnings.[55]

I mentioned earlier that the white lines on the paintings could have suggested a kind of writing. As has been indicated already, each line is far more distinct than the swirls covering Pollock's paintings. A line might be crossed by itself as it loops round, or by another, fresh line dripped on top of it, but each line always remains individual, and has its own shape. This very distinction is what troubled Michael Fried: Louis's lines did not perform the job of line in Pollock's painting, which was to efface its own identity, bounding not shape, but eyesight. But though each white line can be read apart from the other white lines, and from the background, it is also immediately clear that these lines are not recognisable characters from any linguistic script. There are triangles and spirals and crosses, but these configurations are never far from swirls and angled lines that elicit no kind of recognition.

Just beneath the layer of white paint, there are the grid lines, constructed at times by dripping black paint across the surface, at times by removing the layer beneath. If read metaphorically, the grid might have suggested the frame of a pyre, such as the frames that the books were hurled onto in May 1933.[56] This would make of the white lines a kind of burnt writing, akin to the script in the burnt books. We might also recall Louis's painting *The Ladder* and Miró's comments: the ladder was associated with the idea of 'escape' from the conditions of fascism. If a kind of escape ladder, the grid might metaphorically protect the letters from charring, acting as a block between them and the fires. Then, the white lines could have suggested renewed, rather than ruined, writing. The suggestion is strengthened if we return to one of the precise words in the title, 'firewritten'. Just as the words 'Charred Journals' triggered a rich associative constellation of ideas, so too might this phrase.

What does 'firewriting' mean? Some sense is made of this word through Jewish texts about the origins of writing. After the war, there was a growth of interest in mystical texts such as the Midrash and Kabbalah, but Louis himself might have read such texts earlier when working in 1934 on *The History of the Written Word*, a Public Works of Art Project mural for a Baltimore school library, which featured images of a rabbi holding a Torah (fig. 16). In early Midrashim, and Kabbalistic commentaries on them, the origin of the Torah is discussed again and again.[57] The Torah is formulated neither as an historical narrative (that is, the five books describing the story between the creation and the arrival in Canaan), nor is it simply a literal object (a white parchment inscribed with letters of black ink). *Both* these formulations are in play in the myths that surround the original Torah. According to some mystical texts, long before the events it describes took place, the Torah consisted of both the words of the five books, and all the later interpretations of them. Some origin myths concern the ways through which the written Torah (the books) and oral Torah (the future interpretations) became distinct, and it is here that the notion of firewriting emerges: the written Torah was thought to burn before God in letters of white fire on the black fire of the oral Torah. At first, the letters were not recognisable.

Various different Kabbalistic texts describe different versions of these myths, some associating the oral Torah with white fire, the written one with black. It is not important here to pinpoint a precise point of Kabbalistic scholarship, but rather to realise that firewriting is associated – even through a lay understanding – with the *creation* of the book, rather than with its destruction. Indeed, white fire is the original form of writing in the original book; the *medium* of writing. Interestingly, the myths are extremely visual, describing the origin of the book through the distinction of figure and ground that occurs when white fire is seen against black, but also when black ink stands out against white parchment. Turning back to Louis's paintings, the myths seem first to inform the way we could now think about the mark as a figure against a ground. The myths provide an alternative origin for the conception of the 'first mark' with little to do with modernist flatness. More importantly, through these myths, the white lines become suggestive of the renaissance of writing since the Jewish book, though destroyed by flames, was born as flames.

A precarious optimism might have developed as a viewer considered the white lines in this way: the white lines suggested the rebirth of Jewish culture. Looking back at the discourse of post-Holocaust Jewish intellectuals, we can see continual if desperate signs of optimism. In his 1945 editorial for the first issue of *Commentary*, Elliot Cohen hoped that the new journal would be a crucible for a Jewish renaissance, and described the establishment of the periodical as an 'act of faith', the lighting of 'our candle' in 'the midst of this turbulence and these whirlwinds'.[58] In this configuration fire again suggests optimism rather than destruction, but unlike the word 'firewritten', Cohen's is a general, even Catholic allusion, and not a Jewish one. Other Jewish myths help make even more sense of Louis's white lines.

The arrangement of the lines on the canvases might recall a Hasidic text which imagines that, before creation, the Torah 'formed a heap of letters'; an 'incoherent jumble'[59] that arranged itself into words as the events it described took place. Again there is an idea of the origin of books, of rebirth. A third myth is better known to secular Jews. When Moses saw the Golden Calf and destroyed God's tablets, the letters on the tablets flew away, since unlike the stone they were indestructible. Describing the paintings, Louis's wife said he had tried to 'capture the effect of letters and symbols rising like ashes from the surface of a burned page'.[60] Perhaps Louis wished to suggest that like God's letters, the writing burnt by Nazi fires would not be destroyed, but would fly away unharmed. Or conversely, there is the idea that the letters that flew away at Sinai *reappear* after the book burnings across the blackened pages of Jewish history, perhaps to form a new Torah.

Interpretative possibilities abound for spectators familiar with these myths, and well they might given the traditions of Jewish interpretative activities. After all, the biblical commentator Rashi, who, extraordinarily, is listed as a 'prominent maternal ancestor'[61] in Louis's own resumé, likened 'the various interpretations offered by the rabbis for a single biblical verse to the sparks that fly when a hammer is struck upon a rock'.[62] There is another sense of the energetic power of fire here, but in Rashi's metaphor there is also a sense that interpretation does damage. Something is chipped away to make sparks. Perhaps one might also say that the attempt to read Louis's white lines through Jewish texts also does damage. The precise material character and appearance of the surfaces has to be forgotten in order to maintain the readings confidently, and failing to attend to the canvases in this way is a form of damage to them. The layering of paint might suggest moments of creation being superimposed on moments of destruction; the grids might be read as protecting the white lines from the blackness; but when attention is paid once again to the surfaces of the paintings, they pull us back from accepting these readings absolutely. Not only is a spectator unable to see white lines

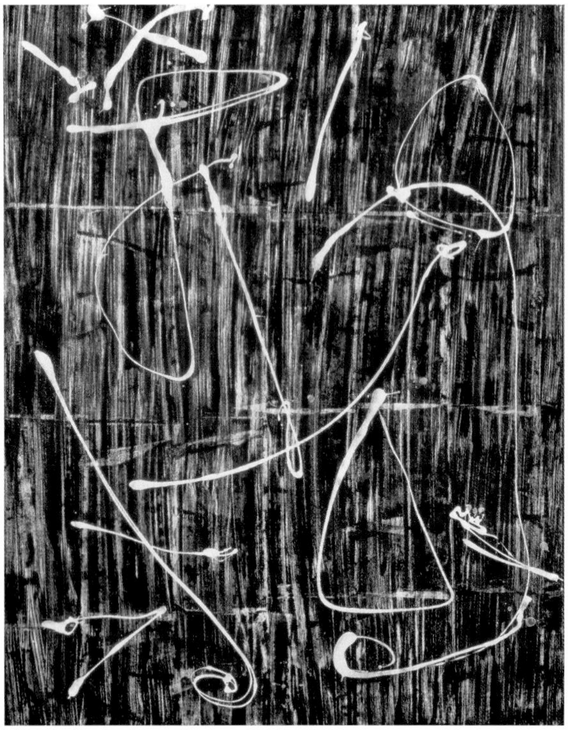

17 Morris Louis, *Charred Journal: Firewritten V*, 1951. Acrylic on canvas, 86.4 × 66.0 cm, The Jewish Museum, New York.

without sensing the blackness around them, but the thin and transparent white acrylic also leaves the blackness visible below.

The sense of optimism is also tempered by the stasis of the various paintings. Like modernist series, there is no narrative or thematic progression from one painting to the next. Spectators might know that God's letters escaped destruction on Sinai, but it is clear that from painting to painting, the white lines do not fly away. They might know that the Torah started as a jumble of incoherence, but then, across the canvases, white lines become no more distinct, no nearer to recognisable letters. The cumulative effect of the various paintings is, then, to tempt the possibility that there might be a progressive movement starting from an originary moment, but to deny a sense of progress. If considered as pages in a journal, the canvases do not show a progression of events, but seem as writings in a diary of an ongoing disaster (fig. 17).

'absent meaning'

In an essay on the history of titles, Stephen Bann quotes Proust, for whom a 'name sanctioned by memory can become [like] "one of those little balloons in which oxygen has been enclosed"'.[63] Proust's simile visualises the potential of the titling name, but also the dangers of staking too much on a title: the balloon can pop. Just so, in front of the *Charred Journals*, the associations and readings a viewer makes might disappear, and for many the interpretations I have been constructing through the titles would not even *begin* to have developed. Michael Fried, for instance, would never have looked at the title in order to explore the possible significance of the works; he would never have begun to read the white lines, even as unreadable or destroyed or proto- writing. He would have seen them simply as figures against a ground. It is possible to imagine another viewer before the paintings at first considering associations and forming readings of the kind suggested in the last section of this chapter, and then suddenly halting, viewing the surfaces anew with the eyes of a modernist critic, and seeing just black and white, paint and canvas, figure and ground.

This scenario would seem to suggest that the readings I developed in the last section are extremely precarious. But what should be made of this precariousness? And what is to be made of the complete opposition of the modernist approach to the one I undertook? We could just conclude that the paintings never quite bear the burden of Louis's ambitions for them, and that his attempt merely witnesses the desperate need at this time to address the Holocaust in any way, no matter how tenuous. The paintings would signal the competing but irreconcilable claims on Louis in 1951 to be an advanced artist, *and*, as a Jew on the left, to address a charged subject. But I want to think more productively about the scenario just described. There is surely something important about the unfixability of the references to the book burnings and to the renaissance of Jewish writing. There is something compelling about the idea that the paintings can encourage interpretations of the kind I have suggested *and* also of the kind made by the modernists. Acknowledging that the paintings prompt and prompted their viewers to generate and empty away interpretations, could it be that this dynamic is the way in which the *Charred Journals* most forcefully – and at the same time most subtly – responded to their post-Holocaust situation?

Maurice Blanchot's book *The Writing of the Disaster* (1980) provides some ways of thinking through many of the features of Louis's work, and especially this dynamic.[64] Blanchot's book is itself a fractured text, consisting of paragraphs sometimes as short as a single sentence, sometimes set in different typefaces as if to give a visual sense of contrasting voices. Blanchot addresses how the disaster impinges on written attempts to represent it. The disaster is at once abstract and specific: at times, it is named simply as 'the disaster', but at other times, it is described as '*The holocaust, the* absolute *event of history – which is a date in history – that utter-burn where all history took fire, where the movement of Meaning was swallowed up*.'[65] As for the writing of the disaster, in the text, the phrase refers both to all writing, and to writing after the disaster. For Blanchot, writing always involves the writer giving up their ability to control meaning: 'to write is to renounce being in command of oneself or having any proper name';[66] 'To write is to be absolutely distrustful of writing, while entrusting oneself to it entirely.'[67] However, Blanchot seems to suggest that 'under the surveillance of the disaster', writing recognises its condition more acutely. After the disaster, 'To write is perhaps to bring to the surface something like absent meaning, to welcome the passive pressure which is not yet what we call thought, for it is already the disastrous ruin of thought.'[68]

As a condition of Blanchot's argument, it is impossible to untangle the general from the specific. However, several strands of his thought seem suggestive in the context of the discussion of Louis's paintings. Blanchot has an interest in the origins of writing:[69] like Louis he was prompted to this interest in origins by the sense of ending imposed by 'the disaster'. For instance, Blanchot discusses the work of the prehistorian Leroi-Gourham, who described 'the first evidence of writing as a series of "small notches" arranged at regular intervals'.[70] Blanchot draws from Leroi-Gourham the conclusion that: 'Design and inscription, art and writing, [are] not distinct from each other. One more affirmation: "If there is a point about which we can now be certain, it is that written signs begin, not as naive representations, but as abstractions."'[71]

Another overlap between Louis's paintings and Blanchot's book involves Blanchot's comments on fragmentation. Blanchot understands that the writing of the disaster is ruined; in fragments. 'The disaster de-scribes'.[72] The white lines on top of Louis's paintings might be a kind of fragmented 'writing of the disaster', whether damaged by the flames of the book burnings, or rising from their ashes. They are a kind of writing that does not accomplish writing's task; they cannot be read. Elsewhere, Blanchot writes that the disaster is what cannot be put into words, '*When all is said, what remains to be said is the disaster. Ruin of words, demise writing, faintness faintly murmuring: what remains without remains* (the fragmentary).'[73] Here, there is the sense that the disaster does not merely challenge attempts to represent it. Representations are not merely in fragments, ruined; rather, the disaster always 'remains to be said'. It is always beyond meaning.

The most interesting strand of Blanchot's thought is his contention that since the disaster was where 'meaning was swallowed up', there is a 'danger that the disaster acquire meaning',[74] and a related injunction to 'keep watch over absent meaning.'[75] The writing of the disaster cannot represent or respect the disaster if it allows it to acquire meaning. Absent meaning must always be guarded. Thinking back to the paintings, through this idea we can *retain* the tension between reading them, and seeing them through modernist eyes; we can retain the idea that in the course of viewing, interpretations are established and collapse. This is the very dynamic that keeps guard over absent meaning.

The *Charred Journal: Firewritten* paintings, therefore, cause their viewers to create meanings while constantly forcing these viewers to witness the breakdown of associative, symbolic and metaphorical suggestions. As the viewer constructs and discards meaning; as the paintings' status as unreadable ruined pages and formalist canvases wavers back and forth, the spectator is increasingly aware of the impossibility of fixed meaning, the absence of secured meaning. The failure of the surfaces to cement *fixed* links to the Holocaust is therefore only a necessary part of the wider success of the series to form a much stronger response to the Holocaust. The *Charred Journal: Firewritten* paintings represented one aspect of the history of the Holocaust but more importantly, the then contemporary significance of that history, its incomprehensibility and its very resistance to straightforward representation. For the viewer of the paintings, the process of making and unmaking interpretations may have been a frustrating one, but perhaps they were put through the lesson Blanchot invokes when he writes '*Learn to think with pain*'.[76]

re-viewing the late work

After showing the *Charred Journals* in the Workshop, Louis was delighted. In a letter, his wife exclaimed: 'It all came out so well that we are more than pleased.'[77] But no matter how well it all came out, Louis was on the cusp of abandoning the kind of painting he had exhibited. Seven days before the Workshop opening, he had made a rare visit to Manhattan where, accompanied by Noland and Greenberg, he had seen Helen Frankenthaler's *Mountains and Sea*. According to Greenberg and Fried, this was the moment of breakthrough. The sight of thinned acrylic stained into the very fabric of the canvas triggered his creation of huge numbers of paintings in a tiny variety of configurations: the 'Veils', the 'Unfurleds', the 'Pillars'. For most critics these paintings would mark Louis's original achievement. No longer would his work merely bear the influence of Pollock or Motherwell. The modernist notion of a breakthrough is in part upheld by Marcella Louis Brenner: the *Charred Journals*, she recalled, marked a caesura, a pause in the progress of a career heading towards proper abstraction. John Elderfield is even more certain about the break. Writing in the catalogue of Louis's posthumous Museum of Modern Art retrospective in 1987, he assumed that at the opening of his show at the Workshop, Louis must have been 'chagrined to see how inconsequential his pictures appeared compared to those he had seen in New York'.[78] Clearly Elderfield was unconcerned with the circumstances of the Washington opening, and Louis's effort to tell journalists about the *Charred Journals* and the book burnings.

After addressing the *Charred Journal: Firewritten* paintings, it is important to look again at both the concept of influence and the idea of a 'breakthrough' moment. It is clear that the *Charred Journals* evoke other contemporary abstract painting: their grids relate to those of Miró and others, their trailed lines to Pollock. Instead of taking these features just as marks of Louis's influences, we could now argue that they witness his attempt to negotiate modernism from within, to turn such painting towards the cultural subject matter of the book burnings. Louis, in other words, put a kind of pressure on the normal autonomy of modernist painting. The *Charred Journals* were not a momentary abandonment of abstraction, but an intelligent manipulation of its conventions and abilities, and of its impossibilities.

What of the idea of 'breakthrough'? For sure, Louis abandoned most of the tactics of the *Charred Journals*, and there might have been many reasons for this. Perhaps Louis thought these strategies too frail, and preferred to develop his formal experiments rather than further pursuing an impossible task. Perhaps, in taking Greenberg's continual advice, he also began to agree with his friend's cautions, expressed in the 1950 essay 'Self-Hatred and Jewish Chauvinism', that 'no matter how necessary it may be to indulge our feelings about Auschwitz, we can do so only temporarily and privately'. We cannot know exactly why Louis ceased making work in the manner of the *Charred Journals*, but we can relax the notion of a breakthrough somewhat, and, revisiting the later works, find them not at the end of modernism's cul-de-sac, but at the beginning of a different path initiated by the works of 1951. Instead of a breakthrough we can come to a more complex formulation of the simultaneous discontinuity and continuity of earlier concerns.

18 Morris Louis, *Beth Chaf*, 1959. Acrylic on canvas, 353.1 × 260.4 cm, National Gallery of Art, Washington D.C.

Curiously, a letter from Louis to Greenberg gives credence to this argument. By 1954, Louis was in regular correspondence with Greenberg, receiving advice on dealers, and discussing issues of painting and 'culture patterns'.[79] In June 1954, Louis wrote that 'I don't care a great deal about the positive accomplishments in [other artists'] work or my own since that leads to an end. I look at paintings from the negative side, what is left out is useful only as that leads to the next try and the next.' In these words, we hear the self-challenging voice of an artist who refuses to rest on any success, fuelled by a ceaseless need to move on. Already, there is a sense that rather than making about-turn changes, or 'breakthroughs', Louis might have worked on each painting project, seeing the faults in each, and moving on to the next. This letter is supposedly written a year after a 'breakthrough' – but the manner of artistic work Louis describes gives no sense that he worked in revolutions, turning his back on his entire career to date. Louis continues: 'I can't help but wish, right or wrong, to take issue with those whose fetish is promoting painting from the stomach, orgasm, or mouth. The psychology becomes a conformity to the mode of bad taste which rivals the good Anglo-Saxons, and the difference adds up to the sameness of focus.'[80]

Reading this private letter, it seems that Louis is describing a division between the culture of gestural painters (De Kooning, for instance), and that of conservative waspish Americans, and placing his way of thinking and mode of painting apart from both. Communicating with another Jewish intellectual, it might be that he was sharing feelings about their relationship to a non-Jewish 'Anglo-Saxon' cultural establishment perceived as closed-minded and conservative. Greenberg wrote to Louis on the headed paper of *Commentary*, but his letters contain no direct discussions about Jewish matters. What is interesting about Louis's letter, though, is that in protesting expressionist machismo (painting from the stomach, orgasm, or mouth), Louis implied as an alternative a painting from the brain. The making of the *Charred Journal: Firewritten* paintings was certainly a cerebral, and not an expressionist or gestural, activity. So too was the painting that came after.

The cerebral work of making the 'mature' paintings could now be considered as the essence of a continued attempt to regenerate culture after cultural destruction: Louis's entire 'mature' work could be treated as his brave project to create after the Holocaust. In its intense seriousness, and in the rigour with which Louis repetitively worked over a very small number of visual 'themes', his 'mature' work manifests the same spirit of hope, the same spirit of a longed-for post-Holocaust Jewish renaissance suggested by the white lines of the *Charred Journal: Firewritten* paintings. Looking at Louis's 'Unfurled' and 'Pillar' paintings, we can agree with Michael Fried that they dramatise the 'impulse to make one's mark', and yet suggest that this impulse is not created by some primeval, essential urge, but by the demands of a particular, post-war historical moment. Looking at a 'Veil' painting such as *Beth Chaf* (fig. 18), the leap from firewriting to its flame-like washes of pigment might not, perhaps, be so great.

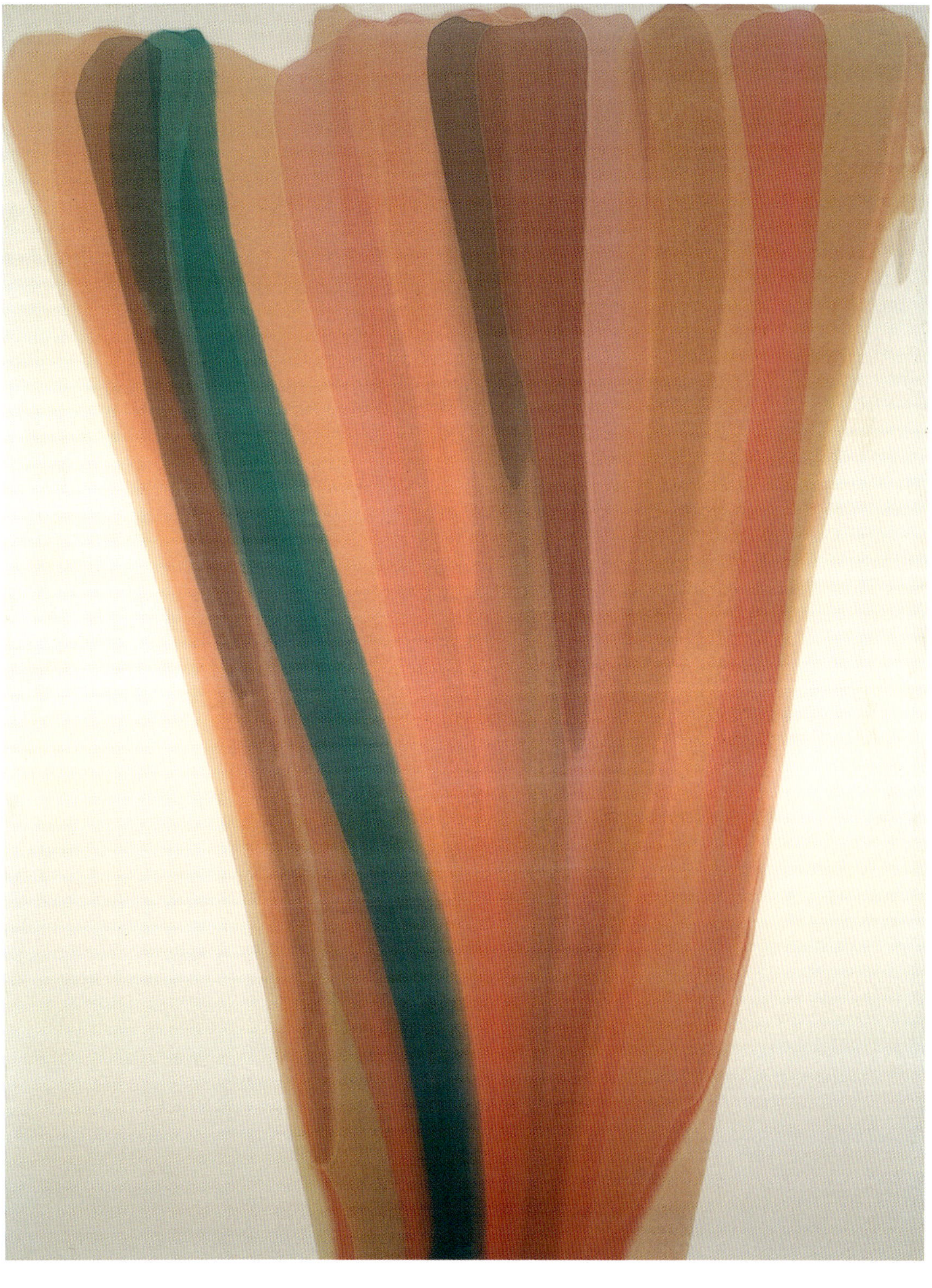

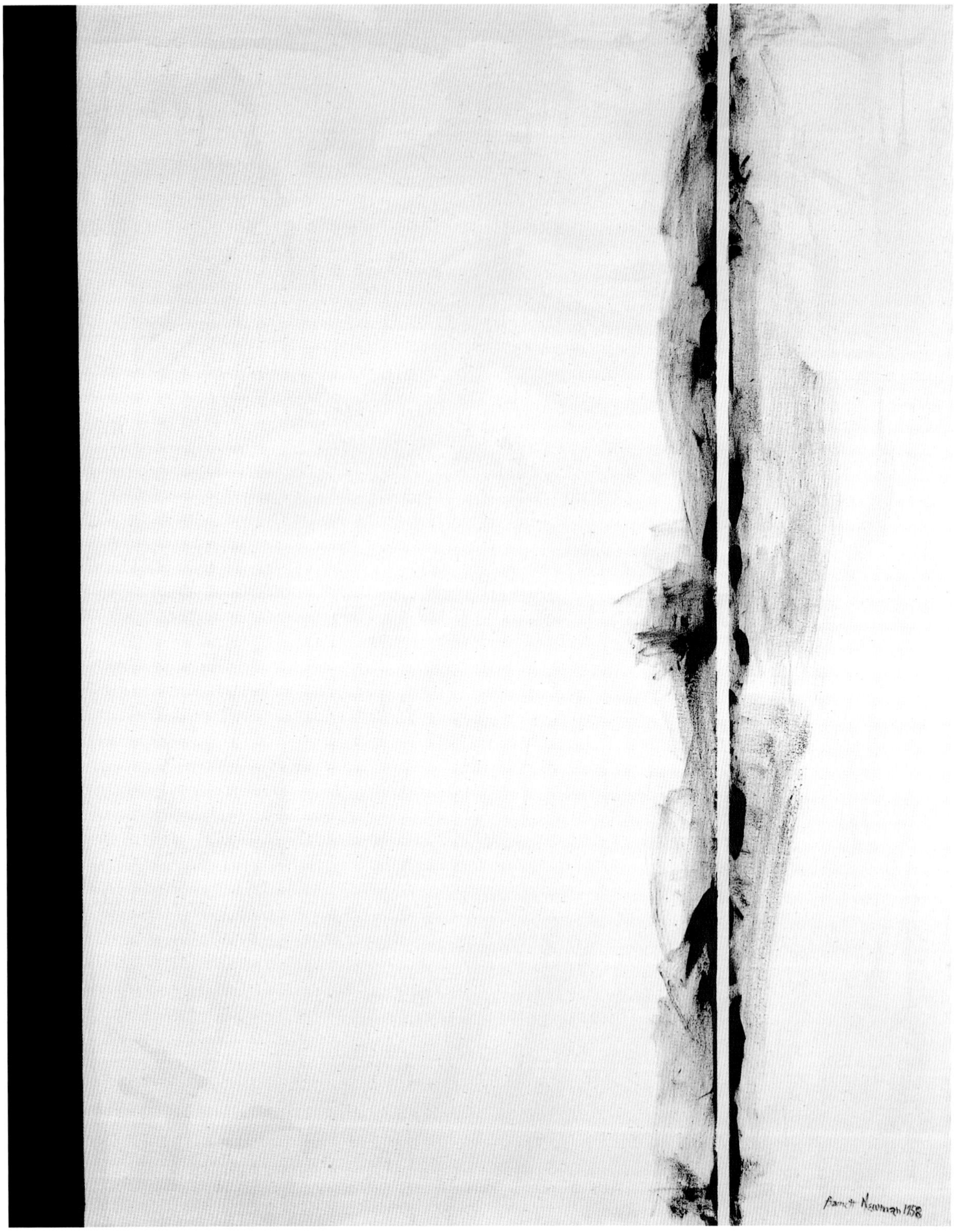
Barnett Newman 1958

three

barnett newman's *the stations of the cross: lema sabachthani*

presenting jewishness

19 Barnett Newman, *First Station*, 1958. Magna on exposed canvas, 198.1 × 153.7 cm, National Gallery of Art, Washington D.C., Collection of Robert and Jane Meyerhoff.

The year after Morris Louis exhibited the *Charred Journal: Firewritten* series in Washington, Barnett Newman titled a painting *White Fire I* (1954; fig. 20). This was the first of four *White Fire* paintings, the last dating from 1968 (Newman also painted *Black Fire* in 1961). As I have demonstrated in the last chapter, the paintings in Louis's series are strongly related to each other and to the ideas suggested by their titles. So is this the case with Newman's *White Fire* paintings too? *White Fire I* is wider than it is high, whilst *White Fire II* (1960) is oriented vertically. *White Fire I* pairs two 'zips', the one pink and clean-edged, the other, blue and fuzzy-edged, since the paint seeped under the masking tape. *White Fire II*, however, features a central zip of reserved canvas between two clean, black borders: Newman stuck a broad band of masking tape down the centre, and dabbed around this before removing the tape to leave a gap surrounded by the very brushy strokes. In contrast to both, *White Fire IV* (1968) is extremely tall and has neither brushy incident, nor any seepage: its centre is an area of raw canvas, flanked by sections of crisp-edged white paint.

Given the visual range of the *White Fire* paintings and the fact that they were made over such a long period, we might well wonder if they were really joined by any specific thinking, and if there is really any significant relationship between the canvases and the ideas around 'firewriting' that Morris Louis explored. Where Louis's references to Jewish myths were largely passed over in early accounts of his work, in the first posthumous text on Newman, Thomas Hess made it his task to account for

Newman's interest, attempting to reveal secret meanings of Newman's paintings through discussion of Kabbalistic texts. This was an extraordinary departure from the Greenbergian, modernist approach to Newman, but when it came to a painting such as *White Fire*, Hess's account was unrevealing: he rather blandly stated that '*White Fire* and *Black Fire*, two of Newman's later titles, refer overtly to Jewish mysticism and to a passage in the Jerusalem Talmud (fourth–sixth century A.D.) which discusses one of the central issues of Kabbalist thought, the genesis of the bible itself.'[1] Indeed to make sense of the *White Fire* paintings it seems that we should place their titles to one side and compare them with contemporaneous works. *Right Here* (1954), like *White Fire I*, is dominated by a white section and flanked towards one side by a leaky blue area; *Profile of Light* (1967), like *White Fire IV*, is divided into thirds and has a vertical axis.

So it seems that the birth of the Torah was a legend to which Newman could return for titles as he wished, whether in 1954 or 1968. Responding to Hess's 'incorrect' interpretation of her late husband's work in 1995, Annalee Newman suggested as much: 'The *only* connection that exists between Barnett Newman and the Kabbalah', she wrote, 'is that Newman used Kabbalistic language for the titles of several of his works. He did so, I am certain, because the language was poetic and fanciful. Let's not forget that Newman also used language from the Old Testament, the New Testament, and Greek epic and myth, and he made reference to numerous other sources, such as American transcendentalism, in his titles.'[2] Newman's *White Fire* paintings should not be considered as attempts to address the specific myths around 'firewriting'. His allusions to the legends seem more casual than Louis's, but is this all we can make of his use of the title *White Fire*? The titles surely hold more interest than Annalee Newman would acknowledge.

At the very least, we can say that through them, Newman wished to present himself as an artist who was interested in Jewish religious and literary traditions. However Newman might have engaged with Jewishness in private is not the issue here – his beliefs, observance, exact affiliations are not under scrutiny. What is important, rather, is that in public, Newman chose, in part through these titles, to present himself in a specific way: as an amateur scholar, comfortable enough with religious literature to be able to use it and to defend his use if necessary (in the pages of *ARTNews* he famously defended his title *Vir Heroicus Sublimis* against the criticism of Erwin Panofsky). Newman's concern with his public image is hardly news: unlike the very private Morris Louis, this was an obsession for the New Yorker. Witness Newman's candidacy for the mayoralty in 1933, his elegant dress sense, his endless and endlessly revised letters to the editors of newspapers and art magazines. Newman's public presentation of *Jewishness* is particularly compelling because it was so far from straightforward, as is indicated by a series of incidents throughout the 1960s.

In January 1965, Newman attended a symposium at New York's Jewish Museum. Titled 'What about Jewish Art?', the event featured Dore Ashton, Arthur A. Cohen, Paul Brach and Peter Selz. Newman knew the institution very well: in 1963 he had exhibited his model of a synagogue in Richard Meier's 'Recent American Synagogue Architecture' show (fig. 21), the only non-architect to be included, and used the

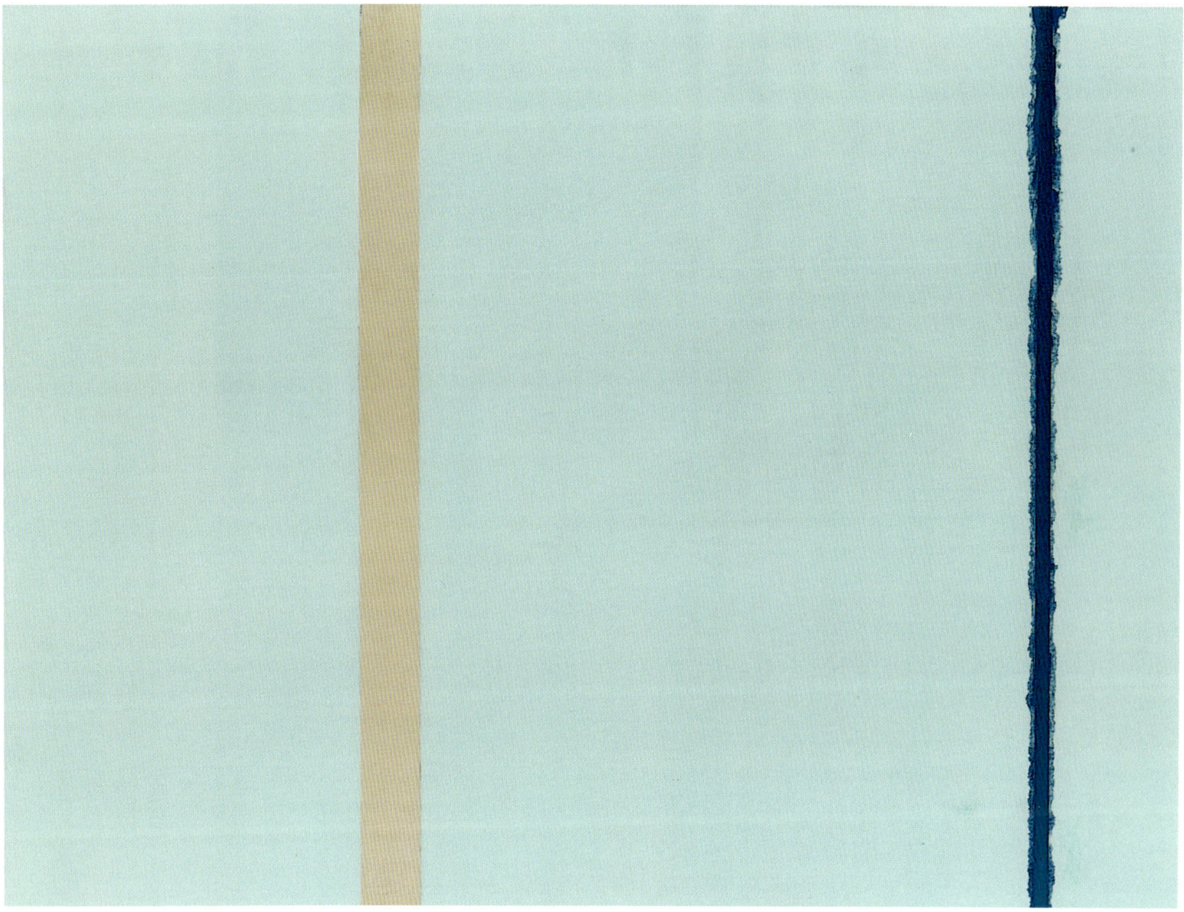

20 Barnett Newman, *White Fire I*, 1954. Oil on canvas, 121.6 × 151.8 cm, Private collection.

catalogue to publish thoughts on synagogue architecture written in 1951 in the immediate post-war context, when the wide-scale revival of the synagogue was routinely described as a response to the European catastrophe.[3] After the synagogue show, Newman's magisterial 1961 painting *Shining Forth (to George)* had been included in the group exhibition *Black and White*, and by 1965 the institution was planning a retrospective of around twelve to fifteen large works – a solo show that would have been Newman's first in a New York museum and the most important exhibition of his to that date.[4] So, prior to the symposium, Newman's relationship with the Jewish Museum seemed to be developing nicely. However, three days after attending, Newman wrote to Hans van Weeren-Griek, then the director, to 'express my disgust at the Jewish Museum's sponsorship of the debate 'What about Jewish Art?' . . . What the Jewish Museum has done is to compromise me as an artist because I am Jewish. Please therefore notify all concerned not to ask me to cooperate ever with any of your shows since you have made it impossible for me to show my work in your Museum.'[5]

There is no complete record of the talks Newman heard, but the notes for the speeches suggest that even those on the panel resisted the title of the discussion: Arthur

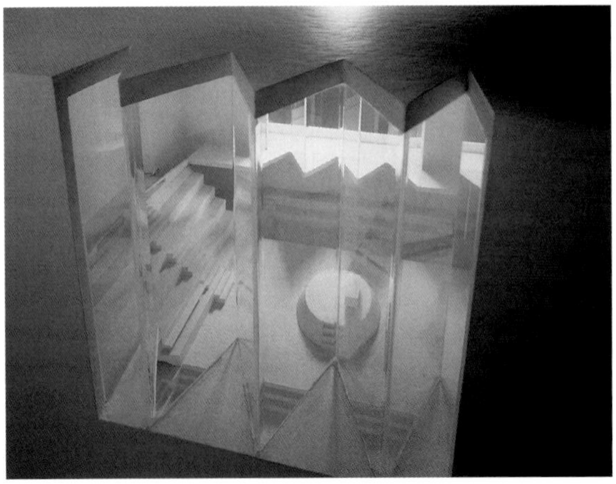

21 Barnett Newman, *Model for a Synagogue*, 1963. Wood, paint, and Plexiglas, 121.9 × 182.9 × 54.6 cm. Estate of the artist; Collection Annalee Newman.

A. Cohen began his presentation re-stating the symposium's question 'What about Jewish art?', only to answer: 'Not very much, not very interesting if there is such a confection, and it is doubtful if there ever was.'[6] Newman's anger about the evening's topic becomes more noteworthy considering Cohen's own hesitation: clearly this had not been an evening affirming 'Jewish art'. What Newman might not have been able to perceive because of his historical moment was that the debate had its own determinants. Against the background of the destruction of Jewish culture in the war, and the post-war claims of its non-existence, it had been imperative for many art historians and critics in the field to proclaim the category 'Jewish art' in various publications and reviews.[7] The Jewish Museum's event was therefore a part of a larger and already existing debate. Nonetheless Newman still felt compelled to object to the possibility of solidifying such a category in connection with contemporary practice, since it carried the risk of pigeon-holing his work within it. He was certainly prescient: five years after his death, once he could no longer resist, Newman's work was displayed at the museum in Avram Kampf's 1975 exhibition *Jewish Experience in the Art of the Twentieth Century*, on which occasion Kampf wrote that 'if there were a Jewish art, Newman's work would be regarded as its most authentic and classic expression'.[8]

Though he objected so strongly and at such great personal cost to the concept of 'Jewish art', Newman by no means let the incident stop him from declaring his interest in Jewish culture. At the symposium, Arthur A. Cohen had alluded to 'Jewish painters who have responded independently of their art to the demands of Jewish existence'[9], and Newman was one such painter who continued to do so. He was more than happy to be a signatory of a letter published in the *New York Times* protesting the 'Arab Threat to Destroy Israel' (June 7 1967), and was a participant – only weeks before he died – in a press conference organised by the 'Conference on the Status of Soviet Jews' (May 28 1970). Comparing the current situation with the story of biblical slavery, Newman read out a simple statement: 'Who would ever have thought that one hundred years after his birth, the mummy in Red Square would turn out to be Pharaoh.'[10] And during all this time he continued to title paintings with Kabbalis-

22 Barnett Newman, *Cathedra*, 1951. Oil and Magna on canvas, 243.8 × 544 cm, Stedelijk Museum, Amsterdam.

tic phrases such as *Voice of Fire* (1967) and biblical names such as *Jericho* (1968–69).

So what can be made of all this? What can be concluded from the seemingly casual, but prominently advertised use of titles such as *White Fire*; the rows with the main secular Jewish cultural institution in his home city; the preparedness to sign public declarations in support of imperilled Jews across the world? Newman's serpentine moves within the organised Jewish cultural sphere might seem to exemplify the idiosyncratic behaviour of this strong minded and often obstinate artist but in fact they witness the more general, compromised position of the post-Holocaust Jewish intellectual. For every compulsion to contribute to the rebuilding and defence of Jewish culture, there would be an equally insistent urgency to distance oneself from unacceptable constructions of Jewish identity. For Newman the key thing was keeping control: 'yes' to Jewish intellectual-artist-architect; 'yes' to scholar; 'no' to maker of 'Jewish art'.

If Newman can now be considered as a post-Holocaust Jewish subject, historical distance allows us also to locate his work in the context of the aftermath of war. None of Newman's early supporters wrote directly of the impact of the Holocaust and Hiroshima on his thinking about the possibility of making art, but then we should not expect them to have done. Strangely, this context was both too obvious to remark upon, and too painful to address. Yet recently there has been a marked turn in the scholarship. At the symposium held at the Philadelphia retrospective in 2002, Benjamin Buchloh referred to Newman's 'skinny' paintings of 1950, arguing that Newman's abstraction represents an acknowledgment of the impossibilities of lyric painting in the wake of the Holocaust.[11] In the recent catalogue raisonné, Richard Shiff places Newman's project as an attempt to face up to his historical moment.[12] Increasingly it seems as if Newman's central statements are his recollections from the mid-1960s about the impossibilities of painting during the War. In 1966 he said that 'the feelings I had at the time of the War in '41 was that the world was coming to an end. And to the extent that the world was coming to an end, the whole issue of painting, I felt, was over because it was impossible to paint flowers, figures, etcetera, and so the crisis moved around the problem of what I can really paint.'[13] This remark comes from a TV inter-

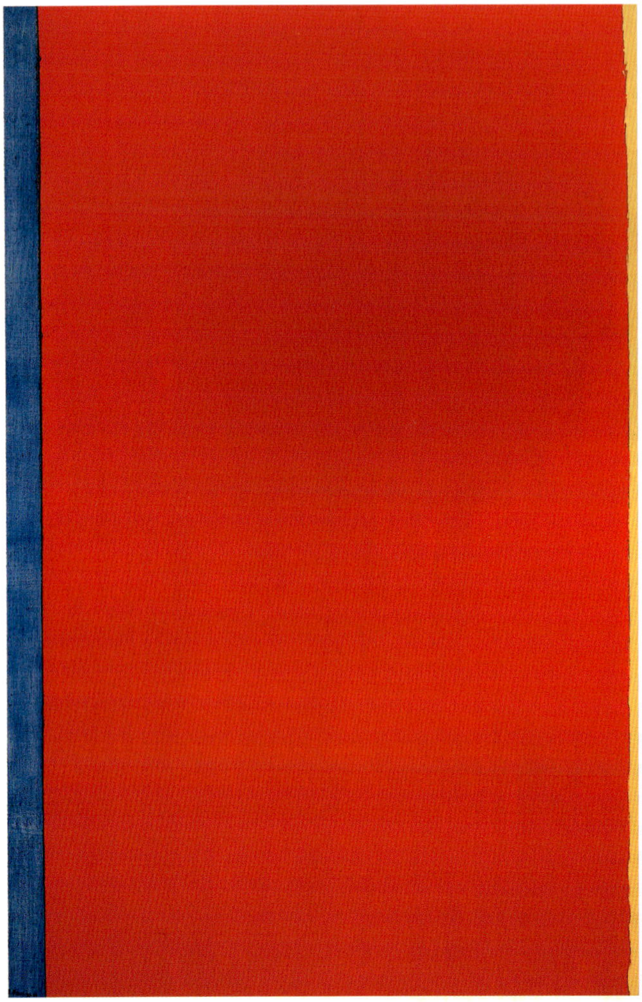

23 Barnett Newman, *Who's Afraid of Red, Yellow, and Blue I*, 1966. Oil on canvas, 190.5 × 121.9 cm, Private Collection.

view with the former Jewish Museum curator Alan Solomon, but the sentiment was often repeated around the mid-1960s in other contexts. Compare the comment to one made in conversation with Thomas Hess, also in 1966: 'The history of my generation begins with the problem of what to paint. During World War II it became nonsensical to get involved in painting men playing violins or cellos, or flowers.'[14] And then to another made the following year, at the symposium on the occasion of the Jackson Pollock retrospective at MoMA: 'In 1940, some of us woke up to find ourselves without hope – to find that painting did not really exist.'[15] Against the backdrop of these sometimes Adornian statements, Newman's work emerges as a serious attempt to rethink painting in the aftermath of the Holocaust, to answer the question of what a serious artist could really paint without recourse to what Newman saw as the bankrupted modes of figuration, symbolism, surrealism, or, his pet-hate, Mondrian-influenced, European-derived formalist abstraction.

Contextualising Newman in this way is certainly welcome, but doing so does little to differentiate the works he made after 1948, when, in front of *Onement*, he first intuited that he had answered the challenge of 'what to paint' in an adequate manner. Newman's post-1948 paintings, though few in number, range in size from the thin bar of *The Wild* (1950) to the eighteen-foot expanse of *Cathedra* (1951; fig. 22); in colour from the white-on-white austerity of *The Name II* (1950) to the exuberance of the *Who's Afraid of Red, Yellow, and Blue I* (1966; fig. 23); and in title from the Kabbalistic *White Fire* to the more descriptive *Yellow Edge* (1968). As so many of his titles affirm (*Genesis – The Break*, *The Beginning*, *Onement*, and, yes, *White Fire*), Newman was thinking about origins and what it meant to begin to make art again after Auschwitz and Hiroshima, but if Newman's entire body of work was a response to the crises of the Holocaust and the War, were all his works equivalent parts of this response? Or were there any points where he specifically addressed what the memory of the Holocaust meant to his viewers? I will now turn to Newman's series *The Stations of the Cross: Lema Sabachthani* and to the exhibition of the series at the Guggenheim between April and June 1966.[16] I will argue that the 1966 installation of *The Stations* constitutes not so much a representation of the Holocaust, as a place set out to compel the viewer to ask the question posed to them by the memory of the Holocaust: Why did you forsake me? This argument would seem strange were we to consider the surfaces of the paintings outside the contingent circumstances of their first exhibition, and indeed it relies on us thinking in detail about those contingencies.

the stations of the cross

The Stations of the Cross: Lema Sabachthani comprises fifteen paintings. The first fourteen are all six and half feet high by five feet wide, painted with various black and white paints, but with large areas of the surfaces remaining as raw canvas. They are individually titled *First Station* to *Fourteenth Station* and they have always been joined by the fifteenth painting in the series, *Be II*, which is slightly larger, and includes a thin band of cadmium red paint at its left edge. Newman made the first two paintings in 1958 after a heart attack but this personal situation interests me less than the moment three years later when, with four paintings finished, he claimed to have realised what he was doing. At this moment some time in 1961 he determined the status of the paintings *as a series* separated from his other paintings, set out to make the other paintings that would complete the series, and decided on a title with profoundly public rather than private resonances. To think about this declared moment of realisation is not just a matter of considering the title; rather, it is to acknowledge that at a certain moment, Newman's paintings meant something to him, their first viewer. This moment of realisation was an important act of interpretation on his part that needs to be taken seriously. To consider the moment, we need to think about what Newman was looking at.

First Station (fig. 19) was made on raw canvas, one of the first times Newman had painted without preparing his ground. On its left edge, he laid down a flat black band. On the right he painted around a strip of masking tape before removing the tape. Some strokes moved upwards around the tape, some traversed it in horizontal swipes. Some were made when the palette knife was freshly loaded, and others seem like the smears of a dried knife. These markings dramatise the white zip of raw canvas left underneath the tape. Unlike those in later paintings, the reserved zip has sharp lines: no paint has seeped under the tape while it was down. In the context of his work, the paint strokes appear extremely gestural. *Within* the zips of former work (such as *End of Silence*, 1949), Newman had employed such strokes, but these had never come outside the zips into the main body of the painting. The *Second Station* (fig. 24) is similar in structure to the *First* (painterly incident on its right side is organised around a removed band of tape), but the paint handling is very different. Black paint has been watered to a browny grey, and applied in consistent, gentle strokes that move down the canvas, following the direction of the band. Either before or after the tape was removed, the very edges of the white space were emphasised by the thinnest of black lines, obviously painted with the kind of care and slowness that serves as counter to the speed of gesture in *First Station*.

24 Barnett Newman, *Second Station*, 1958. Magna on exposed canvas, 198.1 × 153.7 cm, National Gallery of Art, Washington D.C., Collection of Robert and Jane Meyerhoff.

Untitled, these two paintings remained in Newman's studio. Newman made other paintings and drawings between 1958 and 1960, and had an important exhibition at French and Company, and in 1960 he painted two more canvases of the same size. The painting later called *Third Station* (fig. 25) was more complex than the first two. Though there was also a flat band of black on the left, there were now two areas of incident on the right. Nearest to the centre of the painting, Newman taped down two bands of masking tape and painted the gap between them. The exposed canvas was not entirely covered with paint, though: the brush moved deliberately to leave some areas towards its sides unpainted. To the left, the strategy was reversed. He painted around a strip of tape, as in *First Station*, before removing it. Here the strokes were like short jabs, punching the tape at regular intervals down the canvas.

Just as the *Third Station* recalls the *First*, the *Fourth Station* (fig. 26) recalls the *Second*. Once again, Newman painted around masking tape in downward strokes that thin out as they get further from the tape. The paint here is blacker than the *Second Station*, and it has seeped under the masking tape, so the thin white line that appears where it was laid down wavers in thickness and is at points almost bisected. The blackness of the surrounding paint creates an illusion whereby this line of raw canvas appears whiter than the raw canvas elsewhere on the surface. At the left edge, there is a solid black area that recalls the first three paintings, but in this work the paint has separated, so the canvas at its right is stained to a faint yellow.[17] The strangest incident in this painting, however, occurs towards its bottom centre: a small cascade of black drips rains downwards. It is hard to tell if the drips were accidental or if Newman deliberately flicked a loaded brush, but either way he chose not to remove the marks that stand out so clearly against the central expanse of raw canvas.

25 (page 60) Barnett Newman, *Third Station*, 1960. Oil on exposed canvas, 198.1 × 152.4 cm, National Gallery of Art, Washington D.C., Collection of Robert and Jane Meyerhoff.

26 (page 61) Barnett Newman, *Fourth Station*, 1960. Oil on exposed canvas, 198.1 × 152.4 cm, National Gallery of Art, Washington D.C., Collection of Robert and Jane Meyerhoff.

So it was with these four paintings in front of him that Newman determined what he was doing. The paintings certainly looked different from his earlier work. First, they were far more intimate in scale. In contrast to the almost environmental expanses of *Vir Heroicus Sublimis* (1950, 1951), *Cathedra* (1951) and *Uriel* (1954), and to the tall, thin bands of his 1950 'skinny' paintings (whose scale was still large), these were around the

Barnett Newman 1958

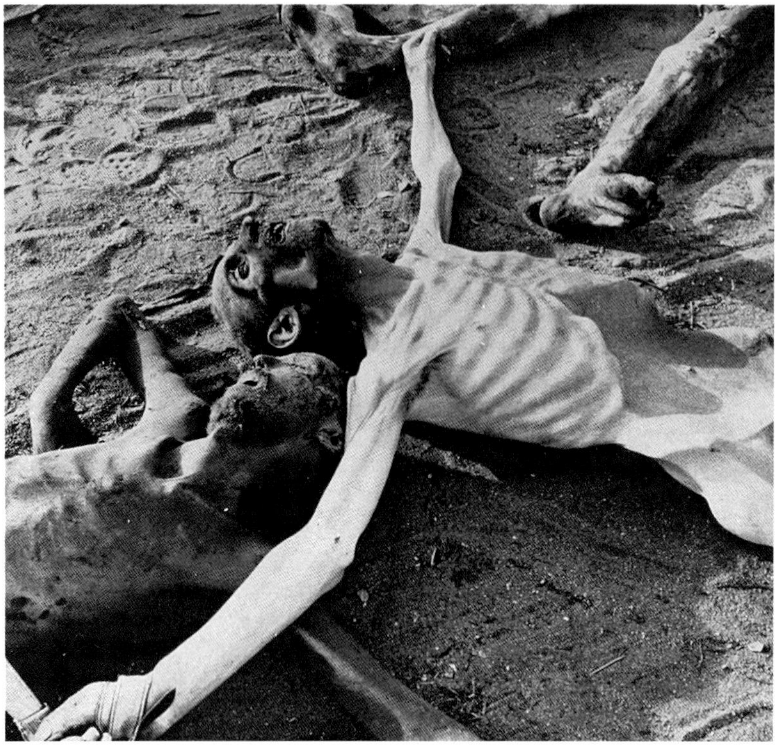

27 The bodies of Holocaust victims at the newly-liberated Bergen-Belsen concentration camp, 17 April 1945. United States Holocaust Memorial Museum, Washington D.C. Courtesy Solomon Bogard.

breadth of an arm-span. Newman had rarely made works so calibrated to the size of the body as here, and after 1966, most of his paintings would be far more expansive. Second, the paintings lacked the chromatic power that had led Clement Greenberg to write that Newman had 'enlarged our sense of the capacities of colour'.[18] But as much as the qualities of earlier works were absent, the four paintings displayed an impressive range of possibilities within a restricted vocabulary. Here were washed out greys and darkened blacks, raw canvas looking dull and raw canvas looking bright; here were expressive brush marks, delicate strokes, filled in zips and shining areas of reserved space.

Newman later gave many accounts of the moment when he realised what he was doing and what the title had to be. He told Alan Solomon that 'the kind of tension and intensity that I thought I was getting was for me the beginning of a series, which I then realised would be the "stations"'.[19] 'When I did the fourth one', he told *Newsweek*, 'I used a white line that was even whiter than the canvas, really intense, and that gave me the idea for the cry. It occurred to me that this abstract cry was the whole thing – the entire Passion of Christ'.[20] The most suggestive statement was written especially for *ARTNews*: 'It was while painting them that it came to me (I was on the fourth one) that I had something particular here. It was at that moment that the intensity that I felt the paintings had made me think of them as the Stations of the Cross. It is as I work that the work itself begins to have an effect on me. Just as I affect the canvas, so does the canvas affect me.'[21]

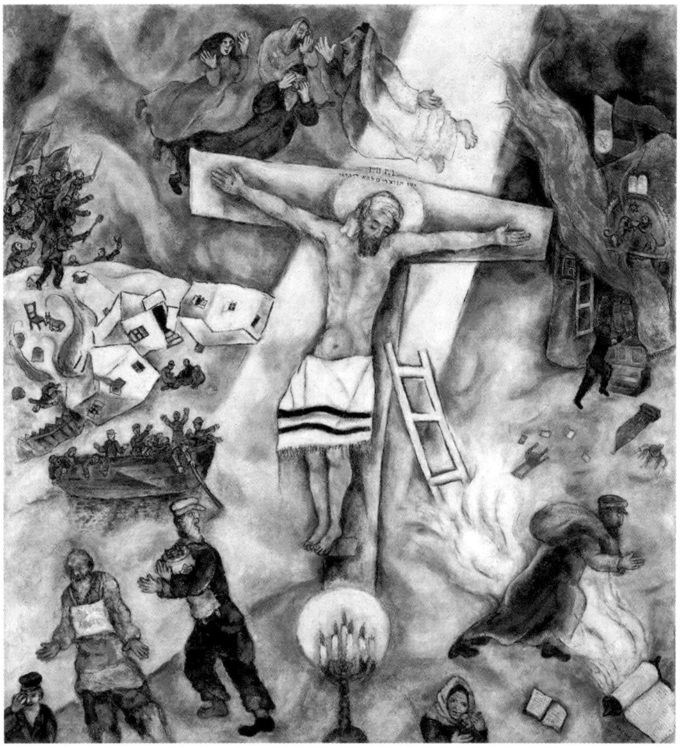

28 Marc Chagall, *White Crucifixion*, 1938. Oil on canvas, 154.3 × 139.7 cm, The Art Institute of Chicago. Gift of Alfred S. Alschuler.

The slight differences in these accounts indicate that Newman was not fully able to give an exact representation about the circumstances around what he termed a moment of realisation of meaning, which is not surprising, since the statements were made some five years after what must have been an intense and private studio moment. Nevertheless, according to these statements, it was 'the intensity' of the paintings that 'affected' him. He equated this intensity with 'the abstract cry'. This 'cry' was equivalent to 'the entire Passion of Christ'. This equivalence prompted the decision to make 'The Stations of the Cross', and to title his series *The Stations of the Cross: Lema Sabachthani*. It was never, then, a matter of iconography, but of affect.

If Newman sensed intensity in the four paintings, by naming them with the allusive title *The Stations of the Cross: Lema Sabachthani*, he was clearly doing more than naming 'intensity'. He could have titled the paintings with Adam's cry of despair, or Abraham's, or with the words of the Psalmist: 'My God, why has thou forsaken me?' These were texts to which he referred in his catalogue statement for the Guggenheim when he wrote that 'Lema Sabachthani', the 'overwhelming question', the 'question that has no answer', 'has been with us so long'. The decision to sidestep these Old Testament texts for the title *The Stations of the Cross: Lema Sabachthani* was made so as to associate the paintings with a chain of ideas associated, at that historical moment, with the intensity of the Passion. Whilst still opening the paintings to universal, non-specific suggestions, through the title Newman was able to partake in an established metaphor that had been used to address the suffering of Jews and other groups under Nazism for almost thirty years.

Ziva Amishai-Maisels has written most extensively about 'Christological Symbolism of the Holocaust', citing numerous examples of artists using crucifixion scenes through this time period.[22] As early as 1933 the German artist Otto Panok had painted *My God, my God, why hast thou forsaken me?*, giving 'Jesus the features of his friend Karl Schwesig, who had been arrested and beaten up by the SS in 1933 for being a Communist and active anti-Fascist' (Panok was later attacked for painting Christ as Jewish). The visual image of the crucifixion was mobilised by artists hoping their works would engage with current events, but the idea of the crucifixion also guided photographers who documented these events. At the liberation of the camps, one represented a corpse as a Christ-figure by composing an image in which the arms spread vertically down the plane of the photograph, like a bright white band against a grey ground (fig. 27). American artists such as Harold Paris were prompted by the re-publication of this image in 1960 to continue using the metaphor of the Passion.[23]

The photograph might have been known by Americans at the end of the war, and may have been amongst those that Newman had seen when he wrote about 'the photographs of German atrocities' in a 1945 text in which he condemned surrealist painters for failing to respond to the horrors of the camps.[24] Though Panok's painting might not have been familiar to Americans, Chagall's use of the crucifixion in paintings such as *White Crucifixion* (1938; fig. 28) had been widely discussed, and the painting had been included in the artist's 1946 Museum of Modern Art retrospective. *White Crucifixion* showed Jesus as Jew, surrounded by burning synagogues, weeping rabbis and shtetl dwellers clutching torah scrolls.[25] Some American critics had failed to note Chagall's metaphor, writing that 'the Christ symbol is foreign to the daily life of Eastern Jewry from which his best works are derived'.[26] But for most, including Newman's friend Harold Rosenberg, Chagall's analogies had been clear. 'In his Crucifixions painted during this tragic period,' Rosenberg wrote, Chagall 'depicts a world flying apart in chaos, houses overturned, ships sinking, Jews fleeing in every direction. The crucified one is a Jew, not the Son of God, but the human victim of violence.'[27] Herbert Howarth, writing in the same publication some years later, was even more insistent: 'Lest there be any doubt about the analogy, Chagall defined his meaning by drawing the Jewish phylacteries on the arms and forehead of the naked Christ on the cross. Christ, being Jewish, comes to stand for him as the Jewish people. His analogy says, as it were: In the European Holocaust Jewry has undergone a new mass crucifixion.'[28]

In the United States, artists such as Abraham Rattner and Seymour Lipton (who, like Newman, showed at Betty Parsons), used 'Christological symbolism'. In 1942, an exhibition of 'Modern Christs' had taken place at the Puma Gallery in New York, and, as Amishai-Maisels writes, by the late 1950s, this 'most obvious [of] symbols' had become 'so common' as to prove problematic to the originality of American Jewish artists, who nonetheless continued to employ it from 1960 to 1961, when 'the Eichmann trial . . . led to a resurgence of clear Holocaust imagery' employing the crucifixion.[29]

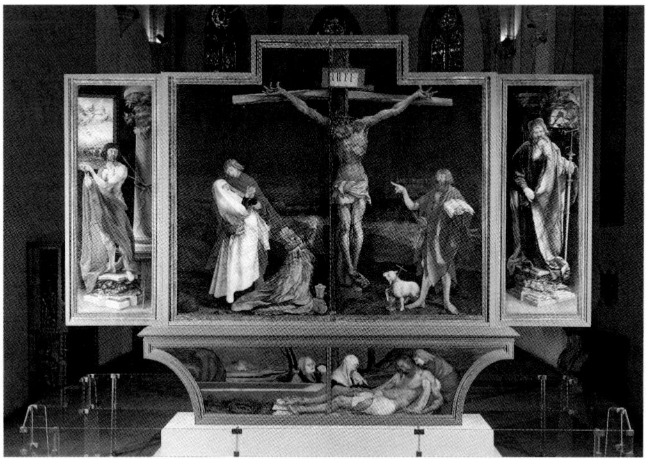

29 Matthias Grünewald, *Isenheim altarpiece*, oil on wood, c.1510–15, Musée d'Unterlinden, Colmar.

The metaphor of the Passion as a means of addressing the Holocaust also had textual currency. The American journal *Contemporary Jewish Record* published a report from Europe in 1943 titled 'The Passion of a People',[30] and in 1945 printed a poem from the Warsaw Ghetto ending with a reference to 'the cry of the crucified'.[31] In his 1960 book, *Christ in Dachau*, the German theologian Johann Maria Lenz recalled that after the American liberation, the SS road had been renamed 'The Way of the Cross'.[32] In 1961, the French philosopher and Talmudic scholar Emmanuel Levinas considered 'the Passion lived out by Judaism between 1940 and 1945',[33] and some years later in Great Britain the Reform Rabbi Ignaz Maybaum wrote in *The Face of God at Auschwitz* (1965) that 'the Golgotha of modern mankind is Auschwitz. The Cross, the Roman gallows, was replaced by the gas chamber.'[34]

So, around 1960–62, at the exact juncture when the Eichmann trial was forcing Americans to witness the events of the Holocaust, the internationally established metaphor of the crucifixion had ongoing currency.[35] Eichmann even referred to himself at trial as Pontius Pilate, an analogy that made 'Christs' of his victims, and his comments were reported by Harold Rosenberg in *Commentary* and, more famously, by Hannah Arendt in the *New Yorker*.[36] The Holocaust posed 'the unanswerable question of human suffering', and the idea of Christ's Passion (the single moment where *he* posed that question), could be used to address the Holocaust. Although Newman refrained from directly relating his idea of the Passion to the Holocaust, there is an illuminating passage in one of his 1966 interviews conducted just after the Guggenheim opening that suggests he was thinking this way.

Newman was speaking to Alan Solomon about a trip he had made to Europe in 1964, once he had already chosen to make use of the metaphor of Christ's Passion. He deliberately avoided going to Germany, but travelled to Colmar near its border to see Matthias Grünewald's Isenheim altarpiece. Newman told Solomon:

> I think Grünewald's *Crucifixion* is maybe the greatest painting in Europe, but one of the things that intrigues me about the Grünewald is the act of active imagina-

> tion on his part. That he was not illustrating so much the Christ in terms of the legend, but since he was doing it for a hospital of syphilitics, that he was able to identity himself with the human agony of those patients, that he was willing to turn the Christ figure into a syphilitic. Now this of course is one of the boldest things that anyone could have done. Yet I think this is part of his genius.[37]

Grünewald's *Crucifixion* (fig. 29) seems to have confirmed for Newman that his own 'act of active imagination' in using the Christian narrative as a means of addressing contemporary suffering had a precedent of 'greatest' importance. Newman also admired the way Grünewald identified Christ's agony with the agony of his work's first viewers – the way Grünewald made his painting with its place of viewing in mind. Later in the interview, Newman stressed the necessity of 'presenting something new in relation to the story of Jesus. It's always been identified with something else'.[38] He argued that 'the nails of the Romans', if compared to events 'going on in Vietnam, or the sort of things that happened in Hiroshima', diminished in their horror, 'so that if we're going to measure the pain, I think the pain was terrible for Jesus, but it somehow – I suppose maybe this is blasphemous – but it seems mild compared to the kind of physical pain people suffer today.'[39] This comment – in which Auschwitz remains unmentioned – was excised from Newman's television interview, and references to Hiroshima and Vietnam do not find their way into Newman's other texts around *The Stations of the Cross: Lema Sabachthani*. It is less the blasphemous nature of the comments, however, than their problematic specificity that accounts for these cuts. In statements about the 'Stations' exhibition, it was preferable to address the work through universal ideas rather than particular ones, opening up associations rather than closing them off.[40]

the guggenheim installation

Newman's exhibition opened at the Guggenheim on 20 April 1966 and was by all accounts an extremely well-attended event. In photographs taken for the press, Newman posed in front of his paintings (fig. 30), but also before a large board on which the title of the series and exhibition was printed (fig. 31). Many of the viewers who came to the Guggenheim over the next few months would have seen these photographs as well as the various statements that Newman published, the interviews he gave, and the lush purple covered catalogue. But if the title and Newman's statements and texts set up a complex of associations mediating viewers' encounters with the canvases, how did the paintings themselves and their arrangement contribute to Newman's ambition to make of his viewers the subjects asking the 'unanswerable question'? In 1962, when he was some way through painting the series, Newman had given another interview to *Art in America* in which he had said that his work was 'full of meaning, but the meaning must come from the seeing'.[41] As the viewers looked at *The Stations of the Cross*, how did they experience its meaning?

In the installation, the paintings were divided between two spaces. The first four *Stations* were on the Guggenheim ramp (fig. 32), and the next ten were in the High

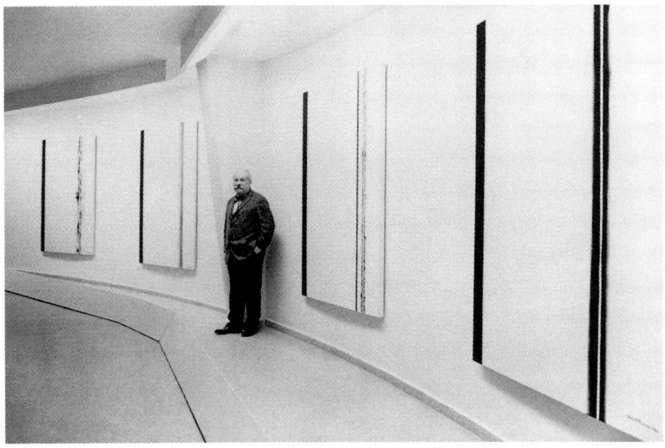

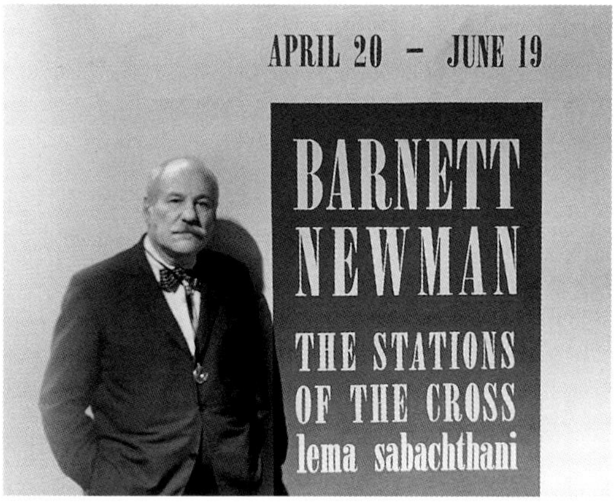

30 (left) Barnett Newman standing between *Second Station* and *Third Station* at the Solomon R. Guggenheim Museum, 1966.

31 (right) Barnett Newman in front of exhibition title for *The Stations of the Cross*, 1966.

Gallery. In this way, the installation separated the four canvases Newman had painted up until the moment when he had realised the meaning of the series, in a way presenting the viewer with what he had had before him in the studio. On the ramp, there was not much space to move away from these paintings, and rather than moving forwards and backwards, viewers would have had to move close by, across them. Newman had always encouraged this kind of close viewing – his statement for his 1951 show at Betty Parsons read: 'The large pictures in this exhibition are intended to be seen from a short distance.'[42] At the Guggenheim, the installation of the first four *Stations* would have encouraged the viewers to sense the differences I described above: the smears of black paint in *First Station*, the pencil-thin line of either side of the zip in *Second*, the repetitive dabs at the right side of *Third Station*, the flicked paint spoiling the otherwise empty white expanse at the centre of *Fourth*. These details witnessed an intensity of process, Newman's meticulous deployment of different brushstrokes from a lexicon of painting modes; for the viewer, the series began to demand an intensity of attention as, on coming to each new painting, previous marks were recalled and differentiated.

In writing of the Passion in the Guggenheim catalogue statement, Newman was keen to assert that it was not the 'terrible walk' along the Via Dolorosa, but 'the question that has no answer'. It was not a succession of events, but 'one event', the single moment where Christ uttered 'Lema'.[43] Newman's insistence on what he elsewhere called in *Newsweek* 'the wholeness of the single event' raises a question about the installation.[44] If the work as a whole comprised various different canvases, if these canvases were organised on various separate walls, and, finally, if a spectator literally had to move around the space over time to view these paintings, how could this temporal dimension of the Passion be manifested? How could a series of paintings create the sense that Newman wanted to achieve of a single intense moment?

On the ramp, as the viewer made sense of each successive canvas, each one just past would be recalled: on coming to the *Third Station*, for instance, the viewer would be reminded of the kind of painting on the *First* as opposed to the more gentle strokes on the *Second*. But next, as they came to the *Fourth*, the *Second* would be called to mind, and this new pair (*Fourth* and *Second*) would appear similar, differentiated from the

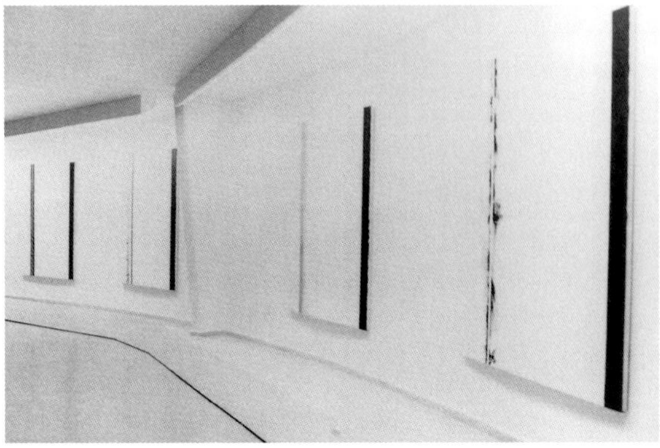

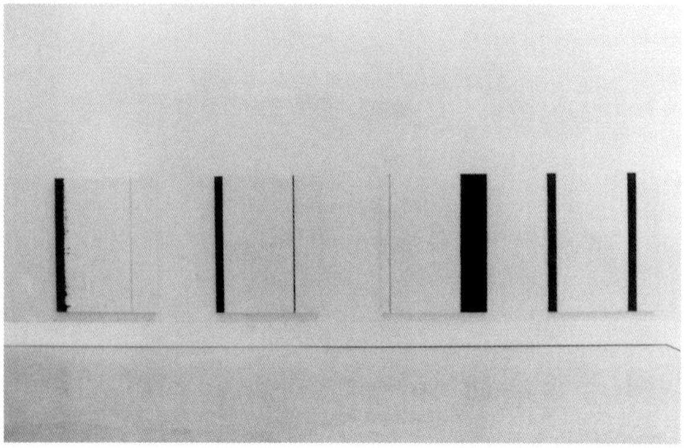

Third and *First*. A web of similarities and differences would be woven, and stepping inside the High Gallery (fig. 33), the web of differences knotted. For the first time in the series, painterly incident occurred to the left side of the *Fifth Station*. This would come as a surprise, marking the canvas as a departure, but only a kind of departure. The dried, smudgy globs of pigment brushed out of the left-hand band would recall the kind of strokes already seen in the *First*, whilst the thin line at the right would evoke the thin lines on either side of the reserved zip in the *Second*. The *Sixth Station* included two straight bands of black with no visible signs of brush or palette work in the expansive sections of raw canvas. If its composition was felt to be new, its contrast to the *Fifth* recalled the way in which the *Second* compared to the *First*. And so on: paintings already seen were recalled as new ones were viewed, and the differences between previously viewed canvases were also called to mind as new contrasts were intuited. As the viewer's memory was returned to former paintings, as they looked at the painting in front of them, the next would be glimpsed at the periphery of vision, pushing itself into view with the paint strokes on the left bar of the stretcher. In these ways, the experience inside the installation was akin to a single moment. Though the viewer might have moved through the room stopping at each *Station*, the linearity of this literal movement would have been utterly scattered by the criss-crossings of anticipation and memory. Though at any time one painting might have occupied the visual field, all were in the mind at once.

32 (left) Barnett Newman, *First Station* through *Fourth Station* on the first ramp of The Solomon R. Guggenheim Museum, 1966.

33 (right) Barnett Newman, *Fifth Station* through *Eighth Station* in the High Gallery, The Solomon R. Guggenheim Museum, 1966.

As well as the 'single moment' of the Passion, the installation also needed to create a sense of place for the viewer. With earlier paintings such as *Vir Heroicus Sublimis* and *Cathedra*, Newman had metaphorically enveloped his viewers, who would sense the flat plane of the canvas bending around them. At the Guggenheim, Newman's viewer would literally be surrounded by *The Stations of the Cross*, with paintings to their sides and behind them. This literal sense of place would have been accompanied by a more psychological sense of place. Since the paintings caused their attentive viewers to construct a web of inter-relationships, the spectator would have felt in the midst of the unified work no matter where they actually stood.

Throughout his career, Newman made several statements about the sense of place that he wished to establish for the viewers of his paintings. 'One of the nicest things

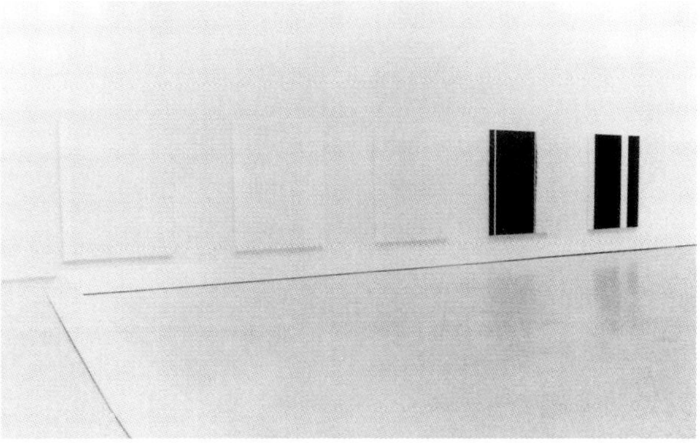

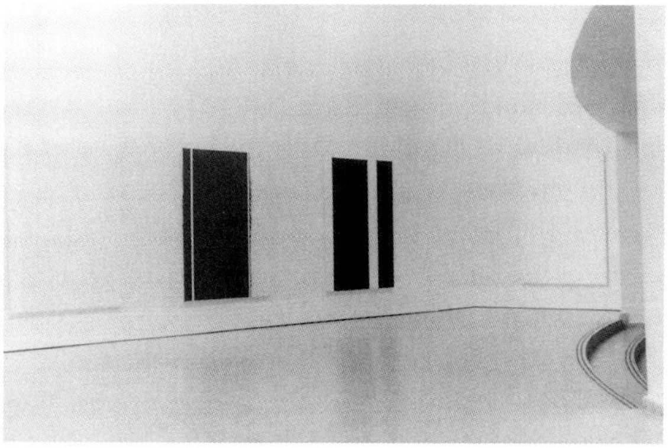

34 (left) Barnett Newman, *Ninth Station* through *Thirteenth Station* in the High Gallery, The Solomon R. Guggenheim Museum, 1966.

35 (right) Barnett Newman, *Eleventh Station* through *Fourteenth Station* in the High Gallery, The Solomon R. Guggenheim Museum, 1966.

that anybody ever said about my work', he told David Sylvester, 'is when you yourself said that standing in front of my paintings you had a sense of your own scale.'[45] Newman also was insistent about differentiating kinds of places: 'Some places are more sacred than others, and that depends, it seems to me, on the quality of the work of art, on its uniqueness, on its rigor.'[46] If the way in which the *Stations* were installed, and the web of connections between them, created a sense of place, the appearance of the latter canvases confirmed the specific kind of place that this was: a place of loss (figs 34, 35). Nuances that dramatised earlier paintings were emptied out of the *Eighth Station*, whose two straight-edged black bands of equal breadth stretched down the canvas without dramatic signs of process. If the residual power of the painting lay in the sharp, clear contrast of raw canvas and black pigment, in the *Ninth*, *Tenth*, and *Eleventh Stations*, even this drama was absent. White paint took the place of black; colour contrast of black and white was replaced by the tonal contrast of white paint and raw canvas. By no means were these the first 'white on white' paintings Newman had shown – he had included *The Name II* and *The Voice* (both 1950) alongside largely red paintings in his second exhibition at Betty Parsons, and Guggenheim viewers familiar with his work might have recalled these reductive canvases. But the white *Stations* had none of the extremely subtle differentiations of the 1950 works. If those earlier paintings rewarded close viewers by showing variances of texture in the whites, the later *Stations* comparatively crudely juxtaposed bright white acrylic with the uninflected yellowish canvas. Clear contrasts returned in the *Twelfth* and *Thirteenth Stations*, the latter almost a mirror-image of the *Eighth*, but disappeared again from the *Fourteenth Station*, alone on its own wall. There was no exposed canvas here, but two kinds of white paint (fig. 36). The main body of the work is free from all brush marks or value contrasts. It is an extraordinarily blank painting, emptied of the minimal incidents that might have engaged the viewer before. Seen with the earlier *Stations* in mind, its spareness is more apparent still.

The installation, I believe, was a place where memory was activated, a place of starkness, a place of loss. Of course, this should not be taken to indicate that the paintings themselves were any *simpler* than Newman's other works: as Carol Mancusi-Ungaro has argued, the *Stations* represent the pinnacle of Newman's technical and material achievement in terms of both the range of paints and their handling.[47] By loss, I mean the loss of the rich chromatic content that prompted Clement Greenberg's critical support, which delighted in Newman's 'exploration of the tensions between different light values of the same color and between different colors of the same light value'.[48] (And Greenberg had acknowledged this kind of loss: in his essay on Morris Louis and Kenneth Noland, Greenberg had mentioned in passing that 'Noland's pictures lose more in black and white than most pictures in our time do; in fact they lose almost as much as Barnett Newman's do.'[49])

36 Barnett Newman, *Fourteenth Station*, 1965–66. Acrylic on exposed canvas, 198.1 × 152.4 cm, National Gallery of Art, Washington D.C., Collection of Robert and Jane Meyerhoff.

Addressing the totality of works in the space, loss also refers to the paring down of viewing possibilities offered by the paintings. While the installation created a complex web of memories (since paintings demanded of their viewers acts of recollection), there was none of the diversity of shape and scale to which Newman's viewers were accustomed. As Ann Temkin has shown, Newman's former exhibitions had been arranged with juxtapositions of thin paintings and wide ones, and tall paintings near short ones, but these paintings were all the same size.[50] More than anyone else, Yve-Alain Bois has described the way in which the different scales of Newman's paintings and the different placements of the zips within them demanded shifts in the position of the viewing subject, who repositioned themselves according to each different painting. In the Guggenheim, the position to be taken in front of each human-scaled canvas was rather more simply central, from which point the viewer could easily see the difference between one side and the other. The regularity and repetition of canvas size would bring with it a loss of one of the pleasures offered by other installations of Newman's work, just as this regularity itself exacerbated differences between works and asked more of the viewer's memory.

Newman's exhibition prompted some extremely hostile responses. Older and younger reviewers found common ground in calling Newman's rhetoric empty. According to John Canaday in *The New York Times*, 'When they are called "The Stations of the Cross", you can't make it work.'[51] For Max Kozloff in *The Nation*, Newman's 'moralistic packaging' of his work was 'unconvincing . . . bombast'.[52] Needless to say, Newman replied to the most damning critics. He attempted to teach Kozloff a 'lesson in art criticism' by sending him a copy of the poet Howard Nemerov's favourable response to his 1958 Bennington College show,[53] and wrote to the publisher of *The New York Times* to accuse Canaday of anti-Semitism, since the critic had extraordinarily compared the black zips in the paintings to 'unravelled phylacteries'. Once again underscoring the connection between the crucifixion and Jewish experience, Newman asked the publisher: 'What do you make of [Canaday's] remarks that turn the ritual phylacteries into an epithet? Is he attacking Jesus because he was a Jew and had to wear them or is he attacking me because he knows that I am also a Jew?'[54] Newman's anger towards his critics is understandable given the seriousness of his approach to his title, and it is unsurprising that he should have reacted so fiercely towards those who expected a facile, iconographic connection between the paintings and the story of Christ's Passion, only to be disappointed by its absence. But some of the comments made in the press were extremely articulate responses, albeit if meant as slurs rather

than as sensitive descriptions. The kind of loss at work in the exhibition was suggested by a phrase of Emily Genauer's from the *Herald Tribune*: she described her experience as 'an adventure in emptiness'.[55] Indeed Newman did hope to create a sense of emptiness and if this was built up both through the appearance and arrangement of the fourteen *Stations*, it was firmly cemented by the final painting in the series, the somewhat larger canvas called *Be II*.

be *II*, awareness, tragedy

Be II was installed outside the Guggenheim's 'High Gallery', further down the ramp (fig. 37 and 38). Though it would have been visible to spectators as they looked at the first four *Stations*, it was placed as an end point – the last painting to which the installation directed the spectator. In size its difference from the *Stations* is quite small, but the painting represents a shift of scale, feeling much broader, certainly now broader than an arm-span. Its central width is white, painted with a somewhat more gloopy paint than the thin white in the *Stations*. To its right there is a very slender band of black, and to the left, a thin strip of cadmium red.

Many commentators considered *Be II* as a final point in terms of the meaning of Newman's work, some even suggesting that it offered a cheerful resolution to the sombre nature of the series, despite the fact that it was placed downwards on the ramp, reached after a slight descent. For the critic Walter Barker, *Be II* 'would certainly have Newman replying to the "Is God Dead?" question with an unmistakable and cheerful "No, not quite!"'[56] But is it really the case that the slight widening of breadth and the mere appearance of red paint offered sufficient visual pleasure to uplift the viewer and bring them away from the bleakness of the *Station* paintings? This was neither a return to the rich pigments of Newman's pre-1958 work nor an announcement for the paintings that Newman would begin after the Guggenheim show – the *Who's Afraid of Red, Yellow, and Blue* series of 1966, 1967 and 1967–68. Rather than a 'happy ending', one might think of *Be II* as a kind of re-beginning, as a moment of confirmation or awareness. Before *Be II*, one painting was seen through the remembered images of the others. With *Be II*, all would be remembered at once. Where chromatic and formal spareness were previously sensed, with the slightest appearance of colour, this spareness would be both remembered and emphasised.

Yve-Alain Bois has written of Newman's paintings as 'a deck of cards in which every work has a particular function and the specific role each plays varies according to the changing context'.[57] *Be II* heightens awareness of the loss experienced in the previous canvases, but at the same time it marks their difference from Newman's earlier works. Specifically, the dabbed downward strokes along the red band of *Be II* recall the brushy texture of the cadmium red zip in *Onement I*, rather than, say, the flatly painted red ground of *Vir Heroicus Sublimis*.

Returning to the moment of *Onement I* (fig. 3), it is interesting to note that in 1948, as he worked on this painting, Newman was also at work on the text called 'The New Sense of Fate'. The text addressed the difference between the Greek artists' attraction to beauty and their poets' interest in tragedy. While prior to the establishment of the term 'Holocaust', many Jews were using the notion of tragedy to describe the recent events (Meyer Schapiro, for instance, referred to the 'tragic experience of the Jewish people' in 1946[58]), Newman argued that American artists must engage in the terrain opened by Greek tragedians rather than artists. Newman contrasted his sense of the tragic with the surrealists', who 'identified tragedy with terror'. He distinguished between the two terms: 'The war the surrealists predicted has robbed us of our hidden terror, as terror can exist only if the forces of tragedy are unknown. We now know the terror to expect. Hiroshima showed it to us. We are no longer, then, in the face of a mystery. After all, wasn't it an American boy who did it? The terror has indeed become as real as life. What we have now is a tragic rather than a terrifying situation.'[59]

For Newman, it was awareness that separated 'terror' and 'tragedy'. Awareness is achieved by the acquisition of knowledge and *produces* a sense of responsibility. We can use Newman's own model to consider what happens to the *Stations* with *Be II*: *Be II* acts in the installation to produce a moment of awareness. In functioning in this way, the painting reveals the schema of *The Stations of the Cross: Lema Sabachthani* to be one modelled on Newman's notion of tragedy. A moment akin to terror (inside the place, and at the single moment) is followed by a moment of realisation or awareness. Newman indeed described *The Stations of the Cross: Lema Sabachthani* to Thomas Hess as having 'a tragic theme'.[60] The spectator is cast as a kind of tragic subject, experiencing the moment of despair before becoming aware. *Be II* might also point to the individual responsibility that this viewer might come to realise.[61]

In 1948, the awareness of recent events prompted a new kind of responsibility, but by 1966, the knowledge of the history of the war had broadened, especially after the Eichmann trial. The idea of responsibility had also changed. Americans were becoming aware of the former irresponsibility that enabled their government to stand by, to use the title of a 'chronicle of American apathy' written in 1965, 'While 6 Million Died'.[62] The remembrance of old wars brought a kind of responsibility in relation to new ones (and we can remember that Newman made reference to Vietnam whilst relating the Passion to contemporary suffering). As a "kind of survivor", to invoke George Steiner's terms of 1965, the American Jew, in addition to remembering the Holocaust and asking the difficult questions imposed by this memory, had now to assume a kind of responsibility in relation to this survival – the responsibility of continued life; the responsibility to 'Be'.[63]

Perhaps Newman's most far-reaching ambition with *The Stations of the Cross: Lema Sabachthani* was to create a place, though an installation of abstract paintings, where a viewer might not only be placed to ask 'Lema Sabachthani?', the question posed by the Holocaust. Aware of their situation, even of their survival, and becoming a tragic subject, they would also be aware of their responsibility in relation to the cause of such despair. Speaking about a 'sense of place' in 1967, Newman prefaced his remarks with the comment that 'it's only after man knows where he is that he can ask himself "Who am I?" and "Where am I going?".'[64] If a viewer was to experience a 'sense of place' before Newman's work, this was never just to be a phenomenological experience, but the grounds of a moral one. Of course, a critic like Max Kozloff distrusted the 'moralistic packaging' of Newman's work, dissuaded perhaps by a pomposity in his rhetoric, but we might now consider Newman's ambitions for the viewer not as a feature of bombast, but as a moral ambition demanded by the necessities of their historical moment. After giving viewers the sense of a place of loss; after pushing viewers to ask questions related to the disaster of the Holocaust, and then making them aware of the conditions of survival, the works set up the possibilities for a responsibility in connection to this awareness. Holocaust memory is at play in *The Stations of the Cross: Lema Sabachthani*, but the project of Holocaust memorial is not constructed as a project involving the acquisition of knowledge about history, nor the recollection of historical detail. Holocaust memorial instead requires the subject's repositioning of themselves with regard to the demands of memory.

37 Barnett Newman, *Be II*, 1961, 1964. Acrylic, oil, pigmented polymer emulsion, and Magna on canvas, 204.5 × 183.5 cm, National Gallery of Art, Washington D.C., Collection of Robert and Jane Meyerhoff.

forms of commemoration

Barnett Newman's use of the metaphor of the crucifixion to place his viewer in the position of the subject asking the question demanded in the mid-1960s by the memory of the Holocaust and war (and we should remember that in his thinking, the two were not separated) might seem to have been a means to avoid a specifically Jewish approach to Holocaust memory. Certainly his strategy makes sense given his documented hostility towards the establishment of a hermetic category called 'Jewish art'. Yet for all the ways in which his rhetoric opened up the universal significance of the memory of the Holocaust, Newman's tactics with *The Stations of the Cross: Lema Sabachthani* recall two modes of Jewish commemoration articulated by Yosef Hayim Yerushalmi in his book *Zachor*.

Yerushalmi describes the ways in which new disasters that befell the Jewish people during the middle ages were remembered not through the initiation of new memorial rituals, but through their superimposition onto old ones. The *Akedah* (binding of Isaac) would be used to describe a Jewish mass suicide during a period of persecution; a fast day commemorating one historical disaster would be used to commemorate another new disaster as well as the older one.

> Medieval Jewish chronicles tend to assimilate events into old and established conceptual frameworks . . . It is important to realise that there is also no real desire to find novelty in passing events. To the contrary, there is a pronounced tendency to subsume even major new events to familiar archetypes, for even the most terrible events are somehow less terrifying when viewed within old patterns rather than in their bewildering specificity.[65]

In a related manner, Newman addressed the 'unanswerable question of human suffering' recently posed by the mid-century through the rhetoric of the biblical complaints. Of course Yerushalmi's account does not map perfectly onto Newman's strategy: Yerushalmi suggests that the use of an archetype was a protective measure, a means of allaying the terror of each new disaster; Newman, by contrast, had no intention of side-

Barnett Newman '61-'64

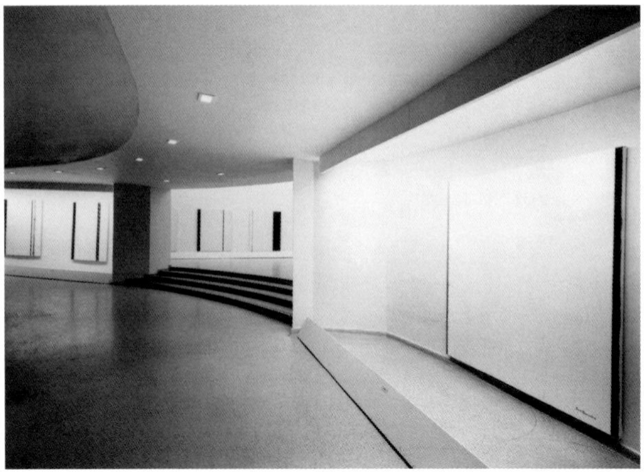

38 Barnett Newman, *Be II* on the ramp at the The Solomon R. Guggenheim Museum, 1966.

stepping the terror he addressed. He spoke rather of using the crucifixion in order to impose some relevance on it.

There is a second way in which Newman's strategies resonate with historically Jewish modes of remembrance. In keeping with the chain of references to the crucifixion, Newman referred in his statements on *The Stations* to 'the first pilgrims [who] walked the Via Dolorosa to identify themselves with the original moment'.[66] The process of identification is the process that the viewer goes through as they become the tragic subject, asking 'Lema?' In the Passover service, this kind of identification occurs too. Rather than remembering that their ancestors were slaves, the celebrant is instructed to tell themselves that *they* had come out of Egypt; that *they* personally have been emancipated. Describing such rituals, Yerushalmi has written that 'whatever memories were unleashed by the commemorative rituals and liturgies were surely not a matter of intellection, but of evocation and identification'. Having survived the foundational catastrophe of Jewish biblical history, Jews remember this catastrophe through telling themselves that *they* survived. I am not suggesting that the viewer of Newman's series was to imagine themselves in the camps – this is not the kind of identification that was either sought or deemed possible. Rather, the viewer identified with the question imposed by the camps; the question imposed *for them*.

In accounting for the ways in which Morris Louis addressed the memory of the Holocaust, I suggested previously that his paintings encouraged an interpretative activity that recalled historically Jewish modes of interpretation (and that this interpretative activity was seen to undo itself). If Louis and Newman both drew on Jewish traditions of interpretation and commemoration, clearly the way in which their abstract paintings generated meanings was very different. Where Louis used black and white paints to produce opposite suggestions about cultural destruction and renewal, Newman never used paints in this way. Black and white never had any kind of symbolic allusions, not even ones which were as deliberately fragile as Louis's. Rather, Newman's use of black, white, and raw canvas was a means of reducing his painterly vocabulary so that the viewer (and we should recall that he was the paintings' first viewer) would be denied the pleasures afforded by colour. Of course, just as Newman's reductions are noticeable within the context of the other paintings in his body of work, Louis's use of black and white becomes compelling especially when considered in the context of his later work.

There are other noteworthy differences between Louis's and Newman's works too. Where Louis used a title to provoke interpretations of specific parts of the paintings, Newman's title operated more affectively, not referring to the surfaces of the individual canvases, but setting up an emotive and allusive context in which the paintings would be encountered. The ways in which the two artists constructed their viewers were also distinct. Louis imagined a viewing subject in mourning, remembering what was lost and attempting to re-begin. Newman's viewers are tragic subjects, thinking about *their* own predicament.

For all these differences though, against the context of the modernist reception of these two artists, the two projects have remarkable commonalities. Where modernist criticism concentrated only on the organisation of pigment on the canvas, in both cases, Louis and Newman treated with extreme care the titling of the works and the ways in which these titles were presented to the public. Whereas for modernists, the only kind of history that counted was the history of the medium, both Louis and Newman undertook to address their paintings to the crises of recent history. It is interesting to note that in 1960, around the time Newman was thinking about this title, another artist prominently associated with modernist painting proposed a Holocaust memorial project. Mark Rothko was approached by the German art historian and curator Werner Haftmann to participate in *Documenta*, but refused because, 'as a Jew, he had no intention of exhibiting works in Germany, a country that had committed so many crimes against Jewry'.[67] Rothko did however agree to make paintings for 'a very small chapel of expiation' to be erected 'in memory of Jewish victims'.[68] The project never came to fruition, but had it done, it would have been fascinating to have seen how Rothko would have changed his painting for this context, and whether he would have deployed allusive titles rather than ones like *Untitled* and *Black on Grey*. Rothko's proposal nonetheless indicates that his paintings would have needed a particular kind of installation to work, and in the same way, for Newman, the installation of the paintings was integral to their meanings. His exhibition worked in tandem with the architecture of the Guggenheim.

This concern with installation in some way predicts the moves away from modernist painting in the late 1960s and the concerns of artists like Beryl Korot, Mel Bochner, Sol LeWitt and Richard Serra, whose works I will look at later; but the dialogue with architecture would be pursued within painting too. The next chapter will concentrate on the work of Frank Stella, also first championed by modernist critics. Though looking in part at work he made in 1959, around the time of the first *Stations*, I will focus on a series painted in the early 1970s. The paintings in the series were never installed in the specific architectural manner that Newman's *Stations* were. Instead Stella used the memory of destroyed architecture as a means of addressing the decimation of the Holocaust.

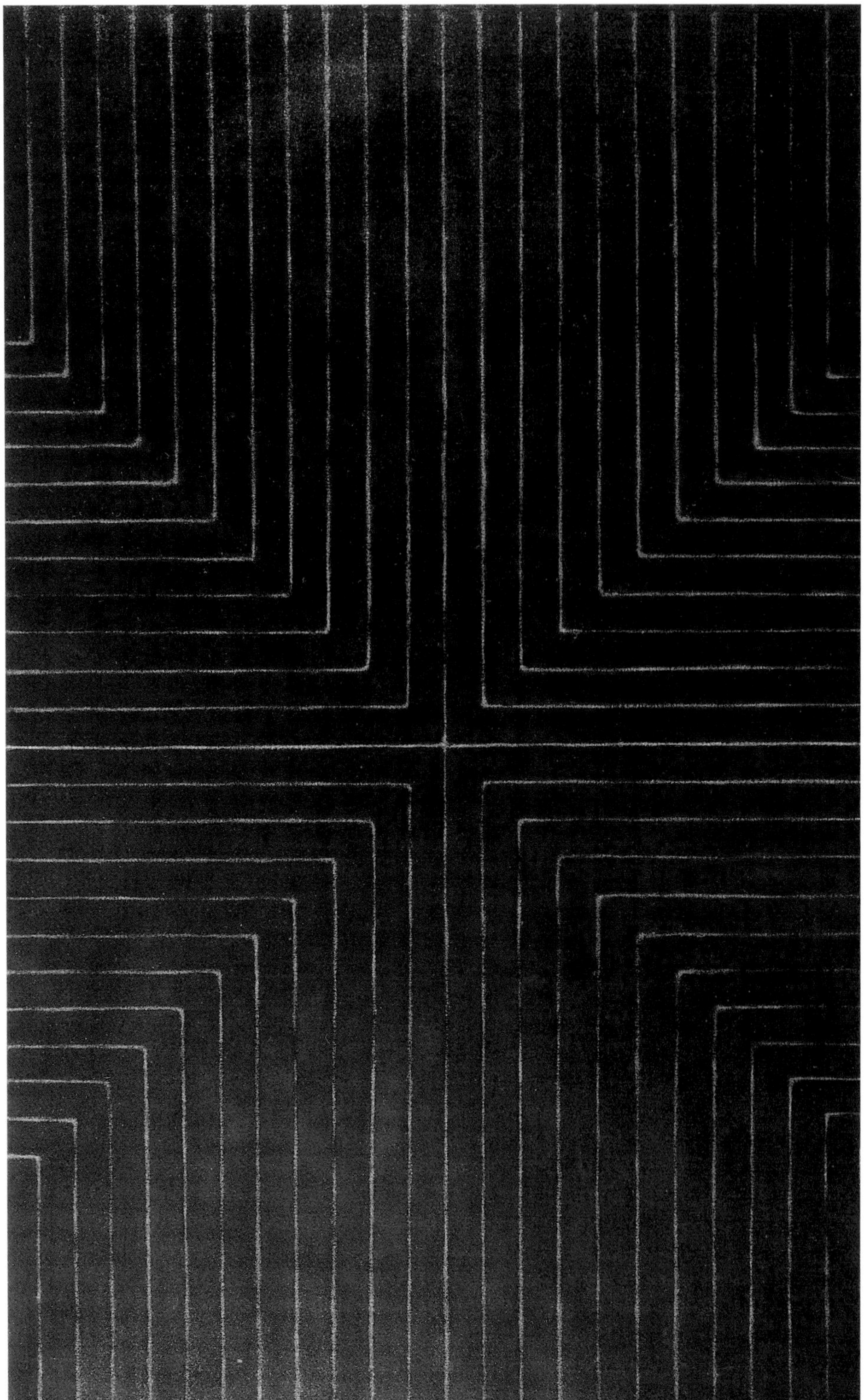

four

frank stella's *polish village* series

summer 1970

By the time of Barnett Newman's death on 4 July 1970, Frank Stella had become the undisputed heir to the throne of modernist painting. In March of that year, the artist, still only 33 years old, had opened his first retrospective at the Museum of Modern Art – an honour not even accorded to Newman during his lifetime (Stella would have his second retrospective there in 1987). The 1970 exhibition was curated by William Rubin, who heralded Stella's 'breathtaking'[1] progress over the past decade, and the show displayed sixty examples from his various series of the late 1950s and 1960s, including the *Black Paintings* (fig. 39), the *Aluminum Paintings*, the *Irregular Polygons* and the *Protractors*. In *The New York Times*, Hilton Kramer applauded Stella's 'phenomenal accomplishment', describing the move away from the visual austerity of the early work towards the 'lush, seductive, and extravagant' character of the recent canvases, but assuring readers that this move was not at the cost of a thoughtful and deductive approach to form: 'the cold hand of reason, of an informed and disabused ratiocination, controls even the most extravagant flights of chromatic invention'.[2] In his magazine, meanwhile, the editor of *Artforum* Philip Leider used more violent language to capture the force of Stella's rise. He described the '*blitzkrieg* manner of Stella's attack' on the shaped canvas – a term which, as we shall see, resonated with some of Stella's own titles.[3] Leider situated Stella's work at the centre of the 1960s debate between the literalists and abstractionists. Precisely because Stella's work could be battled over by sparring figures such as Michael Fried and Donald Judd, 'his shows just get looked at with harder eyes and tougher eyes, because, for almost everyone, taking Stella's measure is more *important*, somehow, than taking anyone else's'.[4]

39 Frank Stella, *Die Fahne hoch!*, 1959. Enamel on canvas, 308.6 × 185.4 cm. Whitney Museum of American Art, New York.

40 *Wooden Synagogues* front cover.

Leider's 'almost' was an important qualifier, though. Not everyone took the questions posed by Stella's paintings to be the crucial ones confronting artists in the summer of 1970; not even everyone working at the Museum of Modern Art. A month after Stella's retrospective closed, Rubin's colleague Kynaston McShine introduced his group show, *Information*, with the following, now famous, jab at painting:

> If you are living in the United States, you may fear that you will be shot at, either in the universities, in your bed, or more formally in Indochina. It may seem too inappropriate, if not absurd, to get up in the morning, walk into a room, and apply dabs of paint from a little tube to a square of canvas. What can you do as a young artist that seems relevant and meaningful?[5]

McShine's question reflected a growing scepticism about the urgency of the formal debates surrounding Stella's exhibition, and indeed this scepticism was made explicit in the work of one of the artists included in McShine's show. John Baldessari proposed to exhibit at MoMA a cadaver lit so as to resemble Mantegna's *Dead Christ* but two years previously he had made *This is not to be looked at* (1967–68), which displayed above this painted text a silk-screened image of the cover of the November 1966 issue of *Artforum*. The cover showed Stella's *Union* (1966) from the *Irregular Polygon* series, and the issue contained Michael Fried's essay 'Shape as Form', a text that had also appeared in the catalogue of Stella's show at the Pasadena Art Museum, which Baldessari must have seen. Baldessari's painted-on title was suitably ambiguous: was *This* Stella's painting, Fried's criticism, *Artforum* itself, or all three? During this period, Stella's work featured on more *Artforum* covers and in more articles than the work of any other artist, and was increasingly affiliated with modernist theory. Baldessari's conflation was therefore an accurate observation as well as a joke.[6] But there is another way to read the sentence: placing the emphasis on the verb, one could posit that the problem Baldessari pointed to was that some painting simply demanded 'to be looked at'. And reading Baldessari's words like this, one might ask whether painting should not be 'thought about' instead?

Taken together, McShine's questioning of the viability of painting and Baldessari's comedic deflation of Stella's own practice and its reception suggest that the summer of 1970 might not have been as comfortable a time for Stella as we might think. When his *Black Paintings* were first shown in 'Sixteen Americans' at MoMA in 1959, Stella's work had been considered controversial and groundbreaking, but now the work was represented at best as a joke, and at worst as irrelevant and aloof.[7] Certainly Stella was not impervious to the political climate that McShine described. On 22 May 1970, a week before its scheduled close, he shut down his MoMA retrospective in sympathy with his 'co-workers' in the 'New York Art Strike against Racism, Sexism, Repression, and War'.[8] Later, after participating in the 'Emergency Cultural Government', a committee trying 'to keep shows out of U.S. government hands during the duration of the war'[9], Stella contributed a silk-screen made 'specifically for Referendum 70', an auction in support of pro-peace politicians.[10] But for all the generosity of these gestures, they did not involve a significant shift in the direction of Stella's *painting*. One might even

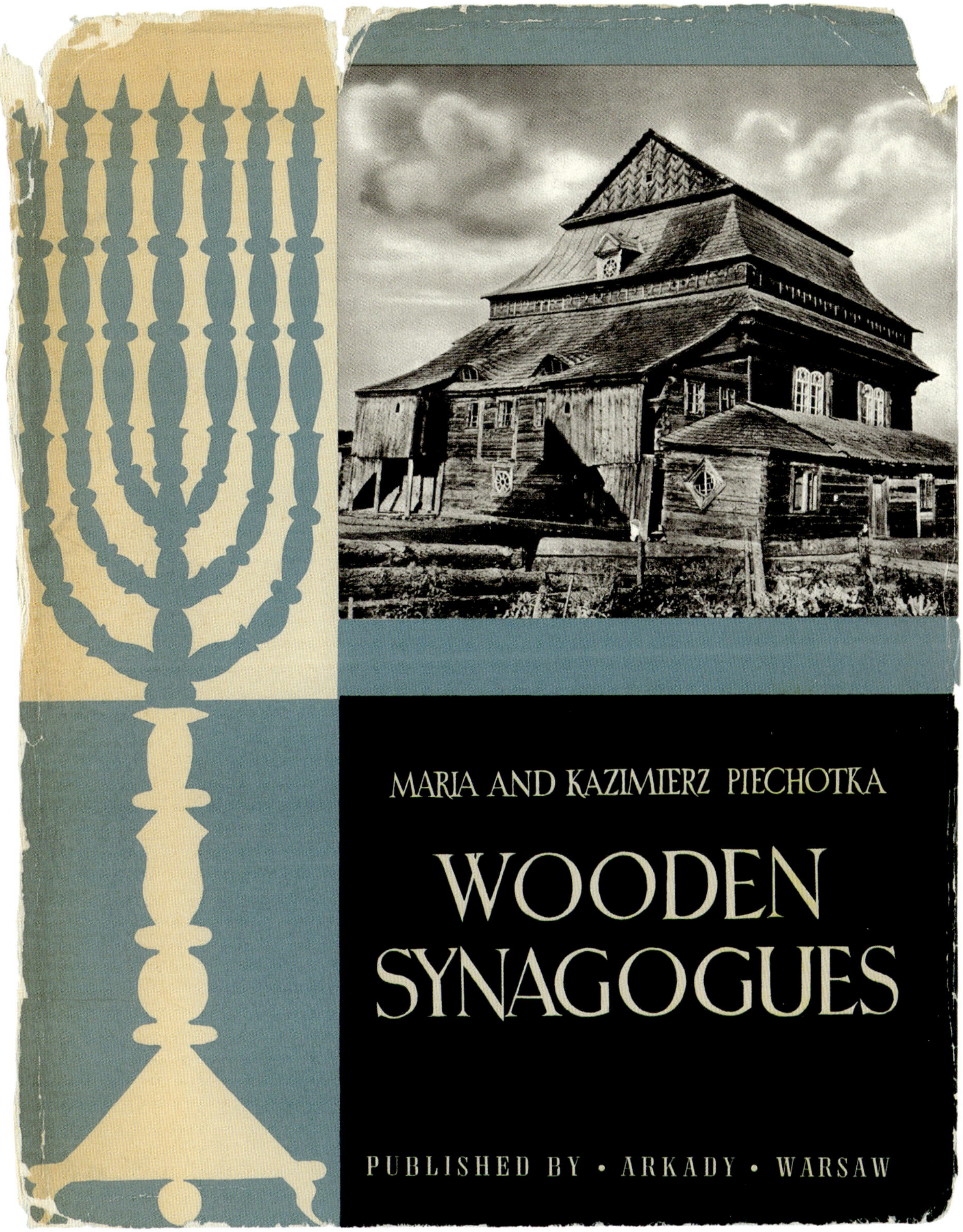
MARIA AND KAZIMIERZ PIECHOTKA
WOODEN
SYNAGOGUES
PUBLISHED BY • ARKADY • WARSAW

say that Stella confirmed McShine's ambivalence about the medium: the only way to make painting's activity critical was to shut down an exhibition, or to use its commercial status to raise funds for 'relevant' causes.

41 Frank Stella, *Chyrow I*, 1972. Mixed media on canvas, 284.5 × 254 cm.

It was in this turbulent context that Stella initiated the series of works with which I am concerned here. At the end of the summer of 1970, Stella sustained a tennis injury which led to an unexpectedly protracted stay in hospital. While there, he was given a book by his friend Richard Meier, the architect who had helped to organise the display of Barnett Newman's *Model for a Synagogue* at the Jewish Museum in 1963. The book, published in 1959, was called *Wooden Synagogues*, and was a beautifully illustrated volume containing the last images of seventy-one 'monuments of Jewish culture', photographed during an architectural survey in the 1920s and 1930s, and destroyed in Poland during the war (fig. 40).[11] The synagogues were ordered alphabetically, without privileging the quality of one building over another. The book interspersed line drawings of plans and elevations with photographs, and where only a sketch of a building existed, this was used to represent it. The English edition contained an introduction by Dr. Stephen Kayser, who had been the curator of the Jewish Museum at the time. 'This book commemorates martyred buildings', he wrote. Remembering the now-destroyed inscription above the portal of the Jablonow synagogue referring to the opening of the gates of Heaven, he continued: 'This book intends to open still another gate, that of remembrance.'[12]

Stella would have read these words in hospital as he spent time leafing through the images of the synagogues. During his convalescence he began to make drawings, and on recovery, he initiated work on a series that would occupy him for most of the early 1970s (figs 41 and 42). The series would be titled *Polish Villages*, with individual works named after forty of the wooden synagogues documented in the book, and by its completion in 1974, the series numbered some 130 works, since some 'Villages' were executed in more than one version. The context I have described so far might suggest that this series could be taken as Stella's reaction to the predicament of painting in 1970, but as well as asking what kind of reaction this was, I want to scrutinise the kind of relationship that exists between the 'martyred buildings' depicted in *Wooden Synagogues* and the canvases and constructions of the *Polish Village* series. But first we should ask how Stella made the works, and how they were initially received.

the *polish villages*, the *wooden synagogues*, and the critical response

Each series of paintings in Stella's 1970 retrospective was unified by distinct formal and material qualities. The *Black Paintings* of 1959, for instance, were all made on rectangular stretchers with lines of black enamel paint running in regular bands from the outside of the stretcher inwards. The eight *Purple Paintings* (1963) were based on regular geometrical figures and each had a central hole that echoed the external shape. The paintings of the *Protractor* series (1967–70) were made on curved supports whose shapes combined circles and half-circles, and were covered by polymer and fluorescent polymer paints. And so on. By contrast the *Polish Village* series was more internally

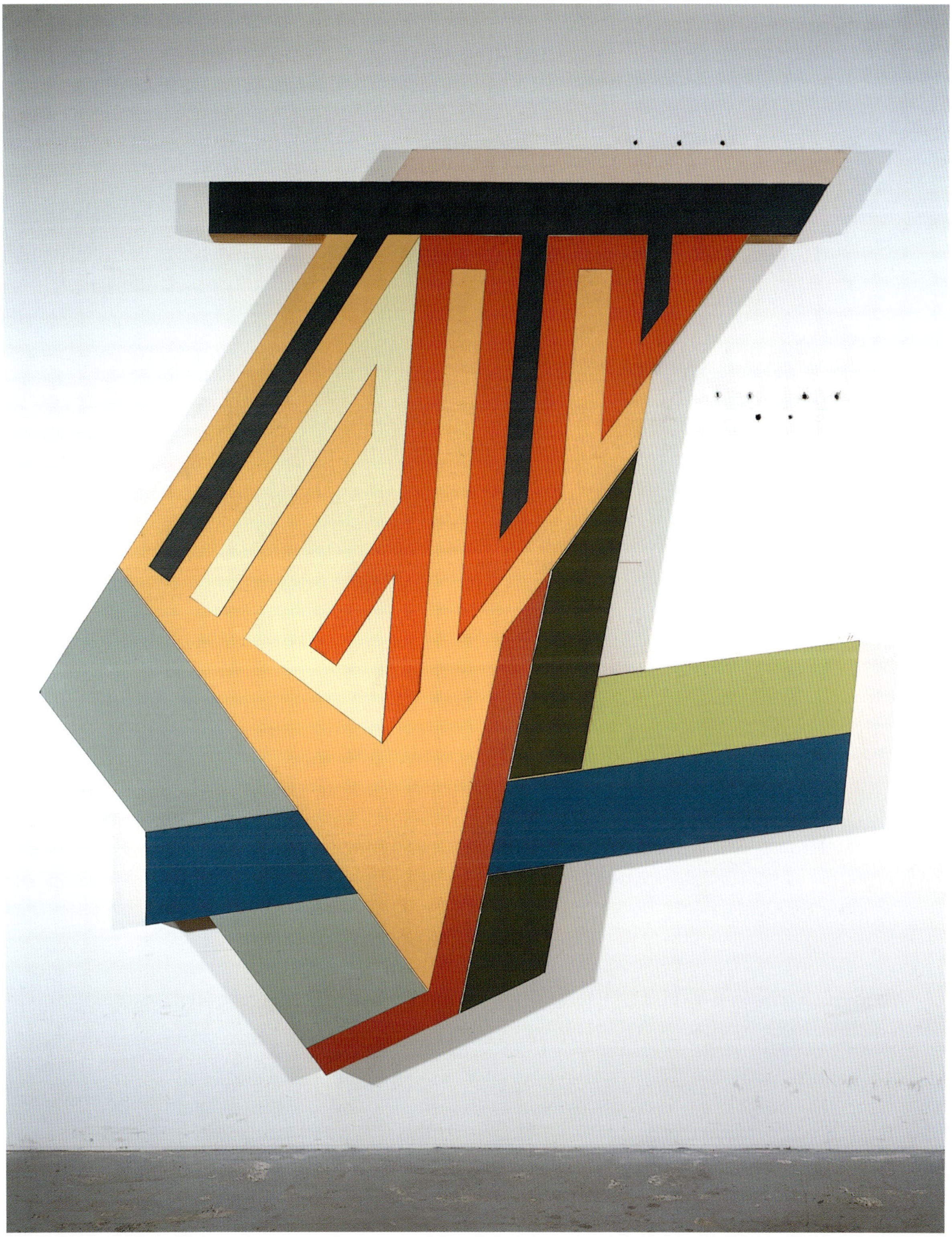

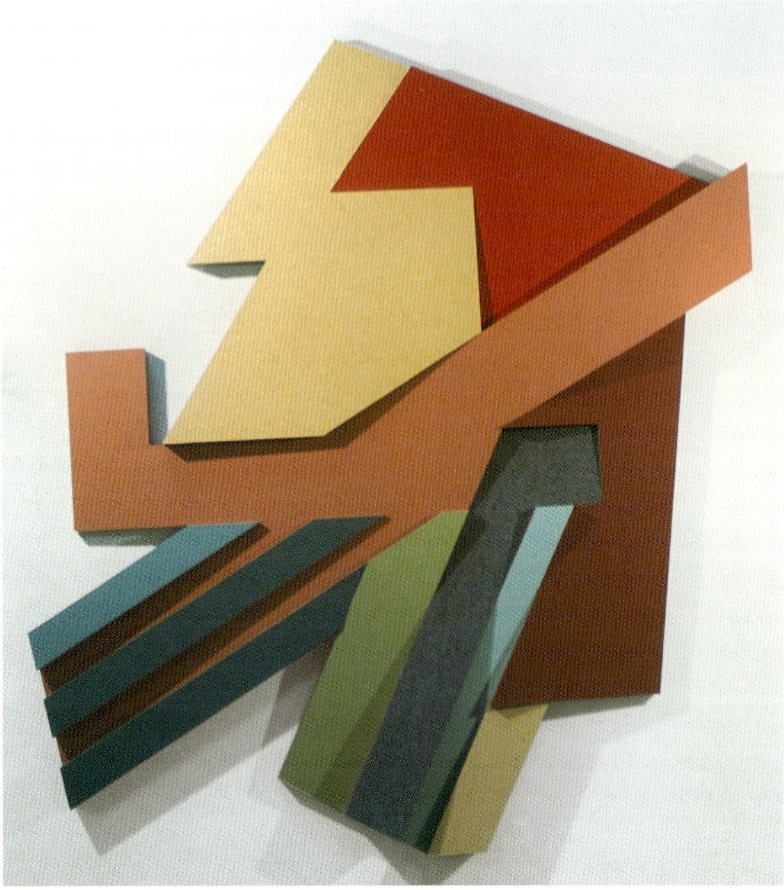

42 Frank Stella, *Ostropol III*, 1973. Mixed media on board, 228.6 × 259 cm.

varied, and as a result it would be impossible to describe any one of the *Polish Villages* as representative of the entire series, in the same way that such a description might have served for works in earlier series by Stella. The only common feature is that each work had an irregular, straight-edged external shape, and was composed internally of a number of connected irregularly shaped, straight-edged monochrome sections.

The relationship of each different work to the axes and orientations of regular, rectangular paintings varied greatly. Some works recalled the orientation of 'normal' paintings quite powerfully. *Felsztyn I* (fig. 43), for instance, had one long vertical edge and one near horizontal edge along its twelve external borders, and *Mogielnica I* had a long horizontal bottom flank. *Lanckorona I* (fig. 44), however, had twenty six edges, of which only one very short one lies on the vertical. And not a single one of the sixteen edges on *Janów Sokólski I* lie on the horizontal or vertical axes (fig. 45). The normal rectangular axis is invoked within the perimeter of some works, such as *Chodorow II* (fig. 46), which contains at its centre a cream rectangle (cut into by a blue diagonal bar), but *Piaski III* has no such invocations, and consists instead of several interlocking bands, almost like the tines of a fork (fig. 47). *Odelsk I* offers the illusion of depth

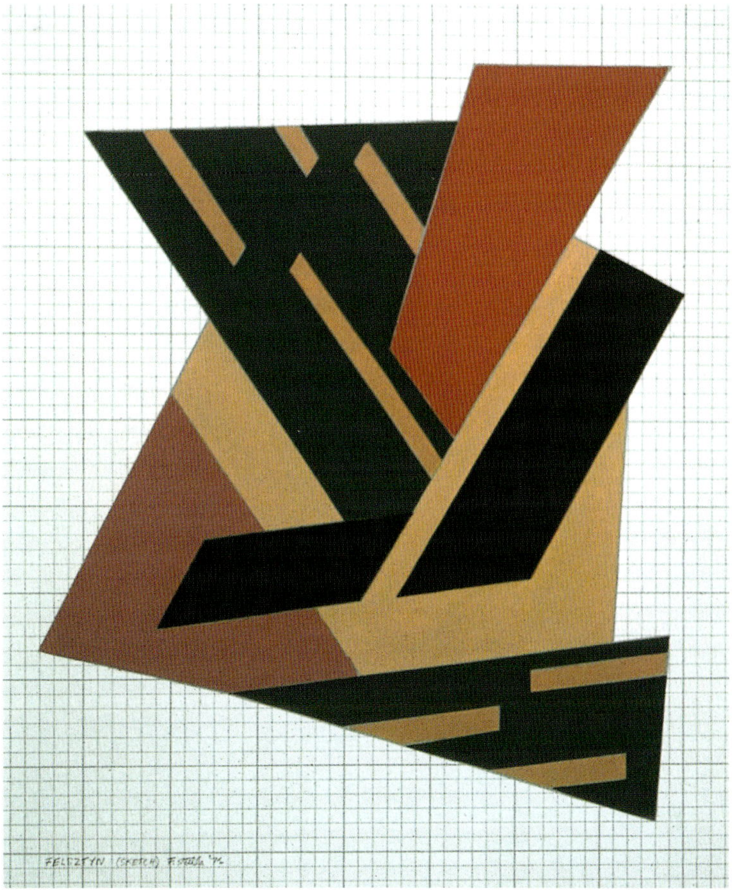

43 Frank Stella, Drawing for *Felsztyn*, 1972. Ink on paper, 79 × 68.5 cm .

(fig. 48): between the central yellow triangle and the underlying black section, a grey strip runs along its left side, suggesting, if this is read as a shadow, that the yellow section lies further away from the wall than the black; such illusionism is entirely absent from other works.

The relationship of internal colours also differed from painting to painting. *Felsztyn III* for instance, had dull colour juxtapositions with sections of beige, olive, orange and brown, so that the entire painting presents a consistent, somewhat autumnal tone. *Chodorow II* features bright contrasts of red, white and blue; *Kamionka Strumitowa III* by contrast brashly juxtaposes a pink next to an orange area that is flanked by grey and surrounded by areas of brown and red paint (fig. 49).

As is indicated by the numbers after each name in the titles, Stella made most works in the series in more than one version. All the versions of a work – *Nasielsk I, II, III* and *IV*, for example – shared both an external outline and an internal arrangement of shaped sections, but there were huge differences between the versions arising from the materials that Stella used and the kind of structures that he built. The clearest accounts of these differences have been provided by Philip Leider in his catalogue essay for the

1978 Fort Worth Art Museum show 'Stella Since 1970', and by William Rubin in his 1987 MoMA catalogue.[13] In most cases, 'version one' would be made on a thick canvas-covered stretcher. Stella collaged onto the sections thin materials such as felt, or second layers of canvas. Apart from the slight differences in the level above the support canvas, all the sections of the versions were on the same plane, parallel to the wall. 'Version two' was made on a wood support, with all the internal sections once again resting on the same plane. A different colour scheme from 'version one' would be employed, as well as a greater diversity of materials. In addition to canvas and felt, Stella mounted various boards onto the sections – pressboard, Homosote, Masonite, Kachina-Board and plywood. Some would be thicker or thinner and so slightly higher or lower off the support than others, providing a low relief. 'Version three' would again replicate divisions while changing the colour arrangements of the previous two versions. However, these works employed a cardboard support and their sections veered off the vertical plane. Looking at *Felsztyn III* from the side, then, it is clear that while some sections lie parallel to the wall, others cut into each other, meeting and tilting away from this plane at oblique angles. But you can sense this from a frontal position too, because the sloping planes cast shadows onto each other in just about any normal lighting condition. Some works, finally, were executed in a fourth version. These, like *Nasielsk IV*, were unpainted wood reliefs, made of different wooden parts, which intersected in the same manner as in the third versions (fig. 50).

Stella did not execute all the versions consecutively. Rather, he first worked on thirteen shapes or 'Villages', which he executed in four versions each, then after completing these he worked simultaneously on the various versions of the next group of shapes. He began to exhibit the works long before the entire series was completed, juxtaposing in each show different versions of the same shape. By the early 1970s Stella was working with a number of private galleries, and he debuted the works in the *Polish Village* series at Lawrence Rubin's in New York (fig. 51) and at Kasmin's in London in 1971, at Leo Castelli's again in New York in 1973 (fig. 52), and then at Knoedler's in New York in 1974. Stella also showed works from the series at public institutions such as the Portland Center for the Visual Arts (fig. 53).

As the first exhibitions of Stella's new work since the MoMA retrospective, these shows were greeted with a great amount of critical attention: long reviews were published in *ARTNews*, *Studio International*, *Art International* and *The New York Times*, and *Artforum* published no less than two feature articles and two review articles on the *Polish Villages*.[14] Some critics devoted their reviews to formal descriptions before attempting to differentiate the quality of the works in a given show: John Elderfield, for instance, felt that '*Raków II* and *Bogoria I* come to look more acceptable than the confusions of *Felsztyn IV* and *Chodorow IV*.' But in general he found the show 'weak', explaining that the 'bewildering' turn the work had taken was a desperate attempt to create a 'radical look'[15].

Other critics spent time differentiating the works in the new series from Stella's earlier paintings. Many drew comparisons with the *Irregular Polygons*, yet as Jeanne Siegel realised, 'the contours are even more irregular and the internal structure – T-

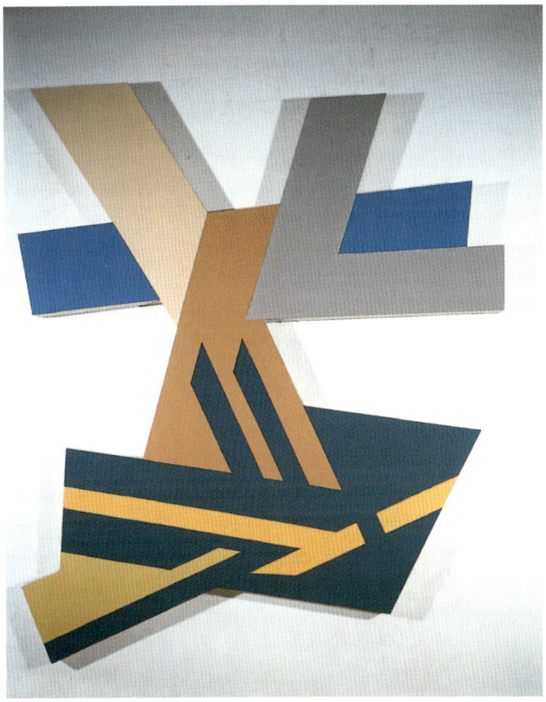

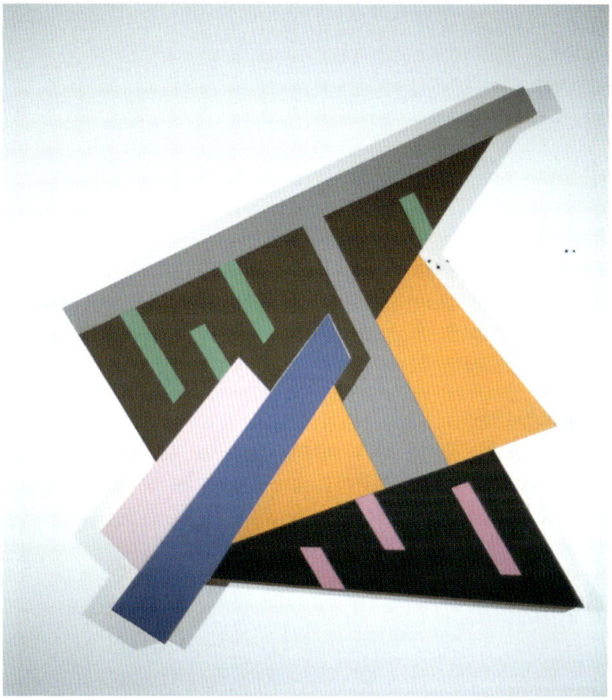

44 (left) Frank Stella, *Lanckororna I*, 1971. Canvas, felt paper, and paint on cardboard. 274.3 × 228.6 cm.

45 (right) Frank Stella, *Janów Sokólski I*, 1972. Mixed media on board, 264.2 × 251.5 cm.

squares, triangles, bars of colour that interlock and occasionally interlace – is more intricate'.[16] (Carter Ratcliff felt it was as if 'two or more irregular polygons. . . . had been placed on top of each other – the irregular becomes slightly crazy'.[17]) Elizabeth Baker noted that, whereas differently coloured areas had previously been separated by bands of unpainted canvas (from the gaps between the black stripes in 1959 to the *Protractor* paintings of 1969), colours now met each other at their very limits. However, where, in a Kenneth Noland painting, such meeting would cause optical fluctuation, in the paintings she described, the dulled colour schemes prevented this from happening.

As well as making comparisons with Stella's own art, some critics chose to reflect on the relationship these paintings struck with contemporary and historical work. While more than one critic drew comparisons with Ron Davis's paintings (Hilton Kramer, Rosalind Krauss), and Roy Lichtenstein's sculpture (Kramer, Jeremy Gilbert-Rolfe), there was little consensus about the most important historical precedents. Some referred to Juan Gris (April Kingsley, Baker), others to Moholy-Nagy (Ratcliff). Baker described the 'sophisticated quotations from Cubism' but also wrote that the paintings 'seem to suggest frozen ideograms of Action Painting's gestural vigor', *and* compared the look of some paintings to 1930s Art Deco architectural details. She maintained that 'they do not break any new theoretical ground',[18] but Irving Sandler felt otherwise. Prompted by the 'three-dimensionality of the components', he inserted the works into a trajectory instigated by cubism, and concluded that they raised 'the important question concerning abstract art now: What is the potential of a relational esthetic?'[19]

By arguing that this was their crucial relevance, Sandler indicated that now, more than before, Stella was moving away from the kind of practice Donald Judd had called for when, in 1965, he had articulated the bankruptcy of the part-to-part relationship. Though Judd had proceeded to eliminate such concerns through the creation of 'specific objects' that were 'neither painting nor sculpture', those artists who sympathised with his critique had justified the continuing production of relational paintings by creating works in series. Through making a series, the painter avoided privileging the choices about the relationship of parts within a given work, staking a work's importance rather on the relationship between its arrangements and those in other works in the series.

46 Frank Stella, *Chodorow II*, 1971. Felt, paper, and canvas collage on canvas, 274.4 × 269.4 cm. National Gallery of Art, Washington D.C. Robert and Jane Meyerhoff Collection.

It was this context that Rosalind Krauss (in her high-modernist youth) mapped out in her account of the *Polish Villages* in a 1971 *Artforum* article titled 'Stella's New Work and the Problem of Series', an article to which it is worth devoting considerable attention. Krauss started by explaining her theory of why it was that so many modernist painters had worked in series. In an effort to produce works 'about painting in general', they came on what she called a particular 'medium', a term she used at this juncture to name what could simply be called a visual idea. Her example of a 'medium' (invoking without naming Morris Louis's 'Unfurleds') was 'pouring rivulets of paint'.[20] Once this 'medium' was discovered, it 'both permitted the generation of a series of objects and *demanded* it'. Only through repetition could the meaning of the 'medium' and its significance for the direction of painting as a whole become evident. 'The series, then, operated as a ground against which the medium became visible', she wrote. If working in series allowed the entire idea or 'medium' of the series to be stated, so the practice allowed each individual work in the series to gain meaning to the viewer and critic, for one could judge it in contrast to the others. Working in series also facilitated a more substantial relationship between viewer and painting that Krauss explained through recourse to Stanley Cavell. Each individual work in the series 'in its absolute difference and absolute connection with others . . . maintains the haecceity (the sheer that-ness) of a material object', and demands in turn that its viewer acknowledges their 'own haecceity', their singularity and incarnation before it.

These arguments supported Stella's early work and could be used to explain the relationship between a viewer and the individual paintings in his early series. But in 1967, the idea of series began to permeate each individual painting. The 'medium' of the *Protractors* was what Krauss called 'serialization': one *Protractor* painting could contain within it six permutations of the semicircular unit that characterised all the *Protractor* paintings, while another might contain two. At this point, a problem arose. A painting that *contained* a series appeared simply as a diagrammatic idea.[21] As a result, the spectator would only encounter the painting as an idea, and not as a singular entity. 'What is being acknowledged is not one's own and the painting's position in space and time, but a metaphysicalizing of the situation'. The point Stella had reached in 1969 was thus 'inimical to painting'.

For Krauss, the *Polish Villages* suggested that Stella had solved the problem in which he had found himself, for no longer did each painting contain a series. Krauss recog-

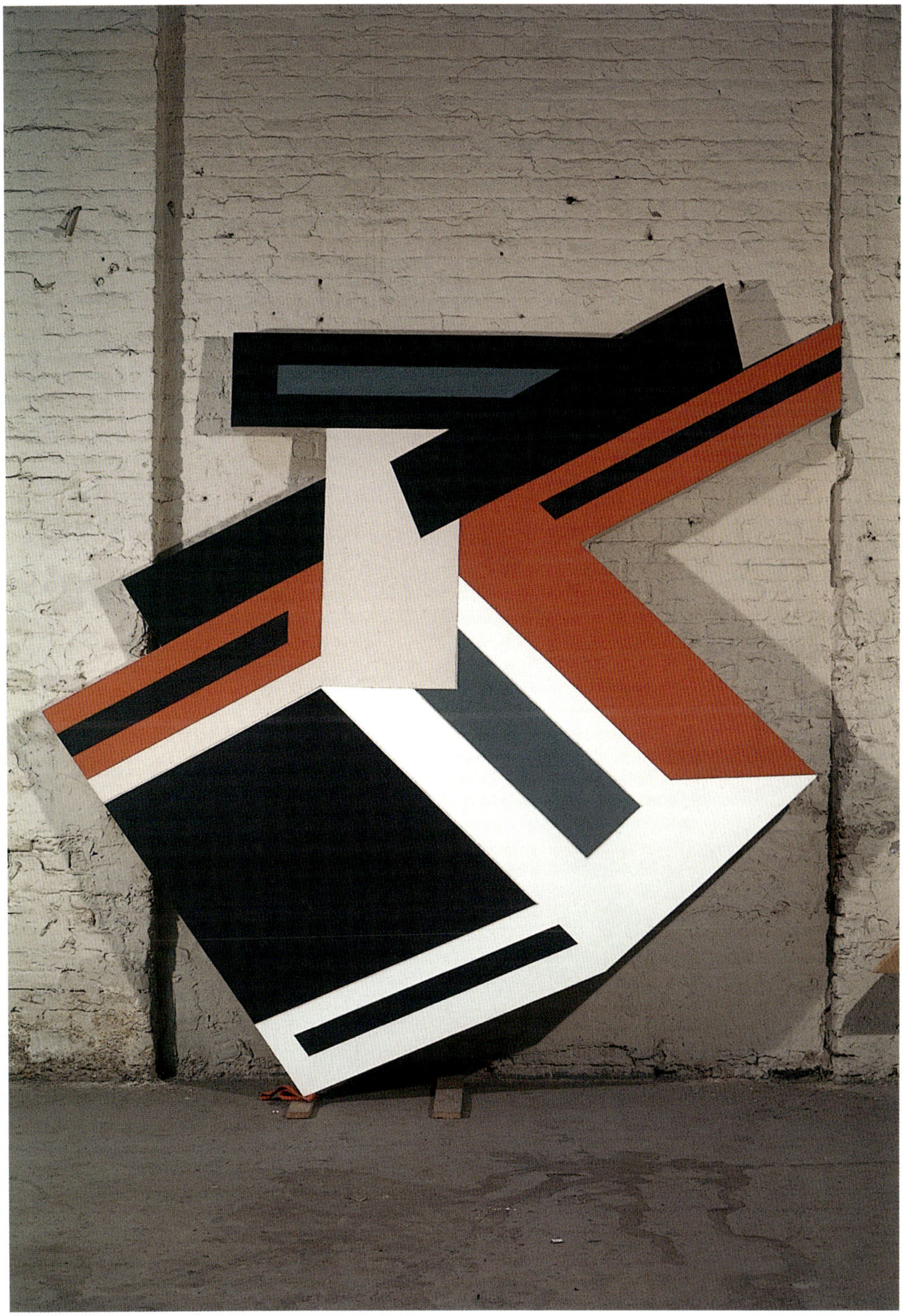

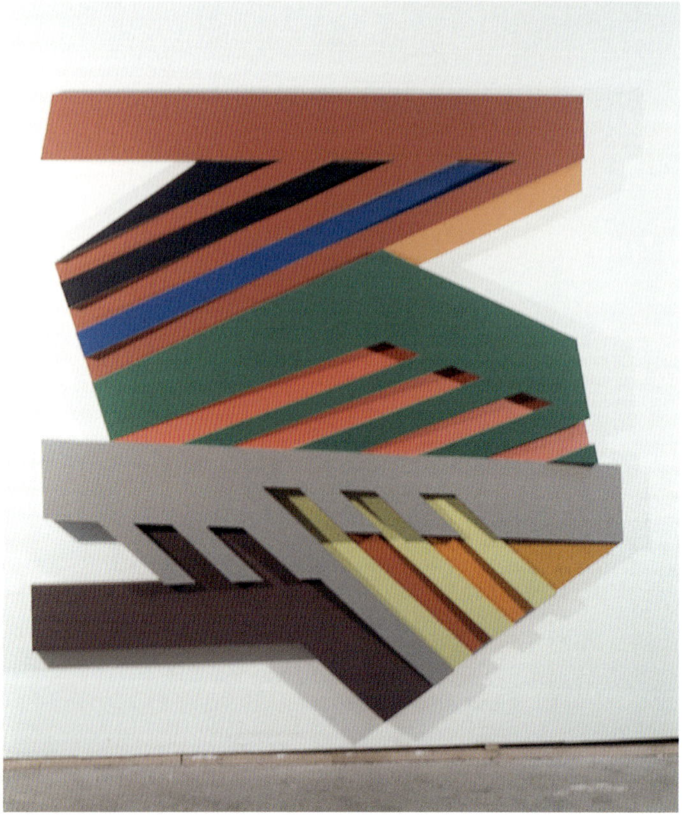

47 Frank Stella, *Piaski III*, 1973. Mixed media on board, 233.7 × 213.4 cm.

nised that the *Polish Villages* raised 'questions about the viability of the very notion of painting in series'. Not only was every 'Village' far more different from each other than each *Protractor* painting; 'from version to version. . . . the coherence implicit in the very idea of 'version' is drained'. Krauss looked carefully at the various works to consider how they restored the relationship between viewer and painting that Cavell had particulated. *Chodorow I*, with its central rectangle, contained a literal centre, and causing a viewer to focus on this midpoint, the work metaphorically demanded that it (as an individual art work) be the centre of attention. *Odelsk I*, meanwhile, created the illusion of depth through various means, including the false 'shadow' of the triangle which I described earlier. It offered the temporary suggestion that it 'had several facets or aspects, not all of which face the viewer, so that the painting in some way is not everywhere equally open and simultaneously available to the viewer'. But in fact it only had one plane, despite the collaged materials of its various sections. The viewer would come to realise that its parts were continuous with one another, but in so doing they would also realise that *their frontal presence before the painting* was necessary for this continuity of surface to be intuited. Therefore, in posing the question of its own orientation and the viewer's orientation towards it, the painting emphasised its own identity as a single, coherent object, and the viewer's singular identity as a viewing subject.

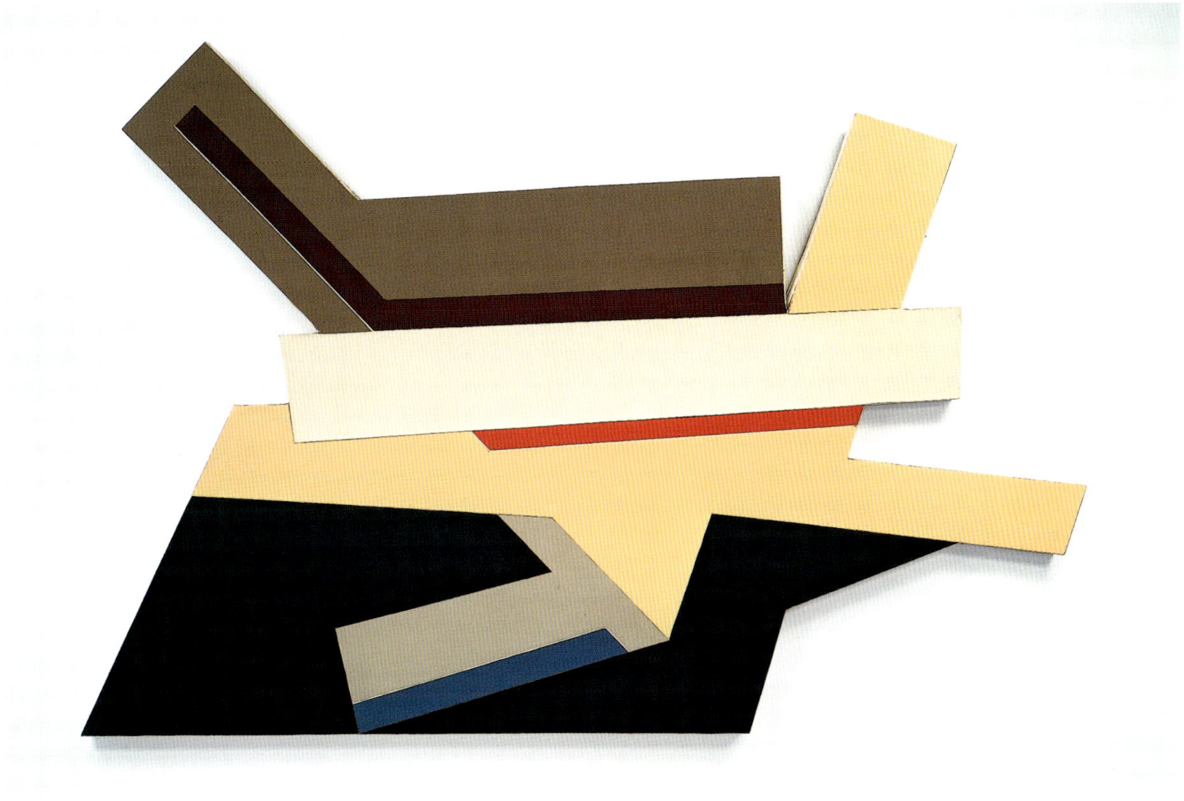

48 Frank Stella, *Odelsk I*, 1971. Mixed media on canvas, 228.6 × 335.3 cm.

With these complex accounts, Krauss made her claim for the significance of the 'best' *Polish Villages*. As a return to proper modernist painting, Stella's new work 'insisted on the singleness-of-aspect of painting itself', and 'asked us to grasp the work of art with the kind of immediacy with which we experience our own inner states. . . . Stella seems to want to ground painting itself in the terms of an experience which is manifestly sensuous.'

Krauss's argument about illusion, orientation and frontality could only work with some of the 'version ones' in the series and it is also noteworthy, I think, that she considered the two 'best' paintings both 'version ones': the 'version threes' and 'fours' questioned the authority and primacy of the frontal viewing position through their tilting planes, and she sidestepped these on terms of insufficient quality. As much as he might have been flattered by her arguments, it was clearly important to Stella to make paintings in the different versions and he continued doing so for years after her essay was published. I will come back to the significance of the versions later, but for now I want to acknowledge the sophistication of Krauss's account of the series and to point out in general once again how seriously these paintings were taken when first displayed. Stella's exhibitions of the early 1970s were covered by critics who went on to become the editors of *Art in America* and *Artforum*, the art critic of *The New Yorker*, the head

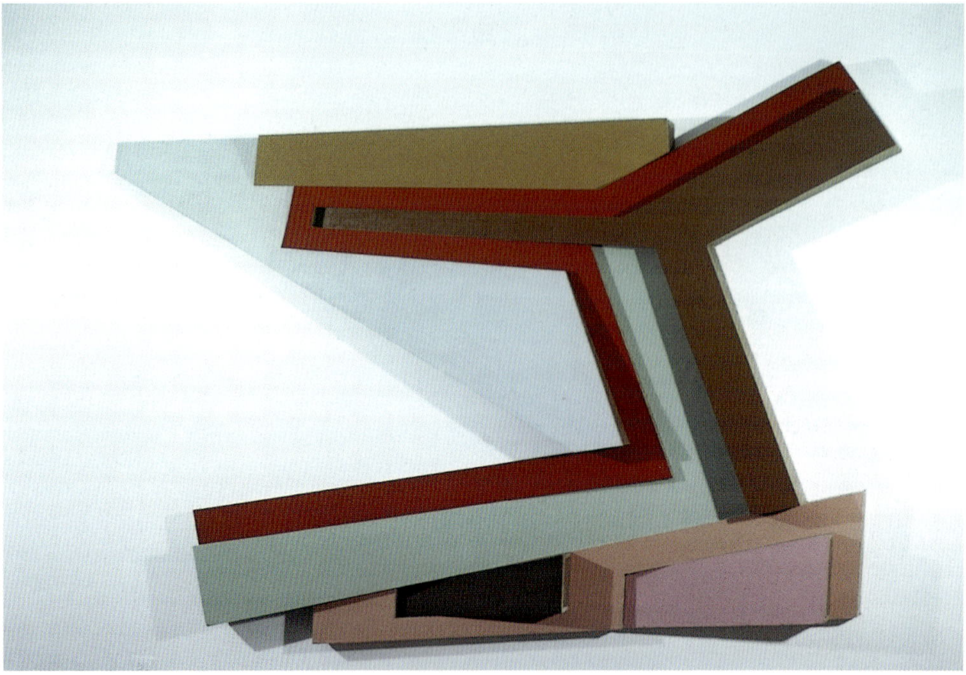

of the department of painting and sculpture at MoMA and the leading modernist art historian of the past thirty years. Many of these writers, moreover, were members of what Max Kozloff would call in a 1976 *Artforum* article the 'oldtime Jewish sect called American art criticism'.[22] Yet not one of these early critics paused before the paintings to ask what it could mean that they were named after Polish villages; what it could mean that Stella had worked from the book *Wooden Synagogues*; what it might signify for a painter to draw from a photographic and architectural archive of edifices destroyed during the Holocaust.

49 (top) Frank Stella, *Kamionka Strumiłowa III*, 1972. Mixed media on board, 223.5 × 315 cm.

50 (facing page) Frank Stella, *Nasielsk IV*, 1972. Unpainted wood, 279.4 × 227.4 cm, The Art Institute of Chicago.

Turning to look at the discourse around the wooden synagogues, this silence in the criticism becomes even more interesting, for the synagogues were hardly considered to have been a minor aspect of the Jewish cultural heritage – they were not interchangeable, in other words, with so many candlesticks, spice boxes, mezuzot or shtetl stories. Far from it: there was in fact a scholarly consensus that the wooden synagogues were 'the only real Jewish folk art in history'[23], the only properly 'Jewish' art to have emerged during the diasporic period.

Why was this? Whereas elsewhere, Jews had built synagogues resembling the religious edifices of their host nations, the wooden synagogues, wrote the artist and scholar Louis Lozowick in 1947, were 'a truly original folk expression' whose 'originality does not lie alone in the exterior architecture, it lies equally in the beautiful and intricate wood carving of the interior'.[24] It was not simply their beauty and originality that accounted for the synagogues' significance, though. In many diaspora countries, Jews had been banned from architectural work, and so had commissioned gentile labourers

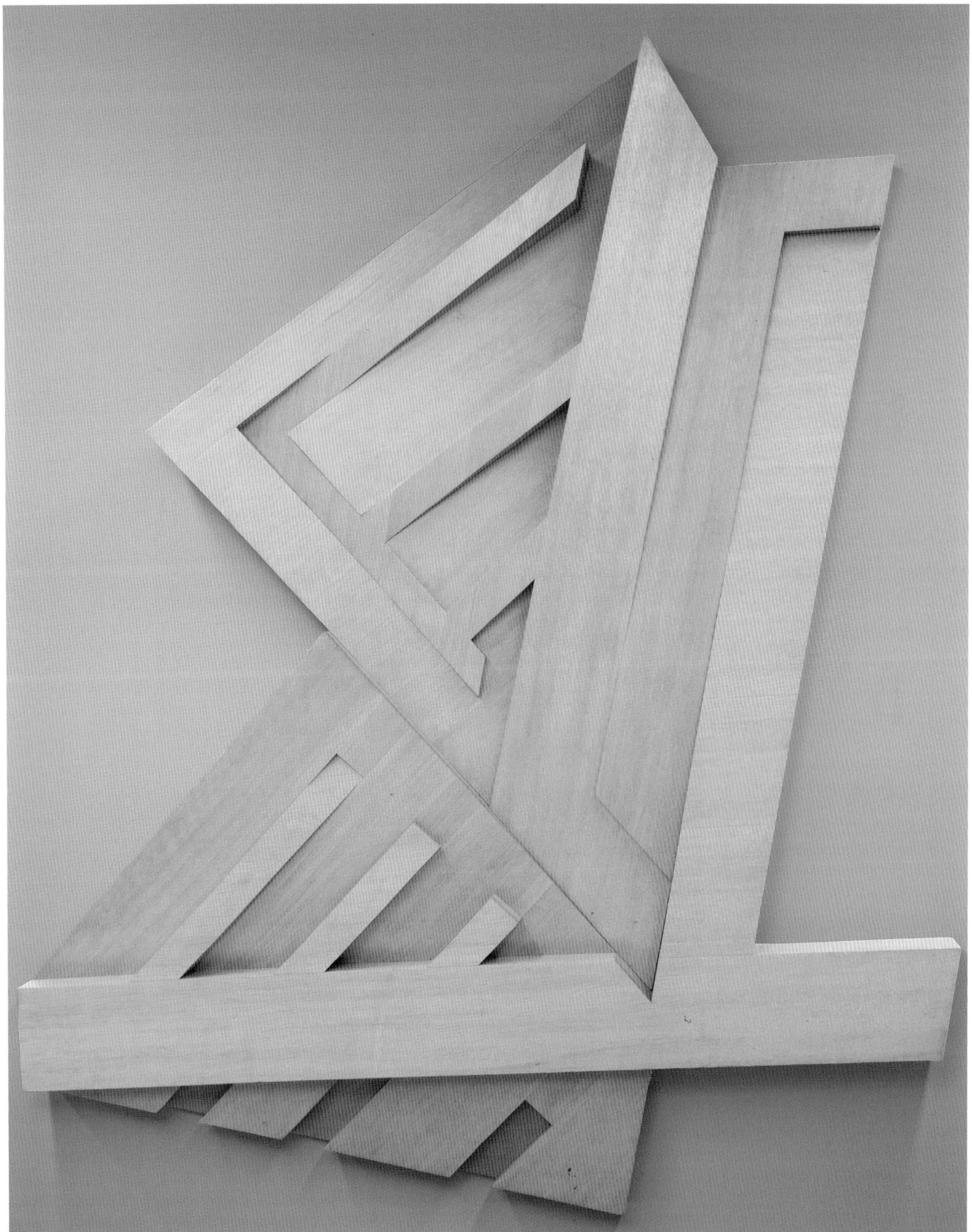

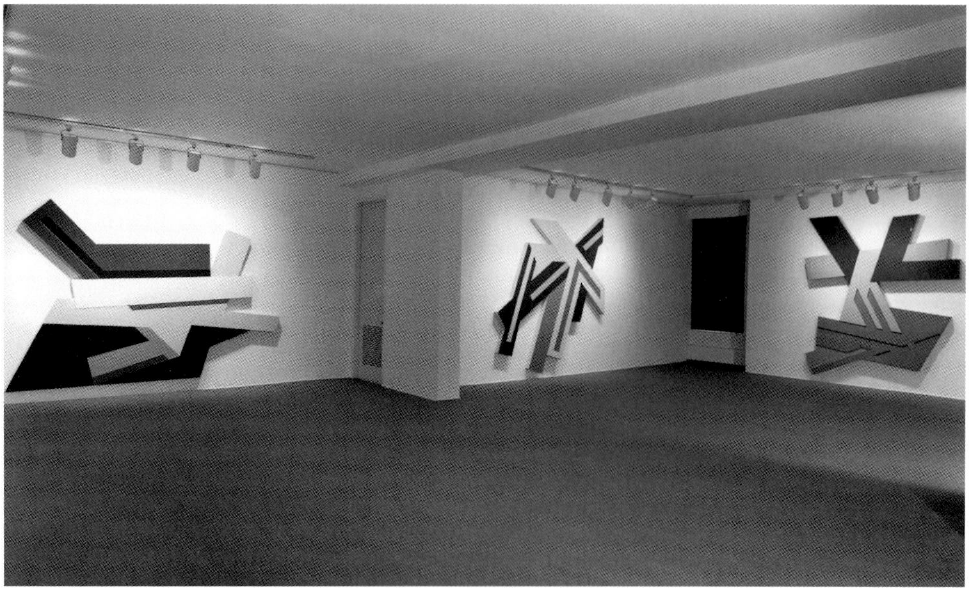

51 Frank Stella, work from the *Polish Village* series, Lawrence Rubin Gallery, New York, 1971. Left to right: *Odelsk I*, *Narowla I*, *Lanckorona II*.

to construct their buildings. The wooden synagogues, however, 'were built . . . from the modest contributions of tailors, carpenters, leather makers, shoemakers'.[25] George Loukomski, who published *Jewish Art in European Synagogues* also in 1947, emphasised that they 'constituted a collective effort. The whole population participated in the construction'.[26] And just as the population of the villages built the edifices, so they came to inhabit them. Introducing *Wooden Synagogues*, Stephen Kayser made this clear:

> If there ever was a truly close relationship between a house of worship and its populace, it lay in the affection which the inhabitants of an Eastern European Jewish country community felt for their synagogues, the home of their souls. Their love and devotion built it, embellished its interior, flocked around it and felt divine protection under its shadow in time of peril.[27]

The synagogues were commemorated in the book Stella had been given, but though they had been destroyed by the time he received it, there had been calls to salvage their remains. Louis Lozowick, reviewing Loukomski's book, recalled that:

> A short time ago I heard a traveller, recently returned from Poland, tell the now familiar tale of Nazi depredation, violence, inhumanity. One thing caught my ear especially. 'From time to time,' he said, 'climbing over the rubble piled high where a house of worship used to be, you discover a piece of wood carving, from the *Aron* perhaps, a twisted metal candlestick, a painted slab. I read of so many millions and tens of millions of dollars spent on charity here and abroad – couldn't some pennies be spared to salvage the few remaining relics of a rich cultural heritage, while there is still time?'[28]

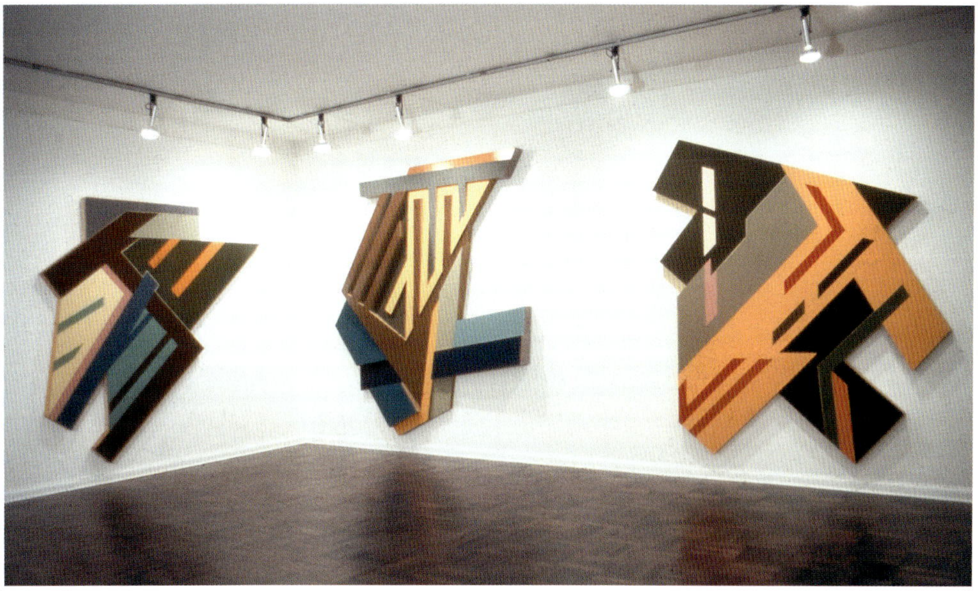

52 Frank Stella, work from the *Polish Village* series, Leo Castelli Gallery, New York, 1973. Left to right: *Lipsko I*, *Chyrow III*, *Bechhofen I*.

Meyer Schapiro might have had the wooden synagogues in mind when in 1946 he urged that the nascent New York Jewish Museum should display 'models of the outstanding buildings of Jewish history',[29] and though this did not come to fruition, when Stella's friend Richard Meier introduced the exhibition of 'Recent American Synagogue Architecture' at the museum sixteen years later, he referred with admiration in the catalogue to the 'marvellous Polish buildings of the seventeenth and eighteenth centuries'.[30]

So, given the affection with which these synagogues were held, there is a real question as to why there was such a lack of early critical attention to the relationship of Stella's paintings and the buildings. But this question is not, in fact, that difficult to resolve. Just as modernist critics hardly stopped to consider what Morris Louis's title *Charred Journal: Firewritten* might have suggested, or what could have been implied by the Barnett Newman's words *The Stations of the Cross: Lema Sabachthani*, so too they halted before probing Stella's titles seriously. Where Newman had always written and spoken about his titles, in the case of Stella, in fact, this reluctance was encouraged by the artist himself: Stella had claimed notoriously in a 1964 interview with Donald Judd and Dan Flavin that before his paintings, 'what you see is what you see',[31] and earlier in the MoMA catalogue 'Sixteen Americans', Carl Andre had written (presumably with Stella's encouragement) that 'Frank Stella's painting is not symbolic.'[32] In print, modernist critics were content to go along with these directives, setting aside any possible relationship between work and title.

However, off the printed page, the issue of the title was discussed in more depth than it might at first appear. In the conversations leading to the catalogue for Stella's 1970 MoMA retrospective, William Rubin had asked the artist several questions about titles. He was particularly surprised when Stella explained that he did not title a work after

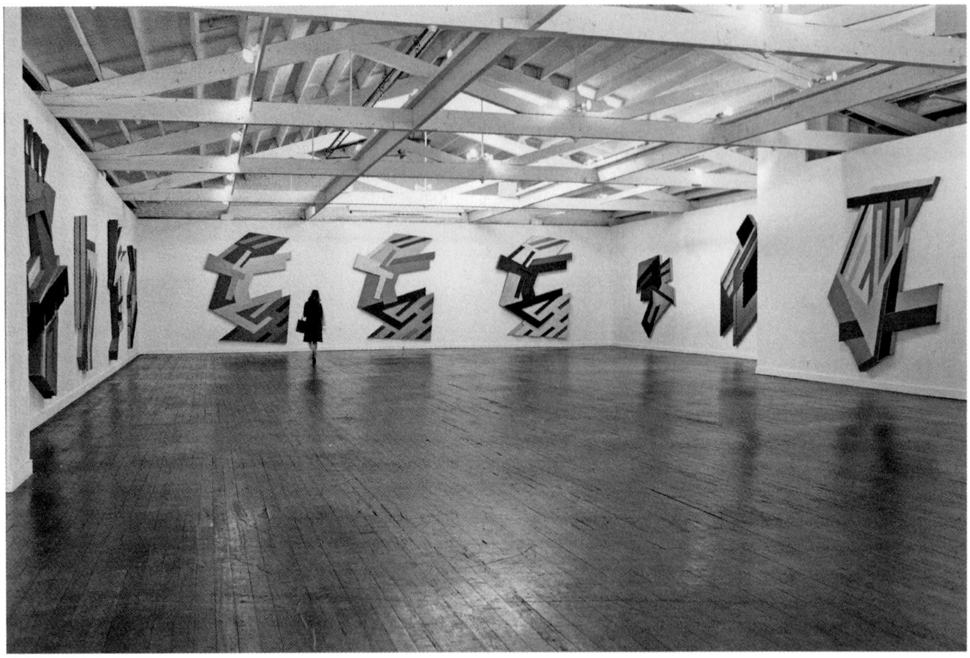

53 *Frank Stella: Recent Paintings*. Portland Center for the Visual Arts, Oregon, 1974. Three versions of *Targowica* are displayed on the back wall.

making it, but during the process, and that though Stella could not always explain why a particular title was given to a particular painting, the process was 'fairly definite'.[33] Should anyone else swap the titles of two works, he would change them back until they were right again. At one point, the discussion attended to the titles of the *Purple Paintings*, all named after Stella's friends. Stella mentioned *Sidney Guberman* (fig. 54):

> Stella: Sidney Guberman. He's a hexagon.
> Rubin: What makes Sidney Guberman hexagonish?
> Stella: He's a Jewish figure, the classic Jewish figure. He's a Jew and Ivy Club [member] at Princeton, and he's a goy Jew and that was a 6-pointed star rounded off, the points had been lobbed off.[34]

If this conversation indicated Stella's familiarity with the culture of assimilating North American Jews, the other titles he discussed with Rubin pointed to a long-standing interest in the Nazi period: three of the *Black Paintings* of 1959 were called *Die Fahne Hoch!*, *Reichstag* and *Arbeit Macht Frei*. Stella had interesting things to say about the relationship between the paintings and Nazism, but however complex the operations of the titles, Stella and Rubin decided to keep their discussion of this matter outside the catalogue. Rubin told Stella that his contention about the specific relationship between a title and a painting 'opens up a possibility of a real misunderstanding about the titles, because people always want to look at a title as if it's a handle to the picture',[35] and Stella conceded that this 'could be a disaster'.[36] Rubin ended up writing in the catalogue that 'Stella would be horrified at the idea that a viewer might use [titles] as a

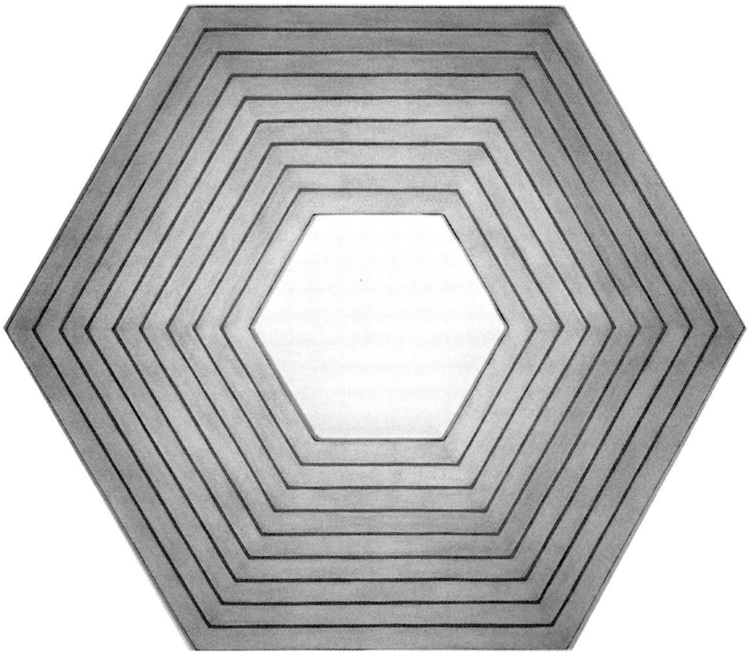

54 Frank Stella, *Sidney Guberman*, 1963. Metallic paint on canvas, 196.2 × 227.3 cm.

springboard to content',[37] and this note of caution stuck. Though Philip Leider had told Stella in a public interview in San Francisco in 1966 that, when looking at *Die Fahne Hoch!*, 'for some reason, I found I could not avoid, by the way, making certain terrible associations',[38] when it was his turn to write a catalogue for the artist, he refrained from exploring these associations himself, and quoted Rubin's words.[39]

And so when it came to the exhibitions of the *Polish Villages* in the early 1970s, the ground simply had not been prepared to enable critics to address these titles with any confidence, nor even to begin to question their possible implications for a treatment of the paintings. The discourse would simply not permit it. If none of the reviewers whose accounts I have examined could have known about Stella's comments on *Sidney Guberman*, all, we can assume, would have known that he had used 'Nazi' phrases as titles for his most famous works and that the 'Polish Villages' were not therefore entirely new terrain. But still, there was silence.

Critical discourses shifted. Curators and art historians began to ask questions about the ideas for the series, and in the early 1980s, the Jewish Museum held an exhibition of six works from the series together with the preparatory drawings. Curiously titled *Frank Stella – Polish Wooden Synagogues – Constructions from the 1970s*, the show was accompanied by a small booklet containing a short text on the work. Carolyn Cohen started by acknowledging that the 'titles for the individual works were inspired by the names of synagogues', but though she described Stella's works in detail, there was no complex treatment of the relationship to the book.[40] If the pamphlet reflected some unease about how to approach the works, there was further institutional wavering: Stella's exhibition extended over Holocaust Day, at which time the museum tra-

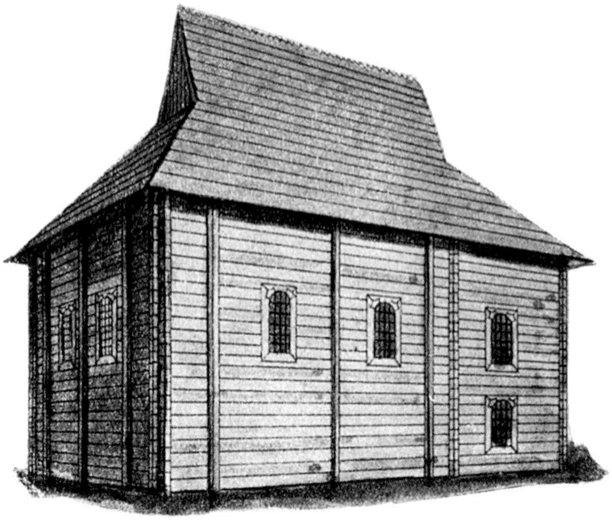

55 (top) Felsztyn Synagogue, Drawing of exterior (from *Wooden Synagogues*).

56 (facing page) Grodno Synagogue, Interior looking towards the Bima and the Ark (from *Wooden Synagogues*).

ditionally held a memorial exhibition. The director, Joan Rosenbaum, drafted a letter to Stella asking if a plaque could be added that day. It would 'indicate that we are honoring the anniversary of the Holocaust with the showing of this exhibition'. Rosenbaum was anxious to assure Stella that she did not 'wish to misconstrue your works . . . as though they were created as a Holocaust memorial'. Her hesitancy seems to have prevailed: the letter was never sent.[41]

Rosenbaum seems to have been correct in her hesitancy: certainly the paintings are not 'Holocaust memorials' in any conventional way. And yet the Jewish Museum's very decision to stage the exhibition shows that their relation to the memory of Jewish culture was at last being considered. Four years later, when he came to curate Stella's second MoMA retrospective, William Rubin would quote the artist, saying that 'The Polish Village series was about more than "the synagogues that were destroyed"; [it was] "about the destruction of an entire culture".'[42] The inclusion of this quote is a stunning reversal of approach, but what exactly is the nature of Stella's 'about'? In what ways *do* the paintings engage the memory of the synagogues, of their destruction, and of the wider historical calamity of which this destruction was a part?

building memories

Despite having argued that the lack of attention to Stella's titles was a critical lacuna, I want to start to answer these questions by stressing that there was no direct relationship between any one painting in the series and the particular synagogue whose name it took. Though such a relationship between painting and title seems to have been present in Stella's mind when he called his purple hexagon *Sidney Guberman*, this was not the case here. Felsztyn synagogue is represented in *Wooden Synagogues* by one small sketch (fig. 55); Grodno synagogue by seven architectural line drawings

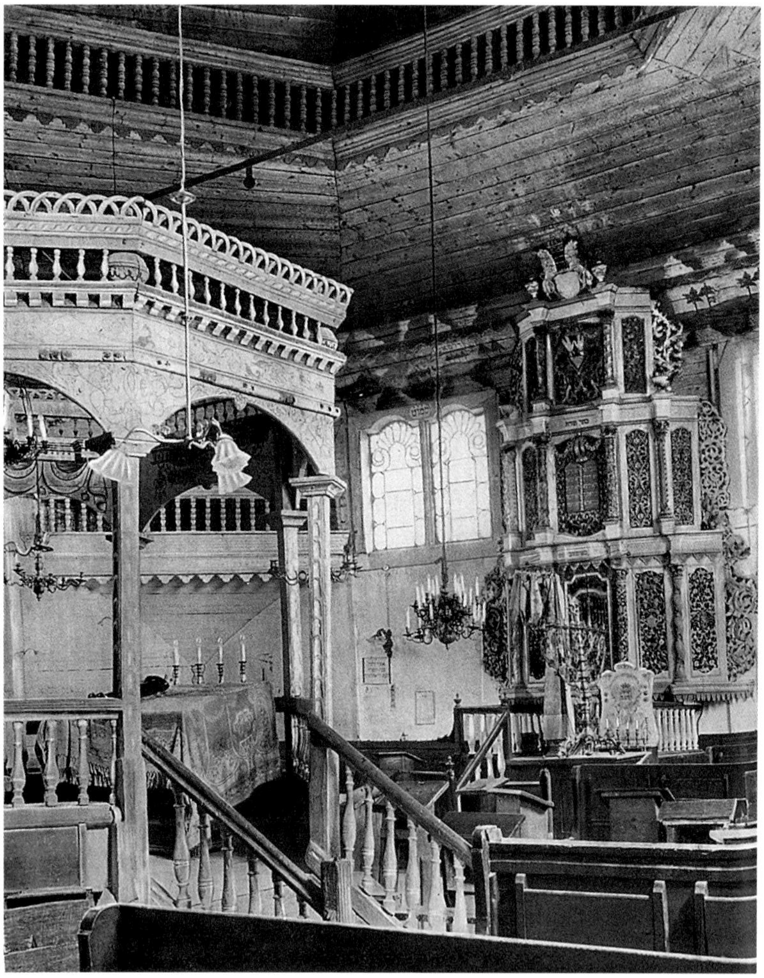

and nine photographs (fig. 56). Stella's *Grodno* looks no more like any one of the sixteen images of the synagogue than *Felsztyn* looks like the single sketch. *Kamionka Strumitowa*, meanwhile, is one of the most irregularly shaped paintings in the series – *Chodorow*, with its central near-rectangle is far more solid, and yet for all the differences between the paintings, both synagogues appear in the book to have looked very similar.

However there are some important general visual connections between the images of the synagogues and the paintings Stella made. From the outside, the most distinctive visual characteristic of the synagogues was their sloping, stilted roofs. The roofs started at a gentle incline quite low off the ground above the main synagogue wall. They would rise up to meet another much shorter vertical wall. Above this, there would tend to be another slope of roof, this time at a steeper angle, before another vertical wall, and finally the sharply angled top slope of the roof ascending right up to its peak. In the images in *Wooden Synagogues*, the vertical reach of the buildings appeared much

57 (following page, top) Zabludow Synagogue, detail of east elevation (from *Wooden Synagogues*).

58 (following page, bottom) Sidra Synagogue, detail of west elevation (from *Wooden Synagogues*).

59 (p. 101, top) Grodno Synagogue, detail of north elevation (from *Wooden Synagogues*).

60 (p. 101, bottom) Janów Sokólski Synagogue, detail of south elevation (from *Wooden Synagogues*).

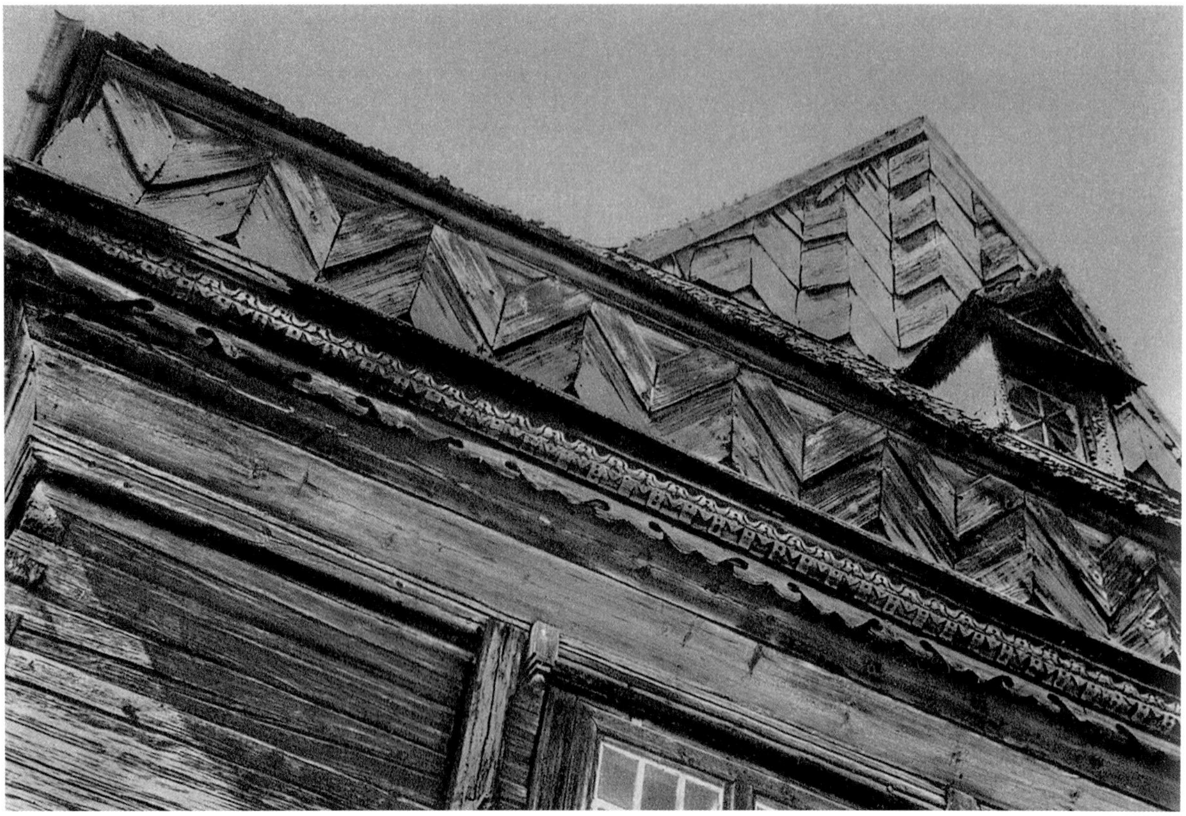
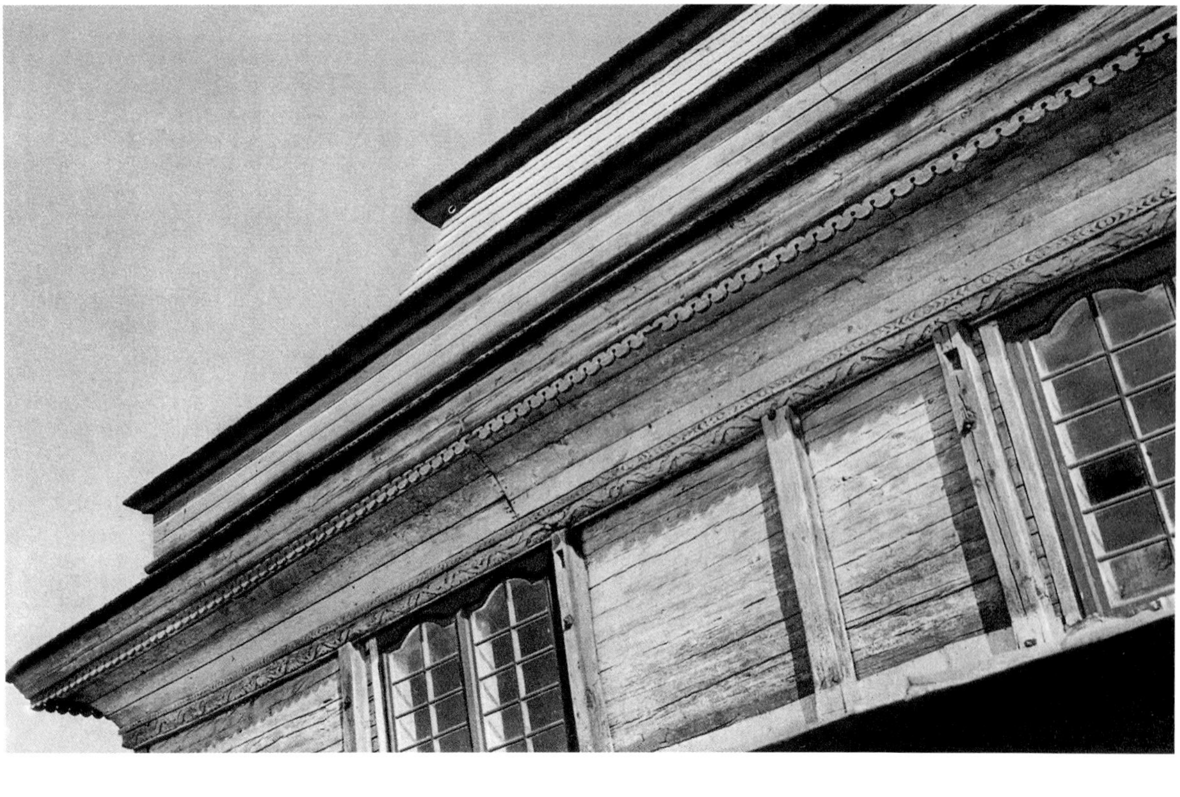

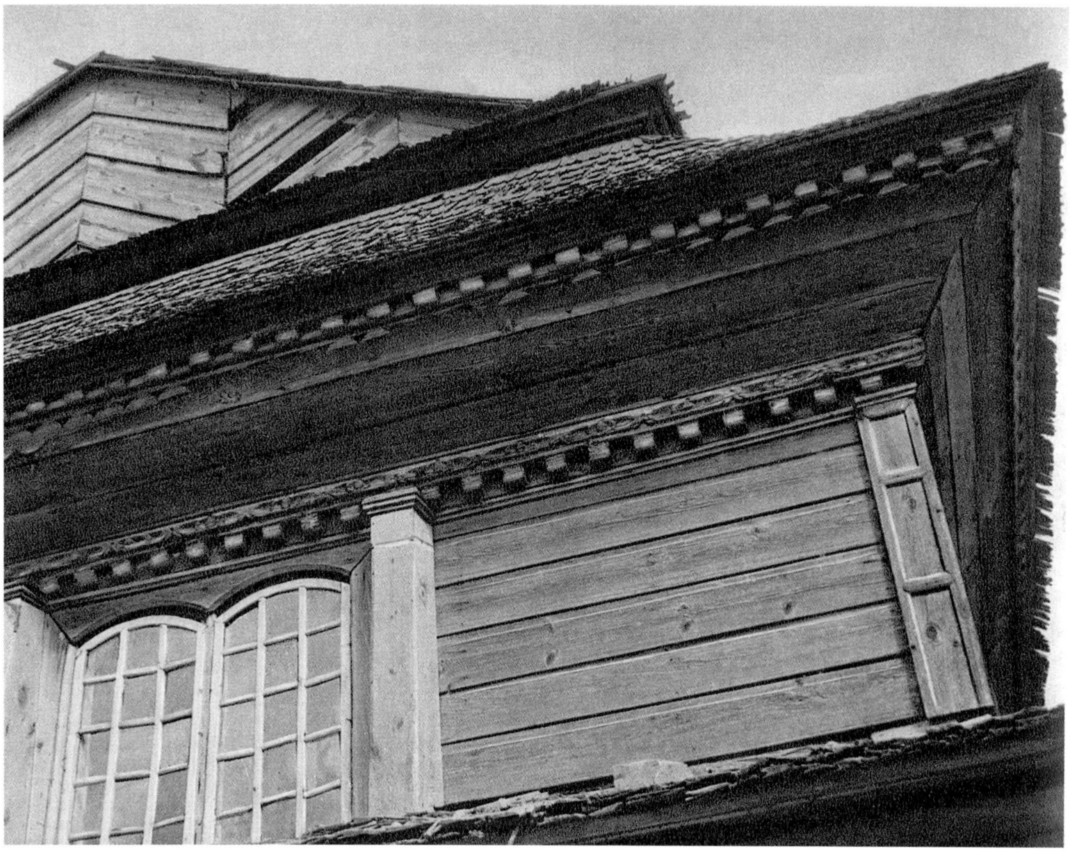

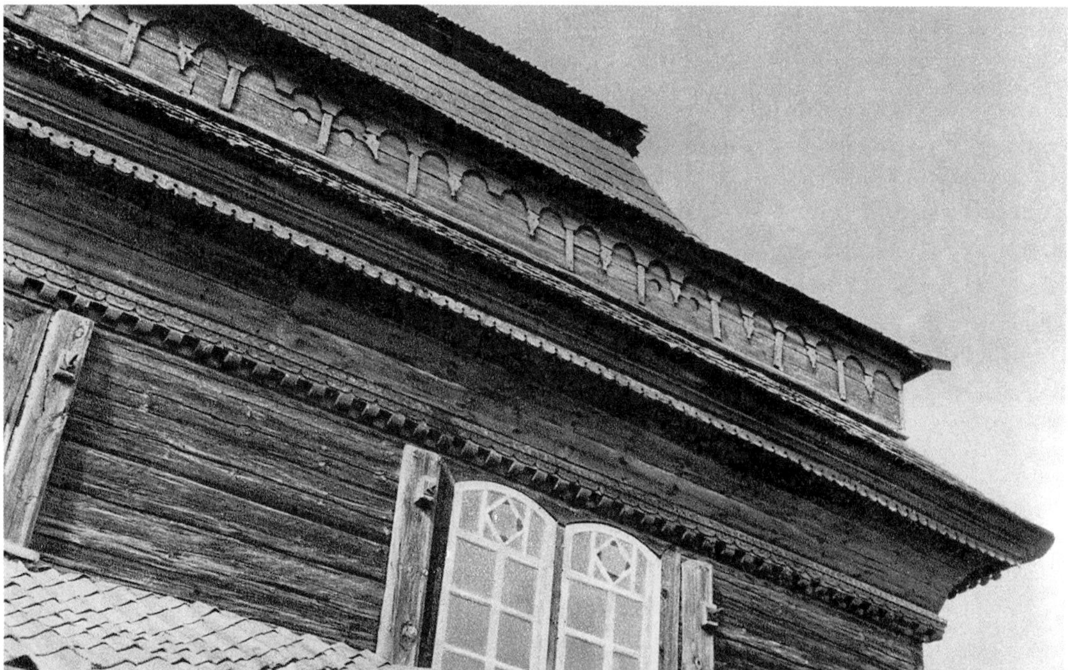

stronger than their horizontal expanse. This verticality is echoed in many of the paintings in Stella's series, but so is the angularity of the synagogues. Even in the most frontal photographs in the book, the diagonal slants of the roofs were extremely prominent, but some detail photographs taken from raking perspectives made such diagonals their subject (figs 57–60). Pitched diagonally across the photographic surfaces, the angles of the architecture were emphasised. In every single work in the *Polish Village* series, this characteristic of the synagogue architecture was recalled.

The more interesting relationships between Stella's works and the synagogues do not rely on such direct visual correspondences, but are more protracted. These photographs were taken in the late 1920s and 1930s by Szymon Zajczyk, an art and architectural historian who was killed in the Holocaust in 1942. Zajczyk's detail photographs were certainly not 'straight' records of the buildings, and though their angled positions might have sympathetically recorded the feel of the architecture, it can also be said with some confidence that they registered the impact of constructivism: Zajczyk might have known the photography of Rodchenko and Moholy-Nagy. In other words, the photographer pictured the synagogues in the recently developed visual language of contemporary art.

If the pictures Stella saw bore the impact of constructivist photography, his paintings in turn recalled the wider visual characteristics of Russian constructivism. As noted earlier, most critics writing at the beginning of the 1970s related the paintings back to cubism, art deco, and even abstract expressionism, but after two important exhibitions of Russian constructivism in New York in 1971, one of which included reconstructions of Tatlin's corner reliefs, the similarities became more apparent.[43] By the time a large number of Stella's series were gathered together in Fort Worth in 1978, Philip Leider could note that 'strong identities with Russian constructivism – materials, relief, dynamic clusters of planes – emerged. Similarities to certain of Malevich's architectural drawings, affinities with Tatlin's painted reliefs, Liubov Popova's 'architectonic paintings', etc., became inescapable'.[44]

As is well known, by this time, a number of American artists had become interested in the work of this period, many reading Camilla Gray's 1962 book, *The Russian Experiment in Art*. Dan Flavin had famously dedicated a series of neon sculptures to Tatlin, and Stella's friend Carl Andre had said in a 1970 interview that 'I would like to think that my work is in the tradition of the Russian revolutionary artists, Tatlin and Rodchenko'.[45] Philip Leider briefly admitted that, like his contemporaries, Stella had been drawn to the 'entire moral, artistic and political ambience for which that period of the history of abstraction has come to stand',[46] but Stella's invocation of constructivism seems to have been more than a loose moral homage and certainly more than a formal allusion.[47] Rather, Stella seems to have tied a complex knot binding the memory of the destruction of constructivism to the memory of the destruction of the *Wooden Synagogues*. If constructivism and the synagogues had already been linked together in the detail photographs in the book, Stella seems to have forged other connections. He might have been thinking about the symmetry between the route an artist such as El Lissitsky had taken from Moscow through Poland to Berlin, and the route the German army took through the Polish villages towards Moscow. He might also have recalled that the Nazis had waged a cultural war on constructivism before the actual war began on Polish soil (Alan Birnholz, writing in *Artforum* in 1969, recalled that 'The Abstract Kabinett like so much of Lissitsky's work, was destroyed by the Nazis in 1936 in their war against "Bolshevist" art'.[48]) He might even have known that before his constructivist work, Lissitsky had produced images of the Eastern European shtetls in his *Had Gadya* drawings of 1919 (a series of works Stella would come back to in the early 1980s). So links existed before Stella began his series, but by simultaneously invoking constructivism *and* the wooden synagogues, Stella suggested that both were the victims of Nazism. It was in this way that he reflected on 'the destruction of an entire culture'.

What is even more interesting is that in order to represent this cultural destruction, Stella produced paintings that not only recalled the angularity of the synagogues and of constructivism, but which conjured the very look of destruction. It is not clear whether or not Stella hoped to replicate the imagined appearance of a flattened wooden building, but he does seem to have created visually chaotic works, and reviewers noted this. April Kingsley contrasted what she considered successful *Polish Villages* to less successful ones: *Nasielsk III* had 'architectural stability' but *Glinne II* appeared to be 'in a state of unsettled flux'.[49] What, though, if this 'unsettled' look was deliberate? Other critical accounts were saturated with the vocabulary of contortion. Elizabeth Baker elegantly described the 'sense of compressed opposing strains' in the paintings before writing that 'their jagged and irregular angularities, filled with non-sequiturs and curious disjunctions, at times have the look of proliferating crystalline structures under heavy metamorphic pressures'.[50] Joseph Masheck, reviewing a later exhibition, captured the feel of the series in his writing: 'With the aggressiveness of [their] sharp, ripsaw lurches, [the third versions] seem like hard-edged painting gone apeshit.' So even though critics failed to describe the invocation of the synagogues and of constructivism, they could not help but articulate the appearance of destruction. The *Polish Villages*, Masheck concluded, were 'exploded paintings'.[51]

So far I have suggested that Stella's paintings visually evoked the memory of the buildings *and* built up chains of memory, connecting the destruction of the synagogues to the fate of constructivism. For all the emphasis on destruction, though, I now want to turn to the idea of construction to suggest a third way in which the series operated: to memorialise building itself. At this point it is worth recalling Rosalind Krauss's arguments about the series. She suggested that Stella moved away from the serialisation that characterised the 'Protractor' paintings to make renewed modernist paintings each of which asserted their individual identity. Krauss considered 'serialisation' in formalist terms only at this date, but in an essay first published in 1986, Hal Foster approached the subject in a different way. In 'The Crux of Minimalism', after describing serial production as the characteristic form of advanced capitalism, he argued that 'not until minimalism and pop is serial production made consistently integral to the technical production of the work of art'.[52] The seriality of pop and minimalism indicated 'the penetration of industrial modes into spheres that were once removed from them'.[53]

If Foster's historical account is coupled with Krauss's contemporary observation that Stella's *Polish Villages* turned away from serialisation, a new consideration of the *process* of making the *Polish Villages* emerges. By deliberately departing from serialisation, Stella distinguished his new working process from serial production, affiliating it instead with a former, pre-industrial phase of manufacture. Rather than relating to then contemporary production, the *Polish Villages* recalled the modes of production that characterised synagogue building: the creation of a unique, handmade, crafted structure. For Krauss, only the 'version one' works declared their uniqueness convincingly, but as I indicated, all the different versions were key to Stella's project and he deliberately displayed them together in the various gallery exhibitions. What lay between versions was *building*, and if we leave Krauss standing in front of *Odelsk I* to step to the side of *Felsztyn III*, we can see how Stella highlighted the affinity with building through emphasising the constructed, material character of the works. Certainly, this quality was palpable for their earliest critics. Jeanne Siegel, focusing on 'version threes', wrote that their 'projections afford an opportunity to expose and highlight a complex array of materials – felt, painted canvas, laminated plywood, corrugated cardboard, construction board'.[54] John Elderfield observed that the works 'cannot help but insist their being carpented'.[55] Hilton Kramer wrote that 'these collages and reliefs seem more like constructions than paintings'.[56]

The main reason why the wooden synagogues were held in such esteem by artists and art historians such as Louis Lozowick, George Loukomski and Stephen Kayser one might now recall, was because unlike the synagogues of Italy, Germany and France, the wooden synagogues were built by the Jewish communities that used them. Jewish labour was somehow marked in the buildings: the processes of their construction signified, and guaranteed their importance. Stella's *Polish Villages* raised process to a subject, retrieving from its annihilation the very memory of building.

the *black paintings*, the *polish villages* and the fate of modernist viewing

This last argument – that the very process of making the *Polish Villages* memorialised the building activities of the architects of the wooden synagogues – relies on a referential and expansive idea of 'process' and such an idea would seem entirely at odds with the status of 'process' amongst the artists with whom Stella had been associated. For if Stella's labour could recall the labour of the synagogue builders, for most artists of Stella's generation, demonstrating the 'process of making' in the final work was precisely a means of restricting that work's potential references. Robert Morris's 1961 sculpture, *Box with the Sound of its Own Making* had also required carpentry, nailing and gluing to come into being, but by playing a tape of the sounds of these activities inside the box, Morris bound such labours to the small object before the viewer. By the late 1960s, Morris had become more interested in the processes of making, as had a number of younger artists including Richard Serra and Eva Hesse. For Serra in particular, in works such as *Cutting Device: Base Plate Measure* of 1969, the demonstration of process was a means of concentrating the viewer's mind on the specific sculpture in front of them. Process was tautological rather than expansive: a means to make the work refer to its own evolution rather than beyond itself to any other object, or activity, or event.

So Stella's move to make process signify was an anomaly given the context of the artists with whom he is usually grouped, even if it anticipated the moves 1970s feminist artists would make when they began to use processes such as stitching for referential purposes. Yet Stella's move was not entirely surprising given his own way of thinking. And it is at this point that we can turn back to the *Black Paintings*, and to the conversation that William Rubin and Stella had about them in the run up to the 1970 retrospective. The common reading of the repetitive processes of Stella's *Black Paintings* has been that they marked a kind of attack on the possibilities of expressive, gestural, compositional painting: Stella simply painted one stripe after another, until the painting was complete. Such a reading would be bolstered by the photographs Stella's friend Hollis Frampton made of the artist painting *Getty Tomb* in 1959 (fig. 61). They showed Stella from behind, face and expression of no concern for the project of recording the making of the painting. Each photograph was taken from the same position, with Stella's body shown workmanlike, just as far from the canvas as his brush required, no nearer or further. Finally, they showed him *still* – there is none of the blur we see in Hans Namuth's famous photographs of Pollock.[57] These photographs supported the literalist reading of early Stella underscored by his own comment: 'what you see is what you see'. But explaining to William Rubin why one painting had been called *Arbeit Macht Frei*, Stella had more to say about process (fig. 62). 'Arbeit Macht Frei' was:

> A Nazi slogan, or maybe just a German slogan that was used unfortunately over in one of the concentration camps, which was [Arbeit Macht Frei] (work makes free), I guess, which is another pun on the whole business – making these kind of paintings is also very laborious. It's very repetitive – four or five coats of doing the same thing and the kind of mechanical process so there's a play, I guess, on also the work process in making the picture.[58]

This comment is obviously quite shocking and perhaps more so because this interview was never cleaned up and edited for publication. Stella's analogy between repetitive painting and the labour that was enforced in Auschwitz seems troublingly casual. But Stella was not the only figure to draw parallels between the work inside Auschwitz and the work outside. For Maurice Blanchot, the labour in the camps at last made evident the previously concealed conditions of labour in industrial modernity. The concentration camps were 'emblems wherein the invisible has made itself visible forever. All the distinctive features of a civilisation are revealed or laid bare'.[59] The false promises of the slogan 'work liberates', as declared in the camps, revealed the false promises of labour at large. The ultimate form of work in the camps, he wrote, 'consists of carrying stones at top speed from one point and piling them up in another, and then

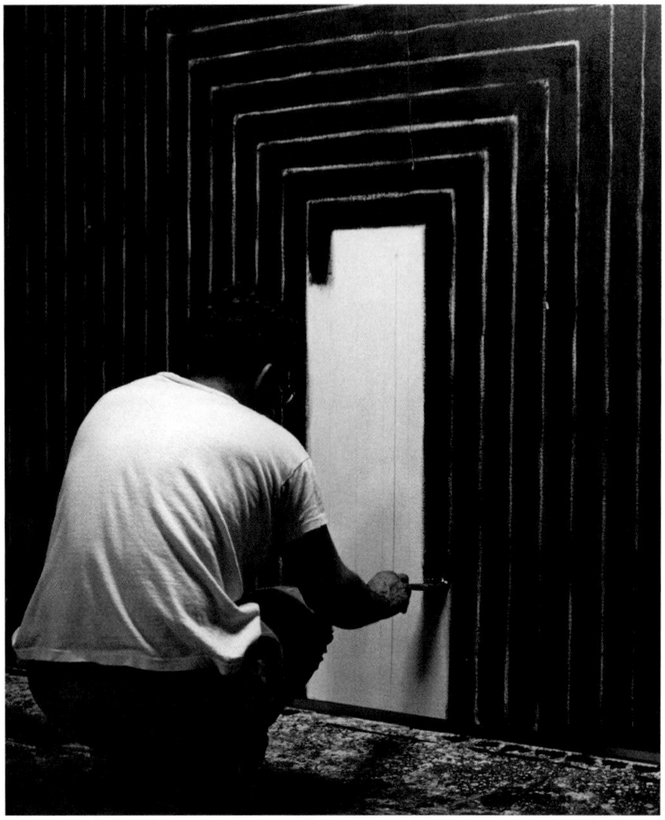

61 Hollis Frampton, *Untitled* from *The Secret World of Frank Stella*, 1958–1962. Black and white photograph, 25 × 20 cm. Collection Walker Art Center, Minneapolis. Gift of Marion Faller, 1993.

in bringing them back at the run to the starting point. . . . [N]o act of sabotage can cancel work, for its annulment is work's very own purpose. And yet labour retains a meaning: it tends not only to destroy the worker, but more immediately to occupy, to harness and control him and at the same time perhaps to give him an awareness that to produce and not to produce amount to the same – that the one and the other alike are work.'[60]

Blanchot's reading of work in the camps might open up a new way of thinking about process in regard to the *Black Paintings*. Stella's comment joined the repetitive process of painting to the work in the camps, but it is possible to go further and argue that process in the *Black Paintings* (and not just the one entitled *Arbeit Macht Frei*) does not simply represent a critique of other ways of making a painting, but represents the absurdity of labour in modernity – an absurdity only symbolised most clearly in the camps. Stella, with house paint and worker's clothes, mimics the form of modern labour, a labour that will never meet its promise to set the labourer free.[61]

If Stella's remarks about the processes of the *Black Paintings* help to cement the argument I am making about the referential possibility of the processes of the *Polish Villages*, his other comments about the 1959 works help us to establish the nature and

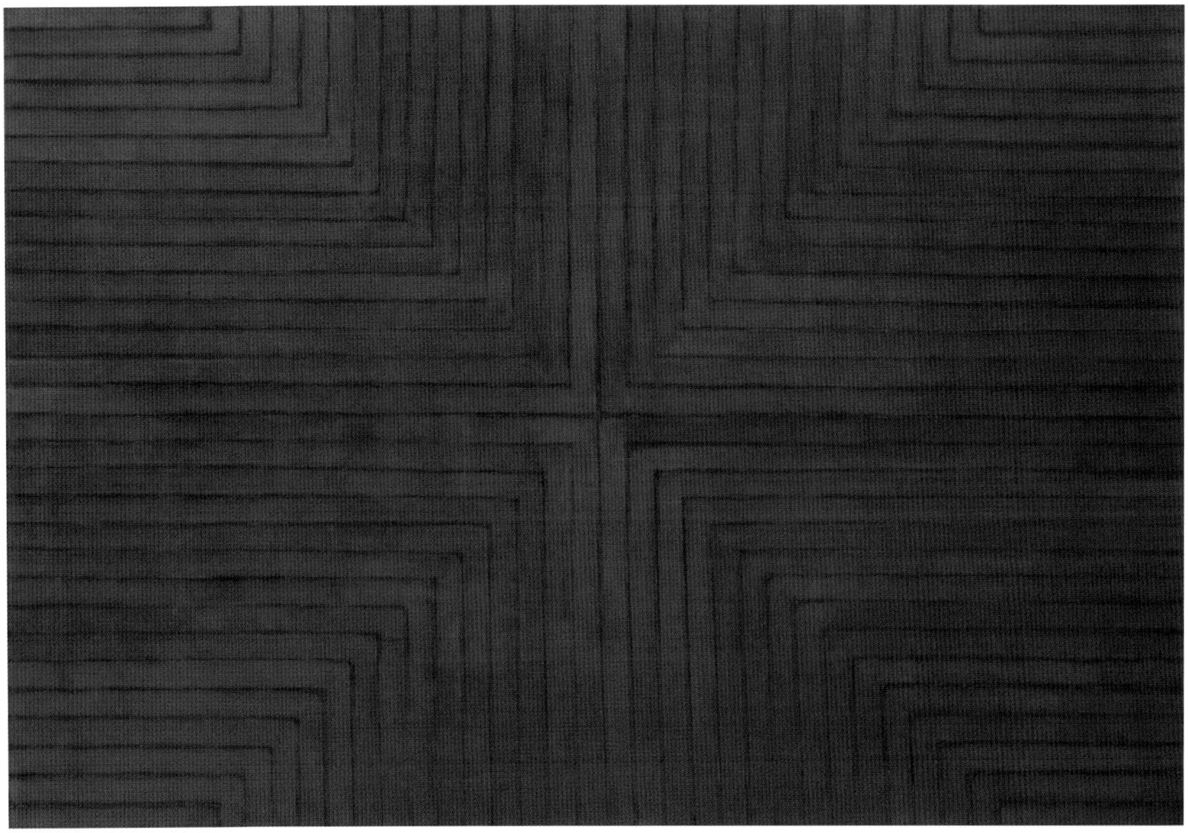

62 Frank Stella, *Arbeit Macht Frei*, 1958. Enamel on canvas, 215.9 × 308.6 cm. Private collection.

importance of the viewing experience that the works of the 1970s created. Much of Stella's and Rubin's conversation revolved around *Die Fahne Hoch!*, a vertically oriented painting that Stella had named after Horst Wessel's Nazi marching song meaning 'The Flag on High'. The painting, Stella said, recalled 'the way the Nazis would drape their flags around the plaza from high up on the buildings. It was the vertical drop idea of a flag being placed that way rather than the flag flying'.[62] Stella spoke of 'wanting to have some of the kind of control that an architectural situation imposes'.[63] He also said that 'what was specifically involved in these pictures aside of certain associative kinds of things was a kind of fairly straightforward aesthetic relationship that the artist bears to a kind of totalitarian thing and particularly a kind of totalitarian esthetics, and by this I mean essentially the question of fascist architecture'.[64]

The paintings – Stella seems to have acknowledged – aimed to exercise a control over their viewers. When looking at *Die Fahne Hoch!*, the viewers place themselves in front of its centre, and their eyes are directed to the meeting place of the cross at its centre. As this is above eye height, they look up, as if standing to attention before a draped flag. Other paintings have different configurations, but Stella's aims are still achieved: the paintings impose one viewing position only, and from that position they yield all

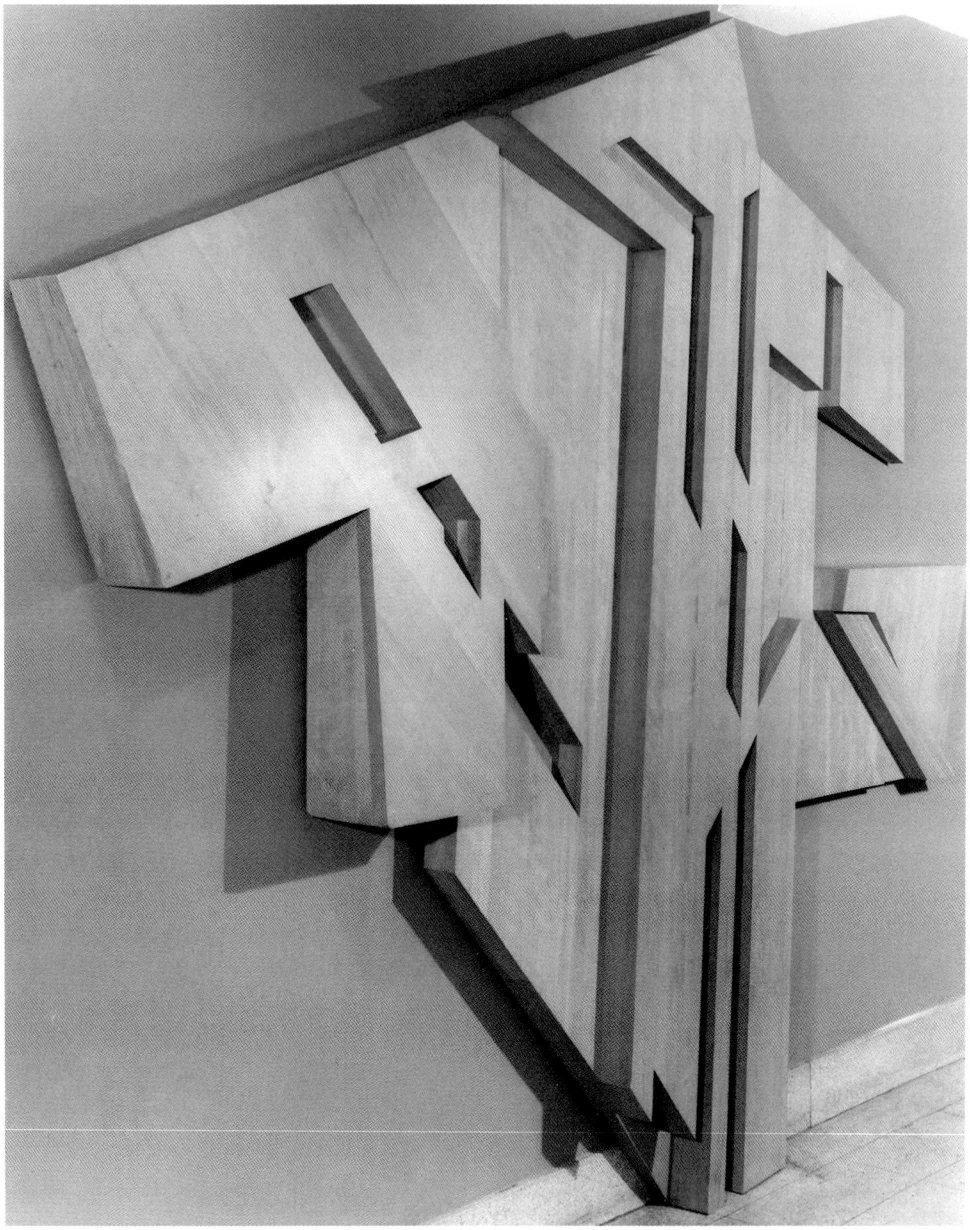

63 Frank Stella, *Bechhofen IV*, 1972. Unpainted wood, 269.2 × 228.6 cm.

their visual content. 'You have limited access . . . the access that the painting gives you. . . . It's a kind of controlled vision, and it's a particularly structured vision.'[65] When we think about these comments, it seems that Stella's 1959 titles, rather than determining specific 'references' of particular *Black Paintings*, exposed the way in which the artist was associating the viewing conditions he created with the power of fascist architecture. The title was thus a moment of transparency in which Stella acknowledged his paintings' ambitions for power.

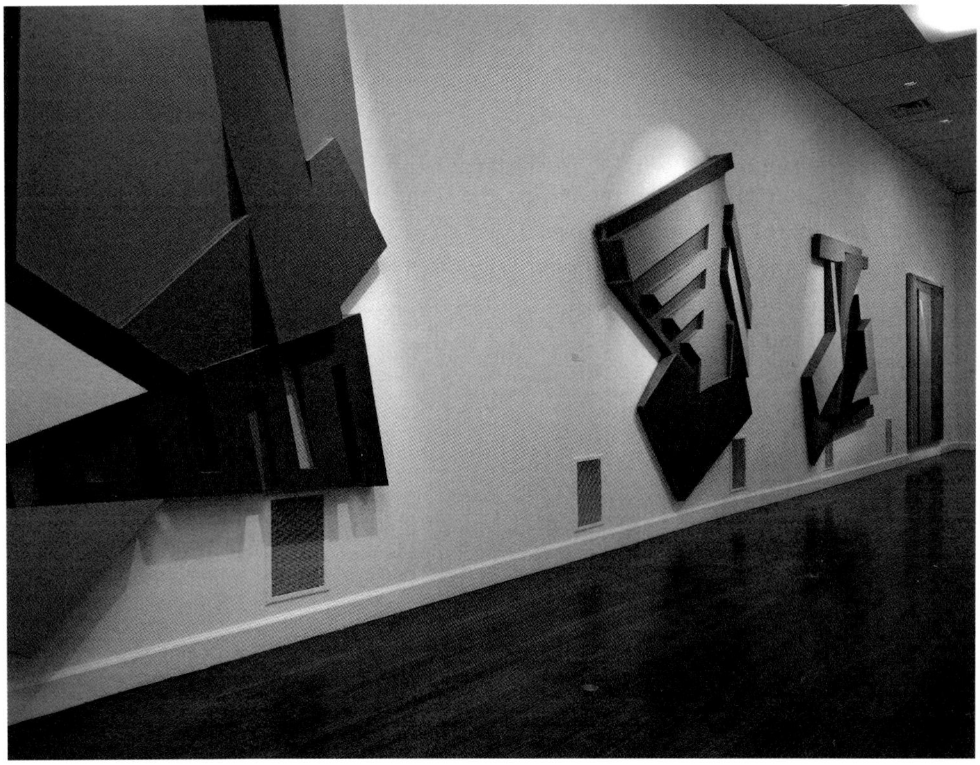

64 Frank Stella, paintings from the *Polish Village* series installed in *Twelve American Painters*, Virginia Museum of Fine Arts, 1974.

If the *Black Paintings* imposed controlled viewing conditions, over the next ten years in the run up to the *Polish Villages* series his paintings relaxed, but never relinquished this authority over the viewer. We might actually say that authority was shared: in the words of Rosalind Krauss, from her 1968 essay 'On Frontality', Stella's paintings began to be 'literally responsive to the same conditions of time and space as was the beholder'.[66] Metallic paint was employed so that the surface of the painting would register and reflect the light source in the room in which it, together with its viewer, was placed. There were increasingly intricate games with the illusions of optical space – the inner squares in the *Concentric Squares* (1962–63) appeared to recede behind the plane of the canvas surface, the *Running Vs* (1964–65) appeared 'as folded planes, buckling away from the wall and projecting into the viewer's space'.[67] What was important, though, was that these were only ever illusions; this was only ever optical space. The paintings, in other words, still controlled how they would be seen, even if the spectator was encouraged to move from side-to-side in front of the surface, rather than remain alert and fixed in one position. The paintings played with frontality, but this play always ended by stressing the secure co-presence of the viewer before the flat surface of the work. So, when Krauss asked in 1968 'when we see a painting, does it occur to us that we are only seeing one aspect?', the answer she intended was a definite 'no'.[68]

In 1971 Krauss maintained her position on frontality when confronting *Chodorow I* and *Odelsk I*, but her confidence before the *Polish Villages* contrasted very clearly with the anxiety that is witnessed in another account of the paintings. John Elderfield wrote that: 'One is never sure whether certain gaps between the applied materials is intentional or not or whether the revealed corrugated paper on the sides is supposed to be part of the painting.'[69] I think that Elderfield's self-questioning, his inability to be sure what he was supposed to be seeing and where he was supposed to be standing, is entirely to the point. A viewer was afforded one aspect from the front, but an entirely different one as they moved around the painting – an aspect seldom recorded in photographs of the works, but evident in the image of *Bechhofen IV* (fig. 63) and in an installation photograph of some of the works at the Virginia Museum of Fine Arts in 1974 (fig. 64). Parts cast shadows over other parts – actual shadows, not illusions of shadows. From the rotated position at their sides, elements of the paintings were visible that were simply unavailable from the front, which is to say that the view that had been seen from in front collapsed like a mirage. In the *Polish Villages*, the control imposed initially by *Die Fahne Hoch!* and then slightly retracted in Stella's later works was completely abandoned. The paintings no longer 'demand[ed] a face-on confrontation by the viewer'[70] as Krauss had termed it; they no longer imposed themselves with the authority that fascist architecture deploys. And, as a consequence, the viewer was thrown into a confused state, knowing neither where to stand, nor what to look at.

Earlier I asked what the appearance and construction processes of the works suggested in terms of the memory of the wooden synagogues. But we can also explore the implications of these viewing conditions further and relate the new viewing conditions that the *Polish Villages* created to Stella's attempt to make work 'about the destruction of an entire culture'. If Stella once had paired the authority of modernist painting with the authority of fascist architecture, now to represent the architecture that fascism had destroyed, he not only took apart the solidity of the modernist plane, but entirely disrupted the securities of modernist viewing habits. Krauss conceived the viewer of these paintings as the modernist subject 'grasp[ing] the work of art with the kind of immediacy with which we experience our own inner states', experiencing their 'haecceity' before the paintings; their co-presence in space and time. But in direct opposition to this formulation, I would argue that the *Polish Villages* construct their viewing subject as a subject in crisis, unable to experience a clear sense of presence before the work, unable to know its limits and unsure of their own position in turn. Stella's paintings constructed their viewer as a post-Holocaust subject: as a subject whose crisis before the paintings might be quite appropriate to a context where, after 'the destruction of an entire culture', all securities are shattered.

painting after 1970

As we have seen, there were several dimensions to Frank Stella's attempt to address 'the destruction of an entire culture'. First, he produced works with some visual resemblances to the photographs of the destroyed synagogues and possibly to the appearance of imagined flattened buildings. Second, he connected the fate of the synagogues to the destruction of constructivist art – another victim of Nazi policy. Third, he treated the process of making the works as a referential activity, one which memorialised the building of the synagogues. Finally, he introduced a viewing encounter that would render his viewers in doubt about the nature of the object before them and the nature of viewing itself.

In all, this amounts to an assault on the flatness of modernist painting, on the non-referentiality of modernist process and on modernist habits of viewing. Stella's invocation of constructivism, meanwhile, recalled an art movement that modernist critics such as Greenberg and Fried sidelined, and the very idea of such recollection countered modernist practice – for if modernist paintings built on the histories of the medium, it was not through this kind of historical reflection. Considering these various assaults together, it could be concluded that if Stella's work was 'about the destruction of an entire culture', this culture was every bit as much the 'culture' of New York modernist theory as the Eastern European culture of the synagogues. Through the assault on modernism, Stella seems to have addressed the situation that I described at the opening of the chapter. If in 1970 Stella's medium was not deemed 'relevant' by Kynaston McShine, and if his practice had been satirised by Baldessari, with the *Polish Villages* Stella retrieved some urgency for his work. Crudely speaking, no longer were these just paintings 'to be looked at', but rather they were to be looked around and thought about instead. Though early critics continued to address them through the frames of modernist theory, Stella's *Polish Villages* proposed that the closed discourses of modernist criticism should be opened up. In this way, Stella's project anticipated the kinds of questions Jacques Derrida would posit when, at the end of the 1970s, he explored the kinds of discourses that frame art works and determine what is properly considered inside and outside them. Derrida asked what a reading of a painting would be like that 'turns its literal limit into an external limit, takes its thickness into account, makes us see the picture from the side of the canvas or the wood'.[71] Whilst undoing modernist discourses, Stella's works literally set this challenge.

Just as in the early 1970s Stella returned to the history that interested him in 1959 (thinking about Nazi history from the viewpoint of its victims rather than its modes of power), so he would return in the early 1980s to the linked histories of Eastern European Jewish culture and constructivism, making lithographs after El Lissitsky's *Had Gadya* drawings. By that time, Stella's constructions had become increasingly complex, leading eventually to the monumental hybrids of painting, sculpture and architecture he has produced in the last decade. In the years that Stella moved away from modernist painting, other artists took up the mediums and practices of video installation, site-specific sculpture and wall drawings. But as we shall see, the ambition continued to address the memory of the Holocaust through the complex means that abstract art afforded. We shall scrutinise these projects in later chapters but the next chapter will stay with the architectural theme of this one. I want to turn now from the memory of architecture to the architecture of memory, and to look at a project that came to its end around the time that Stella's *Polish Villages* were initiated: Louis Kahn's unbuilt *Memorial to the Six Million Jewish Martyrs*.

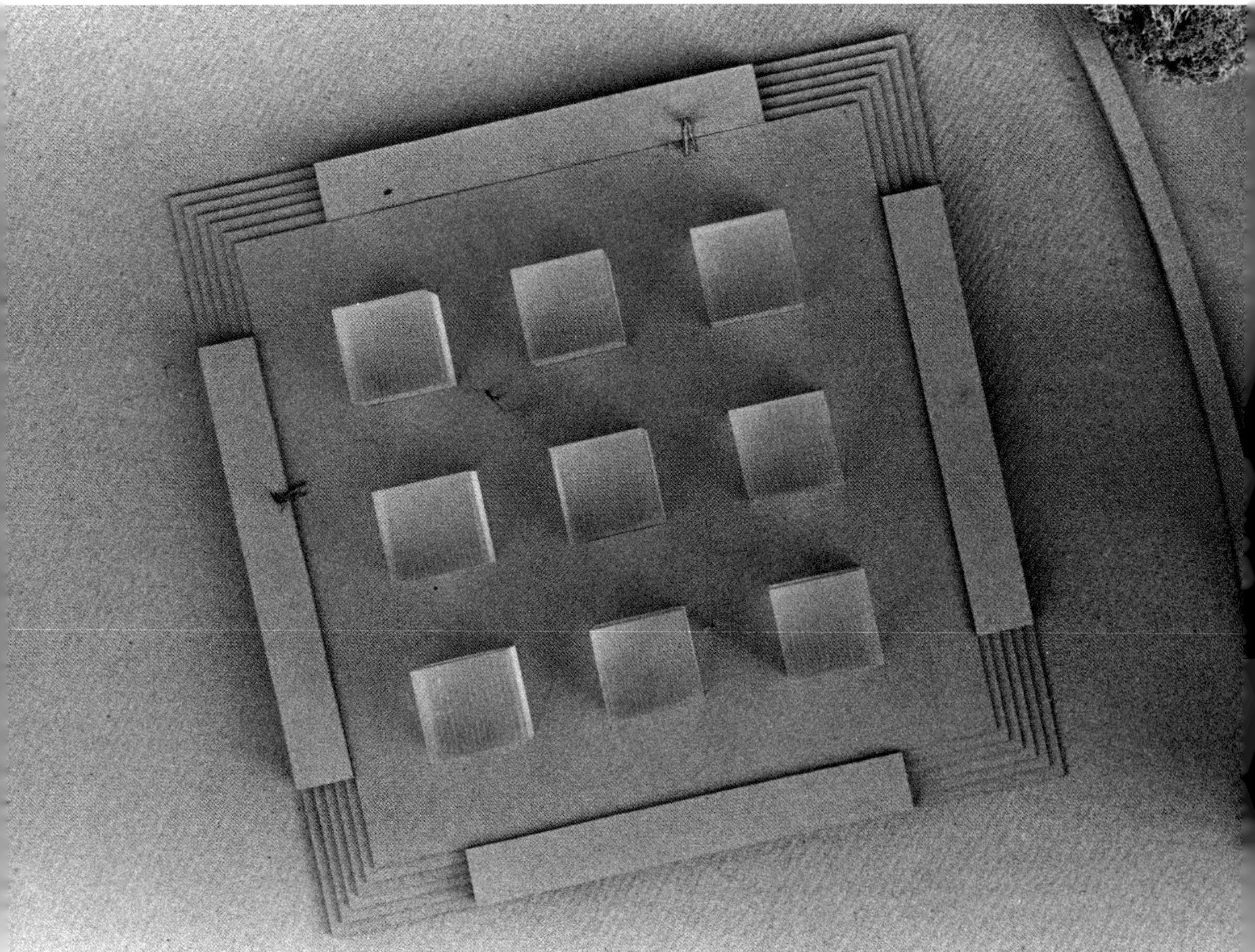

five

louis kahn's *memorial to the six million jewish martyrs*

kahn's memorial

In December 1967, at a meeting of the 'Committee to Commemorate the Six Million Jewish Martyrs', the Philadelphia-based architect Louis Kahn put forward his proposal for the first Holocaust memorial to be erected in New York City (fig. 65). Kahn described a low platform on which would stand nine blocks of solid, transparent glass. The blocks would be twelve feet deep by twelve feet wide, standing a little taller at fifteen feet high. They would be arranged in a regular three by three grid, with the space between the blocks equal to their internal breadth. There were to be no inscriptions on their surfaces, no colouring of the glass and no differentiation between one block and the next. Scholars have described the 'tension between representation and abstraction' in Kahn's work, attending to his frequent references to organic structures and to historical buildings, but little of this tension is apparent here: the plan for the *Memorial to the Six Million Jewish Martyrs* was surely one of Kahn's most abstract designs.[1]

65 Louis I. Kahn, *Memorial for the Six Million Jewish Martyrs*, 1966–72 (Nine-pier model).

To the great loss of New York City, Kahn's *Memorial* was never built, but despite the lack of a physical object of study, I still want to attend to this project in detail. There are two main reasons for this. First, because the story of the project affords the opportunity to see how the coming together of abstraction and Holocaust commemoration was considered at this historical moment by various different constituencies. Unlike the three series of paintings I have discussed so far, Kahn's memorial was commissioned. This means that we can discover not just what Kahn wanted to achieve with his proposal, but what a larger organisation hoped to accomplish by employing him, and supporting and modifying his ideas. Unlike the works of Louis, Newman and Stella, Kahn's proposal was discussed at various stages of its conception by various different kinds of people, not just by art or architecture critics. Kahn's project was debated by the members of the commissioning organisation, by New York's civic authorities, by the architectural press and by visitors to MoMA, where his model was exhibited in 1968. All of these debates are rewarding to examine, and particularly because at the centre of all responses was the question of how the proposal answered the task of representing the Holocaust. The art critics responding to Louis's, Newman's and Stella's works tended to deflect the question of how the paintings represented the memory of the Holocaust, but no commentator on Kahn's proposal could fail to consider how the blocks functioned or failed to function specifically as a Holocaust memorial.

This leads me to the second reason why I want to consider Kahn's proposal. Previous commentators have examined the project's history in order to determine why the *Memorial* was never built.[2] In fact, Kahn's proposal was *accepted* by more institutions and organisations than any proposed Holocaust memorial for New York to that date, but while it is important to understand the reasons for its initial acceptance as well as its eventual failure, it is no less crucial to try to figure out how the original proposal might have functioned *as a memorial* had it been built. Few commentators have given Kahn's initial proposal much attention. The grid of nine blocks, which I take to be the ideal form of the memorial and the form that best expressed Kahn's intentions, certainly did not work as a memorial in any conventional sense. So how could a platform containing only space, glass and light create the conditions for its visitors to remember the Holocaust? This will be the guiding question for the latter half of this chapter, but first I want to turn right back to discover how the commissioning body came to approach Kahn in 1966.

the history of the commissioners

Some historians have suggested that directly after 1945, traumatised Jewish communities were unable to confront the memory of the Holocaust, and were unable to address its impact until the 1960s.[3] But in fact there had been attempts in New York City to erect a Holocaust memorial as early as the late 1940s. These attempts have been well documented in Rochelle Saidel's book *Never Too Late to Remember: The Politics Behind New York City's Holocaust Museum* and James Young's *The Texture of Memory*, but to contextualise Kahn's project it is important to go over some of the ground these scholars covered, in order to give a sense of the various proposals that pre-dated his. Only this way can we get a sense of the shift represented by his abstract proposal, and understand why it was supported. To understand the commission, it is also important to acknowledge the various administrative and political hurdles that a proposal had to straddle in order to be erected in New York. First, the various Jewish organisations from various sectors of the community had to band together to provide administrative, political and financial support. Then the proposal had to be ratified by

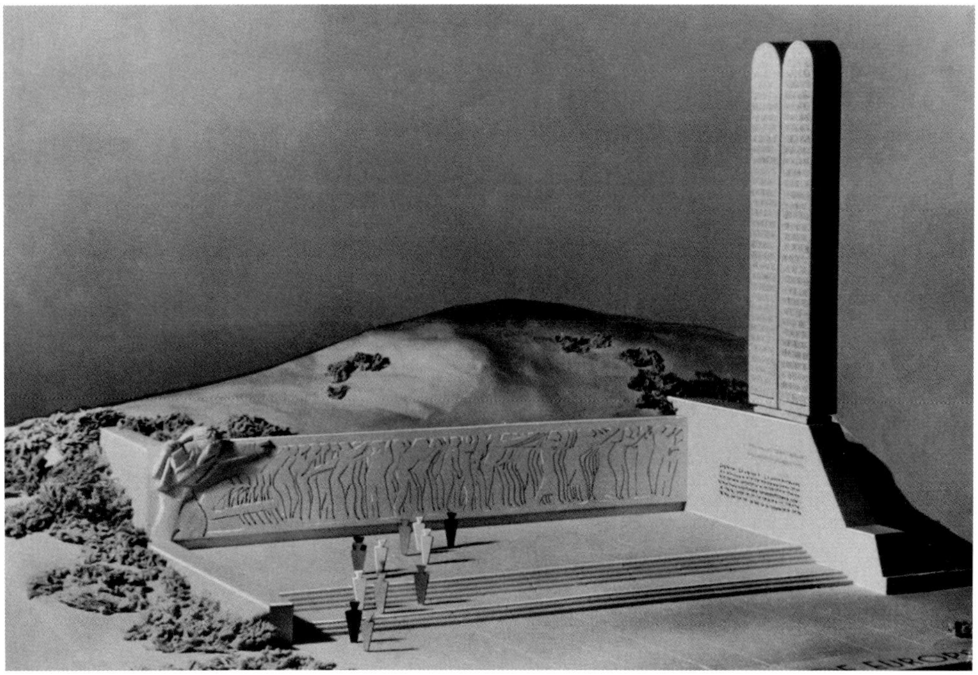

66 Erich Mendelsohn and Ivan Mestrovic, proposal for a Holocaust memorial for Riverside Park, New York, 1951. From the Archives of the YIVO Institute for Jewish Research, New York.

two civic bodies: the Parks Commission (as most proposals envisioned their sites in New York's public spaces), and the New York Art Commission under the control of the Mayor at City Hall. Given these various hurdles it is not surprising that early proposals remained as proposals. As Saidel explains, 'factors that account for the early failures include the inexperience of interest groups in forming political alliances, the political climate, financial problems, lack of interest and other priorities in the Jewish community, the subsequent lack of political benefits for government officials, and the psychological inability of survivors and other Jews to face the issue of the Holocaust, as well as disagreements within the interest group seeking to create the memorial.'[4]

The first proposal for a memorial dates from 1947 and was co-ordinated by Adolph Lerner, a Polish immigrant who had assembled a loose organisation called 'The American Memorial to the Six Million Jews of Europe'. That year, Lerner met with officials in City Hall and the Parks Department, and his organisation commissioned sculptor Jo Davidson and architect Eli Jacques Kahn to design a memorial for a site in Riverside Park on the Upper West Side. The pair conceived a figurative sculpture depicting 'a heroic resistance figure, a religious Jew in supplication, and a man helping an injured comrade, along with a slumping dead figure.'[5] The Jewish Museum, which had opened two years earlier, displayed a model of the piece in November 1948 drawing severe criticism in *Commentary*: art critic Heinz Politzer felt the model 'reveal[ed] all the worst features of sentimental nationalism'.[6] The New York Art Commission also disapproved of the design, whereupon a competition was announced. This drew proposals from a more distinguished group of artists and architects, and in October 1949 the Jewish Museum again hosted an exhibition of models, this time by Erich Mendelsohn and Ivan

Mestrovic, Percival Goodman, William Zorach, Leo Friedlander and Chaim Gross. Initially, Goodman's design was favoured: 'a 60-foot stone pylon topped by a bronze menorah, with a flagstone plaza and a granite wall at the southern end'.[7] But because the Parks Commission perceived that the design would take over Riverside Park, Goodman's proposal was rejected. Instead, the Mendelsohn and Mestrovic proposal was put before City Hall (fig. 66): 'The sculpture was to be an 80-foot pylon of two tablets on which the Ten Commandments would be inscribed, a 100-foot bas-relief wall depicting humankind's struggle to fulfil the commandments, and a giant carving of Moses.'[8] The Art Commission approved the proposal in 1951, but the memorial was never built. The various Jewish organisations could not raise sufficient funds, and it was not in the political interests of the civic authorities to finance the project themselves. There are other reasons for the failure of these initial proposals of the late 1940s and early 1950s to come to fruition but nonetheless it is worth noting the success of the Mendelsohn and Mestrovic proposal in terms of its acceptance by both the Jewish commissioning bodies and the New York civic authorities: this acceptance indicates that figuration and overt Jewish symbolism was not problematic *per se*, so long as that symbolism was honed towards universal goals, and so long as depictions of horror remained minimal.

The next major attempt to establish a Holocaust memorial in New York is particularly interesting in the context of this book because it is connected to the history of an institution associated in the 1960s with the display of abstraction. By the end of the 1950s, the Jewish Museum was gravitating towards an exhibition programme of modernist art, putting on exhibitions such as 'Artists of the New York School – Second Generation', as well as Adolph Gottlieb's first retrospective. At this time, the Jewish Museum and its parent organisation, the Jewish Theological Seminary, began to work with two different patrons in order to develop the institution. The collectors Vera and Albert List agreed to donate $500,000 for an extension to the building on Fifth Avenue to facilitate the modernist programmes, while Michael Zagayski, an immigrant from Europe, offered to donate his collection of silver Judaica – one of the most important in the world. But Zagayski's plan was to have the collection displayed on one floor of the Lists' building, with the other floors dedicated as a Holocaust memorial, including a chapel of sorts.[9] Resisting Zagayski's suggestions, the Lists wrote to the President of the JTS to stipulate that their donation would only go ahead if the extension housed contemporary exhibitions, and if the new wing had no religious space.[10] Zagayski felt this meant minimising the 'Jewish tragedy'. The museum accepted the Lists' donation, and Zagayski withdrew the offer of his collection.

While Zagayski's proposal required the help of the Lists, the Lists' donation did not depend on Zagayski, so in a way the choice the Jewish Museum made was predetermined. Nevertheless, the incident is very telling, since it indicates the priorities of a powerful New York Jewish cultural institution at this time. We do not know what form Zagayski's Holocaust memorial would have taken, but we do know that the space he envisaged for it later housed exhibitions such as *Toward a New Abstraction*, *Black and White* and *Primary Structures*, group shows that included the work of Morris Louis,

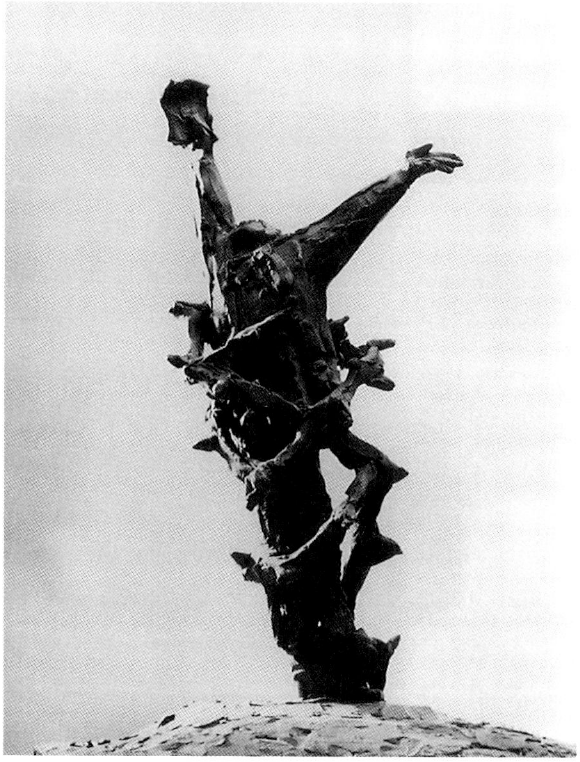

67 Nathan Rapoport, proposal for a memorial to Artur Zygelboim, 1962.

Barnett Newman and Frank Stella. All this suggests that a successful proposal for a Holocaust memorial would have not just had to meet the needs of the communities of survivors in New York, but the cultural ambitions of the longer established American Jewish patrons who gravitated towards modernism and abstraction, and whose interests were exemplified in the 1960s curatorial programme of the Jewish Museum.

By the mid-1960s, there were renewed attempts to erect a memorial in one of New York's parks. The Artur Zygelboim Memorial Committee attempted to commemorate the member of the exiled Polish war-time parliament who had committed suicide in London in 1943 in protest at the allies' incapacity to act swiftly to halt the Final Solution. The Committee proposed a sculpture showing Zygelboim 'with outstretched arms, engulfed in flames and thorns',[11] presumably to symbolise the moment of his suicide (fig. 67). More significant efforts were being spearheaded by Vladka Meed, a survivor of the Warsaw Ghetto. Meed had formed a coalition of 34 Jewish organisations called the 'Committee for the Commemoration of the Six Million Jewish Martyrs' (hence CCSMJM), some extremely small (The United Galician Jews of America), and some, the organisational 'superpowers' of American Jewry – the American Jewish Congress and the American Jewish Committee. The formation of the CCSMJM represented an apparent breakthrough: no longer would the project to erect a Holocaust memorial depend on the massive efforts of tiny organisations of Jewish Holocaust survivors, but proposals could be put forward from a broad base of long-established Jewish organisations. In late 1964, a sculpture by the Polish-born artist Nathan Rapoport was approved by the CCSMJM, a 'Torah scroll with bas-reliefs of Holocaust episodes'.[12] It was also Rapoport who designed the sculpture of Zygelboim, and when both proposals were submitted to the civic authorities in 1965, they were rejected. The Zygelboim figure was deemed a sculpture 'of such distressing and horrifying significance' that it would be unsuitable for a public park. As acceptable as this judgment seems, it should also be noted that memory of Zygelboim represented a kind of accusation of wartime international indifference, including the inaction of the American people and government: such an accusation would obviously be problematic in a memorial. Rapoport's other proposal fared no better: one member of the Art Commission, Eleanor Platt, feared that if erected, the memorial would create a precedent, encouraging other 'special groups' to approach the city in order to have their communities' histories represented. 'In an attempt to treat all equally we could well end up with a profusion of such memorials and become responsible for a progressive violation of the basic concepts for park land use.'[13] Platt's comments severely upset many members of the CCSMJM, who later complained that in calling the Jews a 'special group', she minimised the role of the Jewish communities within the fabric of New York. Perhaps an underlying anti-Semitic sentiment was detected. Whatever the case, the incident indicated that though an iconographical and symbolic memorial could gain the support of the commissioning bodies, at this time a more universal language was required to secure the approval of the city.

And so it was that in 1966, after various other twists (including a proposal for a sculpture showing Cain and Abel, put forward by the City and rejected by the CCSMJM because it implied a brotherhood between Nazis and Jews), the CCSMJM decided to form its own Art Committee. This would be chaired by David Kreeger, a Washington based patron and community leader, and would gather various artists and architects with professionals from museums, universities and publishing houses. The plan was simple: if future proposals put forward by the CCSMJM had already been sanctioned by such a committee, the bodies at City Hall and the Parks Department would be more likely to follow suit. The CCSMJM's Art Committee included the publisher Harry Abrams, museum directors Rene d'Harnoncourt, Sam Hunter, Sherman Lee and Thomas Messer, art historians H. Harvard Arnason and Meyer Schapiro, and architects Percival Goodman and Philip Johnson. On 1 November 1966, Kreeger wrote to Louis Kahn to ask him to join too. Replying the next day, Kahn accepted.

Kahn travelled to a meeting of the Committee on 5 December in New York where attendants discussed some broad aims for the memorial that would be outlined in a letter sent to the members later that month. There is no indication that Kahn put himself forward as a possible designer of the memorial at this stage, but he must have expressed some enthusiasm about the project, for on 12 April 1967, Kreeger wrote to the architect to inform him: 'I am pleased to advise you that the Committee has voted to commission you to prepare the plans and design for a projected Memorial to be created at Battery Park in New York City.'[14]

Why did the Committee select Kahn at this stage? In her account of the project, Susan Solomon indicates that Philip Johnson, who served on a sub-committee of the Art Com-

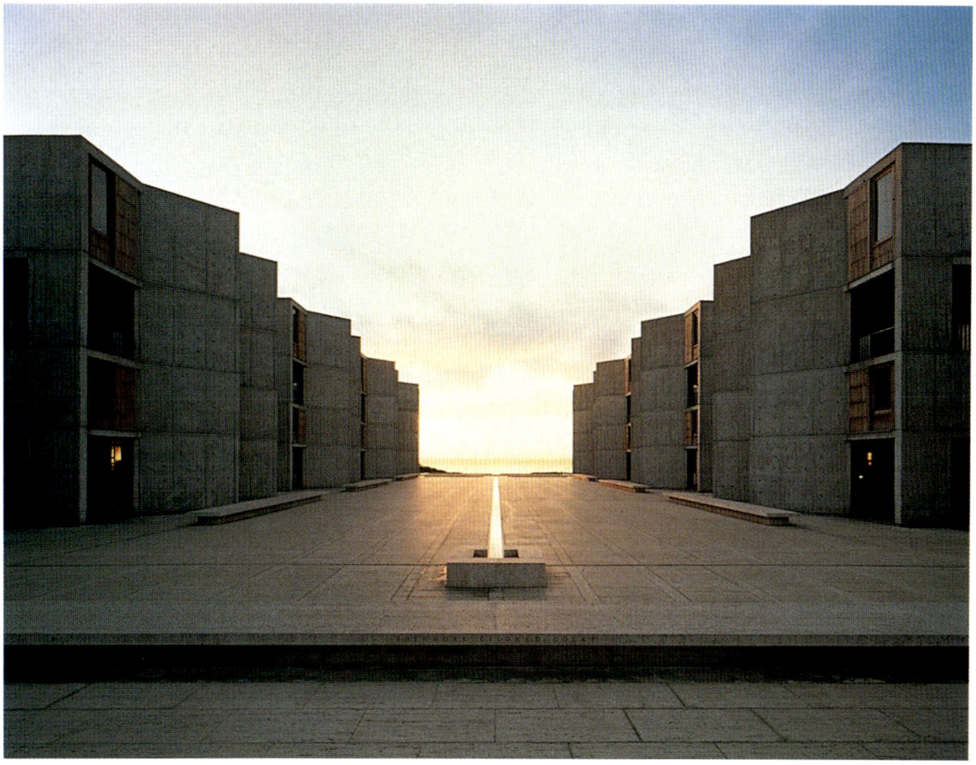

68 Louis I Kahn, Salk Institute for Biological Studies, La Jolla, California, 1959–65.

mittee, suggested the architect to Kreeger. Johnson would have known Kahn's projects well, and we can look briefly at the buildings Kahn had completed by 1966 to understand why he represented an attractive proposition. Kahn's buildings, by the mid-1960s, included The Yale University Art Gallery, the Trenton Bath House, the Richards Medical Research Building and the Salk Institute, and many other public projects were in their early stages. Kahn was known to be an architect concerned with extending the modernism of the pre-war period, yet through remarkably different means from figures such as Gropius and Mies. Kahn tended to prefer more solid-looking materials than steel and glass, making great use of cast concrete in Yale and brick in the Richards Building. Where earlier modernist buildings had shunned all kinds of reference, Kahn explored organic structures to create the forms of early buildings, and later on studied ancient monumental buildings such as the Egyptian pyramids to provide a conceptual basis for his proposals. Perhaps most importantly, Kahn was known for his sensitivity to materials and his concern with social spaces. The Salk Institute in La Jolla, like Battery Park, was a site bordering water. Between the laboratory blocks, Kahn had laid out a concourse intersected by a thin stream (fig. 68). While uniting the terrain of the institute with the vast ocean beyond, the central space encouraged not only contemplation, but crucially, discussion and meeting between the scientists.

Kahn was extremely well respected and recognised in the architectural and intellectual community and certainly not only known in Jewish circles like Nathan Rapoport.

And yet another reason that Kahn's appointment was appropriate was precisely because of his Jewish roots – not that he was by any means an observant Jew. Born in 1901 in Estonia, Kahn had moved to Philadelphia as a child in 1906 and had grown up in an immigrant Jewish community. As Sarah Williams Goldhagen describes, Kahn's 'attitude toward things Jewish was distinctly de-Judaized: he was not an observant Jew, nor was he well informed about the particularities of devotional ritual. His stance toward his heritage resembled that of many immigrants, including many Jewish ones; assimilation without denying one's roots. He spoke no Hebrew, probably never had a bar mitzvah, and knew little of the character of and practice in the congregations of Philadelphia.'[15] And yet still his Baltic background would draw towards him many members of the Eastern European Jewish organisations that made up the CCSMJM.

Kahn also had experience working with Jewish patrons. Kahn had built a synagogue in Philadelphia in the 1930s and had proposed another – the Adath Jeshurun – in 1954. Though the Jewish Community Center of which it was to be a part was never completed, Kahn's bathhouse at Trenton had been acknowledged for its monumentality and use of light, and Kahn had also displayed new plans for the Mikveh Israel synagogue at the Jewish Museum, coincidentally alongside Newman's model in Richard Meier's 1963 show 'New American Synagogue Architecture'. The architectural historian Susan Solomon has studied these various projects in detail, examining why so many failed to come to fruition, and yet we can still be confident that Kahn's longstanding and wide-ranging work with Jewish communities recommended him to the CCSMJM.

From Kahn's various projects, the commissioners could expect a thoughtful proposal that would eschew spectacular imagery for a sensitive approach to site, materials and the eventual visitors to the memorial. Choosing Kahn did not necessarily mean choosing abstraction though: in a much earlier (and unrealised) memorial proposal, his entry to the 1947 Jefferson National Expansion Memorial competition, Kahn had incorporated into his design large-scale narrative paintings and sculptures to give the memorial a didactic power. Despite this precedent of Kahn's use of narrative imagery, the CCSMJM could be sure that whatever Kahn proposed would be as far from Rapoport's figurative designs as imaginable.

the history of the commission

David Kreeger did not supply an extensive brief when he wrote to Kahn to award the commission, but previous letters (including the one he sent following Kahn's first attendance at the Art Committee) give a sense of Kreeger's ambitions for the memorial, and by proxy, those of the CCSMJM. Kreeger's first letter had stated that: 'The sponsors would like to create . . . a monument with educational and artistic value for our generation and future generations, and for people of all faiths and backgrounds.'[16] On 28 December, the aims of the memorial were made clearer:

> The monument is envisioned as one which will reflect and evoke the emotional, psychological, and historical impact of the tragedy of the period, for Jewry as well as for all humanity. It should also deal with man's struggle to retain his dignity

> under the most horrendous circumstances, and express hope for a better future where man will not merely survive but prevail. Because it is meant for the general public, we hope the monument will be of the highest possible artistic integrity and one with which all generations will be able to readily identify.[17]

The CCSMJM's sentiments seem relatively uncontroversial, but on closer inspection problems arise. The memorial should be both 'educational' and 'evocative', but these are two very conflicting modes of address: a didactic memorial would surely function very differently from one that evoked rather than taught its subject. And how possible would it be to 'evoke the emotional, psychological, and historical impact of the tragedy of the period', given the extraordinarily complex and varied psychological impacts that the 'tragedy' had made, and given that the psychological impact was (and is) still unfolding? If the memorial were to reflect a subjective response to the Holocaust, then it should follow that any artist, architect or designer could be faulted by evoking some emotions and not others. Knowing that the New York authorities had favoured designs with universal rather than explicitly Jewish meanings, the CCSMJM stipulated that the memorial should function 'for Jewry as well as for all humanity'. But inevitably a memorial aimed at 'all humanity' might leave some members of the Jewish sponsoring agencies feeling that their particular religious and cultural needs had not been addressed, and a memorial deploying Jewish symbols would alienate a wider public. Furthermore, the memorial should function for 'our generation and future generations', but survivors and children of the future would have starkly different approaches to the memory of the Holocaust. In short, the CCSMJM wanted the memorial to accomplish many ends, some of them conflicting. With the breadth of ambitions in this brief, it was not surprising that Kahn's time with the project was testing. Indeed, many of the problems he encountered were the results of these very contradictory aspirations.

The first stage of the commission lasted between Kahn's appointment on 12 April 1967 and the presentation of his initial proposal at the New York Hilton on 5 November that autumn. To research the project, Kahn was sent various publications. One journal, *Dimension*, included articles by Bruno Bettelheim, Abraham Heschel and Elie Wiesel. The editor, Albert Friedlander, wrote that the texts 'share one hopeful aspect: they stress man's ability to enter the realm of moral action'.[18] The statement is particularly interesting because it closely recalls Kreeger's words that the memorial should deal with 'man's struggle to retain his dignity under the most horrendous circumstances, and express hope for a better future where man will not merely survive but prevail'. These redemptive approaches to the Holocaust were typical at this time, but how far Kahn accepted them remains to be seen. Another document he was sent was a pamphlet by Bernard Postal titled 'Let the World Remember', which featured sixteen images of Holocaust memorials from Los Angeles to Warsaw, most of which depicted figurative images, flames, or inscriptions bearing the names of the dead and the places of their death. One image was not new to Kahn: the recently erected memorial in Philadelphia, designed (again) by Rapoport and depicting an expressionist Rabbi, arms outstretched beneath a burning bush.[19]

We cannot know if Kahn ever read the material he received, but he certainly responded enthusiastically to the task of the project. Vladka Meed, Secretary of the Committee, had sent some of the articles. Kahn met her that summer, and asked about her wartime experience. Meed has recalled that Kahn 'was very serious, very dedicated', that he 'felt very comfortable in the Jewish atmosphere'.[20] Other accounts also suggest his excitement. Kahn met Leonard Meiselman of Collaborative Workshops in May, and Meiselman wrote to Kahn that 'what you were able to communicate verbally about your concept for the Memorial. . . . was very exciting'.[21] The architect saw Moshe Davidowitz of the School of Continuing Education at New York University in August, and Davidowitz followed up to say: 'It was indeed a pleasure to meet with you last week and to discuss the various aspects of your most intriguing proposal for the monument.'[22]

Kahn must have had the idea to make the memorial out of glass blocks earlier in the summer, for at their meeting Davidowitz and Kahn had discussed the use of glass and light in the Jewish tradition. There are no documents outlining how or when Kahn came to this idea, but what is interesting (and typical of Kahn) is that it was only after choosing glass that he researched whether the material had any historical resonances in Jewish architecture and ritual.[23] Davidowitz later posted him the report of a recent archaeological discovery – 'A Huge Slab of Glass in the Ancient Necropolis of Beth She'Arim'. That Kahn checked this reference at all indicates he sensed some kind of Jewish content would be demanded of his proposal. That he checked after making a decision, however, indicates that his concerns with such content were only afterthoughts.[24] Furthermore, Kahn persisted with the idea of using glass for the memorial despite the fact that the discovery in Beth She'Arim revealed no clues as to the actual 'intended use' of the ancient slab.

The authors of the article about the slab found at Beth She'Arim were Robert Brill and John Wosinski of the Corning Museum of Glass, an adjunct of the Corning Glass Works, and Kahn travelled there on 5 September to research how his memorial could be built. Marshall Meyer was the project architect working closely with Kahn on the proposal, and Meyer's memo gives a detailed account of the day.[25] Kahn was shown a variety of glass, and was instructed about cost, casting methods and colour. It is apparent from the memo that Kahn was hoping that his blocks could be absolutely solid, colourless and transparent, but he learnt at Corning that this would not be possible. Total clarity was an option with fused silica, but the material was too expensive. 'Ordinary glass' was cheaper, but too green, and 'optical glass', a 'warm straw color' was 'more acceptable'. A solid block was also out of the question. Not only would it take too long to anneal, but, with its increased density, it would be too highly coloured. The compromise was to make hollow blocks, and to neutralise or decolorise the glass by 'adding ingredients which give complimentary color'. With these added constraints in mind, Kahn returned to Philadelphia.

On 5 November, two months after the visit to Corning, Kahn presented his initial proposal, the nine-block model, to the Art Committee and the other bodies of the CCSMJM at the Hilton in New York (fig. 69). There are no extant minutes of the

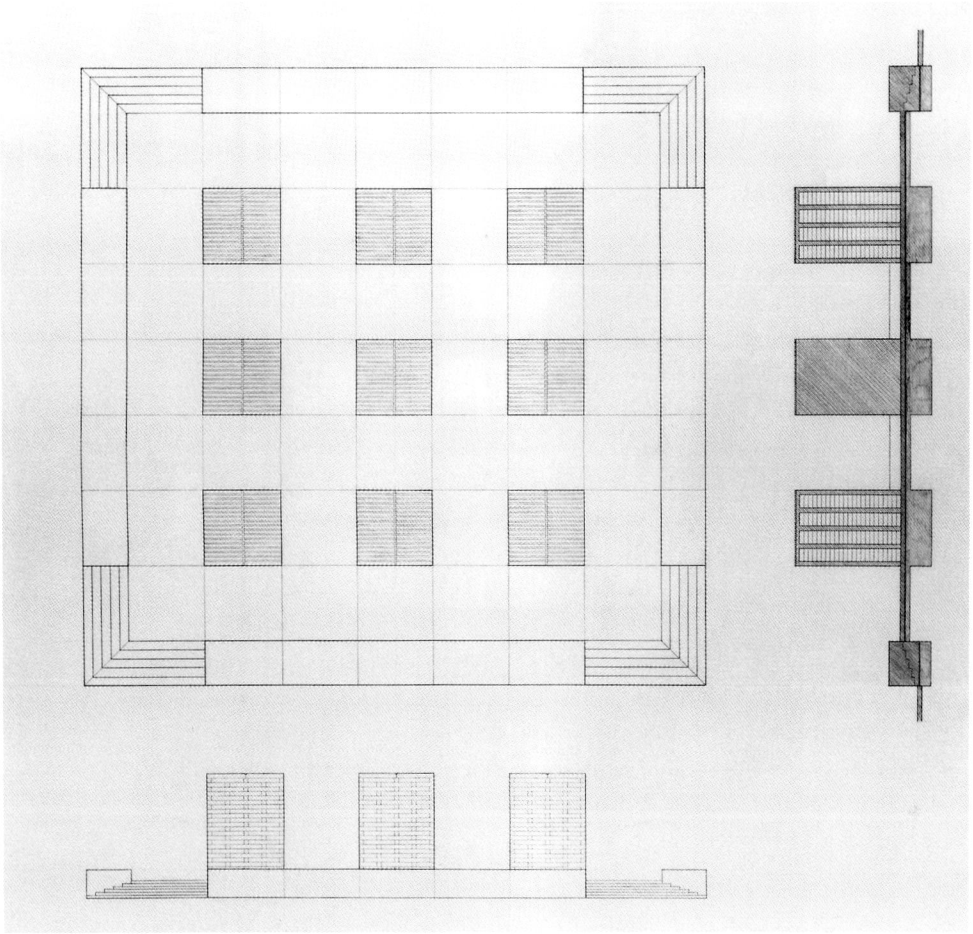

69 Louis I. Kahn, *Memorial for the Six Million Jewish Martyrs*, 1966–72 (nine-pier plan and section).

meeting, but one swift response to Kahn's proposal came in a letter sent the following week by Abraham Duker, Director of Libraries at the Yeshiva University.[26] For Duker, the problem of Kahn's proposal was its abstraction – or what he termed its 'universal symbolism'. Duker conceded that to use 'only Jewish . . . symbolism is unfashionable, and may also be inadequate or parochial'. But 'having decided on the avoidance of specifically Jewish symbols (Menorah, Shield of David), you have found yourself without any Jewish symbols'. This was a great problem, for the visitor to the memorial would not be caused to think about the 'Jewish catastrophe'. Duker pressed for several changes.

First, Duker asked Kahn to change the number of blocks. Kahn would have chosen nine piers simply to achieve a regular small grid, but grounded in Jewish numerology, Duker objected to the connection between the number nine and 'the period of gestation'. Unsurprisingly, Duker suggested that Kahn should rework the proposal using six blocks. Kahn must have considered and rejected such a simplistic reference to the six million, but Duker argued that no other number 'is more pertinent'. The Director of Libraries continued in this vein, requesting the piers should be of different heights 'representing persons of different ages – children, youths, men, women'. His final demand was even less subtle: the colourless transparency of Kahn's glass should go. Instead, the blocks should be made of 'multi-colored glass, solid black for the bottom half, even higher, then changing gradually into grey and ending with white or the color of a flame, signifying a memorial light or hope, as the onlooker would be free to interpret it.'

It is strange that Duker managed to retain any hope for the interpretative freedom of an eventual visitor. His letter evidences a desperate urge for direct symbolism, an anxious fear that Kahn's proposal amounted to a blank. Perhaps Kahn had not presented his ideas compellingly enough, but Duker's propositions completely destroyed the nature of Kahn's work. Kahn did not go on to alter the heights or colours of the blocks, but after the November meeting he did ditch the nine-pier plan. At first the idea was to accept Duker's six-pier suggestion, but when Kahn presented a revised model at a second meeting on 3 December, in addition to the six pillars, he proposed a central seventh (fig. 70).

Eight years later, after Kahn's death, Kahn's engineer August E. Komendant wrote in a memoir that the seventh pier had been his idea. Kahn was unhappy about the connections he was asked to make between the piers and the Jewish dead, so back in Philadelphia, Komendant suggested a seventh pier. 'Six million dead, yes, but from the death and ashes arises new life – the seventh cube symbolises that new life. All the other cubes are dark, lifeless, and the center one should be illuminated.' According to Komendant, Kahn embraced the idea with jubilation: 'Kahn's face brightened and he said: "August, your horse sense solved my dilemma. I knew from the beginning that something was wrong in the six-cube design, so the most important part – the life itself, hope for the future – was missing which makes the memorial of the dead significant." '[27] We might wonder how far this account is trustworthy: Komendant's seamless relay of a long-passed conversation is as self-promoting as it is unlikely. As will become apparent, the inclusion of the central pier seems in many ways to run against the precise character of the earlier model: it is more likely that Kahn integrated the chapel as a means of avoiding the symbolism of six piers, and as a strategic way of satisfying the pressurising demands of his clients.

Kahn presented a revised model with seven piers in December, but at this stage the precise character of the central pier was still undetermined. After the meeting, Kahn received another letter criticising his proposals. This letter came from Joseph Lichten of the Anti-Defamation League of the B'nai Brith. Lichten complained about the mood of Kahn's *Memorial*.[28] Seemingly unconcerned with the fact that Kreeger had asked Kahn to create an environment that would express 'hope for a better future', Lichten worried that Kahn was providing 'a sensation of peace'. Perhaps future generations could look back on the 'events of World War II in a more calm, disassociated manner', and perhaps Kahn's proposal had future generations in mind. But the memorial's initial primary users would be survivors – the generation 'who mourn every third member of their household'. Lichten felt that for such a constituency, the calmness of Kahn's pro-

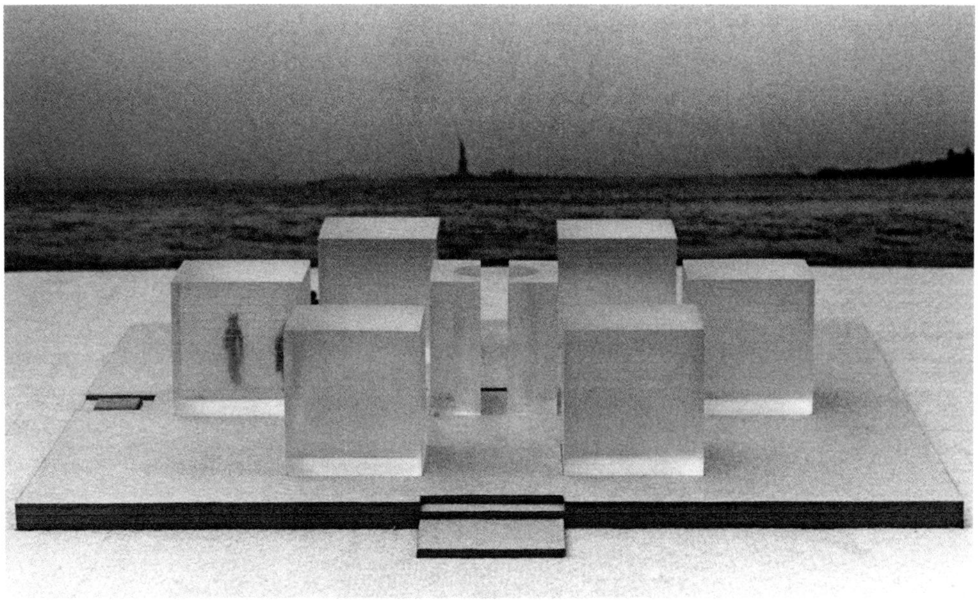

70 Louis I. Kahn, *Memorial for the Six Million Jewish Martyrs*, 1966–1972 (seven-pier model).

posal was inappropriate. He admitted that they would not want to encounter 'a model of horror' – 'Even a genius artist', Lichten continued, 'would not be able, in an art form, to present pulverised human bones or soap made from human bodies'. But those directly touched by the Holocaust would want to see in the memorial 'some expression of their own lives, their own experiences, their seeming humiliation'. Unlike Duker, Lichten did not ask Kahn to make precise changes, but he did ask that the eventual central pillar should give voice to the sentiments of the survivor generation.

The exact character of the central pillar was determined at a meeting on 20 January 1968. It would be hollow, covered with text, and would act as a kind of central chapel space within the memorial. Minutes note that 'The shrine is to be of the same material as the six pillars, but with some lilac in its color. The walls of the shrine are to have several suitable inscriptions in Yiddish, Hebrew and English, both on the outside and on the inside. The ceiling of the shrine is to bear some artistic Jewish symbol.'[29] In conveying these instructions, the members of the CCSMJM were showing how desperately they needed the memorial to present some direct messages. Kahn accepted these requirements, and in May, he wrote a press release explaining the changes the proposal had undergone. Initially he had conceived the monument 'as an environment of light created by nine piers arranged in a square without ritualistic direction', but in response to 'the prevailing desire to give the Monument a sense of the ritualistic', the 'center pier is given the character of a little chapel.' 'The one, then, the chapel, speaks, the other six are silent.'[30] From Kahn's text, it does not appear that the move from the 'non-ritualistic' to the 'ritualistic' was a great loss for him, but it should be remembered that the release was strategically written to placate clients and convince new supporters of the project: as I will argue, the change was fundamental.[31]

During the spring of 1968, the revised *Memorial* was deemed complete enough to put before the civic institutions whose support it relied upon. Unlike previous memorial proposals, Kahn's gained immediate acceptance by the City of New York Department of Parks,[32] and the Art Commission.[33] Arthur Drexler in the Department of Architecture at the Museum of Modern Art agreed to schedule an exhibition of Kahn's model in the autumn, and it opened on 17 October. The model was displayed beside photographs of Battery Park, and a panel above the model contained a text with excerpts of Kahn's press release as well as a list of the distinguished members of the Art Committee (fig. 71).

Kahn's model was applauded in the press. In *The New York Times*, Ada Louise Huxtable wrote that Kahn's 'cool, abstract, poetic, powerful and absolute statement of unspeakable tragedy' was for her one of the 'great works of commemorative art in which man has attempted to capture spirit, in symbol, for the ages.' 'The design is beautiful,' she continued, 'and chilling. There is about it a silent, almost frozen formality, a crystalline sense of the eternal emptiness of death.' The sublime sense of eternity was held in check by the dynamism of light play – the monument was also a site of movement and life: 'The glass rectangles reflect another kind of eternity, the changes of weather, light and season.' 'This is architecture, and at the same time, sculpture,' Huxtable concluded, 'and it is symbolism of the highest order, timeless and contemporary. Mr Kahn weds poetry and philosophy to form.'[34]

This stunning *New York Times* review (which remains the best short description of the *Memorial*) must have delighted the CCSMJM. Huxtable was a significant critic, and had launched severe attacks on other architectural plans for Lower Manhattan.[35] Many other specialist architectural journals also carried short and positive reviews.[36] However, the MoMA exhibition produced responses that equalled with their derision the strength of the architectural critics' commendation. Alexander Raynes visited MoMA and in 'shock', wrote to the magazine *Jewish Currents*. Appalled by the *Memorial*'s lack of narrative, Raynes reported that he had asked a museum official: '"You really believe that these six frozen masses of glass will tell the story of the genocide and tortures committed by the Nazis? Those who will visit this tiny *Ohel* [the chapel] – will they get the full meaning of the inhuman suffering and resistance in those days?"' Arguing that 'nothing would be better' than Kahn's proposal, Raynes feared that: 'History, no doubt, will blame all of us for this sickening situation.'[37] His sentiments were mirrored in a letter sent to New York's Mayor Lindsay by the Independent Jewish Senior Citizens of the Berkeley Area: 'Should the present glass model be erected as a monument to the Six Million Nazi victims it will be to the everlasting shame of the City of New York. It will be a gross insult to American Jewry. It will slander the memory of the dead. Posterity will not believe such callousness possible so soon after the Holocaust. You will not, we trust, permit this to happen.'[38]

After the exhibition, the project continued for six years until Kahn's death in 1974. For my concerns, it is not necessary to look at this last stage of the project in depth. Suffice to say that as work on the *Memorial* continued, the project encountered more and more problems, some financial, some institutional and some tectonic: Kahn

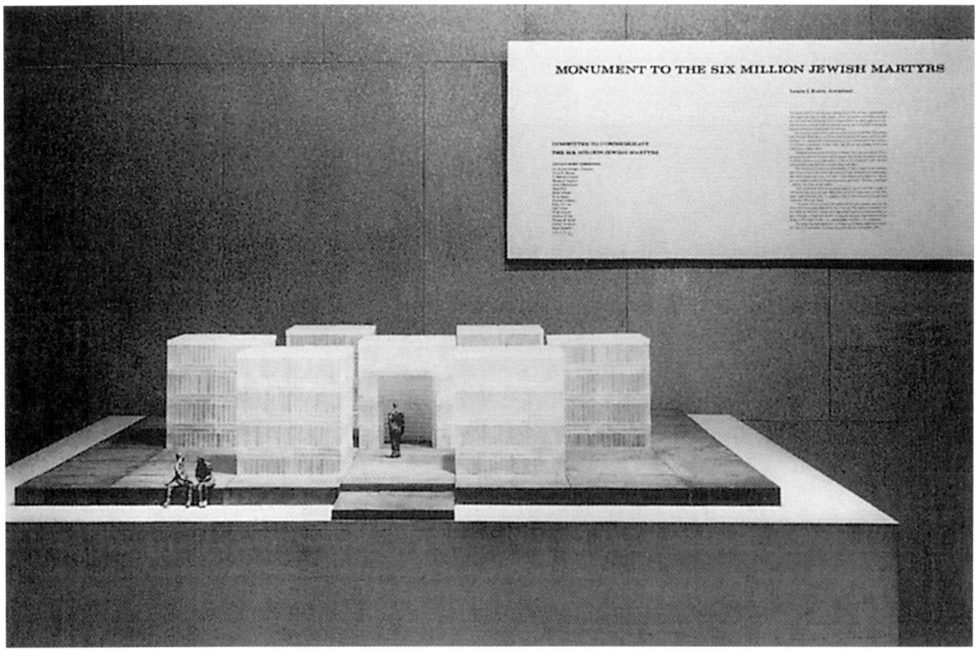

71 Louis I. Kahn, *Memorial for the Six Million Jewish Martyrs*, 1966–1972 (installation of the model at The Museum of Modern Art, October 1968).

searched for ways of reducing construction costs, reluctantly introducing steel frames to hold up the glass piers. Meanwhile, as political circumstances changed, new criticisms of Kahn's plans developed. In 1972, a man called Jesse Reichek wrote to him to urge him to alter plans so as to reflect the calamities of many other victims of oppression. Kahn's press-release text of 1968 had started by stating that 'the architect's thought was that the Monument should present a non-accusing character',[39] but Reichek could not stomach a 'non-accusing' memorial. On behalf of 'the 6 million Jews, 9 million Pakistani refugees, 25 million blacks in Rhodesia, 30 million blacks in South Africa, the millions of American Indians, millions of American black slaves, millions of Vietnamese, millions bombed in Dresden, Regensburg, etc., half a million killed in two days in Hiroshima and Nagasaki, and the twelve thousand arrested in Washington in two days', he demanded that Kahn's *Memorial* 'be accusing'.[40] This letter dramatically indicates the manner in which the Holocaust became a lens through which to focus attention on other contemporary crises.[41] While earlier Kahn had been beseeched to Judaise the *Memorial*, and while in the latter stages some asked him to incorporate a menorah into the roof of the chapel, Reichek asked Kahn to tackle the entire history of global violence in order to 'instruct us as to the meaning of the inhumane'.

Kahn's death terminated the project conclusively, but its collapse by then was complete. The reasons include the aftermath of the six-day war, which deflected funds towards Zionist causes, and a more general shift in the goals of Jewish communal organisations. Around this time, many organisations that had previously supported universalist projects aimed at general audiences now moved towards concentrating on specifically Jewish targets, a shift exemplified by the Jewish Museum's changing curatorial priorities during this time, and its move from modernist exhibitions to exhibitions devoted to Jewish themes. Other more practical reasons for the disintegration of Kahn's project include the structural disunity of the CCSMJM, whose member bodies could barely co-ordinate the payment of Kahn's $18,000 expenses in 1971, let alone raise further funds for construction.[42] However, it is possible to argue that the abstraction of Kahn's proposal scuppered the chances of the *Memorial*'s realisation. As we have seen, there were many reasons why abstraction represented a positive option to some of the constituents of the CCSMJM. First, to recall the terms of Kreeger's letter to Kahn, an abstract memorial could be of 'highest possible artistic integrity', making sense within the context of post-war American art and architecture. Jewish patrons well-versed with modernist art could support an abstract memorial, and it could gain the approval of institutions such as MoMA and critics such as Huxtable. Abstraction would also avoid the problems that previous memorial proposals had encountered, not introducing 'horrifying' images into a park, not being excessively Jewish and not accusing American visitors of historical indifference and inaction in regards to Nazism. So abstraction was right for many in the CCSMJM, but other individuals and organisations involved in the group wanted narrative, Jewish symbolism and obvious didactic content. When members of the Jewish public had the chance to examine Kahn's proposal at MoMA and to voice their own complaints, they would echo the sentiments of figures such as Abraham Duker and Joseph Lichten: internal rifts in the CCSMJM could be mined by those outside it.

Kahn's proposal seems to have been destined to live its existence in the drawings, models, photographs and texts now stored in archives in New York and Philadelphia, rather than as glass blocks by the Hudson. It is to these various texts that I will now return in order to consider how Kahn's proposal made meaning as a memorial. But as I do so, I want to discuss the abstraction of Kahn's proposal in new ways. Abstraction was not just a means of placating patrons and avoiding challenges: rather, Kahn's abstract proposal was a challenge to the very idea of what a memorial could be, and to what its visitors might do in its spaces.

re-reading kahn's *memorial*

There are many different possible ways to address Kahn's nine-pier *Memorial* proposal and to ask about its possible meanings. I want to think about its response to architectural history, the way in which it addresses its site in Battery Park, the manner in which it structured a visitor's passage through its space, and finally the ways in which it might have been experienced by several visitors using it at the same time. But first we can examine how Kahn thought it would function, remembering that the document that expressed his thoughts was a strategically written press release, and therefore hardly a text which expresses all that he might have wished to say.

Kahn did not precisely explain how he thought visitors to the *Memorial* would be caused to remember the Holocaust. Perhaps it was obvious in any case that remembering the Holocaust was not, for him, a matter of recalling particular incidents or individuals through particular didactic symbols or figurative prompts. Instead, Kahn articulated how he hoped to create a 'non-accusing' memorial.[43] As we saw earlier in relation to the failed Zygelboim project, a memorial could easily accuse, and could not only accuse the Nazi perpetrators, but also the politicians and civilians of 'bystander' nations. Kahn refused to indulge in the activity of blaming, so not only did he forsake accusing figures and symbols, but also accusing materials. He reasoned that if a Holocaust memorial were made of stone or brick, it would cast 'defined shadows' over its visitors, and Kahn associated the event of being shaded in this context with the act of being accused. A block of glass, however, could create 'a shadow filled with light', and therefore avoid accusing the viewer. Kahn thought a light-filled memorial would have a 'non-accusing character' because he saw light as a generative and mystical force. As he wrote in several lectures of this period, natural light was for him 'the giver of all presences'.[44] Though his texts do not associate light with a specific divine force, sometimes Kahn echoed ideas found at the beginning of Genesis, where the creation of light precedes the creation of the world. 'Light is the maker of a material,' he wrote, 'and the material was made to cast a shadow.'[45] If Kahn could create an environment where even the shadows would be full of light, not only would it avoid accusation; it would create an all the more powerful sense of generation.

Williams Goldhagen has written about the 'obfuscatory and transcendentalizing terms' of Kahn's late texts, and his quasi-religious sense of light can seem problematically spiritual.[46] Certainly his rhetoric and reasoning was at odds with the literalist approach to light taken by the sculptors of the 1960s who worked with shiny and reflective surfaces or even store-bought fluorescent tubes. But Kahn's use of light as a source of generation does correspond to the ideas expressed by the CCSMJM in Kreeger's introductory letter. The *Memorial* should 'express hope for a better future where man will not merely survive but prevail'. Kahn, it seems, felt that maximising the light play within the *Memorial* was the best way of expressing this hope.

However, while it may seem that Kahn deployed light to create a space that would redeem the horror of the Holocaust by fostering a sense of hope and life, there are other ways of reading his sentiments. In the press release he wrote about the relation of light to site and to time: 'The Monument will get its mood from the endless changes of the light of day and of night, the seasons of the year, the endless play of the weather, and even the sudden light of a flash of lightning. The drama of movement on the river will transmit its life to the Monument.'[47] We could take this as another redemptive statement: the ever-changing light in the *Memorial* would create an ever-renewed sense of life. But equally we could imagine that the changing appearance of the *Memorial* reflected the endless demands of the memory of the Holocaust. Memory could be locked up in a symbol or figure but eventually it would be locked away, opaque to future generations unfamiliar with its references. (This is the fate of most memorials.) An endlessly changing memorial, on the other hand, could insure that the memory of what happened would never cease.

Kahn's text on the use of glass and light in the *Memorial* is therefore more complex and multi-valenced than it first appears, but even so, the text need not delimit the ways of addressing the *Memorial*. Another lens through which to view the proposal is that of architectural history and memory. The concept of 'memory' in architectural discourse at the time referred much more usually to architectural recollection than to the way in which a structure commemorated an event, and Kahn's work was at the centre of this discourse. Where the International Style, in Vincent Scully's words, 'banned history',[48] Kahn deployed it: The Richards Building, for instance, was 'reminiscent . . . of San Gimignano and Siena'.[49] Theorists and architectural historians such as Kenneth Frampton, Manfredo Tafuri and Sarah Williams Goldhagen have contested how exactly these references function in Kahn's architecture,[50] but for my purposes it is neither necessary to determine whether these allusions were fundamental or peripheral to Kahn's project, nor to distinguish Kahn's approach from the kind of eclecticism and post-modern pastiche for which Philip Johnson and Charles Moore would later be criticised. More simply, I want to ask how the *Memorial* remembered or indeed consigned previous kinds of architecture to oblivion.

One argument about such a kind of memory has already been made. In an article looking at various references in Kahn's work to 'Biblical Imagery from Noah's Ark to the Temple of Solomon', the historian Alexander Gorlin argued that 'the nine square plan of the memorial alludes to a reconstruction of Solomon's Temple'.[51] This seems unlikely. As Williams Goldhagen has suggested, in his project for the Adath Jeshurun Synagogue, Kahn changed tack from proposing a six-sided building to a three-sided one precisely 'to avoid all literal references to Jewish symbolism',[52] and there is no indication that Kahn's attitude to Jewish symbolism had changed by the time he proposed his nine-pier model. (If it had changed, then Abraham Duker would have acknowledged Kahn's reference to the Temple when he wrote to the architect to request Jewish symbolism for the memorial). A better starting point would be to ask how Kahn's proposal *forgot* fascist architecture.

Previously I indicated that the lack of symbolism in Kahn's *Memorial* resulted from his ambivalence towards the Holocaust memorials he saw in the literature he had been sent, and especially Rapoport's Philadelphia memorial whose language, argues Susan Solomon, Kahn actively resisted.[53] But equally, eschewing symbols was a means of nullifying the memory of fascism as fascist architects had so frequently deployed them.[54] The memory of fascist architecture would not be eliminated simply by the absence of a symbol, though: an abstract edifice could still wield a kind of authority similar to the command of Albert Speer's parade grounds. In 1966, Philip Johnson published his proposals for the Dallas Kennedy memorial, which would consist of a cube, open at its top and along two facing side slits (fig. 72). Designed to stand thirty feet high, Johnson said of it: 'You can't see Dallas . . . you can't see anything but the sky. You are forced into an attitude of reverie.'[55] Rather than towering over the envisaged visitor and *forcing* their attitude, the height of Kahn's piers related to the human size, as was represented in the drawings showing people moving about the *Memorial* (fig. 73). So through both the abstraction and the scale of the *Memorial*, Kahn defied the architectural memory of fascism.[56]

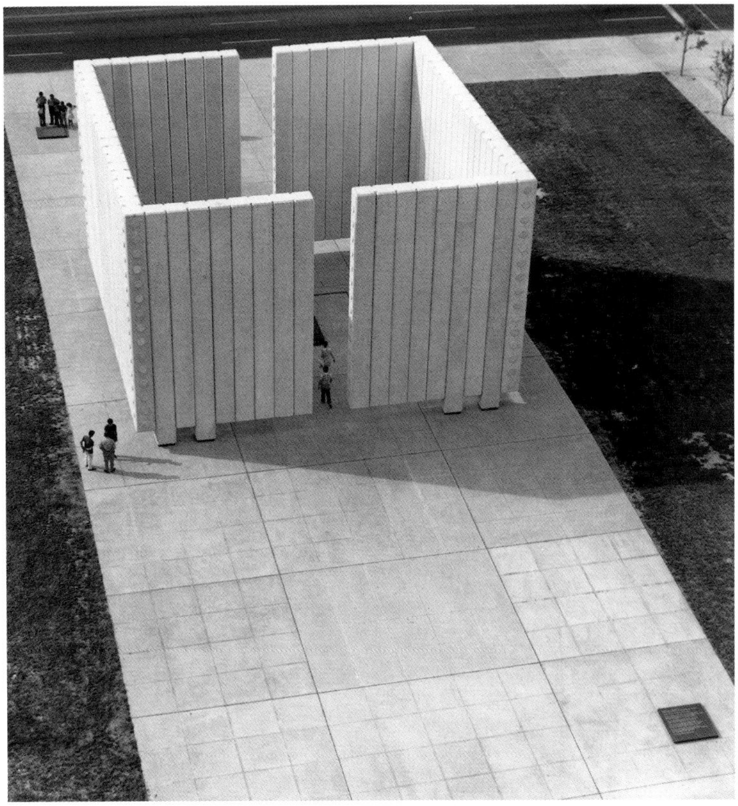

72 Philip Johnson, *Kennedy Memorial*, Dallas, 1970. Courtesy Philip Johnson – Alan Ritchie Architects.

In the place of Nazi architecture, Kahn's *Memorial* remembered the glass architecture of the pre-Nazi Weimar period, and the utopian rhetoric that accompanied the use of glass. In 1914, Paul Scheerbart had urged: 'If we want our culture to rise to a higher level, we are obliged . . . to change our architecture. . . . We can only do that by introducing glass architecture.'[57] 'The new glass environment will completely transform mankind', he hoped.[58] Just over a decade later in 1926, Arthur Korn collected the various uses to which the material had been put in his book *Glass in Modern Architecture*.[59] His rhetoric was not as florid, but many assumptions were intact. In architecture, glass signified and encouraged societal honesty and openness.[60] Such associations would have made glass appropriate to Kahn's *Memorial* and it is even more notable that Kahn planned to use glass given that he had previously tended to avoid the material. Scully wrote that Kahn 'triumphed over the International Style by the subordination of glass or its total elimination' in various buildings of the 1960s.[61] In the *Memorial*, Kahn reversed this trend, and in a manner not dissimilar to Frank Stella's invocation of constructivism, he recalled the dreams of Dessau, and lamented their destruction under Nazism.[62]

Kahn's *Memorial* would have occupied a site in Battery Park on the lower tip of downtown Manhattan. The site was not Kahn's choice (it had been assigned to the

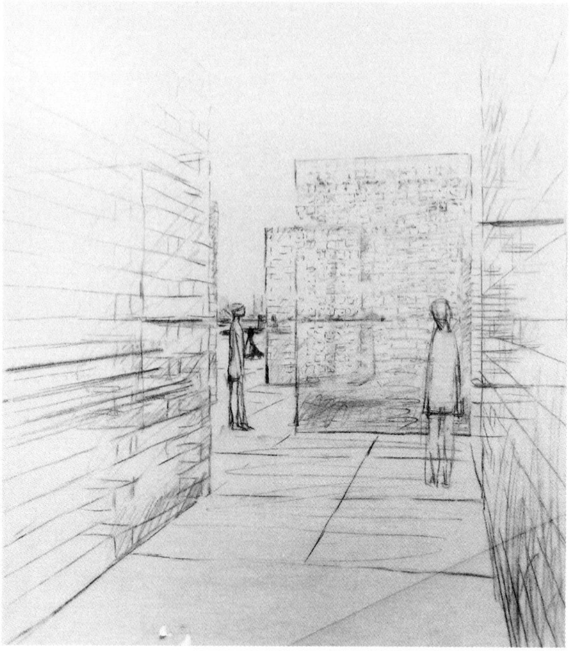

73 Louis I. Kahn, *Memorial for the Six Million Jewish Martyrs*, 1966–72 (Drawing 690.37 showing people inside the memorial).

CCSMJM by the New York authorities before he was commissioned), but it is important to understand what it was like and how he approached it. In the mid-1960s, the park was a kind of graveyard of monuments including what one contemporary guidebook writer called 'a tasteless war memorial which consists of a series of huge granite slabs bearing alphabetical lists of those lost at sea in World War II'.[63] Nearby stood the Wireless Operator's Memorial, the Verrazano Statue, the Castle Clinton National Monument, the Emma Lazarus Memorial, the Walloon Monument, the Ericsson Statue and the Coast Guard Memorial.[64] (Claes Oldenburg's drawing of 1965, *Proposed Colossal Monument for the Battery, New York: Vacuum Cleaner*, shows a giant machine sweeping up these structures; fig. 74.) Battery Park was also the best site in Manhattan from which to view two symbols of immigration: the Statue of Liberty and Ellis Island. Standing by the railings in the park, looking towards the Atlantic horizon, a European immigrant like Kahn might have imagined they were looking back to the east, and to the past. The site was both cluttered and evocative, but however crass he might have found their forms, Kahn did not take an aggressive stance towards the surrounding memorials by surpassing them in height or blocking them from view. Along with the monuments in the bay, he welcomed them into the visual space of the *Memorial*. 'The site,' he wrote, 'in wake of its signs of 'Welcome to America', did much to inspire the use of glass.' Kahn wanted to achieve 'a sense of dematerialization to allow all of these symbolic structures . . . to enter the memorial',[65] and emphasised this by having photographs of the model taken which imaged the surrounding structures clearly. In one particularly beautiful image, the Statue of Liberty is shown sandwiched between the *Memorial* and Castle Clinton (fig. 75). By opening up his structure in this

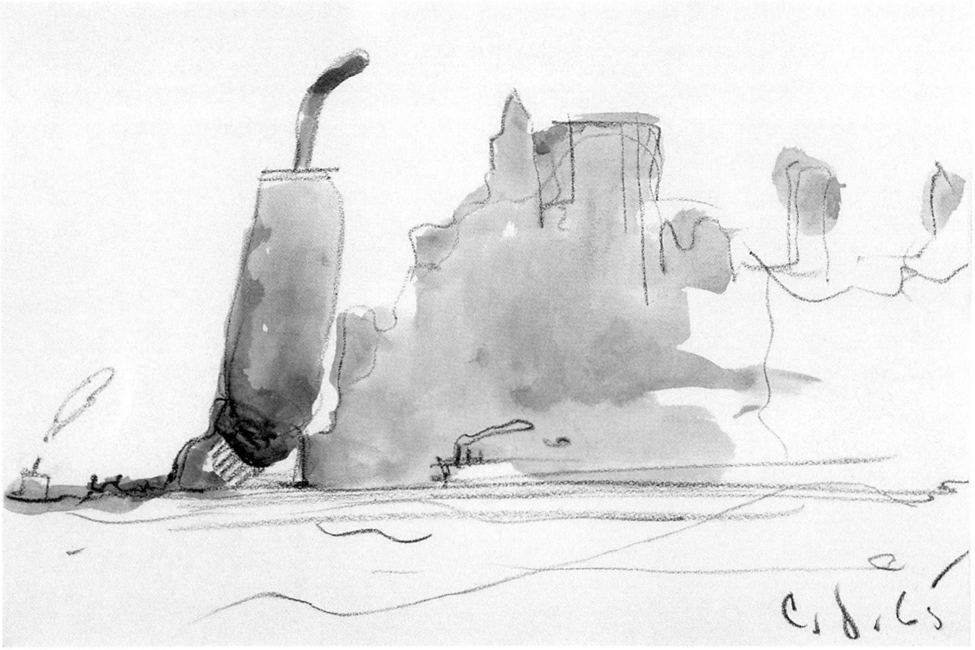

74 Claes Oldenburg, *Proposed Colossal Monument for the Battery, New York – Vacuum Cleaner, East River View*, 1965. Crayon and watercolour, 30.5 × 45 cm, Private collection.

way, Kahn connected the mnemonic focus of the *Memorial* to the subject of immigration. For a future visitor, the activity of remembering the Holocaust would always be connected to pondering their own personal position in relation to their immigrant past – whether or not they were Jewish, and whether or not their families had actually come from Europe or through Ellis Island.[66]

The various monuments in Battery Park could optically penetrate the spaces of the *Memorial* without altering its visual identity. This is because the *Memorial* was comprised of glass and air, both of which are literally transparent. In their important 1963 article 'Transparency: Literal and Phenomenal', Colin Rowe and Robert Slutsky differentiated this kind of literal transparency from phenomenal transparency. Rowe and Slutsky argued that though literal transparency starts off by seeming to offer visual clarity, it allows many optical levels to interpenetrate, and so gives rise to a 'contradiction of spatial dimensions'.[67] When this happens, 'the transparent ceases to be that which is perfectly clear and becomes, instead, that which is clearly ambiguous'.[68] Phenomenal transparency implied spatial ambiguity – the ambiguity of a structure that seemed to suggest a certain spatial order from one perspective, but which exhibited, on experience, a different one.[69]

As much as the literal transparency of its materials was important to the workings of Kahn's *Memorial*, so was the phenomenal transparency of its space. But how was the *Memorial* phenomenally transparent? From a bird's eye view, one would assume that Kahn's *Memorial* would *only* have been literally transparent, and that the structure of its orderly grid would have been evident for anyone visiting the site, from the moment of their approach, through the time they wandered in its spaces, right to the time they left. One would assume, in other words, that a viewer would encounter the *Memorial* at every point as an incredibly ordered and neatly divided environment. However, the phenomenal experience would have been rather more complex, and this was because glass, as well as being literally transparent, was also reflective, depending on the changing light conditions. On account of the endless reflections between them, rather than nine distinct units appearing laid out in a grid, there might have sometimes appeared to have been more, sometimes less, but never a definite number of blocks. Blocks would be seen through each other; they would be reflected in each other's surfaces, and these surfaces would also hold reflections of reflections.

Glass would have dissipated the sense of order of the *Memorial*'s grid, and in fact the nature of this specific grid would also have confounded the initial impression that this was an obviously ordered space. Contrary to the expectations a visitor would have had (given the configuration of most traditional monuments), there was no symbolic centre in the rigorously non-hierarchical nine-pier model, and no one block was differentiated from any other. Rather than envisaging a subject who would walk through the outside towards the centre as if in a ritual, Kahn structured the viewer's journey more loosely. Journeys around the *Memorial* were to continue without a definite sense of direction.[70] The light character of the space would also loosen the journey within it: since the space would not be divided into areas of light and shade, but instead into areas of light and of light-filled shadows, it would seem more unified to the visitor, and their exploration could just persist without an end point.

Kahn eventually bowed to the 'prevailing desire to give the Monument a sense of the ritualistic' and created a ceremonial centre in the middle chapel. For the commissioners, the chapel was a means to guarantee that a visitor would have a place in which to remember the Holocaust. But by introducing such a chapel, the phenomenal transparency of the first proposal would have been lost, and so too, the mnemonic potential of Kahn's design. For Kahn's creation of a non-ritualistic, phenomenally ambiguous space in the initial proposal was actually a crucial strategy to secure the structure's mnemonic function. The first proposal imagined a unified, centreless space that would have seemed to go on and on. Inside it, time would have slowed down. This slowness would have engendered the contemplative attitude necessary to encourage and facilitate the processes of memory. The first proposal did not identify a specific place within it in which to remember, but instead, through its ambiguous spatiality, it created a temporal environment for memory.

Walking into Battery Park off the darkened bustling grid of Manhattan's streets, a single visitor to Kahn's *Memorial* would have found themselves in a more ambiguous and light-filled grid, a slowed-down place in which to remember. But what would it have been like to encounter other visitors there? In her recent book on Kahn, Sarah Williams Goldhagen has placed the creation of communal spaces at the heart of Kahn's entire project. When he worked on the Adath Jeshurun, for instance, rather than creating a building to facilitate 'institutionalized rituals of worship', Kahn wished to encourage 'a spontaneous mode of communing'[71] and hoped the synagogue would 'represent people's connection to each other in a community'.[72] This concern with spaces

75 Louis I. Kahn, *Memorial for the Six Million Jewish Martyrs*, 1966–72 (model showing Battery Park setting and Statue of Liberty).

of congress developed from Kahn's early civic proposals for Philadelphia and persisted in the courtyard of the Salk Institute and the plazas of the National Assembly at Sher-e-Bangla Nagar in Bangladesh. The most important aspect of Kahn's *Memorial* was the way in which it fostered communal remembrance.

Let us imagine many visitors in its space at once. Since they would not be looking up to any figurative images, or reading any texts, visitors would see other individuals through the piers. It might have been quite odd to see others doing what they were doing, which was looking through the glass at themselves. Each visitor would need to make decisions about privacy and space – whether to stand near others, whether to walk different paths through the space, and so on. Such decisions are always made in public spaces but since the proposal did not structure a path of movement towards a centre, moving around and around the piers meant moving around other people, becoming increasingly aware of them, and aware of them as quite strange presences. Where in everyday situations, individuals encounter others in their social roles, within the *Memorial*, one subject would encounter another in a more phenomenologically specific manner, in an unfamiliar way.

As well as its organisation, the materiality of the *Memorial* would also have affected the process of seeing other people. The glass would have been partially translucent, not concealing anything at its centre, allowing the viewer to see inside and through it. It would also have been partially reflective, mirroring the face of the viewer on its surface, even mirroring the reflection of their backs that were cast from the surface of the block behind them, but, crucially, also mirroring everyone around. Contemporary sculptors in the mid-1960s used mirrored surfaces to reflect a *part* of the single viewing subject's body (usually, their feet) to heighten their awareness of their movement around the work, but in Kahn's piers, the reflections would also heighten the viewer's awareness of *other people*. This function of reflectivity has been eloquently articulated by the critic Brian Hatton in his account of an actual structure, Dan Graham's *Star of David Pavilion* in Schloβ Buchberg, which, like Kahn's *Memorial*, makes use of both transparency and reflectivity. 'Our beholding', Hatton writes, 'is no longer a simple matter of contemplating an object, for the object now comprises both the prism itself and that which is seen through it or 'in' it – including ourselves. The "we" is important, for the

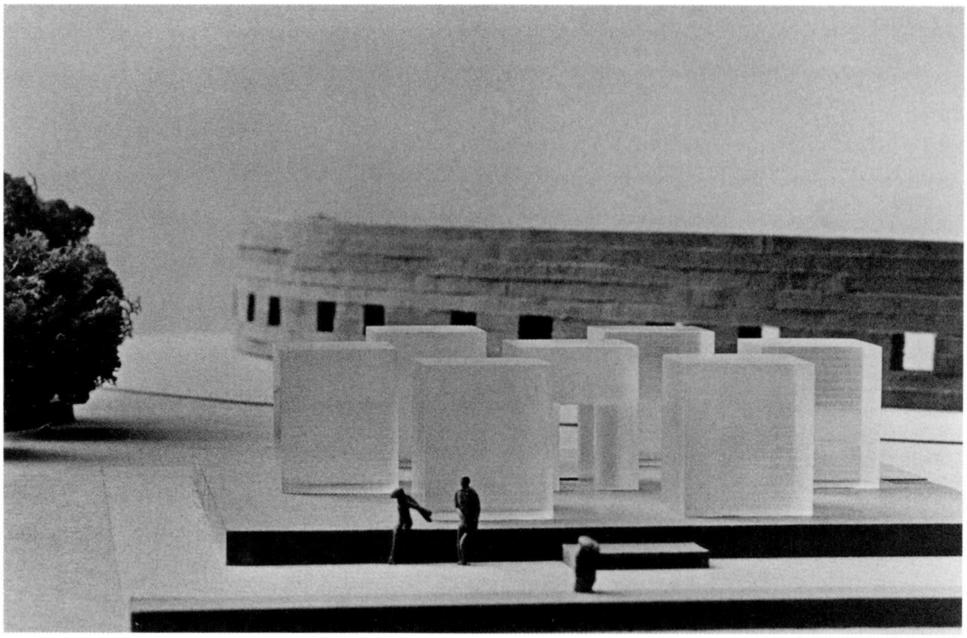

76 Louis I. Kahn, *Memorial for the Six Million Jewish Martyrs*, 1966–1972 (seven-pier model with model visitors).

full valence of the prism is activated in the company – co-attentive, differently engaged, or introspective – of others. The pavilion reminds us how subjectivity is intrinsically reciprocal; we become ourselves through being, *inter alia*, the responsive objects of each others' gaze.'[73]

Hatton's account of Graham allows us to understand how Kahn used glass to create a social space. The reflectivity and transparency of glass would draw visitors' attention to the very activity of looking, to the reciprocal activity of seeing and being seen, to the mutual reliance between one subject and another.[74] Increasingly aware of their presence, one visitor might well greet another, and Kahn's environment would become a place for congress. Would it be too far-fetched to imagine that Kahn hoped his *Memorial* would foster conversation between strangers? The CCSMJM, disturbed by the absence of inscriptions in the initial proposal, demanded that words be legible in the chapel space. But of course, words were to be present in the original *Memorial* – not physically present, but there in the conversation of its visitors. In one model for the seven-pier proposal, Kahn persisted with this idea, positioning two human figures sitting and talking with their backs facing the blocks (fig. 76). The position of the pair suggested that the activity of memory took place in the environment of the whole monument, and not within the confines of the chapel. Their conversation indicated that Kahn conceived memory not just as a private thought process taking place in public, but as a communal activity. Unconditioned by statuary or symbols, stories would flow as memories were shared. The painful past would be recounted and negotiated.[75]

The intended communality of Kahn's proposal was, I believe, the most important reason for its abstraction, and its greatest challenge to the very concept of a memorial.

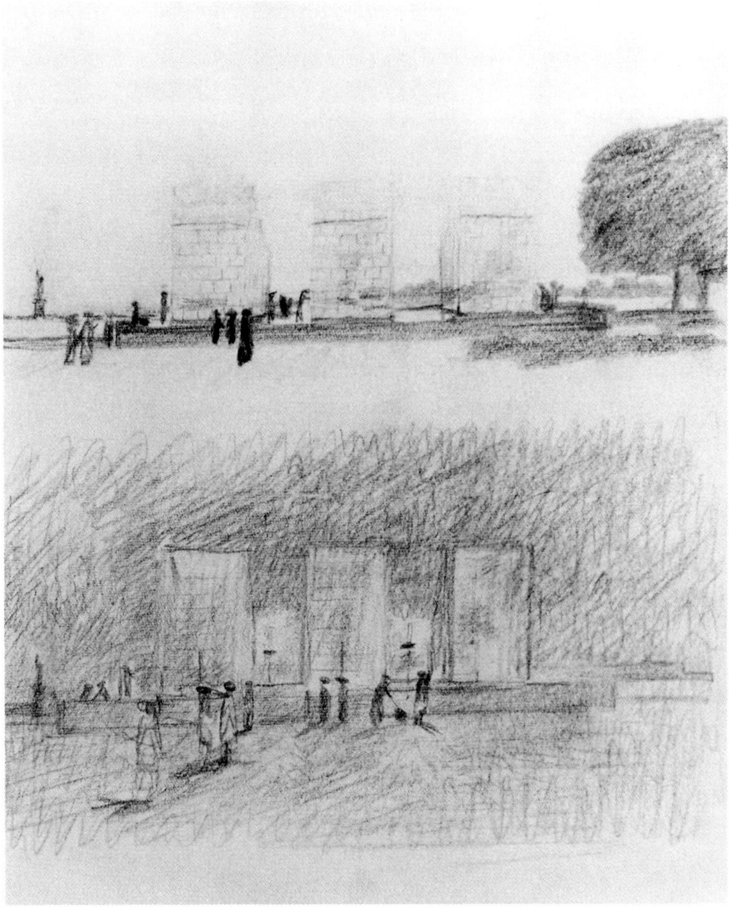

Rather than imagining that a visitor would spend time reading or learning from didactic sources, Kahn proposed that visitors come together in memory (fig. 77). During his work on the *Memorial*, Kahn wrote about the kind of encounters that architecture could foster. 'With only one other person one feels generative. The meeting becomes an event. The actor throws aside the lines of his performance. The residue from all his thoughts and experiences meets the other on equal terms.'[76] Kahn's thinking here (which stresses that the subject must become vulnerable before meeting the other 'on equal terms') and indeed his thinking for the *Memorial* in general, seems to be in accord with Emmanuel Levinas's thought on the ethical (Levinas was another Baltic-born Jew, only five years younger than the architect). Where philosophers like Sartre considered the encounter with the Other as the moment when the subject realised he was placed under threat, for Levinas 'the first revelation of the other, presupposed in all the other relations with him, does not consist in grasping him in his negative resistance and in circumventing him by ruse.'[77] Levinas theorised the moment of the encounter with the Other as the moment of ethics. The subject would intuit the 'infinity' of the Other, their absolute irreducibility, and the absolute and unconditional obligation they had to the

77 Louis I. Kahn, *Memorial for the Six Million Jewish Martyrs*, 1966–72 (drawing 690.8 showing people around the memorial and Statue of Liberty).

Other. This was an asymmetrical responsibility – the subject's obligation to the Other was not balanced by the Other's obligation to them. Levinas described the moment of the encounter with the Other through his idea of the face: 'The epiphany of the face is ethical.'[78]

The rule-less space and the materiality of Kahn's *Memorial* would establish the conditions for the encounter with which Levinas was concerned. Because it would have felt odd to encounter subjects in such an unusual and phenomenologically specific manner, one person would not see another as an equal, but as an unknown entity. Yet in the reflections and between the blocks, one face would be insistently evident to another. Encountering the other as present, the subject would realise their infinite obligation; yet sensing a trace of their unknowability, the subject would not treat the Other as 'same', and would realise the asymmetry of their obligation.

This formulation might seem to take the philosopher's terms too literally and, despite his visual descriptions ('There is first the very uprightness of the face, its upright exposure, without defence'[79]), the idea of *seeing* the face was, for Levinas, metaphorical. In a late interview, Levinas made it clear that he was not simply talking about looking at the Other: 'The relation with the face can surely be dominated by perception, but what is specifically the face is what cannot be reduced to that.'[80] Indeed, Levinas's work implies a critique of the centrality of vision, since vision is associated with control, and panoramic, totalising philosophies.[81] But here too there is another connection to Kahn's ideas. We have seen how Kahn's *Memorial* relinquished the control fascist monuments assume, and how the ambiguous visuality of the proposal destabilised order to foster memory. So, like Levinas, Kahn both criticised problematically totalising forms, and questioned the ambitions of vision to achieve clarity.

All this notwithstanding, Levinas's description of the encounter does seem appropriate to theorise Kahn's communal ambitions for the *Memorial*. By creating the conditions for an ethical encounter of subjects, Kahn hoped memory would be generated for the sake of the present and the future. What was remembered would be as much the past – the experience of the individual – as the obligation of the present: the individual's responsibility for the Other. In the remembrance of this responsibility, the visitor would re-establish the bond that Nazi ethics destroyed.[82] After all, as Primo Levi recalled, 'Our feeling that we exist depends for a large part on the gaze of others directed at us: we can thus characterize as non-human the experience of those who lived through those days when Man was an object of men's gaze.'[83]

a 'throwing into question'

Some five years after Kahn's death extinguished all hope of the *Memorial* being built, the French writer Georges Perec came to the site that the architect wanted to make visible through his glass blocks. Perec made a film on Ellis Island, and found himself addressing what 'being a Jew means'. He wrote: 'It's not a sign of belonging, a religion, a praxis, a culture, a folklore, a history, a destiny, a language. It is an absence rather, a question, a throwing into question, a floating, an anxiety, an anxious certainty behind which there is the outline of another certainty, abstract, heavy, insupportable: that of having been designated as a Jew, and therefore as a victim, and of owing my life simply to chance and to exile.' Though Perec might be at home in many countries including America and France, 'one thing alone in this almost limitless range of possibilities was forbidden to me, that of being born in the land of my ancestors, in Poland, in Lubartow, Pulawy or Warsaw, and of growing up there in the continuity of a tradition, a language and an affiliation.'[84]

Rather than conceiving a memorial with the texts and symbols of a decimated Jewish culture, so many compensatory signs of belonging and tradition, Kahn aimed to reflect the condition of the post-Holocaust Jewish subject as Perec described him, a subject for whom, in the absence of a secured home, everything was thrown into question. But in 'throwing into question' everything about a Holocaust memorial, Kahn avoided the raw pessimism of Perec's vision. His *Memorial* did not aim simplistically to redeem the horror of the Holocaust through the peaceful beauty of glass and light, but it did propose that memory be a communal and a restorative activity (fig. 77). All of its ambitions were to be achieved through its abstraction. This abstraction should neither be understood as a means of placating sensitive New York authorities, nor of wooing culturally ambitious Jewish patrons. The abstraction of Kahn's *Memorial* was instead problematic and challenging, and though a clear departure from the textual and figurative memorials proposed before it, Kahn's *Memorial* would have dramatised the presence of real figures, and encouraged the beginnings of real spoken language in the place of texts. As well as the needs of 'future generations', Kahn took seriously the predicament of survivors and immigrant Jews in post-war America, but his proposal could never fully gain their support. The community would only ever properly back a didactic, obviously Jewish memorial that could assuage the anxiety of dislocation that Perec so eloquently described. This is why the 'central chapel' became so important to the CCSMJM. Eventually, in 1997, a Holocaust memorial was erected in Battery Park, and unsurprisingly, it took the shape of a six-sided, six-tiered museum, a kind of ultimate version of the chapel. The 'Museum of Jewish Heritage – A Living Memorial to the Holocaust' displays a conventional exhibition about the Holocaust between other exhibits on Jewish life before and after the Holocaust. A visitor to the museum spends time looking at maps and photographs, films and artefacts, rather than looking at themselves looking, and looking at other visitors.

It was those latter activities that Kahn proposed take place in his *Memorial*. In the years his proposal was debated, activities such as looking at yourself looking became the concern of many New York artists and especially those who began to use video. Video allowed artists to watch images as they taped them, and as a result, most early video artists imaged their bodies. But one among them, Beryl Korot, turned her camera away from her body, and towards a didactic Holocaust memorial. However, this was unlike the one the CCSMJM had envisaged, and unlike the 'Museum of Jewish Memorial', for Korot made her film away from New York, and in West Germany. Her video was recorded at the recently opened museum in the concentration camp in Dachau.

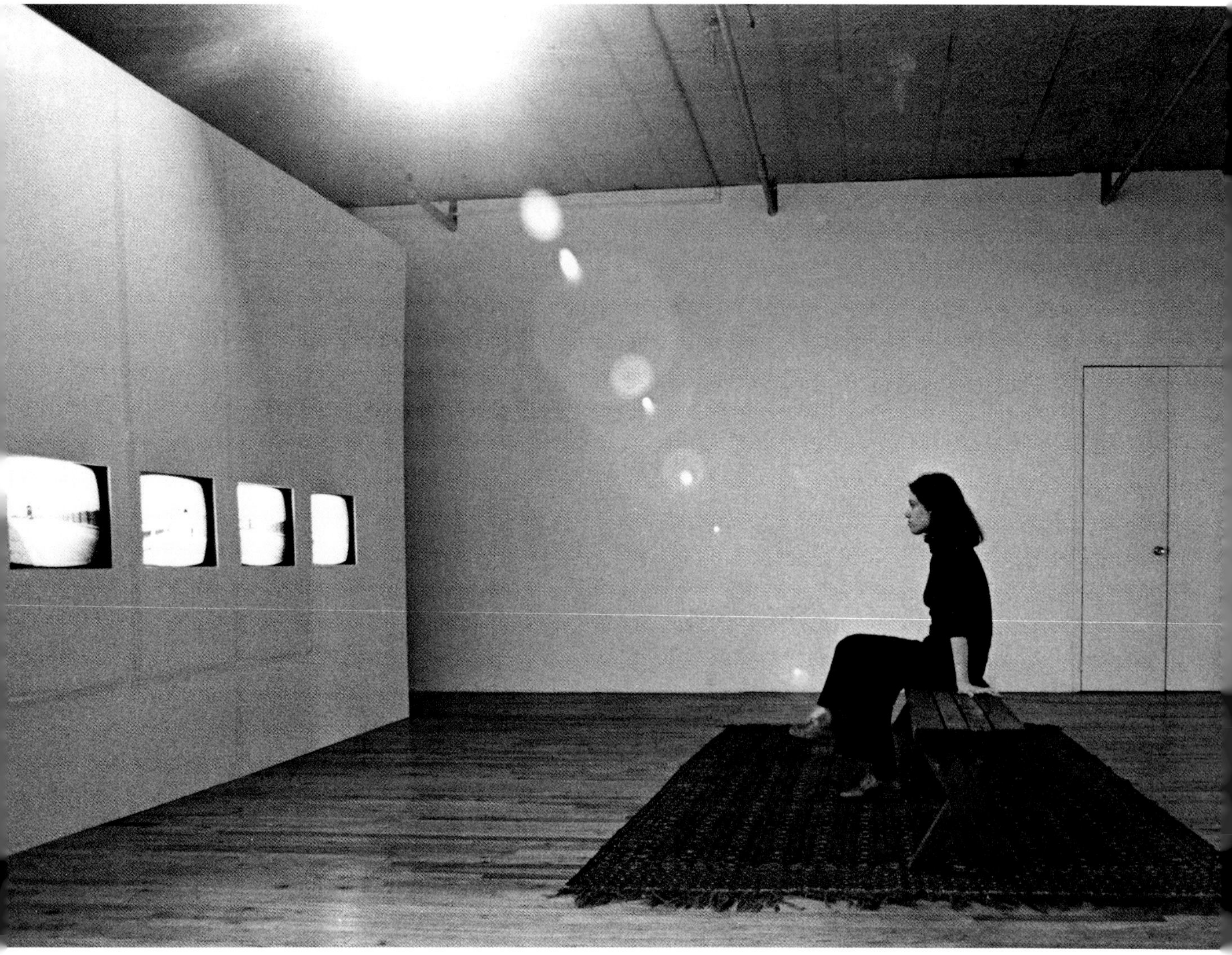

six

beryl korot's *dachau 1974*

video, abstraction, memory

In the summer of 1974, the twenty-nine-year old video artist and editor Beryl Korot travelled from her home in New York to Germany, following an invitation to join him from her partner, the composer Steve Reich, who was then on the DAAD fellowship in Berlin. Older artists such as Newman and Rothko had refused to go to Germany during the 1950s and 1960s, but by the early 1970s more and more Americans were travelling there through programmes such as the DAAD and the country's expanding network of public and private galleries. Though the *Artforum* editor Philip Leider reacted to Mel Bochner's travels by saying 'Mel, you're Jewish . . . Your grandmother will turn over in her grave',[1] the artist was happy enough to show in Düsseldorf at Heiner Friedrich's and in Bern in *When Attitudes Become Form*. Korot was of Bochner's generation but the trip was still difficult for her. 'Being a Jew', she said, 'going to Germany at that time for me was a very big step'.[2] In order, it seems, to justify her visit, Korot set herself some conditions. 'If I'm going to go with Steve to Berlin,' she recalled, 'I'm going to go to Dachau.'

78 Beryl Korot, *Dachau 1974* installed at The Kitchen, New York, 1975. Korot is sitting on the bench. © Beryl Korot.

Korot's visit resulted in a new work that she premiered at The Kitchen in New York in 1975, a video installation called *Dachau 1974* that presented her footage of the concentration camp. Korot used four monitors, each showing different passages from this footage, each flashing on and off at regular intervals (fig. 78). I will be asking how she derived the complex structure of the work and what effect this structure had on the viewer's encounter with the subject and memory of Dachau. But before I come to Korot's work, its making, editing and presentation, I need to ask what it means to consider a video installation that shows pictures of a concentration camp as an 'abstract' work. Does the category 'abstraction' make sense here? Could any video art work really be 'abstract', or continue the pursuits and investigations of 'abstraction'?

If some histories of the medium are examined, the answer seems to be a definite 'no'. In the early 1990s, Korot's work was included in an exhibition called 'The First Generation: Women and Video, 1970–1975', and writing in the catalogue, Anne-Sargent Wooster specifically set video against abstraction, arguing that the tapes in the show 'were an essential part of the attack on modernist art in the late 1960s and early 70s', by which she may well have meant the work of painters such as Newman and Stella.[3] Martha Rosler, recalling the early days of video art in 1984, noted that it had 'displaced the expressive models of art that had held sway in the West since the early postwar period.' Video artists, she continued, 'saw themselves as carrying out an act of profound social criticism, criticism specifically directed at the domination of groups and individuals epitomized by the world of television and perhaps of all mainstream Western industrial and technological culture'. Video art also targeted 'the institutions of art . . . , regarded as another structure of domination': no longer did artists require the gallery and museum to distribute and exhibit their work.[4]

Rosler's own journey from her early abstract expressionist paintings to her videos such as *Semiotics of the Kitchen* (1975) indicated that abstraction was no longer tenable for her, but even those artists who were at the same time developing the language of abstraction in other parts of their practice would relinquish it when it came to making video works: in 1973 Richard Serra made the polemical *Television Delivers People* whose titles, rolling down to the accompaniment of muzak, inform its viewer that: 'You are delivered to the advertiser who is the customer . . . You are consumed . . . You are the product of television.'[5] Looking at works by Rosler and Serra one might well conclude that abstraction was impossible in video: the medium demanded a confrontation with the commercial function of television and the corporate control of the networks.

However, another view onto early video art practices would yield another answer about the viability of 'abstraction' in the new medium. Nam June Paik was one of the initiators of video art, famously buying the Sony Portapak on the very day of its commercial release in 1967. Paik had been working with televisions long before this, drawing inspiration from figures such as John Cage and George Macunias, and in 'prepared television' works, such as *Magnet TV* (1965), he had distorted television signals to produce abstract patterns on the screen. Steina and Woody Vasulka also created a host of abstract video works using various other technologies to manipulate images, such as their *Calligrams* (1970). Another example of an artist making 'abstract' images was Mary Lucier. In part taking off from her husband, the composer Alvin Lucier's work *I am sitting in a room* (1969), Lucier became interested in the way a video image deteriorated over time and through repetition, and in the fact that when a camera was exposed to extreme light, it would burn away the vidicom tube and thus null its sensitivity. The damage was a material kind of memory. Discussing her work *Fire Writing* (a piece that showed at The Kitchen in the months after Korot's show), Lucier wrote

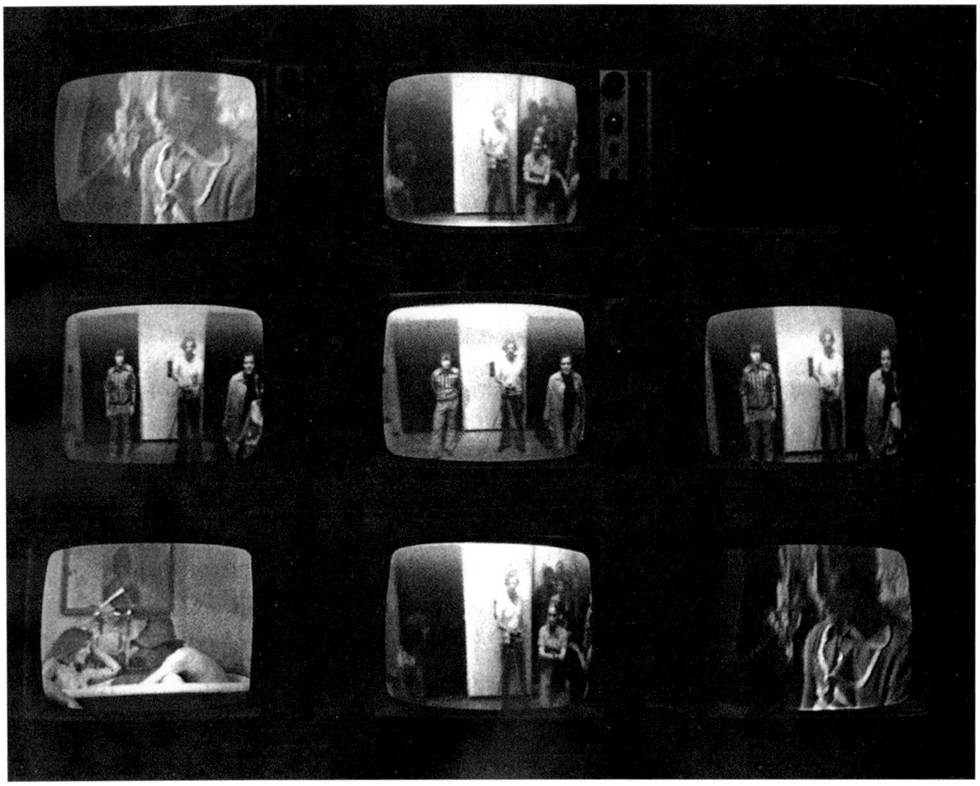

79 Ira Schneider and Frank Gillette, *Wipe Cycle*, 1969. © Ira Schneider and Frank Gillette.

'The result of this primal encounter [the filming of extreme light] is a trauma so deep that its scars cannot be erased but, instead, accumulate on the image surface as a form of memory, and any picture subsequently recorded by that camera must be viewed through the scar tissue of the prior trauma.'[6]

Paik's, the Vasulka's and Lucier's work in many ways recalled traditions of twentieth-century abstraction: Piet Mondrian's early abstractions from nature, the op-art patterns of Victor Vasarely, and in Lucier's case, Lucio Fontana's damaged paintings. While never only interested in optical effects (their manipulations would cause the viewer to rethink their everyday encounter with television), Paik and the Vasulkas in particular approached technology with optimism, viewing it (in contrast to Rosler and Serra) as an exciting resource for artists rather than as a weapon of the media state. These artists' works are grounds to support the use of the term 'abstraction' in relation to early video art, but nevertheless I would like to posit other connections between abstraction and video that do not rely simply on the presentation of a distorted, patterned, 'abstract' image.

For instance, if Barnett Newman and Frank Stella had been interested in making their viewers conscious of the activity of looking at their paintings by positioning zips at particular intervals or by using slightly reflective metal paint, so too did many early video artists create works that dramatised the way a video addressed the viewer. Rethinking Vito Acconci's *Centers* (1971), a video in which the artist points towards the centre of the screen (and therefore at the viewer) for over twenty minutes, Anne Wagner has written that 'video art aims to summon you into the present moment, as an audience, and sometimes, under selected circumstances, to make you all-too-conscious of that fact.'[7] There were also connections between minimalist sculpture and video art.[8] If, in the classic analysis, minimalism aimed to alert the viewer to the physical conditions of their encounter, making them conscious of their movement, so did some early video installations. Where Robert Morris used mirrors to reflect the viewer's passing feet, Peter Campus deployed video's facility to simultaneously record and transmit an image, taping his viewer entering a space and throwing this very picture onto the wall of the gallery before them, often at oblique angles to create anamorphic images as in *Mem* (1974–75). Finally, if artists such as Sol LeWitt and Mel Bochner had, during the 1960s, used serial rules to determine the position of units in compound abstract art works (LeWitt's *Serial Project ABCD* of 1966 and Bochner's *Sixteen Isomorphs (Negative)* of 1967), so too video artists worked with multiple monitors and constructed rules to predetermine what each monitor would present.

One work of great importance to Korot which brings together many of the shared concerns of abstraction and video art (enquiries about how a viewer sees, how they move around an exhibition space, how different parts of a work are arranged) was Ira Schneider's and Frank Gillette's 1969 *Wipe Cycle* (fig. 79). This was presented at the first gallery show of video art, 'TV as a Creative Medium', held at the Howard Wise Gallery in 1969, and 'consisted of a bank of nine monitors and a closed-circuit video camera that recorded live images of viewers as they approached. These fragments of footage were played on eight- and sixteen-second delays, jumping from monitor to monitor and interspersed with periods of live-broadcast TV and prerecorded segments.'[9] Schneider said that 'the most important function of *Wipe Cycle* was to integrate the audience into the information'.[10] Seeing themselves moving around a gallery, between images that were broadcast on the regular TV networks, a viewer would come to realise that they were as much a maker as a receiver of television content; that their normal position – at home in front of a single monitor – was a position of passivity and subservience that they could now disturb and contest. The enquiries of abstraction continued, but video's connection to television meant confronting questions of information delivery, and therefore politics, in more obvious ways than before.

Hopefully 'abstraction' now seems to be a category that *can* usefully describe a video installation, and even one that deploys what I call abstract strategies and forms of organisation rather than 'shapes'. Certainly, Korot used many different abstract strategies to present her footage of Dachau. But before we come to this footage, we should acknowledge the major challenge that faced her. Video might well address the current conditions of network television, but how could video be used to confront a subject such as Dachau? Where a video artist interrogated history, it was art history, as in Hermine Freed's *Art Herstory* (1974), for which Freed taped herself in the poses of canonical paintings, questioning the former representation of women in art. Where a video artist investigated memory, it was the material memory of the medium, as in Mary Lucier's *Fire Writing*. But a confrontation with the history and memory of the

Holocaust seemed impossible – impossible because of the very properties of the video medium.

Continuing Greenbergian enquiries to explore a distinctly non-Greenbergian medium, many early writers on video investigated these essential properties, and often described them in relation to film. Video was intertwined with TV where experimental films confronted Hollywood; the video image was delivered by electromagnetic signals where film was indexical; video was transmitted onto glass from behind where film was projected onto a surface from in front of it; and most important of all, video had the technical facility to play back an image at the very same time as it was recorded whereas film played back footage recorded in a previous time. This last technical facility was crucial: where film was a means of imaging the past, video was the art of 'The Present Tense'. In his 1976 essay of this title, the critic Bruce Kurtz clearly stated that 'Newness, intimacy, immediacy, involvement, and a sense of the present tense are all characteristics of the medium.' 'The presentness of the medium is probably its single most consequential feature.'[11]

Different writers have continued to reach different conclusions about video's 'presentness', but all concur that this is the essential feature of the medium. In 1976 Rosalind Krauss argued that video's technological facilities meant the new medium would be better characterised not by an account of its physical apparatus but through the psychological idea of narcissism: artists were videoing themselves looking at their own images as these images were recorded by their cameras and simultaneously relayed onto monitors placed beside their cameras.[12] In the mid-1980s Fredric Jameson found that 'video has a powerful claim for being the art par excellence of late capitalism',[13] and this because video, with its facility of instant playback and total flow, was an amnesiac medium. 'Memory', he wrote, 'seems to play no role in television, commercial or otherwise (or, I am tempted to say, in postmodernism generally) . . . A description of the structural exclusion of memory, then . . . might well lead onto . . . a theory of video itself.'[14] In 1990, Mary Ann Doane wrote that: 'The temporal dimension of television would seem to be that of an insistent "present-ness", a "*This is going-on*" . . . a celebration of the instantaneous.'[15] And in 2002, David Joselit posited that 'video and history would seem to be incompatible, since the former is permanently locked in the present tense.'[16]

These various comments helpfully describe the situation that faced Beryl Korot when she took her video footage of Dachau and began to mould it into a new work. If Korot, like other video artists, could draw from the various activities of abstract artists, a massive challenge remained: how could she use a medium that was 'locked in the present tense' and whose structure guaranteed the 'exclusion of memory' to explore the history and memory of a concentration camp?

beryl korot and *radical software*

With this challenge in mind, I want now to step back from the theory of the video medium in order to introduce Beryl Korot and to consider what she would have seen

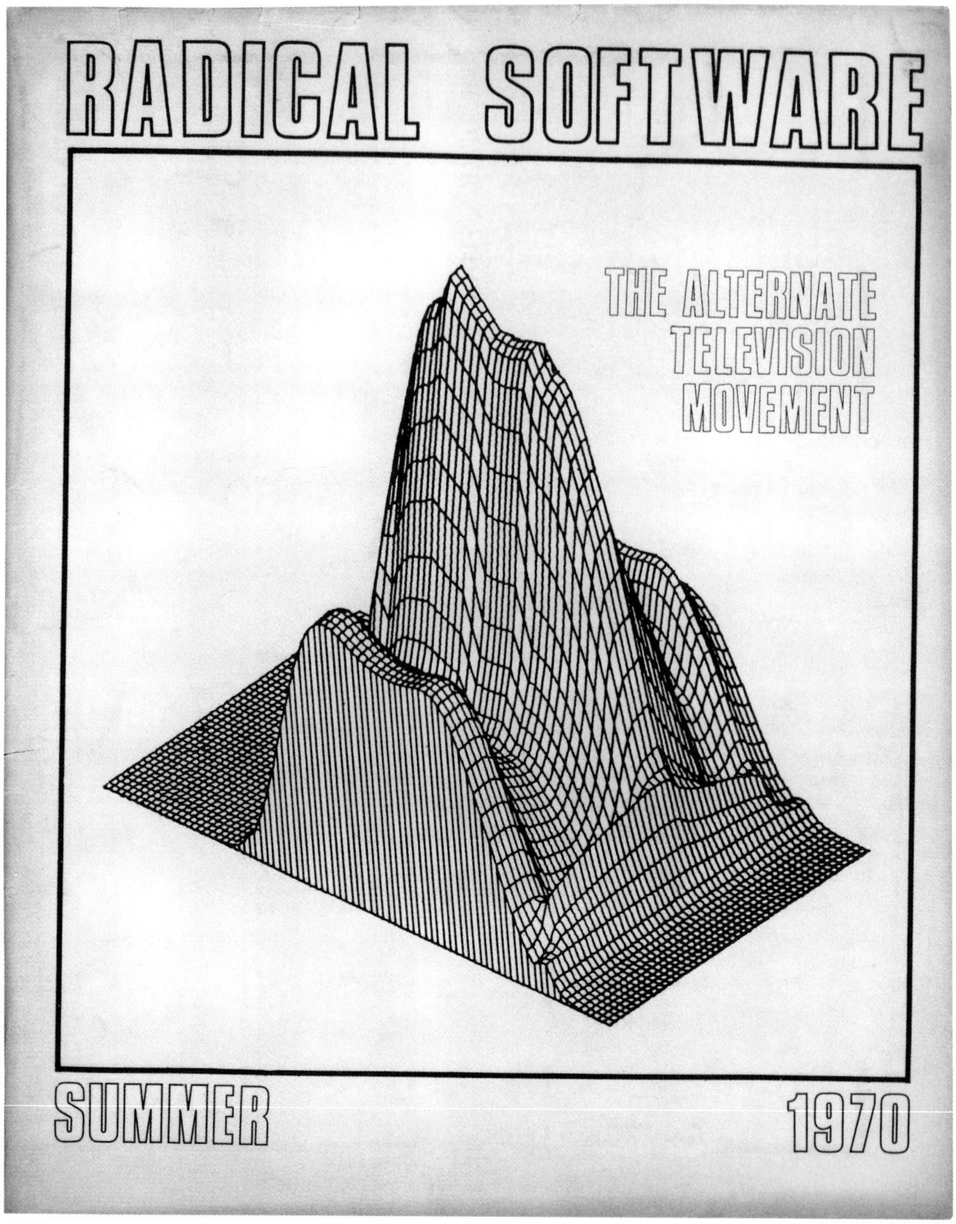

80 *Radical Software*, Issue 1, Summer 1970.

during her visit to Dachau in 1974. Today, Korot is less well known than other figures associated with early video art such as Paik, Acconci, Dan Graham, Bill Viola or Joan Jonas, but in the early 1970s she was at the centre of the video art community, and in 1976 she co-edited the anthology *Video Art* in which projects by all these artists were published alongside texts such as Bruce Kurtz's essay on the medium. Korot had studied literature at the University of Wisconsin and after arriving in New York in the late 1960s and taking a job at the *New York Review of Books*, she had begun to make her own work, attuned to the possibilities of video through her contact with figures such as Ira Schneider and Frank Gillette, and her encounter with *Wipe Cycle* at 'TV as a Creative Medium'. Korot knew Schneider from her university days and in late 1969, she met the artist Phyllis Gershuny, who had also recently been introduced to video. Over the spring of 1970, the three friends began to work on a project to publish a newsletter that would be distributed to the video community in New York, a publication that would contain technical information as well as analytical articles and that aimed 'to bring together people who were already making their own television, [and to] attempt to turn others on to the idea as a means of social change and exchange'.[17] The project culminated in *Radical Software*, first published in June 1970, and terminated in the summer of 1974 after eleven issues (fig. 80).

Korot's and Gershuny's opening editorial for the inaugural issue gives a clear sense of the reasons for their politicised commitment to video.[18] Writing at the height of the Vietnam War, they declared that: 'Power is no longer measured by land, labor, or capital, but by access to information and the means to disseminate it. As long as the most powerful tools (not weapons) are in the hands of those who would hoard them, no alternative cultural vision can succeed. Unless we design and implement alternative information structures which transcend and re-configure the existing ones, other alternate systems and lifestyles will be no more than products of the existing process.' Television, the primary contemporary source of information, was controlled by the networks, but video technology enabled any user to make their own TV, creating their own information and broadcasting it. 'Videotape can be to television what writing is to language . . . Soon accessible VTR systems and videocassettes will make alternate networks a reality.'[19] As Korot more recently put it, the aim was allow people 'to write in the medium, not just read it.' *Radical Software* would deliver to those interested the necessary skills and advice about how to create alternative television so that eventually the activated audience would have 'access to the informational tools they need to shape and reassert control over their lives'.[20] The magazine's readers were encouraged to send in their own advice and responses to the magazine in a section called 'Feedback', and Korot and Gershuny directly implored them to photocopy the articles and distribute them as widely as possible.

Though the editors included an article and a project of Nam June Paik's in this inaugural issue, *Radical Software* departed from what Benjamin Buchloh has termed his 'technocratic idealis[m]'.[21] Korot and Gershuny realised that artists could not meaningfully experiment with and deploy new media unless they first acknowledged the ways in which technology was used by and served the network corporations and the state. Nonetheless, the magazine was infused with optimism about the capacities to reply to those in power through video's 'feedback' facilities.

In a recent introduction to *Radical Software*, its instigators are termed 'media activists'[22] and it is notable that the words 'art' and 'artist' were palpably absent from the magazine's opening editorial. But if editing this activist journal was her primary occupation at this time, what of Korot's own 'art' work? In 1973, she produced two short videos, each using one channel: *Lost Lascaux Bull* and *Invision*. The first has been described as her comment on 'the notion of the transmission and reproduction of

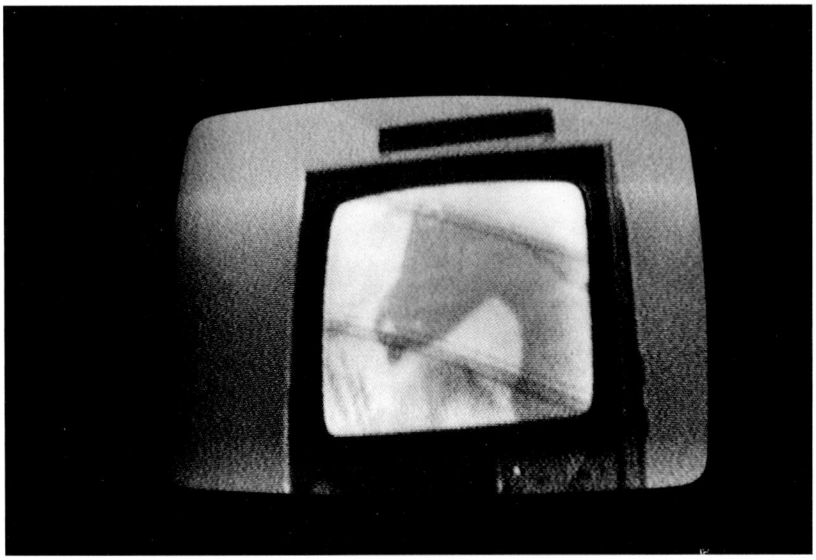

81 Beryl Korot, *Lost Lascaux Bull*, 1973. © Beryl Korot.

information through the ages'.[23] We see first an image of the bull on the caves at Lascaux through flames. This direct image makes way for the image of a monitor, a screen within the TV screen before the viewer (fig. 81). The bull reappears now on the internal screen at two removes from the viewer. Various distortions subsequently interrupt the image on the internal monitor: the bull is broken up by static and vertical roll, so that eventually what started as a primal image is mediated and lost. If *Lost Lascaux Bull* appears to have been a poetic meditation on the technological mediation of images, *Invision* was much more subjective. In Korot's words, it consisted of 'an alternation between somebody sitting in front of a TV set and a very abstract section that follows in which somebody could be daydreaming or just going off in their imagination. The abstraction represents that. And then there are external shots that were made on a mountain top that take you outside the inner self.'[24]

Korot's video practice seems to have developed some of the interests she explored in her *Radical Software* writings. As well as these single channel works, she also assisted Ira Schneider in making *Manhattan is an Island* in early 1974 (fig. 82) – an installation that used seven video channels on up to twenty-three different monitors, and which therefore 'took the viewer out of a traditional environment [and] into a public space.'[25] But really neither her activist editorial practices (the second issue of the magazine contained her informative report on Cable television), nor her single channel works, nor her commitment to the radical possibilities of multiple channel work give any indication that she would, in 1974, create a video installation featuring images of a concentration camp. Nonetheless when she joined Steve Reich in Berlin that summer, she was determined not just to visit the site near Munich but to make work, for she took on her trip to Dachau her Sony Portapak video camera.

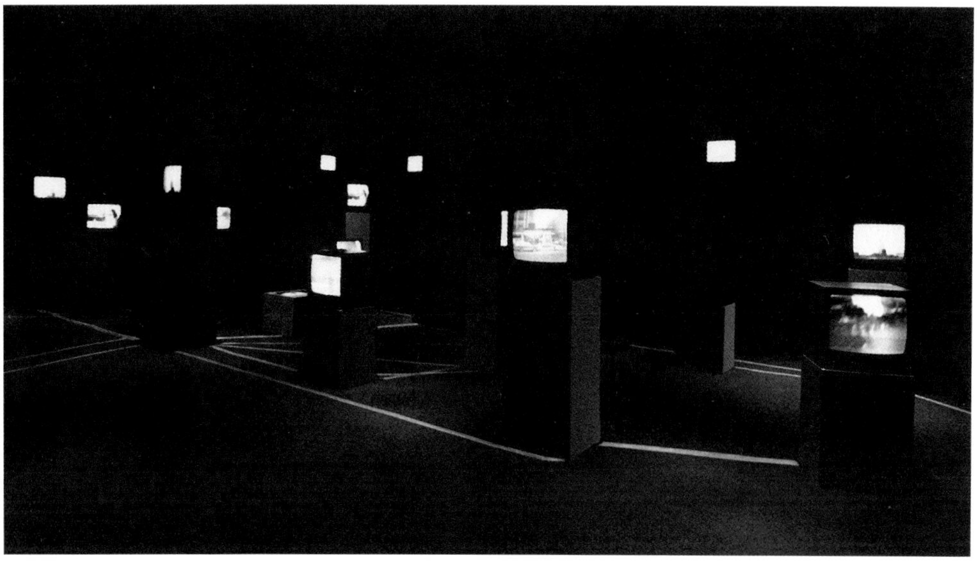

82 Ira Schneider with Beryl Korot, *Manhattan is an Island*, 1974. © Ira Schneider.

dachau in 1974

There are various published accounts by American visitors to Dachau dating from around this period that give both a sense of why people visited the camp and what they saw there.[26] There were those, such as Alfred Werner who returned to see the camp where they had once been imprisoned,[27] but some, like Korot, made the journey in order to justify a first visit to Germany: the critic Midge Decter, wife of *Commentary* editor Norman Podhoretz, joined a group of nine intellectuals travelling around Germany in 1967, all there to write reports for *The Atlantic Monthly*.[28] Before her trip Decter had been sent a form by her German hosts asking which places she wished to visit, and in a similar way to Korot, she insisted on including Dachau in her tour. The writer Irving Halperin was spending time in Germany in the mid-1960s to research his book *Here I Am: A Jew in Today's Germany*, published in 1971. In the midst of a relatively unproblematic sojourn, '[a] day comes when something in you cries out: My God, did it really all happen here – Crystal Night, the burning of the synagogues, the camps? . . . I had spoken abstractly about the Holocaust in lecture halls, and now I had the need to *see* it. So in mid-April I visited Dachau.'[29]

Halperin's memoir indicated that, for visitors such as himself, Dachau had come to actually stand for the Holocaust. At a time when travel to the Polish death camps was bureaucratically as well as emotionally challenging, Dachau would serve metonymically as the very site of the Holocaust. Another writer, Sylvia Tennenbaum, published an account of another visit in an American journal in 1976 and described her distraction in front of what she described as a 'second-rate' memorial sculpture. She found herself judging this memorial and asked: 'Why can I not stay with the thing at hand? What is the thing at hand? The death of six million Jews, some of them my relatives.'[30] These various comments indicate how over-determined any visit to

Dachau was, and so it is unsurprising that the site itself was often deemed to be disappointing.

Dachau was quite a modest place. For Decter, this in itself was a surprise: 'I was taken aback by how unimpressive it was . . . The camps, I realized, had come to loom in my imagination as vast, seemingly endless places . . . But Dachau is small, one might almost say cozy – in any place, completely and terribly accessible, traversable, at a brisk pace, in ten to fifteen minutes.'[31] While buildings in some of the death camps had been destroyed, the buildings of Dachau were preserved, and had actually been used after liberation to house displaced persons. Visitors would see some of these barracks ('equi-spaced, equisized, monotonously alike', in Halperin's words[32]), together with the roll call ground, the four ovens and two gas chambers that had never been used. They would also see a makeshift museum that had been set up immediately after the liberation in 1945.[33] The displays changed over time, but many visitors found them too orderly, and felt they detracted from the emotional experience of the camp. When Halperin visited in 1964 and saw 'exhibition cases, documents, photographs, data, statistics . . . Wall charts list[ing] how many died from illness, from medical experiments, from hanging . . .', he asked: 'Is it appropriate for a museum to be at Dachau . . . ? Rather it seems to me that in such a place, where the ovens were, the visitor ought to confront empty rooms and silence – a silence in which one might reflect on what he knows, even at second remove, from having read the literature of the Holocaust.'[34] Tennenbaum reacted similarly: museums, she wrote, 'exist to collect objects, to sift information, and classify statistics. The museum rooms at Dachau through which I walk like a sleepwalker yield nothing more.'[35] For some, the whole camp felt over sanitised. 'Dachau,' Decter wrote, 'like the other camps in West Germany, has been "cleaned up" . . . its mass graves marked with tasteful memorial plaques, planted with good lawn, and bordered with neat flower beds; its gallows replaced with a marker; its administration building converted into a modern, well-lighted museum of horrors.'[36] By the mid-1970s, this 'cleaning-up' was so advanced that Tennenbaum complained on her arrival that 'it is no different here than at any other tourist attraction in Europe.'[37]

Whatever her expectations, Korot came to Dachau belatedly – the camp had been sanitised and prepared for foreign visitors such as herself. She drove with Reich to Munich on Wednesday 25 September 1974 and spent the following rainy day – which happened to be Yom Kippur – wandering through Dachau's spaces. The next day was fine weather and she returned with the camera and shot approximately four and a half hours of footage. From a number of carefully chosen positions throughout the camp's museum, inside its buildings and on its peripheries, Korot taped predominantly static shots, often using a tripod and barely moving the camera, showing the tourists moving through the spaces, but not focusing on any particular visitor. Though she would have seen a number of artefacts, some brutal, some poignant, she trained her Portapak on the architecture of the camp, concentrating on its present status as a tourist venue. 'In making this piece, I chose not to use anything about what happened there except the architecture which spoke for itself', she later said.[38] The day after the shoot, she returned to Berlin with Reich. In the following weeks, there would be DAAD gatherings, exhibition openings and social events, and frequently Korot would be asked how she was spending her time. Provocatively, she would quip 'I just spent the weekend visiting Dachau'. 'It would produce the thickest silence', she recalls. Nowadays, many DAAD artists probe the histories of Berlin and Germany (Susan Hiller is but one example[39]), yet in 1974, Korot's activity was unprecedented. But if the news of the trip was problematic for Reich's hosts, the footage she had taken in the former concentration camp posed a greater problem for Korot, for when she looked over it, the video seemed to her pretty lifeless – and lifeless in a bad way.

editing and structuring the footage

Korot had taped Dachau from thirteen still positions in various parts of the camp and had also made a single panning shot moving from one of these viewpoints to another. The first shot had been taped outside the perimeter fence and showed a road that borders the camp, inevitably recalling the opening of Alain Resnais' *Night and Fog* (1955), though Korot had not seen it at the time. A tall fence stretches away from the front right of the frame to the back left where a watchtower rises. The road is asphalted and, during the shot, various cars and vans move towards and away from the camera. In addition, a cyclist is riding along towards the front of the frame. The second shot showed another road, this time rough and covered by gravel, and this time bordered at either side by a barbed wire fence. At the back of the image, there is another watchtower between the fences. This is the view of 'no man's land', the area between two fences set out to trap the potential escapee. Korot's tape showed two women walking along it, calmly approaching the camera.

The next two images were shots of the symmetrical grid of the barracks – a close up, and a long shot in which the building lies in the mid-point of the image between a foreground of grass and the sky above. The fifth and sixth views were taped inside the barracks, showing beds and rooms and museum exhibits, and visitors walking through these. The fifth is a view down a darkened corridor, the sixth a view from a low point up to an image affixed to the wall (one guesses Korot was kneeling down) which is interrupted by the heads of the passing visitors. Then from inside the barracks, Korot taped a view out of the window towards another watchtower in the distance.

The eighth shot was taken from outside again, and showed visitors crossing a bridge spanning the Wurm Canal which ran through the camp. They are all moving from left to right and in the only pan in Korot's footage, she repeated this movement by following the visitors from the bridge towards a gate. The view to the gate was then held as the next, still shot – the ninth. Korot's video camera at this moment also pointed towards the sun, and so this image is slightly burnt out by white circles and rings of light. It seemed that the movement showed a direction away from the camp through the open gate and towards the fields beyond, but the tenth and eleventh shots returned to its bleak interior: a view of the gate of the crematoria building, and then a frontal shot into the ovens themselves. The final two shots returned outside: the penultimate showed a fence and watchtower to the left and, to the right, a tall row of cypress trees that stretch way beyond the top of the frame, and the last showed the surface of the canal with sunlight glinting off the slow moving water.

These views had been filmed in order as Korot had walked through the camp. Though she had followed an obvious path through Dachau's site, the sequence this journey had generated might have suggested a kind of narrative that echoed the historical fate of the camp inmates: Korot's footage moved, like the prisoners, from the world outside into the camp, into its recesses, and eventually to the place of death. The final sequence moved from fire to water and to the light reflecting off it, and could have appeared as a coda to this narrative, almost offering the consolation of natural beauty and flowing movement.[40] When Korot played back her footage on a single monitor, she might have felt that her sequence of long static shots appeared too objective a documentation of the camp. Indeed the first filmmakers after the liberation of the camps had used long shots precisely to document the settings in what Nicolas Losson has called the 'least manipulated (and manipulable)' way, knowing that the 'spatiotemporal continuity [of long shots] would authenticate these macabre scenes'.[41] Korot might also have found the last passage of the flowing water too redemptive and symbolic, even though Dachau's prisoners had been drowned in the stream.[42] Perhaps Korot read her tape in this way, but whether or not she did, we know that she was dissatisfied with the footage when she watched it back. As she later told a journalist, in its raw state, the footage was 'so deadpan it was boring'.[43] Korot had wanted to avoid emotional, expressive camera movement, but had never aspired to make a 'boring' video. How, she wondered, 'was I to bring life to those images?'

Korot's first decision when she began to work with the material she had taped was to show it on more than one monitor. As I have already indicated, she was familiar with early installations of video art which used many monitors: Schneider and Gillette's *Wipe Cycle*, as mentioned, but also works by Paik including *TV Garden* (1974) in which plants interspersed a floor on which monitors had been randomly positioned, all screens facing up. But though there were political reasons for using more than one channel, the risk of using multiple monitors here was that the installation could become spectacular. A viewer encountering an abundance of bright screens might well be overwhelmed and desensitised to the images on each particular television. In comparison to then contemporary multi-channel installations, Korot determined on a sober arrangement of four monitors placed in a horizontal row. For the purposes of the following account, I will designate these monitors from left to right simply as A, B, C and D.

Korot chose the number four because this would be the least number of monitors necessary for her to work with a weaving structure. The footage would be broken up into clips derived from the thirteen shots she had taped: A and C would show similar images, while B and D presented different images, so that the image appearing on A appeared to thread under B returning on C, while the image on B thread under C returning on D (fig. 83). (As we shall see later, though they were paired, the two monitors in

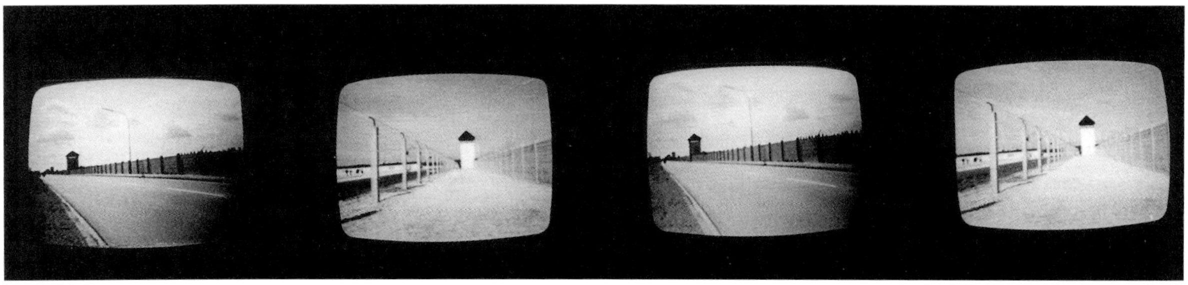

each pair showed slightly different images at any given moment). Monitors A and C would start with clips derived from one shot, switching to clips from another after a set time (starting with the 'Road shot' and switching to the 'Barracks Close-up shot', for instance); B and D would similarly move together from one shot to a new one but after a different amount µof time (switching from the 'No-Man's Land shot' to the 'Barracks Long-shot', for instance). In this way, the sequence of shots Korot had taken in the camp would be played out, the entire work lasting twenty-four minutes. At any one moment of the video, the viewer would see an 'image block' consisting of four different moving images, and in total there were eighteen image blocks (fig. 84). This arrangement was clearly depicted in a drawing Korot made that was eventually exhibited with the videos: each shot is represented by a symbol, and one can see how the pairs move from one shot to another together (fig. 85). The idea of weaving is emphasised by the way the warp lines continued at the top and bottom.

83 Beryl Korot, *Dachau 1974*. This image shows the opening images on the four monitors. © Beryl Korot.

To work with weaving was perhaps the most important and certainly the most distinctive of Korot's formal decisions. This was, as she has said, 'a time when randomness and the ephemeral (live feedback) were the focus of much work', but a random arrangement of images from her footage would not be suitable for her intentions. The idea of weaving would provide a 'strong structural framework' as opposed to a random one, but while being tight, weaving would allow her to present the narrative of her journey through Dachau in a 'non-linear' manner.[44] Later she wrote about using weaving for 'the creation *of nonverbal narratives*'.[45] Korot's interest in weaving predated her work with the Dachau footage. She had spent time with Navajo weavers before travelling to Germany,[46] and had long been interested in the work of Anni Albers.[47] Korot's attraction to weaving was prompted by a powerful insight that took the emphasis away from the 'newness' of her chosen medium, and de-fetishised video technology: She saw weaving as a parallel technology to video:

> 'Weaving technology is the first computer on earth,' she has said. 'Because I was involved in video, and [only later] became interested in weaving, I immediately viewed it as the technology it was, not in terms of the objects it created, but what it was doing. This ancient tool had imbedded in it this incredible sophistication to program patterns according to a numerical structure, and that really interested me enormously. My first epiphany was that each of these [media] had the infor-

84 (following pages) Beryl Korot, *Dachau 1974*. © Beryl Korot. These three pages represent the eighteen 'image blocks' that unfold through the work. Each horizontal row of four rectangles represents one 'image block'. These three pages do not give an accurate impression of how the work looks when installed. For an illustration of how a particular 'image block' looks on the rounded monitors, see fig.83.

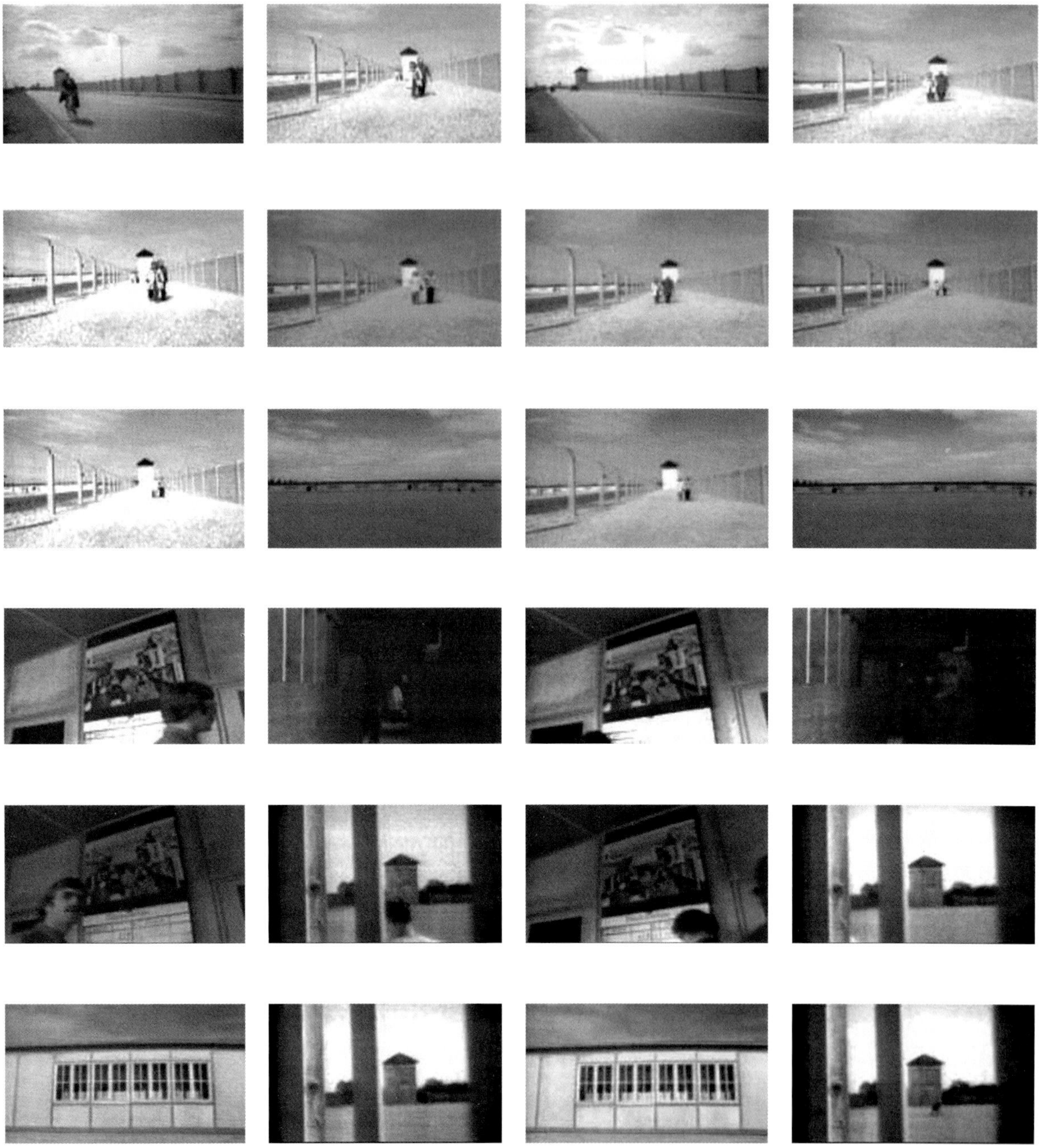

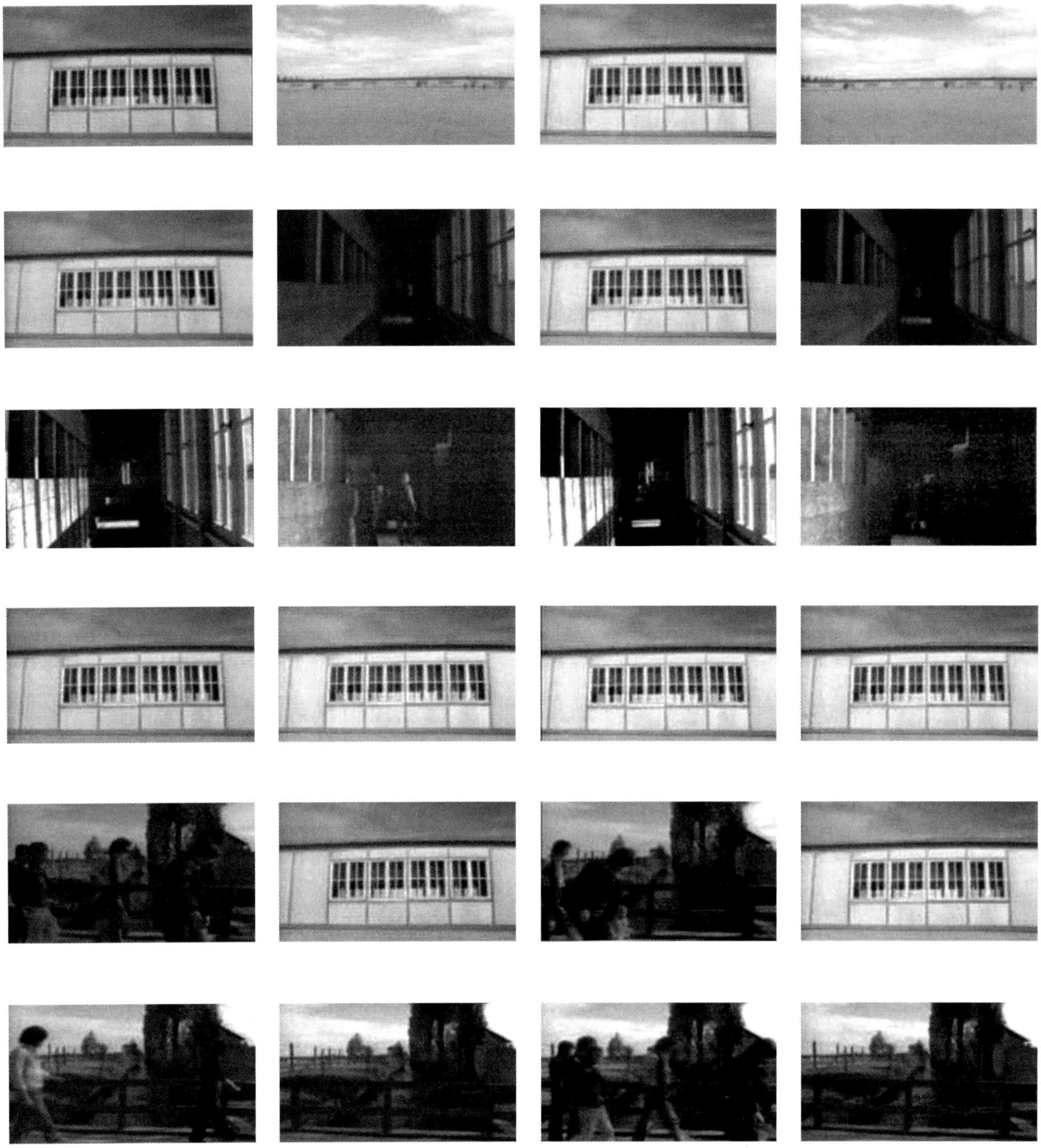

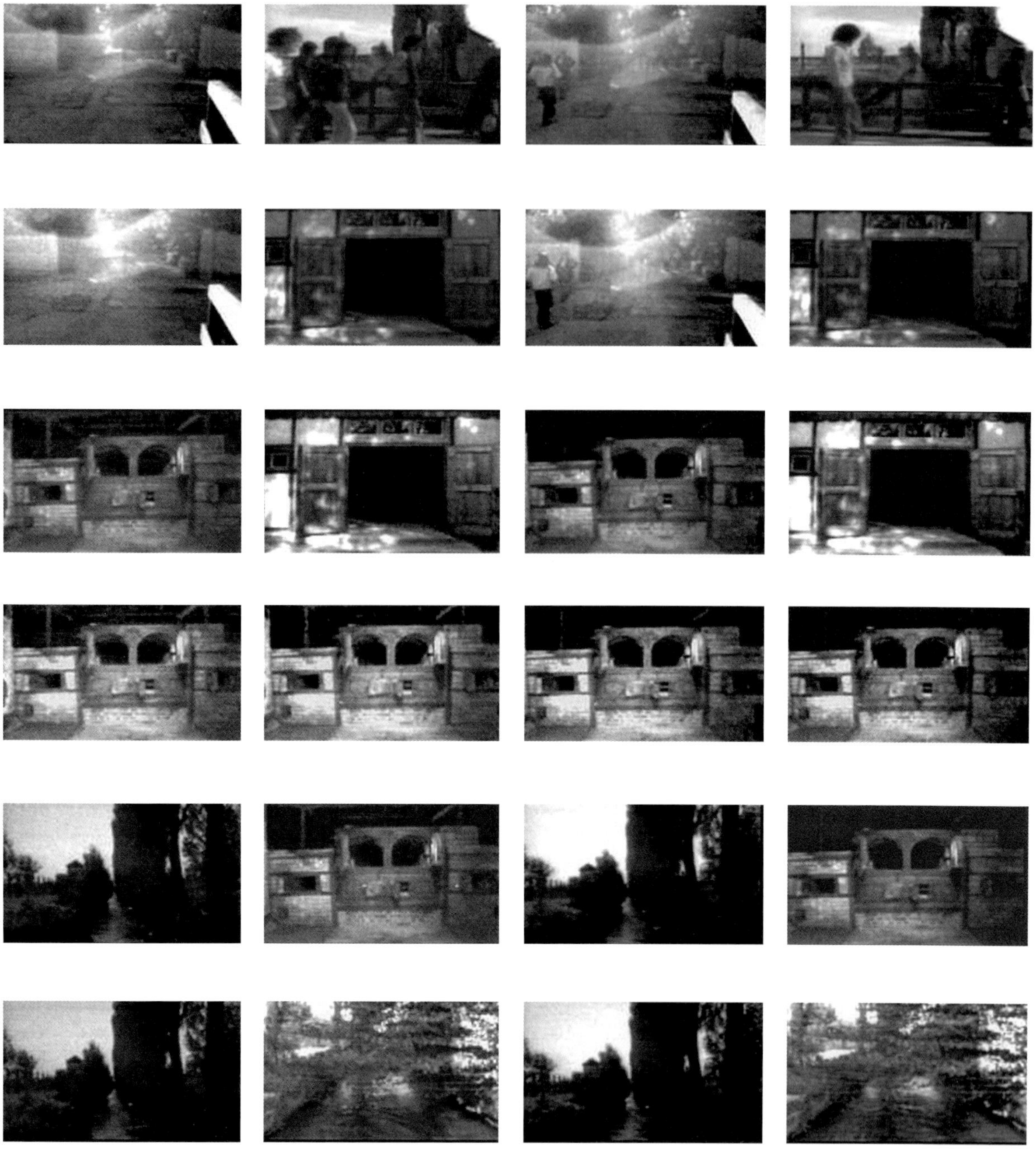

mation embedded in lines. And that seemed to me no coincidence. How the embedding took place and how it was retrieved by the viewer were earmarks of whether it was an ancient or modern technology but the fact that this existed was a clue to how the human mind functions in terms of putting information together and creating tools.'[48]

Korot's interest in the connection of weaving to video motivated her decision to use four monitors arranged in pairs, but what about her editing of each shot, and the arrangement of the edits on each individual monitor? Korot copied each one of the thirteen shots she had taped around the camp several times, and then broke each shot into clips. A single five minute still shot that Korot had taped in one location (No Man's Land, say) could generate clips of different lengths (for instance, clips of 10 or 15 seconds) but also different clips of the same length, from different parts of the five minutes. Korot determined each monitor would play clips of the same duration over and over again, each clip separated by a one second black pause. What I will call the 'clip structure' worked as follows: monitor A would always play clips of 15 seconds before a blank, black pause of 1 second, after which another clip from the same shot of the same length would follow; B would play clips of 11 seconds with 1 second pauses; C, clips of 7 seconds, and D, of 15 seconds. Because A and C were a pair, the clips on them would always be derived from the same shot, but because they were showing these clips for different amounts of time (15 and 7 seconds) and from different parts of the shot, the 'action' on A as often followed the action on C as preceded it. (In passing we can note that Korot's drawing did not represent the division of shots into clips.)

The formal decisions to arrange the repeating clips for pre-set different lengths on each monitor, so that each monitor had its own rhythm, indicated other interests of Korot's besides weaving. In many ways, Korot operated in the edit suite as LeWitt and Bochner had done when arranging their serial works of the mid-1960s. In his essay 'The Serial Attitude' of 1967, Bochner had outlined some tendencies in serial practice: '1. The derivation of the terms or interior divisions of the work is by means of a numerical or otherwise systematically predetermined process (permutation, progression, rotation, reversal). 2. The order takes precedence over the execution. 3. The completed work is fundamentally parsimonious and systematically self-exhausting.'[49] Korot's structure was not self-exhausting, but it would be true to say that 'the order took precedence over the execution', in as much as once she determined that monitor A would always show clips of 15 seconds, this rule would be followed regardless of the nature of the shot from which the clip derived. In his 'Paragraphs on Conceptual Art', Sol LeWitt had famously written that 'to work with a plan that is preset is one way of avoiding subjectivity',[50] and LeWitt's account could usefully explain why Korot edited her material using a serial structure of sorts: it was a means of working with all the footage without immediately emphasising more emotive or shocking passages.

Korot's arrangement of different clips from the same shot running slightly out of synch with one another on the paired monitors suggests the influence of another formal device, and one particularly well known to her, namely phasing. Since 1966, Steve Reich (who had always been deeply involved with visual artists) had been working with phasing, a compositional technique that at its simplest meant two identical instruments playing the same repeated passage of music over a long period of time, moving in and out of synch with one another.[51] The disconcerting effects of phasing have been elegantly described by Pamela Lee in an essay comparing Reich's forms with those of LeWitt. 'In spite of its structural (even mathematical) legibility,' Lee writes, 'phasing produces the paradoxical condition of *non-comprehension* . . . As musical loops or words are repeated seemingly ad infinitum, the consequence is not so much reduction or perceptual clarity (however stripped down the process, there is nothing minimal about it), but expansion, a shuddering of sound felt like an echo. What is produced in the slippage of two identical passages is all at once shimmering, austere and cacophonous, the effect only increased by increments as the work is apprehended in time.'[52]

85 Beryl Korot, Drawing to accompany the installation of *Dachau 1974*. © Beryl Korot.

Lee's account of phasing would also describe the effects of the slight disjunctions between the repetitions and the non-synchronisation between the paired monitors in Korot's work, but it should be emphasised that Korot's structure in *Dachau 1974* was not exactly like Reich's form. 'Phasing,' she has said, 'is something that goes on and on and on', whereas her structure imposed various kinds of endings. The relationship between monitors A and C might for a while approximate to the relationship between two identical phased musical phrases because an identical passage appears to proceed on each screen, the one moments before or after the other. But the images on the two monitors will soon stop and change.

Korot therefore put to work many of her interests while transforming her footage of the concentration camp into what would become the installation *Dachau 1974*: her engagements with multi-channel video installations, with weaving, seriality and phasing. A final formal decision was made during the installation of the four monitors in The Kitchen in March 1974. Instead of placing the monitors in the centre of the exhibition space Korot placed them against the long wall of the room and then constructed a large screen running parallel to the wall. Recalling the shape and dimensions of cinema screens, it was punctured with four holes for the monitor screens. This meant that the bodies of the monitors were not present and treated as sculptural objects as they had been in so many other video installations. While the decision to conceal the monitor boxes focused the viewer's attention on the displayed images, Korot's invocation and interruption of the cinema screen foregrounded her commitment to the video, as opposed to cinematic medium. If the cinema screen set up expectations of a particular kind of narrative structure, her video installation refused this entirely.

dachau 1974

The edit over and the installation set out, some six months after her trip to Dachau, Korot opened a show on March 15 1975 at The Kitchen, the Soho home of avant-garde performance and video art, the venue that would host exhibitions by Peter Campus, Mary Lucier, Philip Glass, Laurie Anderson and later Cindy Sherman. The

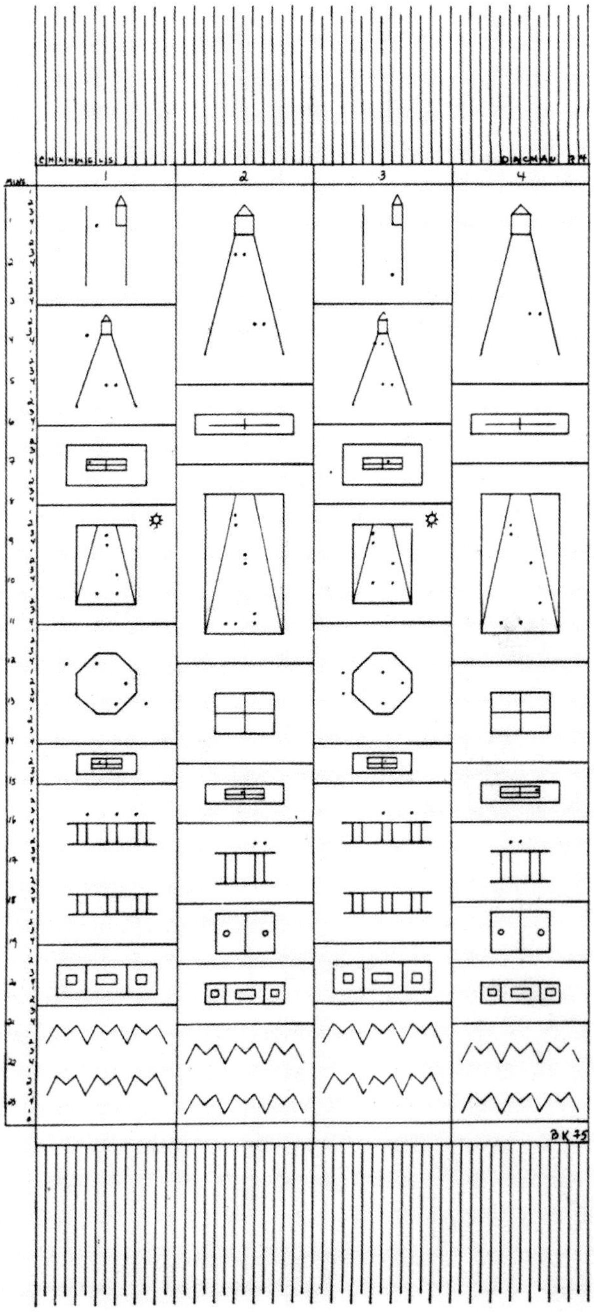

Structural Diagram to 4 channel video work -- DACHAU 1974

show was simply titled 'Beryl Korot: Video', but Korot's drawing and other available material explained that the footage had been recorded in Dachau. Though it would last for a mere two weeks, Korot's work was reviewed in *Artforum*, *Arts Magazine* and *The Soho Weekly News*,[53] and within the next few months discussed in essays on video art by curators and critics including David Ross, John Hanhardt and Bruce Kurtz.[54] Many of the early video artists already mentioned here visited, an indication both of the intimacy of the video community at the time and of Korot's significant position within it. Nam June Paik, Korot recalls, 'spent a week at *Dachau* [sic] lying on a bench'. Mary Lucier came and photographed Korot on this bench for what would become the main installation document of the exhibition. Hermine Freed came and later reviewed the show. Richard Serra's enthusiasm was so great that he recommended Korot to Joyce Nereaux, then director of Castelli/Sonnabend tapes and film, paving the way for an exhibition of new work by Korot that took place at Castelli's two years later.[55]

I want to ask now how the abstract structure affects the viewer's encounter with the images and how the abstract structure itself is an encounter with Dachau – questions that were not explored in any great detail by these early viewers. Everyone watching *Dachau 1974* comes to sense that a narrative and a structure are progressing on the screens, though the narrative and structure cannot be 'read' at once. The narrative charts a journey through the camp that starts outside, moves into the barracks, to the ovens, and then to the stream, unfolding through the succession of eighteen image blocks of clips from the thirteen mostly still shots that Korot taped. The structure, meanwhile, is in some respects apparent from the beginning (the viewer cannot help but recognise that the monitors are paired and that short clips of footage are repeating), but its precise organisation only becomes evident over time, and only to those who concentrate on it.

Because of its complexity, the structure inflects different viewers' encounters with the subject of Dachau in different ways, and can even affect the same viewer's encounter in different ways over the 24-minute course of the work. Seeing watchtowers and barbed wire fences, some viewers might recognise that this is a concentration camp right from the start, and the structure can re-enforce the impact of this image. Obviously the image occurs four times, but more significantly, the action within it repeats. In the clips derived from the first shot, cars, vans and bicycles ride by the concentration camp fence, their passage announced by the crescendo of their motors. It would be unlikely for these mundane road scenes to be read in allusive and metonymic ways were the car to drive past Dachau once (as Korot had seen it), but because the same vehicles are shown driving past again and again, the scene moves from a literal to a more metaphoric register. Just as the image might recall the ease with which Germans lived alongside Dachau in the 1930s and 40s, so it could suggest the tendency of modern West Germans of the 1970s to speed by the Nazi past without stopping to confront it.[56] Likewise later in the work, one hears a visitor to the camp laughing in the museum display rooms. This undoubtedly inappropriate laugh would hardly be noticed were it not for the structure of *Dachau 1974*: the recurrence of the sound makes it galling, an indication of a nonchalant and disrespectful treatment of the site. Just after this passage, all four screens turn to show frontal views of the crematoria: here the repetition acts very simply to amplify the visual presence of the ovens, eight (two on each screen) appearing along the same horizontal axis as the monitors. The sound of laughter makes way for the tolling of what sounds like a funeral bell – so that relationship of sound and image moves from one of offensive dissonance to one of mournful harmony.

The repetition of *particular* scenes and sounds can make them particularly disturbing and emotionally powerful, but the abstract structure of the work as a whole can also re-enforce the impression of the camp, whether or not one intuits its precise organisation. 'Sometimes', Korot recalls, 'people would come [into The Kitchen] not knowing even what Dachau was and not looking at the [drawing] on the wall and they would say to me, was this a prison camp?' Just as prisoners had been policed by absurd but rigorously enforced rules, so too the material Korot recorded had been cut up and edited into a strict structure. The rhythms, she said, were 'relentless and solid . . . [they] created the feeling of the place.' For Susan Heineman, who reviewed the work in *Artforum* and who seems to have attempted to convey the stilted rhythms of the work with her prose, 'watching the tapes what comes across is a sense of endless time, repetition and sameness punctuated by the blinking on and off of the image. A kind of relentless rhythm which complements the scene of Dachau, the memories of Dachau'. 'One by one the monitors turn off,' she concluded. 'What remains is not a comprehension of or even an interest in the formal structure of the piece. But a sense of its coincidence with its subject. The way in which the regularized, monotonous yet emphatic, recurrence of the selected shots recreates the impact of Dachau.'[57]

Yet while the structure could be re-enforcing and mimetic, it could also have entirely different effects on the viewer's encounter with the images of Dachau. Noting a certain regularity (rather than randomness) in the repetitions of clips, one can be drawn to fathom how these repetitions are ordered. Since the 'clip structure' tempts the viewer to work out its organisation, there can be a point where rather than echoing the 'feeling' of the camp, the structure diverts attention away from the images. For instance, one might try to fathom the relationship between the two paired monitors at any given time. At the start, the footage displayed on A recurs on C with a slight delay: a van driving along the road leaves the frame on A seconds before it leaves on C. However, soon after, a cyclist riding towards the camera leaves the frame on C *before* leaving the frame on A, indicating that the 'delay' works both ways. The temporal relationship of the pairs is relatively easy to tell when there is movement in the image (for instance in these road shots, but especially in the eighth shot showing a group of people walking over a bridge). However, during those clips that show the architecture devoid of human presence, there is no way of telling whether one sequence from the footage precedes or follows the other. To determine the workings of the piece, the viewer might concentrate on individual monitors, even timing the length of clips on each.

As this happens, the structure begins to act as an interruption, as a veil, distancing the view onto Dachau and protecting the viewer (and the artist, who was the first viewer of the material) from a direct confrontation with the difficult sight. To see the work is always to see interruptions: not only is Korot's footage broken up into clips and between the monitors, but the monitors too break the flattened surface of the white screen. Korot seems to have indicated that the structure was in some ways protective: 'I was taking very loaded material [and letting] formal elements be as strong. That was the only way that I felt I wanted to confront this very painful and unspeakable material . . . The only way to talk about it would be through the silence of structure.'

So the abstract structure can both re-enforce the impact of the images and deflect this impact. Another way of thinking about the structure is that it is itself an encounter with the subject of Dachau, and a concrete formal acknowledgment that Dachau could not be fluidly represented with a coherent sequence of images like any other place. Only broken images and fractured narratives would be appropriate: Korot's structure deliberately destabilises what would otherwise be too facile a presentation of the camp. During her visit, Korot might have seen tourists passing through Dachau as if it were just another tourist location, and indeed at times we see their unfettered passage from the barracks over the bridge and beyond. The broken structure of *Dachau 1974*, however, renders impossible any viewer's attempt to treat the concentration camp as a tourist location that they can visit and consume vicariously.[58]

Furthermore, the structure through its opacity serves as a representation of the incomprehensibility of the subject. Even when the ordering systems of the structure are fathomed (for instance, by timing the repetitions on each monitor, or by looking at Korot's diagram), they can neither be seen nor sensed. Before the monitors, an accurate sense of the structure remains elusive due to the movement on the screens and between them as they flash on and off. This formulation might well recall the perceptual effects of phasing. Pamela Lee has written that while structurally 'legible', phasing produces a sense of 'non-comprehension'. What is remarkable here is that Korot deployed phasing's facility to engender a sense of 'non-comprehension' in order to represent a site that defies comprehension.

But if the structure is an encounter with Dachau, it never presents itself as a fully resolved solution to the problems of its representation. Towards the end of the work, there is a period of one-and-a-half minutes where all four screens present frontal views onto the crematoria. Whilst the accompanying sound of tolling bells gives the scene an even more sombre character, as the screens flash on and off at their regulated intervals, the viewer can begin to wonder whether this formal disturbance is really adequate as a means of representing the image of the crematoria before them. At this juncture, one begins not only to experience the structure, but to question it. The structure no longer appears as Korot's complex but fully adequate solution to the problem of how to work her footage, but almost as an interim solution with inevitable shortcomings: here, the repetitions come across as somewhat fussy. Since the structure during this brief moment of the work becomes problematic, Korot raises within the work questions about the adequacy of the form she has created, pressing the viewer to address critically more general questions about Holocaust representation.[59]

Korot's structure functions in various ways, then. The repetitions can mime the sense of the camp's brutality, and emphasise the offensiveness of some of the sights and sounds Korot recorded. At other times or for other viewers, the structure can draw attention to itself and act as a veil. The structure acknowledges the impossibility of a casual representation of the camp and indicates through its own opacity the incomprehensibility of the subject; the structure even serves as a self-consciously problematic device. In many ways the effects of *Dachau 1974* recall the effects of Andy Warhol's 'disaster' paintings in which images of car crashes, suicides and electric chairs were repeated in a grid. Hal Foster has written that: 'Somehow in these repetitions, several contradictory things occur at the same time: a warding away of traumatic significance *and* an opening out to it, a defending against traumatic affect *and* a producing of it.'[60] Just so, there is no singular impact of the form of *Dachau 1974*: Korot's abstract structure instead emerges as an extraordinarily serious and complex means of representing Dachau, and even of raising the question of how it could be represented.

While the comparison with the disaster paintings suggests yet another of the artists whose work informed Korot's, there are two very obvious differences between Korot's work and Warhol's series of paintings. Where Warhol was primarily working with images of contemporary events, or of still-functioning penal mechanisms (the electric chair), Korot was treating images of an historical nature, or more accurately, images of a museum on the site of an historical concentration camp. Where a viewer sees the repetitions of suicides and crash victims across the surface of Warhol's paintings at one moment, Korot's viewer becomes aware of repetitions over time.

Noting these points, we come to two of the most salient features of Korot's work. Korot always conceived her project as an encounter with Dachau specifically as she found it in 1974. This was never a project to represent what had taken place within its fences, and so neither archival footage nor survivor testimony would be useful to her (to evoke the two most famous films of concentration camps, *Night and Fog* and *Shoah*). Rather she was interested in the camp's present-day status, hence the importance of her title *Dachau 1974*. As I remarked earlier, visitors to Dachau in 1974 as often felt under-whelmed as emotionally over-powered, usually became their visits were over-determined by expectations formed by their reading and general knowledge about the Holocaust. Their visits were mediated even before they arrived, and once they entered the camp, they could only view it through the mediation of the museum and the various sanitising 'improvements' that had taken place since liberation. Korot's footage documented the museum displays and the way in which visitors toured around in groups, but the sense of this mediation was conveyed most powerfully through her structure. Just as her visit to Dachau was framed by the activities of all those who had planned out the displays before she arrived, so too the visitor to The Kitchen in 1975 could only see Dachau through the structure Korot had determined since her visit.

The history of Dachau 'as it had been' was always out of reach: Korot acknowledged this not only through filming particular images showing the contemporary life of the camp, but also by presenting the footage in a highly structured way, emphasising the way all encounters with the place now were mediated. As it played out over time, the form of *Dachau 1974* also represented the ways in which memory processed the site – and here, I am thinking both about the memory of single subjects and of entire cultures. As Korot knew, the memory of the Holocaust was compelling and insistent (it had drawn her to visit Dachau), but also deceptive and fragile (she had experienced at first hand her German hosts' repression of any discussion of her project). The structure of *Dachau 1974* represents both aspects of memory. In its repetitiveness, we can sense the inescapable demands that Dachau makes on memory, but in its fragmentation, we sense the fragility of memory.

This point can be made most clearly if we consider how the 'weave structure' set up expectations that the 'clip structure' defied. In an actual woven cloth, the weft disappears under the warp, and when the thread reappears, a 'later' section of it emerges. And so we expect that a clip seen on A will return on C at a later moment. But as we have seen, a visual event starting on A often disappears from view only to return on C at an earlier moment. The weave structure promised to unite, but the clip structure served to untie images. Through placing two formal structures at odds with one another, Korot found a way to represent in a spatial and temporal way the fragile workings of memory. Like memories, her images appear and disappear, interrupt and are interrupted, surface and resurface – but out of time and at some degree of distortion, never fluidly.

What now emerges very clearly is that Korot forged a structure through which video could not only represent an object to be remembered, but the very processes of memory. This was really a remarkable achievement and all the more so in 1974 when the various articles about video's purchase on 'The Present Tense' were being penned. Korot's work also stands in direct opposition to Fredric Jameson's claim that a 'description of the structural exclusion of memory, might well lead onto a theory of video itself'. But if *Dachau 1974* addressed video to a subject that would have seemed impossible for it, it should nonetheless be acknowledged that Korot simultaneously relied on the most well-remarked features of the medium. Because of the ways in which she structured her footage of Dachau, her viewers would always be kept alert, aware of the changes occurring *in the present tense* around them. As she said, 'I sought to work in such a way that carefully composed image/time relationships would seen live and present to the viewer.'[61] A viewer responsive to the work would be responsible for making sense of its form. In this way the structure served to emphasise that the responsibility of memory is in the present.

the legacy of the work

Dachau 1974 was presented in many different locations after its first showing at The Kitchen. Two exhibitions were held in New York State in the mid-1970s, and the work was shown at *Documenta 6* in Kassel in 1977. Sometimes, Korot would present the work at art schools in less than ideal screening situations, where, for instance, the monitors would be arranged in a line but without the screen that she had built at The

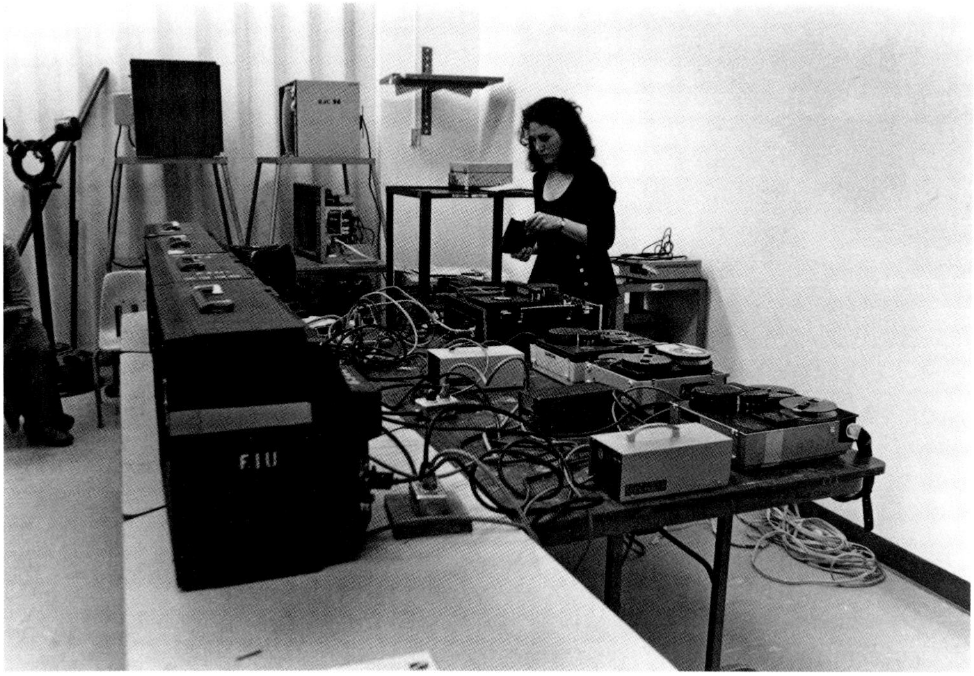

86 Beryl Korot at Broward College, Florida, 1976 setting up *Dachau 1974* on four monitors.
© Beryl Korot.

Kitchen. In the image of the screening at Broward College in Florida in 1976, the complex machinery of an early multi-channel video installation is apparent, and it is also clear that Korot needed to move from one machine to another to set each tape running (fig. 86). After another presentation at the Whitney in 1980, American museums from Long Beach to Pittsburgh installed the piece. It was one of only nineteen works to be selected for inclusion in what, to date, has been the main historical overview of moving and projected image work from this period: Chrissie Iles's 2002 Whitney show 'Into the Light'. And yet curiously, despite this institutional recognition and the impact that it had on other artists such as Mary Lucier,[62] *Dachau 1974* has not been discussed in many histories or critical reviews of video art. It gets no mention from David Joselit in his *Artforum* review of 'Into the Light', despite his interest in history and mnemonic representation, and none too in Janet Kraynak's *Documents* review of the same show.[63]

Perhaps this is because Korot's work was so unlike the other video works of its period: the work was neither an activist examination of the power of the television networks, nor a formal examination of video's specific facilities for instantaneous recording and playback. Instead, this was a work that harnessed video's particular capabilities to address an historical and mnemonic subject in an entirely new way. Though Korot's work had no parallels when it was made, today many artists are working in the terrain that Korot first explored. The Israeli-born, American-educated and Berlin-based artist Omer Fast, for instance, made *Spielberg's List* in 2003. Fast filmed the material for the work in and around Krakow, recording interviews with Poles who had played extras in *Schindler's List* and also taping guides as they took tourists around the still-intact sets of Spielberg's film. The context of this work is the Hollywoodisation of the Holocaust, and the tourist industry around Auschwitz. Korot addressed the mediation of Dachau at a much earlier stage, taping the camp before blockbuster Holocaust films existed, and before Dachau had been replicated as a movie set. Nonetheless, Fast's work shares a crucial formal feature with Korot's. He shows identical footage on his two screens but subtitles the voices with alternative translations, one often referring to the events of the 1940s, and one to Spielberg's reconstructions of them in the 1990s. This means that the viewer is never sure which period the Polish people on the screen are addressing. Fast's viewer must look from screen to screen in the instants the subtitles appear, choosing between alternative meanings, just as Korot's viewer is activated by the 'image/time' relationships proceeding before them.

While this contemporary parallel suggests *Dachau 1974* was 'ahead' of its time (and indeed there are other works one could mention alongside *Spielberg's List*, such as Marine Hugonnier's *Anna Hasunova*), it is important to note the ways in which Korot's project was very much marked by her historical moment, and the ways in which the work signalled a different relationship to Holocaust memory than the one that had persisted for older artists. Newman, Louis and Kahn were all born in the early part of the century and were adults by the 1930s. As they came to learn about the events in Europe after the war, they had to face up to the contingencies of their survival (had it not been for their parents' immigration, they would have been killed), and to the implications of their association with the general American inactivity during the war years. Furthermore, they had all practised as artists and architects before, during and after the Holocaust, and this meant that they had to scrutinise their practices, asking what it meant to pursue their art in a radically changed cultural context. These general conditions to some extent determined their entire post-war practice and the way in which they addressed the Holocaust in the projects I have examined, but Korot faced the memory of the Holocaust in an entirely different context. Born during the 1940s, she would have grown up knowing about it, never learning through the relatively direct channels such as the eye-witness press reports and just-published photographs of the liberation of the camps that Newman once wrote about. Furthermore, Korot could never ask what it meant to continue making art in the aftermath of the Holocaust with the personal agony of someone who had made art *before*. Both the images she taped of a camp seen thirty years after liberation, and the structure she created for the presentation of these images as the work *Dachau 1974*, witness these conditions. *Dachau 1974* is a work that explores the ways in which the memory of the Holocaust affected those who lived after, rather than during and after, its historical terminus.

Korot was one of the first artists of her generation to address Holocaust memory, but later many of her contemporaries would explore the ideas she had investigated. Indeed *Dachau 1974* was hugely important to her partner Steve Reich, who in 1988 composed *Different Trains*. Unlike Korot, Reich addressed the memory of the Holocaust through very personal memories. As an infant in the early 1940s, Reich had travelled with his governess by train from his father in New York to his mother in Los Angeles, and he began the work with the realisation that had he been born in Europe, he would have travelled on very different trains. Like Korot, though, Reich used repetitive forms: he recorded the sounds of European and American locomotives, and interviews with his elderly governess and with Holocaust survivors, and then broke these recordings into fragments which repeated over the length of the work. Also, like Korot's video installation, Reich's composition was self-initiated. By contrast, the projects I will turn to now came to being as a result of commissions. Most of the artists I will be concerned with were also of Korot's post-war generation, and the first I will look at is Mel Bochner. Korot's video had been taped in a concentration camp in Germany in 1974; almost twenty years later, Bochner installed his work in an SS prison in Rome.

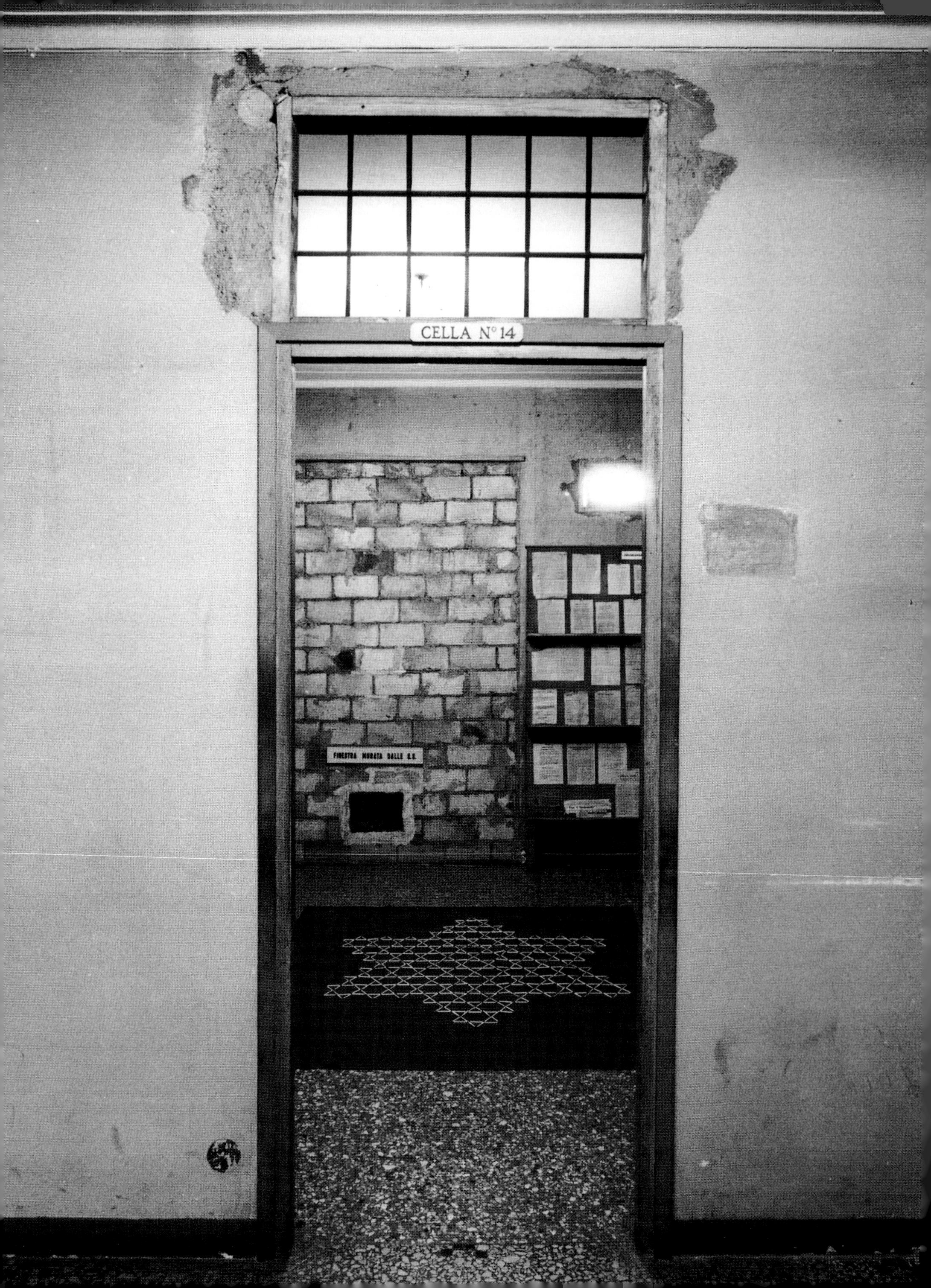
CELLA N° 14
FINESTRA MURATA DALLE S.S.

seven

mel bochner's *via tasso* project

mel bochner, italy and the via tasso

87 Mel Bochner, *Via Tasso* installation view, 1993. © Mel Bochner.

In 1992, almost twenty years after Beryl Korot's visit to Dachau, one of the artists whose earlier serial strategies had informed her own, Mel Bochner, received from the Italian-American curator Carolyn Christov-Bakargiev an unexpected invitation to make a work in a former Nazi prison in Rome. Christov-Bakargiev had been teaching in a school there, and was at this time extremely concerned with the rise of Alleanza Nazionale and the Italian right. Tackling national amnesia in the most local and direct of ways, she decided to include in her syllabus a lesson on the Nazi occupation of the city. Amazed to find out that her pupils knew nothing of the period, she took them to the Museo Storico della Liberazione di Roma on the Via Tasso.

The apartment building which then housed the museum had been built in the 1930s. Owned originally by Prince Francesco Ruspoli, between 1943 and 1944 it had served as the Roman base of the Gestapo. Political and Jewish prisoners had been incarcerated there, many later taken to their murder at the Ardeantine caves, others deported from Via Tasso to death camps. Some had been tortured to death in the prison – a fate represented at the end of Roberto Rossellini's *Roma, città aperta* (Open City; 1945) when the resistance fighter Manfredi and the priest Don Pietro are taken to Via Tasso. As is shown in the film, to convert the apartments into their prison, the Nazis had bricked up the windows with breeze blocks, and had fixed cell number plates above the door to each of the rooms, but had changed little else (the floral wallpaper stayed up in some of the spaces). After the liberation, the first three floors were dedicated as a museum. Some rooms had been converted to house displays about the resistance, the anti-Semitic policies of the Nazis and the history of the prison. Other cells

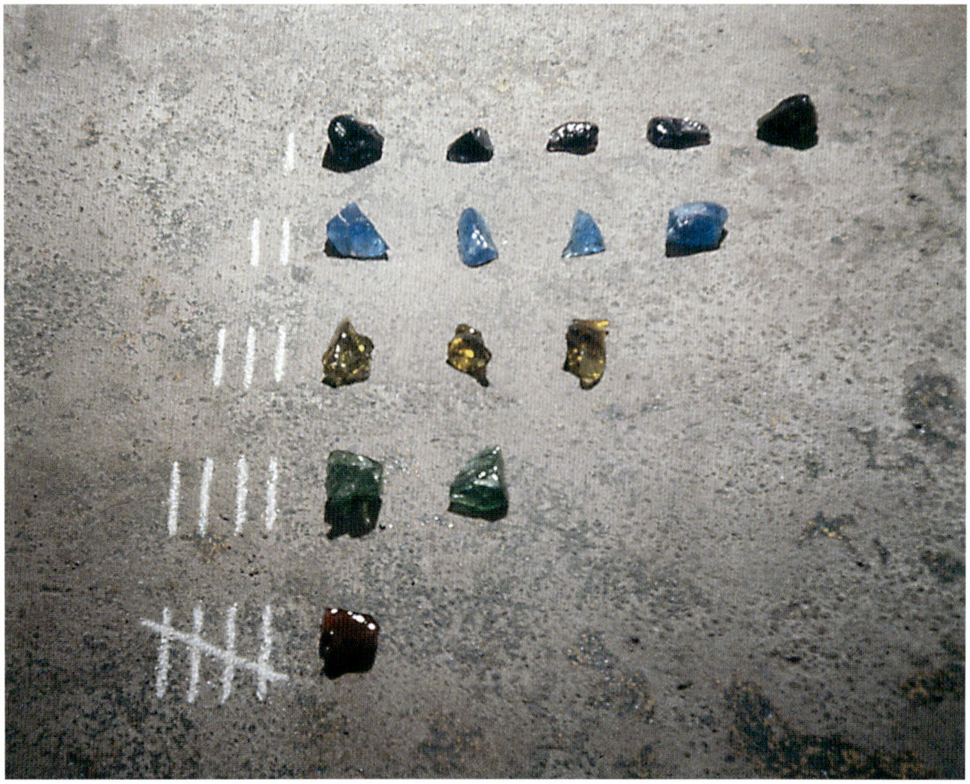

88 Mel Bochner, *Cardinal vs. Ordinal 5*, 1972/91. Glass and chalk on floor. © Mel Bochner.

had been left to stand as they had been found at the liberation. Prisoners had scrawled graffiti over many of the walls, and these had been left for all to see, protected under glass. One inscription read: 'It is better to die heroically at twenty than of old age at one hundred' – a canny twist of Mussolini's famous saying: 'Better live one day as a lion than one hundred years as a lamb.'[1] Hardly a regular tourist stop, Christov-Bakargiev found the museum extremely impoverished. She decided to initiate an art programme with the intention of bringing attention to the building and remembering its past at this precarious moment of neo-fascist resurgence. The art works, she hoped, would 'offer a homage to the prisoners of via Tasso'. The building was 'a banal place that history has turned into something extreme', but artists 'can add a new chapter to a violent and dramatic past'. They can 'act with respect and care, so that abuse and torture are not the last words said'.[2] Mel Bochner was the first of the artists she contacted.[3]

Bochner was neither a stranger to Carolyn Christov-Bakargiev, nor to Italy. The previous year, in fact, he had put together a show with her at the Studio Casoli in Milan called *Fontana's Light: Omaggio a Lucio Fontana* where he had remade pieces from the twenty-year old body of work called *Theory of Sculpture*. The sculptures had originally been made using chalk, stones or hazelnuts, but in Milan, Bochner used chunks of coloured Murano glass that he had found in Fontana's studio (fig. 88).[4] Bochner's

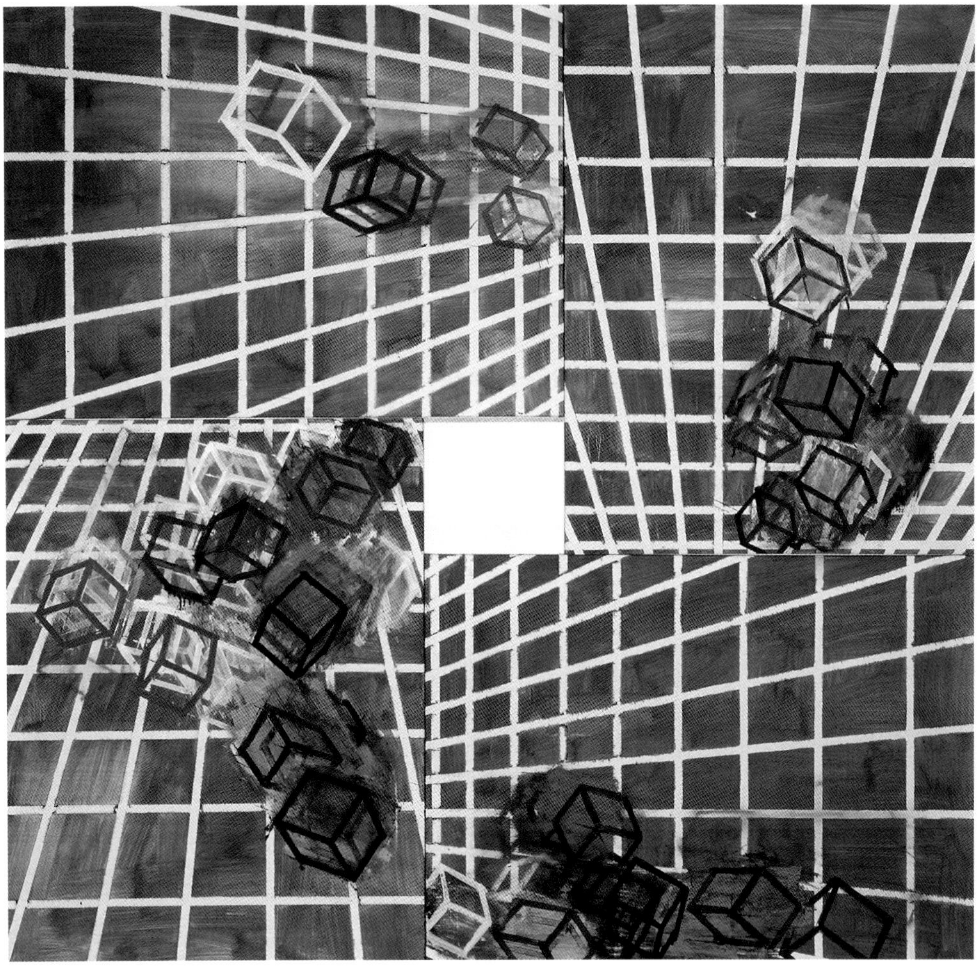

89 Mel Bochner, *Rome Quartet II*, 1991. Oil on four canvases, 140 × 140 cm. © Mel Bochner.

Italian connection went right back to the earliest years of his career when, in 1970, he had shown wall drawings at the Studio Toseli in Milan, and at the Sperone Gallery in Turin. Though the austerity of these works must have seemed at odds with their Italian setting, Bochner's engagement with the country and its art history soon resulted in a shift in his work. A trip in 1974 changed his attitude to both shape and colour. Impressed with the irregularity of the layout of Siena and 'the colours of Italian painting of the early Renaissance'[5], Bochner removed grids and primary colours from his drawings. Pentagonal compound shapes of rich maroon and orange danced around the walls in their place.

This body of work resulted in his turn to painting, the medium that has preoccupied Bochner from the 1980s onwards, and in many works, Bochner would signal his interest in Italy – in the four-part painting *Rome Quartet II* (1991; fig. 89), and in the series of drawings that had been titled after Roman streets (for instance *Via Della Penitenza* of 1987). So Italy and Rome in particular were exceptionally generative places for Bochner – far more so than for most American artists of his generation. Yet despite the longstanding importance of the country to the artist, Christov-Bakargiev could hardly have been confident that he would comply with her request to place work in a location so strongly associated with Italy's wartime history and with the murder of its Jewish population.

Back in New York, Bochner contemplated the invitation. Though never one to put his work 'in the service of anything', this was not a commission he had sought, but an invitation extended to him. Christov-Bakargiev carefully explained the history of the site, and he accepted the proposal and began to work on ideas for the show. Bochner initially planned to recreate an early work, making 'the connection very abstract'.[6] In time however he decided against installing an existing work, and began to work on drawings for a new piece. The new piece became two pieces, and two became three. All three sculptures went on show in 1993.

The *Via Tasso* project represents another example of an abstract artist attempting to engage the memory of the Holocaust, and in what follows, I will pursue the same interpretative enquiries I have used to study Newman, Korot and others. How did Mel Bochner deploy his abstract language to address this memory? What meanings can we make of the *Via Tasso* sculptures, and in what ways did the work problematise the very act of interpretation? Despite the longer lapse of time between Bochner's *Via Tasso* project and the works I have discussed previously – all of which date from the mid-1960s to the mid-1970s – there is a clear continuity of concerns. But before addressing Bochner's work in detail, it is worth noting several shifts signalled by his commission in relation to the projects examined so far.

First, some shifts can be noted in the wider political and cultural negotiation of the Holocaust between the 1970s and 1990s. Frank Stella's attempts to represent 'the destruction of an entire culture' had been met with critical silence, and a different kind of silence greeted Beryl Korot when she spoke about her project to video Dachau in 1974 with her DAAD hosts. The first scenario witnesses art criticism's limited abilities to discuss the relation of painting and the Holocaust in the 1970s; the second suggests the German cultural establishment's unwillingness to confront the memory of Nazism around the same time. Christov-Bakargiev's approach to Bochner testifies to a partial shift in these situations. Following the widespread cultural commemoration of the Holocaust through the building of museums, the making of Hollywood films and the writing of more and more histories, by the early 1990s an art critic or curator could not only write about an artist's attempt to confront the Holocaust, but could commission artists who had given no previous indication that they would accept such a task to create new works at a site of former suffering. (Christov-Bakargiev went on to commission Lawrence Weiner, Enzo Cucci and Fabio Mauri to make work at Via Tasso.) Such curatorial activities might be a welcome result of the wider cultural engagement with the Holocaust, but the precise circumstances in which Christov-Bakargiev operated indicate that not everything had changed since the 1970s. Between the 1970s and 1990s, there had been (in some quarters) a move from the repression to the denial of the Holocaust, and in others, a continued unwillingness to face up to the events of the 1930s and 1940s. This unwillingness in part constituted the political circumstances in Italy to which she responded.

A second change that occurred between the time of Korot's and Bochner's work can be explored just by noting the different places in which their works were displayed. While Korot taped her footage in Dachau but showed it in a New York art institution, Bochner was asked to show his work in the Gestapo prison itself. Unlike any of the projects discussed so far, Bochner's was situated at a site touched by Nazism. Christov-Bakargiev's project to commission work not just to respond to this site, but to be shown *at* it, is but one example of a number of similar projects begun in the 1990s in which historic sites became spaces for temporary art installations; another was the programme at the synagogue at Stommeln where Richard Serra installed *The Drowned and the Saved.*[7] These projects indicate a shift in the nature of site-specific practices since the 1970s. Initially, site-specificity denoted works that responded to the architectural features of the container and whose identity would therefore change if installed elsewhere. Bochner had been among the first artists to make works that explicitly dealt with the architecture in which they were placed: his *Measurement: Room* series of 1969 mapped the dimensions of the Heiner Friedrich gallery in Munich onto its very walls.[8] By the 1990s, critical site-specific projects responded to the history and cultural meanings of a site as well as its architecture. Christov-Bakargiev's project to commission site-specific works for Via Tasso was in some ways, then, indebted to Bochner's own earlier practice, but still the idea of situating a work in a place such as Via Tasso was relatively new for him, and it considerably affected the way he went about the project.

One other difference between Bochner and the previous subject of my discussion (not so much a shift in the wider conditions determining the circumstances for the work, but something worth pointing out) concerns Bochner's age at the time of the commission, or rather the longevity of his career at that moment. While Korot made her work soon after she began to use video, Bochner accepted the *Via Tasso* commission some twenty-five years after he had started showing his work. By the early 1990s, he had a highly developed language of his own. Just as Frank Stella looked back at his *Black Paintings* whilst embarking on the *Polish Villages*, so Bochner looked back to his own work as he considered the history of Via Tasso. As much as I will be investigating Via Tasso and the work Bochner placed there, I will also attempt to explore the position of the 1993 project within the context of Bochner's wider work, and not just in terms of his long-standing interest in Italian art and in the city of Rome.

five properties of *via tasso*

Mel Bochner's *Via Tasso* project consisted of three sculptures made of burnt cooks' matchsticks arranged on the ground of the prison cells on the third floor of the Museo

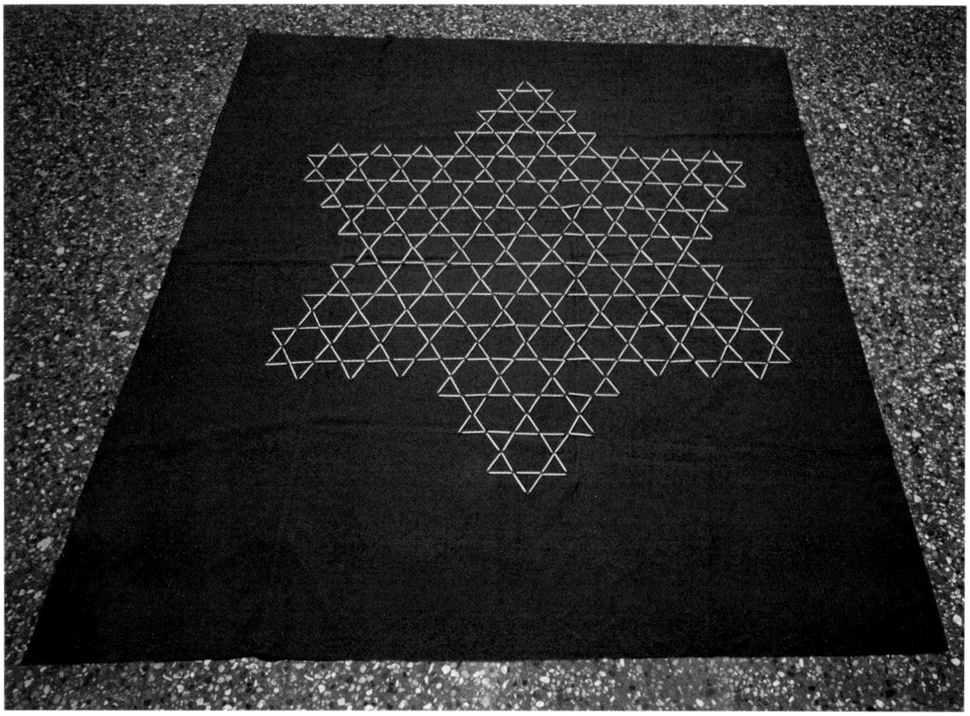

90 Mel Bochner, *Yisgadal (for the Jews of Rome)*, 1993. 365 burnt matchsticks on army blanket on floor. © Mel Bochner.

Storico della Liberazione di Roma (fig. 87). To reach the work, one had to pass through the museum. The rooms on the first floor housed a research library and the museum offices, and on the second floor, there were a set of cells, some given over to displays, others left bare to allow the prisoners' graffiti to be seen. By the time the Bochner work was visible, a visitor would have had a powerful impression of the history of the prison but also an increasing sense of the banality of the site. For this was just the normal third floor of an apartment block in the heart of Rome, not a stereotypical out-of-the-way, underground, rat-infested dungeon. As it had done in the mid-1940s, everyday life continued outside on the street and in the neighbouring buildings, but though the sounds of Rome were audible, the bricked-up windows blocked everything from sight. Bochner's work could not be disassociated from this heavily atmospheric context that was particularly upsetting because it was so ordinary. The sculptures looked relatively ordinary too, each comprised of one material laid down in ways that anyone could have followed. In fact all of the components of the work might have seemed simple, but I want now to scrutinise the five properties of the work in turn to explore how together they created a project with a complex range of suggestions. So let us consider the 'five properties' of *Via Tasso*.

The most obvious property of the works was their shape. In all three sculptures, the matchsticks were arranged into a six-pointed star. Though now taken for granted as a Jewish symbol, as Bochner would have known, this had not always been the case. The six-pointed star was to be found in ancient synagogues including the syn-

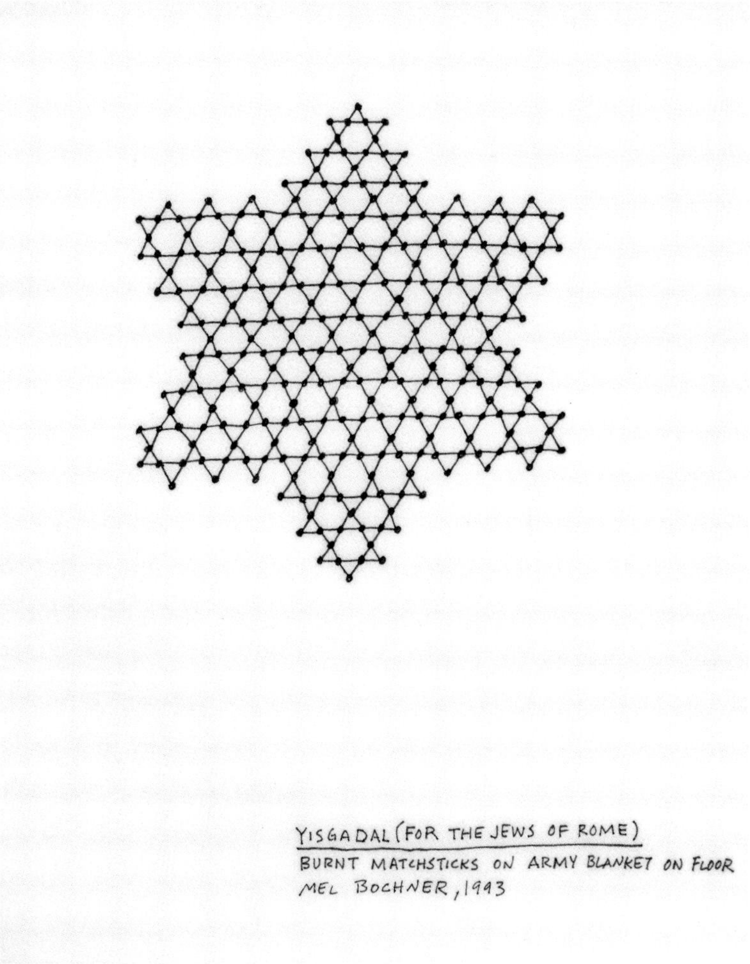

91 Mel Bochner, Drawing for *Yisgadal (For the Jews of Rome)*, 1993. Ink on paper, 27.9 × 21.6 cm. © Mel Bochner.

agogue of Capernaum (second or third century CE), but, as Gershom Scholem wrote in an essay of 1949, only as a decorative pattern alongside swastikas, 'and certainly no one will contend that this makes the swastika a Jewish symbol'. Not far from the Via Tasso building, the relief carved into the Arch of Titus showed the Jews carrying the Menorah from the temple, a symbol that historically *had* been associated with Judaism. There were no Stars of David on the Arch, nor within the Great Synagogue of Rome that remained intact throughout the period of the German occupation. The adoption of the star as a symbol had only taken place in the nineteenth century when early secular Zionist leaders sought to use a symbol unconnected to any religious signification. No matter how recent its use, however, no matter its non-biblical origins, the star had been chosen by the Nazis for the Jews to wear. One of the displays on the third floor of Via Tasso was a collection of badges worn by various groups persecuted under Nazism, including the yellow star. Bochner's decision to use a 'Magen David' shape points first of all to its use in the Nazi period,

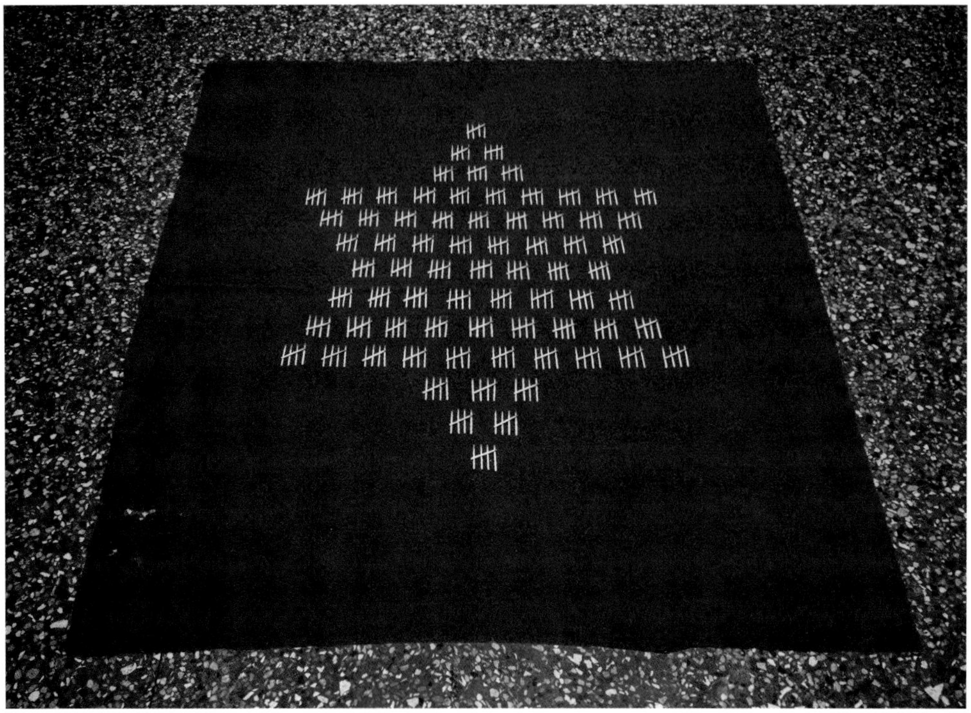

92 Mel Bochner, *Yahrzeit (for the Jews of Rome)*, 1993. 365 burnt matchsticks on army blanket on floor. © Mel Bochner.

but those knowing what Scholem had called 'The Curious History of the Six-Pointed Star' would have recognised that the shape was not essentially 'Jewish'. Bochner's matches could equally be said to describe a regular geometrical figure made of two overlaid triangles.

If the first property of the sculptures was shape, the second was material. The works were made from burnt wooden cooks' matches. Looking closely it would have been clear that the matches had been struck and then quickly blown out because only their heads were charred. Bochner could have allowed the flame to consume the match almost to its end, and had he done this, each match would have looked more singular, and each would have been so fragile as to risk crumbling on contact with the ground. Such a work might well have encouraged a viewer to imagine the artist holding each brief flame in his hands, as if each time remembering a life. However, Bochner seems to have lit and extinguished more than one match at once, making the work with a certain economy, so the matches are more impersonal. Nonetheless, they certainly remain allusive. In this way they recall an approach to materials associated with Arte Povera rather than with minimalism – Jannis Kounellis's use of coal in his *Untitled* coal piece from 1969, for instance. Kounellis used coal not just as a literal substance, but to generate an imaginative response: the work prompts its viewer to think of the energy stored up in the material; its potential to generate heat and fire. But unlike Kounellis's coal, Bochner's matches were used up, and could not allude to a potential future state.

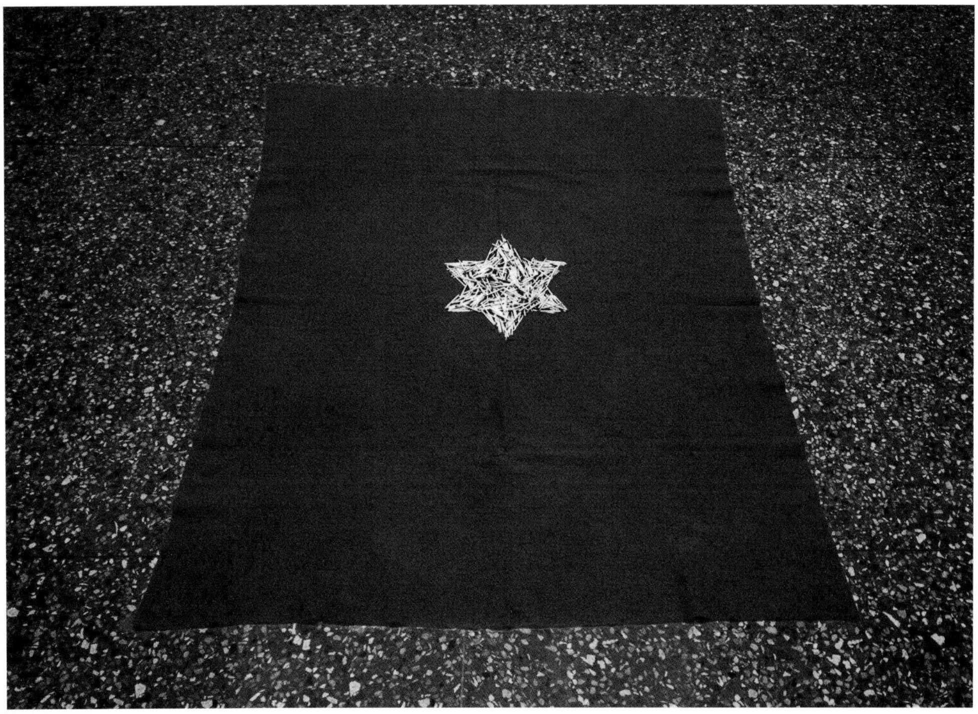

93 Mel Bochner, *Yiskor (for the Jews of Rome)*, 1993. 365 burnt matchsticks on army blanket on floor.

The burnt matches would have provoked many thoughts – about the burning of books, and synagogues, about the extinguishing of lives, and about Jewish mourning candles. They are a burnt offering, which in Greek, is a Holocaust. The matches were all the more resonant in the darkened space of Via Tasso: this was already a place where daylight had been extinguished by the blocking-up of the windows. The burnt matches repeated this darkening.

The third property of the works was number. Though it would have been clear that each sculpture utilised a large number of matches (certainly more than were necessary just to describe the external form of the six-pointed star), it was also apparent that this was not a crass attempt to allude to the figure of six million (and there have been art works that attempt to do just this). The number of matches in Bochner's sculptures was closer to the number of Roman Jews killed in the Holocaust (2164)[9], but in fact Bochner worked with a specific number of matches without such an allusion in mind. The central work was arranged into 73 gates of 5 matches which allowed a viewer to count precisely: 365. In fact in each of the three sculptures, Bochner used 365 matches. The German occupation of Rome did not in fact last as long as a year (it lasted 270 days) but the period of Jewish mourning is one year, during which time immediate relatives of the deceased recite daily memorial prayers.

Shape; material; number; arrangement. All the sculptures were positioned on top of army blankets on the floor of the cells. By placing the sculptures on the floor, Bochner

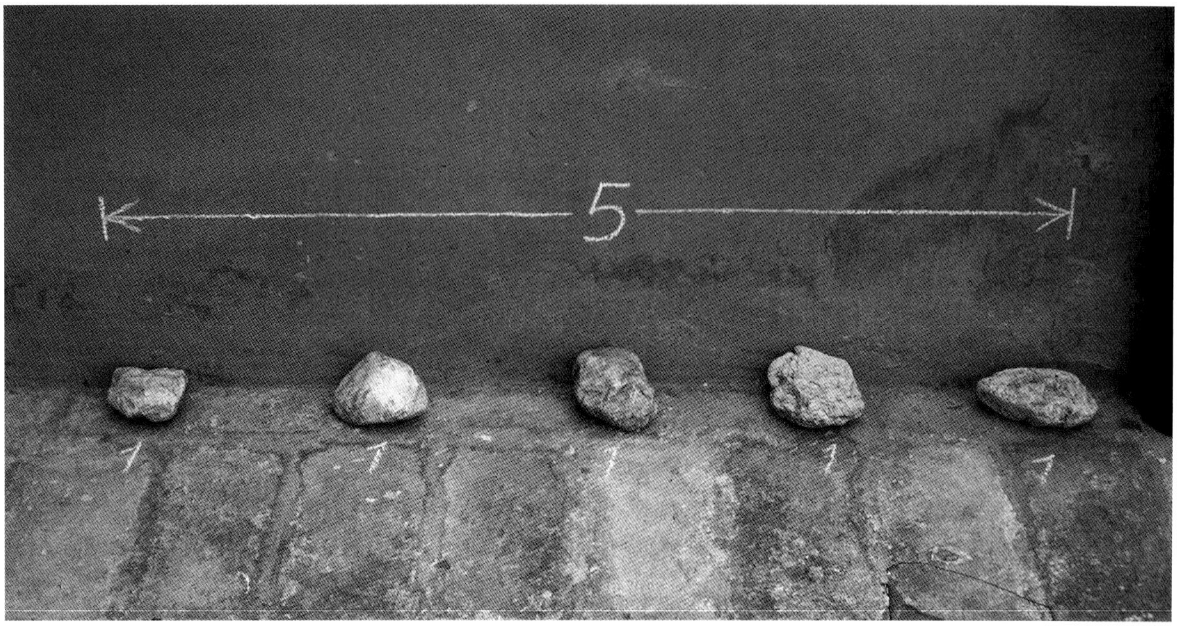

94 Mel Bochner, *Measurement Five*, 1969/71. Stones and chalk on floor. © Mel Bochner.

deferred to the displays on the walls, allowing the exhibition panels to remain visible for all the visitors. The sculpture also occupied the abject area once populated by the prisoners: in Rossellini's film, as he is brought into the cell, we see Don Pietro slung down to the ground, and later the prisoners squat down, there being no benches, of course. While each of Bochner's sculptures was floor-bound, they were differentiated by the way the matches were deposited. In the first, the individual matches were placed along the horizontal and diagonal axes of the star, forming a grid of tessellated mini-stars (fig. 90). The internal arrangement reiterated the outside shape and this repetition had two effects. First, it emptied out the religious symbolism to produce a merely decorative pattern, and in so doing, returned the star to its original status not as a Jewish symbol but as one decorative shape amongst many others. But the external shape could also be said to be unified through internal repetition, or strengthened. Interestingly, in the preparatory drawing for this sculpture, Bochner imaged the match heads as nodes, bonds or points of contact between lines (fig. 91). As mentioned already, the matches in the second work were arranged in gates (fig. 92). Four verticals were crossed by a diagonal fifth, forming a primitive counting system, and one often associated with prisoners who number their days of captivity. There were grids and other counting systems scratched into the Via Tasso walls amongst the other graffiti, and though there were no gates, Bochner's sculpture still echoed those inscriptions. For the last work, the matches were piled askew on top of each other, under and over themselves (fig. 93). It seemed that they had been dropped randomly like pick-up-sticks and only then pushed together into the shape of the star. Matches were scattered and crowded. Perhaps this suggested the crowding of prisoners in small cells such as the ones at Via Tasso. Or maybe even the piles of corpses in the gas chambers where many of Via

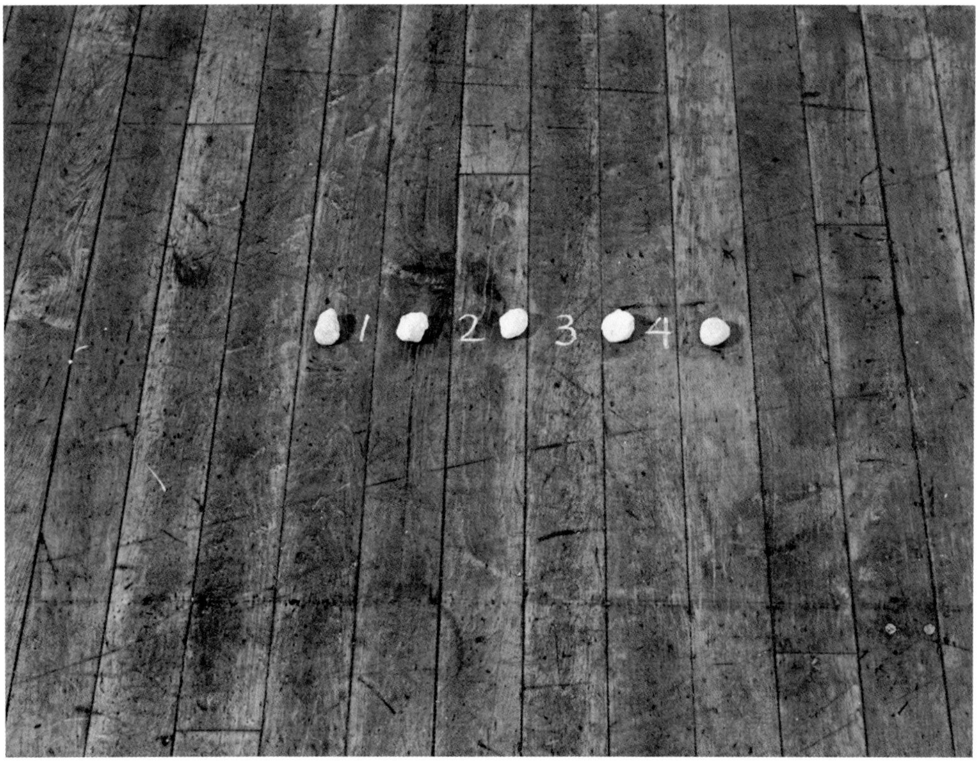

95 Mel Bochner, *Four Spaces*, 1972. Stones and chalk on floor. © Mel Bochner.

Tasso's prisoners eventually died. Or the scattering alluded to the dispersal of the Italian Jews, from ancient communities to the various places of their murder or of their post-war life.

All of the properties of the sculptures invited interpretation, and so did their inter-relationship. In Bochner's earliest multi-part works, serial principles had determined the different arrangements of each part but no serial principle operated in Via Tasso. Obviously by making more than one arrangement, Bochner could produce a greater range of associations, as we have seen, but would it also be possible to posit a kind of narrative link between the pieces? In a text dating back to 1973, Bochner had written that: 'Narrative fiction as a model yields a history of sequences . . . If A then B, if B then C, if C etc.'[10] Perhaps there was a kind of sequence ordering the Via Tasso sculptures, charting the different periods of the lives of the Jews – the first sculpture recalling the communal bonds between the Jews before the Holocaust; the second, the period of their incarceration; the third, their death and dispersal.[11]

One: shape; two: material; three: number; four: arrangement; five: sequence. Each of these five properties of the work invites different associations, but as we think these through, there is a sense that these sets of associations do not really slot together to produce a coherent reading of the whole work. Bochner's own work might help to analogise this interpretative impasse. A sculpture called *Measurement Five* from 1969 consisted of five pebbles arranged at the corner of a floor and wall (fig. 94).

An arrow on the wall stretched from one end of the row to the other, bisected by the number '5', and each pebble had the numeral '1' inscribed in chalk before it on the floor. This sculpture juxtaposed two ways of measuring the stones: either they could be taken as a unified group, or counted as separate units. The *Via Tasso* work might have invited a singular and total interpretation, but contemplating it, one sensed that instead of an accumulation of meaning, entirely separate associations were produced by its shape, material, number, arrangement and sequence. We do not get to '5' but are left with '1 1 1 1 1' instead. *Four Spaces* from 1972 (fig. 95) might also describe this situation: for the work, Bochner chalked numbers in each of the spaces in a row of five pebbles. Thinking about the five properties of the *Via Tasso* sculptures, we are more conscious of the space between each of their associations than of their addition.

Each of the 'five properties of *Via Tasso*' invites interpretation, but as the five sets of associations fail to add up to a whole, there is a growing sense that if the work does have a cumulative reference, it is to the very conventionality of the kind of associations it provokes, which is to say that the work seems 'about' the established language of Holocaust memorials. *Four Spaces* was part of a series called *Theory of Sculpture*, so titled because the individual works were not so much discreet sculptures as parts of an investigation of how all sculpture works – Bochner took as his subject sculptural principles such as extension, un-levelling and counting. The *Via Tasso* project in turn might be read as a 'Theory of Memorials', a demonstration and implicit comment on the way 'number', 'shape' and 'material' have been used in so many Holocaust monuments to produce quick associative possibilities. In interview, Bochner has said that most Holocaust memorials he knew during the time at which he made this work were 'really kitsch', but this antipathy towards a certain kind of symbolic work had firm roots in his thinking. As early as 1966, he had written about the clichés of memorial art, reviewing an exhibition by Michael Mazur in *Arts Magazine*. It was, he wrote, 'another tedious exhibition celebrating man's inhumanity to man . . . The tenacity of this genre (and its implicit "liberal" outlook) is astounding. Mr. Mazur's sincerity is not in question, but his remarkably superficial content and contrived posturing are. Such tired clichés as floating hands, amputated limbs, vanishing figures and segments of hospital beds are devices of the illustrator.'[12]

'Tired clichés' could also describe Stars of David, burnt matches and prisoners' gates. If so, the following question emerges: why would Bochner (who would be conscious of this tiredness) have chosen to make the *Via Tasso* work? It was surely not his intent to use Christov-Bakargiev's invitation as an opportunity to scrutinise the conventionality of Holocaust memorials – and to do so would have been to degrade the memory of those who suffered where his matches were placed. It is fair to suggest that Bochner accepted the invitation with some 'scepticism' about the project, given what Andreas Huyssen described the year after the exhibition as 'the excess of Holocaust imagery everywhere in our culture',[13] but much less generous to assert that his response was merely an ironic offering of a cluster of clichés, as if to say: 'You want a Holocaust

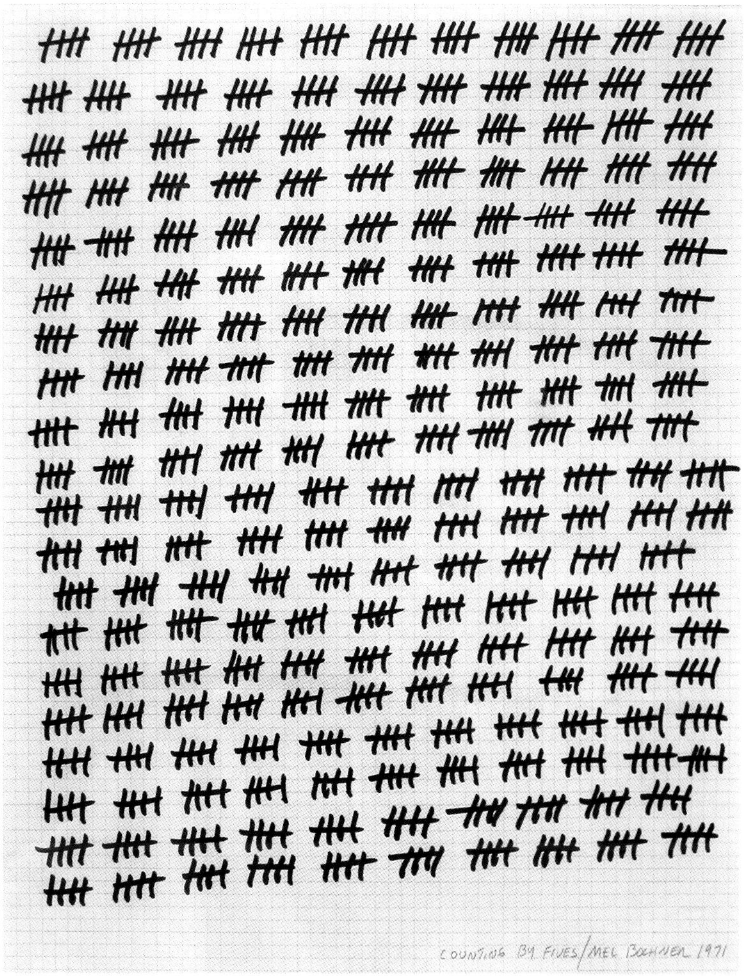

96 Mel Bochner, *Counting by Fives*, 1971. Ink on graph paper, 30 × 22.9 cm. © Mel Bochner.

memorial? Here's one readymade.'[14] Rather, as we shall see, it seems that Bochner managed to acknowledge the conventionality of the allusions he created with the work, while deploying them with absolute sincerity.

crosses and swastikas

I have already made brief references to Bochner's work of the late 1960s and early 1970s in order to consider the disconnected nature of the allusions produced by the properties of the *Via Tasso* sculptures. It might be clear already from such references that Bochner approached the task of addressing Via Tasso and making what would be his first new sculptures since the early 1970s by using the well-established language of his own work.[15] But what is not yet evident is just how many elements of the *Via Tasso* sculptures derived from this language. I now want to look back to this work of the late 1960s and 1970s.

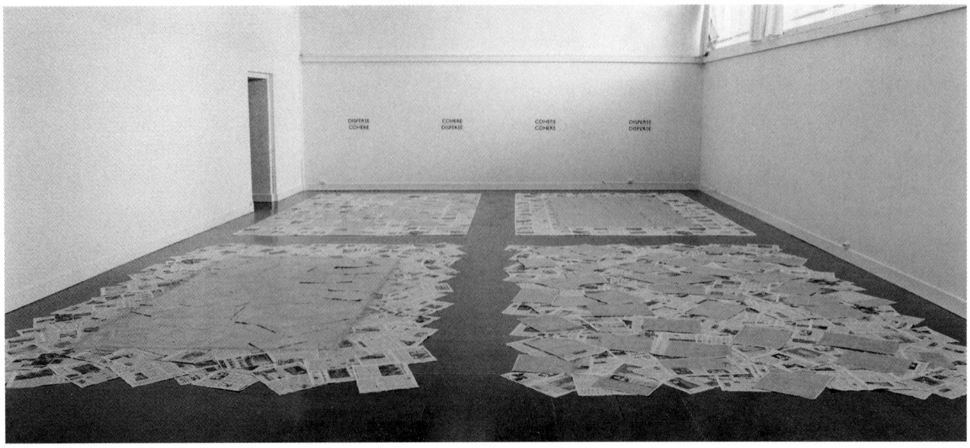

97 Mel Bochner, *Theory of Painting*, 1969–70. Blue spray paint on newspaper on floor, vinyl letters on wall. Collection of The Museum of Modern Art, New York. © Mel Bochner.

Doing so not only helps to show precedents for Bochner's *Via Tasso* sculptures, but helps to indicate the complex positions of *Via Tasso* in a more nuanced manner.

On looking at Bochner's work of this earlier period, the familiarity of the elements of *Via Tasso* are immediately apparent, as is the vast gulf separating the piece from the earlier work. Properties that read so allusively in Via Tasso had previously functioned in much more literal ways. Matches were matches, numbers were numbers, shapes shapes. Bochner's literal approach to materials is close to, but not best described by Frank Stella's comment 'what you see is what you see'. For Bochner, it was rather the case that materials were more simply functional, provisional and 'expedient'. As he told Ellen Johnson in 1972, 'I don't want the viewer to become involved with *specific* physical qualities in a work.'[16] With *Via Tasso* in mind, certain early works stand out – and not just those with similar materials.

Gates, for instance, appeared in the drawing *Counting by Fives* of 1971 where Bochner contrasted the pre-given ordering system of the graph paper grid with the gates' comparative messiness (fig. 96). Though the gate is the simplest means of grouping pen marks, the inconsistency of their arrangement in this drawing is striking. The rows spill over the horizontal lines; the vertical stacks of gates are entirely askew. There are sometimes ten, and sometimes eleven gates in each row, and the immediate appearance of the length of the row will not always reveal how many gates it contains: vision gives rise to doubt.[17] The individual strokes might be captive to the system of the gate, the gates liberated from the geometry of the grid; but there is certainly no allusion to actual captivity as in *Via Tasso*.

In *Theory of Painting* from 1969–70 there is a precedent of sorts for the dispersed and scattered arrangement of the matches in the third floor sculpture (fig. 97). To make the work, Bochner laid out newspaper on the floor, spraying some areas with blue paint. There were four arrangements in the work, corresponding to the word groups 'Cohere/Cohere', 'Disperse/Cohere', 'Cohere/Disperse' and 'Disperse/Disperse' that were written on the wall. Rosalind Krauss has argued that Bochner posits and suspends the theories of figure/ground and figure/frame: the horizontal spread of the work pre-

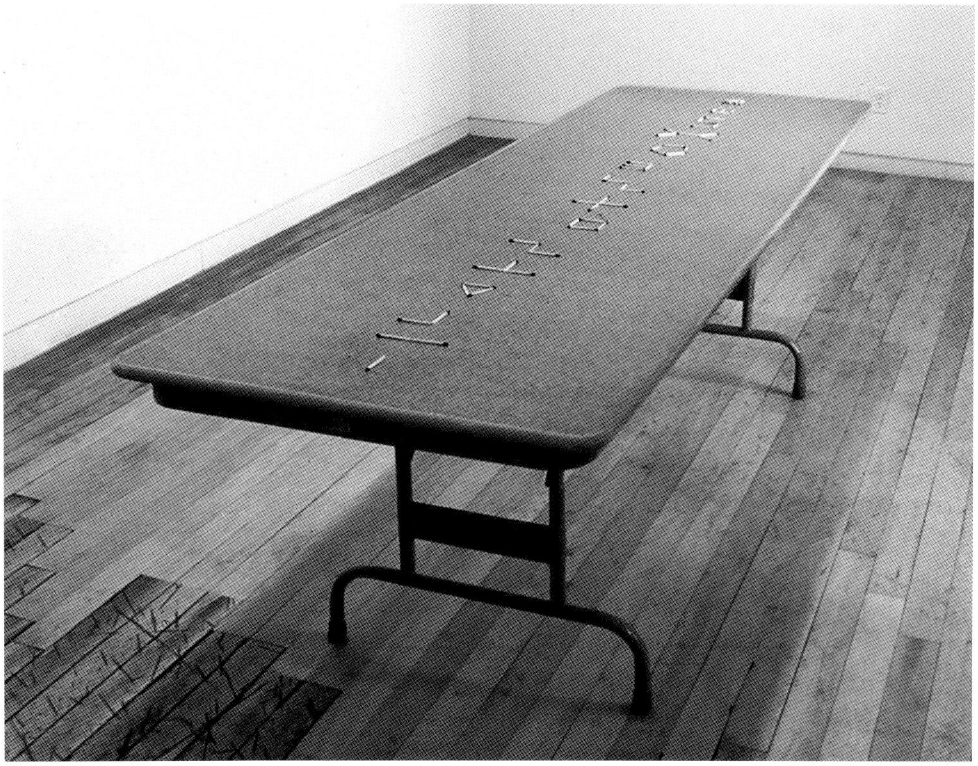

98 Mel Bochner, *To Count: Transitive*, 1973. Matchsticks on table. © Mel Bochner.

vented the viewer from learning lessons purely as conceptual theories.[18] Addressing its floor placement, she situated the work in the context of artists following Pollock, who would investigate what she elsewhere called the medium of horizontality.[19] And indeed the work does call to mind other floor-bound practices such as Carl Andre's and Barry Le Va's: certainly the dispersal of sheets and of colour in *Theory of Painting* are in no way related to the abjection of prisoners on cell floors, the dispersal of populations, or of refugees – even though such subjects might well have been a pressing concern artists responding to Vietnam in 1971.[20]

Perhaps no one work anticipates the elements that would eventually comprise *Via Tasso* more than *To Count: Transitive* of 1973, where burnt matchsticks were arranged end to end in groupings of one, two, three, and four, making straight lines, triangles, zigzags and squares (fig. 98). Initially, *To Count: Transitive* seems like a very simple serial arrangement. The work 'begins' with all the ways of arranging matches in groups of one, then in groups of two, in groups of three, and so on. But no serial logic is at work. *To Count: Transitive* instantiates the collapse of numerical thought under the pressure of actual, physical perception. It is reasonable to imagine that looking along the top row, the concept or word 'one' comes to the viewer's mind. But does this concept describe the 'one match', the 'one line' or the 'one right angle' as in the configuration furthest to the right, or 'row one', where all these possibilities coexist? These kinds of questions persist as we continue to look at the work. In *To Count: Transitive*, matches were used as convenient, cheap items that are clearly differentiated between one end and the other. The critic Lizzie Borden distinguished Bochner's 1973 match sculptures from earlier ones using pennies and stones, writing that: 'The choice of matchsticks is particularly opportune because they provide both point (head) and line (stick) which form actual shapes or diagrams; the rocks in earlier works had remained as points.'[21] In no way were matches allusive in the same way as they would be in *Via Tasso*. The idea of extinguished lives or of burnt offerings could not have been farther from Borden's or Bochner's minds.

When we return to thinking about *Via Tasso* from this brief foray into Bochner's previous work, though we can see how Bochner deployed his vocabulary more clearly, *Via Tasso* actually becomes more opaque. For the earlier works put considerable strain on the former reading of the Rome project as a series of highly allusive sculptures, or even as a work acknowledging the conventionality of such allusions. *Counting by Fives*, *Theory of Painting* and *To Count: Transitive* make us hesitate in associating 'burnt matchsticks' with extinguished lives, 'scattering' with dispersed communities, 'two overlapping triangles' with the Jewish star. They invite us instead to detach these associations from the Rome sculptures, to bracket out all allusions.[22] But in a darkened prison, matchsticks cannot just remain matchsticks for long: allusions flood back in.

*

The notion of bracketing has always been important to Bochner. Speaking with the artist in the months immediately after *Via Tasso* was installed, but referring to his paintings, James Meyer asked whether Bochner's 'current work hasn't betrayed the anti-subjectivist, anticompositional commitments of your early work and writings.' Bochner replied: 'I don't at this point find the words you're using – "subjective", "compositional" – pejorative. They were in the sixties; they were what I bracketed out.'[23] Earlier in the conversation, talking about his return to painting in the 1980s, Bochner reflected on the position of the medium in his work, and on the way it had seemingly disappeared between 1966 and 1980: 'In my own mind, my project has always been a kind of research based on the idea of bracketing and *unbracketing*. When you bracket or set something aside, you don't eliminate it.' Along with painting, the 'subjective', and the 'compositional', we should ask if the 'allusive' was something else just bracketed out from Bochner's earliest works to be taken up for the first time in Via Tasso, or whether indeed these brackets always permeable.

Looking back again, through *Via Tasso*, to Bochner's work of the 1960s and 1970s, we cannot help but note another Italian installation. In 1972, Bochner placed *Four, Four, Four, Four*, a sculpture of stones forming a cross, in the Church of San Nicola in Spoleto (fig. 99).[24] Whereas Bochner made the *Via Tasso* sculptures only after the invitation to work in the prison, a drawing called *Four, Four, Four, Four* existed before any opportunity to make a sculpture in the church – it was one among the twenty-one drawings that comprised the book *Primer*. However, when the Spoleto opportunity did come up, Bochner specifically chose to make this sculpture rather than any other. In

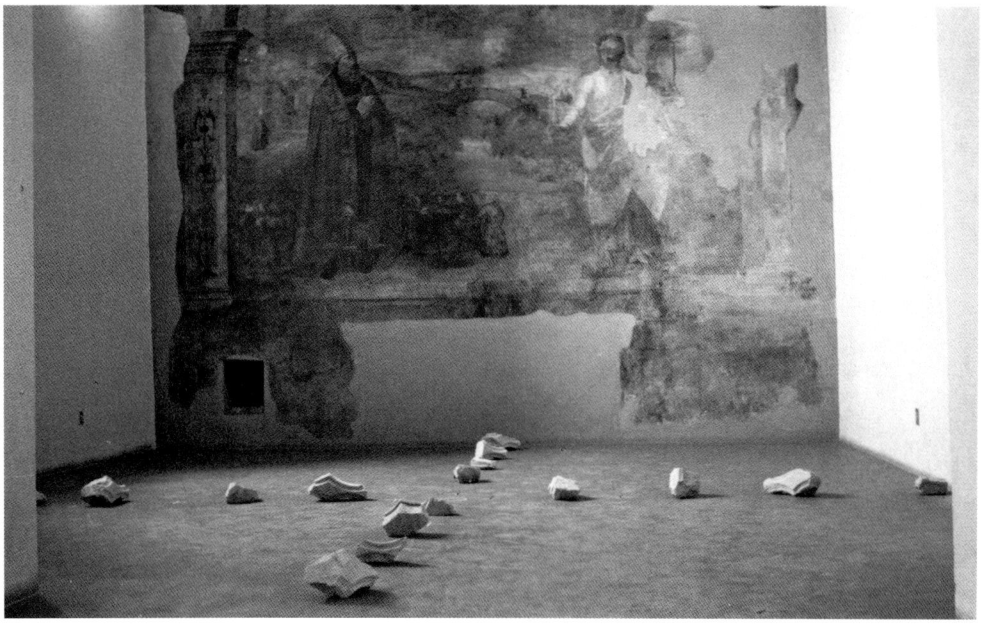

99 Mel Bochner, *Four, Four, Four, Four*, 1972. Stones and chalk on floor. Installation in Church of San Nicola in Spoleto. © Mel Bochner.

the drawing, he had not specified the kind of stone that might be used to execute the sculpture, but when he came to Spoleto, Bochner found fragments of Roman stone 'which had been dug up in an excavation and left lying in a courtyard'. According to Barry Schwabsky, he used these stones to make the piece because he was interested in the way in which Romanesque churches 'incorporate found pieces of earlier architecture, particularly fragments of the Roman ruins on whose sites they were frequently constructed'. 'I always wanted to find some way to incorporate that idea into my work . . . the idea that it would be the stone that had already been manipulated or changed or altered or even better, carved', Bochner said.[25]

So Bochner's materials had a reflexive relationship to context: the sculpture, like the church, was made out of the materials of a ruin. Nothing was added to the site, apart, that is, from 'addition', and 'nothing', for at the centre of the four axes, Bochner chalked a 'zero', and along them, various 'pluses'. The number of pluses differed on each axis, and the position of the viewer around the piece would determine how the sums were read: one axis might from one place bring to mind the idea 'three plus one', but from another place, 'one plus three'. The physical encounter with the work caused some doubt about how to read it: this much the Spoleto piece shared with other contemporaneous works. But as Schwabsky has shown, the installation was unusual for in Spoleto, the cross gained meaning from the context. While the shape was appropriate to the church's religious history, equally Bochner's use of it acknowledged the church's current deconsecrated status: the internal echo of the cross in the plus signs suggested a non-symbolic, non-sacred meaning.[26] The Spoleto installation is clearly a kind of precursor of the *Via Tasso* project, a place where the brackets to 'allusiveness' were opened. But as well as the 'cross', there is another shape lingering in Bochner's early work that pre-figures his use of the 'Star of David/six-pointed star' at Via Tasso: a swastika.

The swastika appears towards the top right of *36 Photographs and 12 Diagrams* (fig. 100). The work was made in 1966 when Bochner was invited to contribute to Virginia Dwan's show 'Scale Models and Drawings' that was planned for January 1967. At the time Bochner was arranging blocks in his studio in configurations on a seven-by-seven grid, in stacks up to four blocks high. Each configuration related to the square outline of the grid and contained a strong bilateral symmetry. Not willing to privilege any particular arrangement as definitive, Bochner decided to exhibit photographs and diagrams describing some of the configurations he had built. The images were taken by a professional photographer and, seeing them, Bochner was struck less by their documentary quality than by their difference from the diagrams. The photographs recorded shadows, and in them the blocks seemed oddly placed, because the square edges of the configurations bowed out and caved in. These quirks in the photographs resulted from the contingencies of the lens shape, the shutter speed and the aperture setting, and Bochner explored these oddities of the medium of photography in one of the two bodies of work that followed *36 Photographs and 12 Diagrams*, as Scott Rothkopf has shown.[27] In the other, he used the *36 Photographs and 12 Diagrams* to develop his approach to seriality. He took a photograph of a new arrangement of blocks, cut it up, reprinted it as a negative, and arranged the four corners in every possible configuration using the serial principles of rotation and reversal to make *Sixteen Isomorphs (Negative)* of 1967, which he later illustrated alongside works by Donald Judd, Sol LeWitt and Eva Hesse in his *Artforum* article 'The Serial Attitude'.[28]

As well as being a very generative work for Bochner, *36 Photographs and 12 Diagrams* is increasingly recognised as having a crucial place in late 1960s American art – it was one of only two photographic works recently included in a survey of minimalism.[29] Little attention has been paid to the swastika though, and in order to pursue an enquiry into the *Via Tasso* project, I now need to think it through. The swastika *fits in* with the other arrangements, but it is not predicated by them because of a serial rule. Yet we would have trouble bracketing the swastika from view, and this is only exacerbated when we discover a drawing also made in 1966 where the word 'swastika' rests uneasily between the brackets of its deliberately worded title: *Untitled (Number Drawing with Swastika)* (fig. 101). Why not just 'Number Drawing'? The title fixes our focus on one arrangement out of the ten shown on the paper. We hardly see the cross below the swastika, for example.

What exactly was Bochner doing with these swastikas? The answer lies earlier in Bochner's career. Having graduated from the Carnegie Technical Institute in 1963, Bochner enrolled in the Department of Philosophy at Northwestern University in Chicago where an old friend was writing a PhD on Heidegger. Elisio Vivas, one of the American New Critics, was teaching there – his publications then included *The Moral Life and the Ethical Life* (1950) and the edited collection *The Problems of Aesthetics* (1960). Bochner signed up for Vivas's course but 'The first day at that class, we got into this horrendous argument.'

100 Mel Bochner, *36 Photographs and 12 Diagrams*, 1966. 36 Gelatin silver prints and 12 pen and ink drawings, 20.3 × 20.3 cm each; 185.4 × 139.7 cm overall. Collection: Staedtische Galerie im Lenbachhaus, Munich. © Mel Bochner.

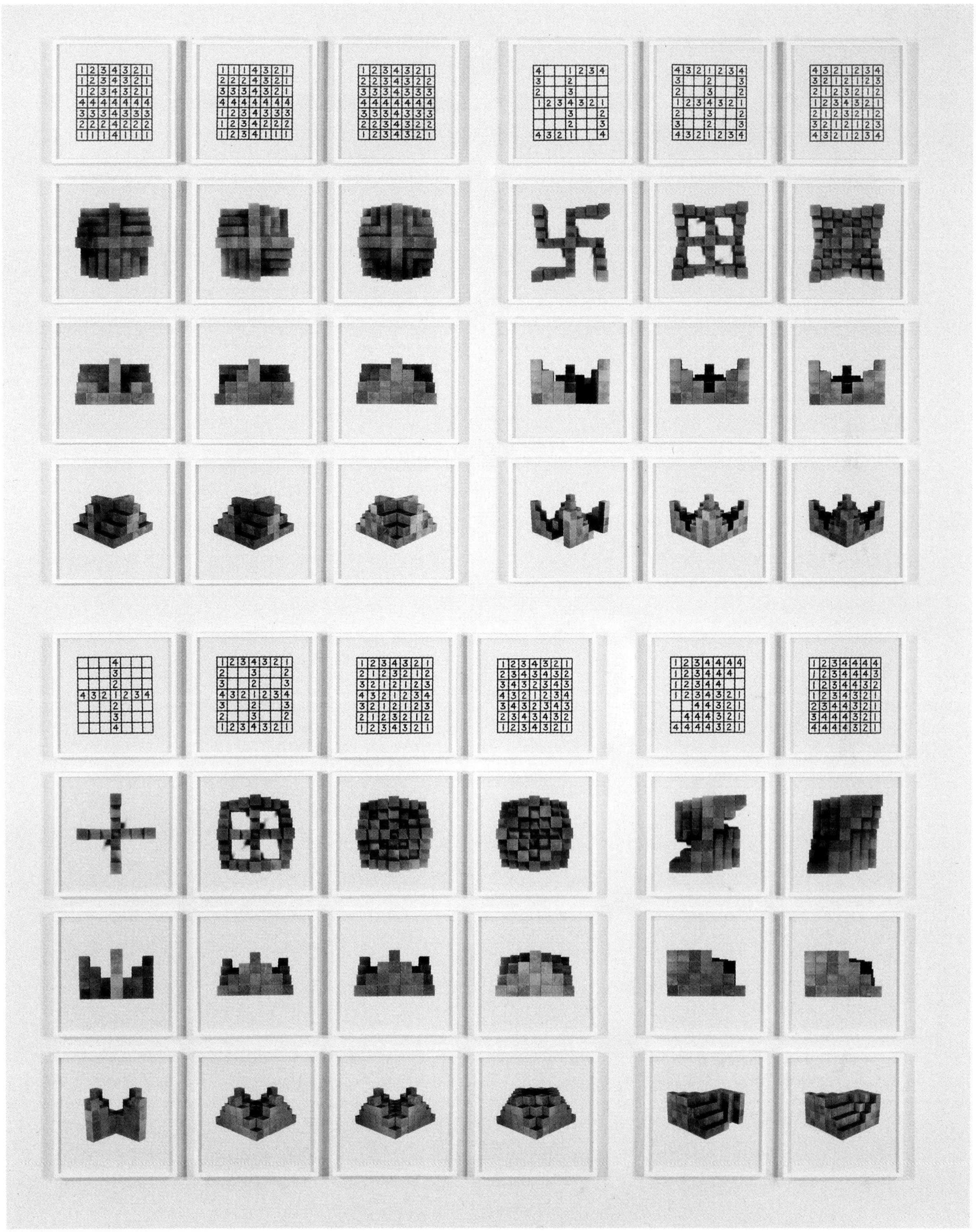

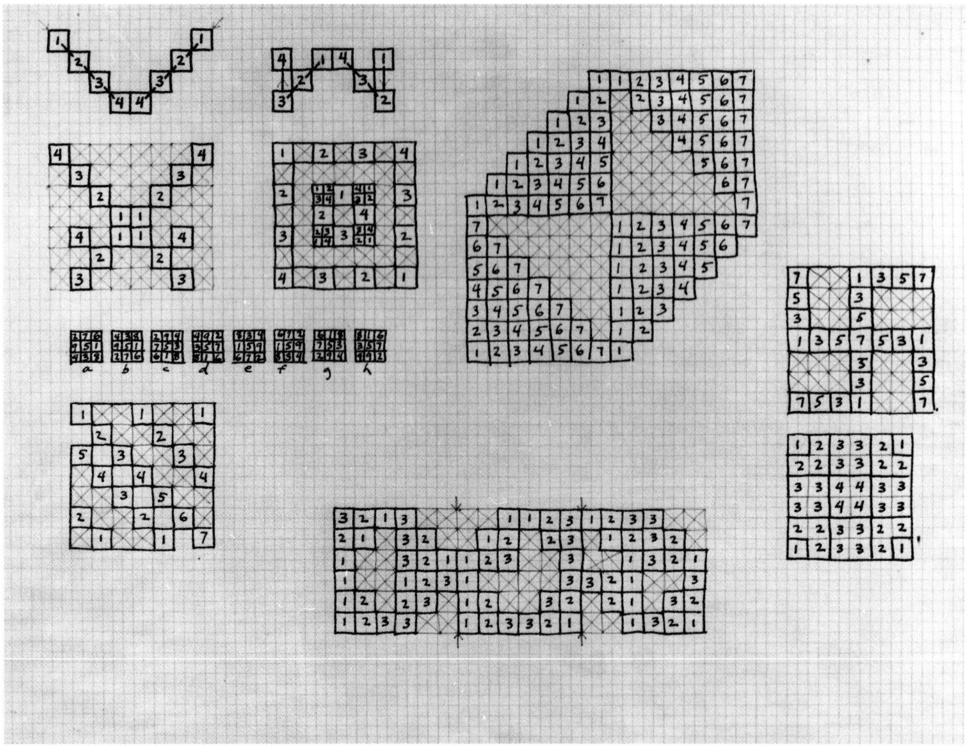

101 Mel Bochner, *Untitled (Number Drawing with Swastika)*, 1966. Colour inks on graph paper, 40.6 × 53 cm. © Mel Bochner.

> [Vivas] began the class with the premise that there is no such thing as an unethical work of art. In order to be a work of art, every work has to represent an ethical or moral position. I said I disagreed with that. He said there's no grounds on which you can possibly disagree, because you can't have a work of art that represents an odious philosophy. And I said, well, I can think of one. I brought up Leni Reifenstahl. It's very hard for me to say that that's not a work of art, and yet it represents a totally odious philosophy. He got very angry, and accused me of being a Skinhead and a neo-fascist. How could I possibly bring this up? Didn't I know what the Nazis had done? On and on and on. And I kept saying, no I'm not defending Nazism, I'm just trying to see why you would not call that an art work.

Realising that Vivas and he would never see eye to eye, Bochner left the course. In time he also left Chicago, returning to Pittsburgh and eventually coming to New York in 1964, where he found a job at an institution that would have hardly employed a neo-fascist: Bochner became a guard at the Jewish Museum.

Around two years later, Bochner came to make the two works with swastikas. He was living near the Jewish Museum, in Yorkville, an area heavily populated with immigrant Germans, and he did visit bookstores that he recalls had 'offbeat' material. The debates he had with Vivas remained pressing for him. He had come to know Stella's *Black Paintings*, and was impressed by the way that through titles like *Die Fahne Hoch!* and *Reichstag*, Stella had been able 'to import some kind of basically unethical reading into an art work'. Bochner had also met Dan Graham and Sol LeWitt, like him, young Jewish intellectuals. Recently, Graham has recalled that at that time, his friends were very interested in fascist culture and Speer and Riefenstahl. Graham explained that this interest was fostered in opposition to the politics of their parents' generation, a liberal humanism that itself gave rise to what he calls 'corporate fascism'. 'What was being used to support liberal humanistic corporate fascism was a hatred of Nazi icons,' he said.[30] According at least to Graham, it made sense that an artist would flirt with 'Nazi icons' in order to attack liberal humanism and stake a position against 'corporate fascism'. This is the principle that my enemy's enemy is my friend.[31]

Graham's fascinating recollection certainly complicates particular art historical arguments which suggest that the employment of forms associated with fascism makes art works fascist.[32] But this position does not really account for Bochner's swastika, for the artist was hardly flirting with the provocative potential of the Nazi icon, nor taking a position against liberal capitalism. Rather, for very sophisticated reasons, Bochner seems to have been pulling the terms 'Nazi' and 'icon' apart. In fact, to use different semiotic terms, he was treating a symbol as a sign. To return to the *36 Photographs and 12 Diagrams*, the initial way to understand the presence of the swastika is that it is simply a shape like the others, determined by the broad formal idea behind all the arrangements. In their presence, its identity as a 'Nazi icon' falls apart. On a Nazi flag, the swastika would have had one meaning, but here, it has another. There is nothing inherently fascistic about the shape: its meaning is determined by context. The work seems to say, at least for a moment, 'here is a swastika, but it is not a Nazi icon here.'

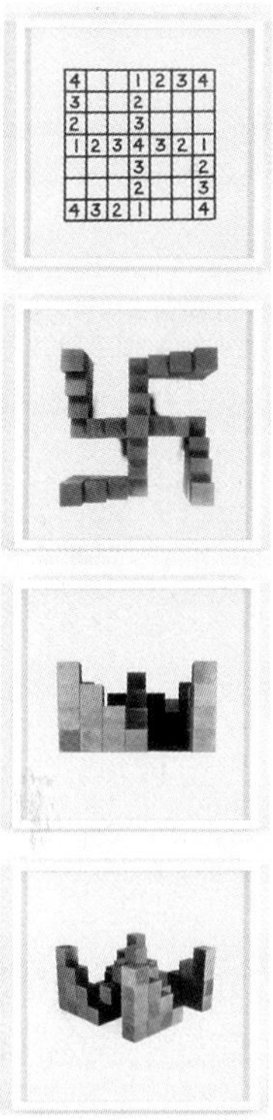

102 Mel Bochner, *36 Photographs and 12 Diagrams*, 1966. (Detail: Row D) © Mel Bochner.

Yet it would be ludicrous to suggest that the shape towards the top right is equivalent to the other shapes (fig. 102). Memories haunt it that cannot be pushed away: inevitably, that shape makes the viewer uncomfortable. Which is to say that any time you want to see it as a Nazi icon, you see it as one arrangement of wood blocks amongst others; any time you want to see it as such an arrangement, it is a Nazi icon. *36 Photographs and 12 Diagrams* invites the viewer to interpret the shape through two competing systems. The first could be named as 'formalism' and the second, 'political symbolism' – the swastika has one identity if seen as a shape amongst others, and another when seen in terms of Nazi history. The two approaches to the shape cannot be resolved: doubt as to its 'meaning' will always remain in the mind.

This analysis be rephrased to say that the swastika has an aesthetic identity (albeit in its functioning in the anti-aesthetic mode of the austere *36 Photographs and 12 Diagrams*[33]), and an ethical identity (or rather an unethical one). It can never be purely 'aesthetic' not purely 'ethical'. With this rephrasing, it is now clear how the work allegorises Bochner's new and revised position in 1966 vis-à-vis his 1963 debate with Elisio Vivas. In class in Chicago, Bochner had taken a firm line against an equally firm one. Vivas was certain that aesthetics and ethics were connected, Bochner equally sure they were not. Three years later (and notably, the year in which Adorno, in *Negative Aesthetics*, called for 'thinking against itself'), Bochner must have felt that both protagonists in the debate had been too assured. A more considered response to Nazism and the Holocaust (which lay at the root of his and Vivas's disagreement) was not certainty but doubt. Bochner was now embracing a position of doubt, and demonstrating it in and through his work.

This exploration of doubt would continue. In the *36 Photographs and 12 Diagrams*, Bochner brought 'formalism' and 'symbolism' or 'ethics' and 'aesthetics' into difficult contact (as well as 'photographs' and 'diagrams', which is the obvious pairing in the work). In later works he would create other oppositions: between language and materiality in the wall drawing *Language is not transparent* from 1970; measurement and perception in the drawing *Eye Level: Estimated/Measured* of 1971 (fig. 103); numbers and a viewer's physical orientation in *Axiom of Exhaustion* also of 1971; and mathematics and sculpture in *Meditation on a Theorem of Pythagoras* of 1972 (where Bochner discovered only 47 pebbles were required instead of 50 to describe in sculpture the equation $3^2 + 4^2 = 5^2$). In all of his works, the viewer would be made aware of the fragility of meaning as one system of knowledge contacts another so that its authority contracts before it. All of his works would instantiate doubt.

The artist's endeavour was recognised very early on when, in 1974, Rosalind Krauss wrote that: 'In describing Bochner's enterprise, then, one might say that he is constantly mapping the axiomatic principles of a particular system onto the physical facts of the visual world in order to point to the way that what appear to be the "givens" of one field crumble before the "givens" of another.'[34] Previously Krauss had differentiated Bochner from 'conceptual' artists because he refused the model of knowledge they assumed in their work – a model of knowledge as pure, transparent and certain.[35] Other historians have attended to Bochner's demonstrations of doubt by suggesting other contexts for them: Richard Field, for instance, argued that Bochner's 'devotion to uncertainty, the uncertainty of both language and experience and their interface' marked 'the real inheritance of Jasper Johns'.[36] As these art historians indicate, there are many sources for Bochner's interest in doubt, but with the debate he had engaged in with Vivas, and the *36 Photographs and 12 Diagrams* in mind, it becomes clear that another source for his thinking was his acknowledgment of a post-Holocaust epistemological crisis. Not only did this acknowledgment cause Bochner to rethink Vivas's and his own earlier certainties about the relation of ethics and aesthetics, but the certainties of any system of knowledge.

Keeping this context in mind, we can also begin to reconsider Bochner's approach to materials. In the *36 Photographs and 12 Diagrams*, the uncertainty about the meaning of the swastika is achieved in part by the fact that the swastika is only clearly represented in one photograph (which is actually only one of the three photographs that document this particular configuration of blocks). The medium intensifies the sense of its contingency: no fixed model of a swastika was ever built and instead the arrangement of blocks only formed a swastika for the duration of the photograph and from one point of view. Bochner thus embodied within the materiality of the work its underlying principle of doubt, and in later projects he found other ways to make materials underscore his devotion to uncertainty. As we have seen, he would use paper, masking tape, pennies, chalk, stones, hazelnuts and matches. These materials would only ever find temporary form in the studio or at exhibition, before being gathered together and

103 Mel Bochner, *Eye Level: Estimated/ Measured*, 1971. Pencil and red pencil on paper, 30 × 45.72 cm. Collection: Suzanne F. Cohen, Baltimore. © Mel Bochner.

probably thrown out (except for the coins). And even at exhibition, chalk could be rubbed away, stones kicked out of place.

Bochner never denied the materiality of his works, and this is another reason why he resisted labels like 'dematerialisation' or 'conceptual art'.[37] It was precisely the materiality of the work that counted (often against a system such as 'counting'), but the materials would be expedient and provisional. It was also never the case that the materials would literally disappear or (to pick up Krauss's phrase) 'crumble', in the manner of say Robert Morris's *Steam* or Eva Hesse's latex sculptures. Nor was Bochner really concerned with mobile transportability, which seems to have motivated LeWitt's Wall Drawings. In 1973 he described his materials to an Italian journal as being 'parsimonious', but this was nothing to do with the poverty of Arte Povera (where there was often a sense of the alchemical, of the possible redemption of low materials).[38] It was rather a sense of sparseness and vulnerability that was important. Bochner's was a provisional, fragile materiality that embodied doubt and his hesitancy to make anything permanent and monumental.[39] In short, Bochner's approach to materials was absolutely intertwined with his acknowledgment of a post-Holocaust cultural and epistemological landscape where all certainties were shattered.

for the jews of rome

The *Via Tasso* project can now be considered in detail once again. Initially, it had seemed that the memory of Bochner's works from the 1960s and 1970s would have caused us to hesitate in reading the 'five properties of *Via Tasso*' in the highly allusive manner

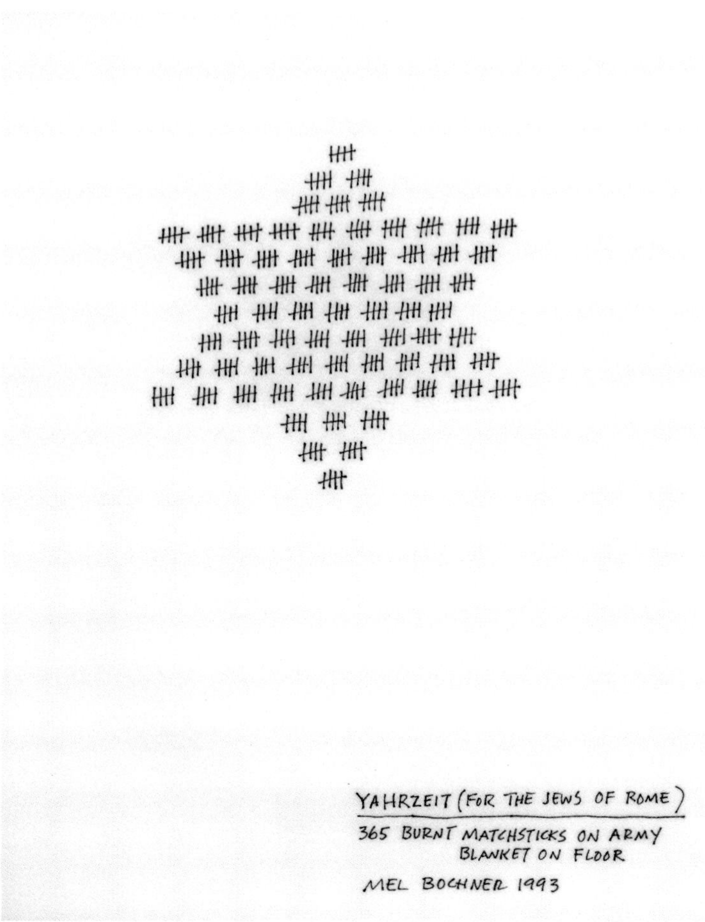

104 Mel Bochner, Drawing for *Yahrzeit (for the Jews of Rome)*, 1993. Ink on paper, 27.9 × 21.6 cm. © Mel Bochner.

described earlier. After all, Bochner had used gates, matchsticks and triangles early on without ever invoking imprisonment, spent lives or Jewish stars. But once the swastika within *36 Photographs and 12 Diagrams* has been acknowledged, there arises a more complex situation. First, it becomes clear that Bochner had been thinking about the memory of Nazism in his work long before 1993, and in fact right from the beginning of his practice. Second, the tension he created at Via Tasso (between a viewer's inclination to read the work allusively and to see it in more literal terms) appears to be one he had created and explored from that time too. And third, it becomes apparent that his commitment to instantiating the doubt that arises from this tension was in part a result of his acknowledgment and exploration of a post-Holocaust intellectual crisis. Rather than seeming an aberrant commission totally out of line with Bochner's work, *Via Tasso* now emerges as entirely appropriate for the artist's ongoing project. The Gestapo prison in Rome could be the most suitable place to demonstrate a condition of meaning and of materiality that the artist had explored through his work from the mid-1960s onwards.

Bochner's work was always a meditation on questions posed in part by the history of fascism, and so it was appropriate to a site associated with fascism's victims, but it

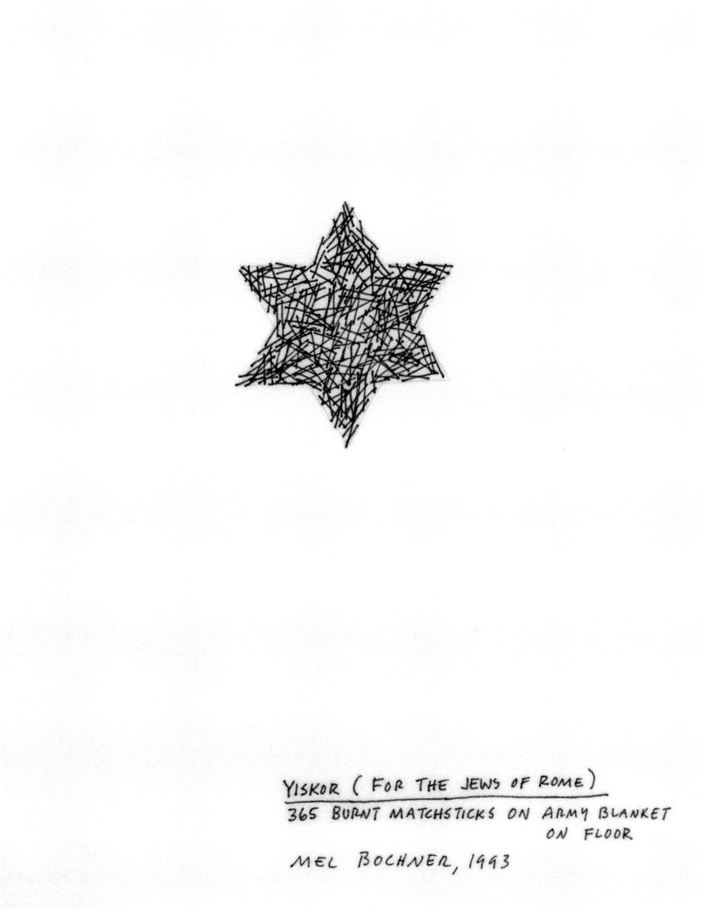

105 Mel Bochner, Drawing for *Yiskor (for the Jews of Rome)*, 1993. Ink on paper, 27.9 × 21.6 cm. © Mel Bochner.

is possible to think about the relationship between the *Via Tasso* project and its site in a more specific manner. To do so, it is necessary to look at the various textual supplements of the work. The project was accompanied by a very humble looking pamphlet with a grey card cover. At the top of the inside page, Bochner printed a suggestive quotation from the Ba'al Shem Tov, the eighteenth-century founder of Hassidism, 'Nel ricordo sta il segreto della redenzione', which could be translated as 'In remembrance lies the secrets of redemption'. This was printed without explanation, but asks the reader to question who was being remembered, and what was being redeemed. I will return to these questions soon; first I wish to look to the texts printed below the words of the Ba'al Shem Tov: the two-part titles of the three sculptures.

The tessellated star was listed as *Yisgadal (for the Jews of Rome)*; the gated one *Yahrzeit (for the Jews of Rome;* fig. 104), and the piled one *Yiskor (for the Jews of Rome;* fig. 105). Yisgadal, Yahrzeit and Yiskor are Hebrew and Yiddish words associated with Jewish mourning prayers and ceremonies. Yisgadal, which actually means 'May his name be magnified', is the first word of the Kaddish, an ancient hymn now mainly recited as a prayer in memory of the departed. Yahrzeit, which means 'year time', is the name for the anniversary of a death, an occasion on which one lights a Yahrzeit candle in memory of the departed. Yiskor is the name of the service held three times a year but most famously on Yom Kippur for the memorial of the dead. All three words are extremely familiar even to the most secular of Jews, since the last religious rituals abandoned by secular Jews tend to be the rituals of mourning. Bochner chose these titles carefully, but they did not specifically name the three individual sculptures: 'Yahrzeit' could equally have named the scattered one as the gated one, for instance. Bochner was interested in these words because in the Jewish memorial prayers to which they referred, the word 'death' is never mentioned. These words acted, as Bochner said, 'as the counterweight to the burned matchsticks imagery'. Yisgadal, Yahrziet and Yiskor indicated that the artist's interests were in celebrating the life of the sculptures' dedicatees rather than simply remembering the circumstances and places of their deaths.

These dedicatees were named in the second part of the title, '*(for the Jews of Rome)*'. This form recalled Dan Flavin's career-long use of brackets and his tendency to dedicate untitled works to friends, dealers, artists and thinkers. Before *Via Tasso*, Bochner had not used a bracketed dedication, but the show he had made with Christov-Bakargiev had itself been called *Fontana's Light: Omaggio a Lucio Fontana*. The phrase '*for* the Jews of Rome' (my emphasis) is a reminder that the work is not in any crude way 'about' them, and so should not be scrutinised for a portrayal or representation of Roman Jewish life, but at the same time, it announces that Bochner was not making this work as a generalised response to the Holocaust and to the kind of violence perpetrated in prisons and camps such as the Via Tasso. Many of the allusions I explored earlier were appropriate in such general ways to the setting of a Nazi prison (for instance, Jews across Europe had been made to wear the yellow star, and all victims of the Holocaust might have been invoked by the 'burnt offering' of the matchsticks), but in two important respects, the *Via Tasso* work addressed its specific dedicatees.

The first way in which it did this was by acknowledging, rather than denying, the peculiar political history of the Italian Jewish community. When first approached about the *Via Tasso* commission, Bochner began to research the history of the Italian Jewish community by reading Alexander Stille's book *Benevolence and Betrayal: Five Italian Jewish Families Under Fascism*, and had learnt that one in every three Jewish adults had been members of the fascist party. Fascist Jews saw absolutely no conflict between their religion and their nationalist political allegiance, and their conflicts instead were with Italian Zionists who undermined their claim that Judaism and Italian nationalism were compatible.[40] Mussolini's policies did not include racial laws until he faced pressure from Germany in 1938, and even then fascist Jews continued to be loyal to Il Duce, trying to prove their allegiance by burning down the headquarters of the Zionist press.

In his introduction, Stille had described the pressures placed on him *not* to write on Jewish fascism and his decision, despite these pressures, to go ahead with his research. Though the invading Germans made no distinction between fascist and anti-fascist Jews, during the process of *his* research, Bochner might have also felt that the history of the Italian Jews set particular challenges to representation: could the Italian victims of Nazism be remembered if the fascist sympathies of members of this community were simply brushed aside? Fascism had employed symbols like no prior political force, the very term 'fascism' deriving from symbol of the party (the fasces is 'the ancient Roman symbol of imperial authority' – 'a bundle of wheat with an axe emerging from the top'[41]). Unlike other artists who in their confrontations with the Holocaust refused to deploy symbols at all (recall Louis Kahn resisting pressures to turn his *Memorial* into a collection of symbols), Bochner employed the symbol of the Jewish star in a blatant way, even if, as I have shown, his earlier work put some pressure on the reading of the star as a symbol and not a shape. By making use of the star, Bochner managed in a canny way to acknowledge Italian Jewish fascism, but at the same time, this was the only symbol that united Italian Jews – the one chosen as their badges by their Nazi oppressors.

Bochner thus avoided the easier amnesiac option of disavowing the complex political affiliations of the Italian Jewish community, but we should recall that his work was not dedicated to the Jews of Italy, but more specifically to the Jews of Rome. The Roman Jews were distinguished from the other Italian communities not by their politics (for in Rome, too, there were fascists and anti-fascists) but by their economic situation. Jews in Ferrara, Turin and Genoa were assimilated, affluent professionals; Roman Jews were 'the poorest, the least educated, and the most insular in Italy'. Bochner would have learnt this from Stille's book, which had been divided into chapters about Jewish families in these four cities.[42] Right up to the thirties, Stille writes, 'The families of the [Roman] ghetto were poor and numerous, often living six or seven people to a room . . . The majority of the city's Jews remained rooted in or near the old ghetto and continued to scratch out a living as itinerant peddlers, rag pickers, salesmen, tailors and shopkeepers.'[43] Stille researched and described the fate of the Di Veroli family, whose poverty worsened after 1938, when the new racial laws caused Giacomo di Veroli to shut the fabric store he had set up some years before. 'Just as he had done some forty years earlier,' Stille wrote, 'Giacomo took to the streets with needles, thread, pins, ribbons, buttons, and thimbles, the instruments of the tailor's trade, on which Jews of the ghetto had depended for centuries.' The situation deteriorated in 1940 when the withdrawal of the peddling licence terminated the already meagre income of his and other Roman Jewish families.

Needles, thread, pins, ribbons, buttons, thimbles; chalk, nuts, pennies, stones, matches. Naming the materials of Giacomo di Veroli's trade and Mel Bochner's sculptures, it is finally clear how the *Via Tasso* work suited its Roman Jewish dedicatees. Bochner's materials had always been parsimonious, but at Via Tasso the humility of his sculptures were absolutely fitting to the memory of the historical impoverishment of the Jews of Rome.

'In remembrance lies the secrets of redemption.' If it is now clear how the works specifically remembered the Jews of Rome, it is equally evident that Bochner avoided the redemptive language of other Holocaust memorials: this was not a work of light and beauty, but of austerity and darkness. The artist did not presume he could redeem the deaths of the Jews of Rome, so what, then, was being saved? Perhaps Bochner used the words of the Ba'al Shem Tov to think about the future as well as the past. Christov-Bakargiev had initiated the *Via Tasso* project against the context of rising neo-fascism – perhaps, Bochner suggested, through the remembrance of the Jews of Rome, the present might be redeemed.

the story of the blankets

One of the features of the *Via Tasso* works that I have not discussed is their supports – the 'army blankets' on top of which the matches rested. There was a practical reason to use some kind of support for the sculptures: the Museo Storico della Liberazione di Roma had a kind of salami marble floor with flecks of dark and light stone, and the matches, had they been placed directly on top of it, would have been rendered invisible. The blankets thus acted as a ground against which the matches could be seen clearly, but a tablecloth or towel would have served the purpose adequately enough, and Bochner had initially considered using paper and even canvas, rejecting these supports because they would have brought in problematic references to other mediums of art. Eventually, he decided upon using army blankets (which he found in the Army and Navy store on Canal Street in New York) because their materials would add another allusive facet to the work. They would suggest the kind of blankets the prisoners might have been apportioned in the prison; rough replacements for the smooth sheets of their homes.

But when the exhibition opened, Bochner discovered that the blankets he had brought with him evoked quite different memories.

> An elderly woman came up to me in tears. A woman who lived across the street, who had lived across the street for seventy years. She said she hadn't seen a blanket like that since after the war, when the American army had distributed blankets to everyone since nobody had coats. Right after the war everyone was making their coats out of these blankets. So the whole thing flooded back to her – the way in which the blankets had been part of her life and what they meant in the war. Protection, the American army, warmth, security, the end of the war: all those references that I could have never anticipated.

A simple cloth placed on the ground to evoke wartime discomforts reminded one viewer of post-war protection: the 'story of the blankets' exemplifies what I have been arguing about *Via Tasso* – that it was not only a work whose suggestions were incredibly diverse but one whose competing meanings were intentionally insecure. Bochner made the sculptures knowing that they would generate allusions both to the prison setting and to their dedicatees, but he also knew that the sculptures could be read simply as literal arrangements of plain materials. The moment any one set of meanings seemed stable, other suggestions would compete with them to unfix them. And if the sculptures were taken to refer beyond their materials and shapes to events and individuals and experiences, Bochner also knew (as he would have been reminded by the elderly woman) that there was no way to predict the flow of these references. If it can be said, after all this, that meaning at Via Tasso was a fragile thing, it is also clear how the blankets helped to express fragility in a material way: they tempted one to imagine pulling them away from the floor, so that in one instant the fragile forms of the sculptures would be ruined, and matches would be sent cascading around the cells.

I have explored the origins of Bochner's explorations of doubt and fragility already and the way in which the *Via Tasso* project extended these explorations: if early on in his thinking, the memory of the Holocaust had prompted the artist to question the authority of any system of thought, addressing this memory directly at Via Tasso meant making a work whose suggestions were delicate rather than authoritative, a work that generated allusions even as it undid them. While it is possible that Bochner would always have created a work of material and interpretative fragility no matter where or when he had been asked to address the Holocaust, I believe there is more to say about the appropriateness of the fragility of the *Via Tasso* work in relation to its context.

First, the fragility represented the situation of Holocaust memory in this precise place and time. While by the early 1990s, few in New York would have contested the events of the Holocaust (even if many contested its implications) the same was not always the case in Europe, where neo-fascist political tendencies still erupted. Second (and as I have intimated earlier), the fragility of the work was appropriate to the setting: Bochner did not show this work in a New York gallery or an American Holocaust museum, but at a place of former suffering, and the humble nature of the sculptures deferred to their site. Finally, the fragility of the work was appropriate to the brevity of its existence. Bochner was not asked to create a monument that would last for generations, but to make a short intervention. Rather than treating the commission as if it called for a permanent addition to the prison, Bochner acknowledged through the materiality of his sculptures the brief life of the installation. The sculptures had been constructed (though not conceived) in a matter of hours, and could be cleared away in minutes. In many ways, the project was all the more powerful because it was short-lived and because its brevity was materially expressed.

Around the same time that Bochner worked on the project, Sol LeWitt, Joel Shapiro, Richard Serra and Ellsworth Kelly were installing works in the United States Holocaust Memorial Museum in Washington D.C. Some of these artists were personal friends of Bochner's, and all had shown their work in various contexts alongside his over the decades before, since like Bochner, these artists were, in different ways, associated with the history of abstraction in the United States. There were some other connections between the *Via Tasso* and Washington projects: like Bochner, the four artists were approached to make works for the setting rather than nominating themselves. And like Bochner, they confronted the memory of the Holocaust at a relatively advanced stage of their career, looking back to the language of their past work to forge their responses. But in every other way, the Rome and Washington commissions were dissimilar: where Bochner confronted a site touched by Nazism, the four artists worked in the context of a brand new American museum. Where Bochner was asked to create a temporary installation, the four were asked for permanent works, and where in Via Tasso Bochner could dedicate work to the small and ancient community of the Jews of Rome, in Washington, the artists had to confront the entirety of the Holocaust as documented in the myriad photographs, films, maps, artefacts and wall panels all around.

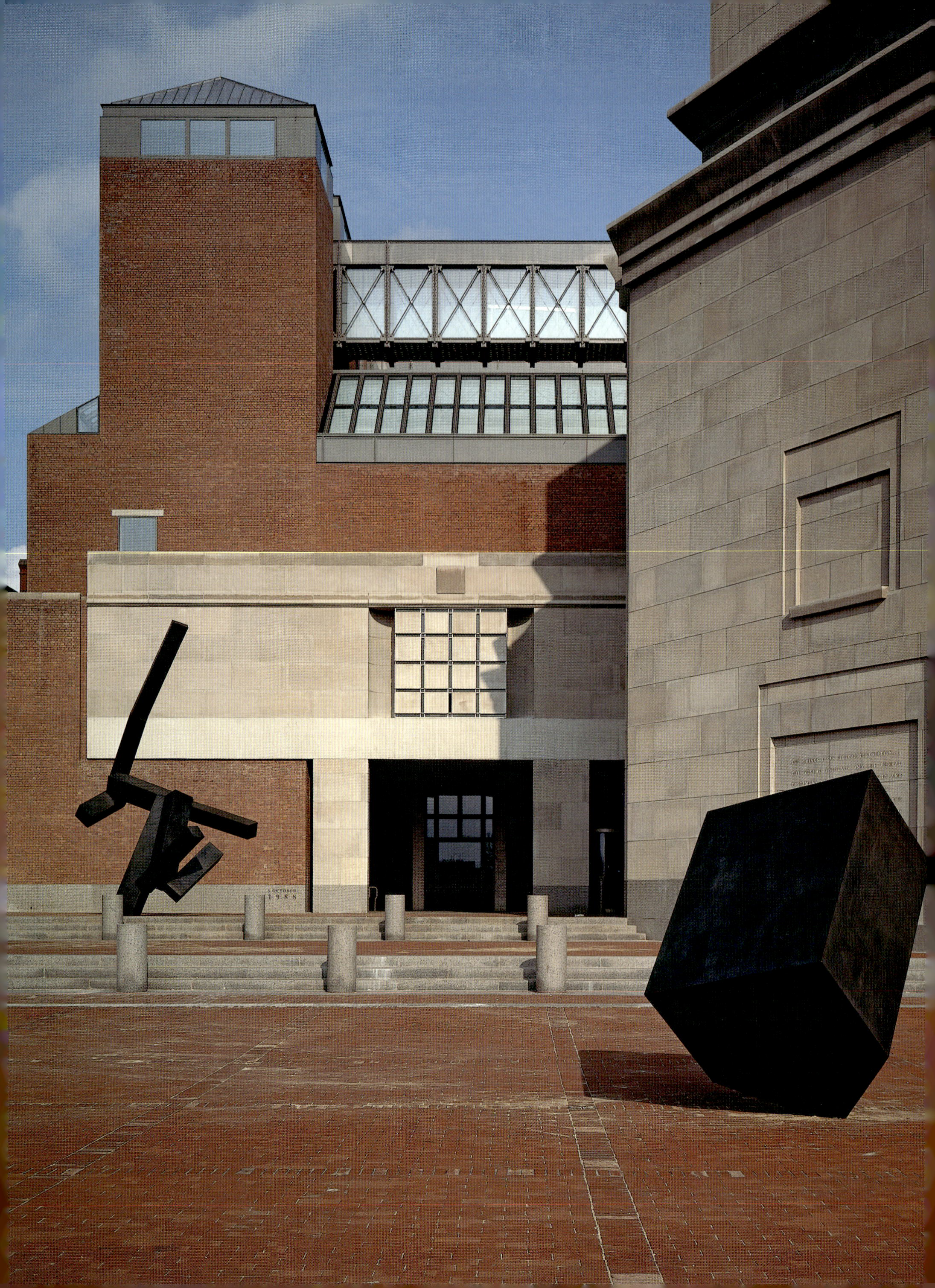
OCTOBER
1 9 8 8

eight

the commissions in the united states holocaust memorial museum

the inauguration of the united states holocaust memorial museum[1]

On 22 April 1993, President Clinton, Elie Wiesel and numerous other dignitaries gathered in Washington D.C. to open the United States Holocaust Memorial Museum (USHMM; fig. 107). The inauguration was the culmination of fifteen years of research, fundraising, planning and building: Wiesel had been appointed by President Carter back in 1978 to head the 'Commission on the Holocaust' and to make recommendations as to how the Holocaust should be represented and commemorated by the state.[2] The eventual opening of the USHMM confirmed the centrality of the Holocaust in American civic life: it was an immense museum right on the Mall, set to draw millions of visitors, nothing like the smaller memorials discussed with regard to Kahn at the beginning of chapter four, all of which, despite their formal differences, had been envisioned for sites on the peripheries of New York.

106 Joel Shapiro, *Loss and Regeneration*, 1993. Bronze, 784.9 × 538.5 × 233.7 cm (figure); 274.3 × 233.7 × 233.7 cm (house). Collection USHMM. © Joel Shapiro.

The USHMM was an institution with many components. It occupied a new building specially designed by James Ingo Freed of Pei, Cobb and Freed, situated between 14th and 15th Streets (fig. 108), with the latter entrance looking straight onto the Washington Monument.[3] The building included a massive atrium, named 'The Hall of Witness' (fig. 109), two theatres for screenings and symposia, and a temple-like memorial space, 'The Hall of Remembrance', a structure built to recall the verticality of the Polish wooden synagogues once so dear to Frank Stella.[4] Most visitors would spend the bulk of their time in the suites of exhibition galleries reached from the Hall of Witness by a series of lifts, spiralling downwards over three floors. Here, the history of the Holocaust was represented through narrative displays of artefacts, films and photographs. The USHMM also featured an archive and research centre, and organised a 'Committee on Conscience' to advise the government of the United States about future genocidal issues. Finally, the museum included four art installations, the result of an Art for Public Spaces Programme (AFPSP). During the years of its formation, new works had been commissioned by Joel Shapiro, Richard Serra, Ellsworth Kelly and Sol LeWitt. These were positioned outside the 15th Street entrance, inside the 'Hall of Witness' and at two different points between the three floors of the narrative exhibition. If the foundation of the museum had demonstrated a shift in the civic attitude towards the representation of the Holocaust, this programme indicated an equally massive change in the preparedness of institutions to consider the possible relationship between abstraction and the Holocaust. I have already commented on the phenomenon of curators commissioning abstract artists to make works for Holocaust sites in relation to Mel Bochner's project in Rome: the Washington commissions were even more startling, for here, artists were being asked to make works to be shown in perpetuity, right at the centre of the largest Holocaust museum on the American continent, and right alongside other institutions devoted exclusively to art where their work would be regularly displayed.

In recent years, the USHMM has drawn a number of critical responses, some by writers who have attended to the way in which the museum frames the Holocaust through the story of the American liberation of the camps,[5] some by writers who have doubted it can fulfil its aims to 'improve' visitors through the learning about the Holocaust,[6] but at the time of its opening, the USHMM was positively reviewed. Nevertheless, right from the start the art programme drew significant criticism, and from diverse quarters. Michael Kimmelman attacked the commissions on the front page of *The New York Times*, arguing that 'no artwork related to the Holocaust can equal in its visceral impact the sight of an actual railroad car on which Jews were transported to Auschwitz'.[7] Paul Richards, writing in *The Washington Post*, started his article 'Obscene Pleasures: Art Amongst the Corpses' with the line 'There is art in the USHMM. There needn't be.' The art, he continued, was 'unnecessary. No, it's worse than unnecessary. It distorts and misguides'. Richards complained that the works diluted the 'central theme' of the museum and that if such dilutions were needed, it would have been better to have included representations of slavery and other historical atrocities instead.[8] These critical reports were exceptionally visible, but in private the art programme caused problems for the institution too: one donor to the USHMM withdrew support when she learnt of the commissions. ' "Distractions" of any kind have no place in such a building', she wrote. The presence of art reminded her of the orchestras playing Mozart in the camps.[9]

For these opponents of the AFPSP, the very presence of any kind of art was distracting, diluting and disrespectful. Other figures complained not so much about the programme as about the choice of *abstract* works. Herzl Emmanuel wrote to the museum's chairman insisting that: 'There is no way this kind of purist art can logically cohabit with the Museum's staggering array of artefacts.'[10] Mark Strauss, a survivor who had offered his own work to the museum, 'appeal[ed] to the public, to

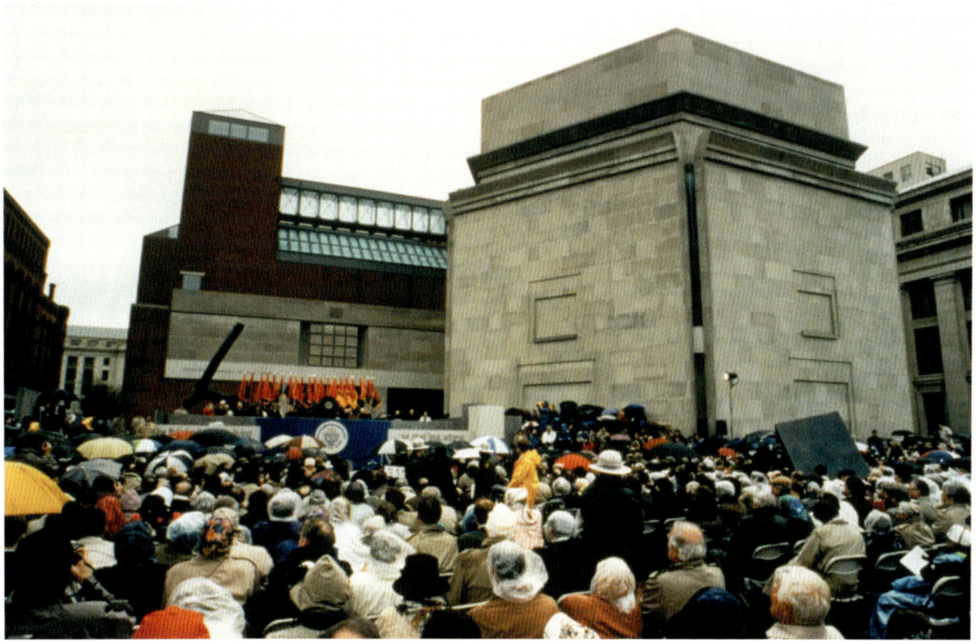

107 The inauguration of the United States Holocaust Memorial Museum, 22 April 1993.

whom the Museum belongs, to see "white-on-white" rectangles and other minimalist nothings and decide for themselves whether these have relevance to Holocaust [sic] or any meaning at all.' He later took his complaints to a congressman and a senator.[11] Related criticisms were made in the press: Ken Johnson, writing in *Art in America*, posited that abstraction, 'a mode of art that normally focuses on formal, perceptual or immediately cognitive concerns may not be the most appropriate approach for creating a genuinely convincing memorial'.[12] Johnson wondered why the commissioners had not selected Barbara Kruger or Hans Haacke (artists 'who have combined interests in issues of politics and morality with innovative ideas about the possibilities of public art') or Christian Boltanski or Anselm Kiefer (artists who he said 'have directly addressed the Holocaust in their work'). Not really thinking whether the work of artists such as Boltanski might be rendered invisible amongst the displays of photographs in the museum, and not knowing that there had in fact been discussion at an early point of inviting Boltanski to help in the design of such displays,[13] Johnson put the choices of Shapiro, Serra, Kelly and LeWitt down to the lamentable caution of the commissioners. But by the time Johnson's article appeared, six months after the opening of the USHMM, it was increasingly clear that whether or not he was right in this last respect, the caution of the commissions had not managed to stave off controversy and complaint.

In these various criticisms of the art programme, writers, whether they were donors, survivors or art critics, appeared to want to protect the memory of the Holocaust from the art in the museum, which they considered to be irreverent and irrelevant. But another criticism of the art programme could be formed by asking whether abstrac-

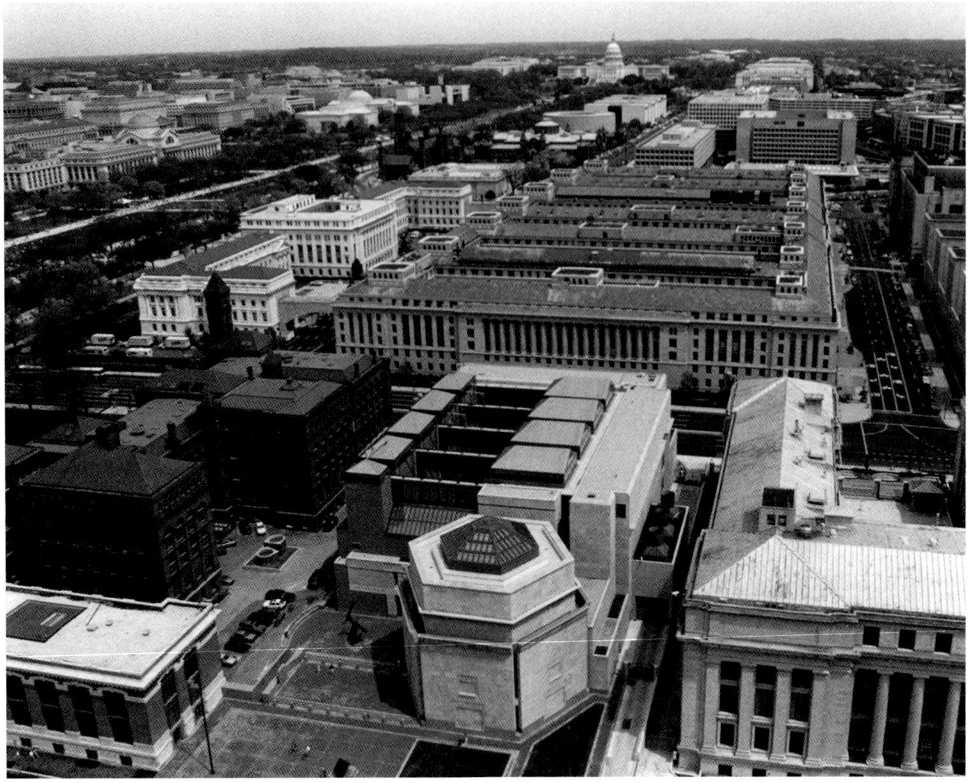

108 Aerial view of the USHMM looking from 15th Street in the direction of the U.S. Capitol.

tion itself was not co-opted in the USHMM. This argument would protect 'abstraction' as much as 'the Holocaust'. The very same year as Kelly, LeWitt, Shapiro and Serra were commissioned, Rosalind Krauss (who has written monographic essays on the latter three[14]) argued that the display of art from the 1960s in the Panza collection amounted to 'an historical recoding of Minimalism in the direction of privacy, interiority, spirituality . . . an act of redefinition [which] fails to do justice to the aspiration of the sixties.'[15] She has not addressed the Washington commissions, but her comments from this time might also speak to the situation there. Were ' "white-on-white" rectangles and other minimalist nothings' too easily introduced into the ceremonial and memorial spaces of the institution? Were art works *used* to create space for spiritual reflection; to nuance the moods of spectators as they passed through the exhibitions; to condense narratives into easily consumable symbolic forms; or even to uplift viewers by reminding them of the creativity of the human spirit? If so, was abstraction asked to function in ways that these artists had never expected, and even in ways they had previously resisted?

So the study of the USHMM commissions begins with two related questions: to what extent were the criticisms of the art programme justified? And to what extent did the programme represent a co-option of abstraction and a negation of its once radical aspirations? These questions will only be answered by thinking about the individual works

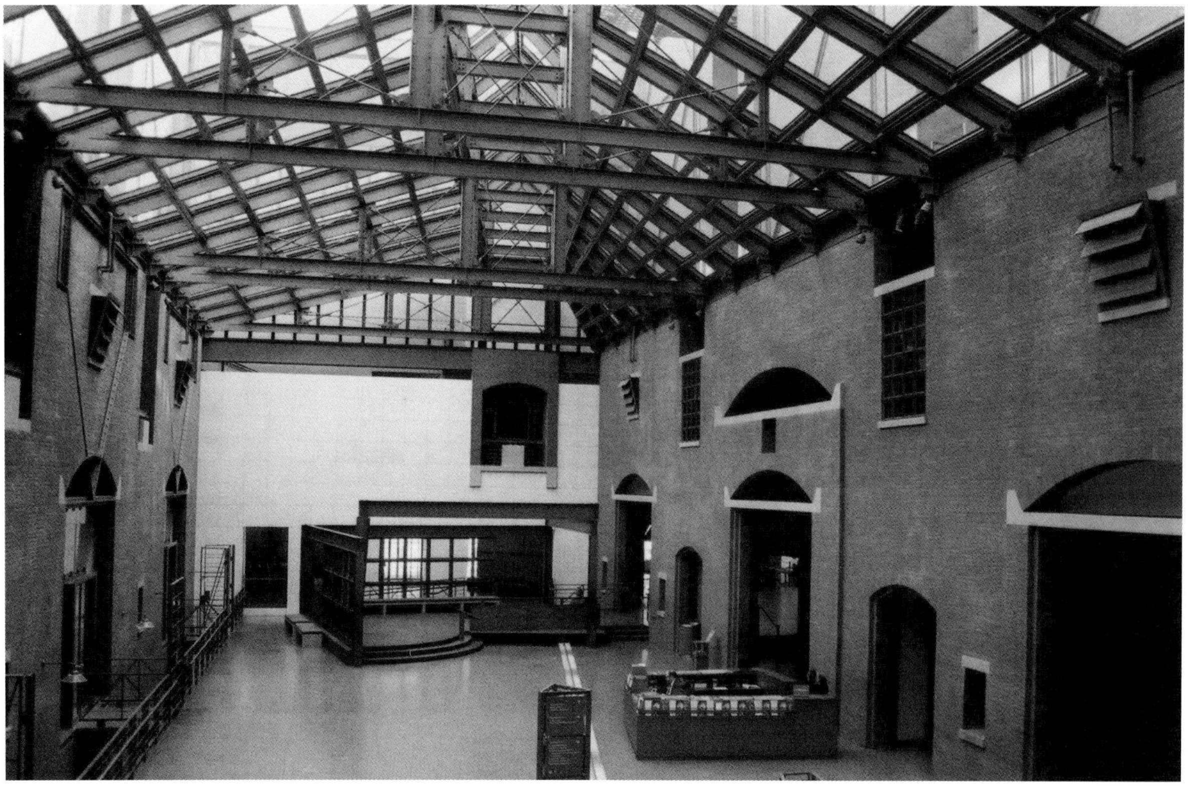

109 James Ingo Freed, The Hall of Witness in the USHMM.

in some detail and by attending to their placement in the contexts of the museum's architecture and displays, but first it is necessary to scrutinise the commissioning process and to see how works by these four artists came to be integrated into the fabric and exhibitions of the United States Holocaust Memorial Museum.

the beginnings of the art for public spaces programme

From reading some of the criticisms that were made of the art programme in the USHMM, it might seem that four well-known American male abstract artists had been brought in at the last minute to decorate the museum. It might also seem that contemporary art was never supposed to have been displayed there. Both impressions are wrong. The commissions of LeWitt, Kelly, Serra and Shapiro took place gradually through carefully planned processes. And long before their names were ever mentioned in connection with the museum, there had been plans for the Washington Holocaust memorial, in whatever shape it would take, to include contemporary art.

Indeed at this point, it should be pointed out that the final outcome of Carter's 'Commission on the Holocaust' – a new building housing a narrative exhibition – was by no means determined from the beginning of the process in 1978. There was no indication early on that a museum would be formed, nor that an architect would be approached to construct a new building, nor even that the memorial would be housed in a building. Between Wiesel's appointment by Carter in May 1978 and his report in September of the following year, he approached various figures to sound out what shape a memorial might take. Julius Schatz of the American Jewish Congress (who had been involved in Louis Kahn's commission, and who would later play a role in the AFPSP) conceived the institution at this moment as a park rather than a building. 'In the park', he wrote, 'I see a place of public gathering, exhibition and performance, where the year around art may be displayed, music, drama and dance performed, and symposia held in memory of those who fell.'[16] So even before the notion of a museum and building took shape, there was the aspiration that art should be part of the memorial.

When Wiesel reported back to Carter, the 'park' proposal was not carried forward. The idea of a building had taken shape, and though no specific mention was made of the display of art, Wiesel did recommend that the 'museum must be of symbolic and artistic beauty, visually and emotionally moving in accordance with the solemn nature of the Holocaust', and that the 'museum would present the Holocaust through pictorial accounts, films and other visual exhibits within a framework that is not merely reportorial but analytic, encouraging reflection and questioning.'[17] These suggestions clearly paved the way for the later commission of art as a complement to the architecture, countering the more straightforwardly narrative or 'reportorial' components of the museum.

By 1979, it was also clear that the museum would be situated in Washington D.C. Initially, there had been some debate over the different merits of a site in the capital versus one in New York, the city with the largest Jewish population in the country.[18] Though the final location of the museum between 14th and 15th Street was only determined in 1981, and though James Ingo Freed was only introduced to the project five years later, staff involved in the institution's 'Committee for Collections and Acquisitions' began through the early 1980s to collect artefacts for eventual display in whatever architectural container would emerge. As they did, they also began to archive art proposals in a registry of Holocaust-related art. This registry would serve as a possible source of work for eventual inclusion in the museum, and as an educational resource for Holocaust art researchers. Susan Morganstein, Director of Special Exhibitions from 1986, had a key interest in visual arts, and began to develop the AFPSP. Quite early on, she faced a problem: as well as acquiring works made in the camps, without invitation the museum was being donated art works made subsequently by survivors and other artists. Whereas the first kind of works were to be accepted by the museum as artefacts without consideration of aesthetic quality, it was less clear how to respond to the second grouping. These works presented 'a unique and difficult dilemma. Are we to treat these works strictly as historical records, as memory pieces, aesthetically, or by all the above criteria?'[19]

This discussion took place as museum staff began to consider how and where art works would be placed in the museum building. The sense of what this building would be like was emerging by 1988 as James Ingo Freed began to present his plans. Having worked with artists in previous projects, Freed was enthusiastic about including art works in the building. Though his ideas about the role of art changed over time, in 1989 he indicated that he saw art works as having a ceremonial function in the museum – they might be focal points in wreath laying ceremonies, for instance.[20] Committee minutes from this moment suggest Freed's predilection for overtly symbolic art ('he foresaw something representative of life, such as a tree of life'), but also indicate that 'he was not necessarily recommending representational works'.[21] Freed's ideas about the function of art works should be understood in the context of his ideas about the museum's architecture: the building would communicate through several means at once. As much as he proposed overtly referential uses of architectural structures (such as the 'watch towers') and materials (such as red brick strapped by iron – a feature he related to the ovens in the death camps), Freed also hoped to communicate through less symbolic and referential registers, creating awkward atmospheres with space and light, as with the twisted skylight in the Hall of Witness. Freed also considered very carefully the relationship the building would have with its neo-classical architectural context, in some ways unifying the building with those surrounding it, and in some ways disturbing the unity of these streets. Many different modes of architectural communication were proposed at once, each offered as a possible response to the task of building a Holocaust memorial museum. So if it seems that Freed's sense of the symbolic and ceremonial role of art in the museum was initially quite traditional, it should be recalled that he considered the communicative potential of space and materials in other more radical ways at the very same time.

By July 1989, seven places within Freed's building were proposed as possible sites for art works.[22] Over the following year, in order to decide how to proceed, members of the Committee for Acquisitions and Collections conducted research on various models of public art acquisitions and commissions, such as those used by other federal institutions, Holocaust museums and art museums.[23] At the same time, the Committee formed a 'Subcommittee for Art for Public Spaces' to address the question of 'Art for Public Spaces' exclusively. The subcommittee began to compile long lists of possible candidates, and though it is clear from these lists that the artists were to be well-known figures differentiated in terms of stature from amateur artists such as some of those who had donated works to the museum as mentioned above, there was neither any consensus at this point that all chosen works would be newly made, nor even that they would be by living artists: Louise Nevelson and Eva Hesse were discussed.[24] While it was a general premise that a new work of art would only be commissioned if the artist had previously shown some interest in addressing the Holocaust,[25] no clear distinctions were made at this point between modes of address: Jim Dine, George Segal, Anselm Kiefer, Christian Boltanski, Louise Fishman and Jonathan Borofsky were mentioned alongside Serra and Shapiro, whose names were actually removed from the long list at one meeting.[26]

As well as naming possible artists, members of this subcommittee also discussed their ideas about the purpose of the art programme, offering different perspectives from Freed's. In March 1990, Hadassah Rosensaft, a survivor, hoped for a narrative work of sculpture that would 'come from the heart and express emotion'.[27] Anita Reiner 'suggested that when the artists were selected, the Committee should meet with them, tell them stories, and they could translate the stories into art. She recommended deleting Richard Serra from the list.'[28] The museum director Jeshajahu Weinberg disagreed with her general approach: 'there will be a lot of narrative in the Museum', he said, arguing that art was needed 'to balance the narrative – a counterpoint. . . . We shouldn't rule out non-figurative art just because some people would not understand it – that it would still have emotional impact.'[29] As these comments suggest, the discussions about artists raised the question of accessibility, but it was by no means evident that abstract works would be more or less accessible choices. One committee member suggested that children 'react to abstract art',[30] while another argued that 'most of the visitors to the Museum would not know a lot about abstract art', and asked 'if the Museum wanted to speak to 1% of the visitors or 99%'.[31] The notion of percentages was raised once more at a later meeting on 16 May. Ms. Lauder, underlining the fact that 'this project will be *very* visible', stressed that 'we must aim toward the top 10% of museum visitors'.[32]

This sounds like an elitist remark, but rather than read it as such, we might consider this 'top 10%' as those who would spend time in the museum rather than rushing through it as one more tourist stop in the mall, and who would be open and sensitive to all its eventual components – from gruesome photographic images, to precise architectural details, to art works. Nevertheless, though they were not thinking about catering for art critics and art-world insiders, it is clear from the various minutes that the museum staff and committee members felt considerable cultural pressure to acquire the work of artists that could equally be included in the collections of the nearby National Gallery and Hirshhorn. As Anita Reiner commented, 'we want the acquisitions for our public spaces . . . to be of a quality consistent with and equal to our neighbours.'[33] The main aim of the programme was to match the import of the institution with the serious work of serious artists, but these kinds of pressures cannot be forgotten.

In their research into equivalent commissioning processes, the members of the Committee had discovered that other institutions employed art professionals to run procedures, and independent juries to choose artists.[34] Recognising their own lack of experience in the task of commissioning or acquiring art works, and also wanting to conform to the procedures that worked well for other institutions, the staff of the USHMM began to delegate the organisation of the art programme, though of course they continued to attend all subsequent meetings.[35] The curator and consultant Nancy Rosen was appointed as an independent administrator of the programme in June 1990, with the role of mediating between the museum, the jury, and later, the artists and installation teams.[36] In the autumn, possible names for this jury were nominated and invited, including Nan Rosenthal of the Metropolitan Museum, Gary Garrels then at the Dia, and many other museum curators.[37] Ziva Amishai-Maisels was the only juror to be invited who had extensive research interests in Holocaust related art, and this suggests that the USHMM were seeking guidance from figures who had worked with living artists rather than with the subject that the museum would commemorate. Much later on, critics of the AFPSP would complain that 'this group [of curators and scholars] evidently had great powers of persuasion for they succeeded in prevailing on the committee to completely disavow their own convictions'.[38] However, while the external curators did shape the eventual commissions, they did not overturn an already coherent set of plans for the art works. As we have seen, prior to this point, there were no homogenous 'convictions' about the kind of works that would be brought into the museum. The jury was hardly a rubber stamp for the selection of abstract works. The curators Gary Garrels and Marc Rosenthal later organised major exhibitions of abstract art, but all the curators on the jury had experience working with a range of different artists.

Jeshajahu Weinberg introduced the first jury meeting on 17 April 1991. 'Art for Public Spaces was not an integral part of the story,' he said, 'but a counterpoint to the story. It was not complimentary but compatible with the character of the museum.'[39] The jury were being told that the narrative of the Holocaust would be conveyed by the exhibition displays, and not by the art work, even though some of the art work would be positioned in the midst of those displays. In order to give them a sense of these displays and of the architecture of the museum, the jury were then taken around a mock-up of the exhibition, and then around the construction site, and shown where the art works would be sited.[40] They began considering artists for each of the sites, but first an interesting general discussion took place concerning artists' nationalities. Though jurors had been told that they would be choosing artists 'without regard to religion, race or nationality',[41] an immediate debate sparked up over a possible approach to Rebecca Horn and Anselm Kiefer, whose names were on the shortlist that had been prepared for the meeting. Some members felt that nationality should not, indeed, be a factor in their considerations; others suggested the positive value of commissioning German artists. Though Kiefer was approached later and asked to propose a work for the museum (he declined to submit a proposal), a decision to restrict commissions to American artists eventually prevailed. Though this was not finally confirmed at this meeting, it was suggested here as a path of sensitivity, since any commission of a German artist was said to risk offending survivors. The eventual choice of American artists might be said to accord with the ideological character of the museum, whose displays open with an image of G.I.s liberating camps, but it would be extremely crude to suggest that LeWitt, Serra, Kelly and Shapiro were figures standing for American nationalistic ideology: when he was contacted by the USHMM, Serra had only recently published his text 'Art and Censorship', whose opening line read 'The United States government destroyed *Tilted Arc*.'[42]

the specific commissions[43]

From this point onwards, it is necessary to think about the way the individual commissions took place rather than about the programme as a whole. The jury began to consider five different locations for art works, and each involved a different process. The first site under deliberation was not, in fact, designated for an actual art work, but rather for a collaborative project. At the 15th Street end of the Hall of Witness, Freed

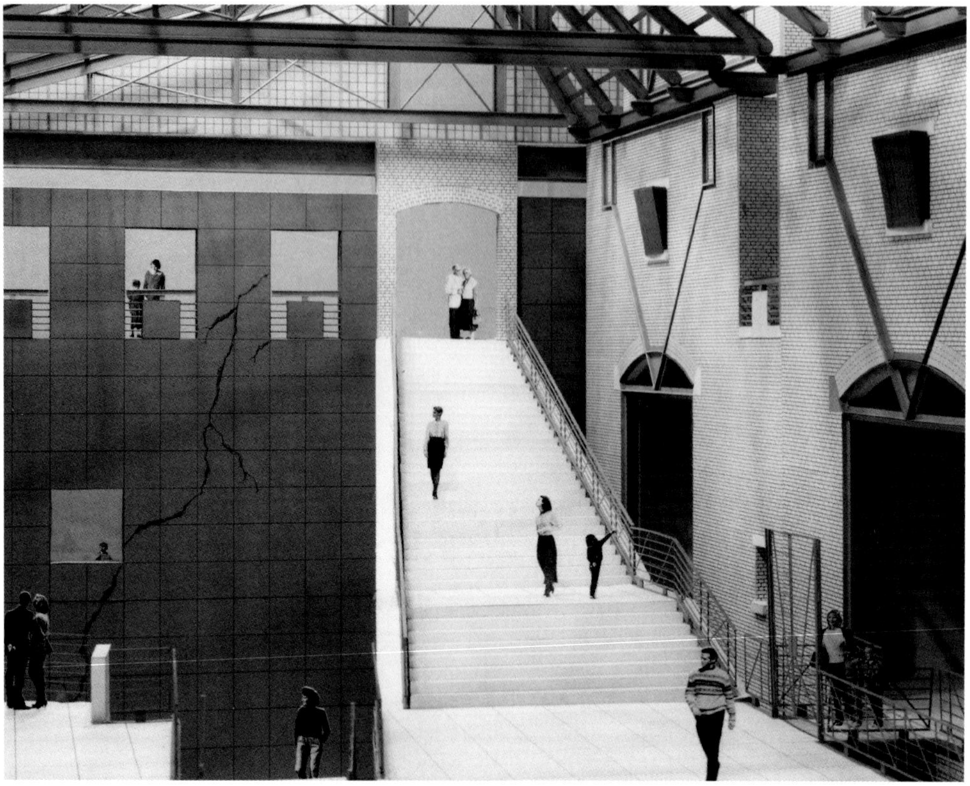

110 James Ingo Freed, sketch for The Hall of Witness at the USHMM showing 'crack' in black granite wall, 1988–90.

was building a black granite wall. From early on, he had hoped that this wall would contain a crack (fig. 110). This would be one of the more brutal metaphoric elements in the building, and Freed seems to have been quite ambivalent about it. In 1989 he had written that 'The crack in the granite wall is a bit banal. I'm bothered by the literality, but I think we have to go through with it. We intend to take hammers and go at it with them. I don't want to make a drawing. I want to go ahead and smash it.'[44] Later, not knowing how such a crack might effectively be implemented, Freed asked the jury to suggest an artist who would be contracted as a 'design consultant/collaborator'.[45] Prior to the April jury meeting, it had been decided that three names of possible 'collaborators' be proposed.[46] The jury was asked to rank these, and the highest ranked individual would be approached and invited to meet Freed. If the meeting went well, this artist would be enlisted. If not, the second preference would be invited. At the April meeting, the jury were told that 'Mr. Freed absolutely felt there had to be some depiction of moral breakdown.'[47] Hearing this, they decided first to approach Richard Serra.

Serra came down to Washington to meet Freed, despite quite a troubled history of working with architects in the city.[48] 'I don't know if I would have done it if I wasn't Jewish', he has said.[49] This project came at a moment between the artist's work on *The Drowned and the Saved* and his later participation on the proposal with Peter Eisen-

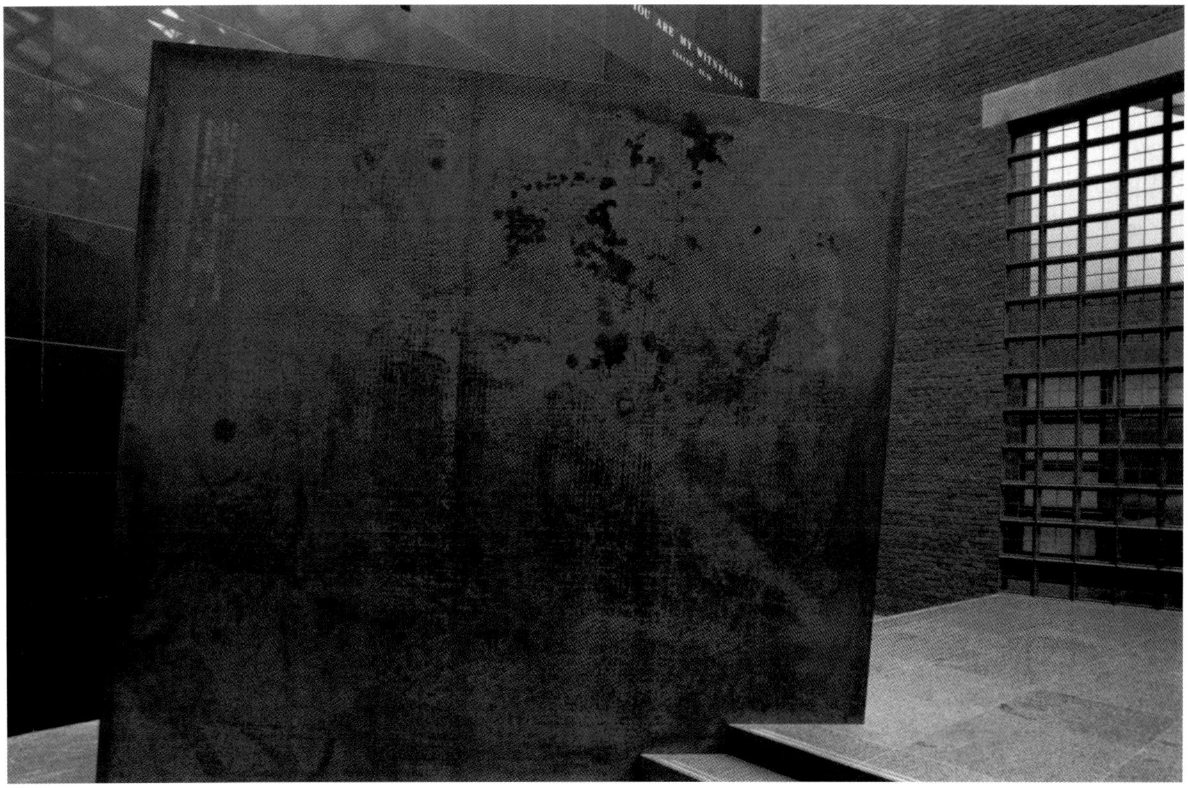

111 Richard Serra, *Gravity*, 1993. Weatherproof steel, 366 × 366 × 305 cm. Collection USHMM. © Richard Serra.

man for the Berlin Holocaust memorial. But though Serra was certainly thinking through the Holocaust and its impact on his upbringing during these years, it is still quite surprising that he accepted the approach of the USHMM jury, for his work had never deployed the kind of symbolism that Freed was seeking from the crack. Serra did not feel that he could provide the technical solutions sought ('I didn't really understand how you could, without cracking the piece after it was up the wall, construct a crack and then put it together'[50]), but more importantly, he was sceptical about the project: 'It was going to be an artifice that would not ring true in terms of what it was supposed to symbolically represent. Nor did I think that you could make a symbol or a sign for the memorialisation of the Holocaust by making a crack in the wall. It just seemed to be a pseudo-art convention that wasn't going to fly.'[51] Serra's scepticism must have reinforced that of Freed, but others working on the project were also dubious:[52] Nancy Rosen has suggested that this doubt was exacerbated by the architectural activity at that time, when postmodernists were employing brash symbols (such as cracks) in projects with far less serious goals.

Serra's scepticism seems to have been the necessary catalyst for Freed to abandon his plans for the crack. But rather than leave the institution alone, Serra proposed a way in which he could contribute to the building that would also allow him to 'stay within [his] language'. He walked around the building with Freed, located a staircase in the

Hall of Witness, and decided that he wanted 'to impale a large weight into the bottom of the staircase to give that whole shaft a kind of ballast to it' (fig. 111). Working actively in collaboration with the architect, Serra 'simply tr[ied] to figure out what the dimensions had to be. In terms of its size, Freed and I, with poles and strings, in the shaft, figured out how big it ought to be. At one point we thought that 13, 14, 15 feet was too big, and so finally we got it down to what it ought to have been – which was 12 by 12 feet and 10 inches, and that was all worked out in a couple of days of actually visibly on site making a mock-up.'[53] The idea for the work was presented to the jury by Freed and Serra together at their second meeting on 24 June, a presentation widely described by the AFPSP participants as the most exciting moment of the commissioning processes. The idea was accepted, and the fabrication began. On 19 September, Serra ordered steel from his usual suppliers, and the slab was delivered to Washington and eventually lowered into place through a gap in the skylight of the Hall of Witness, deliberately left open for this installation.

The commissioning process for the work outside the museum on the 15th Street plaza was entirely different. Barbara Diamonstein-Spielvogel had called this space 'an antenna to the world', and in a committee meeting she 'reiterated the central role the sculpture would play in the public identification of the Museum'.[54] Because of its external location, any proposal needed to be accepted by the Washington D.C. Commission on the Fine Arts, the body responsible for ratifying public art proposals. Before the jury was convened, the members of the museum's art subcommittee had decided that there would be a closed competition for this site, and that four artists should be invited to prepare maquettes. They prepared a shortlist that was discussed at the June jury meeting.[55] Four artists (some of whom had not been on the shortlist) were approached in the summer.[56] Some travelled to Washington to see the building, others visited Freed's model in the Pei, Cobb and Freed offices in New York, and all four presented proposals with maquettes at the third jury meeting on 11 November. Jonathan Borofsky's proposal was quickly rejected (a monumental pair of hands holding a ruby, under which the visitors would pass), and debate centred on the other three, less symbolic proposals.[57]

Joel Shapiro's proposal was chosen, a two-part sculpture consisting of an overturned 'house' and a collection of welded metal oblongs that from some viewpoints might read variously as a tree or as a falling figure (later, I will look at the work in detail; see fig. 106). Like Serra, Shapiro had also recently worked on a different Holocaust-related project, having participated in a competition for a memorial in Düsseldorf for which he proposed a tiny model of a burnt house to be sited in a large neo-classical courtyard.[58] Like Serra, Shapiro also accepted the invitation of the USHMM jury enthusiastically. Rather than working out the proportions of his sculpture on-site, however, he built a model of the museum's façade in his studio, and began to position maquettes in relation to it. In an early model, Shapiro positioned the 'house' on the wall of the Hall of Remembrance, but when this was presented to Freed, the architect was unwilling for a sculpture to be affixed to his building. Shapiro modified the proposal,

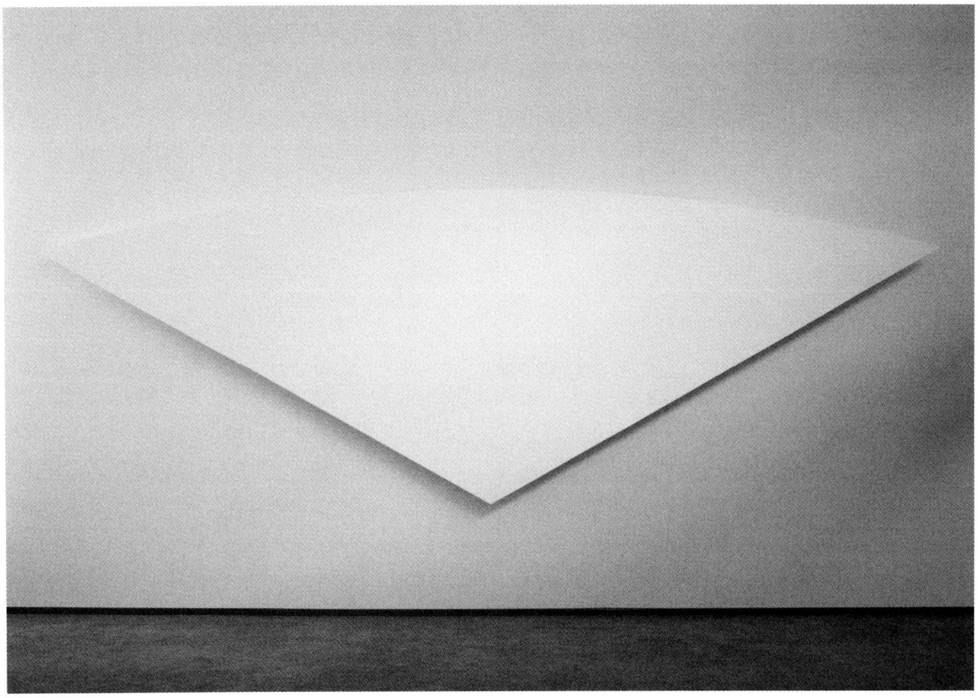

112 Ellsworth Kelly, *Memorial*, 1993. Enamel on wood and composite in four parts. Fan: 289.6 × 838.2 × 5.1 cm. Collection USHMM. © Ellsworth Kelly.

and in April 1992, presented it alongside Freed to the Commission on Fine Arts in Washington D.C. The work was accepted, fabricated and installed.

The third and fourth spaces were equivalent, placed above one another in rooms at the 14th Street end of the building. The museum's exhibition galleries circled around the Hall of Witness in a downward spiral, and these two spaces were situated at the foot of the two staircases where visitors descended from one floor to the lower one. Both these spaces interrupted the exhibition narrative, and in museum documents, they had variously been described as 'lounge' spaces, as 'passages' and as 'important place[s] to pause and pass through'.[59] While the precise contents of the exhibition either side of both these points were not known when the work for these spaces was being considered, it was clear both to the jury and to the artists that the first space would follow displays on the rise of Nazism, and the second, displays about the Final Solution.

Since the works for these rooms neither affected the architectural structure nor required external ratification, the final decisions on the artists were less urgent. At the June meeting, the jury short-listed three artists for each room and nominated a small number of alternatives.[60] All these individuals would be invited to submit proposals which would then be decided upon at the November jury meeting. During the summer, attempts were made to approach the artists. Some immediately declined,[61] while others began to work on proposals.

When asked to submit a proposal, Ellsworth Kelly's first response was to question why the museum approached him when he would obviously not be providing a work with narrative or symbolic content. As he recalled, he was told that such content was

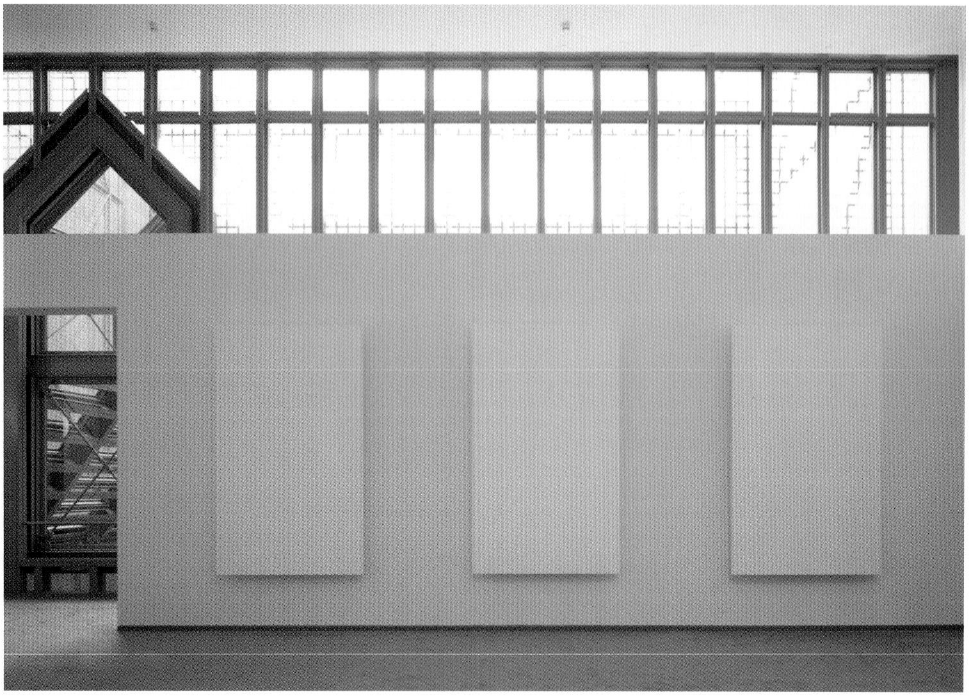

113 Ellsworth Kelly, *Memorial*, 1993. Enamel on wood and composite in four parts. Each of three panels: 274.3 × 162.6 × 5.1 cm. Collection USHMM. © Ellsworth Kelly.

not expected, and that the museum wanted something that 'would apply to a more "spiritual" context'.[62] Sara Bloomfield wrote to him to say that the space for his work was set aside for 'quiet conversation, silence, or contemplation'.[63] Kelly's first idea was to make three monochrome panels painted red, yellow and blue, but he relinquished this plan because, as he explained, 'colour was too personal, too [much] about me. Colour has its own memories.'[64] Eventually, Kelly chose to propose a white monochrome arc and three white monochrome panels (figs 112 and 113). Though he explained his refusal of colour in favour of white as a means of emptying out his subjective associations, there is a very long history of white monochromes in Kelly's practice, dating back to *Window III* (1949) and *Neuilly* (1950), and including the sculpture *White Angle* (1966) and the painting *Diagonal with Curve* (1978). For whatever reason, Kelly did not associate the white monochrome with personal memories. In November, Kelly's proposal was accepted for the first lounge, and fabrication and installation work ensued. Kelly chose to call his work *Memorial*.

The second space proved more difficult. Initially, two proposals had been offered, one by Sol LeWitt, and another by Jackie Winsor. Neither were accepted, and in early 1992, Rosen conducted discussions with jury members about this room. Some jurors hoped for 'work that might be more "readable"/accessible than the Serra and Kelly, which are so pure-abstract', while Nancy Rosen herself encouraged the jury to think of new names 'to get away from the established male candidates'.[65] A new list of possible artists was compiled, and the jurors were asked to indicate which of these should be invited to submit proposals.[66] As it happens, LeWitt was invited once again, and his work was chosen: so there was neither a move away from abstraction, nor from 'established' male artists.

LeWitt's first proposal had been for 'a wall-like sculpture with an irregular ("broken") top edge, made of black, concrete blocks to be stacked along the long diagonal wall of the room' (fig. 114).[67] Though there are no documents that specify the reasons for its rejection, we might surmise that without knowing it, LeWitt had offered a work that recalled Freed's plans to crack the black granite wall of the Hall of Witness, plans by this stage already overturned by Richard Serra. LeWitt's initial proposal suggests that his first inclination was towards a symbolic use of both colour and shape. Though it is difficult to say much about this proposal, it does seem to relate to his earlier use of black concrete blocks in his work *Black Form: Memorial to the Missing Jews* of 1987, first installed in Münster in 1987 and subsequently relocated to Hamburg-Altona in 1989 (fig. 115).[68] The earlier work functioned both as symbol/image (the gravestone), as a visual blockade (the sight lines to the baroque building behind were interrupted), and a physical one, interrupting movement across the space. His proposed broken wall, however, could not be circumnavigated. It would just have been encountered as an image alone.

It was the artist himself who approached the museum again to offer alternate suggestions when this broken wall was rejected.[69] The jury specified that he propose a wall drawing rather than a structure;[70] LeWitt submitted four maquettes[71], and one was chosen for the space – a work LeWitt initially titled 'Progression of Coloured Squares', but that came to be known by the museum as *Consequence*. LeWitt supplied detailed instructions for the priming of the wall[72], and sent his assistants to install the work (fig. 116).

Though the work was never installed there, the jury also considered a fifth site for a new art commission. Lawrence Weiner was invited to propose a work that would be situated inside the Hall of Witness. Like Serra, Weiner came to Washington to meet Freed, and decided during his visit both the work he wished to make, and where and how he wanted to install it. Weiner proposed a sculpture which would be lettered onto the raw I-beams towards the 14th Street entrance of the space using puddling, a technique of melting the metal of a welding rod straight onto another metal. 'The sculpture is built with steel upon the steel of the platform of the architect James Ingo Freed', Weiner wrote, describing the technique as 'a scar'. The proposed sculpture read:

> BREAD CAST UPON THE WATER
> WINE POURED UPON THE SEA
> STONES PLACED UPON EACH OTHER
> WOOD THRUST INTO BRINE

Like Serra, Shapiro and LeWitt, Weiner had also at this point recently made a work in Europe that elusively addressed the history of Nazism: SMASHED TO PIECES (IN THE STILL OF THE NIGHT), installed on the side of the Flakturm building in Vienna in 1991.

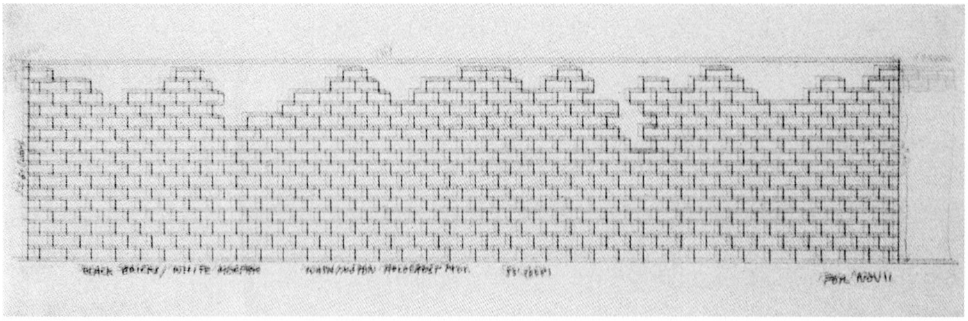

114 Sol LeWitt, *Working Drawing for Cinderblock Structure for USHMM* (never realised), 1993. Ink, pencil on vellum, 20.5 × 60.5 cm. © Sol LeWitt.

When Benjamin Buchloh later suggested to Weiner that the work should be read in the context of 'the Holocaust history of the city', the artist replied that 'I knew damn well it had a metaphor'.[73] But Weiner also insisted that the work emerged from his thinking at the time about the sounds of night and day, and stressed that it would have a 'totally different metaphor' if placed on a desert island, where dropping coconuts shatter the still of the night. Considering the work Weiner proposed for the USHMM, it is important to keep in mind Weiner's insistence that his works do not 'make a metaphor',[74] but instead provoke metaphoric readings from viewers that are different in different contexts.

Weiner has explained that his sculpture, which would have been part of the very fabric of Freed's building rather than an added substance, was 'a way to place some parts of the material reality of the world in the midst of what was terror and horror'.[75] In the middle of the Holocaust museum, visitors would be provoked to think about materials and 'definitive actions' different from those that they learnt about in the exhibition, and through this they would come both to connect their time in the museum with their lives outside it, and to realise that their responsibilities lay as much towards the present as the past. Seeing the sculpture, viewers would come to a 'realisation that they *did* have a life to live, and that life had to stop at some point only discussing what other people did [by which Weiner meant people in the 1930s and 1940s], and look in terms of what [their] possibilities were.'

According to this line of reasoning, any materials and actions might have fulfilled this role: Weiner's materials might have been 'Big Stones' as in the 1990 work BIG STONES MOVED HERE & THERE BETWEEN THE HEAVENS & THE EARTH, or 'Sandstone' as in the 1993 work SOME LIMESTONE SOME SANDSTONE ENCLOSED FOR SOME REASON. But the four phrases in the sculpture he proposed to the USHMM used materials and activities which in the context would have produced particular suggestions. The guiding intention for the entire work (that the visitors should think about the activities and responsibilities of their own lives rather than just learning about the activities of the past) is in some ways figured by the first phrase, which is close to the verse from Ecclesiastes 11:1: 'Cast thy bread upon the waters: for thou shall find it after many days.' The biblical commentator Rashi described the text as a suggestion that people should help their brethren even when they do not expect to see them again, and that rewards

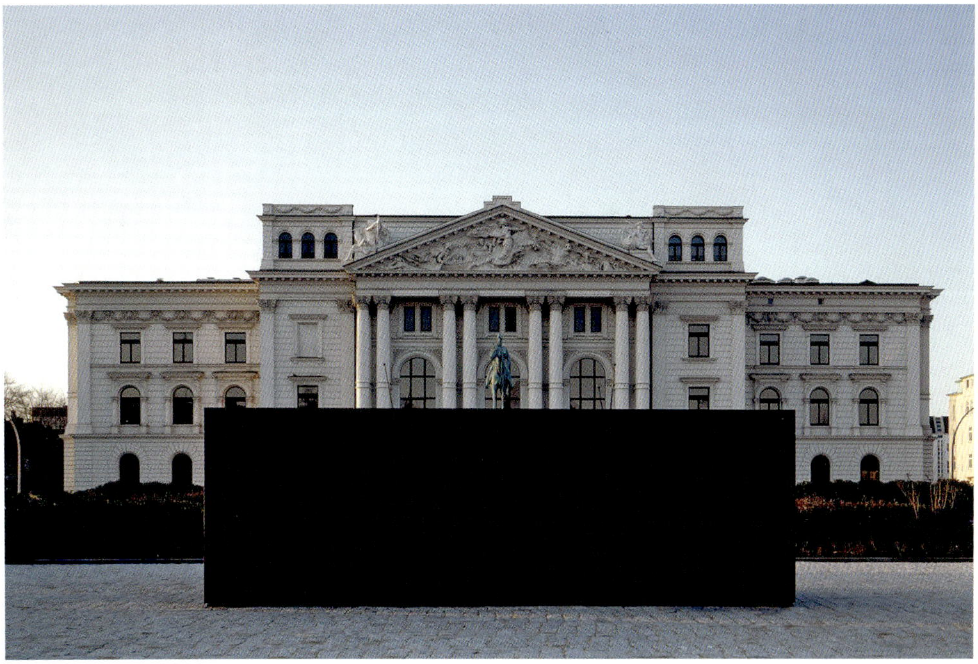

115 Sol LeWitt, *Black Form: Memorial to the Missing Jews*, 1987. Painted concrete block, installed in Platz der Republik, Hamburg-Altona, Germany. Collection of the Freie und Hansestadt Hamburg, Kulturbehörde. © Sol LeWitt.

would come later. Weiner's phrase actually withholds the idea of belated rewards, so the act of generosity and responsibility that we might imagine becomes an act carried out for no reason other than itself.

While BREAD CAST UPON THE WATER invokes a biblical phrase of universal familiarity, the second line, WINE POURED UPON THE SEA suggests a Christian event (or rather, the inversion of Christ's turning water to wine). STONES PLACED UPON EACH OTHER, by contrast, would have invoked for some the Jewish practice of laying stones (rather than flowers) on graves. In fact, STONES PLACED UPON EACH OTHER at once conjures this act of mourning, and suggests the very activity of building, which could be considered more extensively as rebuilding, or moving on after a period of mourning. A less culturally specific notion of moving-on is invoked as well by WOOD THRUST INTO BRINE, which could suggest the launching of a ship.

Weiner has mentioned that he deliberately chose to avoid exclusively Jewish connotations because he distrusted the museum's almost exclusive concentration on the Jewish victims of Nazism. By invoking material activities not associated with Judaism, the work could also more easily allow visitors to think about the external world and their activities within it. Though Freed was very enthusiastic about it, the work was not installed, and its rejection can be put down to a number of factors. The most prosaic is that it would have been illegible as a work of art in the space, given the number of other wall texts, including a quotation from Isaiah on the black granite wall ('You are my witnesses') and Eisenhower's remarks made at a concentration camp in 1945, carved into the exterior wall near the Shapiro sculpture. The artist himself has suggested that survivors and relatives of survivors involved in the commissioning process

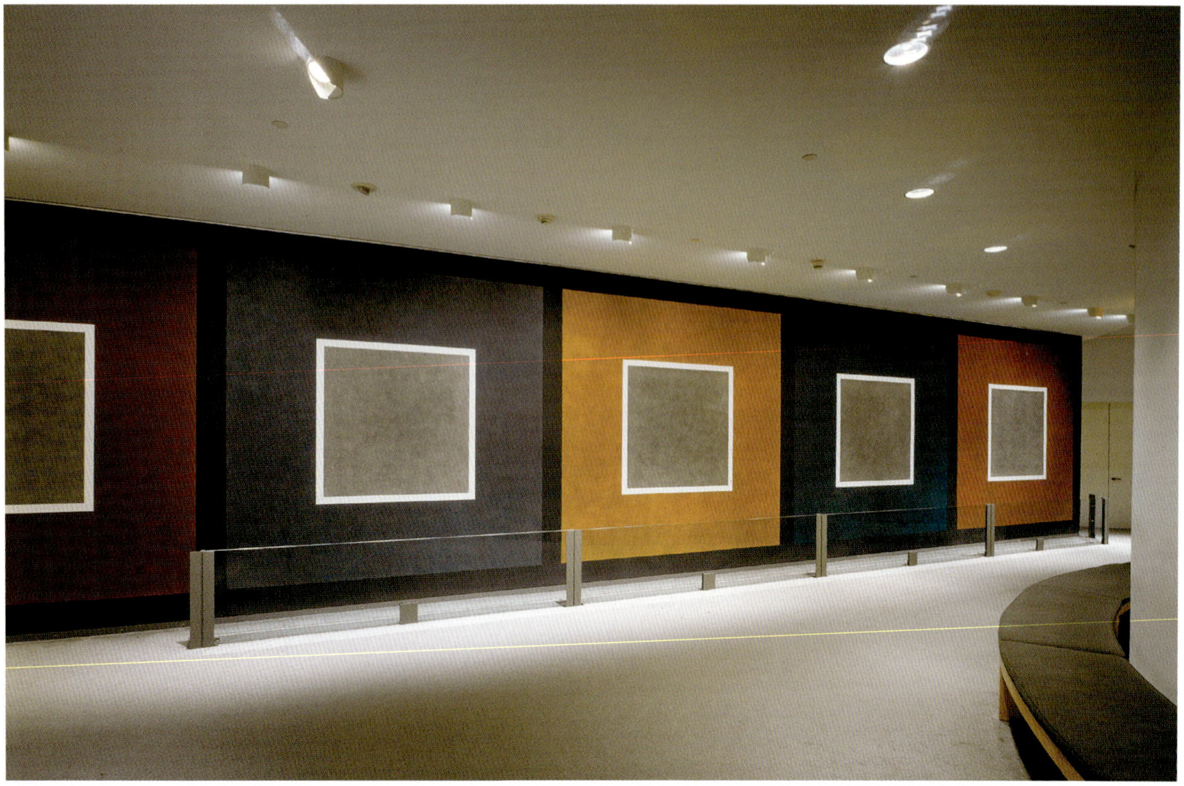

116 Sol LeWitt, *Consequence*, 1993. Wall drawing with colour ink wash. Collection USHMM. © Sol LeWitt.

did not feel that their relatives' deaths were adequately addressed by the work. Most interestingly, one jury member has suggested that some people felt that the sculpture 'could be read as a text [indicating] that somehow the Jews might have been responsible for their own fate'.[76] Though the juror did not mention this, we might guess that Weiner's first phrase for some recalled the practice of *tashlich* when Jews cast bread upon the water at Rosh Hashanah, a ritual connected to casting away the sins of the previous year. Though unintended, the invocation of Jewish sinning and atonement was troublesome. The openness of Weiner's work at this moment was at a great cost, but it was later installed elsewhere, in a place utterly unconnected to the history of the Holocaust.

*

By early 1993, the four works successfully commissioned in the process of the AFPSP were being installed. The progress of the programme had been reported to the museum's Council by Julius Schatz at bi-annual meetings, and payments for artists' fees and materials had been raised.[77] When details of the programme had been announced to the press the previous November, the *Washington Post* headline ran 'Abstract works secretly commissioned'.[78] However sensationalist the headline, it is worth pausing here to ask how it had come to pass that all four of the works were 'abstract'. I have already noted that the jury were given no specific instructions to select abstract artists: indeed amongst those who were approached were Kiefer, Borofsky and Ann Hamilton. No specific discussion regarding abstraction had taken place at the jury meeting in April 1991, and because minutes of the June and November jury meetings were not taken,[79] it is impossible to know if there was a conversation about abstraction then. This seems unlikely – the jury appear to have deliberated about which serious artists might respond to an approach to make a proposal. That the majority of these worked primarily with abstraction seems to have been a result of what jurors had been told about the museum, the architecture and the hopes for the AFPSP. It was only after proposals such as those of Borofsky were rejected that the preferences for abstraction could be confirmed as a trend, and had Lawrence Weiner's been approved (it seems to have been favourable to the architect and the jury), the *Washington Post*'s notion of abstraction, at least, would have been tested.

The four works were formally revealed at a press viewing on 13 April 1993. Though Serra's and Shapiro's sculptures would be visible outside the exhibition, Nancy Rosen was concerned that the programme as a whole might not make sense to the press if journalists were taken straight to the other art works, so she requested that they be led through the museum, replicating the experience of future visitors. 'The choice of abstract art for those rooms was so centrally based on the impact of the permanent exhibition and its images, documents, archival objects. I really feel that people will not really understand the choice of Kelly and LeWitt without at least a bit of that experience.'[80] Following Rosen's caution, I will now address the works themselves by considering their placement within the architecture and exhibition narratives. While it will be important to ask how the surrounding locations affect (and infect) the possible meanings of the works, I will also look at the ways in which the artists negotiated this location. 'My problem,' according to Richard Serra, 'was to stay within my language, knowing that it was going to be subverted by the context, to deal with my content as sculpture, even knowing that it was going to be misinterpreted.'[81] If content risked being 'subverted by the context', we might also ask whether the invitation to place work in the USHMM caused the artists to shift their working processes, keeping to their 'language', but altering their vocabulary.

a tour through the museum

Joel Shapiro's two-part *Loss and Regeneration* stands at the 15th Street entrance of the museum. Furthest away from the entrance, and just in front of the large, windowless facade of the Hall of Remembrance, there is a geometric form resembling a toppled 'house', with only one corner of its 'roof' in contact with the ground. Beyond it, some two steps up, a larger structure rises: a more complex form assembled from nine oblongs of different thicknesses. From some perspectives, the shape appears as an angular tree, and from others, it resembles a falling 'stick man' whose 'head' tips downwards towards the left, and whose 'arm' is raised upwards to balance the fall (fig.

117).[82] The 'off-balance' look is most powerful in front of the work. Both parts of the work are large in size, but their scale diminishes next to the rise of the museum behind.

117 Joel Shapiro, *Loss and Regeneration*, 1993. © Joel Shapiro.

Of the four works made for the museum, Shapiro's work has prompted the most interpretative comment.[83] Critics have been drawn to search for the symbolic meaning of the two parts, taking the work as an illustration of an idea about the Holocaust. The first form has been interpreted as a symbol for domestic destruction – an introduction to, and a reminder of the displays that the visitor encounters about the loss of home suffered by the victims of the Holocaust. But questions remain as to the identity of the house: 'While it could signify an overthrown Jew's house (or a sort of upended Ark of the Covenant),' writes James Hall, 'it might equally represent an overthrown building in a concentration camp.'[84] Hall does not explain that this second possibility might involve a bizarre fantasy, since few camp buildings were in fact 'overthrown'. The meaning of the 'tree/figure' is similarly hard to pin down. Not only is it impossible to tell if the form is a tree or figure, but if the latter, the meaning of the gesture is unclear. According to Peter Schjeldahl, 'The lurching motion of the figure has something gallantly balletic about it, and something painfully awkward . . . The desperate gesture of the figure's raised arm can be seen as imploring or angrily defiant.'[85] Shapiro's title also encourages questions: does *Loss* refer to the 'house', and *Regeneration* to the figure/tree, or does the 'figure/tree' embody both of these ideas?

These kinds of interpretative speculations seem as traditional as the work itself. It is, after all, a large bronze sculpture adorning the entrance space of an institution, held in place by unseen tectonic supports. It is a sculpture that teeters on the border of figuration, and one that invites questions as to the possible narrative links of its two components. In the text he submitted when proposing the sculpture to the USHMM, Shapiro wrote that 'the "tree" embodies cycles of life, death, anguish, the overcoming of anguish – and possibilities of a future,'[86] a comment that could cement a reading of the work as a traditional, symbolic monument. Shapiro later said that he was 'trying to find some form that would communicate',[87] and certainly this seems to be a work attempting to communicate in an obvious manner through the provision of easily graspable and coherent images.

Without wishing to deny this character of the work, I would like to rethink it slightly and to suggest a greater degree of complexity than might be evident from the account of it thus far. One context for the work would be an overtly figurative memorial, of which the most obvious and recent example at the time of its making was George Segal's *The Holocaust* (1984), for which Segal cast human bodies and arranged them after looking at images of the liberation of the camps. Shapiro has said that the presentation of a 'series of corpses' is something you 'can't do',[88] and *Loss and Regeneration* represents as much a resistance to figurative sculpture as a tentative recuperation of its potentialities. Another context is geographic rather than art historical. Though in most cases it was photographed with the USHMM behind, from another vantage point, one sees Shapiro's sculpture with the white needle of the Washington Monument stretching above it (fig. 118). Shapiro's work refers to the language of this monument but overturns it: the artist offers a work in two fragments rather than a unitary form, and

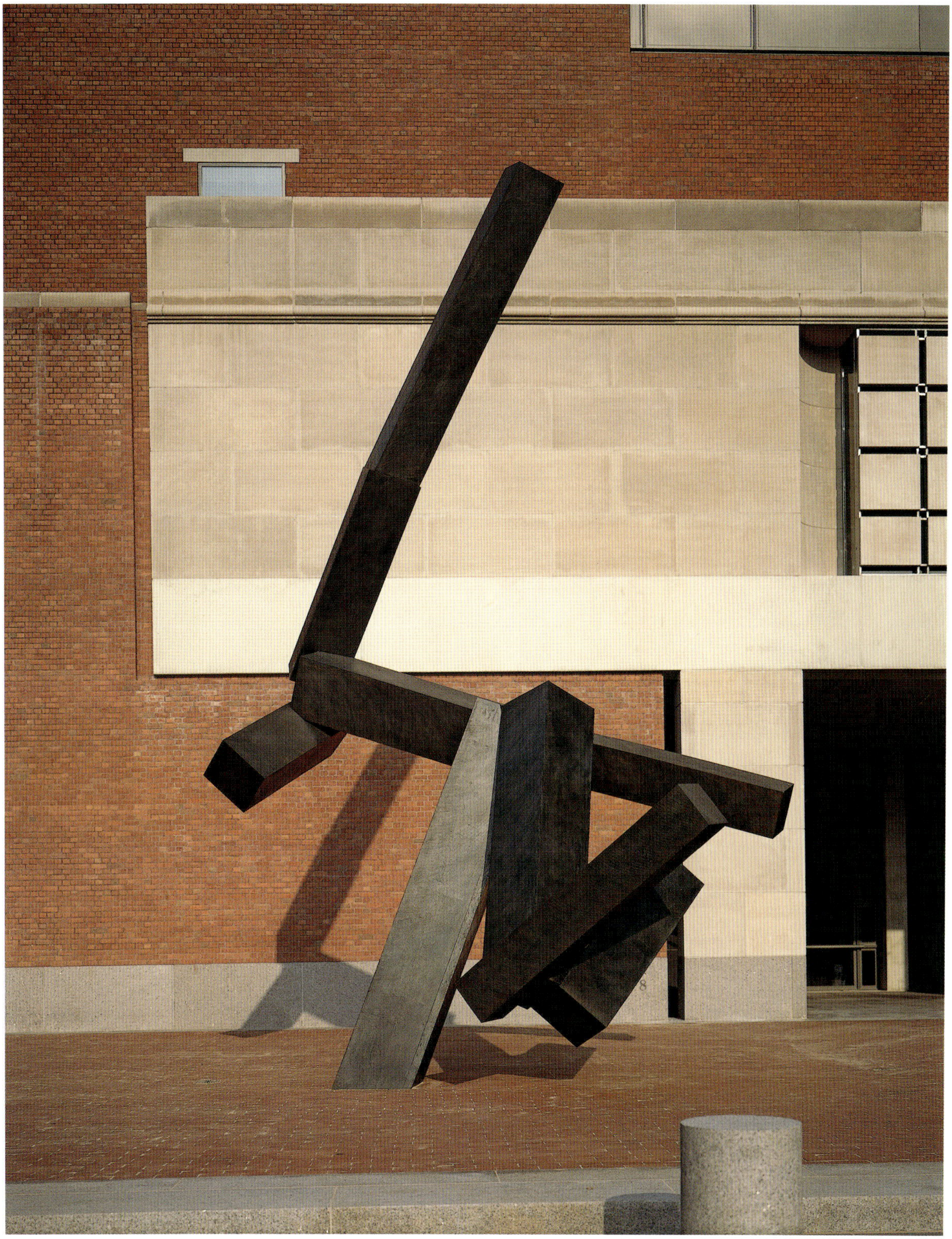

eschews the verticality of the obelisk for the lurch and fall of his work. Where the apex of the obelisk reaches towards the sky, the tip of Shapiro's 'house' touches the ground. Shapiro has said that he saw his work as a 'foil' to the Washington Monument, but I would go further and suggest that his work dramatises the post-Holocaust impossibility of a traditional language of commemoration right in front of one of the largest commemorative monuments in the country.

118 Joel Shapiro, *Loss and Regeneration*, 1993. View towards Washington Monument.

Another way into the work is to attend more closely to the dynamics of viewing that it organises. I have already mentioned that the larger part of the work coheres as a rudimentary 'figure' from some aspects, but as one walks around, this 'figure' quickly loses its coherence and the oblongs appear as just that: a collection of welded geometric shapes. If one begins to simultaneously approach and walk around the sculpture, a second kind of disintegration occurs to make the 'symbolic' or 'figurative' reading even harder to sustain. One begins to notice the surface of the metal. Shapiro could have made the sculpture with clean, smooth metal surfaces, but instead he cast it from wood. The figure was made at a sawmill by assembling cut logs into oblongs, and casting from them, so its surface is traversed by the regular curving lines of the saw's teeth (fig. 119). By contrast, the house was made by building a plywood model, filling it with plaster, and then casting from that mould, so its surfaces show the thin striations of the plywood's grain (fig. 120). These surfaces look extremely different, and might invite comparison. What seems crucial is that they do not help to secure any of the speculations as to the 'meanings' of *Loss and Regeneration* in terms of the identity of the 'house', or the character of the 'figure' and its gesture. Instead, the surfaces refer back to two different modes of fabrication, rooting the sculpture in Shapiro's activity rather than in that of the 'figure'.

This way of attending to the work also roots it in Shapiro's history rather than in the history of the Holocaust. Shapiro's first works explicitly dramatised their materials and the processes of their making, and he showed alongside other post-minimalists (including Richard Serra) at exhibitions such as 'Anti-Illusion: Procedures/Materials' at the Whitney Museum in 1969. At this time, Shapiro was making work by stapling dyed nylon directly to the wall, or by repetitively printing his inky thumb on lengths of paper. With the move to bronze sculpture and the near-figuration, Shapiro would seem to have abandoned the radical abstraction of his early practice, but the marks on the two parts of *Loss and Regeneration* recall this moment.

Loss and Regeneration can be read quite quickly as a falling figure and an overturned house, a pairing that forges an obviously symbolic condensation of the museum's content, and that acts as a concise introduction to the narrative exhibition. While the work does function in this way, a more considered approach would need to take account of the way it questions monumental forms, and would need to emphasise the precariousness of any figurative reading and the abstraction of its cast metallic parts. These parts neither refer through their materiality nor through their making to the events that the museum will present. *Loss and Regeneration* therefore by no means acts as a simplistic introduction to the museum, but almost as a challenge to look at the

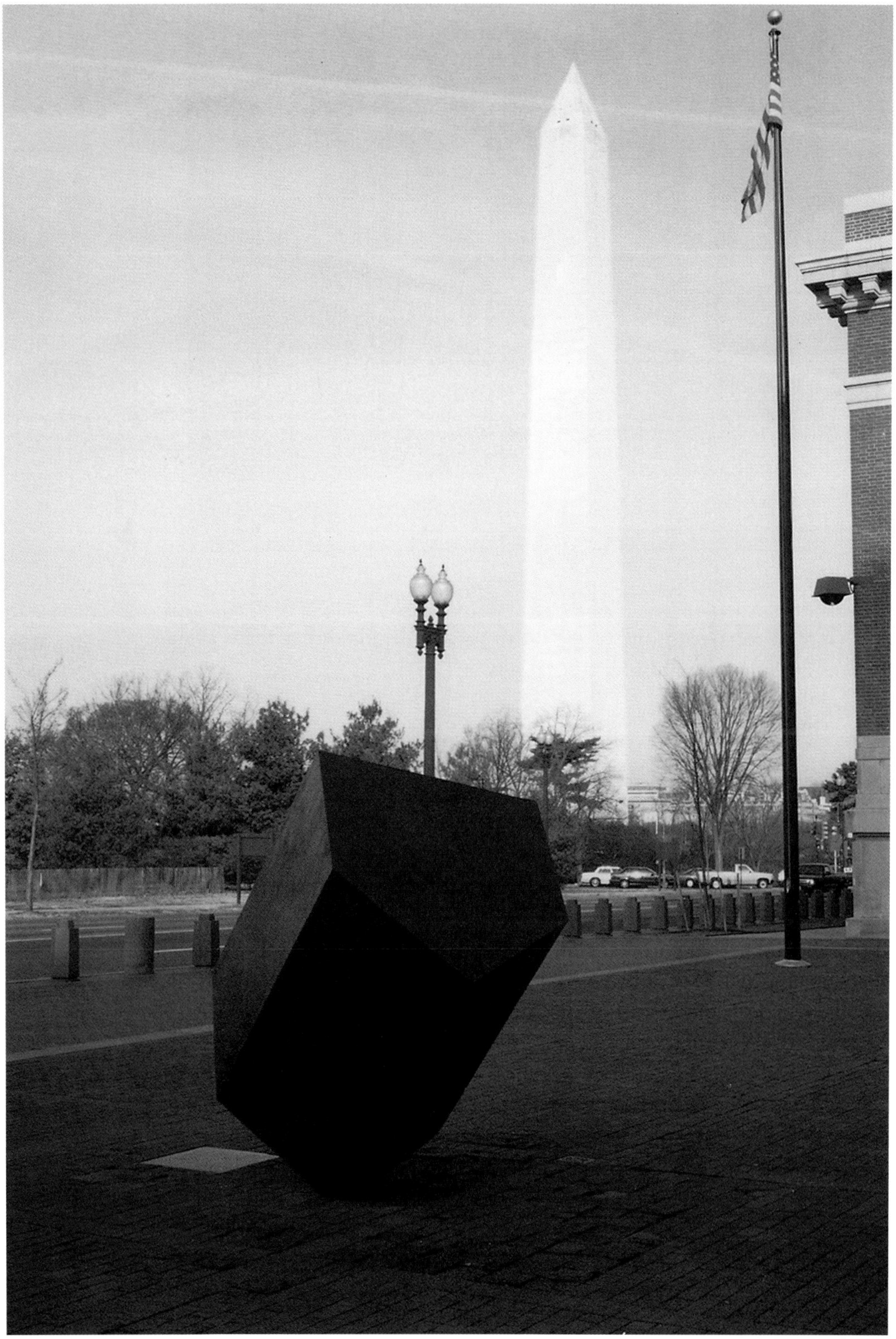

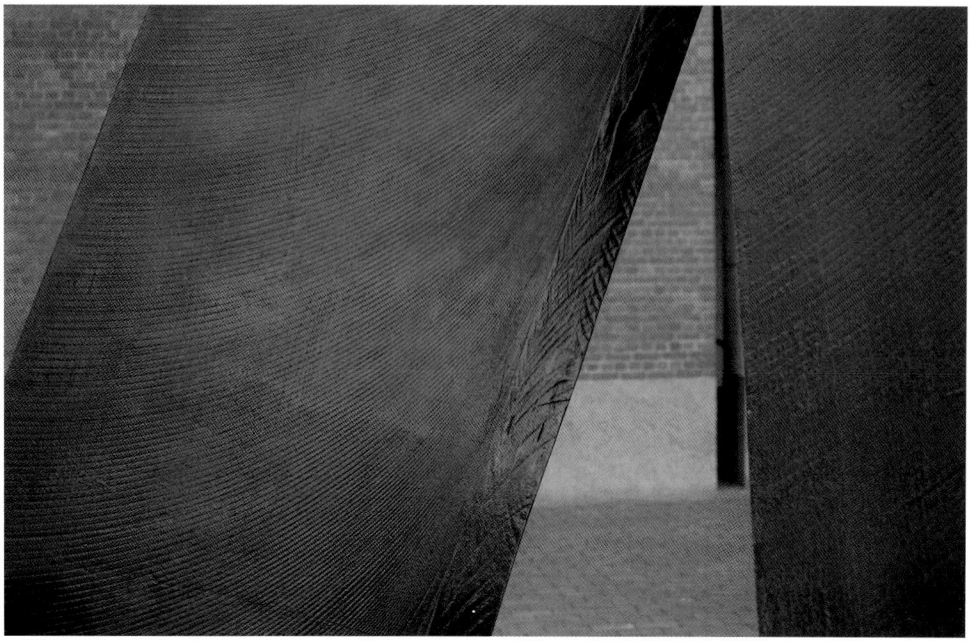

119 Joel Shapiro, *Loss and Regeneration*, 1993. Detail of 'figure' showing surface.

material within from multiple angles, and to attend to precise details rather than just attempting to gain an overview of a history of calamity.

*

Beyond Joel Shapiro's sculpture, one enters the Hall of Witness. This is a huge atrium topped by a twisted skylight and flanked by red-brick walls with black and white granite walls at its ends. From the Hall, visitors enter lifts which ascend while an audio recording plays the voice of an American GI describing the discovery of a concentration camp. The doors open onto a huge black-and-white photograph of American soldiers standing by a pile of charred corpses, and a grey wall inscribed with the words 'The Holocaust' (fig. 121). Its story is being told through the conventions of Hollywood (starting at the end with the arrival of the Americans) and through the devices of theatre (the doors of the lift mime the opening of the stage curtains). Stepping to the side of the photograph, visitors move back in time to the beginnings of Nazi terror.

Ellsworth Kelly's *Memorial* is positioned after the first lap of the narrative. By this moment, visitors have seen artefacts and images documenting the period leading up to the beginning of the war. Most of the space they pass through has been darkened, but to travel from one half of the exhibition galleries on the south side of the building to the other on the north, they have passed over a bridge affording a view down onto the Hall of Witness and its skylight. The narrative proceeds through exhibits representing the response of Americans to early news from Nazi Germany – reports of the book

120 Joel Shapiro, *Loss and Regeneration*, 1993. Detail of 'house' showing surface.

burnings, for instance. Visitors then enter the 'Tower of Faces', a photographic installation of hundreds images of Jewish families from the ghetto of Eishishok. Steps beyond descend to Kelly's room.

The first visible part of the work is a huge arc stretching from the end of the wall at which viewers enter, right over to the exit through which they will proceed to rejoin the museum's story (fig. 122). The arc is situated opposite a wall which backs onto the Hall of Witness, and on which are placed three rectangular panels, spaced at even intervals. Like the arc, the fibreglass panels are very thick, and are held out from the wall by around six inches by circular bolts visible from the sides. As reliefs, the works are separated spatially from the walls, though in colour they are almost identical to it: all four parts of the work are white, slightly brighter than the wall against which they are seen. Were they lit as Kelly desired, the works would almost disappear into the walls and, unlike Kelly's other work, hardly announce their presence.[89]

What can possibly be said about a work which visually offers so little? There are neither signs of brushwork nor making, nor nuances nor fluctuations of tone or colour, nor contrasts of materials, and not even the consistent pattern of a canvas's weave. Of all the works I have discussed so far, Kelly's *Memorial* would seem to give the least to vision – far less, even, than Newman's *Fourteenth Station*. And yet because of its situation, writers have been tempted towards allusive accounts of these white slabs. Linda Nochlin, for instance, mentioning the work in an article published on the occasion of Kelly's Guggenheim retrospective, suggested that its 'whiteness refer[s] to loss and memory: the always blank page of history'.[90] The trouble with such a comment is that

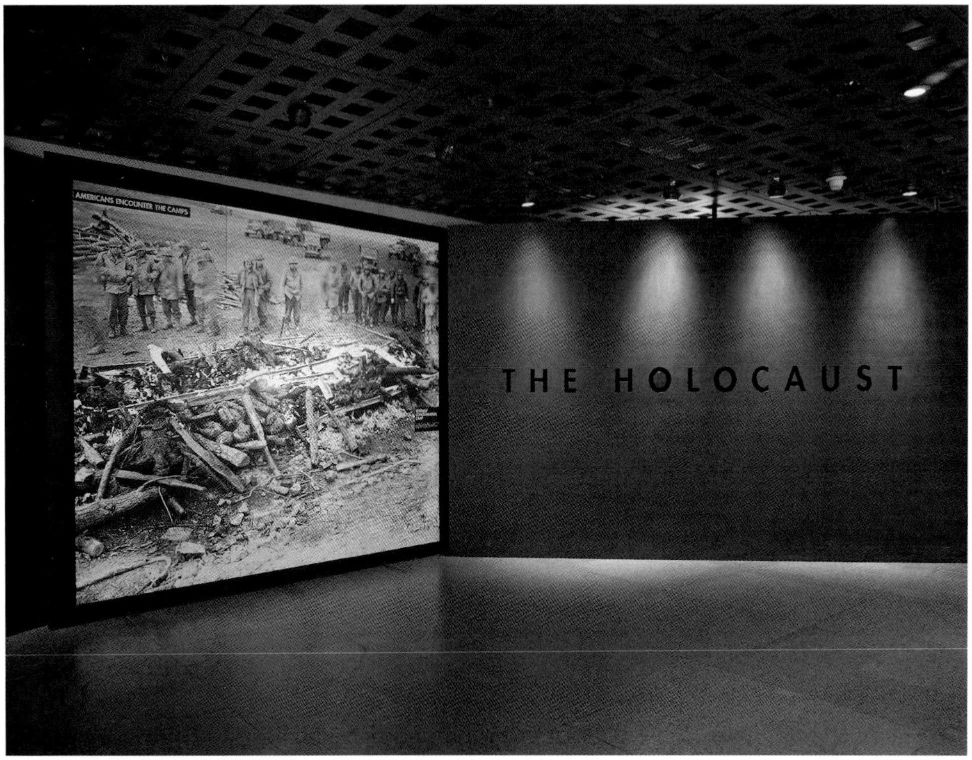

121 (top) USHMM, View from elevator of the beginning of the Permanent Exhibition.

122 (facing page) Ellsworth Kelly, *Memorial*, 1993. Enamel on wood and composite in four parts. Fan: 289.6 × 838.2 × 5.1 cm. Collection USHMM. © Ellsworth Kelly.

it forgets the art history of blank pages, so to speak; the history that would compare the work with Malevich's *White on White* (1918), Newman's *The Voice* (1950), Manzoni's *Achromes*, Robert Ryman's entire oeuvre, and, of course, Kelly's own white monochromes. Whiteness in these works does not refer to 'loss and memory', or at least not in the way Nochlin meant. But the second floor of the USHMM is not equivalent to a room in the Museum of Modern Art charting different approaches to the white monochrome, and by placing such works here, Kelly knew he could invite a different set of readings. He has also relinquished a literal account of *Memorial*. 'My paintings are memorials to the suffering, [to] the concentration camps',[91] he has said. 'When I made them blank, they looked like memorial tablets that don't have names on them.'[92]

So there is a tendency to read the works as 'blank pages' and as empty 'memorial tablets', a tendency enforced for Kelly by the commission, and for Nochlin by the circumstances in which the works are found. These allusive readings are inevitable, and occur even when attempting to restrict a reading to what is visible in the space. Despite the lack of colour, texture, and so on, the work does provide a set of contrasting forms. On the one wall there is a single curving structure, and on the other, three repeated, regular and straight forms. What might the viewer make of these shapes, their arrangement and their contrasts? The repetition of the rectangle could be taken as an articulation of the impossibility of narration. While the exhibition structures images in a narrative sequence, Kelly's rectangles offer no sense of forward or backward move-

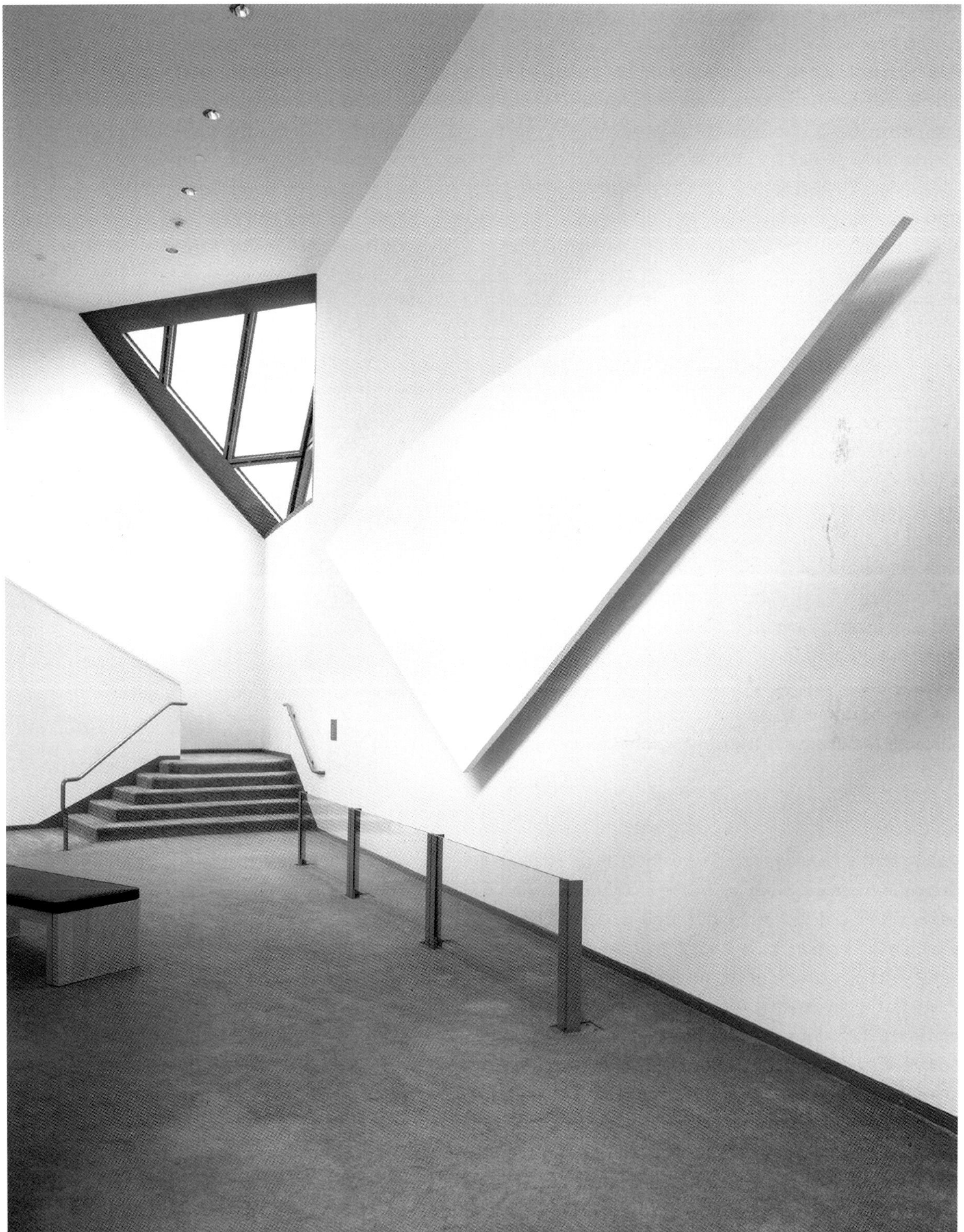

ment, but just a blank restatement of an uninteresting shape. We might even read repetition here as a kind of stutter: faced with the images all around it, the work is tongue-tied with nothing to say. By contrast, the arc offers not just a different and more unusual shape, but a different sense of movement. Instead of static repetition, it suggests the movement from one end of the room to the other, and also a release from the geometric and angular features of the architecture and most of the display panels.

Kelly was asked to make a work that would provide the setting for 'quiet conversation, silence, or contemplation'. While some have found the work 'very spiritual',[93] Kelly has mentioned its 'mystery'. As I will argue later, these terms seem problematic given the history and radicality of Kelly's once decidedly anti-spiritual abstraction. Though it might seem that the USHMM has used Kelly's work (with his full participation) to provide a space for contemplation, I think that the work nonetheless dramatises an interesting problem as to what kind of contemplation could possibly occur here. The work seems to articulate two irreconcilable positions. On the one hand, it suggests the impossibility of representation: the impossibility of using colour, texture, or material contrasts in this place. Through the repetition of the rectangles, there is the added sense of the impossibility of movement or narrative. On the other hand, the work suggests the possibility of transcendence, since the arc suggests a release and an escape from the order of the museum. On the one hand, that is to say, the work argues that art can do nothing when faced with the history of the Holocaust, nothing other than articulate its own impossibility. On the other, it suggests that art (in its most reduced form) can still function in one of its most ancient roles, to allow space for spiritual contemplation and memory. This is a fascinating problematic and one that the work manages to pose vividly. In the room, there are few vantage points where one can see both the panels and the arc. These contradictory ideas are thus expressed through the arrangement of the panels in the space.

*

Sol LeWitt's *Consequence* is positioned in a space below Kelly's *Memorial*. It comes after the most gruelling leg of the exhibition which covers the concentration and elimination of Nazi victims. Exhibition designers organised a physical as well as a visual experience: visitors pass over a replica bridge of the one in the Lodz ghetto beside a wall-size photograph of the original. Some time later, after viewing an expansive plaster model of a gas chamber (complete with miniature dying figures), they walk through a cattle truck. Soon after, they cross back to the north galleries to find displays of Roman Vishniac's photographs of Polish Jews. Behind a barrier is a wall-sized image of a room whose floor is a field of hair. Visitors pass through the bottom section of the 'Tower of Faces' – more and more photographs from Eishishok – but this time, a wall panel describes with cutting brevity how, in two days, an SS mobile killing squad destroyed the nine-hundred year old community. Just after this point, stairs lead down to the last level of the museum's exhibition display. LeWitt's wall drawing covers the entire left wall of the space at the bottom of the steps (fig. 123).

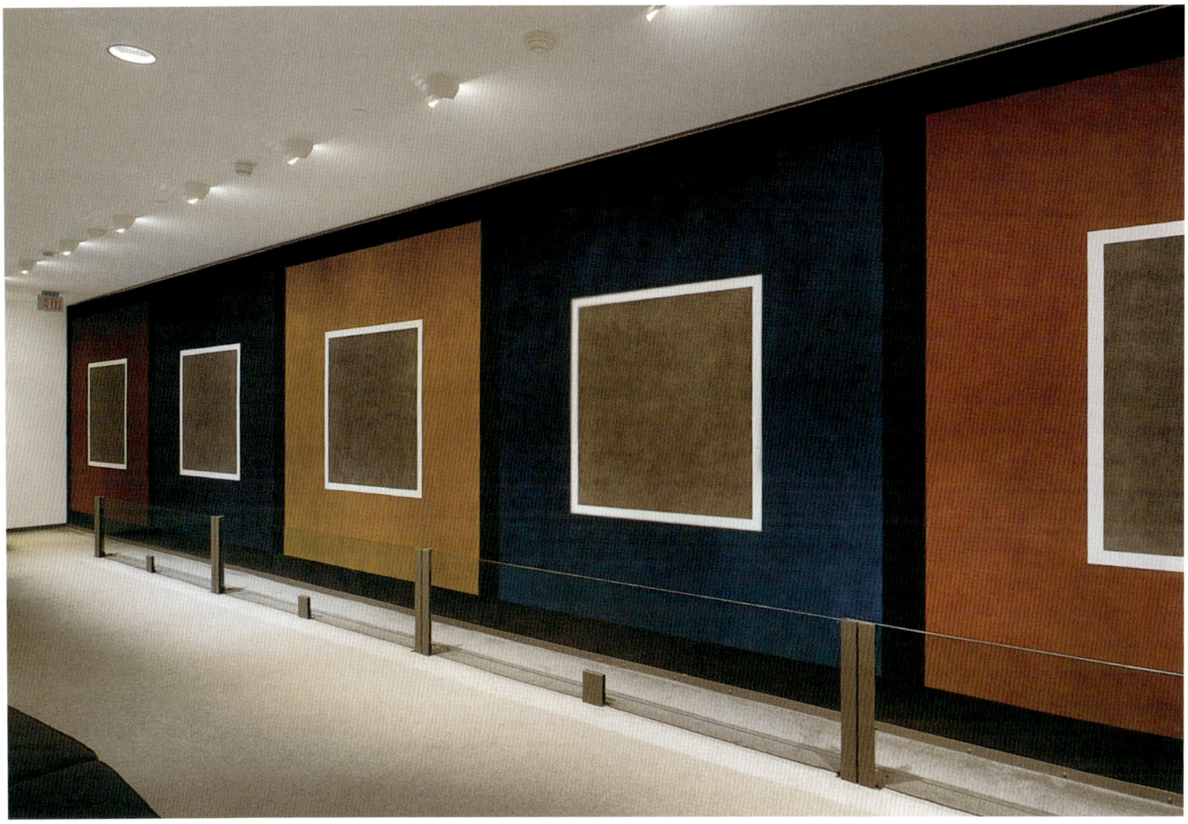

123 Sol LeWitt, *Consequence*, 1993. Wall drawing with colour ink wash. Collection USHMM. © Sol LeWitt.

Consequence runs just over 16 metres, reaching 3.4 metres high. It has five square sections, each separated by a thin black border which also runs along the top and bottom of the wall. In the middle of each section is a grey square, just over a metre wide. These squares are framed by thin white lines, which in turn are framed by broader coloured sections reaching to the black border. Each is coloured differently – from left to right, the colours run a browny red, purple, mustard, blue and orange. Each colour is a result of a different layering of washes of four inks: the primary colours, plus grey. These washes were applied onto the wall with rags, and since the rag drags across the wall unevenly, the colour surface is slightly differentiated, or mottled.

As I have mentioned, *Consequence* was not LeWitt's first idea for the space, and even the choice of this particular drawing cannot be attributed to him: he sent in a selection of maquettes from which this was chosen (another was similarly divided into five sections, but each contained a different shape). Nevertheless, this does seem to be the drawing the artist preferred. 'I thought I would prefer myself to have the squares all the same,' LeWitt has said, 'to have the progression be less diverse . . . to keep the area in a calm and not very aggressive mode. I thought it would be more apt to have the same figure in each one – which is a square within a square – and then just change the colour from square to square.'[94]

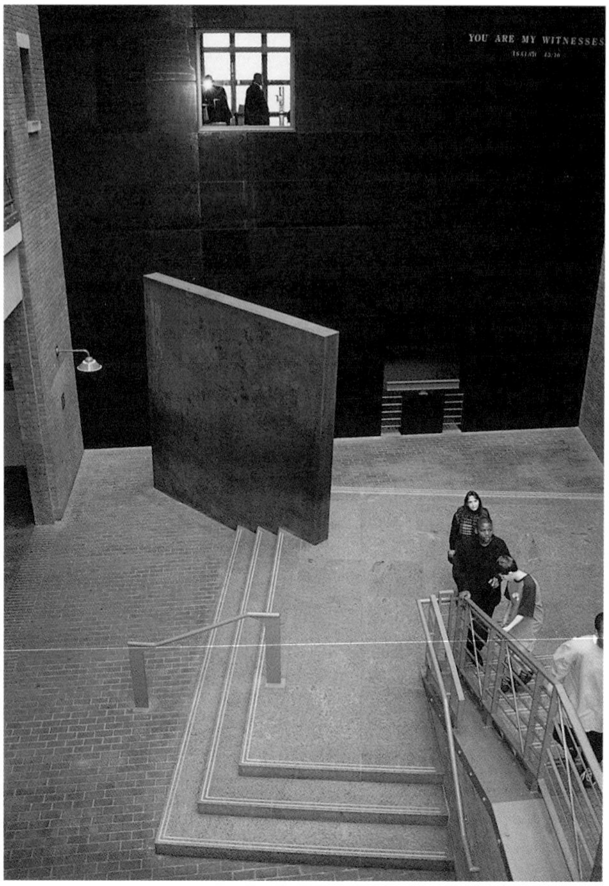

124 Richard Serra, *Gravity*, 1993. © Richard Serra.

LeWitt suggests here that the work is 'apt' because the repetition of forms keeps the space calm rather than jolty or quirky (the possible effect of juxtaposing triangles, pentagons, etc). Certainly compared to other contemporaneous wall drawings by the artist, *Consequence* establishes a sombre rather than a joyous mood. This is as much a result of the repetition of shapes as of two other features: its colour and its frame structure. Central grey squares dominate the drawing. Repeated over its length, each is emphasised by the bright (but thin) bordering band of white. Greyness also permeates the surrounding colours: the only ink present in each coloured section was grey, and its presence is evident, spoiling and muddying what would be bright reds and oranges. Though colour almost never had such a function in LeWitt's previous work, here grey takes on referential potential.[95] From the opening image in the museum's display, viewers have encountered black-and-white photographs, and in the displays leading up to *Consequence*, they have thought about fires, charring and ash.[96] Susan Morganstein has said that 'Coming where [the drawing] does in the exhibition, it is almost like the smoke has poured out.'[97] As she acknowledged, such associations are not those that usually accompany a LeWitt wall drawing, but are inevitable here.

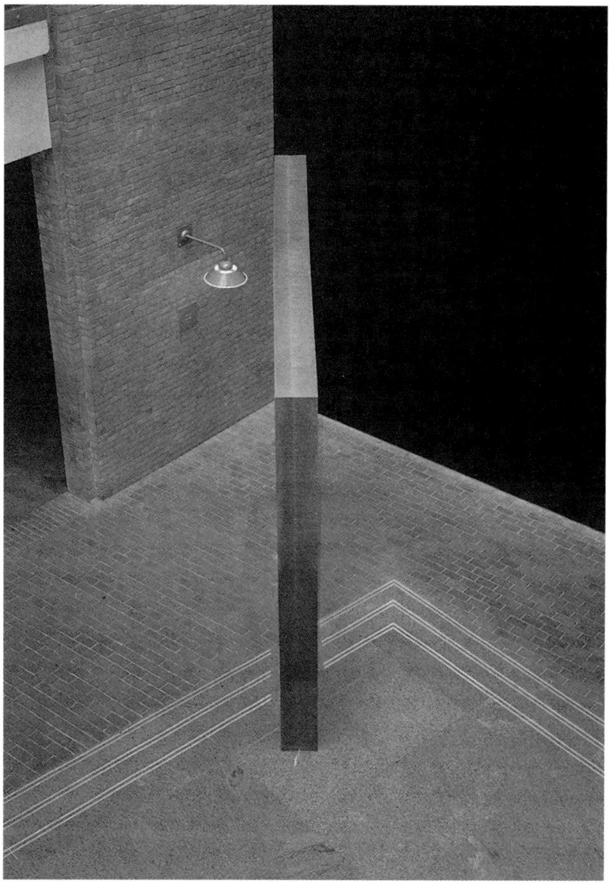

125 Richard Serra, *Gravity*, 1993. View of *Gravity* from staircase indicating its position off the corner point of the bottom stair.

The form of the work also invites consideration. *Consequence* is neither a progression of even 'squares within squares' (such a drawing would use concentric squares whose bands were of equal thickness) nor of serially ordered bands, whose thicknesses would change according to a given system. Instead the work uses two thin parts (the white and the black) and two thick parts (the grey and the coloured section). The context imposes a reading of this form: coming to the work straight after seeing the photographs in the 'Tower of Faces', and having just learnt how the subjects of these photographs have been killed, one is tempted to see LeWitt's frames as a series of emptied portraits where, in the absence of the sitter, only greyness can be framed.

So in three important aspects, LeWitt's work suits the space in which it is encountered. One could also argue (as I did with regard to Kelly's three rectangular panels) that the repetition of LeWitt's forms resists the narrative progress of the exhibition. In this respect, it is important to recall that LeWitt preferred the title *Progression of Coloured Squares* over the museum's *Consequence*. The latter title superimposes onto the work the idea of a sequence of causes and effects such as those the exhibition documents, where for instance the Final Solution is a consequence of Nazi anti-Semitism. But the work actually holds off this idea of narrative. The artist's own 'pro-

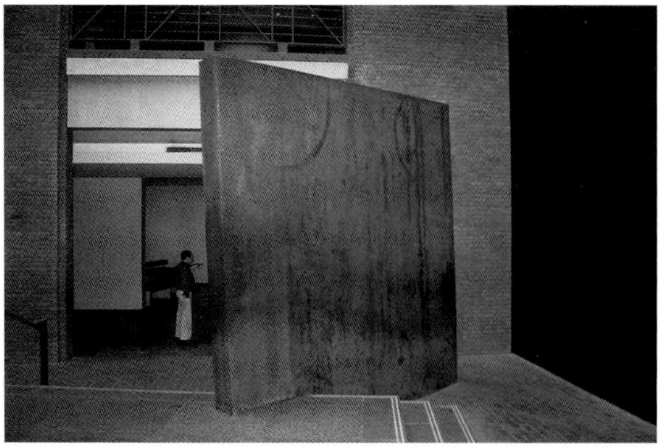 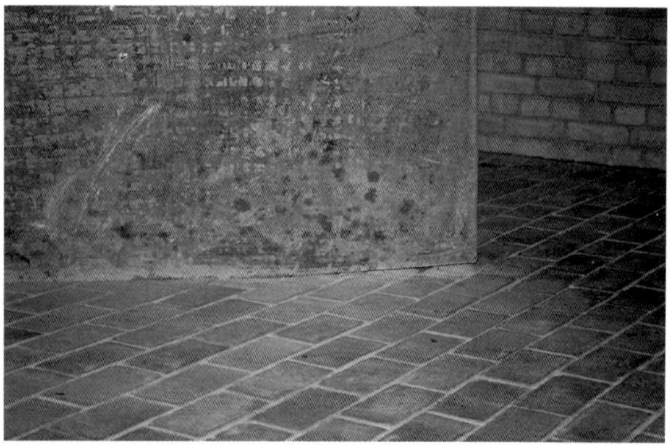

126 (left) Richard Serra, *Gravity*, 1993. View of *Gravity* from near bottom of staircase indicating how it seems to tilt to left.

127 (right) Richard Serra, *Gravity*, 1993. View of *Gravity* from ground showing how the lower right edge is slightly above floor level.

gression of coloured squares' implies no sense of movement or of causality, and looking at the drawing, there is no sense that any colour is the consequence of the one before. In contrast to the idea of 'consequence', the artist's title (as well as the work's appearance) suggests a kind of stasis. The wall drawing could be seen as acting against the onward pull of the exhibition's displays, inviting the visitors to stay a while in this space of calm and reflection. The work's invitation is particularly poignant given that it is placed in what would seem to be a passage-way, merely connecting two parts of the display: for the most part, this invitation is ignored.

*

The final section of the exhibition returns visitors to the content of the first photograph of the liberation of the camps, and to the Hall of Witness. Visitors pass by a wall made from facsimiles of Eastern European Jewish gravestones, and can stop to watch films of survivor testimonies in an amphitheatre whose walls are built with Jerusalem stone.[98] After emerging from the exhibition, the visitor's passage is no longer so strictly structured. They can proceed towards the Hall of Remembrance whose benches surround an open and empty floor, and there they can light candles underneath inscribed biblical texts and the carved names of prominent death sites. Alternatively, or after a time there, visitors return into the hulk of the Hall of Witness. They come out at the top of a staircase which descends into the main concourse, and doubles back on itself to go further down to a services area. At the bottom of this staircase, intersecting it, an apparently square, large steel slab rises up: Richard Serra's *Gravity*.

Viewers tend not to approach the sculpture from below, and they cannot walk up to it along a horizontal plane from afar: the architecture organises a route towards and around it from the top of the staircase, and the work was plotted with this route in mind. From the top of the stairs, the first effect of the work is to exacerbate the sense of descent (fig. 124). This happens in part because the weight of the sculpture appears as an image: indeed, Serra wanted to give the 'whole shaft a ballast'. The emphasis on descent is also due to the weight being 'impaled'. The slab appears as if it has fallen into the stairs, slicing into them from above. This imagined 'fall' becomes a kind of surrogate for viewers' movements – not only is the sculpture in the location to which they are headed, but it appears to have got there through the same downward movement that they are making.

But the sculpture works in more peculiar ways too. At first, and from above, it is hard to determine what position is actually occupied by the piece. *Gravity* appears small in scale, dwarfed both by a huge black granite wall that rises the full height of the west end of the Hall of Witness. The sculpture seems to stand upright, but as the viewer descends, the sculpture appears to be tilt downwards to the floor to the right. Further down, the illusion is corrected: there is a place on the stairs where viewers face *Gravity* along the axis of its diagonal direction, so they can tell that it is, indeed, perpendicular to the floor (fig. 125). At this point, the viewer gains an accurate sense of its spatial position, and understands why it has appeared to lean. This is because the corner of the stairs is angled away from the corner of the walls beyond it, and *Gravity* is (unexpectedly) aligned along the intersecting axis of the wall's corner, while cutting into the staircase off *its* corner.

A few steps down, the viewer reaches the sculpture's edge. Now *Gravity* seems to tilt to the left. (fig. 126) The edge is marked by horizontal scrapes showing where the slab was cut. The surface of the square plane is polychrome and complex. Though, in the main, a dark grey, there are areas of rusty brown. These areas seem to have been made by scratches or by unknown eroding agents. At the top right corner of the left side is a digital print of numbers. These details might sustain attention, although none are the result of any activity carried out by Serra. The most dramatic aspect of *Gravity*'s placement is perceived at ground level: the sculpture pitches into the floor. This has not been visible during the descent but looking at the work from the side, it is clear that the slab is sunk into the ground. Its bottom edge does not lie flush with the floor – the bottom corner of the piece is just above ground, by around a mere centimetre (fig. 127). The sense of sinking is strongest from a position away from the slab to its right, since the downward pitch is set against the vertical rise of the walls. The stairs also make this pitch seem more pronounced: the stairs are a 'rising' ground level, and make more of the corner appear to lie under the ground.

The confusions caused by the sculpture build up an overwhelming sense of spatial insecurity, working both against and with the architectural context. *Gravity* unsettles the rectangularity offered by the grids of the granite wall, the rectangular windows, and those other elements of the Hall of Witness which regulate space. At the same time, the effect of *Gravity* is heightened by, and heightens the effects of elements of the setting such as the diagonal skylight, and offset angles, which, without *Gravity*, would have already created a strange space. Together, *Gravity* and The Hall of Witness fix viewers in a warp.

Gravity has been described as a gravestone, and the digital marks on its surface have been said to symbolise the tattoos imprinted on the skin of concentration camp prisoners.[99] This second reading is as crude as it is unsurprising: Serra has always left factory stamps on his works so as to leave the industrial processes of fabrication visible, but as James Ingo Freed noted, Serra could have expected the reading: 'You put that stamp on [in] 20,000 places and nothing would happen. You put it there, and you expect it to happen. If [Serra] didn't want it there, he would erase it.'[100] Other readings have been prompted by the way in which the work structures movement around it. Ralph Grünewald wrote that: 'Like those unfortunate family members who were forced to separate from one another, so too will visitors need to separate as they move around the massive steel sculpture.'[101] *Gravity* certainly tempts analogies, some less problematic than others. As it pitches down, wedging into the steps, there is the impression that the steps are holding it in place, and that, were they not to clamp it, it might pitch further down, or even topple to one side. Susan Morganstein (who was involved in the commission) suggested that: 'If you and I could jump on it enough, it would smash down, and the whole building would be destroyed. It's a piece about the fragility of the stasis we have.'[102] So here the work serves as an analogy for the memory of the Holocaust rather than for an event at the camps: just as the sculpture could collapse, so could the attempt of the museum to commemorate.

Such readings are available, but like the descriptions of Kelly's paintings as 'memorial tablets', or LeWitt's sections as 'empty frames', they seem prompted by contingencies, and are not the kind of descriptions that usually accompany Serra's work. Even historians who have provided such accounts see *Gravity* in new ways. Hal Foster suggests the work represents 'a manifestation of the co-presence of the sacral and the secular'.[103] The viewer moves around the piece, experiencing it spatially (the mode of secular sculptural experience all of Serra's work enables), while they are also 'stilled by the plane'. This leads to 'an arresting of the viewer before the work' (a 'sacral' experience).[104] Foster suggests that with *Gravity*, 'there is another icon in play: the memorial wall'.[105]

However, while Foster argues for a 'sacral' dimension to the work, the achievement of *Gravity* is that it *maintains* the secular *against* the pull of the sacral, and this is particularly noticeable when one considers the materiality of the sculpture. Surrounding *Gravity* are other walls made of heavily allusive materials. Jerusalem stone is used in the exhibition and granite (reminiscent of Maya Lin's Vietnam memorial) is used in the Hall of Witness, alongside red brick chosen to conjure the sense of the cities of once-Jewish Europe. Then there are the walls made out of copied Jewish gravestones, and the reconstruction of the wall of the Warsaw ghetto. In the context of these walls and these materials, Serra's steel is resolutely literal, and nothing like a 'memorial wall'.[106]

In other ways too, what is intriguing and ultimately successful about *Gravity* is that Serra kept to his 'secular' principles and contributed to the setting without compromising his language. Freed has said that Serra '[didn't] want any reference to the Holocaust',[107] and the artist explained that 'in confronting the site I wish to create a field force so that the space is discerned physically rather than optically'.[108] *Gravity* functions like all Serra's other sculptures, achieving its effects for the viewer as they move between the sculpture and the existing architecture, but of course the effects that are produced by the work speak not just of space in a general sense, but to the context.[109] The sculpture affirms and heightens the 'gravity' of the USHMM. Serra's title, though a

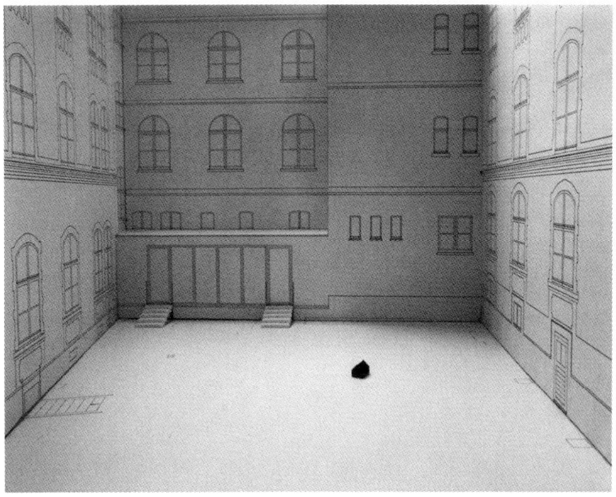
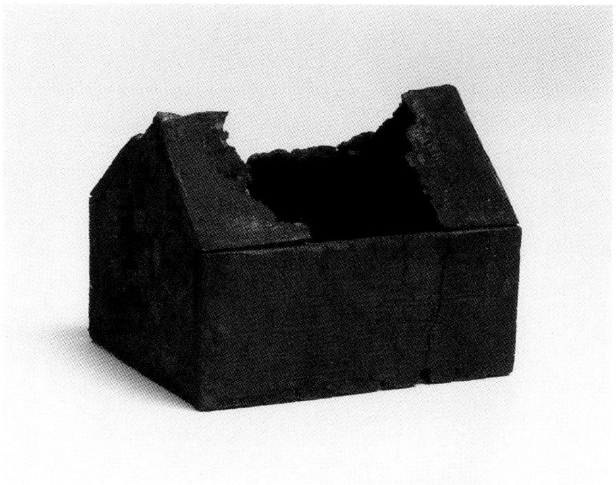

pun, is not flippant – it emphasises the way in which the metaphoric notion of 'gravity' is conveyed through the physical. The artist twisted his exploration of gravity, pursued through his entire career, in order to engage subject matter and context through sculpture. The work started with Freed's hopes for 'some depiction of moral breakdown', and though his granite wall was never cracked, Serra's intervention did manage to represent the breakdown that was the Holocaust. Though the artist once said that his sculptures 'do not relate to the history of monuments. They do not memorialise anything',[110] here, through abstract means alone, a memorial atmosphere is emphasised.

128 Joel Shapiro, Model of site with proposed sculpture and location for the Stadhaus, Düsseldorf, Mühlenstrasse 29, 1989 (left); and detail of proposed sculpture (right). Burnt wood, 17.5 × 23.2 × 18.1 cm. No longer extant.

in defence of the AFPSP?

I opened this discussion with two questions: to what extent were the criticisms of the AFPSP at the USHMM justified, and to what extent did the programme represent a co-option of abstraction and a negation of its once radical aspirations? Having attained a sense of how the commissions proceeded, how the artists responded to the invitations from the museum, how their works are encountered in the context of the museum's architecture and displays and how their works have been considered by various writers, I can finally attempt to address these questions.

In order to establish whether or not abstraction was co-opted, I would like to begin by thinking about the commissioners. Did they seek to (ab)use abstraction in order to soothe the visitors' way through the displays, and to offer the redeeming reminder of post-war human creativity, or was their thinking about art in line with the once radical aspirations of the artists they selected? There is no way of answering this question one way or the other. Some people working for or with the USHMM did indeed hope that the works would allow moments of respite, giving spiritual content to the narrative and even functioning as proofs of the 'aesthetic genius of the human imagination'.[111] Yet others were aware of the 'aspirations' of artists of this generation and might have hoped that the works would not just serve an audience proceeding through the main part of the museum, but shape that audience, so that they emerged with a multifaceted approach to what Holocaust memory might mean. What is certainly clear is that despite the fact that some people associated with the museum strongly disapproved the choice of work, those who supported it could come to a consensus about the work even if they had divergent attitudes towards its purpose and effect.

The second part of the response to the question needs to consider the possibility that the artists let the language of their art be twisted in ways that seem entirely contrary to their practice. Serra suggested that the problem of placing work in the USHMM was that it would inevitably be 'misinterpreted', but were any of the artists party to this misinterpretation? The circumstances of LeWitt's commission mean that it is impossible to determine whether or not he intended or supported the reading of grey in *Consequence* as an allusion to ash, or frames as an allusion to emptied photographs, but such readings are nonetheless hard to stomach when recalling his earlier serial approaches to shape and colour. Kelly had used white in non-associative ways since the late 1940s, and in the 1952 work *Red Yellow Blue White*, he had even deployed the white of the wall as an essential part of the non-composition. As Yve-Alain Bois has demonstrated, during this period he had derived the shapes of his paintings from 'already made' forms encountered on the streets of Paris. The paintings were therefore indexical traces of the forms, in some ways memorials of them. Kelly at that time promoted an art with 'no metaphor (no transformation), no transcendence (no abstraction), no representation (only presentation).'[112] Given these roots of Kelly's art, it is hard to swallow the reading of *Memorial*'s white as a reference to loss, its rectangles as 'memorial tablets', and the work as a whole as spiritual – all readings that the artist has encouraged. Instead of the work giving a sense that Kelly struggled with what it meant to use the well-established language of his abstraction to confront the space of the USHMM, it can seem that he grafted the 'loss of the Jews' too easily onto the meanings of his white monochromes. And yet at the same time, with the arc, Kelly deployed an idea of transcendence developed in his work in a completely new and productive way. As Benjamin Buchloh has argued, Kelly's arcs 'convey to the spectator a sense of spatial expansion [and] the curve's seductive sinuation promises to transcend the limited parameters of the spectators' spatial and perceptual confinement'.[113] In the USHMM, in fascinating contrast to the rectangles, the arc promised to transcend the particular confinement of the angular architectural setting.

This question – whether the artists let the language of their art be twisted in ways that seem contrary to their practice – requires a different response when considering Shapiro and Serra. Shapiro's contribution to the USHMM did not amount to a major shift away from the main direction of his work at this time. Indeed his previous commission for a Holocaust project for Düsseldorf had involved more of a break – or at least a shift back to the language of his 1970s sculpture. In 1973, Shapiro had exhibited tiny cast-iron houses on the floors of otherwise empty galleries in order to provoke the viewer to consider the difference between their scale and that of the models. As Rosalind Krauss articulated at the time, this strategy already involved the idea of memory, for just as events become distant to us in memory, so the familiar figure of the house would be distanced by scale from the viewer.[114] For the Düsseldorf commission, Shapiro planned to revisit his radical approach to scale in order to address a new idea of memory (fig. 128). But this approach to scale was largely absent from the USHMM work, despite the interesting relationship of the work to the Washington Memorial. Instead, *Loss and Regeneration* fitted in with Shapiro's large welded oblong sculptures of the 1980s and early 1990s which had already signalled a movement away from some of the most interesting characteristics of his earlier work. Nonetheless, as I suggested, the traces of process and the literalness of materiality persisted in the USHMM project from Shapiro's earliest work. Shapiro did not encourage a metaphoric reading of process as Kelly had encouraged an allusive reading of whiteness. In this way, his contribution was comparable to Serra's, which (as I have suggested) was the most satisfying of the contributions to the AFPSP. By no means at all a misuse of his work, *Gravity* was absolutely characteristic of Serra's abstraction, but at the same time absolutely appropriate to the setting.

And so with regard to the artists rather than the commissioners, the response to the problem of abstraction's possible co-option in the USHMM is complex. On the one hand, it can be said not only that the circumstances caused problematic and unusual readings of the works, but that artists twisted their language in conformity with their expectations about the setting's requirements without much difficulty. On the other hand, it can be argued that the AFPSP was a unique opportunity for these artists to put their language to work without compromise and in a completely new way as to let abstract art confront Holocaust memory in extremely subtle and complex manners. But what of the first question I raised: to what extent were the vociferous criticisms of the art programme justified?

These criticisms took two forms. There were those who opposed the presence of any kind of art in the USHMM, and those who objected to the inclusion of abstraction. As far as the first case is concerned, it should be very clear that the commissioned works never occupied so much space that they could ever have prevented viewers from learning about the incidents of the Holocaust documented in the displays. Nor did they provide the 'obscene pleasures' that one critic complained about: the works were neither easy to look at nor to contemplate. As for the second criticism, it is futile to wonder whether Christian Boltanski or Hans Haacke (to cite two of the alternative artists named by the critics) would have provided 'better' solutions. Not only do we not have concrete proposals to compare with the works realised by Shapiro, Kelly, LeWitt and Serra, but it is hard to imagine how work by such artists would have fared in the midst of the photographic and text-based displays of the USHMM exhibition. Because if this, it is difficult to meet the objections to the AFPSP head-on, but I do wish to cite three arguments in defence of the programme. The first of these was formulated by James Freed.

As I mentioned earlier, the architect had initially argued that art would function in two ways in his building. A crack implemented in conjunction with an artist would provide a symbol of breakdown, and in other places, art works would serve as sites for ceremonies. By the time the museum was opened, Freed had changed his attitude. The architect argued that when visitors encountered the art works, they came into contact with contemporary cultural production as it exists *outside* the museum. It was not so much that the presence of art works illustrated the difference between 'civilised' art and the 'depravity' of the Holocaust. Rather, by causing the viewers to remember the world outside the museum, Freed felt that the art works disqualified the possibility that the museum might become a hermetic environment cut away from reality. This was a threat that had been considered right through the planning of the institution: the Holocaust should not be represented as an ahistorical bad dream that one might enter and leave, or as Freed put it, an 'abstract world'.[115] Freed came to believe that the art works gave the museum 'a kind of legitimacy'.[116] Viewers would know that the art works were a real product of contemporary culture, and because of the juxtaposition, the Holocaust would be shown to be real too; a proper subject of historical enquiry and thought.

I have described how Richard Serra persuaded Freed to abandon his symbolic crack. In so far as *this* argument goes, Freed seems to have assimilated the thinking of Lawrence Weiner. Weiner had suggested that his work would introduce 'definitive actions' and the 'material reality' of the world into the museum, thus connecting the museum to the world outside and reminding visitors of their responsibilities to their world as much as to the world they learnt about. Though Weiner's work was never installed, Freed came to see the art works fulfilling this purpose. But just as Weiner's argument did not necessitate the precise materials of the sculpture he proposed, so Freed's new argument did not explain why the art works needed to be abstract. Nonetheless the abstraction of the works in the AFPSP can also be defended.

In the text he published during the building's planning, Freed had described another fate that the museum needed to avoid. Summarising the 1979 report to President Carter, Freed wrote that the USHMM 'must not be a reconstruction because that would devalue the Holocaust; a reconstruction would be a Disneyland – clean, cute, no tension'.[117] But though his architecture resisted such a reconstruction, the displays it housed often became spectacular and theatrical. Probably without realising that Freed had used the term, Richard Serra described the museum as 'Disneylandia'. I would like to argue that abstraction works against the insistent lure of the narrative, and against the spectacle of the displays. In some ways, the works *take on* specific aspects of the exhibitions to recast them: Shapiro's 'figure' against the clay figures in the gas chamber model, Kelly's and Serra's walls against the facsimiles of ghetto and gravestone walls, LeWitt's passage against the passages over the 'ghetto bridge' and through the cattle truck. The abstract works interrupt the narrative and puncture it, refusing to represent the Holocaust through graphic images and steady narratives. They might afford an important opportunity for contemplation, but rather than merely soothing visitors, the works encourage a more complex response. In part this is precisely because of the lure of symbolic readings imposed by contingencies: Shapiro's sculpture as a body, Kelly's paintings as a cemetery, LeWitt's wall drawing as empty frames, Serra's slab as a gravestone. The context tempts all of these readings, but despite any intention one way or the other on the part of the artist, the works do nothing to secure them and everything to resist securing them. The works are difficult, and because of their abstraction, they unsettle the very notion of Holocaust memory. Unlike the artefacts, photographs, films and texts, they neither control the object nor the means of memory. They leave one asking, indeed, 'what am I supposed to remember *here*?' In revealing this to be such a difficult question, they ruffle the smoothness of the very notion of a memorial museum.

The last defence of the AFPSP would need to set the programme in the context of the religious spaces within the museum and the rhetoric of Elie Wiesel, whose voice was so important to its foundation. In an unrelenting attack, Norman Finkelstein has scrutinised Wiesel's 'sacralization of the Holocaust': 'The Holocaust is effectively a "mystery" religion', Finkelstein wrote. 'Wiesel intones that the Holocaust "leads into darkness", "negates all answers", "lies outside, if not beyond, history", "defies both knowledge and description", "cannot be explained nor visualized", is "never to be comprehended or transmitted", marks a "destruction of history" and a "mutation on a cosmic scale".'[118] Though it might seem that abstraction would be precisely the mode of art that could complement this approach to the Holocaust – that abstraction refuses to explain or visualise the Holocaust, and so sanctifies it – in the USHMM this could not be further from the case. Rather than seeing these works as avoiding representation, I want to conclude by remembering the ways in which they invite physical and material responses, and encourage close observation of details, the ways in which they pose contradictory ideas about the relationship of art and the Holocaust rather than neat platitudes. In all these ways, the works of the AFPSP resist the sacralisation of the Holocaust in favour of more concrete and complex forms of commemoration.

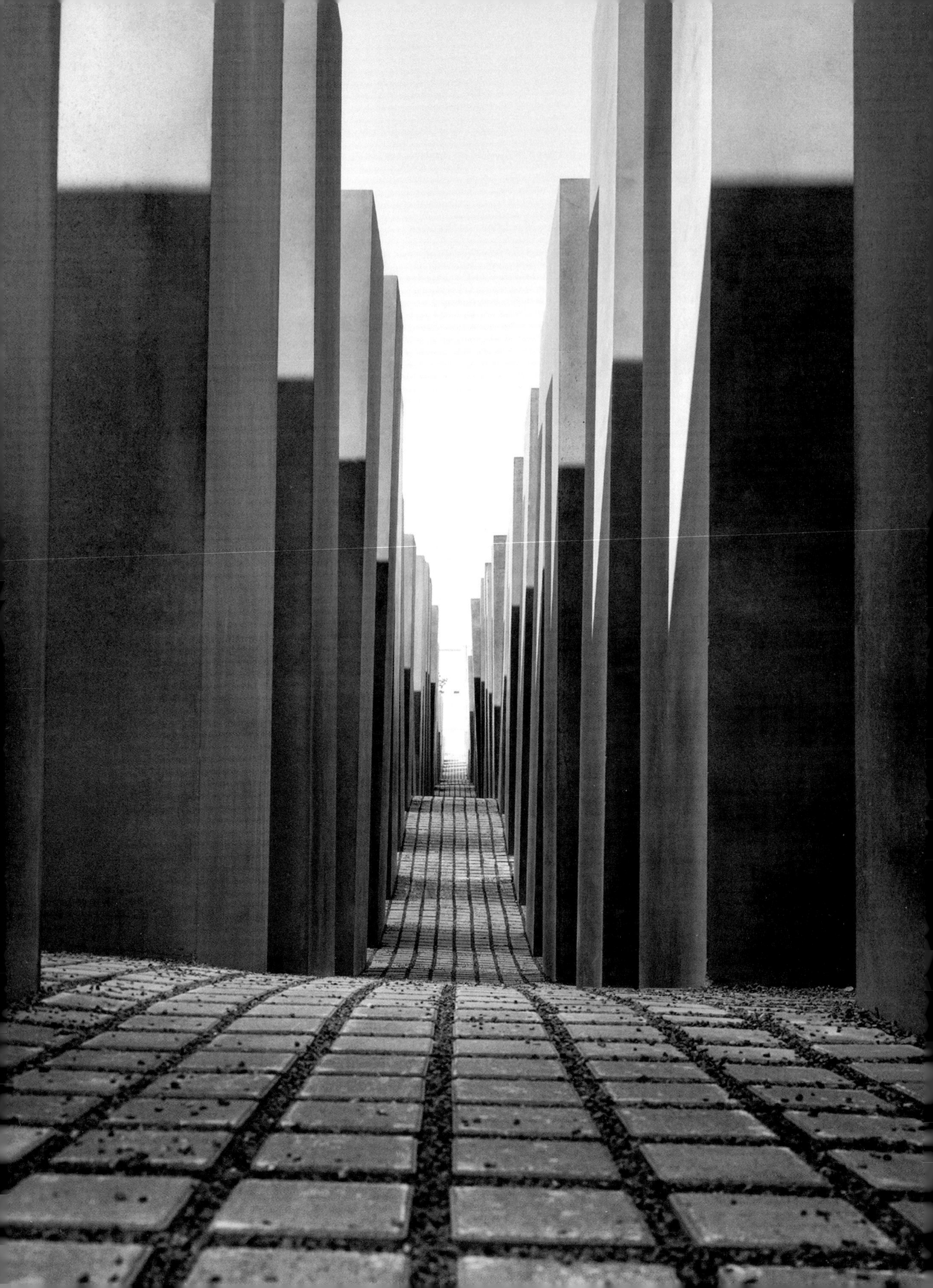

nine

peter eisenman's *memorial to the mudered jews of europe* and susan hiller's *the j.street project*

the two memories

On a cloudy day in May 2005, I paid a second visit to Berlin in order to attend the inauguration of Peter Eisenman's *Memorial to the Murdered Jews of Europe* (fig. 130). Numerous officials gathered and dignitaries spoke; photographers bustled around at the perimeters of the field eager for a glimpse of the architect; news reporters grabbed elderly Holocaust survivors who had been invited to the event and probed them on their reaction to the new monument. A scaffold had been built on one of the roads flanking the field, allowing TV cameras to film the expanse of the memorial from above. The action took place outside the field itself, but once the media had departed, I was able to enter the completed memorial for the first time.

129 Peter Eisenman, *Memorial to the Murdered Jews of Europe*, view along north–south axis.

The first surprise on stepping into the memorial was the amazing speed of my transition from outside to within the field. The field comprises a grid of some 2,700 rectangular-sectioned stelae or pillars, and those on the uneven periphery are low-lying, around the height of benches (fig. 131). As I entered the space of the memorial, my body rose above these blocks, but with only five or so strides, the pillars towered above me – as the pillars rise, the ground level simultaneously dips. It had not seemed from the periphery that the blocks would rise up so quickly, but there is an obvious reason for this drama – initially, I had been looking at the top of the field and at the Berlin landmarks beyond. I had not thought to look at the ground level, and had not anticipated the drop. So, quite suddenly I moved from a position where I could see all around me, to a position where I was enclosed by the memorial and unable to have

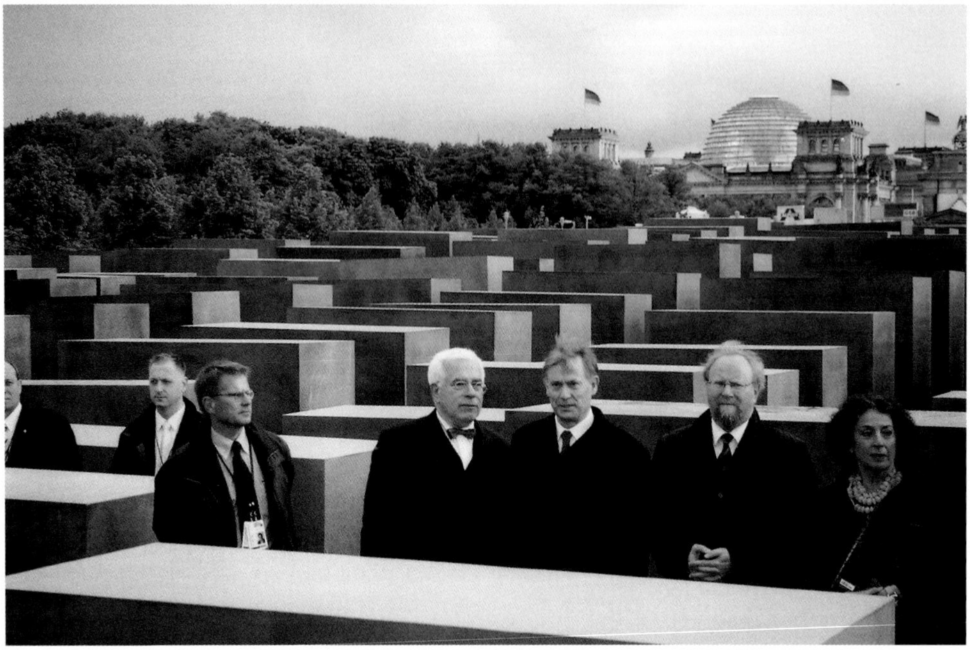

anything approximating to the viewpoint of the TV cameras just mentioned. With the rapid immersion, it seemed as if time had suddenly slowed down. On the periphery, I encountered the memorial distracted by the fast temporality of city. There had been cars driving around, the sound of distant sirens, the Potsdamer Platz skyscrapers beyond. But with these few steps into the pillars, it seemed that I began to walk more slowly; and surrounded by the stelae, the bustle of the city made way for the slow time of remembrance.

130 Peter Eisenman, President Koehler, Wolfgang Thierse, Lea Rosh and others at the inauguration of the *Memorial to the Murdered Jews of Europe*, Berlin, May 2005.

With this quick move from bustle to slowness, the journey inside the memorial began. Yet to call the movement within the memorial a 'journey' is misleading. Journeys imply directions from one place to another, and it was immediately clear that there was no route to follow here. The memorial had no centre, no point of focus. With every step I took, I was brought to a kind of crossroads: I could move forward, backwards, left or right: no one direction was privileged, nothing would be more or less appropriate. This produced both the sense that the memorial offered more routes through it than I, or anyone, could ever take – its space was inexhaustible – and the sense that all routes were equally valid. Though it was always up to me which way to turn, and though any direction I took would be adequate, I also knew that the memorial would exceed my attempt to fathom it.

To walk within the memorial was to become at once conscious of the random nature of my own navigation, and of the uniformity of the directional choices available to me. But though I was immediately aware of repetition, both in terms of the choice of routes and in terms of the pillars themselves (each was made of the same concrete, each had a similar texture, each had the identical width and breadth), the field did not

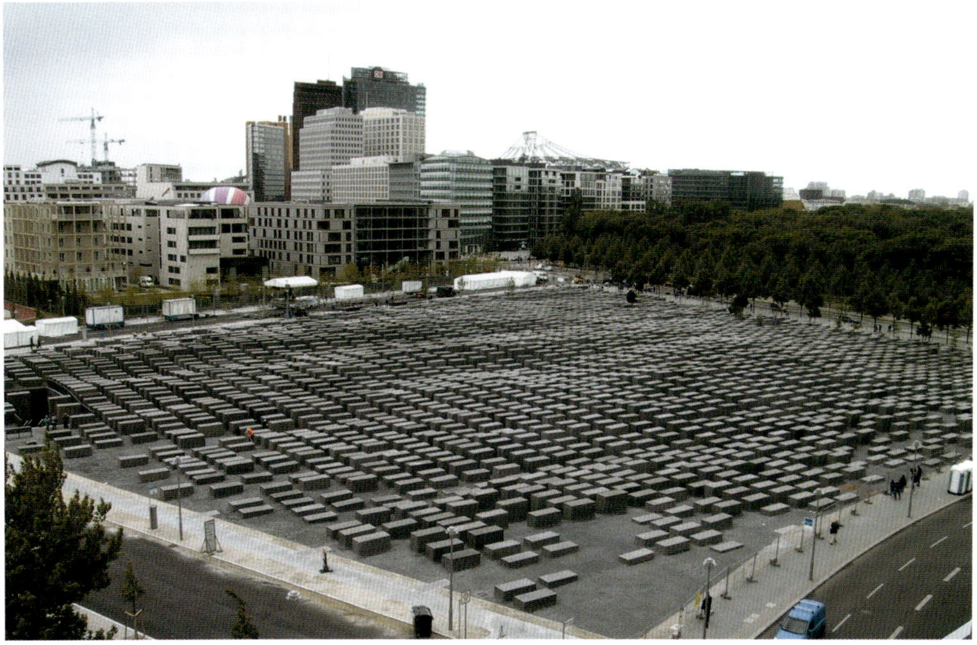

131 Peter Eisenman, *Memorial to the Murdered Jews of Europe*, View looking southwest from the roof of the Hotel Adlon towards Potsdamer Platz.

feel at all homogeneous. Of course, as I had perceived from the outside, though arranged on a grid, the pillars varied in height, but from within, two more kinds of difference were palpable. First, there was the extreme contrast between the sightlines along the north-south and the east-west axes. Facing east or west, I looked into a cold corridor whose oppressiveness was forged not just by the repetition of the pillars but by the constancy of the ground level (fig. 132). Looking north or south, however, there was more of a sense of disturbance because the ground undulated before me (fig. 129). The second kind of difference was that while most of the pillars rose up perpendicular to the ground, as pillars elsewhere do, some lurched at unexpected angles, tipping into the corridors or away, so enclosing or opening up the space in which I moved. Another kind of surprise awaited: from time to time, other attendants of the inauguration appeared also pacing through the field. Much as I knew I was not alone, the sight of these people was always disturbing: suddenly someone would come out from a few pillars beyond me, and one of us would change our direction. I might lose this person for a time, but then they would reappear, now far beyond me along the same corridor, now right beside me to my left or right.

The May clouds shifted towards the late afternoon, and raking sunlight hit the pillars. Their blank, grey concrete was now divided into areas of light and dark, with stelae throwing sharp shadows across each other's faces. The play of light and shadow further tempered the repetition of the field but this light play was elegant rather than spectacular, with no special effects or phenomenal surprises. Unlike monuments that serve to frame or give focus to their contexts (as nearby, for instance, the Brandenburg Gate frames a view down Unter der Linden, and the Siegessäule gives focus to the

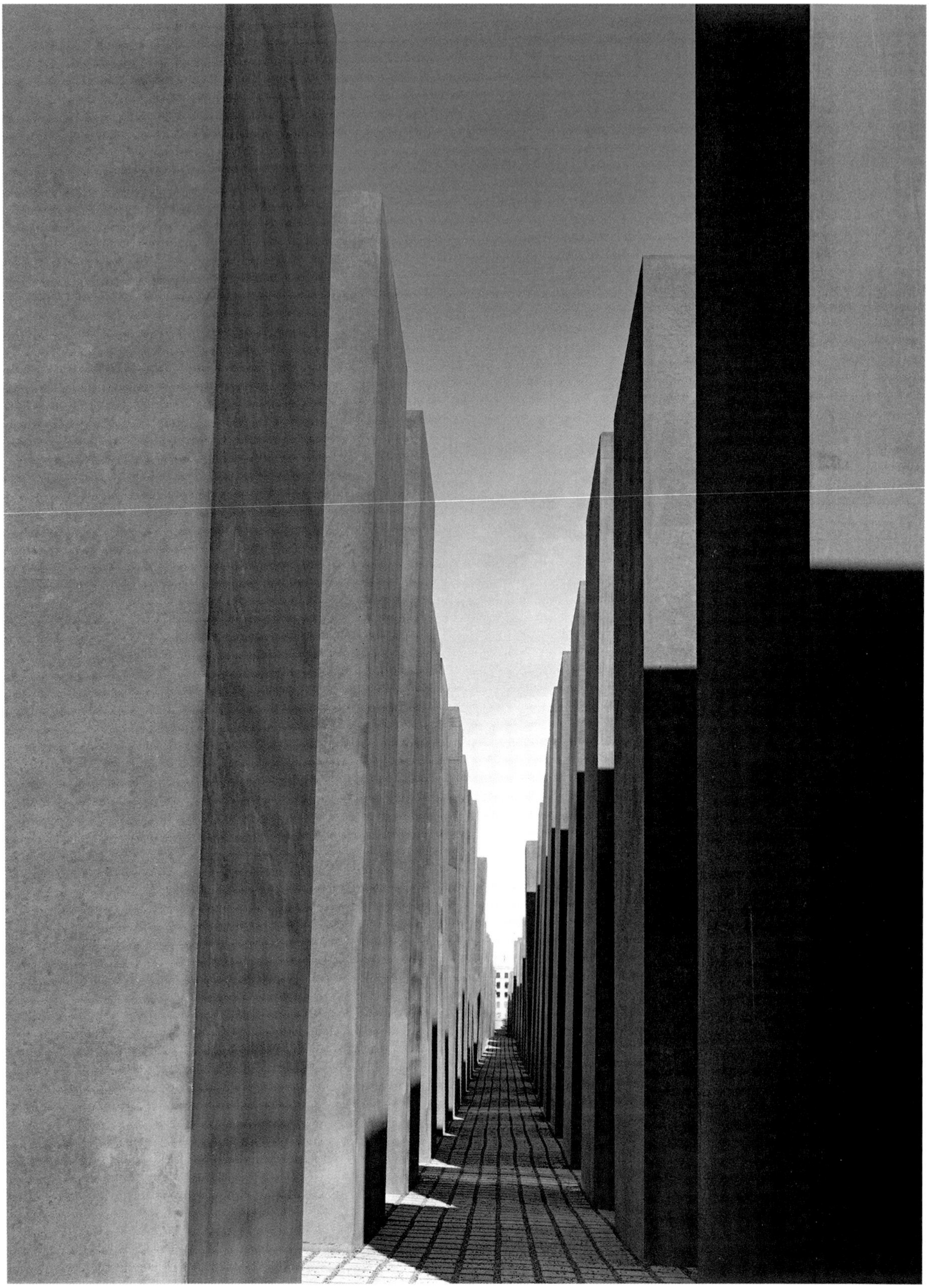

Tiergarten), I had sensed that this memorial fractured Berlin as I had paced around, slicing up its landscape to produce partial, jagged views such as that of the Bundestag dome between the pillars (fig. 133). But approaching another periphery, Berlin suddenly unified again. Now I was outside once more, looking from above, over the field in which I had paced. It was time to leave the memorial behind, but there was more to see. Though Eisenman had intended the memorial to comprise the field of pillars alone, pressure had been brought on him to accompany the field with an exhibition centre in which the history of the Holocaust would be communicated by conventional displays. The size and precise location of the display centre – called the 'Ort' – had been debated, and the decision to place it under the field had prevailed. And so, re-entering the field towards the south-east corner, I descended the steps to see the displays.

132 Peter Eisenman, *Memorial to the Murdered Jews of Europe*, view along east–west axis.

The Ort comprised one corridor and four large rooms. Rather than attempt to reprise the kind of chronological narrative told, for instance, at the USHMM, the exhibition designers here had decided to memorialise the Holocaust in four different manners. In the first room, the floor was punctuated by a grid of illuminated panels, each showing last letters and testimonies of victims (fig. 134). In the second room, pre-war photographs of Jewish families were displayed next to texts describing their fates. In the third, the names of the dead were projected onto the walls while spare biographical accounts sounded from loudspeakers. In the last, displays recorded information about the camps and various other sites of death. Thus narrative was eschewed in favour of four contrasting modes of memorial, so that individual lives were recorded alongside collective deaths, and victims were given a voice as perpetrators' acts were recorded.

As sensitive as this exhibition was, the attempts to integrate the architecture of the field into the Ort felt strained. In the first room, the illuminated panels were the same dimensions as the stelae's footprints. In the second, the stelae appeared to protrude from the ceiling but stopped before reaching the floor, providing suspended walls on which the family photographs were displayed (fig. 135). Of course, though grey, these protrusions were obviously not made of concrete, and were hollow and tinny when tapped. The third room was wide open, with the field's forms replicated as a grid in the ceiling, while finally in the fourth room, a pattern of columns defined its uneven perimeter. While the decision to use four methods to represent the history of the Holocaust felt convincing, by contrast, the decision to use four devices to combine the upper architecture with the lower space was aggravating. The problem of how to integrate the field and the Ort together had not been solved.

That week, Eisenman's memorial was greeted by a host of reviews in the German and international press, and the most compelling text, 'The Two Memories', was written by Giorgio Agamben in *Die Zeit*.[1] Agamben strongly supported both parts of the memorial, writing eloquently about their differences. In his text, he distinguished the 'memorable' from the 'unforgettable'. The 'memorable' referred to information that could be conveyed by texts, photographs, maps, numbers and documents: this was the preserve of the Ort. The 'unforgettable' was that part of the memory of the Holocaust that could not be so contained; that which exceeds the archive. This was the preserve of the field. At first, Agamben seemed to indicate that Eisenman's achievement was his insistence on the 'unforgettable'. Where most traditional monuments and museums function through the provision of texts and images, Eisenman had constructed a 'book of stone' whose 'absolutely illegible' pages 'can neither be inscribed nor read'. By doing this, Eisenman not only did justice to this dimension of Holocaust memory, but also avoided the likely effect that a purely museum-based memorial would have: it would 'cover up with heaps of memories that which needs to remain unforgettable', ultimately serving those who wished to forget. Agamben championed the illegibility of the stelae, but in the end, he suggested that both the 'memorable' and the 'unforgettable' needed to be acknowledged, as they were by the Ort and field respectively. Both parts of Eisenman's memorial were necessary to each other. The 'true place' of the memorial he defined as the 'immaterial threshold' between the field above and Ort below.

Though intriguing, Agamben's account did not attend to specific architectural details: the threshold between the field and Ort might have been conceptually 'immaterial', but in terms of architecture it was excessively physical – as I have mentioned, there were four different material strategies deployed to integrate the architecture above with what lay below. But I want to contest Agamben's account on other grounds. Comparing the field with the Ort is ultimately unhelpful, I think, because it makes the field seem too monolithic, just a place of emptiness in contrast to the Ort as a place of information. For all the elegance of Agamben's distinction between the 'unforgettable' and 'memorable', the field is made to seem too silent, too illegible. Certainly, as Agamben noted, the pillars were not inscribed as might be Chinese stelae (a comparison he made), but the field does suggest more than just an absence or impossibility of meaning. Eisenman, after all, had confidence that the field could serve on its own as a memorial.

To explore this argument I would like to think about Eisenman's specific strategies in making the field, and then ask how these strategies can be read, how they create affects and meanings.[2] From my opening description, it might seem that Eisenman simply placed a grid of pillars on the uneven ground of Berlin, deciding at random which should stretch straight up, and which should rise at an angle. In fact, the form of the field was determined in an entirely different manner, through a process that really is the core of Eisenman's work on the memorial. Eisenman invented two topographies, each a plane like a wavy sheet, each undulating differently (fig. 136). Each topography was then divided into an identical grid of rectangular sections, with narrow pathways between them. One topography was placed above the other, so that the one grid lay above the other. All this was done on computers in order to plot out the position the columns would occupy. The columns simply joined the rectangular sections in the top grid to those in the bottom grid. The columns vary in height and tilt because the two topographies were not parallel sheets, but differently irregular. Eisenman, as we shall see, has a particular term to describe the process of determining height and tilt, but its simplicity should hopefully be evident already, and it should also be clear that this is an impersonal system rather than a subjective or random decision-making process. It is also important to note, at this point, why the simplicity of this

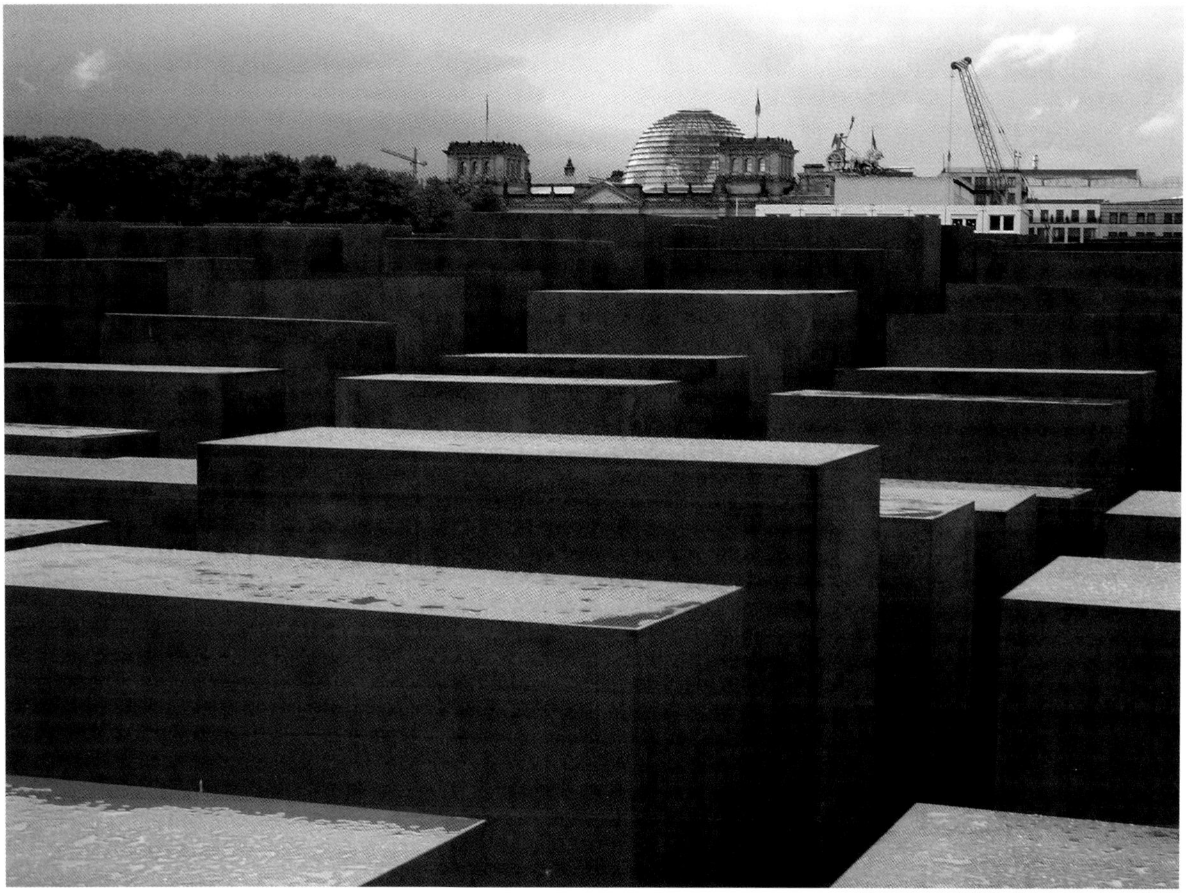

133 Peter Eisenman, *Memorial to the Murdered Jews of Europe*, View towards Bundestag and Brandenburg Gate.

process remains illegible when walking through the field. This is because it is not possible to see the two topographies at once. From outside and above, the top topography is visible – the wavy top of the field. From inside, it is the bottom topography that is seen, or felt – the bumpy ground of the paths. Their relationship is not something that can be seen. It is described by the tilt of the columns, but when confronted with this tilt – when looking ahead at a tilting column – the viewer neither looks to the ground, nor sees the column's top face.

The process that formed the field involved the superimposition of two invented topographies and their joining by a grid of columns, but for all its supposed simplicity and neutrality, it is a process replete with suggestion. What did it mean to invent a topography in the first place? Eisenman could have placed the pillars on the bare ground of Berlin as he found it when the site was turned over to him. Equally, he could have engineered a flattened and neutral plain on which to position the blocks. He decided to invent a topography of bumps and low valleys for particular reasons. Not only would the ground of the memorial, positioned in the centre of Berlin, feel entirely distinct

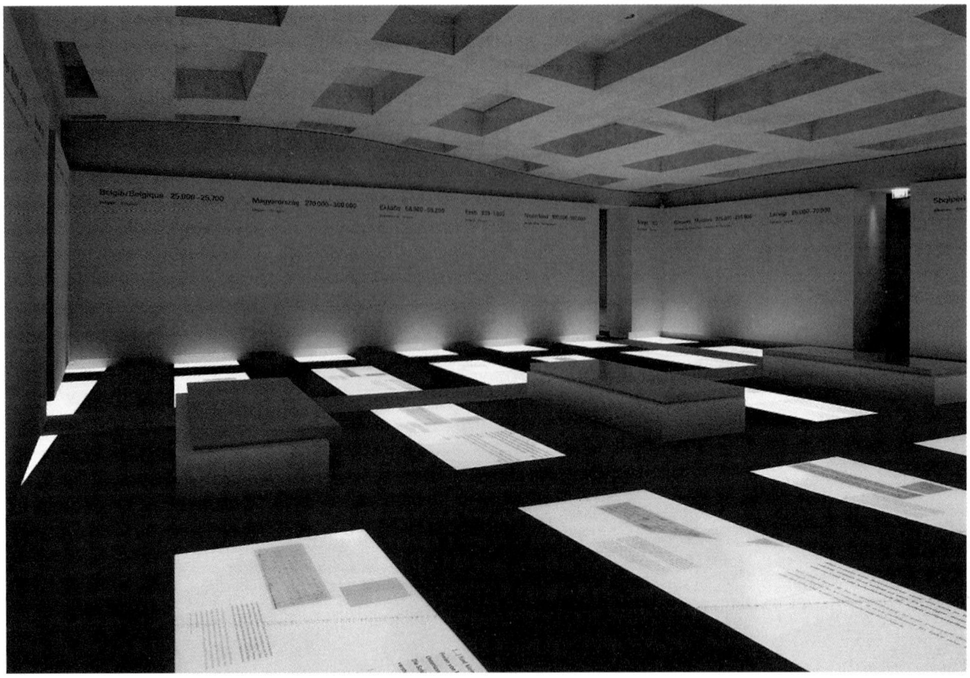

134 Interior view of the first room of the Ort of Information in *Memorial to the Murdered Jews of Europe*.

from the ground outside; the fabrication of a new ground would also serve to oppose one of the principles of Nazism. As Eisenman has noted, one of Nazism's core ideologies involved the sanctity of the German ground. His memorial replaced the firmness and fixity of the German ground with a fictitious, unpredictable, newly invented topography, one that is 'other than stable', as he said.[3]

By inventing *two* topographies and having a grid of pillars to connect them, Eisenman in addition produced a reading of Nazism. The architectural strategy that Eisenman deployed causes a particular sensation in the field. Walking through it, a visitor knows that the columns are plotted on a grid, but cannot tell why there are odd undulations above and below, and why pillars ahead lean and lurch. What is sensed is that a rational system has produced disturbing and unpredictable results. Eisenman's strategy sets up this sensation, and this experience in turn serves as an analogy for Nazism: Nazism is also a disturbing product of a rational system. Nazism is conceived here not as an interruption of medieval madness in modernity, but as a product of modernity – as a moment in which modernity's rationality gives rise to calamity, a moment where modernity's industrial and economic means are put to horrific use. Eisenman thus reads the Holocaust as have others before him – Adorno and Horkheimer, Zygmunt Bauman, for instance – as 'an exquisitely modern form of genocide.'[4] By reading the Holocaust in this way, Eisenman also turns the memorial into a warning. The memorial not only reads history, but suggests that there is no reason why contemporary industrial capitalism cannot produce another Holocaust. Reason and order, in other words, can once again give rise to chaos and violence.

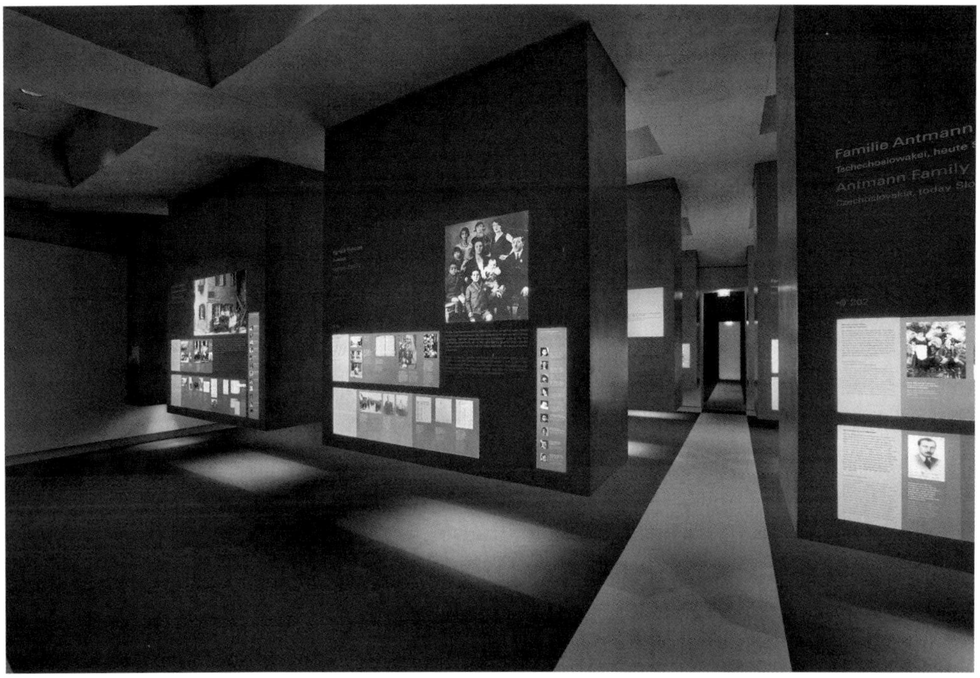

135 Interior view of the second room of the Ort of Information in *Memorial to the Murdered Jews of Europe.*

All this is to argue for the legibility of the field. The field enacts a reading of Nazism, and serves as a warning against a recurrence of totalitarianism. Hopefully it should be clear that this interpretation of the field results from a combination of my personal experience of the memorial, together with an understanding of Eisenman's architectural strategy. But there are other interesting ways to read the memorial. Because Eisenman used grey concrete as the material of his wavy pillars (rather than glass or steel, for instance), the memorial comes to resemble, albeit rather loosely, a premodern graveyard, such as the famous Jewish Cemetery in Prague. This is to say that Eisenman's field conjures not only a space of death, but a famously Jewish space, and one belonging to a community destroyed by the Nazis. This allusion to Prague cemetery starts as a formal resonance, but becomes more nuanced. If, when navigating the field, one thinks of a distant graveyard, then one has to compare a graveyard in which the dead are named on the graves (such as Prague's), and this field of stelae, in which such naming does not take place. In his book *Remnants of Auschwitz*, Agamben showed how the very concept of death was eliminated in the camp.[5] Death was no longer a privileged event, since the destruction of the human had taken place before the moment of death. As others have commented, it is impossible to name all the victims of Nazism, as entire communities, and all records of individuals, were destroyed. Making the comparison between a graveyard and the stelae, a visitor is given cause to ponder these dimensions of the Holocaust within Eisenman's field. Once again, this is to say that the field generates readings and meanings. It is not the case that the pillars are blank stones simply void of inscription. Rather, this

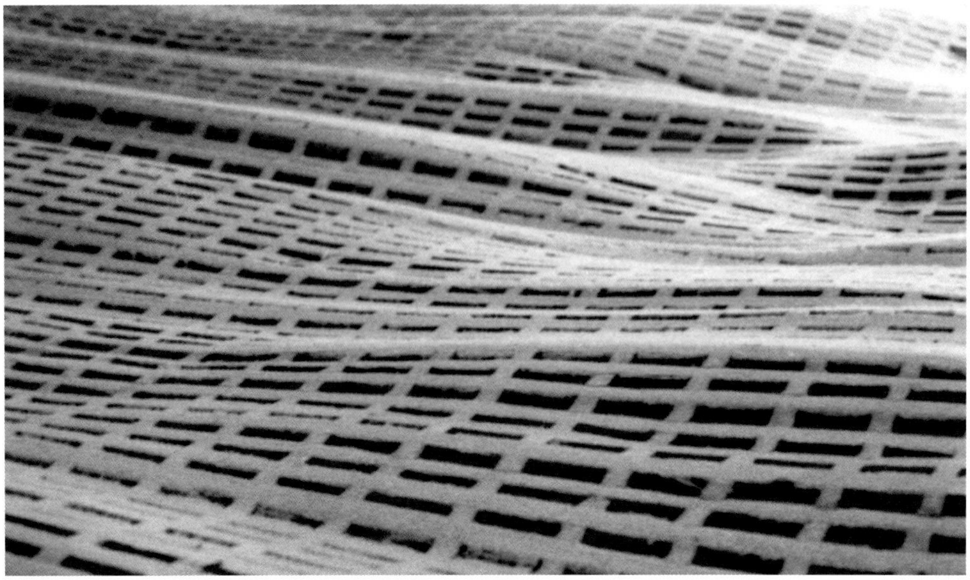

136 Peter Eisenman, Original topography model for ground of the *Memorial*. Black rectangles indicate the place of the stelae.

absence of inscriptions *signifies* as a reflection on the nature of the death in the Final Solution.[6]

Earlier, I described my initial visit to the memorial, and the sense of disorientation and solitude within the field. I felt disoriented first because of the speed of the transition from outside to within, and this feeling continued because all places within the field seemed similar – there were no set routes, no markers to distinguish one particular junction point from another. I felt solitary because the paths only allowed me to walk by myself, and also because the field prevented me from seeing other visitors for any length of time – they kept disappearing and reappearing as they took their own path. These senses were part of the affective dimension of the memorial, and are, as such, other parts of its meaning. I should be clear at this point that such affects were very much intended by Eisenman, and once again, for specific reasons relating to his understanding of the subject of the memorial. As he recalled at interview, part of the research he had undertaken for the project had involved talking to survivors who recalled, more than anything else, the loneliness of prison life, its disorientations. Although he in no way aimed to recreate the camp with his memorial – such an ambition would stretch the limits of empathy and would risk the accusation of banalising the experience of the victims – he did hope that the physical encounter with the memorial would generate affects that were appropriate to the subject being commemorated.

As I mentioned in the introduction, to address Eisenman's memorial fully means to engage important questions: what does it mean for Berlin to build a Holocaust memorial at all? Who is the memorial for? What does it mean for an American Jew to be its architect? What is its relationship to other memorial sites in Berlin, and Daniel Libeskind's Jewish Museum in particular? These questions have been, and continue to be tackled elsewhere.[7] What concerns me here, however, is to ask how the field *works* as a memorial, a question that some who have pursued these debates leave aside. It should by now be clear that the field alone functions in various ways. It enacts a conceptual critique of the Nazi idea of 'ground' while physically interrupting the centre of Berlin; it reads Nazism as a product of modernity and as an ongoing threat; it alludes to other architectural sites such as the Prague graveyard in order to suggest the difference between the lives commemorated there, and the manner of death in the Final Solution; and it creates a sense in the visitor of disorientation and solitude. Of course the field involves many renunciations – it refuses to glorify its architectural context; it refuses to provide a central focus of memory or a route towards a centre; it refuses to provide a symbol or text to steer thought towards the subject of memory. All these renunciations register the impact of the Holocaust on architectural and memorial language, but to think about the field only as an acknowledgment of the impossibility of traditional forms of commemoration, and as an illegible form in contrast to the informational Ort, will not do. It is just that the field produces its meanings without recourse to texts, photographs or maps. It represents the Holocaust through the devices that I insist on calling those of abstraction.

'there is no abstraction there. . . .'

At one of the press conferences before the opening of the memorial, Eisenman faced a questioner who asked him if the memorial was abstract. 'Anyone who thinks this is abstract art should take a walk in those piers', he replied. 'There is no abstraction there. There is a lot of feeling . . . You will feel what it is like to be lost in space. When you walk in this it is not an abstraction.'[8] Somewhat surprised by his thrice-articulated resistance to the term abstraction, when I met Eisenman, I asked if this reply had been strategic – a means of combating critics who would see the field only as a gesture of refusal to represent the Holocaust. The architect insisted again that the memorial was not abstract, but this time explained that it was not abstract because it was indexical. 'Indexical' was the term that he used to describe the process that I accounted for above, whereby the columns join the grid of the top topography to the lower one. Initially described by Charles Peirce, and famously deployed by Rosalind Krauss to theorise art of the 1970s, the index is the kind of sign that is caused by its referent, without necessarily resembling it – a shadow of a body, or a footprint in the sand.[9] This kind of cause-and-effect relationship accounts for the vertical orientation of the pillars: their tilt is determined by imprinting the upper topography on the lower.

Eisenman had used indexicality elsewhere, and it is one of the core strategies in a particular phase of his architecture, but usually, the form that is imprinted on a ground has some basis in history. A very clear example of this indexical process is his 1996 proposal for the 'Memorial for the Victims of the Holocaust' in Vienna (fig. 137).[10] Here, Eisenman planned to trace the outlines of two historical maps of the Viennese ghettos of 1421 and 1678 on the ground level of the Judenplatz. Three metres above, he imagined another outline – this time, a 1938 map of Austria/Germany after the Anschluss. The outline above would be connected to the two below by a series of slanting planes, and in this way a form would be produced connecting two sets of shapes, both resonant of different moments in the history of Austrian anti-Semitism. I raise this proposal here not to initiate a discussion of the ideas within it, but to stress the contrast with the memorial that Eisenman would propose for Berlin just a couple of years later. Like the Vienna proposal, the Berlin memorial is formed by imprinting a form on another, but unlike in Vienna, the Berlin forms are neither determined by any historical shape, nor map, nor image. Rather, the topographies and their external boundaries were invented. So why, I asked, did Eisenman – in the space of two years – move from proposing a Holocaust memorial shaped by combinations of maps, to proposing another whose forms had no basis in history? The architect explained that the Vienna proposal was too literal, and literal symbolism risked banalising the Holocaust. When it came to working in Berlin, he wanted to work in a manner that was, as he said, 'more *abstract*'.[11]

Clearly Peter Eisenman has some ambivalence about the term 'abstraction'. His memorial, he says, is not abstract because it generates real feelings; but it is 'abstract' in relation to other architectural work in which walls and boundaries have been determined by maps, or the footprints of other buildings. Eisenman's hesitancy towards 'abstraction' is understandable given his need to defend his memorial against the charge of emptiness, but others without such investments have also wavered in their use of the term. For instance, in a short text that appeared as a foreword to one of the books on the memorial, Jürgen Habermas wrote that 'the abstract formal language of modern art' is the only medium to 'portray a breach in civilisation', because its 'brittle self-containment is more likely than any other to guard against solecisms and trivialisations'. But at the same time, he stated that: 'Anything more tangible would risk the pitfall of false abstraction.'[12] I think that what Habermas meant is that a memorial that represented the Holocaust through a symbol or image would trivialise it by reducing it to such a symbol in the way that (in one vein of the tradition of abstraction) some early twentieth-century painters reduced a form in the visual world down to its essence, abstracting it. This would be 'false abstraction': by contrast, the abstraction of Eisenman's memorial was effective precisely because it was made out of the language of architecture (its self-containment) rather than out of an abstracted idea or form taken from the history of the Holocaust.

Peter Eisenman is not the only artist I have discussed who resists the term 'abstraction'. Indeed, discussing his work in general (rather than thinking about *The Drowned and the Saved* and *Gravity*), Eisenman's one-time collaborator Richard Serra concluded a text of 2004 by emphasising that 'I am not interested in form as pure abstraction', and went on to say that instead he wanted 'to direct the consciousness of the viewer to the realities of these conditions: private, public, formal, ideological, economic, psychological, commercial, sociological, institutional – or any of these combined'.[13] In some way, Serra echoed Barnett Newman's earlier scepticism about 'abstraction': for Newman, this meant the rarified world of Platonic forms. Meanwhile other artists have distinguished the works that I have discussed in this book from earlier works which

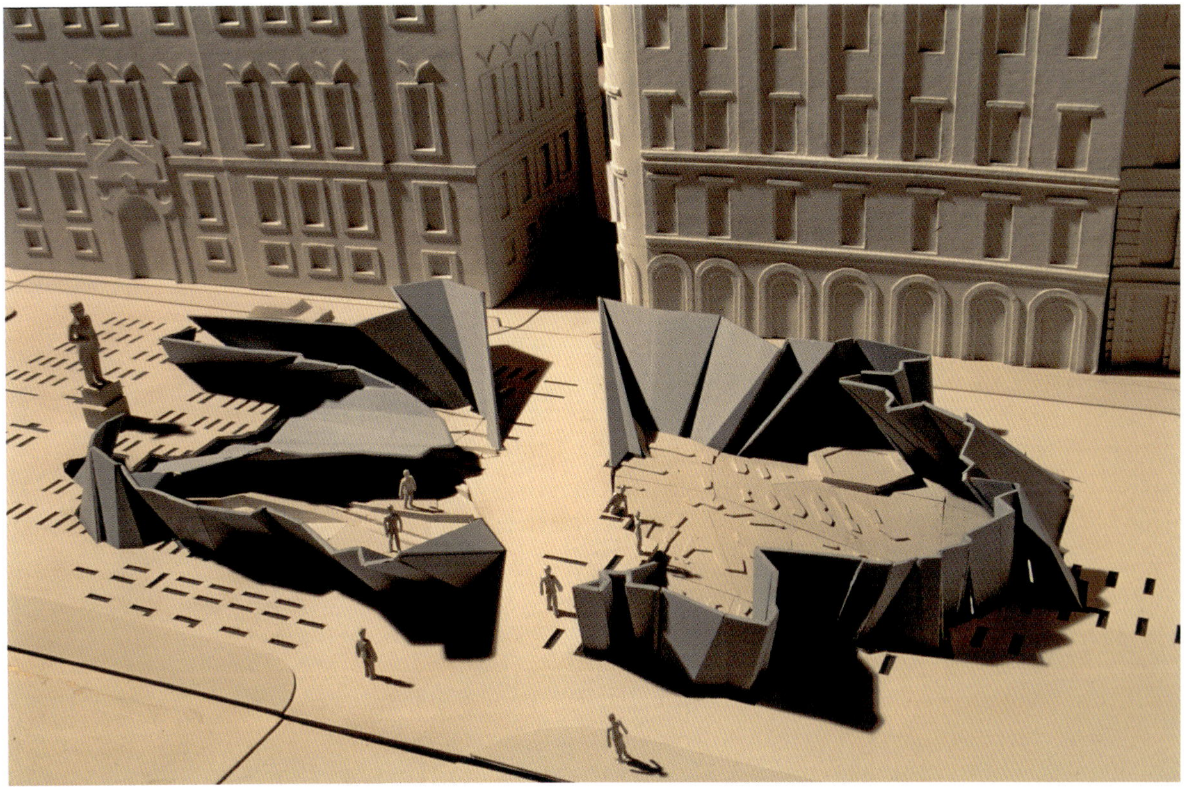

137 Peter Eisenman, Model of the Monument and Memorial Site Dedicated to the Jewish Victims of the Nazi Regime in Austria 1938–45, 1996.

were, in their words, more 'abstract': Beryl Korot, for instance, called the work she made before *Dachau 1974* 'abstract', which suggests she did not think this an altogether appropriate term for the later piece; Mel Bochner, similarly, talking about his initial ideas for Via Tasso, described his plans to make a 'more abstract' connection with the site than that which he eventually formed.

All of this points to the rather fraught status of the term at the heart of this book. But as important as it is to register the ambivalence of artists and architects whose work I have addressed under the title 'Abstraction and the Holocaust' towards the very word 'abstraction', it is also essential to defend my use of the term. Quite simply, I do not see abstraction in the pejorative way that Eisenman and Serra (and others before them) do; rather, I see abstraction in an expanded way, precisely as an art that can address all the realities that Serra lists, but that does so in distinctive ways. In the context of the representation of the Holocaust, it is particularly important to recognise this: if abstraction were taken as an art of 'purity', of 'form', then it would be possible to say that it only ever functions to express the unrepresentability of the Holocaust. However, if abstraction is taken to be an art that addresses reality, then it can – as I have argued – represent the Holocaust in real ways, but in ways distinct from other art forms.

Though I have insisted that each work or group of works discussed in this book represents the Holocaust and its memory in specific and unique ways, in concluding the book, at the risk of over-simplification, three primary operations can be isolated. And what is so interesting about Eisenman's memorial is that all three are at work in it. First, the abstraction of an art or architectural work allows for meanings to be suggested by it, and interpretations to be formed by its viewers, while at the same time insuring that such readings are never fixed, never asserted didactically, and that they remain fragile and contingent. In the case of Eisenman's memorial, the field could be read as an indication of Nazism's roots in rationality and modernity. This reading of the memorial's form is tenable, but even for those who interpret the memorial in this way, it is never taken as anything like the simplistic 'message' of the memorial, and one might as easily think about the random nature of the stelae's tilts in other ways. We can think back to similar operations of abstraction: Morris Louis's paintings might have prompted thoughts about the destruction and regeneration of Jewish culture, but would have also appeared literally as white lines on a black ground; Frank Stella's carpented constructions could be taken as oblique representations of shattered buildings, or equally as invocations of constructivist art that was also ruined in the mid-century; Mel Bochner's match sculptures suggested the extinguishing of Jewish lives and the poverty of the Roman Jews, but were also mere materials simply laid out in geometric shapes; Joel Shapiro's sculptures appeared like falling bodies and upturned houses but also as cast sheets of metal imprinted with the grain of wood. In sum, in this first operation, abstraction does not name a condition whereby a work is empty of meaning, but a condition in which meanings are fragile, contingent, sometimes even transient.

The second way in which abstraction operates in connection to the Holocaust is in the creation of mnemonic environments. Each environment will be differently shaped according to its media and materiality and setting, and each environment will function in different ways, setting up different encounters with the memory of the Holocaust, but what is common between such environments is that memory is never marshalled or directed towards a specific image or symbol. Eisenman's memorial does not tell its visitors what to remember, but it does construct a space for the visitor in which time feels slowed down, and in which they wander alone through an occasionally oppressive and chaotic environment. The very activity of memory is encouraged, and the kind of memory is suited to this particular place and historical period (Berlin, at the time when most visitors did not live through the 1940s). Other mnemonic environments I have looked at function in related ways, but in manners that were appropriate to their historical date and their location: Barnett Newman's installation of paintings set the viewers' mnemonic faculties to work as they considered the inter-relationships of paintings so that a space of loss was constructed in which the implications of their own survival could be confronted. Louis Kahn's memorial formed a place where viewers would connect their memories to the surrounding institutions and locations, and come together, sensitised to each other's presence, to consider what the Holocaust meant to them. Beryl Korot's video installation set out an environment in which the insistence of memory would be dramatised at the same time as its imprecision was enacted.

Richard Serra's sculpture in the Holocaust museum worked in co-ordination with James Ingo Freed's architecture to forge a physical and affective sense of gravity.

The third operation that I want to isolate is the way abstract works effectively recognise the difficulties of Holocaust representation, acknowledging the bankruptcy of former modes of commemoration, but never proposing fixed solutions to the task. Eisenman, for instance, recognises that 'the enormity and horror of the Holocaust are such that any attempt to represent it by traditional means is inevitably inadequate.'[14] His memorial thus neither has a focal point, nor images of suffering, nor symbols of hope; but nor does it suggest that the field is a perfect solution. As many have recognised, there are always visitors who completely fail to register that this is a memorial, and their welcomed presence in the field only serves to throw the field's resolution and efficacy into relief. Thinking in this way, we can look back to Beryl Korot's editing of her video footage, which at once recognised the inadequacy of narrative to represent Dachau in 1974, and at the same time would have been encountered as an at times problematic treatment of the footage, as worthy of praise as of the charge of obfuscation. Ellsworth Kelly's installation at the USHMM, as I have argued, suggested at once that art had no means to represent the Holocaust, and that art could offer some opportunity for reflection and transcendence. These two suggestions did not cancel each other out, but by being posited on opposing walls in the same space, dramatised the problematic of Holocaust representation in a vivid and physical way.

If by describing these three operations, I have condensed the way that abstraction works to represent the Holocaust and shown how all these operations persist in Eisenman's memorial, it has also been clear that each art work's operation cannot be reduced to these three strategies. The question now remains as to whether I am arguing that abstraction is somehow a more appropriate form of visual representation than other art forms. Before responding to this, I want to register two points. First, it is important to remember that the artists whose work I have considered never shouldered the burden of describing the events of the Holocaust for audiences who did not know about them, nor were they bearing witness to events that they suffered directly. This point sounds obvious, but it is important to recall it, because doing so helps us to realise why the kind of debates we would bring to bear on works that do have this burden are not relevant here (for instance, the burden shared, but differently managed, by Alain Resnais and Claude Lanzmann). A comparison between informative or documentary art works and abstraction will not illuminate either category, for each has a different kind of task.[15] The second point is to recall that it has been more important to me to note (as an historian) when and how abstract artists have confronted the Holocaust than to argue (as a theorist) whether or not their works constitute a more complex, respectful and considered response to this event than the works of other artists from Nathan Rapoport to Luc Tuymans.

Nonetheless, it should be clear by now that I believe that the works I have discussed not only approach the representation of the Holocaust in compelling ways, but also in ways that are appropriate to the intellectual and ethical post-war condition. These are not works that attempt to disavow the challenges the Holocaust set for representation, nor are they works that attempt to provide false consolations, nor do they offer the redemptions of artistic beauty. While it has never (or rarely) been the case that the artists I have examined retreat into positions of piety, respecting the sublime unrepresentability of the Holocaust, they do forge responses to the Holocaust that acknowledge not just the catastrophic violence of its history, but the violence it did to post-war thought. In some cases, abstraction works not just by responding to this violence, but by creating situations of doubt: I am thinking of the way Frank Stella's constructions upset the viewer's ability to know what to look at and where to stand; the way Mel Bochner's installation made its viewer unsure as to whether to treat the sculptures as allusive or literal material. In all cases, abstract works form *difficult* responses to the Holocaust in which easy meanings are withheld. They provide the opportunity for what Adorno called 'thinking against itself'; they are instructed by the lesson that Blanchot described in his aphorism 'learn to think with pain.'

new roads of memory

Over the course of this discussion, I have charted various shifts in the reception of 'abstraction' and 'the Holocaust', and in the reception of their relationship. Where once the responses of abstract painters to the Holocaust were completely ignored and sometimes denied (interestingly by Jewish New York art critics), more recently (but with Kahn's commission serving as a precedent), curators and institutions have commissioned artists and architects working with abstraction to respond to Holocaust-related settings and to make Holocaust memorials. Where once the Holocaust was only tangentially addressed in a handful of cultural journals, more recently, a memory industry has spawned, leading to the creation of museums, films, university departments dedicated to the study of the Holocaust, and countless publications such as this one. For some critics of this situation, the memory of the Holocaust is abused by representations that are mystical and spectacular and sometimes both at once.

In very recent years, several artists have addressed this latter situation not by making work about the Holocaust but about this troubling turn in its cultural negotiation, criticising the abuses of memory and thinking in particular about the 'Hollywoodisation' of the Holocaust. Sometimes this kind of work can be politically and formally astute (Omer Fast and Piotr Uklanski, for instance);[16] at other times, it seems to create the same kind of spectacle that it criticises – but without intending to do so (artists such as Santiago Sierra and Tom Sachs).[17] With reference to the works in the USHMM, I have already suggested that abstraction can serve to counter a 'spectacularisation' of the Holocaust. I believe this argument is also relevant to Eisenman's memorial, particularly because the ever-shifting views within the stelae never approximate to the newspaper-friendly aerial views of the entire field that have come to represent it. The question I want to pose, in concluding, is whether abstraction still serves an important role for artists thinking about the memory and cultural representations of the Holocaust.

In tackling this question, it strikes me that it would be misguided to look to a new generation of painters and sculptors working with abstraction to forge complex

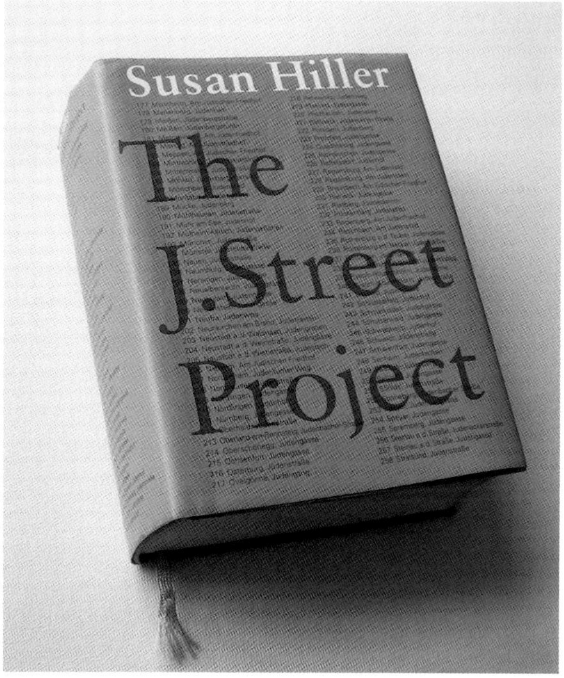

138 Susan Hiller, *The J.Street Project*, book.

responses to the ongoing shifts in Holocaust memory, even though such a generation *has* emerged over the past ten years with artists revisiting the practices of colour-field painting, post-minimalist sculpture and so on. These younger artists 'choose' abstract painting and sculpture as historically available forms and mediums amongst other equally viable forms and mediums (internet art, multi-screen video projections, for instance), and their situation is therefore quite different from that of the artists I have treated who started to make abstract work between the 1940s and 1960s when abstraction was the dominant, and for some, *only* viable form of art practice. For younger abstract painters and sculptors, their choice of abstraction makes it rather unlikely that they will want to address shifts in the reception of the Holocaust; the older generation, as I have argued, needed to confront the Holocaust, and did so despite the fact that the discourses that surrounded abstraction seemed to preclude their attempts to address history and memory. So instead of finishing with the work of an abstract painter or sculptor, I want to end by considering a photographic and video-based project which does not 'look' abstract, but in which *strategies* of abstraction are at work, just as they were in Korot's *Dachau 1974*. Importantly, this new work was initiated and completed in Berlin during the same period that saw the erection of Peter Eisenman's memorial. The work in question is by Susan Hiller, and is called *The J.Street Project* (2002–5).

The J.Street Project began while Hiller was in Berlin as a DAAD scholar. One day, walking in Mitte, she came across a street sign reading 'Jüdenstraße' (fig. 139). Though most would pass by, the sign caused Hiller to halt, as for her it pointed not so much to the street below as to the absence of Jews from Berlin and from Germany. Though Hiller was well aware of the history of the Holocaust, it is easy to imagine why this incident was so affecting, and the sign, so perplexing. Mitte is an area undergoing rapid gentrification, where new commercial and residential buildings can seem to eclipse the material evidence of Berlin's recent past. In contrast to the new architecture, this humble street sign witnessed not only the history of the local Jewish community, but the compulsion of the post-war German state to re-inscribe this history onto the city: 'Jüdenstraße' was clearly not a relic from the pre-1933 city, but a newly fabricated sign that must have been restored and possibly re-restored at some dates since 1945. Though this act of restoration was respectful, perhaps the street was originally named as an act of racist segregation; perhaps the restorers were, against their intentions, repeating an offence. The sign would not say, of course.[18] Perhaps most significantly, the sign was touching because it was so very ordinary. It was neither a massive Jewish edifice (like the nearby synagogue) nor a deliberately placed Holocaust memorial (such as Eisenman's), but instead a blank marker whose everyday purpose was quite removed from its chance effect on Hiller.

139 (facing page) Susan Hiller, 'Jüdenstraße, Berlin Mitte, Berlin' from *The J.Street Project*, 2002–5. © Susan Hiller.

140 (page 258) Susan Hiller, 'Jüdenstraße, Kempen, Nordrhein-Westfalen' from *The J.Street Project*, 2002–5. © Susan Hiller.

141 (page 259) Susan Hiller, 'Jüdenstraße, Osterburg, Sachsen-Anhalt' from *The J.Street Project*, 2002–5. © Susan Hiller.

This poignant moment of accidental and sudden confrontation with the history of Jewish Berlin life, its destruction and its post-war commemoration, initiated a massive research project. Working in collaboration with her husband David Coxhead, Hiller located all the streets in Germany with the word 'Jüde' in their names – so many Jüdenstrasses, Jüdenallees, Jüdengasses, and Jüdenwegs (to cite only the most common terms). In all, some 303 streets were discovered, from the south-western French border to Görlitz near Poland in the north-east. Over a three-year period, Hiller travelled to each site to take photographs. The photographs were not attempts to document the streets and the surrounding areas objectively by following any one consistent visual regime: unlike the Bechers, for instance, Hiller photographed the streets in many different ways, sometimes including passers-by (fig. 140), sometimes showing streets empty of people (fig. 141), sometimes centring the street sign, sometimes not. Nor were the photographs particularly subjective: odd viewpoints were avoided, no 'artful' effects were deployed, and the same amount of contextual information tended to be supplied (the streets were shot without zoom or wide-angle lenses, so there is always a sense of the surrounding architecture and vegetation, but never an indication of the wider landscape). While most photographs included street signs and often not just the 'J-Street' sign (fig. 142), in many places that Hiller visited, all signs were absent. This was the case particularly in rural settings where Hiller tended to photograph down the centre of a road: these streets often lay outside towns because Jews had been prevented from walking through town centres (fig. 143). Since the completion of the project, the photographs have been displayed in a gallery in a grid formation, each one named by a number, with a large map on a facing wall on which the numbers are positioned in the appropriate locations. The photographs have also been collected in a short but wide grey book, seven inches high and two inches thick, the sculptural volume of which indicates the magnitude of its content (fig. 138).

Hiller also shot some footage in each location, sometimes a few brief seconds, sometimes for several minutes, and most of the time, filming from a different position to that of the still camera. In certain situations, the footage showed daily life around the

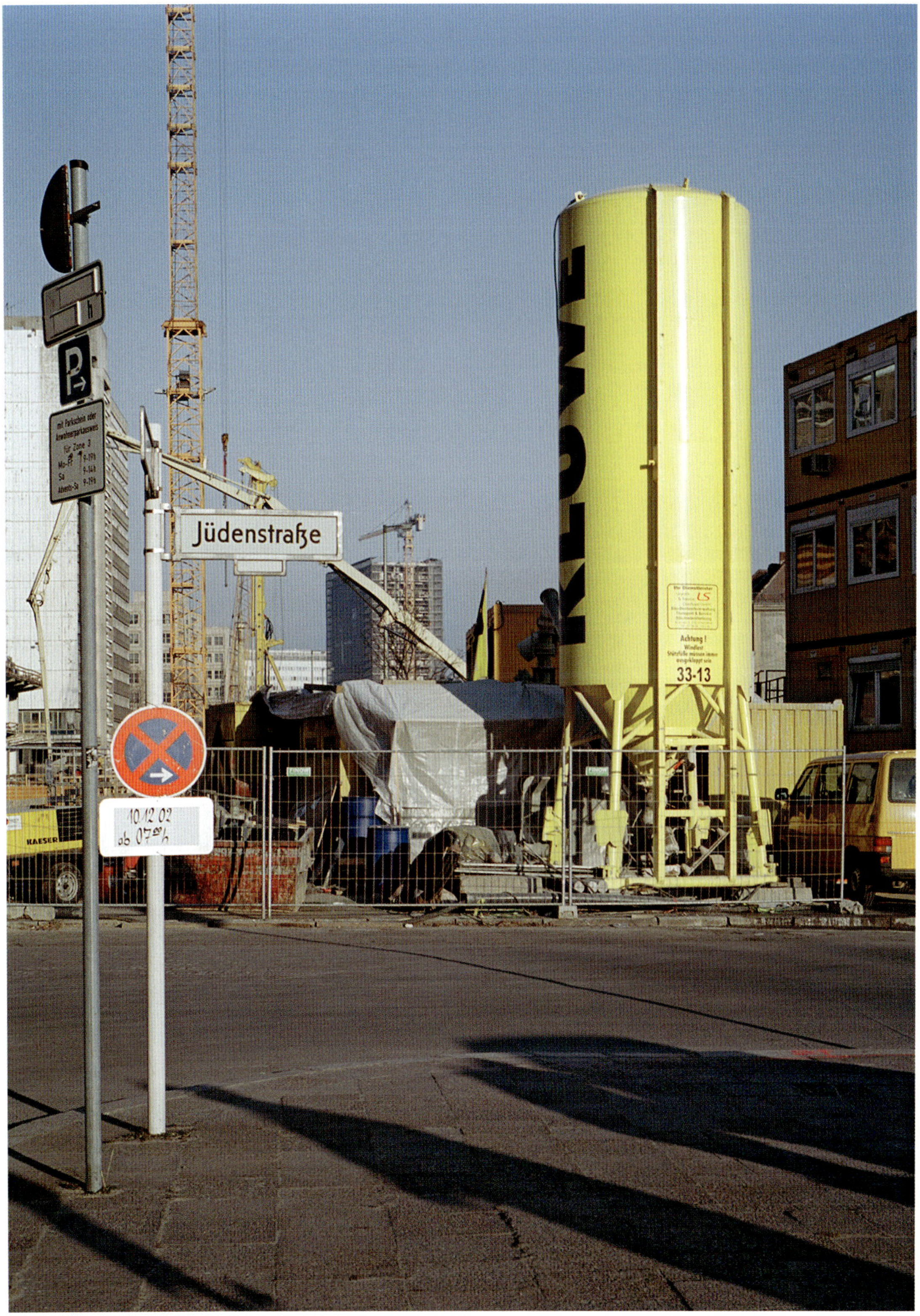
Jüdenstraße
Achtung !
33-13
KAESER

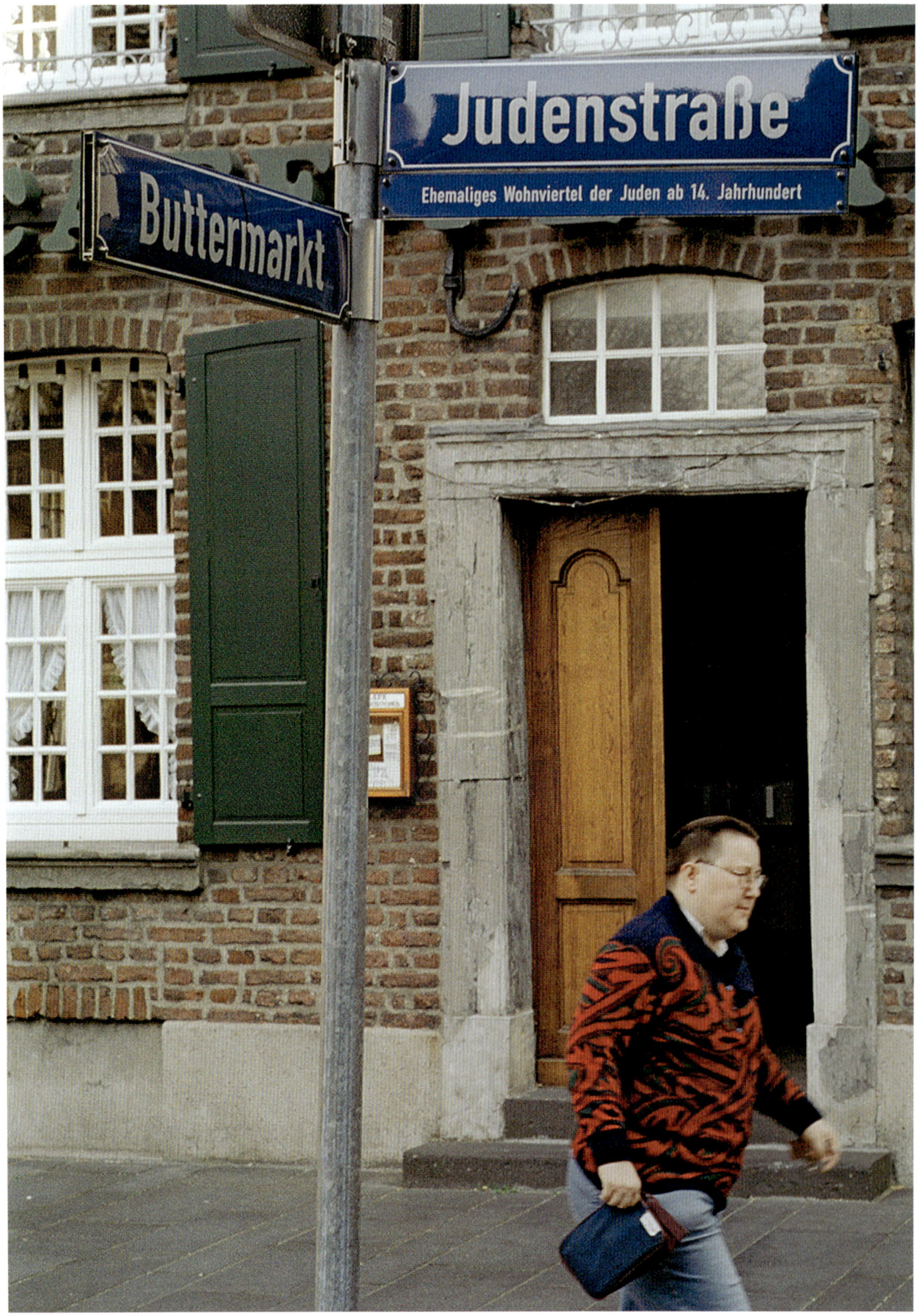
Judenstraße
Ehemaliges Wohnviertel der Juden ab 14. Jahrhundert
Buttermarkt

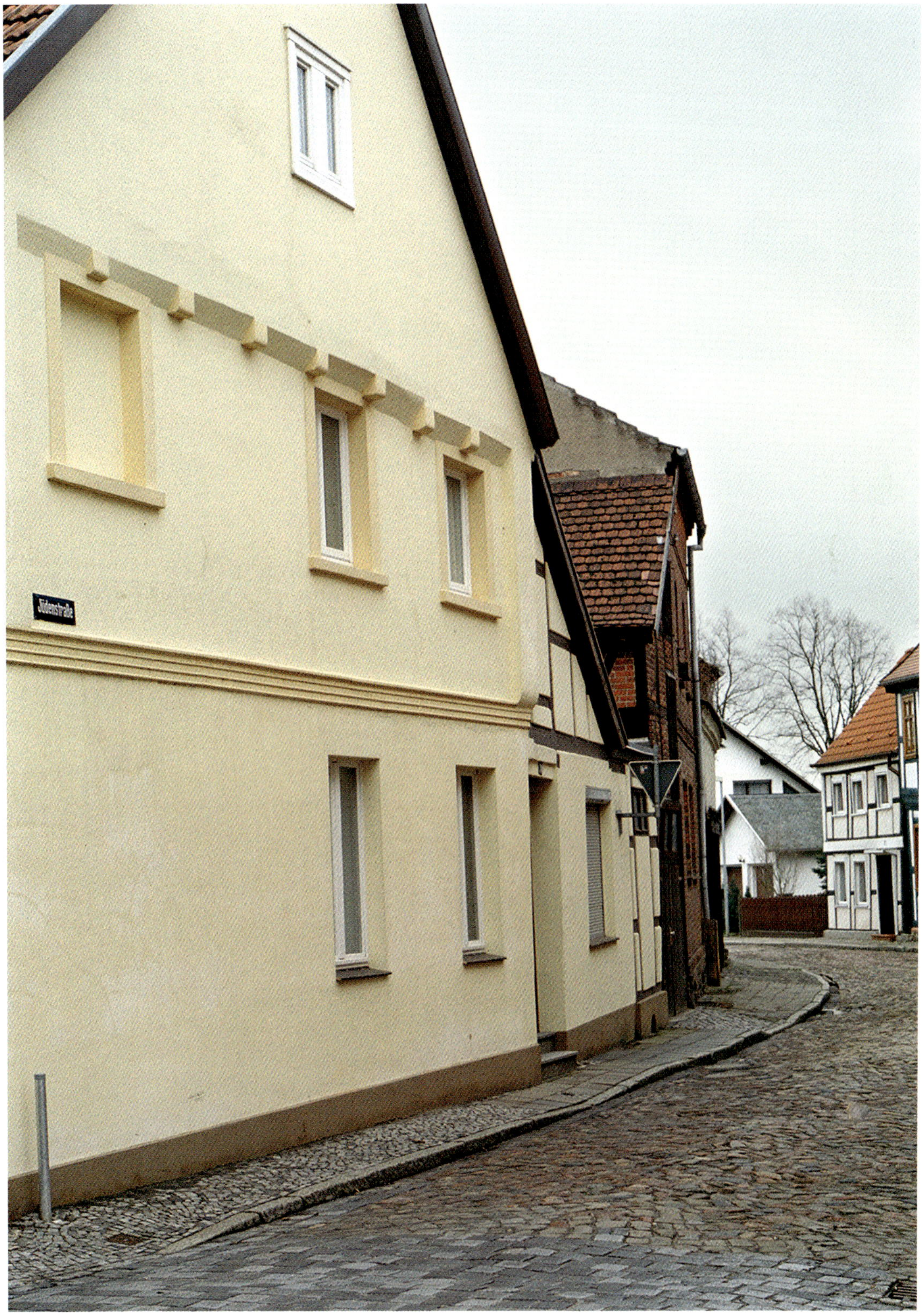
Jüdenstraße

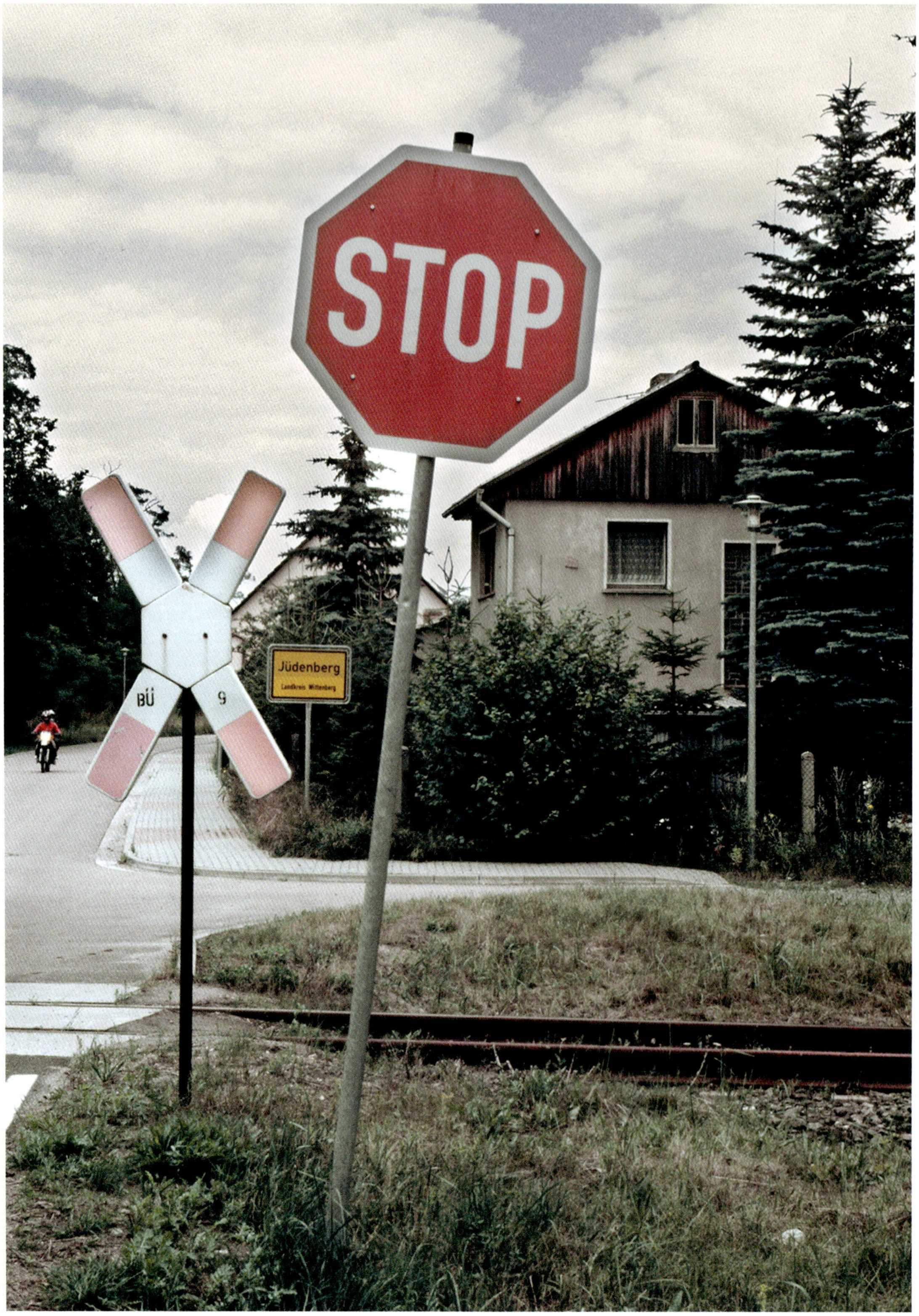
STOP
BÜ 9
Jüdenberg

street; in quieter places, the only movements are those of the wind and trees. The clips were edited but not to a consistent length, and then arranged according to several ordering principles into a 67-minute video. The dominant structuring principle was to arrange clips according to the seasons in which they were filmed, but going in reverse: the video starts with streets filmed in winter, then others filmed in autumn, then summer, then spring. Within each season, clips were sometimes randomly juxtaposed, but sometimes placed together because of visual similarities: for instance, at one point there are several clips in which the views of the street are occluded by passing vehicles, and at another point there is a sequence of shots of rural streets. Hiller used sounds and music recorded on location as well as an added soundtrack. Sometimes a video clip is only accompanied by the sound recorded at the location, but elsewhere, a piece of music recorded in one place stretches over a period of a few minutes, as if binding together several geographically distant streets. While this 'binding' music came from a range of disparate sources (a busker playing Nirvana; a musical box; some overheard Klezmer music), the added music was a segment of a string quartet composed by Lejaren Hiller, a modernist American composer with no relation to the artist who pioneered the use of computers in composition.[19] This music recurs at the start of every new season section, and while it plays, there is always a sequence of relatively short clips in which the street signs are particularly central.

142 Susan Hiller, 'Jüdenberg, Sachsen-Anhalt' from *The J.Street Project*, 2002–5. © Susan Hiller.

So in what ways are strategies of abstraction at work in *The J.Street Project*? First, I would like to consider Hiller's visual subject (the street sign) as a quasi-abstract image because of its double status: it is at once brimming with suggestion, and totally banal. To make just one comparison with the more obviously abstract work discussed earlier, this status strikes me as in some ways equivalent to the status of Morris Louis's white lines, which at varying moments suggested the biblical legends of Jewish writing and the plain matter of paint. This ambiguous character was apparent even in Hiller's initial encounter as the Mitte sign was both a dumb piece of street furniture, and the prompt for all sorts of questions. Hiller's *representation* of the sign concretised this double character: on the one hand, the single photograph was totally mute, failing to supply any information about the exact history of the Berlin Jewish community. On the other hand, the image was intensely suggestive, since Hiller shot the sign against a background of building works, as if to indicate the gulf between an ongoing material reconstruction of Berlin, and a demographic reconstruction that will never be possible.

In continuing her project in the way she did, Hiller maintained the ambiguous, abstract character of her subject. By visiting and imaging *all* the streets, Hiller emphasised the ideas raised by the first photograph, underlining the extensiveness and diversity of the historical Jewish population of Germany, and also asking questions that could not have been posited in Berlin: what, for instance, does it mean for a German community to restore or not restore a 'J-street' sign in a remote corner of the country out of the view of Jewish and other tourists, where not even a trace of a Jewish population remains? However, by extending the project from one photograph to 303, Hiller at the same time emptied the meanings of the first encounter, and the power of the initial photograph. By imaging *all* the signs, and confronting the viewer with *all* of them, Hiller made it impossible for each sign to touch the viewer as she had been touched in Berlin. Necessarily, some photographs are poignant and demand attention and thought; others are flicked through, and passed by. In sum, then, Hiller's first encounter, her first photograph, and her entire project, all share an ambiguous status: like the more abstract-looking works I have considered throughout this book, the meaning and effect of these encounters and images cannot be fixed.

143 Susan Hiller, 'Judenweg, Frauenau, Bayern' from *The J.Street Project*, 2002–5 © Susan Hiller.

In the video, a handful of shots occurring at separate moments over the 67 minutes feature street cleaners. These scenes (together with other ones in which dogs bark at the camera) cannot help but appear as particularly resonant given the history marked by the project. There are also many long shots such as one near the beginning in which the camera looks over a market place (fig. 144). Here nothing much happens, and growing bored, one hardly registers the street sign in the corner of the screen. So just as in the book and the installation of photographs, the proliferation of video shots serves both to emphasise and empty away the implications of the street names. However, in addition, the repetitive structures of the video create what I have called a mnemonic environment, and the formation of this environment is the second reason why I insist that abstraction is at work in *The J.Street Project*. As I have described, several repetitive structures play out simultaneously. Some of these structures function very precisely to divert thought away from the street names (for instance, the repetition of clips that share a banal visual feature such as a passing car). Other structures really serve to focus memory – most importantly, the repetition of Lejaren Hiller's rather mournful music, and its coupling with a sequence of close-up shots of street signs. Over the course of 67 minutes, Hiller's structures cause her viewer to remember and forget the street names, to contemplate the erasure of Jewish communities and to erase this erasure from the mind, so that the work comes to address not only the history of the communities, but the very workings of memory itself.[20]

We might get a sharper sense of *The J.Street Project* by comparing it to Peter Eisenman's *Memorial to the Murdered Jews of Europe*, and in so many ways, Hiller's work stands in direct opposition to Eisenman's memorial. Where Eisenman built 2700 concrete stelae, adding to the fabric of Germany, Hiller used photography and film, just documenting matter that already existed. Where Eisenman's memorial is located in a ceremonial capital and is symbolically cut off from this central location owing to his fictitious ground topography, Hiller shows how the traces of the murdered Jews permeate the existing topography of Germany; how they are dispersed all over the country. Where Eisenman's memorial is a designated space in which the activity of memory is cut off from everyday life, Hiller shows how memory can be prompted by the most everyday of objects, but also how such objects can equally be passed by.

There are important differences, but then in many other ways, Eisenman and Hiller approach the Holocaust in related manners. Both address the memory of the Holocaust in the present tense: Eisenman's field is only ever activated as the visitor walks through it; Hiller shows the contemporary situation of the streets. Both hope to address the Holocaust to the present crises: Eisenman, when he suggests how the memorial can serve as a warning; Hiller, when she writes that the project allowed her to 'reflect not

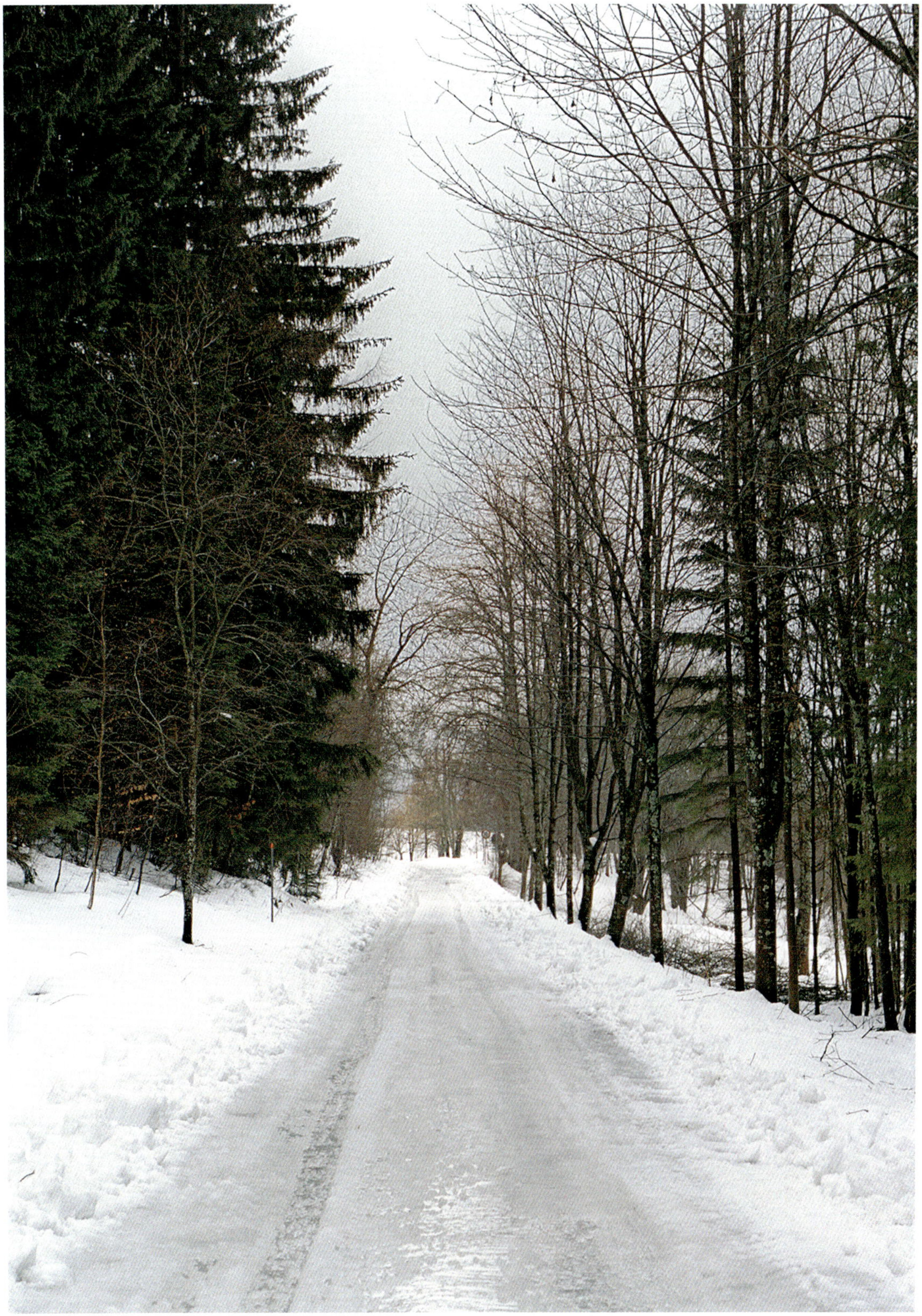

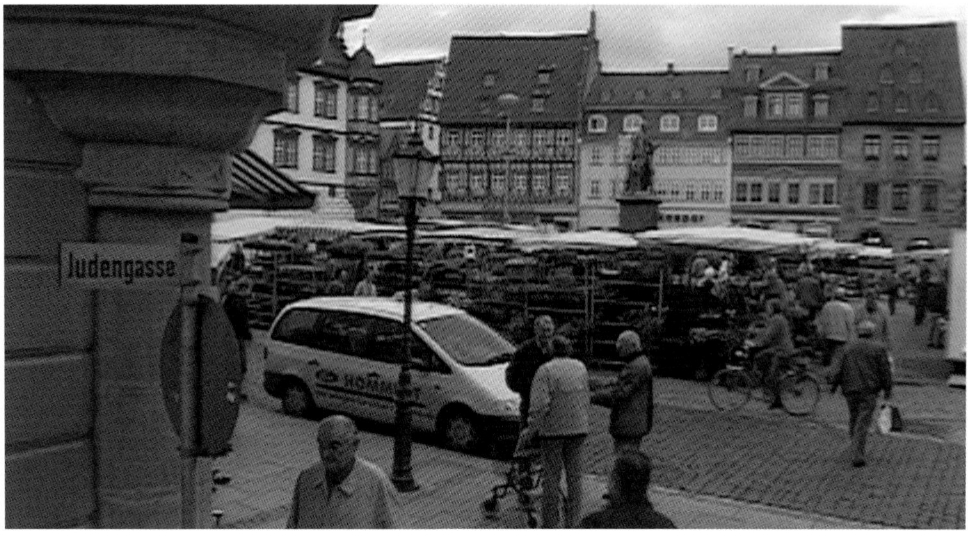

144 Susan Hiller, *The J.Street Project*. Still from video showing market place. © Susan Hiller.

only on one unique, incurable, traumatic absence, but also on more recent attempts to destroy minority cultures and erase their presence.'[21]

Crucially, many of the connections between the two projects pertain to the abstraction of their approaches. Obviously, both Eisenman and Hiller refused to picture suffering, to use symbols of destruction or regeneration, and to provide information about the Holocaust. Neither made use of archival images or testimonies (the Ort's display, remember, was not planned by the architect). Within the field itself there is no centre point, just as Hiller's grid, book and video refuse to posit a point of origin or conclusion (the initial photograph is never placed at the beginning). Both addressed the Holocaust through ambiguous forms and images that can suggest Jewish graveyards (in Eisenman's case) or point to vanished communities (in Hiller's case) but that can also be encountered much more literally as blank concrete and near-invisible street signs. Both Eisenman and Hiller used repetition to a variety of ends, letting it trigger the very processes of memory and forgetting. Finally, for Hiller as for Eisenman, the path of memory is an empty road. The viewer or visitor enters this road literally (in Eisenman's field) or imaginatively (before Hiller's photographs and video). They embark upon a mnemonic journey, but their choice to reflect on the history and implications of the Holocaust is only offered, and never determined by the work before them.

the two abstractions

Some way into Hiller's video, there is an image of a street sign before a field (fig. 145). At the back of the field, the sun is setting. The shot is held for a particularly long time, while the fading light causes the words on the sign – 'Am Jüdenfriedhof' – to become more and more illegible. Eventually, the sign is reduced to a silhouette, but the colours behind it grow more intense, and the scene more beautiful. This street sign was once

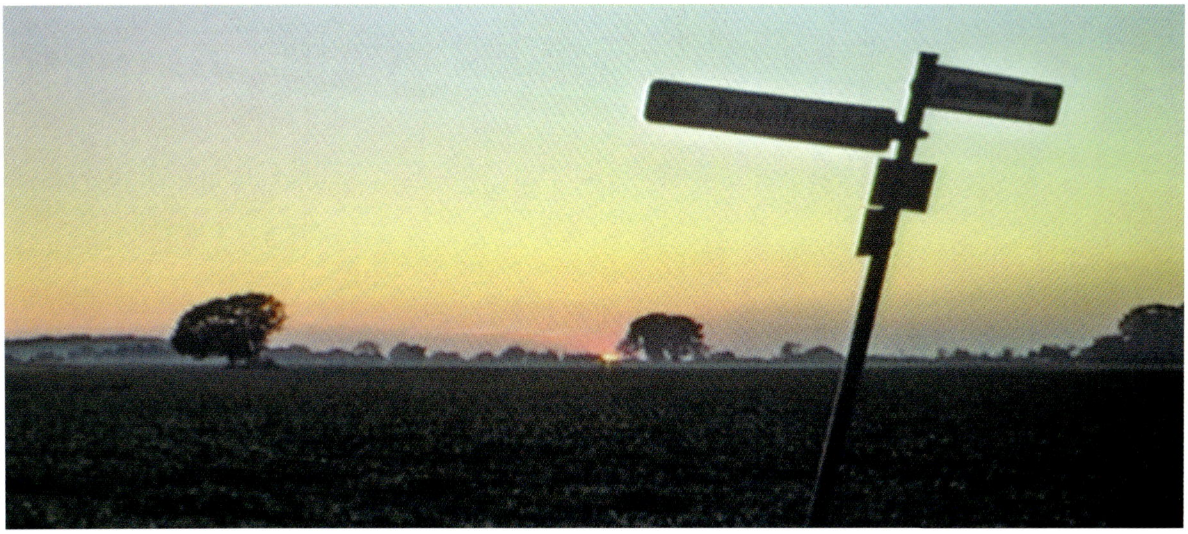

145 Susan Hiller, *The J.Street Project*. Still from video showing sunset behind sign. © Susan Hiller.

the record of a community's loss, for it pointed the way to the Jewish cemetery. Now, it marks the loss of that community. As the sunset renders it black and blank, there appears a loss of these two losses, but with a consequent gain: the reminder of eternal natural beauty of the dying day.

As I watched the video for the first time, I supposed this was its final image. Had this been the case, Hiller would have been concluding *The J.Street Project* in quite a clichéd manner, offering the wondrous colours of the twilight sky as consolations for the loss her project recorded. She would also have concluded with an obviously abstract image – for the sign becomes an abstract form, its diagonal rectangles reminiscent of a Malevich painting. Hiller would have aligned a traditional form of abstraction with natural beauty as if to indicate that abstraction cannot work in the cause of memory. As the sign becomes abstract, its signified is forgotten. Abstraction therefore can only be an art of amnesia and blankness, or an inert part of a scene of consolation.

But I was wrong: this was not the final shot. The colours of the night sky darkened, and the shot gave way to another, and another, and so on. A minute or so later, the refrain of Lejaren Hiller's composition recurred, and with it another succession of street-sign shots. The video had entered the final section and season, and strangely, I then realised, it had proceeded backwards, from winter through autumn and summer to spring. Perhaps this reverse structure indicated the desire to travel back in time, while the repetition within the season blocks served as a constant reminder of the impossibility of this desire. Perhaps this tension indicated that for all the research and travel undertaken by the artist, for all the completeness of her archive, the loss of 303 Jewish communities remained totally irreparable. Hiller's various repetitive structures worked to suggest so many different ideas about the Holocaust and its memory. These structures were forms of abstraction, and it was clear that these new forms of abstraction were anything but blank.

notes

1 introduction: abstraction and the holocaust

1 For details of this, see Young 2000, chapter seven.

2 I am not here concerned with the general impact of the Holocaust on artists or their unconscious reactions. Part of the reason for this is scope – were I interested in such impacts, it would be necessary to think not just about émigrés such as Eva Hesse whose life had been touched by the Holocaust, but all American artists who had heard news of the camps. Another reason is that unconscious reactions are often hard to specify. I do not believe that in any extant work Mark Rothko attempted to address the Holocaust, but all of his work was made in its shadow. A third reason not to look at unconscious reactions is that they sometimes produce an absence of work, and I am concerned with the study of physical objects. For instance, in the mid-1940s Lee Krasner found herself unable to paint anything but grey monochromes. Robert Hobbs has recently argued that this impasse registers the impact of news from Europe. But since Krasner destroyed the works, it is impossible to enquire how this impact materialised. See Hobbs 1999, pp. 64–69.

3 There is a growing attention to the negotiation of the Holocaust in the work of European artists as diverse as Arman, Joseph Beuys, Jean Fautrier, Simon Hantai, Anselm Kiefer, Gustav Metzger and Gerhard Richter, to name but a few, and in some cases, this work was abstract. I restrict my study to American examples for reasons of scope but also so as to be able to think about the reception of the Holocaust in specific conditions. The American artists I discuss shared an artistic tradition, and a nationality, and to an extent, the reception of the Holocaust was contingent upon nationality. What it has meant to think about the Holocaust as an American is very different from what it might mean as a German or French citizen.

4 See Fer 1997, p. 5.

5 See Van Alphen 1997, p. 4.

6 Claude Lanzmann, 'Seminar on *Shoah*' in Nouvet 1991, p. 82.

7 Claude Lanzmann, 'Seminar on *Shoah*' in Nouvet 1991, p. 92.

8 Bauman 2000, p. 227.

9 In passing, it is worth mentioning that many cultural historians have, to my opinion, falsely argued that 'the Holocaust' was not dealt with until the mid-1960s. But if one looks for articles on 'the tragedy', 'recent events in Europe', 'the catastrophe', 'Auschwitz', 'the camps', they appear aplenty. For more on the history of the term 'Holocaust' see Novick 1999.

10 Agamben 1999, p. 29.

11 Agamben also notes a use of the term 'Holocaust' in an English twelfth-century text celebrating a pogrom: after the coronation of Richard I, Londoners massacred Jews perpetuating 'a Holocaust [that] could not be completed before the next day' (Agamben 1999, pp. 30–31). This celebratory use of the term by anti-Semites is another reason for his resistance to it.

12 Agamben 1999, p. 30.

13 The theoretical literature on Holocaust literature is of course expansive and in discussing Adorno and Lyotard here, I by no means wish to suggest that other accounts have not been important to my thinking. In the years during which Eisenman's memorial had been planned, a huge body of literature has arisen drawing from psychoanalytic theories of trauma, criticising the realist and narrative representations of the Holocaust in historiography, popular films, TV series and novels. Saul Friedlander is particularly concerned with the opacity of the Holocaust to historical understanding, noticing how it 'could well be inaccessible to all attempts at a significant representation and interpretation' (Friedlander 1993, p. 113). Eric Santner has criticised the 'narrative fetishism' of German films such as Edgar Reitz's *Heimat*. Such films offered undisrupted stories of German history. Like the fetish object that disavows the trauma of sexual difference, narrative in such cases was a device to refuse to mourn and come to terms with traumatic history. Narrative fetishism is a 'strategy of undoing, in fantasy, the need for mourning by simulating a condition of intactness, typically by situating the site and origin of loss elsewhere' (Eric Santner, 'History Beyond the Pleasure Principle: Some Thoughts on the Representation of Trauma' in Levi and Rothberg 2003, p. 214). In part building on Santner's writing, Hayden White argued that 'the kinds of antinarrative nonstories produced by literary modernism offer the only prospect for adequate representations of the kind of 'unnatural' events – including the Holocaust – that mark our era.' (White 1999, p. 81). The theoretical literature on Holocaust representation based on psychoanalysis and trauma theory might be helpful in formulating an approach to some of the works I discuss. For instance, through its refusal to provide a narrative (even the direction of the viewer though the piers is uncontrolled), Eisenman's memorial refuses to disavow the traumatic character of the Holocaust. However, in the main the objects of my study have suggested different approaches to me. None of the works I am concerned with tackle narration, and so the literature on traumatised narrative will not speak to them. But the main reason why trauma studies will not help me is that they often assume the possibility of two alternative modes of representation – the narrative realist (whether this be a piece of history writing, a film, a monument) and the traumatic. But this choice did not present itself to the artists whom I cover: it was never the case that they decided on abstraction as an appropriate representational tool for the purpose of negotiating the Holocaust in their work. The artists were working with abstraction already, a mode of practice that predates the Holocaust even if it does not predate modernity.

14 Theodor Adorno, 'Cultural Criticism and Society' in Adorno 2003, p. 162.

15 Rothberg 2000, pp. 34–36.

16 Theodor Adorno, 'Metaphysics and Culture' in Adorno 1973, p. 365.

17 Adorno 1973, p. 367.

18 Adorno 1973, p. 367.

19 Theodor Adorno, 'Commitment' in Arato and Gebhardt 1978, p. 312.

20 Theodor Adorno, 'Commitment' in Arato and Gebhardt 1978, p. 312.

21 Adorno 1973, p. 362.

22 This has been Lisa Saltzman's suggestion. See Saltzman 1999, p. 23.

23 Rothberg 2000, p. 46.

24 Adorno 1973, p. 365.

25 Adorno, quoted in Rothberg 2000, p. 46.

26 Lyotard 1988, p. 13.
27 Lyotard 1988, p. 13.
28 Lyotard 1988, p. 13.
29 Debra B. Bergoffen, 'Interrupting Lyotard: Whither the We?' in Silverman 2002, pp. 127–39.
30 Dominick LaCapra has disagreed with Lyotard's 'appropriation of "the jews" ' because it 'obliterates the specificity of the Jews as a complex historical people'. Lyotard's entire theorisation of the Holocaust is questionable: 'Lyotard . . . intensifies Lacoue-Labarthe's tendency to "trope" away from specificity and evacuate history by constructing the caesura of the Holocaust as a total trauma that is un(re)presentable and reduces everyone (victims, witnesses, perpetrators, revisionists, those born later) to an ultimately homogenizing yet sublime silence.' LaCapra 1994, p. 97.
31 Žižek writes that the predominant feature of today's academic Holocaust industry is the 'elevation of the Holocaust into metaphysical diabolical evil, irrational, apolitical, incomprehensible, approachable only through respectful silence. . . . the Holocaust is referred to as mystery, the heart of darkness of our civilisation; its enigma negates all (explanatory) answers in advance, defying knowledge and description, noncommunicable, lying outside historicisation – it cannot be explained, visualised, represented, transmitted, since it marks the Void, the black hole, the implosion, of the (narrative) universe.' Žižek 2001, p. 66.
32 Lyotard 1990, p. 26.
33 Lyotard 1990, p. 26.
34 Lyotard 1984, p. 37. See also the essay 'Newman: The Instant' in *The Inhuman*, where Lyotard writes: 'A canvas by Newman draws a contrast between stories and its plastic nudity. Everything is there – dimensions, colours, lines – but there are no allusions. So much so that it is a problem for the commentator. What can one say that is not given? It is not difficult to describe, but the description is as flat as a paraphrase. The best gloss consists of the question: what can one say? Or of the exclamation "Ah". Of surprise: "Look at that". So many expressions of a feeling which does have a name in the modern aesthetic tradition (and in the work of Newman): the sublime. It is a feeling of "there" (*Voilà*). There is almost nothing to "consume", or if there is, I do not know what it is. One cannot consume an occurrence, but merely its meaning. The feeling is instantaneous.' Lyotard 1991, p. 80.
35 Lyotard 1990, p. 36.
36 Solomon interview p. 13.
37 In the following pages, especially in the chapters on Morris Louis, Barnett Newman and Frank Stella, the terms 'modernism' and 'modernist' refer to the critical discourse of figures such as Clement Greenberg, Michael Fried and the young Rosalind Krauss. All these critics agreed on the importance of artists such as Jackson Pollock and Morris Louis. Formal accounts of art prevailed over other kinds of enquiry. there were, ofcourse, differences between these critics' positions, but nonetheless, they used the terms 'modernism' and 'modernist' refer in much more specific ways than they are used today. In recent books and exhibitions, modernism sometimes describes a huge range of art forms emerging between 1860 and 1960, including for instance dada and surrealism. 'Modernism' can also be used to describe the architecture of Le Corbusier, or the designs of the Bauhaus, along with such movements as De Stijl and constructivism. I am not conerned here with debating the way the term should be used. Rather, it is simply important to specify that when I write about 'modernist painting', for intsance, I am using the term to refer to these crites' accounts, and not invoking a wider notion of modernism.
38 This meant Greenberg could even write about Picasso's painting *The Charnel House* without discussing what it meant for Picasso to have used photographs of the camps.
39 Though Greenberg's art criticism is more well known than his 'Jewish' cultural criticism, there is a growing body of literature that examines his 'Jewish' texts and indeed the question of Jewishness in relation to Greenberg's modernism. This literature includes Noyes Platt 1989; Bloom 1994; Margaret Olin, 'C[lement] Hardesh [Greenberg] and Company – Formal Criticism and Jewish Identity' in Kleeblatt 1996, pp. 39–59; Steyn 1999; and Louis Kaplan, 'Reframing Self-Criticism – Clement Greenberg's "Modernist Painting" in the Light of Jewish Identity' in Soussloff 1999. Kaplan's essay has a useful overview of the previous literature. At times, this literature suffers from an imbalance: the subtleties of Greenberg's art criticism are reduced in order to comment on his prescription of abstraction, or on his tendency to sidestep the Jewishness of modernist artists. Louis Kaplan notes how writers examining the question of Jewishness discussed Greenbergian modernism without paying attention to the concept of self-criticism: in a fascinating article, he notes how the 'war-torn' language of early essays such as 'Towards a Newer Laocoon' takes on 'ghastly overtones when one considers the precarious situation of European Jews around 1940' (pp. 183–84), and how this language is replaced by the idea of self-criticism, a concept then displaced from essays on Jewish identity to essays on modernist art. My own interest is in the nuanced effect of the Holocaust on Greenberg's criticism.
40 Cohen 1945, pp. 1–2. Greenberg is listed as Managing Editor on the masthead of *Commentary*. The literature on the Jewishness of the 'New York Intellectuals' includes discussion of their reactions to the Holocaust. See for example Bloom 1986, chapter eight.
41 Greenberg 1955, pp. 242–43.
42 Greenberg 1950, p. 430. In his chapter 'Silences in the Doctrine' (in de Duve 1996), Thierry de Duve has discussed this essay, thinking about the Greenberg's relationship to Jewishness in parallel with his relationship to kitsch. Though de Duve's discussion is fascinating, my interest focuses on its concern with the psychological effects of 'Auschwitz' on Jewishness.
43 Margaret Olin, for example, has argued that Greenberg sought to describe artists such as Rothko or Gottlieb as 'definitively American' (Kleeblatt 1996, p. 50), and that Greenberg's reluctance to articulate how their Jewishness might affect them should be seen as part of a 'post-Holocaust scenario, in which Jews sought to demonstrate their American identity' (p. 50–51).
44 When Leo Steinberg had to defend the initiation of a programme of abstract art exhibitions at the Jewish Museum in 1957 he offered some bland comparisons between modern art and 'Jewry', seemingly unconvinced of his own words: both modern art and Jewry are 'masters of renunciation', Jewry is an 'abstract nation, proving, as did modern art, how much was dispensable'. See Steinberg 1957, pp. 7–8.
45 Faison 1950, p. 299. Faison's article 'What is Jewish Art' was a review of Karl Schwartz's *Jewish Artists of the Nineteenth and Twentieth Centuries*.
46 It should be noted that Schwartz's book appeared in the wake of Jean-Paul Sartre's 1948 publication *Anti-Semite and Jew*, a text that prompted many Jews to defend the existence of authentic Jewish culture; Sartre 1995. For an early American response to Sartre's book, see Rosenberg 1949. See also the special edition of *October* 87 (Winter 1999).
47 We might couple these questions with a statement from the third Kafka essay, where Greenberg writes: 'Religion dissolves into culture, and culture is seen as humanity's effort to keep the formless at bay. Culture is also illusion: illusion piled upon illusion.' Clement Greenberg, 'At the Building of the Great Wall of China', in Greenberg 1993b, p. 51.
48 Anna Chave's 1990 essay 'Minimalism and the Rhetoric of Power' was a crucial intervention in the scholarship around post-war American abstraction. Chave was one of the first art historians to look seriously at the titles of Frank Stella's *Black Paintings*, and bravely explored the ways in which associations triggered by the titles and by the appearances of abstract art works complicated their reception. With this approach, she convincingly countered the claims that some minimalists put forward about the non-associative, purely literal character of their work. While I follow Chave in attending to such associations and in looking at titles, I have a different understanding to her of the relation of abstraction to fascism. Chave criticised minimalist work for its 'domineering, sometimes brutal rhetoric', writing that 'The Minimalists effectually perpetrated violence through their work – violence against the conventions of art and against the viewer – rather than using their visual language to articulate a more pointed critique of particular kinds or instances of violence.' In making this argument, she looked at moments where artists referred to Nazi culture and architecture. Her examples were Stella's *Black Paintings* (1958–59), Walter de Maria's swastika-shaped *Museum Piece* (1966–67) and Tony Smith's account of the Nuremberg Parade Ground (1966). While I agree with Chave that these artists were attracted to the power of fascist symbols and structures (indeed I will discuss Stella's Black Paintings in more detail in chapter three), I want to argue that abstraction can actually serve in impor-

tant ways to memorialise the victims of Nazism. This argument in some ways runs counter to Chave's, particularly in relation to our differing accounts of Richard Serra's work, but in many ways, my argument actually extends one line of thinking in her essay. Despite what Chave argues about the power of minimalism, she also suggests that once works are reconsidered against the grain (for instance, by taking in the associations of titles), they 'occupy unstable symbolic space' (p. 50). It is precisely the instability of meaning in abstraction that makes it a mode of art appropriate to the negotiation of Holocaust memory.

49 Benjamin Buchloh has been particularly attentive to these artists. See the essays collected in Buchloh 2000 and other publications on Martha Rosler, Allan Sekula and Raymond Pettibon.

50 Richard Serra, catalogue statement in Serra 1993, unpaginated.

51 Foster 1998, p. 26.

52 See section on *Gravity* in chapter seven.

2 morris louis's *charred journal: firewritten* paintings

1 The notion of a 'breakthrough' was first posited by Greenberg. Louis's experience of Frankenthaler's painting 'led [him] to change his direction abruptly'. See Clement Greenberg, 'Louis and Noland' in Greenberg 1993b, p. 96. Michael Fried was more concerned with theorising the breakthrough, since he saw it as emblematic of the typical career path of many modernist painters. He wrote of Louis's pre-1953 work as a 'term of apprenticeship', necessarily longer for modernist artists than for traditional artists. Louis had made a 'radical departure from his previous work' – his post-breakthrough works 'amount to a repudiation of [previous] work and its underlying assumptions.' In a passage particularly emblematic of his concerns, he wrote that it was tempting 'to describe Louis's breakthrough as one in which *painting itself* broke through to its future.' Fried 1971, pp. 12–13.

2 Rose 1971, p. 62.

3 Fried's earlier texts on Louis included 'The Achievement of Morris Louis', *Artforum* 6 (February 1967), an essay which had accompanied the first major retrospective of Louis's work, organised by the Los Angeles County Museum of Art in 1967.

4 Greenberg 1993b, p. 97.

5 Fried 1971, p. 13.

6 Fried 1971, p. 22.

7 Fried 1971, p. 32.

8 Fried 1971, p. 32.

9 Fried 1971, p. 33.

10 Fried 1971, p. 33.

11 Fried 1971, p. 40.

12 Fried 1971, p. 40.

13 Fried 1971, p. 40.

14 Fried 1971, p. 32.

15 Fried 1971, p. 35.

16 As I argue, Fried's account of the first mark keeps out the consideration of that mark as writing. A different response to Fried's position would be suggested in Michael Newman's account of the relation of drawing and memory. In his essay on Avis Newman, Newman, following Derrida, thinks through another originary story about drawing – Pliny the Elder's story of Butades' daughter. Before her lover departs on a journey, she draws his silhouette on the wall behind him. In contrast to Fried's sense of drawing as an activity of new creation in which the artist seizes the empty plane as his or her own, here, drawing is an act of preservation at a moment of loss. Newman Michael 1995.

17 In addition to Fried, other writers have discussed the paintings without sustained comment. Dore Ashton has written that the series shows 'Louis brooding on a highly charged emotional theme'; Ashton 1990, pp. 18–19. The exception is Mira Goldfarb Berkowitz, who organised an exhibition of the paintings for The Jewish Museum, New York, in 1998. Berkowitz published a small exhibition pamphlet, based on her MA thesis on these paintings, *Sacred Signs and Symbols in Morris Louis: The* Charred Journal *Series, 1951* – CUNY 1993, copy from CUNY library, New York. While her research and mine make use of many of the same documentary materials (indeed her biographical attention to Louis's early career is much greater than mine), our procedures are very different. Berkowitz treats the series as a 'statement in support of all victims of social injustice' (p. 31) with a 'pervasive theme' (p. 79). Titles are treated straightforwardly, with no attention to the idea that they might not guarantee meaning, and 'signs and symbols' are read with ease. Little attempt is made to reconstruct the encounter with the paintings, nor to probe how the surfaces might generate and frustrate the development of associations. Rather than seeing the paintings as a statement, I want to understand the ways in which they play out the problematic of making straightforward meaning. Berkowitz also claims that abstraction functioned for Louis as a means of universalising the theme of the Holocaust. Although, like her, I claim that the series relates not just to the past but to the time of its making, and to McCarthyite censorship in particular, I see abstraction not as a language that allowed the Holocaust to be generalised, but as the language of the most advanced art of 1951, and the language that allowed the artist to create objects without fixed meaning.

Goldfarb Berkowitz also adopts a problematic idea of Jewish identity, writing, for instance, that the series indicates how Louis 'may have been seeking to re-identify with his roots', and that it 'attests to the fact that he was proud of and devoted to his heritage, and considered his Jewishness a fundamental part of his identity' (p. 58). I do not conceive Jewish identity as monolithic and secure, and nor do I argue that a Jewish subject can establish a secure allegiance to 'Jewish identity'. Jewishness is constantly re-negotiated, a fraught area of subjectivity, and particularly so after the Holocaust.

18 Upright Headley 1979, p. 51.

19 Morris 1968, p. 35.

20 Morris 1968, p. 35.

21 See 'The Technique of Morris Louis' in Upright 1985.

22 Archives of American Art, Morris Louis files, reel 4990, 0153. Marcella Louis Brenner to Mr. Foster, 31 August 1970. Foster had written to enquire about Louis's working methods.

23 Archives of American Art, Morris Louis files, reel 4994. Interview with Marcella Louis Brenner for WETA television documentary, 11 January 1966.

24 Tannous 1978, p. 78.

25 Upright 1985, p. 37.

26 Louis had been offered teaching at the Workshop after Jacob Kainen had recommended he see Leon Berkowitz. Shortly before he died, I interviewed Kainen, who had few memories of Louis.

27 Upright 1985, p. 36, quoting William Rubin, 'Letter to the editor' *Artforum* (March 1971) p. 8.

28 Reviewing a posthumous exhibition at Lawrence Rubin, Joseph Masheck wrote 'surely the very title of such a work as Louis's *Saraband* (1959) is meant to suggest the irrevocable dance gesture in time quite as much as a *Nijinsky* by Kline, or any Pollock 'polka' (Masheck 1970a, pp. 78–79). Some months later, Masheck posited that 'the "Veils" . . . may, in their collective title, refer not only to their appearance but also to a concept of Schopenhauer's which was taken up by American artists around the turn of the century (it appears many times in John La Farge's *Considerations on Painting*: the "veil" of Maya, which separates the self from the selves of others)' (Masheck 1970b, p. 78). Rubin replied that *he* had coined the term 'Veil', and insisted that Louis had not been interested in titling work. Masheck was unfazed: this only proved the appropriateness of the title (Masheck 1971, p. 10). In passing it is important to note that the 'Veils' were titled after Hebrew letters (*Dalet Kuf, Beth Tet*, and so on), but only because Louis's widow needed a system of non-associative designation – the 'Unfurled' series uses Greek letters. (Upright 1985, p. 37). Though they seem unimportant in the terms of this chapter, these debates indicate why the 1951 paintings were not studied.

29 Berkowitz 1953, unpaginated.

30 Portner 1953, p. L3.

31 Greenberg 1986b, p. 286.

32 Greenberg 1986b, p. 229.

33 Greenberg 1986b, p. 188.

34 Johnson Sweeney 1948, p. 67.

35 The configuration of interlocking triangles had emerged in many of Louis's drawings of the period. This is unsurprising as Louis's drawings contain all sorts of lines and shapes. What is important, though, is that having made these drawings, some of the shapes were recognised as holding specific meaning, and one with a particularly nuanced meaning was painted onto canvas. See catalogue entries D159–63, D353, D418, D420, D482 in Upright Headley 1979.
36 Scholem 1949, p. 251.
37 Varnedoe 1996, p. 124.
38 Marcella Louis Brenner interview.
39 Upright 1985, p. 11.
40 Greenberg 1986b, p. 229.
41 See 'Black or White', in Motherwell 1992, pp. 71–72.
42 Robert Rauschenberg quoted in Joseph 2003, p. 86.
43 See Associated Press 1933, p. 5; Birchhall 1933, p. 1, and Editorial 1933, p. 12. Birchhall, writing in *The New York Times*, quoted Goebbells' proclamation that 'Jewish intellectualism is dead', but seems to have underestimated the significance of the event, calling it 'childish', and writing of the 'ripples of amusement that went through the outside world'.
44 Editorial 1933, p. 16.
45 Sartre 1995, p. 24.
46 Rosenberg 1949, pp. 8–18.
47 *Commentary* 1949, p. 363.
48 *Commentary* 1949, p. 368.
49 Fiske 1959, p. 48.
50 Marcella Louis Brenner interview.
51 George Dondero, quoted in Boswell 1949, p. 7.
52 Boswell 1949, p. 7.
53 Strauss 1952, p. 25.
54 Archives of American Art, Morris Louis Files, reel 4993, p. 1434. During this interview, Bocour tried to recall if Louis had been a member of the John Reed Club. Bocour did not think so, and indeed, there are no precise records to indicate the specific political affiliations of Louis in this period.
55 Mira Goldfarb Berkowitz also used the Heine quotation in the pamphlet produced for the Jewish Museum exhibition to draw attention to the connections between burning books and burning bodies.
56 My thanks to Dr. Tom Gretton for this suggestion.
57 See Scholem 1996, pp. 44–50.
58 Cohen 1945, p. 1.
59 This is discussed in Scholem 1996, p. 76.
60 Upright Headley 1979, p. 52.
61 Archives of American Art, Morris Louis Files, reel 4988, p. 0021.
62 See Boyarin 1992, p. xvii.
63 Bann 1985, p. 178.
64 Blanchot 1995.
65 Blanchot 1995, p. 47.
66 Blanchot 1995, p. 121.
67 Blanchot 1995, p. 110.
68 Blanchot 1995, p. 41.
69 Blanchot 1995, p. 107–13.
70 Blanchot 1995, p. 111.
71 Blanchot 1995, p. 111.
72 Blanchot 1995, p. 7.
73 Blanchot 1995, p. 33.
74 Blanchot 1995, p. 41.
75 Blanchot 1995, p. 42.
76 Blanchot 1995, p. 145.
77 Archives of American Art, Morris Louis Files, reel 4988, p. 0076. Marcella Louis to unspecified person ['You all'], 15 April 1953.
78 Elderfield 1987, pp. 13–14.
79 Archives of American Art, Clement Greenberg files, N70–7R 0502–3. Morris Louis to Clement Greenberg, 1 June 1954.
80 Archives of American Art, Clement Greenberg files, N70–7R 0502–3. Morris Louis to Clement Greenberg, 1 June 1954.

3 barnett newman's *the stations of the cross: lema sabachthani*

1 Hess 1971, p. 82.
2 Newman 1995, p. 117. Annalee Newman was responding to Matthew Baigell's article, 'Barnett Newman's Stripe Paintings and Kabbalah, A Jewish Take' in Baigell 1994. Baigell had argued, as I do, that Newman's use of titles did not spring from a religious Jewish scholarship.
3 Armin Zweite gives the fullest account of this project; Zweite 1999, pp. 236–54. Zweite assumes that Newman's text was written after Richard Meier approached him to make a model for the exhibition, but in the Barnett Newman Foundation, the file containing Newman's text is labelled 'Project for a Synagogue, 1951', and the typed text inside is dated 1951. Two years previously, Paul and Percival Goodman (who also contributed to the 1963 exhibition) described the opportunities for Jewish artists to make works for the many synagogues being planned across the States, and the impetus for these new buildings. 'Suddenly there occurred the fact that six million Jews were slaughtered in three or four years, just because they were Jews. We do not know in what ways other groups would react to such a happening, but among the Jews it seems to have had the following effect: they became aware of themselves as a physical community, a congregation. . . . The reaction has been the sense of the co-presence of a certain identity and certain rudiments of a tradition, what we are calling the sense of being a physical congregation.' Goodman 1949, p. 52. The article was one of many that addressed the relation between the effects of recent history, and the growth of interest in the synagogue. In his 1950 article 'The Postwar Revival of the Synagogue', Will Herberg noted that arguments connecting 'the shattering experience of demonic anti-Semitism' to the revival of the synagogue were 'commonplace' (Herberg 1950, p. 315). Janay Jadine Wong has written an account of the commissions of works by painters and sculptors for these new synagogues. See Wong 1994.
4 Jewish Museum archives, 'Proposals of the Exhibition Committee', Box: Director/Admin, Subjects A–Z, 1962–66, File: F–G General 1964.
5 Barnett Newman Foundation, Hans van Weeren-Griek files. Letter from Barnett Newman to Hans van Weeren-Griek, 18 January 1965.
6 Arthur A. Cohen, notes for talk. Arthur A. Cohen archive, courtesy Elaine Lustig Cohen. My thanks to Mel Bochner who enabled me to access this archive.
7 See for instance Landsberger 1946, Wischnitzer-Bernstein 1946, Lozowick 1947, Loukomski 1947, Lozowick 1948, Namenyi 1957, Roth 1961.
8 Kampf 1975, p. 46.
9 Arthur A. Cohen, notes for talk. Arthur A. Cohen archive.
10 Barnett Newman Foundation, 'Conference on the Status of Soviet Jews' files.
11 Benjamin Buchloh, 'Lines of Abstraction in 1948', unpublished paper given at the symposium 'Reconsidering Barnett Newman', held at the Philadelphia Museum of Art, April 2002.
12 For instance, Shiff writes that 'the evolution of [his] art is best understood in the light of Newman's moral stance, which deepened in reaction to his experience of World War II', and later that 'The concept of the tragic acquired topical urgency for the generation of World War II. Perhaps that in itself explains why Newman invoked the tragic so insistently.' (Shiff 2004, pp. 14 and 43).
13 Alan Solomon was interviewing Newman for a television programme broadcast on 12 July 1966 as part of the USA Artists series on National Education Television. The interviews with Solomon were heavily edited before being broadcast, with several of the comments most interesting for my purposes cut. Archives of American Art, Alan Solomon files. Transcript of Barnett Newman interview, 20 March 1966 (Henceforth 'Solomon interview').
14 Newman 1992, p. 274.
15 Newman 1992, p. 191.
16 The relation of Holocaust memory to Newman's series has not been discussed in previous accounts of the works (Alloway 1966; Hess 1971; Rosenberg 1978).
17 In many of the paintings, the separation of black Magna paint causes an oily yellow stain on the canvas adjacent to a black area. Tom Learner, a

Tate conservation scientist who has written a paper called 'Magna', stated in conversation with me that this separation would have occurred quite quickly, and certainly before the paintings were exhibited in 1966. Considering the subtle tonal shifts in all the paintings, it is likely that these accidental changes contributed to the desired visual content rather than detracting from it. Certainly Newman would have seen these changes, and he did not choose to conceal them.

18 Greenberg 1993b, p. 55. Newman later commented 'I had been working a lot with color, and I felt that perhaps I was being intoxicated and beguiled with what happens with color for me.' (Solomon interview, p. 2). Elsewhere, he remarked 'If you examine the problem of color, it's interesting to me that with a large, tragic theme of this kind – for example, when Picasso did *Guernica*, he couldn't do it in color, he did it in black and white and gray. I couldn't make a green Passion or a red one. You wouldn't have me make a purple Jesus or something like that. It had to be black and white. The compulsion was absolute.' (Newman 1992, p. 277). Though interesting the second statement seems to contradict other accounts of the series because Newman suggests here that he painted in black and white *because* he was painting the Stations; where elsewhere he was at pains to say that he only realised that the black and white paintings were the Stations when looking at them.

19 Solomon interview, p. 3.

20 Newman 1992, p. 188. This seems to be a misquote: Newman did not 'use a white' paint on this canvas: rather, the raw canvas between two black bands looks whiter than the raw canvas in the centre of the painting.

21 Newman 1992, p. 189.

22 Amishai-Maisels 1989, pp. 1657–71; and Amishai-Maisels 1993.

23 Schoenberner 1960, p. 196. One of the figures in George Segal's 1984 sculpture *The Holocaust* mimics the pose of this victim.

24 'Surrealism and the War' in Newman 1992, pp. 94–96.

25 *White Crucifixion* had been presented to the Art Institute of Chicago after the 1946 exhibition. Newman might have seen the painting again when he visited Chicago in 1955.

26 Klonsky 1945, p. 91.

27 Rosenberg 1945, pp. 26–33. Considering the confidence with which Rosenberg described Chagall's use of the crucifixion in this text, written for a Jewish readership, it is fascinating how reticent he was when he recalled his friend Newman's use of the crucifixion: 'To my mind, the title *The Stations of the Cross* was a mistake, and I argued against it with Newman on the ground that an event held sacred by a cult . . . ought not to be appropriated by outsiders and given changed meanings.' Rosenberg 1978, p. 73. Somehow (perhaps mindful of his readership) Rosenberg had changed his attitude on how 'an event held sacred by a cult' might be used. Needless to say, he did not relate Newman's use of the Passion to the 'tragic period' of the Holocaust.

28 Howarth 1948, pp. 16–17.

29 Amishai-Maisels 1993, pp. 192–93.

30 Shuster 1943, pp. 23–36.

31 From 'The Funeral' by M. J. This was one of the handful of poems collected by A. Glanz-Leyeless, and published in the article 'Poems from the Warsaw Ghetto', in *Contemporary Jewish Record* (April 1945), pp. 129–36.

32 Amishai-Maisels 1993, p. 187.

33 Emmanuel Levinas, 'Jewish Thought Today' in Levinas 1990, p. 162.

34 Maybaum 1965, p. 36.

35 There are many reasons for the use of this metaphor, stretching beyond its most obvious suggestion that Jews suffered unjustly as did Christ. In the early period of Nazism, the presentation of Jesus as a Jew might have served to remind Christian Germans of their bonds with Jews. Speaking at a Rabbinical conference in New York in 1964, the theological scholar Jacob Agus suggested that Jews died 'as the initial sacrifice of an anti-Christian crusade' (Agus 1964, p. 13). With this in mind, the metaphor would have warned Christians that the object of Nazism's attack was not only Judaism, but actually, the entire Judeo-Christian tradition. Another dimension of the metaphor, more appropriate when considering its function after the war, is described by Shoshana Felman in her account of Paul Celan's *Todesfuge*. Felman writes that Celan 'forces the language of Christian metaphorics to *witness* in effect the Holocaust, and be in turn witnessed by it.' Felman 1992, p. 30. This formulation would make Christianity a kind of guilty party. Newman's use of the metaphor of the crucifixion does not seem to partake in this project.

36 Rosenberg 1961, p. 370; Arendt wrote that 'Eichmann felt like Pontius Pilate and washed his hands in innocence.' Arendt 1963, p. 135.

37 Solomon interview, p. 7.

38 Solomon interview, p. 23.

39 Solomon interview, p. 8.

40 As Richard Shiff has recently argued, this practice of opening up, rather than tying down meanings, was typical of Newman's approach, and characterised his writing as well as his painting. Shiff writes that Newman's work was 'safe from being converted into lessons' and that 'like his paintings, many of Newman's written statements, despite their reasoned argumentation, are more likely to affect readers emotionally than provide a definitive solution to a problem.' (Shiff 2004, p. 31).

41 Newman 1992, p. 251.

42 Newman 1992, p. 178.

43 Barnett Newman, 'Statement' in Alloway 1966, reprinted in Newman 1992, p. 188.

44 *Newsweek* 1966.

45 Newman 1992, p. 257.

46 Newman 1992, p. 289.

47 Carol Mancusi-Ungaro, 'Barnett Newman's Pilgrimage in Paint' in Ho 2005.

48 Greenberg 1993b, p. 55.

49 Greenberg 1993b, p. 99.

50 Ann Temkin, 'Barnett Newman on Exhibition' in Temkin 2002.

51 Canaday 1966.

52 Kozloff 1966, p. 598.

53 Archives of American Art, Thomas Hess files. Barnett Newman to Carey Williams, Editor, *The Nation*, 8 June 1966.

54 Barnett Newman Foundation, *The Stations of the Cross: Lema Sabachthani* files. Letter from Barnett Newman to Mr. Arthur Ochs Sulzberger, President, *The New York Times*, 28 May 1966.

55 Genauer 1966.

56 Barker 1966.

57 Bois 2002, p. 103.

58 Meyer Schapiro, 'Memo for conferences', 26 June 1946 (Ratner Center R.G.25 1/3). This memo, which outlined several possible themes for conferences, was prepared by Schapiro as he worked as a consultant to the newly established Jewish Museum in 1946.

59 Newman 1992, p. 169.

60 Newman 1992, p. 277.

61 In *Remnants of Auschwitz*, Agamben writes that 'After Auschwitz it is not possible to use a tragic paradigm in ethics' (Agamben 1999, p. 99). This sentence concludes a section of the book in which he considers whether the model of the Greek tragic hero can account for the situation of the camp survivor or indeed the former SS prison guards. Agamben elegantly indicates how the model cannot fit either subject. Agamben's arguments here might trouble the idea that the indirect survivor (the 1960s American, for instance) can take the position of the tragic subject, but nonetheless, I believe that *Newman*'s notion of tragedy was at play in *The Stations*.

62 Arthur Morse published his research in a series of articles in *Look* magazine, later collected in Morse 1967.

63 Steiner 1967, pp. 119–35.

64 Newman 1992, p. 289.

65 Yerushalmi 1989, p. 36. Yerushalmi is also interested in the way 'the rabbis [in the Talmud] seem to play with time as though with an accordion, expanding it and contracting it at will. Barriers of time can be ignored and all the ages placed in an ever-fluid dialogue with each other' (p. 17). This suggests another correspondence with Newman's idea of the Passion. For Newman the Passion was a temporal construct in which moments of history are squeezed together. The notion of temporal compression also accords with the temporality of the experience of the installation.

66 Newman 1992, p. 188.

67 Haftmann 1971, p. viii.

68 Haftmann 1971, p. ix.

4 frank stella's *polish village* series

1 Rubin, William 1970, p. 149.
2 Kramer 1970, p. 34.
3 Leider 1970, p. 50.
4 Leider 1970, p. 47.
5 McShine 1970, p. 138.
6 Amy Newman counts three Stella covers and seven solo feature articles on Stella between 1965 and 1974. Newman, Amy 2000, p. 530.
7 Peter Plagens has commented recently that 'I didn't have any conscious idea that what was needed now, at this moment in the early 70s, is a criticism of the institutions with a broader, more political, sociological take, and let's get outside Michael Fried telling us "what stripe in Stella goes over what" sort of thing.' (Newman, Amy 2000, p. 377). Even in retrospect, then, Stella's work and Fried's criticism of the mid–late 1960s are conflated as representing everything that the political situation did not require.
8 *New York Times* 1970, p. 40.
9 Baker 1970, p. 64.
10 This is illustrated in the advert for the auction. *ARTNews* (September 1970) p. 65.
11 Jan Zachwatowicz, 'Introduction' in Piechotka 1959, p. 8. In the 1920s, Oskar Sosnowski of the Polish Institute of Architecture instigated a project to record the rural synagogues. Many photographs were taken and archived, mostly by the art historian Szymon Zajczyk. Though (along with the buildings) some of these documents were destroyed during the war, there were still enough photographs to assemble *Wooden Synagogues*. The main text, by Polish architects Maria and Kazimierz Piechotka, was written in the 1950s.
12 Stephen Kayser in Piechotka 1959, pp. 5 and 6. Kayser later worked with Richard Meier on the 1963 Jewish Museum 'Recent American Synagogue Architecture'.
13 Leider 1978, pp. 10–12 and Rubin, William 1987, pp. 32–34.
14 The reviews included, in order of publication, Kramer 1971, Baker 1971, Ratcliff 1971, Krauss 1976b, Sandler 1972, Elderfield 1972, Schjeldahl 1973, Siegel 1973, Masheck 1973, Kingsley 1973, Finkelstein 1973 and Gilbert-Rolfe 1974.
15 Elderfield 1972, p. 30.
16 Siegel 1973, p. 78.
17 Ratcliff 1971, p. 60.
18 Baker 1971, p. 88.
19 Sandler 1972, p. 33.
20 Krauss 1971, p. 41. All the following quotations come from this article.
21 Krauss here might have made an implicit reference to Rubin's diagrams of the *Protractors* on pp. 136–37 of his 1970 catalogue.
22 Kozloff 1976, p. 44.
23 Kayser in Piechotka 1959, p. 5.
24 Lozowick 1947, p. 107.
25 Lozowick 1947, p. 107.
26 Loukomski 1947, p. 37.
27 Kayser in Piechotka 1959, p. 5.
28 Lozowick 1948, p. 384.
29 Meyer Schapiro, quoted in Minutes of the Museum Committee of the Jewish Museum, 1 October 1946. Ratner Center, R.G.25, 1–2. Schapiro was involved with plans for the Jewish Museum between 1946–47.
30 Meier 1963, p. 7.
31 This was from a 1964 radio broadcast with Dan Flavin, Donald Judd and the critic Bruce Glaser. Reprinted in Meyer 2000, p. 199.
32 Miller 1959, p. 76.
33 The Museum of Modern Art, New York, Department of Painting and Sculpture: Frank Stella Collection File [Interview] [Henceforth 'Stella/Rubin interview']. The papers documenting Stella's conversations with Rubin before the 1970 retrospective are in disarray. They are unpaginated, stapled together out of order. Some are simply transcripts of Stella talking; others include Rubin's questions.
34 'Stella/Rubin interview'.
35 'Stella/Rubin interview'.
36 'Stella/Rubin interview'.
37 Rubin William 1970, p. 45.
38 The Museum of Modern Art, New York, Department of Painting and Sculpture: Frank Stella Collection File. Typescript of interview of Frank Stella by Philip Leider at San Francisco Art Institute, 15–17 April 1966.
39 Leider 1978, p. 102.
40 Cohen 1983.
41 Letter from Joan Rosenbaum to Frank Stella, 4 November 1982. Marked 'Never Sent'. Jewish Museum Archives, Frank Stella file.
42 Rubin William 1987, p. 40.
43 'Russian Art of the Revolution' showed at the Brooklyn Museum of Art in the summer of 1971. 'Art in Revolution: Soviet Art and Design since 1917' was held in the New York Cultural Center in the autumn. The latter included reconstructions of Tatlin's corner reliefs.
44 Leider 1978, pp. 102–3.
45 Andre 2005, p. 229.
46 Leider 1978, p. 102.
47 In 'Some Uses and Abuses of Russian Constructivism', an essay of 1990, Hal Foster criticised Stella for abusing constructivism. 'Often when [constructivism] is treated, it is not as a semiological analysis of art forms, much less a supersession of art, but rather another style to be manipulated in a *posthistoire* pastiche. Specific examples of this fetishism of the sign of Constructivism are the constructions of Stella.' (Foster in Andrews and Kalinovska 1990, p. 249). Foster does not refer directly here to the *Polish Villages*, and he might well have had in mind Stella's entire work between 1970 and 1990. For sure, Stella's work of the 1970s did not question the production and distribution systems of bourgeois art as did many constructivists, and as would many other artists of Stella's generation. However, Foster's criticism suggests that Stella's interest in constructivism was a matter of simple visual and material quotation: I am arguing by contrast that Stella was specifically interested in acknowledging the connected fates of constructivism and the synagogues.
48 Birnholz 1969, p. 73.
49 Kingsley 1973, p. 54.
50 Baker 1971, p. 88.
51 Masheck 1973, pp. 80–81.
52 Foster 1996, p. 63.
53 Foster 1996, p. 66.
54 Siegel 1973, p. 78.
55 Elderfield 1972, p. 31.
56 Kramer 1971, p. 25.
57 In dialogue with Frampton, Carl Andre argued that 'Frank Stella is a Constructivist. He makes paintings by combining identical, discrete units. These units are not stripes, but brush strokes. We have both watched Frank Stella paint a picture. He fills in a pattern with uniform elements. His stripe designs are the result of the shape and limitation of his primary unit.' (Andre and Frampton 1981, p. 37). Andre's invocation of constructivism here relied on the importance of deductive and repetitive processes. Whilst Stella's forms and processes of 1959 recalled some of Rodchenko's *Spatial Constructions*, I am interested in a different relationship to constructivism: the ways in which his work of the early 1970s deployed constustivist form and materiality.
58 Stella/Rubin interview.
59 Blanchot 1995, pp. 81–82.
60 Blanchot 1995, p. 81.
61 This reading of Stella's process could be contrasted with interpretations of the working methods of sculptors such as David Smith and Anthony Caro. Hal Foster argues that Smith assumed the role of the 'proletarian producer' but that his working methods never analysed the forms of labour in industrial society. Rather, his 'gestures can be seen as compensatory to the reified routine of actual labour in capitalist industry' (Foster in Andrews and Kalinovska 1990, p. 247). In other words, Smith hoped to redeem processes such as welding, turning them from mundane functional processes into refined, high art procedures. By contrast, in the *Black Paintings* Stella painted work as it was: repetitive and mundane.
62 Stella/Rubin interview.
63 Stella/Rubin interview.
64 Stella/Rubin interview.
65 Stella/Rubin interview.
66 Krauss 1968, p. 44.

67 Krauss 1968, p. 44.
68 Krauss 1968, p. 43.
69 Elderfield 1972, p. 31.
70 Krauss 1968, p. 43.
71 Derrida 1987, p. 74.

5 louis kahn's *memorial to the six million jewish martyrs*

1 Williams Goldhagen 2001, p. 210. Elsewhere (p. 135), Williams Goldhagen refers to the 'abstract, minimalist forms' of Kahn's Trenton Jewish Community Centre.
2 Saidel 1996, pp. 70–79, and Solomon 1997, chapter five. Susan Solomon's work has been invaluable. In her PhD thesis she considers the memorial in the context of Kahn's other proposals for the Jewish community, paying particular attention to his communication failures with Jewish clients. Solomon also published an historical account of the proposal in Brownlee and De Long 1992. Her comments in interview have also been helpful. Like Solomon, my research makes use of Kahn's archives. Though this means that we address some of the same material, I am much more interested in probing the meanings of Kahn's proposal as an abstract memorial, in particular in the penultimate section of this chapter.
3 Deborah Lipstadt, for instance, has stated that 'An examination of Jewish periodicals [in the 1950s and 1960s] reveals few articles on the Holocaust.' (Lipstadt 1996, p. 195). Saul Friedlander writes of 'the 15 or 20 years of "latency" that followed the war in regard to talking or writing about the Shoah, particularly in the United States'. ('Trauma, Memory, and Transference', in Hartman 1994, p. 259).
4 Saidel 1996, p. 44.
5 Saidel 1996, p. 49.
6 Politzer 1949, p. 590.
7 Saidel 1996, p. 50.
8 Saidel 1996, p. 50.
9 The earliest document of contact is Dr. Louis Finkelstein's letter of 16 June 1958 to Jakob Michael, in which he notes that 'the Seminary has committed itself to the concept of creating a Yizkor memorial for the martyred Jews of Europe', and that the Seminary was working with Michael Zagayski to raise funds for this. Letter from Dr. Louis Finkelstein to Jakob Michael, 16 June 1958, Ratner Center, Zagayski papers 1–10.
10 Letter from Albert List to Dr. Louis Finkelstein, 7 September 1960. Ratner Center, Zagayski papers 1–11.
11 Saidel 1996, p. 60.
12 Saidel 1996, p. 58.
13 Saidel 1996, p. 60.
14 The Architectural Archives, University of Pennsylvania. Louis I. Kahn Collection, University of Pennsylvania and Pennsylvania Historical and Museum Commission. Box P–36 (Hereafter 'LIK36'), File E, Letter from David Kreeger to Kahn, 12 April 1967.
15 Williams Goldhagen 2001, p. 91.
16 LIK36 File E, Letter from David Kreeger to Kahn, 1 November 1966.
17 LIK36 File E, Letter from David Kreeger to Kahn, 28 December 1966.
18 Albert Friedlander, 'Editor's Page', *Dimension* (Spring 1967), p. 3. This was sent to Kahn by Moshe Davidowitz of New York University. (LIK36 File E, Letter to Kahn, 15 May 1967).
19 Susan Solomon quotes Sybil Milton's description of Rapoport's work: 'The florid and heavy-handed work combines biblical motifs with the Holocaust: an unconsumed burning bush, a dying mother, Jewish resistance fighters, a child with a Torah, and a blazing menorah.' Solomon 1997, p. 344.
20 Interview with Vladka Meed, New York, 23 February 2000.
21 LIK36 File E, Letter from Leonard Meiselman to Kahn, 15 May 1967.
22 LIK36 File E, Letter from Moshe Davidowitz to Kahn, 14 August 1967.
23 In a similar manner, whilst planning the Adath Jeshurun synagogue, Kahn had conducted research about Jewish religious and cultural practices only after coming up with a formal idea for the building. Kahn planned out a building which would be supported by clusters of tree-like columns, and had later justified his plans by arguing that the earliest synagogues came into being when biblical Jewish communities came to gather together under trees. See Williams Goldhagen 2001, pp. 94–95.
24 Manfredo Tafuri wrote that history, for Kahn, 'is only an *ingredient* to be manipulated', and that 'he uses it to justify choices', an argument that seems to have some backing here. See Tafuri 1980, p. 56. However, while Kahn might have sought to use Jewish history to justify a choice, his invocation of architectural history is integral to the function of the memorial.
25 LIK36 File E, Memo, 6 September 1967.
26 LIK36 File B, Letter from Abraham Duker to Kahn, 13 November 1967.
27 Komendant 1975, p. 172.
28 LIK36 File E, Letter from Joseph Lichten to Kahn, 8 January 1968.
29 LIK36 File B, Minutes of meeting, 20 January 1968.
30 LIK36 File D, Kahn's press release, 3 May 1968.
31 Susan Solomon has argued that the press release evidences Kahn's repeated failure to communicate his ideas successfully to his Jewish clients. Kahn gives insufficient support to his choice of abstraction, articulating his ideas instead according to his expectations of criticism, and therefore losing the opportunity to celebrate the proposal for its merits (Solomon 1997, pp. 357–61).
32 LIK36 File E, Letter from August Heckscher to Kahn, 22 March 1968.
33 LIK36 File E, Letter from Elliot Willensky to Kahn, 19 April 1968 enclosing copy of Art Commission resolution dated 17 April 1968.
34 Huxtable 1968.
35 See in particular 'Singing the Downtown Blues' in Huxtable 1972, pp. 56–60.
36 Eckhardt 1968, p. B2; *Time Magazine* 1968, p. 78; *Architectural Record* 1968, p. 36; *Architectural Forum* 1968, p. 89; *Progressive Architecture* 1968.
37 Raynes 1969, pp. 38–41.
38 Art Commission Files, City Hall, New York. Letter to Mayor Lindsay, 22 May 1969.
39 LIK36 File D, Kahn's press release, 3 May 1968.
40 LIK36 File B, Letter from Jesse Reichek to Kahn, 1 February 1972.
41 As we have seen, Holocaust memory was also intertwined with contemporary concerns for Louis and Newman, whether related to McCarthyism, Hiroshima or Vietnam.
42 Material regarding these payments is in the American Jewish Committee files in their archives in New York. In co-ordination with David Kreeger, the AJC Executive Vice President Bertram Gold spearheaded the drive to collect promise monies from the various organisations that had made up the Committee. There are also some letters in LIK36.
43 LIK36 File D, Kahn's press release, 3 May 1968.
44 Kahn 1991, p. 235.
45 Kahn 1991, p. 235.
46 Williams Goldhagen 2001, p. 2.
47 LIK36 File D, Kahn's press release, 3 May 1968.
48 Scully 1993, p. 97.
49 Scully 1962, p. 28.
50 Frampton 1996, p. 217, Tafuri 1980, p. 56 and Williams Goldhagen 2001.
51 Gorlin 1985, p. 87. Gorlin also argued that Kahn's 'solid cubes [were] echoing with the form of the ovens at Auschwitz', an even more ridiculous contention.
52 Williams Goldhagen 2001, p. 98.
53 Solomon 1997, p. 344.
54 In a 1944 symposium in which Kahn had taken part, Philip Goodwin had highlighted the use of easily accessible symbols in monuments: 'The use of a *trade-mark* in countless repetition has proved valuable with the eagle, the swastika, the fasces, the hammer and sickle, politically speaking.' Philip Goodwin, 'Monuments' in Zucker 1944, p. 599.
55 *Architectural Record* (January 1966), p. 42.
56 Though Kahn clearly resisted the controlling forms of fascist architecture, he had always hoped to create monumental structures. However, 'monumentality' did not mean for him anything like what it had meant to architects such as Speer. Kahn had written an essay entitled 'Monumentality' in 1944 for a symposium chaired by Paul Zucker. Monumentality was 'a spiritual quality inherent in a structure which conveys the feeling of its eternity'. Monumentality should serve civic needs ('the school, the community or culture centre'), and was to be achieved through the use of new materials ('steel, the lighter metals, concrete, glass, laminated woods, asbestos, rubber, and plastics'). 'Structural perfection' must be sought in order to

achieve 'impressiveness, clarity of form and logical scale'. A monumental building would respect 'the meaning of a wall, a post, a beam, a roof and a window and their interrelation in space.' (See 'Monumentality' in Kahn 1991, pp. 18–27).

In his text on the *Memorial*, Kahn used the terms 'monument' and 'memorial' interchangeably, but not the term 'monumentality'. Was the proposal 'monumental' in Kahn's sense of the word? Perhaps the question is misleading, for monumentality was achieved in Kahn's work through the way in which a building used materials and engineering to achieve essential architectural functions (the provision of a roof, a window, and so on) and these functions were irrelevant in this project. If the aim of monumentality for Kahn was to create a sense of community amongst the users of a structure, then this *Memorial* was certainly 'monumental', for as I argue later, this was its aim. But at the same time, it could be suggested that because of its materiality, Kahn's *Memorial* refused the monumentality and solid appearance of his other buildings. Rather than asserting itself as a structure, the *Memorial* allowed other edifices to be seen in it and through it. In this way Anthony Vidler's judgment of the transparency of Rem Koolhaas' 1989 competition entry for the French National Library seems apt as a comment on Kahn's proposal: just as in Koolhaas's proposal, transparency in Kahn's suggested 'a crisis of confidence in monumentality' (Vidler 1992, p. 220).

57 Scheerbart 1972, p. 41.
58 Scheerbart 1972, p. 74.
59 An English translation was published in 1967. See Korn 1967.
60 In a recent essay on Gerhard Richter's 2002 series of grey painted glass panels, Benjamin Buchloh has considered the changing approaches to, and evaluations of glass in German architectural discourse of the first half of the twentieth century. Buchloh considers Walter Benjamin's critique of Scheerbart and shows how by the late 1920s, Mies was more interested in the reflective than transparent qualities of glass. Buchloh 2002, pp. 21–24.
61 Scully 1993, p. 98.
62 The memories of Bruno Taut's Glass Pavilion (1914), Gropius' Dessau Bauhaus (1925–26), and Mies' Barcelona Pavilion (1929) seem far more significant than any memories of the Jewish use of glass.
63 Kaplan and Tauber 1966, pp. 338 and 404.
64 Hepburn 1964, pp. 112–15.
65 LIK36 File D, Kahn's press release, 3 May 1968.
66 By connecting the memory of the Holocaust to these sites of immigration, Kahn linked the freedom and life won after the Holocaust with the freedom offered to its immigrants by America. The 'better future' Kreeger had mentioned in his letter was to be found precisely in the USA. Some Holocaust survivors (including individuals on the CCSMJM) had found a haven in America, so for them this connection was literal, but Kahn seems to have hoped that the link would make sense for all eventual users of the *Memorial*. Therefore despite the absence of any images of American flags and symbols, the memorial still espoused a nationalistic ideology.
67 Colin Rowe and Robert Slutsky, 'Transparency: Literal and Phenomenal' in Rowe 1995, p. 160.
68 Rowe 1995, p. 161.
69 Their central example was Le Corbusier's villa at Garches, whose facade suggested a spatial order contradicted by its plan.
70 Kahn had long been interested in creating what he called 'nondirectional' spaces, for instance in his 1954 designs for the public spaces and ground floor of the Philadelphia City Tower. See Williams Goldhagen 2001, p. 77.
71 Williams Goldhagen 2001, p. 95.
72 Williams Goldhagen 2001, p. 100. Introducing his work on the Trenton Jewish Community Centre, for instance, she describes Kahn's 'long-standing desire to create an architecture that would become a symbol of communal identity and encourage communal participation. His self-appointed task was to design buildings and civic spaces that would revitalise what he perceived to be an endangered public realm' (Williams Goldhagen 2001, p. 122). Later she writes that Kahn 'hoped that his communal sentiment, when combined with self-awareness, would encourage individual social responsibility' (p. 207).
73 Hatton 1997, pp. 45–46. Dan Graham's pavilion took the shape of a Star of David. Though this form was completely intentional, there is little indication that Graham intended the pavilion to be taken as any kind of Holocaust memorial. Rather it seems he chose the form because of the uneasiness of making work for an Austrian institution. See Graham 1999, pp. 180–81.
74 In the context of post-war architecture, Kahn's approach to glass seems even more significant. The reflective properties of glass tended to be used in corporate architecture so as to prevent people seeing inside offices. Kahn used reflection to entirely different political ends, encouraging people to pay attention to each other's presence, rather than disabling communication.
75 Despite Kahn's ambivalence towards using symbolic Jewish forms, the notion of memory in his *Memorial* resembles the oral memorial traditions of Judaism. At calendar festivals, for instance, Jews tell stories to each other. Yerushalmi has been particularly interested in oral rather than visual mnemonic processes in Judaism (Yerushalmi 1989). Since the time of Kahn's proposal, oral memory has been in play in other Holocaust memorial projects. This has been due to the ageing of the survivor population, and the threat of Holocaust denial.
76 Kahn 1991, p. 249.
77 Levinas 2000, p. 197.
78 Levinas 2000, p. 199.
79 Levinas 1999, p. 86.
80 Levinas 1999, pp. 85–86.
81 Adriaan Peperzak has written that 'Western thought and practice in [Levinas's] view are marked by a striving for totalization, in which the universe is reduced to an originary and ultimate unity by way of panoramic overviews and dialectical syntheses.' Adriaan Peperzac in Levinas 1996, p. x.
82 Tamra Wright has described Levinas's description of the encounter between the Self and the Other as a kind of post-Holocaust ethics. See Wright 1999.
83 Primo Levi quoted in Losson 1999, p. 35.
84 Georges Perec, 'Ellis Island: Description of a Project' in Perec 1997, p. 136.

6 beryl korot's *dachau 1974*

1 Newman, Amy 2000, p. 243.
2 Interview with the artist, 8 September 2003. All subsequent quotes of Korot's, unless otherwise attributed, come from this interview.
3 Hanley and Wooster 1993, p. 21.
4 Rosler 2004, pp. 53–54.
5 Richard Serra, 'Television Delivers People' in Korot and Schneider 1976, p. 115.
6 Mary Lucier, 'Light and Death' in Hall and Fifer 1990, p. 457.
7 Wagner 2000, p. 69.
8 Wagner also explores these. See Wagner 2000, pp. 73–74.
9 Joselit 2002b, p. 155.
10 Schneider quoted in Bruce Kurtz, 'The Present Tense' in Korot and Schneider 1976, p. 240.
11 Bruce Kurtz, 'The Present Tense' in Korot and Schneider 1976, pp. 234–43.
12 Krauss 1976a.
13 Jameson 1992, p. 76.
14 Jameson 1992, pp. 70–71. As David Joselit has summarised, 'video [for Jameson] is a primary tool in accomplishing [the] massive evacuation of memory through the constant replenishment of mediated experience.' Joselit 2002a, p. 135.
15 Mary Ann Doane, 'Information, Crisis, Catastrophe' in Mellencamp 1990, p. 222.
16 Joselit 2002a, p. 135.
17 Untitled editorial, *Radical Software*, 1:1, Summer 1970. The journal is now available at www.radicalsoftware.org.
18 Michael Shamberg, the publisher of *Radical Software*, also contributed to this opening editorial.
19 Untitled editorial, *Radical Software*, 1:1, Summer 1970.
20 Untitled editorial, *Radical Software*, 1:1, Summer 1970.
21 'Typical of the technocratic idealists who fostered the cult of the gadget in the field of video art is Nam June Paik.' See Buchloh 1985, p. 217.
22 http://www.radicalsoftware.org/e/volume1nr1.html.
23 Hanley and Wooster 1993, p. 70.
24 Hanley and Wooster 1993, p. 71.
25 Beryl Korot, correspondence with the author, May 2006.

26 For a detailed account of the history and post-war history of Dachau, see Marcuse 2001.
27 See Werner 1951.
28 Decter 1967.
29 Halperin 1971, p. 106.
30 Tennenbaum 1976, p. 42.
31 Decter 1967, p. 52.
32 Halperin 1971, p. 108.
33 Werner described the museum as 'a large room filled with photographs, a model of the camp, and maps showing the location of the cemeteries . . .'. Werner 1951, p. 545.
34 Halperin 1971, pp. 109–10.
35 Tennenbaum 1976, p. 43.
36 Decter 1967, p. 52.
37 Tennenbaum 1976, p. 42.
38 Korot, quoted in Wiegand 1975. (It is worth noting that Korot did not film the chapel, which many visitors quoted above found objectionable.)
39 See the section in the conclusion on *The J.Street Project*.
40 Hollis Frampton's *Zorns Lemma* of 1970 ends with a similar elemental progress.
41 See Losson 1999, pp. 27–28.
42 Alfred Werner wrote about the stream in these terms: 'We drove to what looked like a nice fast flowing brook . . . The little moat, bluish and clear . . . nobody will know what anguish it once caused so many human beings.' Werner goes on to describe how an old man had been kicked into its waters by SS guards. See Werner 1951.
43 Korot quoted in Glueck 1977.
44 Korot quoted in Wiegand 1975.
45 Korot 1988, p. 369.
46 The weaver was Noel Bennett, and Korot had attended her workshop at Mills College in California.
47 Korot she was unaware that Albers had made a work, *Six Prayers* (1966–67), as a commission for the Jewish Museum to commemorate the 'six million'. For an account of Albers' commission, see Karen Feeney, 'Anni Albers: Devotion to Material' in Fox Weber and Tabatabai Asbaghi 1999, pp. 120–22.
48 As well as determining the number of monitors and division into two intersecting pairs, Korot's interest in weaving also inspired the way she broke up the footage. Though she worked with the most up-to-date technology affordable, Korot edited with a stopwatch, primarily because she was interested in working with video editing in a very manual way, just as a weaver worked with their hands. 'Just as the spinning and gathering of wool serve as the raw material for a weaver, so the artist working with video selects images to serve as the basic substance of the work. All technology, in its capacity to instantly reproduce, store, and retrieve information, has moved continually in a direction that seeks to free us from labouring with our hands by giving us conceptual freedom to organize, select, and judge. For myself, it's become clear that the greater my understanding of the role of craftsmanship in working with the video medium, and the more manually active I remain in the selection process, the greater the possibility for making a technological work true to my intentions.' Beryl Korot, 'Dachau 1974', in Korot and Schneider 1976.

Albers's texts on weaving emphasised the importance of the physical contact of hand and material at a moment when most textile production was industrialised. 'Some hand-weavers have been trying to draw attention to weaving itself as an integral part of textile work . . . These weavers are bringing back the qualities that result from an immediate relation of the working material and the work process. Their fresh and discerning attempts to use surface qualities of weaves are resulting in a new school of textile design.' Albers, 'Constructing Textiles' in Fox Weber and Tabatabai Asbaghi 1999, p. 94. Albers did not fetishise tactility and was wary of the 'romantic overestimation of handwork', and of weavers who turned away from modernity and industry, secluding their work in a protected space of craft. Rather, Albers felt that hand-weaving could inform and improve the industrial production of textiles.

49 Bochner 1967, p. 28.
50 Sol LeWitt, 'Paragraphs on Conceptual Art' in LeWitt 1995, p. 79.
51 'The underlying process in all of Reich's earlier music is the simultaneous repetition in two or more voices of a pattern with self-regulating changes. Normally this consists of a melodic/rhythmic pattern, which at any given moment appears fixed and static but full of energy. Through various techniques a process of gradual change is established, which the ear soon recognises as the work itself in progress. The unfolding of this process constitutes the work's fulfilment.' See Paul Hillier, 'Introduction' in Reich 2002, p. 4.
52 Pamela Lee, 'Phase Piece' in Baume 2001, p. 56.
53 See Heineman 1975; Wiegand 1975; and Freed 1975.
54 See David Ross, 'The Personal Attitude'; John Hanhardt, 'Video/Television Space'; and Bruce Kurtz, 'The Present Tense' in Korot and Schneider 1976.
55 This was *Text and Commentary*, shown at Leo Castelli in 1977.
56 It is a strange coincidence that in two of the four accounts of Dachau referred to above, writers mentioned seeing people riding bicycles just outside the camp. In both cases, the figure on the bicycle is made to stand for the 'German people'. Halperin saw a young boy on a bike who approached him to say hello, prompting the American to write 'I wanted to believe in the young of Germany.' (Halperin 1971, p. 113). Tennenbaum saw 'a small blonde girl riding her bicycle down the wide path between the poplars' and wondered 'surely no one has told her about the history of this place' (Tennenbaum 1976, p. 45). Korot's bicyclist just rides by, but his or her presence might generate similar readings. Passing by without paying any special attention to the site to her side, the cyclist might seem either ignorant of or freed up from the weight of the past.
57 Heineman 1975, p. 76.
58 I take this idea of vicarious tourism from Griselda Pollock. In her essay 'Holocaust Tourism', she confronts the problem of day trips on which tourists are taken to Auschwitz and other sites of death, and also writes of the way 'vicarious tourism is created through representation, and especially through film'. Nevertheless, Pollock then gives three examples of films which 'refuse and even refute the dominant terms of cinema' and thereby disable vicarious tourism. Her examples are *Kitty Returns to Auschwitz*, Chantal Ackerman's *D'Est*, and Lanzmann's *Shoah* (Griselda Pollock, 'Holocaust Tourism' in Crouch and Lübbren 2003, p. 179 and p. 186). As I have indicated, Korot visited Dachau long after it had opened for tourist visitors, but long before the phenomenon of day trips. Nonetheless, Pollock's formulation is useful to think about *Dachau 1974*.
59 In many ways this moment in Korot's work parallels the effects, at least for myself, of a near-contemporaneous project, the twentieth panel of Gerhard Richter's *Atlas*, which dates from 1967. Famously, Richter has never painted images based on the photographs he has collected of concentration camp victims, but in this panel, he coloured over three black and white photographs with lurid orange, green, blue and yellow tones. The panel acts not as a resolved answer to the question of how an artist might work from such photographic material, but as a question itself, asking its viewer to answer why such colouring is so problematic.
60 Foster 1996b, p. 42.
61 Korot, 'Dachau 1974' in Korot and Schneider 1976.
62 Mary Lucier's multi-channel works *Ohio at Giverny* (1983) and *Wilderness* (1986) used similar paired structures to *Dachau 1974*, but the paired channels showed the same images. Lucier also wrote an article in 1978 after coming across an eight-part video installation in a fashion store on 57th Street. The shop designer, she realised, had taken the weaving structure of his installation from Korot. See Lucier 1978.
63 Joselit 2002a; Kraynak 2002.

7 mel bochner's *via tasso* project

1 Cited in Pugliese 2002, p. 44.
2 Carolyn Christov-Bakargiev, 'Artists at Via Tasso: A New Chapter' in Christov-Bakargiev 1993 (unpaginated).
3 Carolyn Christov-Bakargiev, 'With Mel Bochner', in Christov-Bakargiev 1991, p. 7.
4 Brenda Richardson quotes a lecture Bochner gave at CUNY in 1975: 'The time spent in Italy in the spring of 1974 had been influential: "Siena deeply impressed me. Not a right angle in the entire city. The streets swung out from the Campo like the arms of a starfish. And the Campo itself was a

shape without measurable dimensions . . . The space seemed to rotate on every axis. I could not find its coordinates. It had a purity beyond intellection and prior to the grid".' Richardson 1976a, p. 48.

5 Interview with Mel Bochner, April 2002. All quotations by Mel Bochner that are not separately footnoted are from this interview.
6 See Clement et al. 2000.
7 Miwon Kwon mentions Bochner's early work in this context. See Kwon 2002, pp. 14–15.
8 See 'Rome' entry, *Encyclopaedia Judaica* (Jerusalem, 1972), p. 253.
9 Bochner 1973, p. 75.
10 In interview, Bochner mentioned that he saw the work 'sequentially'. However, he described the sequence as starting with the order of *Yisgadal*, moving through the disorder of *Yiskor* and then back into the order of *Yahrzeit*.
11 Bochner 1966, p. 68.
12 Andreas Huyssen, 'Monument and Memory in a Postmodern Age', in Young 1994, p. 13.
13 Apparently Bruce Nauman has proposed such an ironic memorial. When the city of Hanover asked him to propose a Holocaust Memorial for the city, he proposed a piece with the text: 'We are sorry for what we did, and we promise not to do it again'. See http/www.deckchairs.net/weblog/2002_03_24_deck_archives.html.
14 By 'new', I mean entirely new, both in form and material. As mentioned already, Bochner had remade sculptures from the early 1970s using materials he had never previously used.
15 'Art = Idea +/- the Object: Talking with Mel Bochner, 18 April, 1972' in Johnson 1995, p. 210. In a similar vein, Bochner told Flash Art in 1973: 'Believe me, I have no vested interest in pebbles or masking tape or chalk.' See Haller 1973, pp. 14–15. According to Ulrich Wilmes, 'the non-materiality of these elementary components advances Bochner's contention that the object itself is insignificant'. See Ulrich Wilmes, 'A Theory of Sculpture', in Field 1995, p. 263.
16 James Meyer differentiates Bochner's approach to vision from Judd's and Morris's but links it to his friends', describing 'the problematized vision of LeWitt, Bochner, Smithson, and Hesse, a vision that failed to grasp its object.' See Meyer 2001, p. 205.
17 Rosalind Krauss, 'Theory of Painting' in Field 1995.
18 See Rosalind Krauss, 'The Crisis of the Easel Picture' in Varnedoe and Karmel 1999, pp. 155–79.
19 Bochner has objected to simplistic discussions of the politics of postminimalism: 'What I'm very nervous about are some of the exceedingly facile statements that have been made that postminimalism is the "art of the war in Vietnam". Things like that curdle my blood. Because it demeans not only what was at stake in the Vietnam War but what was at stake in the art, and it trivializes them both.' Newman, Amy 2000, pp. 400–401.
20 Borden 1973, p. 75.
21 It is as if, to use Krauss's phrase from 'Theory of Painting', the 'materiality of the signifier' intrudes to put pressure on signification.
22 'How Can You Defend Paintings Now? A Conversation between Mel Bochner and James Meyer' in Melville 2001, p. 203.
23 This installation is discussed by Barry Schwabsky in detail in his chapter 'Rubble – Representing Mel Bochner's Early Work'. See Schwabsky 1997, pp. 179–90.
24 Schwabsky 1997, p. 185.
25 As Schwabsky makes clear, the relation of the work to its setting is even more complex, particularly because the fresco shows 'Jesus presenting the church to St Peter with the statement, "On this rock I build my church".' Schwabsky 1997, p. 188.
26 See Rothkopf 2002.
27 Incidentally, in the article, between the illustration of a Bochner photograph related to *None Tangent* (1967), and Eva Hesse's *Addendum* (1967), there is a picture of a model by Bernard Kirschenbaum in the shape of a six-pointed star. See Bochner 1967, p. 33.
28 This was the exhibition *A Minimal Future* organised by Ann Goldstein at Los Angeles Museum of Contemporary Art in 2004. See Goldstein 2004. The other photographic work in the exhibition was Dan Graham's *Homes for America* (1966–67).
29 See Benjamin Buchloh/Dan Graham, 'Four Conversations: December 1999 – May 2000' in Brouwer 2001, p. 82. Perhaps the most famous example of an artist using Nazi regalia during this period is the advert for Robert Morris's poster for his Leo Castelli show of 1974.
30 Graham outlined his thinking in a 1981 text called 'The End of Liberalism'. 'In Nazi propaganda, new techniques of mass psychological or product representation (swastika, national flag, corporation logo) replaced traditional forms of representation. And, following the war, these techniques would spread to corporate advertising.' See Graham 1993, p. 70.
31 See for instance Chave 1990.
32 Bochner has commented on the anti-aesthetic quality of seriality while recalling *ARTNews*' refusal of his article 'The Serial Attitude'. *ARTNews* rejected the piece because it 'was a direct assault on their whole system of values. Not just because it presented art that they didn't like, but because of the attitude it took – *trans-stylistic* and *meta-critical*.' See Newman, Amy 2000, p. 233.
33 See Krauss 1974, p. 21.
34 See Krauss 1973.
35 See Field 1995, p. 64.
36 See Bochner 1973 and many of the texts collected in Bochner 2003.
37 Haller 1973, pp. 14–15.
38 If this reading suggests an ethical character to Bochner's work despite his resistance to Vivas's contention that art and ethics were absolutely inseparable, then we should also acknowledge Bochner's own critique of Michael Fried's ethical criticism. The problem with Fried's 1960s writing was that 'In his partisanship for one type of art, he saw an *ethical* issue at stake. To equate the art you like with the "good" is very suspicious, because it's too easy to slide from aesthetic terms into ethical judgements, and demonize the art you don't like, which is what he does' (See Newman Amy 2000, p. 203). Hopefully it is clear that my understanding of the ethics of Bochner's restraint is distant from Fried's ethical criticism.
39 Stille 1993, p. 22.
40 Stille 1993, p. 36.
41 In Stille's introduction, he had also explained that the diversity of the Italian community had led him to decide that the only way to write a history of Jewish life under fascism was through specific stories of families in different communities. As he wrote, 'If there is a virtue to the collection of individual stories, perhaps it is as an antidote to overbroad generalizations.' 'The complexity of individual experience, with all its rough, solid three-dimensionality, can be a useful touchstone for the abstract, linear theories of history.' See Stille 1993, p. 16.
42 Stille 1993, pp. 171–72.

8 the commissions in the united states holocaust memorial museum

1 The archival material on the Art for Public Spaces Programme is stored in two places in the USHMM. A) The 'Art for Public Spaces' files. This is a filing cabinet full of documents, and the principal source of my archival material. B) The USHMM institutional archive. This is the formal institutional archive of the museum. This contains boxes of documents. Those that I have consulted include Jeshajahu Weinberg's files, Michael Berenbaum's files and the Council Files.
The minutes of different meetings of a particular museum committee are not collected together in these archives. For instance, one might find the January 1991 minutes of a 'Committee for Collections and Acquisitions' meeting in the Art for Public Spaces files, and the February 1991 minutes of this same committee in Jeshajahu Weinberg's files.
Unless specified as coming from 'Weinberg files', 'Berenbaum files', or 'Council Files', all museum documents come from the Art for Public Spaces files.
Between November 2000 and January 2001, I conducted interviews with artists Sol LeWitt, Richard Serra, Ellsworth Kelly, Joel Shapiro and Lawrence Weiner; architect James Ingo Freed; USHMM director Sara Bloomfield; AFPSP project administrator Nancy Rosen; former Director of Special Exhibitions Susan Morganstein; and Jury members Gary Garrels and Nan Rosenthal. Unless otherwise stated, all quotations come from these interviews.

2 Carter announced the 'Commission on the Holocaust' on 1 May 1978, on the thirtieth anniversary of the establishment of the State of Israel. Edward Linenthal has discussed the links between the initiation of the institution, Carter's desires to satisfy American Jews sensitive both to his pro-Palestinian approach to Middle East questions, and the non-existence of a national Holocaust memorial. Linenthal's study *Preserving Memory: The Struggle to Create America's Holocaust Museum* (Linenthal 1995) is the most complete history of the institution, and I will not rehearse this history here, other than where it bears on the history of the Art for Public Spaces Program. Curiously, Linenthal looks at many issues relating to architecture, changes in personnel and artefacts, but makes no mention of the AFPSP.

3 See Dannatt 1995; Muschamp 1993; Murphy 1993.

4 James Freed commented that the wooden synagogues were 'very beautiful, very articulate. These structures were not like cathedrals, but more like working spaces. These images and others that we saw [while researching] had a residual, lingering presence in our minds, and that's partially what our building is about.' See Freed 1993, p. 91.

5 See chapter six in Cole 1999.

6 Peter Novick writes that the museum's founders 'assumed that a visit to the museum would produce a moral transformation, that the visitors would be inspired to work for a "deepening of [the] quality of American civil and political life and a strengthening and enrichment of the moral fiber of this country." . . . There are surely those who are turned around by the experience [of the museum], emerge with altered values or perspective . . . But how many? It is difficult to imagine anyone leaving this magnificently designed museum less overwhelmed by the horror of the Holocaust, and, as with *Schindler's List*, it's usually the reverse. But to go from that to the notion that visitors are in any sense different after the encounter – that they have in any worthwhile sense "learned lessons" – seems to me to confuse an admirable aspiration with actual or attainable accomplishment.' Novick 1999, pp. 260–61.

7 Kimmelman 1993.

8 Richards 1993.

9 Letter from Brenda Levenson to Sarah Bloomfield, 6 December 1992.

10 Letter from Herzl Emmanuel to Harvey Meyerhoff, 9 March 1993.

11 Letter from Mark Strauss to Jeshajahu Weinberg, Director, 6 June 1993. Strauss publicised his complaints: Weinberg's files contain letters from US Congressman Frank R. Wolf and Senator John Warner, both of whom wrote to the museum on Strauss' behalf to pursue his objections. Weinberg's replies laid out the history of the AFPSP, defending the commissioned works. (Weinberg files, 1997–014 Box 3 Director of the Museum. Records of the Museum Director Jeshajahu Weinberg 1979–94. Permanent.)

12 Johnson 1993, p. 95.

13 Committee on Collections and Acquisitions, 1 June 1989, p. 5 (Berenbaum files).

14 See Krauss 1976b, Krauss 1986, 'LeWitt in Progress' in Krauss 1985 and 'The LeWitt Matrix' in Iles 1993.

15 Krauss 1991, p. 140.

16 Julius Schatz, 15 February 1979, quoted in Linenthal 1995, p. 59.

17 From 'Section III. Proposals and Projects: Specific Recommendations' in Report to the President – President's Commission on the Holocaust', 27 September 1979. Reprinted by the USHMM, July 1999, p. 9 (this is a small pamphlet known as 'The Brown Book').

18 See Linenthal 1995, p. 58.

19 Minutes, Committee of Collections and Acquisitions, 1 December 1988.

20 Minutes, Committee on Collections and Acquisitions, 1 June 1989, p. 4 (Berenbaum files).

21 Ibid, p. 5. Freed also suggested at this point that Christian Boltanski assist the exhibition designers on the arrangement of an installation of photographs taken in the Ejszyszki ghetto, an installation through which the visitor passes twice, and which is followed in the journey around the museum by the rooms containing the works of Kelly and LeWitt. Though Boltanski was never directly involved in this installation, its arrangement recalls his practice.

22 A document dated 14 July 1989 names these sites, together with the kinds of works sought. In addition to the three places where work was put (the Serra space was not named), this document names four other places, with suggestions for kinds of work. These were 'A monumental bas-relief in the Hall of Witness, on the upper part of the wall to the right of the 14th Street entrance'; 'A work of art on glass, on each of the two grid walls in the Hall of Witness, in front of the 14th Street entrance (etchings?)'; 'A vertical sculpture with small circumference on the bottom platform of staircase [sic] leading from Hall of Witness to Concourse'; and finally, 'A work of art inside the tower space from 5th floor down to 3rd floor.'

23 Minutes, Committee on Collections and Acquisitions, 1 June 1989, p. 7 (Berenbaum files).

24 Minutes, Committee of Collections and Acquisitions, 3 April 1990, p. 5; Minutes, Committee of Collections and Acquisitions, 16 May 1990, p. 11.

25 Previous Holocaust-related works did help Serra, Shapiro, and LeWitt gain commissions. However, the choice of Kelly suggests this kind of background was no longer, at that later stage, considered a prerequisite for the commission.

26 This 'long list' was presented and discussed on March 8, 1990.

27 Minutes, Committee for Collections and Acquisitions, 8 March 1990, p. 4.

28 Minutes, Committee for Collections and Acquisitions, 8 March 1990, p. 6.

29 Minutes, Committee for Collections and Acquisitions, 8 March 1990, p. 7. At a later committee meeting, Weinberg added to this argument, hoping that 'art would provide visual relief to people going through the exhibitions . . . this art will almost be like a part of the interior architecture.' Committee of Collections and Acquisitions, 16 May 1990, p. 11.

30 Minutes, Committee for Collections and Acquisitions, 8 March 1990, p. 8.

31 Minutes, Committee for Collections and Acquisitions, 8 March 1990, p. 5.

32 Minutes, Committee for Collections and Acquisitions, 16 May 1990, p. 11.

33 Minutes, Committee for Collections and Acquisitions, 1 June 1990, p. 7. This particular document is incomplete and undated.

34 See Minutes, Committee for Collections and Acquisitions, 8 March 1990, p. 9, and 3 April 1990.

35 A proposed procedure for these delegations was submitted to the Ad Hoc Committee from the Committee on Collections and Acquisitions on 28 June 1990. This recommended procedure was largely followed from then on.

36 Rosen worked as a curator during the 1970s before starting to work as 'an independent curator and fine arts advisor to corporations, developers, private collectors and non-profit organisations' (Nancy Rosen C.V., Weinberg files).

37 By 16 November 1990, the following had been invited onto the jury (then current institution listed): Nan Rosenthal (National Gallery of Art); Susan Delahanty (Contemporary Arts Museum, Houston); Howard Fox (Los Angeles County Museum of Art); Gary Garrels (DIA Centre); Ziva Amishai-Maisels (Hebrew University, Jerusalem); Ned Rifkin (Hirshhorn Museum); Marc Rosenthal (Guggenheim Museum). The letter confirming the acceptance of a jury position was unspecific about the purpose or kind of art sought, stating simply that 'the Museum complex will be distinguished by a number of contemporary art works conceived and commissioned expressly for this site and context.' (Letter from Barbara Diamonstein Spielvogel to Susan Delahanty, 11 January 1991). This is the earliest dated document I have found which makes clear that all works for the AFPSP will be newly commissioned. However, the jury did still discuss briefly the possibility of acquiring Barnett Newman's *Zim Zum* for the programme.

38 Letter from Herzl Emmanuel to Harvey Meyerhoff, 9 March 1993.

39 Jury Minutes, 17 April 1991, p. 2.

40 By this time, the number of sites under consideration had been reduced to five. Plans for a 'bas relief' and an 'etched glass' work had been abandoned. The Tower Space (which became the 'Tower of Faces') was to be filled by the exhibition design team.

41 Jury minutes, 17 April 1991, p. 8.

42 Serra 1994, p. 215.

43 The four chosen artists were also all men, and all but Kelly were Jewish. The jury considered proposals by Ann Hamilton and Jackie Winsor, but chose not to commission them. It is hard to determine whether the ques-

tion of Jewishness played a part in the choice of Serra, LeWitt, and Shapiro. Though Nancy Rosen, Susan Morganstein, and jury members have said that this was not a factor, Nan Rosenthal admitted that this 'probably didn't hurt' (Rosenthal interview). While their Jewish background might not have been a significant factor for those that chose them, undoubtedly it played a part in the artists' decisions to accept commissions.

44 Freed 1993, pp. 93–4.

45 Memo from Susan Morganstein and Nancy Rosen to Albert Abramson and Jeshajahu Weinberg, 30 January 1991 (Weinberg files).

46 In a fax to the jury members dated 8 February 1991, Nancy Rosen named these as Robert Morris, Richard Serra and Rebecca Horn.

47 Albert Abramson to the jury, Jury Minutes, 17 April 1991, p. 15.

48 Serra encountered related architectural tendencies in Washington D.C. in 1978 working with Robert Venturi on a proposal for Pennsylvania Avenue. His proposal for Federal Plaza was rejected, and Venturi proposed two pylons that would frame the Treasury building. Withdrawing from the project, Serra compared these pylons to fascist architecture. See 'Richard Serra's Urban Sculpture' (interview with Douglas Crimp) in Serra 1994, pp. 138–39; Gilbert-Rolfe 1978, pp. 66–67 and Forgey 1978, p. D2.

49 Serra interview.

50 Serra interview.

51 Serra interview.

52 Minutes from a 1991 meeting report that 'there was concern that the "crack" might [. . .] look either contrived or fashionably "deconstructed".' (Minutes, Subcommittee for the Art in Public Spaces of the Committee on Collections and Acquisitions, 18 January 1991).

53 Serra also described working with Freed while being interviewed by Chuck Close. 'I ended up having total admiration for [Freed]. [He is] doing his best work. He's a very open, sincere, generous guy, and I had a very good time working with him. We went to the museum together to mock-up the piece. We were trying to figure out how big it should be, and we played the game "it's too small, it's too big" . . . So we both decided how big it should be. And how thick it should be. There aren't many architects who want to climb around with sticks and strings in the middle of the foundation doing that, right? He was completely into it, totally into it, and it probably wouldn't have gotten built the way it did, or be as tuned to the space, without his input. He was completely willing to play.' See Close 1998, pp. 70–71.

54 Minutes, Subcommittee Meeting of the Committee on Collections and Acquisitions, 18 January 1991, p. 2.

55 A shortlist dated 18 January 1991 names Magdalena Abakanowicz, Anthony Gormley, Robert Morris, and as alternatives and other consideration, Jonathan Borofsky and Mark di Suvero; and Tony Cragg, Sol LeWitt and Ursula von Rydinsvald.

56 These were Jonathan Borofsky, Martin Puryear, Walter de Maria and Joel Shapiro.

57 Gary Garrels mentioned debating between Walter de Maria and Joel Shapiro (Garrels interview).

58 See Teicher 1998, pp. 18–19.

59 Letter from Susan Morganstein to Ann Hamilton, 1 August 1991. In a draft letter to Ellsworth Kelly dated 24 October 1991, the purpose of the space is described 'It is the intention of the Council that Room A provide an opportunity for visitors to sit and to reflect within their circulation of the Museum's permanent exhibition and to serve as a place for quiet conversation, silence, or contemplation' (Weinberg files).

60 For 'Room A' (the upper lounge), the jury invited proposals from Ellsworth Kelly, Anselm Kiefer, Richard Long, and listed Martin Puryear and Frank Stella as alternates. For 'Room B', they invited proposals from Sol LeWitt, Ann Hamilton, Dan Flavin, and listed as alternates, Jackie Winsor, Richard Hamilton, and Mel Chin (memo from Susan Morganstein to Albert Abramson, 6 August 1991).

61 Anselm Kiefer and Dan Flavin declined to participate (memo from Susan Morganstein to Albert Abramson, 6 August 1991).

62 Kelly interview.

63 Letter from Sara Bloomfield to Ellsworth Kelly, 24 October 1991.

64 Kelly interview.

65 Memo from Nancy Rosen to jurors, 17 April 1992.

66 This list included Helen Frankenthaler, Vija Celmins, Susan Rothenberg, Robert Morris and again, Sol LeWitt, though this time, a wall drawing, rather than a structure, would be invited (memo from Nancy Rosen to jurors, 17 April 1992).

67 Memo from Nancy Rosen to Albert Abramson and Jeshajahu Weinberg, 9 June 1992.

68 See Young 1993, pp. 17–19. The memory of this piece might have been one of the factors that played into the jury's decision to contact LeWitt. His decision to accept the invitation might have been affected by the contrast with the history of his German work and expectations around this more friendly project.

69 LeWitt 'asked several times if he could submit alternate proposals'. Memo from Nancy Rosen to Albert Abramson and Jeshajahu Weinberg, 9 June 1992.

70 Memo from Nancy Rosen to Albert Abramson and Jeshajahu Weinberg, 9 June 1992.

71 Letter from Nancy Rosen to Ann Farrington, 29 October 1992 (Weinberg files).

72 See 'Memo from Nancy Rosen: Re Art for Public Spaces, Installation Schedules and Specifications', 12 January 1993 (Weinberg files).

73 Buchloh 1998, p. 27.

74 Lawrence Weiner quoted by Iwona Blazwick, 'Labyrinth', in Weiner 1993.

75 Weiner interview.

76 Garrels interview.

77 Julius Schatz reported to the Council on the development of the AFPSP. On 13 November 1991, he had told the Council that: 'We hope it [the AFPSP] will enhance the Museum aesthetically. More importantly, we hope that it will make a contribution of speaking to the larger American community about the Holocaust through an artistic medium.' (Minutes, Unites States Holocaust Memorial Council, 13 November 1991, p. 63; Council Files). The following spring, Schatz reported that 'I have found this [overseeing the AFPSP] to be one of the most rewarding aspects of my own personal life in the many years that I have served in public and Jewish public service.' (Minutes, United States Holocaust Memorial Council, 13 May 1992, p. 50; Council Files).

78 Lewis 1992, p. D1.

79 The decision not to take minutes was made to guarantee the privacy of the jury deliberations.

80 Fax from Nancy Rosen to Ann Farrington and Susan Morganstein, 29 March 1993.

81 Serra interview.

82 In Shapiro's studies for the work, the 'figure' did not have this outstretched arm and appeared to be falling rather than righting himself. By adding the outstretched arm, Shapiro made the figure's gesture more ambivalent.

83 See the section 'Memory' in Teicher 1998, pp. 18–21.

84 Hall 1999, p. 13.

85 Schjeldahl 1993, p. 5.

86 Joel Shapiro, 'USHMM Proposal'.

87 Shapiro interview.

88 Shapiro interview.

89 At the time of my research in 2001, the lighting cast a strong shadow onto the wall below the works. Meanwhile, their top edges were less distinct, appearing to blend into the wall behind. Kelly was not content with the present lighting, which, unknown to him, had been installed before his works were positioned. He said that he would have preferred an even lighting that eliminated the downward shadow and that gave an equal distinction between work and wall at bottom and top (Kelly interview). James Freed, however, let me know at the time that he would happily change the lighting to suit Kelly's wishes (Freed interview).

90 Nochlin 1997, p. 77.

91 Kelly interview.

92 Kelly interview.

93 Nancy Rosen, for instance, has said that while the panels have 'very strong connotations [with] monuments', the fan is the 'more graceful element' and is 'very spiritual' (Rosen interview).

94 LeWitt interview. With LeWitt's contemporary work in mind, it becomes both harder and easier to make specific claims about *Consequence*. Other drawings are made by the same inks, but *Consequence* uses colour (specifically, grey) differently. Though the 'square within a square' structure is

also used in other drawings (e.g. *Wall Drawing 665*, 1991, Castello di Rivoli, Turin), this structure can be differentiated from the less sober 'continuous form' works of the later 1980s, and the 'loopy' works of the late 1990s.

95 Though LeWitt had not used grey in this manner before the USHMM commission, subsequently, in 1995, he created an installation of cinder blocks at the Ace Gallery in New York. Encountering the 'tank of greyness', wrote Yve-Alain Bois, 'more than anything one thought of Auschwitz's grim chimneys. This was no paean to logic as a means to debunk the claims of reason, but rather a stark recognition that the dreary reunion of the two had been one of the main sources of human disaster in recent history.' Bois's comment indicates that LeWitt's forms and colours could even be allusive outside a setting as over-determined as the USHMM. See Bois 2000, p. 97.

96 The first photographic image, we might recall, shows a pile of charred corpses. While LeWitt might not have known the precise content of the exhibition, he knew that it would, primarily, be photographic, and that these photographs would picture such images.

97 Morganstein interview.

98 This wall is a replica of a Holocaust memorial made in the Remu synagogue cemetery in Krakow. Gravestones used by the Nazis for various purposes were reassembled to form the memorial.

99 Dannatt 1995, p. 15.

100 Freed interview.

101 Ralph Grunewald, 'Architectural Symbolism and Other Features of the USHMM' (Internal museum document), 23 March 1992. Adrian Dannatt, combining an account of the work's appearance with a description of the movement around it, has articulated a different analogy: 'Around this metal wall the visitor is faced with another decision, to go one way or the other, to avoid its headlong violence. The wall is openly cold and cruel, an elemental force that cannot be negotiated with or appeased' (Dannatt 1995, p. 15). Here, the work becomes itself a symbol for the Holocaust: it is cruel and must be confronted, just like the Holocaust in this place.

102 Susan Morganstein interview.

103 Foster 1998, pp. 26–27.

104 Foster 1998, p. 26.

105 Foster 1998, p. 26.

106 It should be said that Foster also sees the work as refusing to raise the Holocaust 'to the oppressive status of the sublime or the divine' (Foster 1998, p. 27). As far as a conclusion is concerned, then, my reading of the work is in agreement with Foster's. However, by paying more attention to the precise context, it has been possible to contest aspects of his argument.

107 Freed interview.

108 Serra, quoted in Dannatt 1995, p. 15.

109 Such spatial effects are not offered by Serra's contemporaneous works. *Intersection* (Basel, 1993) or *Snake* (Bilbao, 1996) are much more concerned to generate spatial play through their own means only (rather than through their relation to nearby walls or steps). As well as this, the surprises that mark the passage through these works amount to a joyous, exciting experience, rather than to a grave one.

110 Serra 1994, p. 135 (interview with Douglas Crimp).

111 Report to the President - President's Commission on the Holocaust, p. 11.

112 See Bois 1992 and Bois 1999, p. 18.

113 Buchloh 2003, p. 25.

114 See Krauss 1976b.

115 Freed interview.

116 Freed interview.

117 Freed 1993, p. 91.

118 Finkelstein 2000, p. 45 discussing Novick 1999, and quoting Elie Wiesel, *Against Silence* (New York, 1984) and *All Rivers Run to the Sea* (New York, 1995).

9 peter eisenman's *memorial to the murdered jews of europe*, and susan hiller's *the j.street project*

1 Agamben 2005, p. 45.

2 Eisenman describes some of these in his text 'Memorial to the Murdered Jews of Europe', published in Eisenman 2003 and Eisenman 2005.

3 Eisenman interview.

4 Bauman 2000, p. 228.

5 'In Auschwitz, people did not die; rather, corpses were produced. Corpses without death, non-humans whose decease is debased into a matter of serial production. And, according to a possible and widespread interpretation, precisely this degradation of death constitutes the specific offense of Auschwitz, the proper name of its horror.' Agamben 1999, p. 72. In the next sections of the book, Agamben goes on to think through this interpretation.

6 Esther Da Costa Meyer has also discussed the memorial's other architectural associations – for instance, to 'quarries exploited by the Nazis using slave labor', and to Bruno Taut's unbuilt *Stadtkrone*. See Da Costa Meyer 2006, p. 48.

7 See the various texts on the memorial listed in the bibliography, and Young 2000, chapter seven.

8 Peter Eisenman, Berlin Press Conference, 16 August 2003, p. 4. This document is courtesy of Michael Blackwood, and was sourced at the Eisenman Architects office.

9 See 'Notes on the Index' parts 1 and 2 in Krauss 1985.

10 Eisenman's plans were published in a special issue of *El Croquis*. See Eisenman 1996, pp. 144–51.

11 Eisenman interview.

12 Jürgen Habermas in Rauterberg 2005, unpaginated.

13 Richard Serra, 'Questions, Contradictions, Solutions: Early Work' in Foster 2005, p. 54.

14 Peter Eisenman, 'Memorial to the Murdered Jews of Europe' in Eisenman 2003, p. 314.

15 It may well be the case that the distinctions that I have implied as existing between abstract memorials such as Kahn's and realist ones such as Rapoport's, map onto distinctions between reflexive and self-questioning documentary works such as *Shoah*, and other films which unquestioningly deploy narrative, acting, and so on (*Schindler's List* being only the most famous example). To pursue this line of thinking further is beyond the scope of this book.

16 See Godfrey 2006, pp. 130–33.

17 Many of the artists responding to the spectacularisation of the Holocaust were included in the Jewish Museum exhibition of 2002, *Mirroring Evil: Nazi Imagery/Recent Art*. See Kleeblatt 2002. Santiago Sierra's project dates from 2006: working in the same site in Stommeln in which Richard Serra had installed *The Drowned and the Saved*, Sierra turned the synagogue into a gas chamber by parking cars outside and passing tubes from their exhausts through openings in the synagogue walls. Sierra was hoping to raise awareness about the 'banalisation of the Holocaust' but the project became a media event. The rather predictable controversy that the work sparked seems to have precluded a genuine reflection on this banalisation.

18 In his essay on *The J.Street Project*, Jorg Heiser has discussed this point, writing that some signs and street names are 'clear evidence of centuries of segregation and stigmatization' (Hiller 2005, p. 620).

19 The music is Lejaren Hiller's *Quartet No. 4 for Strings* (1957), also called the *Illiac Suite*, and comes from his recording *Computer Music Retrospective*.

20 Heiser has convincingly suggested that the work addresses two equally 'inappropriate' approaches to memory common in Germany. On the one hand, there is the tendency to be lost in the everyday and to ignore the past. On the other, there is the temptation to dwell on sites associated with Nazism, but doing so often generates a perverse 'pleasure in guilt'. The work keeps both these approaches in some tension by causing the viewer to linger on images and to pass others by: in this way, the work refrains from positing a resolved answer to the question of how to handle memorialisation.

21 Hiller 2005, p. 7.

bibliography

Adorno 1973 — Theodor Adorno, *Negative Dialectics,* trans. E. B. Ashton (London: Routledge, 1973)

Adorno 2000 — Theodor Adorno, *The Adorno Reader*, ed. Brian O'Connor (Oxford: Blackwell, 2000)

Adorno 2003 — Theodor Adorno, *Can One Live After Auschwitz: A Philosophical Reader*, ed. Rolf Tiedemann (Stanford: Stanford University Press, 2003)

Agamben 1998 — Giorgio Agamben, *Homo Sacer: Sovereign Power and Bare Life*, trans. Daniel Heller-Roazen (Stanford: Stanford University Press, 1998)

Agamben 1999 — Giorgio Agamben, *Remnants of Auschwitz: The Witness and the Archive*, trans. Daniel Heller-Roazen (Stanford: Stanford Univerity Press, 1999)

Agamben 2005 — Giorgio Agamben, 'Die zwei Gedächtnisse', trans. Charlotte Schepke, Die Zeit (4 May 2005), p. 45

Agus 1964 — Jacob Agus, 'God and the Catastrophe', *Conservative Judaism* (Summer 1964)

Alloway 1966 — Lawrence Alloway, *Barnett Newman – The Stations of the Cross: Lema Sabachthani* (New York: Guggenheim Museum, 1966)

Améry 1980 — Jeam Améry, *At the Mind's Limits: Contemplations by a Survivor on Auschwitz and its Realities* (Bloomington: Indiana University Press, 1980)

Amishai-Maisels 1989 — Ziva Amishai-Maisels, 'Christological Symbolism of the Holocaust', in Yehuda Bauer, ed., *Remembering for the Future II: The Impact of the Holocaust on the Contemporary World* (Oxford: Pergamon Press, 1989), pp. 1657–71

Amishai-Maisels 1993 — Ziva Amishai-Maisels, *Depiction and Interpretation – The Influence of the Holocaust on the Visual Arts* (Oxford: Pergamon Press, 1993)

Andre 2005 — Carl Andre, *Cuts: Texts 1959–2004*, ed. James Meyer (Cambridge, Mass.: MIT Press, 2005)

Andre and Frampton 1981 — Carl Andre and Hollis Frampton, *12 Dialogues – 1962–1963* (Halifax and New York: The Press of the Nova Scotia College of Art and Design and New York University Press, 1981)

Andrews and Kalinovska 1990 — Richard Andrews and Milena Kalinovska, eds, *Art Into Life: Russian Constructivism 1914–1932* (Seattle: The Henry Art Gallery, University of Seattle and New York: Rizzoli, 1990)

Arato and Gebhardt 1978 — A. Arato and E. Gebhardt, eds, *The Essential Frankfurt School Reader* (Oxford: Blackwell, 1978)

Architectural Forum 1968 — Anon, 'Lest We Forget', *Architectural Forum* (December 1968), p. 89

Architectural Record 1968 — Anon, 'Louis Kahn designs a Memorial to Six Million Jews', *Architectural Record* CXLIV: v (November 1968), p. 36

Arendt 1963 — Hannah Arendt, *Eichmann in Jerusalem – A Report on the Banality of Evil* (New York: The Viking Press, 1963)

Ashton 1990 — Dore Ashton, *Morris Louis* (Milan: Padiglione d'arte contemporanea, 1990)

Associated Press 1933 — Associated Press, 'Germans Set Fire to Liberal Books', *Washington Post*, 11 May 1933, p. 5

Baigell 1994 — Matthew Baigell, 'Barnett Newman's Stripe Paintings and Kabbalah', *American Art* IX:i (Spring 1994) pp. 32–43

Baigell 1997 — Matthew Baigell, *Jewish-American Artists and the Holocaust* (New Brunswick: Rutgers University Press, 1997)

Baker 1970 — Elizabeth Baker, 'Pickets on Parnassus', *ARTNews* LXIX:v (September 1970), pp. 30–33, 64–65

Baker 1971 — Elizabeth Baker, 'Frank Stella, Revival and Relief', *ARTNews* LXX: vii (November 1971), pp. 34–35, 87–89

Bal, Crewe and Spitzer 1999 — Mieke Bal, Jonathan Crewe, and Leo Spitzer, eds, *Acts of Memory: Cultural Recall in the Present* (Hanover and London: Dartmouth College and University Press of New England, 1999)

Bann 1985 — Stephen Bann, 'The mythical conception is the name: Titles and names in modern and post-modern painting', *Word and Image* I: ii (1985) pp. 176–90

Barker 1966 — Walter Barker, 'The Passion without the Image', *St. Louis Post Dispatch*, 12 June 1966, p. 5C

Battcock 1995 — Gregory Battcock, *Minimal Art: A Critical Anthology* (Berkeley: University of California Press, 1995)

Bauman 2000 — Zygmunt Bauman, *Modernity and the Holocaust* (Cambridge: Polity, 2000)

Baume 2001 — Nicholas Baume, ed., *Sol LeWitt: Incomplete Open Cubes* (Cambridge, Mass.: MIT Press, 2001)

Bédard 1994 — Jean-Francois Bédard, ed., *Cities of Artificial Investigation: The Work of Peter Eisenman 1978–1988* (Montreal and New York: Canadian Centre for Architecture and Rizzoli International, 1994)

Benjamin 1997 — Andrew Benjamin, *Present Hope: Philosophy, Architecture, Judaism* (London: Routledge, 1997)

Berenbaum 1990 — Michael Berenbaum, *After Tragedy and Triumph: Essays in Modern Jewish Thought and the American Experience* (Cambridge: Cambridge University Press, 1990)

Berkowitz 1953 — Leon Berkowitz, *Paintings by Morris Louis* (exhibition pamphlet, Washington D.C.: Washington Workshop for the Arts, 1953)

Birchall 1933 — Frederick Birchall, 'Nazi Book-Burning Fails to Stir Berlin', *The New York Times*, 11 May 1933, p. 1

Birnholz 1969 — Alan Birnholz, 'El Lissitsky's Prouns, Part II' *Artforum VII: iii* (November 1969), pp. 68–73

Blanchot 1995 — Maurice Blanchot, *The Writing of the Disaster*, trans. Ann Smock (Lincoln, Nebraska: University of Nebraska Press, 1995)

Bloom 1986 — Alexander Bloom, *Prodigal Sons: The New York Intellectuals and Their World* (Oxford: Oxford University Press, 1986)

Bloom 1994 — Lisa Bloom, 'Ghosts of Ethnicity: Rethinking Art Discourses of the 1940s and 1980s', *Socialist Review*, XXIV: i–ii, (1994), pp. 129–64

Bochner 1966 — Mel Bochner, 'Michael Mazur', *Arts Magazine* XL: vii (May 1966), p. 68

Bochner 1967 — Mel Bochner, 'The Serial Attitude', *Artforum* VI: iv (December 1967), pp. 28–33

Bochner 1973 — Mel Bochner, 'Review of Lucy Lippard's Six Years: The Dematerialization of the Art Object from 1966 to 1972', *Artforum* XI: x (June 1973), pp. 74–75

Bochner 1988 — Mel Bochner, *Drawings* (New York: David Nolan Gallery, 1988)

Bochner 1998 — Mel Bochner, *Mel Bochner: Drawings 1966–1973* (New York: Lawrence Markey Gallery, 1998)

Bochner 2002 — Mel Bochner, *Mel Bochner: Measurements – Works from the 1960s/1990s* (Dijon: FRAC Bourgogne, 2002)

Bochner 2003 — Mel Bochner, *Spéculations: Écrits, 1965–1973*, ed. Christophe Cherix and Valérie Mavridorakis (Geneva: Musée d'art moderne et contemporain, 2003)

Bohm-Duchen 1995 — Monica Bohm-Duchen, *After Auschwitz: Responses to the Holocaust in Contemporary Art* (Sunderland: Northern Centre for Contemporary Art, 1995)

Bois 1998 — Yve-Alain Bois, *'Perceiving Newman'* in *Barnett Newman* (New York: Pace Gallery, 1988)

Bois 1990 — Yve-Alain Bois, *Painting as Model* (Cambridge, Mass.: MIT Press, 1990)

Bois 1992 — Yve-Alain Bois et. al., *Ellsworth Kelly: The Years in France, 1948–1954* (Washington D.C.: National Gallery of Art, 1992)

Bois 1999 — Yve-Alain Bois, *Ellsworth Kelly – The Early Drawings* (Cambridge, Mass.: Harvard University Art Museums, 1999)

Bois 2000 — Yve-Alain Bois, 'Sum and the Parts: LeWitt in Retrospect', *Artforum* XXXVIII: vi (February 2000), pp. 92–97

Bois 2002 — Yve-Alain Bois, 'Here to There and Back: Barnett Newman in Retrospect', *Artforum* XL: vii (March 2002), pp. 100–108

Borden 1973 — Lizzie Borden, 'Mel Bochner', *Artforum* XI: viii (April 1973), pp. 75–76

Boswell 1949 — Peyton Boswell, 'A Plea for Tolerance', *Art Digest*, 1 June 1949, p. 7

Boyarin 1992 — Jonathan Boyarin, *Storm from Paradise: The Politics of Jewish Memory* (Minneapolis: University of Minnesota Press, 1992)

Boyarin 1996 — Jonathan Boyarin, *Thinking in Jewish* (Chicago: The University of Chicago Press, 1996)

Bradbury 1953 — Ray Bradbury, *Fahrenheit 451* (Ballantine: New York, 1953)

Brouwer 2001 — Mariann Brouwer, ed., *Dan Graham: Works 1965–2000* (Porto: Museu de Arte Contemporânea de Serralves and Düsseldorf: Richter, 2001)

Brownlee and De Long 1992 — David Brownlee and David De Long, eds, *Louis I Kahn: In the Realm of Architecture* (The Museum of Contemporary Art, Los Angeles and Rizzoli: New York, 1992)

Buchloh 1985 — Benjamin Buchloh, 'From Gadget Video to Agit Video: Some Notes on Four Recent Video Works', *Art Journal* XLV: iii (Fall 1985), pp. 217–27

Buchloh 1989 — Benjamin Buchloh, 'A Note on Gerhard Richter's *October 18, 1977*', *October* 48 (Spring 1989), pp. 88–109

Buchloh 1998 — Benjamin Buchloh, Alexander Alberro, Alice Zimmerman, David Batchelor et. al., *Lawrence Weiner* (London: Phaidon, 1998)

Buchloh 2000 — Benjamin Buchloh, *Neo-Avantgarde and Culture Industry: Essays on European and American Art from 1955 to 1975* (Cambridge, Mass.: MIT Press, 2000)

Buchloh 2002 — Benjamin Buchloh, *Gerhard Richter: Eight Gray* (Berlin: Deutsche Guggenheim, 2002)

Buchloh 2003 — Benjamin Buchloh, *Ellsworth Kelly: Matrix* (New York: Matthew Marks Gallery, 2003)

Canaday 1966 — John Canaday, 'Art: With Pretty Thorough Execution', *The New York Times*, 23 April 1966, p. 26

Celan 1996 — Paul Celan, *Selected Poems*, trans. Michael Hamburger (London: Penguin, 1996)

Chave 1990 — Anna C. Chave, 'Minimalism and the Rhetoric of Power', *Arts Magazine*, LXIV, (January 1990), pp. 44–63

Chave 2000 — Anna C. Chave, 'Minimalism and Biography', *The Art Bulletin*, LXXXII: i (March 2000), pp. 149–63

Chevlowe and Goldfarb Berkowitz 1997 — Susan Chevlowe and Mira Goldfarb Berkowitz, *Morris Louis: The Charred Journal Series, 1951; Rico Lebrun: The Holocaust Paintings* (exhibition pamphlet, New York: The Jewish Museum, 1997)

Christov-Bakargiev 1991 — Carolyn Christov-Bakargiev, *Mel Bochner – Fontana's Light, Omaggio a Lucio Fontana* (Milan: Studio Casoli, 1991)

Christov-Bakargiev 1993 — Carolyn Christov-Bakargiev, *Mel Bochner: Via Tasso* (Rome: Museo Storico della Liberazione di Roma, Edizioni Carte Segrete, 1993)

Clark 1999 — T. J. Clark, *Farewell to an Idea* (London and New Haven: Yale University Press, 1999)

Clearwater 2000 — Bonnie Clearwater, *Frank Stella at Two Thousand: Changing the Rules* (Miami: Museum of Contemporary Art, 2000)

Close 1998 — Chuck Close, *The Portraits Speak: Chuck Close in Conversation with 27 of his Subjects* (New York: ART Press, 1998)

Cohen 1945 — Elliot Cohen, 'An Act of Affirmation', *Commentary* (November 1945), pp. 1–2

Cohen 1983 — Carolyn Cohen, *Frank Stella: Polish Wooden Synagogues: Constructions from the 1970s* (New York: The Jewish Museum, 1983)

Cohen 2003 — Josh Cohen, *Interrupting Auschwitz* (London: Continuum, 2003)

Cole 1999 — Tim Cole, *Images of the Holocaust: The Myth of the 'Shoah Business'* (London: Duckworth, 1999)

Commentary 1949 — Commentary roundtable, 'The Jewish Writer and The English Tradition, Part II', Commentary (October 1949), pp. 361–70

Cooper 2006 — Harry Cooper, *Frank Stella 1958* (New Haven and Cambridge, Mass.: Yale University Press and Harvard University Art Museums, 2006)

Crouch and Lübbren 2003 — David Crouch and Nina Lübbren, *Visual Culture and Tourism* (Oxford and New York: Berg, 2003)

Crow 1996a — Thomas Crow, *Modern Art in the Common Culture* (New Haven and London: Yale University Press, 1996)

Crow 1996b — Thomas Crow, *The Rise of the Sixties* (London: George Weidenfeld & Nicolson Ltd, 1996)

Da Costa Meyer 2006 — Esther Da Costa Meyer, 'Speak, Memory: On Peter Eisenman's Holocaust Memorial', *Artforum* XLIV: v (January 2006), pp. 47–48

Dannatt 1995 — Adrian Dannatt, *United States Holocaust Memorial Museum: James Ingo Freed* (London: Phaidon, 1995)

Decter 1967 — Midge Decter in 'Germany Through American Eyes', *The Atlantic Monthly* (May 1967), pp. 50–3

De Duve 1996 — Thierry De Duve, *Clement Greenberg Between the Lines*, trans. Brian Holmes (Paris: Dis Voir, 1996)

Derrida 1987 — Jacques Derrida, *The Truth in Painting*, trans. Geoff Bennington and Ian McLeod (Chicago: The University of Chicago Press, 1987)

Diederichsen, Baghramian, Demand and Piper 2005 — Diedrich Diederichsen, Nairy Baghramian, Thomas Demand, and Adrian Piper, 'The Memorial to the Murdered Jews of Europe', *frieze* 91 (May 2005), pp. 90–111

Eaglestone 2004 — Robert Eaglestone, *The Holocaust and the Postmodern* (Oxford: Oxford University Press, 2004)

Eckhardt 1968 — Wolf Von Eckhardt, 'A Memorial to Slain Jews That's Fashioned of Light', *The Washington Post*, 10 November 1968, p. B2

Editorial 1933 — Editorial, 'Book-Burning Day', *The New York Times*, 11 May 1933, p. 12

Elderfield 1972 — John Elderfield, 'UK commentary', *Studio International* 183: CLXXXIII: 940 (January 1972), pp. 30–31

Elderfield 1987 — John Elderfield, *Morris Louis* (New York: The Museum of Modern Art, 1987)

Eisenman 1987 — Peter Eisenman et. al., *Houses of Cards* (New York and Oxford: Oxford University Press, 1987)

Eisenman 1996 — Peter Eisenman, *El Croquis Special Issue: Peter Eisenman 1990–1997* (Madrid: El Croquis, 1996)

Eisenman 2003 — Peter Eisenman et. al., *Blurred Zones: Investigations of the Interstitial* (New York: The Monacelli Press, 2003)

Eisenman 2004 — Peter Eisenman, *Eisenman Inside Out: Selected Writings 1963–1988* (New Haven and London: Yale University Press, 2004)

Eisenman 2005 — Peter Eisenman et. al., *Materials on The Memorial to the Murdered Jews of Europe* (Berlin: Foundation for the Memorial to the Murdered Jews of Europe, 2005)

Faison 1950 — S. Lane Faison, 'What is Jewish Art', *Commentary* (March 1950), pp. 299–300

Felman 1992 — Shoshana Felman and Dori Laub, *Testimony – Crises of Witnessing in Literature, Psychoanalysis and Literature* (New York: Routledge, 1992)

Fer 1997 — Briony Fer, *On Abstract Art* (London and New Haven: Yale University Press, 1997)

Fer 2004 — Briony Fer, *The Infinite Line* (London and New Haven: Yale University Press, 2004)

Field 1995 — Richard Field, ed., *Mel Bochner: Thought Made Visible 1966–1973* (New Haven: Yale University Art Gallery, 1995)

Finkelstein 1973 — Louis Finkelstein, 'Seeing Stella', *Artforum* XI: X (June 1973), pp. 67–70

Finkelstein 2000 — Norman Finkelstein, *The Holocaust Industry* (London: Verso, 2000)

Fiske 1959 — Marjorie Fiske, *Book Selection and Censorship: A Study of School and Public Libraries in California* (Berkeley: University of California Press, 1959)

Flanzbaum 1999 — Hilene Flanzbaum, ed., *The Americanization of the Holocaust* (Baltimore and London: The Johns Hopkins University Press, 1999)

Forgey 1978 — Benjamin Forgey, 'The Continuing Battles of Pennsylvania Avenue', *Washington Star*, 11 April 1978

Foster 1985 — Hal Foster, ed., *Postmodern Culture* (London: Pluto Press, 1985)

Foster 1987 — Hal Foster, ed., *Discussions in Contemporary Culture* (New York: Dia Art Foundation and The New Press, 1987)

Foster 1996a — Hal Foster, *The Return of the Real* (Cambridge, Mass.: MIT Press, 1996)

Foster 1996b — Hal Foster, 'Death in America', *October* 75 (Winter 1996), pp. 37–59

Foster 1998 — Hal Foster, *Richard Serra – Sculpture 1985–1998* (Los Angeles: Museum of Contemporary Art, 1998)

Foster 2002 — Hal Foster, *Design and Crime* (London: Verso, 2002)

Foster 2005 — Hal Foster et. al., *Richard Serra: The Matter of Time* (Bilbao: Guggenheim Museum, 2005)

Fox Weber and Tabatabai Asbaghi 1999 — Nicholas Fox Weber and Pandora Tabatabai Asbaghi, eds, *Anni Albers* (New York: Guggenheim Museum, 1999)

Frahm 2005 — Klaus Frahm, *Memorial to the Murdered Jews of Europe* (Berlin: Foundation for the Memorial to the Murdered Jews of Europe, 2005)

Frampton 1996 — Kenneth Frampton, *Studies in Tectonic Culture: The Poetics of Construction in Nineteenth and Twentieth Century Architecture* (Cambridge, Mass.: MIT Press, 1996)

Frascina 1985 — Francis Frascina, *Pollock and After: The Critical Debate* (London: Paul Chapman Publishing, 1985)

Frascina 1999 — Francis Frascina, *Art, Politics and Dissent: Aspects of the Art Left in Sixties America* (Manchester: Manchester University Press, 1999)

Freed 1975 — Hermine Freed, 'In Time, Of Time', *Arts Magazine* XLIX: X (June 1975), pp. 82–84

Freed 1993 — James Ingo Freed, 'The United States Holocaust Memorial Museum' *A+U* 278 (November 1993), pp. 90–94

Fried 1971 — Michael Fried, *Morris Louis* (New York: Abrams, 1971)

Fried 1998 — Michael Fried, *Art and Objecthood* (Chicago: The University of Chicago Press, 1998)

Friedlander 1992 — Saul Friedlander, ed., *Probing the Limits of Representation: Nazism and the 'Final Solution'* (Cambridge, Mass. and London: Harvard University Press, 1992)

Friedlander 1993 — Saul Friedlander, *Memory, History, and the Extermination of the Jews of Europe*

(Bloomington and Indianapolis: Indiana University Press 1993)

Garrels 2000 — Gary Garrels, ed., *Sol LeWitt: A Retrospective* (San Francisco: San Francisco Museum of Modern Art, 2000)

Genauer 1966 — Emily Genauer, 'Christ's Journey on Canvas', *New York Herald Tribune*, 20 April 1966, p. 20

Gilbert-Rolfe 1974 — Jeremy Gilbert-Rolfe, 'Frank Stella', *Artforum* XII: vi (February 1974), pp. 67–68

Gilbert-Rolfe 1978 — Jeremy Gilbert-Rolfe, 'Capital Follies' *Artforum* XVII: i (September 1978), pp. 66–67

Glueck 1977 — Grace Glueck, 'Art People', *The New York Times*, 18 March 1977

Godfrey 1999 — Mark Godfrey, 'Keeping Watch Over Absent Meaning: Morris Louis's *Charred Journal* series and the Holocaust', *Jewish Quarterly* (Autumn 1999), pp. 17–22

Godfrey 2000a — Mark Godfrey, 'The Gates of Remembrance: An Oblique Look at Frank Stella's *Polish Villages*', *Object* 3 (Autumn 2000), pp. 5–30

Godfrey 2000b — Mark Godfrey, 'A Space for Public Memory: Re-reading Louis Kahn's 'Memorial to the Six Million Jewish Martyrs', *New Voices in Jewish Thought* 3 (Autumn 2000), pp. 88–117

Godfrey 2002 — Mark Godfrey, 'Burnt Books and Absent Meaning: Morris Louis' *Charred Journal: Firewritten* series and the Holocaust' in *Image and Remembrance: Questions of Representation and the Holocaust* (ed. Florence Jacobowitz and Shelley Hornstein) (Bloomington: Indiana University Press, 2002)

Godfrey 2004 — Mark Godfrey, 'Barnett Newman's *Stations* and the Memory of the Holocaust', *OCTOBER* 108 (Spring 2004), pp. 35–50

Godfrey 2005 — Mark Godfrey, 'Barnett Newman's Stations and the Memory of the Holocaust' in Melissa Ho (ed.), *Reconsidering Barnett Newman* (Philadelphia: Philadelphia Museum of Art, 2005)

Godfrey 2006 — Mark Godfrey, 'Omer Fast', *frieze* 97, March 2006, pp. 130–33

Goldfarb Berkowitz 1993 — Mira Goldfarb-Berkowitz, *Sacred Signs and Symbols in Morris Louis: The Charred Journal Series*, 1951 (MA dissertation, CUNY, 1993)

Goldstein 2004 — Ann Goldstein, *A Minimal Future? Art as Object 1958–1968* (Los Angeles: The Museum of Contemporary Art and Cambridge, Mass.: The MIT Press, 2004)

Goodman 1949 — Paul and Percival Goodman, 'Modern Artist as Synagogue Builder', *Commentary* (January 1949) pp. 51–55

Gorlin 1985 — Alexander Gorlin, 'Biblical Imagery in the Work of Louis I. Kahn – From Noah's Ark to the Temple of Solomon', *A+U* 176 (May 1985) pp. 83–92

Graham 1993 — Dan Graham, *Rock My Religion – Writings and Art Projects 1965–1990* (Cambridge, Mass.: MIT Press, 1993)

Graham 1999 — Dan Graham, *Two-Way Mirror Power*, ed. Alexander Alberro (Cambridge, Mass.: MIT Press, 1999)

Green and Seddon 2000 — David Green and Peter Seddon, eds, *History Painting Reassessed* (Manchester: Manchester University Press, 2000)

Greenberg 1950 — Clement Greenberg, 'Self-Hatred and Jewish Chauvinism – Some Reflections on "Positive Jewishness"' *Commentary* (November 1950), pp. 426–33

Greenberg 1955 — Clement Greenberg, trans., 'Paul Celan: Death Fugue', *Commentary* (March 1955), pp. 242–43

Greenberg 1986a — Clement Greenberg, *Perceptions and Judgments – The Collected Essays and Criticism, Volume 1, 1939–1944*, ed. John O'Brian (Chicago: The University of Chicago Press, 1986)

Greenberg 1986b — Clement Greenberg, *Arrogant Purpose – The Collected Essays and Criticism, Volume 2, 1945–1949*, ed. John O'Brian (Chicago: The University of Chicago Press, 1986)

Greenberg 1993a — Clement Greenberg, *Affirmations and Refusals – The Collected Essays and Criticism, Volume 3, 1950–1956*, ed. John O'Brian (Chicago: The University of Chicago Press, 1993)

Greenberg 1993b — Clement Greenberg, *Modernism with a Vengeance – The Collected Essays and Criticism, Volume 4, 1957–1969*, ed. John O'Brian (Chicago: The University of Chicago Press, 1993)

Guilbaut 1983 — Serge Guilbaut, *How New York Stole the Idea of Modern Art* (Chicago: The University of Chicago Press, 1983)

Güse 1987 — Ernst-Gerhard Güse, *Serra* (New York: Rizzoli, 1987)

Haftmann 1971 — Werner Haftmann, *Mark Rothko* (Zurich and New York: Kunsthaus in association with the Marlborough Gallery, 1971)

Hall 1999 — James Hall, 'Joel Shapiro: The Art of Over-Stretching' in *Joel Shapiro – Sculpture 1974–1999* (Litchfield: Yorkshire Sculpture Park, 1999)

Hall and Fifer 1990 — Doug Hall and Sally Jo Fifer, eds, *Illuminating Video: An Essential Guide to Video Art* (New York: Aperture in association with the Bay Area Video Coalition, 1990)

Haller 1973 — Lisa Haller, 'Interview with Mel Bochner', *Flash Art* XLI (June 1973), pp. 14–15

Halperin 1971 — Irving Halperin, 'Dachau 1964' in *Here I Am: A Jew in Today's Germany* (Philadelphia: The Westminster Press, 1971)

Hanley and Wooster 1993 — JoAnn Hanley and Ann-Sargent Wooster, *The First Generation: Women and Video, 1970–75* (New York: Independent Curators Inc., 1993)

Hartman 1994 — Geoffrey Hartman, ed., *Holocaust Remembrance: The Shapes of Memory* (Oxford: Blackwell, 1994)

Hatton 1997 — Brian Hatton, 'Star of David Pavilion' in *Dan Graham – Architecture* (London: Camden Arts Centre, 1997)

Heineman 1975 — Susan Heineman, 'New York', *Artforum* XIII: x (Summer 1975), p. 76

Hepburn 1964 — Andrew Hepburn, *Complete Guide to New York City* (New York: Doubleday, 1964)

Herberg 1950 — Will Herberg, 'The Postwar Revival of the Synagogue', *Commentary* (April 1950), pp. 315–25

Hess 1969 — Thomas Hess, *Barnett Newman* (New York: Walker and Company, 1969)

Hess 1971 — Thomas Hess, *Barnett Newman* (New York: The Museum of Modern Art, 1971)

Hiller 2005 — Susan Hiller, *The J.Street Project* (Compton Verney and Berlin: Compton Verney House Trust and DAAD, 2005)

Ho 2005 — Melissa Ho (editor), *Reconsidering Barnett Newman: A Symposium at the Philadelphia Museum of Art* (Philadelphia: Philadelphia Museum of Art, 2005)

Hobbs 1999 — Robert Hobbs, *Lee Krasner* (New York: Independent Curators International and Harry Abrams, 1999)

Hornstein and Jacobowitz 2003 — Shelley Hornstein and Florence Jacobowitz, eds, *Image and Remembrance: Representation and the Holocaust* (Bloomington & Indianapolis: Indiana University Press, 2003)

Howarth 1948 — Herbert Howarth, 'Chagall's Christ', *Jewish Frontier* (May 1948)

Huxtable 1968 — Ada Louise Huxtable, 'Plan for Jewish Martyrs' Monument Here Unveiled', *The New York Times*, 17 October 1968, p. 108

Huxtable 1972 — Ada Louise Huxtable, *Will They Ever Finish Bruckner Boulevard?* (New York: Collier Books, 1972)

Iles 1993 — Chrissie Iles, ed., *Sol LeWitt: Structures 1962–1993* (Oxford: Museum of Modern Art, Oxford, 1993)

Iles 2001 — Chrissie Iles, *Into the Light: The Projected Image in American Art 1964–1977* (New York: Whitney Museum of American Art, 2001)

Jameson 1992 — Fredric Jameson, *Postmodernism: The Cultural Logic of Late Capitalism* (London: Verso, 1992)

Johnson 1993 — Ken Johnson, 'Art and Memory', *Art in America* LXXXI: xi (November 1993), pp. 90–99

Johnson 1995 — Ellen Johnson, *Modern Art and the Object* (New York: Icon Editions, 1976/1995)

Johnson Sweeney 1948 — James Johnson Sweeney, 'Miró: Comment and Interview', *Partisan Review* XV: i (1948)

Joseph 2003 — Brandon Joseph, *Random Order: Robert Rauschenberg and the Neo-Avant Garde* (Cambridge, Mass.: OCTOBER books and MIT Press, 2003)

Joselit 2002a — David Joselit, 'Into the Light: The Projected Image in American Art, 1964–1977', *Artforum* XL: v (January 2002), pp. 135–36

Joselit 2002b — David Joselit, 'Tale of the Tape', *Artforum* XL: ix (May 2002), pp. 152–55, 196

Kahn 1969 — Louis Kahn, *L'Architecture D'aujourd'hui Special Issue*, no. 142, Feb–March, 1969

Kahn 1991 — Louis I. Kahn, *Writings, Lectures, Interviews*, intro. Alessandra Latour (New York: Rizzoli, 1991)

Kampf 1975 — Avram Kampf, *Jewish Experience in the Art of the Twentieth Century* (New York: The Jewish Museum, 1975)

Kaplan and Tauber 1966 — Samuel Kaplan and Gilbert Tauber, *The New York City Handbook* (New York: Doubleday, 1966)

Kimmelman 1993 — Michael Kimmelman, 'Making Art of the Holocaust: New Museum, New Works', *The New York Times*, 23 April 1993, p. 1, 24

King 1985 — Elaine King, *Mel Bochner 1973–1985* (Pittsburgh: Carnegie-Mellon University Art Gallery and Carnegie-Mellon University Press, 1985)

Kingsley 1973 — April Kingsley, 'New York Letter', *Art International*, XVII: iv (April 1973), pp. 53–54

Kleeblatt 1996 — Norman Kleeblatt, *Too Jewish – Challenging Jewish Identities* (New York: The Jewish Museum, 1996)

Kleeblatt 2002 — Norman Kleeblatt, *Mirroring Evil: Nazi Imagery / Recent Art* (New York and New Brunswick: The Jewish Museum and Rutgers University Press, 2002)

Klonsky 1945 — Milton Klonsky, 'Review of Marc Chagall by Lionello Venuri', *Commentary* (December 1945), pp. 90–91

Komendant 1975 — August Komendant, *Eighteen Years with Architect Louis Kahn* (Englewood, New Jersey: Aloray Publishers, 1975)

Korn 1967 — Arthur Korn, *Glass in Modern Architecture* (London: Barrie & Rockliff, 1967)

Korot and Schneider 1976 — Beryl Korot and Ira Schneider, eds, *Video Art* (New York: Harcourt Brace Jovanovich, Inc., 1976)

Korot 1988 — Beryl Korot, 'Language as Still Life: From Video to Painting', *Leonardo* XXI: iv (1988), pp. 367–70

Kozloff 1966 — Max Kozloff, 'Art', *The Nation*, 202, no. 20, 16 May 1966, p. 598

Kozloff 1969 — Max Kozloff, *Renderings: Critical Essays on a Century of Modern Art* (New York: Simon and Schuster, 1969)

Kozloff 1976 — Max Kozloff, 'Jewish Art and the Modernist Jeopardy', *Artforum* XIV: viii (April 1976) pp. 43–47

Kozloff 2000 — Max Kozloff, *Cultivated Impasses: Essays on the Waning of the Avant-Garde 1964–1975* (New York: Marsilio Publishers, 2000)

Kramer 1970 — Hilton Kramer, 'Art: A Retrospective of Frank Stella', *The New York Times*, 25 March 1970, p. 34

Kramer 1971 — Hilton Kramer, 'Art: Two Uses of the Shaped Canvas', *The New York Times*, 16 October 1971, p. 25

Krauss 1968 — Rosalind Krauss, 'On Frontality', *Artforum* VI: ix (May 1968), pp. 40–46

Krauss 1971 — Rosalind Krauss, 'Stella's New Work and the Problem of Series', *Artforum* X: iv (December 1971), pp. 40–44

Krauss 1973 — Rosalind Krauss, 'Sense and Sensibility', *Artforum* XII: iii (November 1973), pp. 43–53

Krauss 1974 — Rosalind Krauss, *Line as Language: Six Artists Draw* (Princeton, New Jersey: The Art Museum, Princeton University, 1974)

Krauss 1976a — Rosalind Krauss, 'Video: The Aesthetics of Narcissism', *October* 1 (Spring 1976), pp. 51–64

Krauss 1976b — Rosalind Krauss, *Joel Shapiro* (Chicago: Museum of Contemporary Art, 1976)

Krauss 1981 — Rosalind Krauss, *Passages in Modern Sculpture* (Cambridge, Mass.: MIT Press, 1981)

Krauss 1985 — Rosalind Krauss, *The Originality of the Avant-Garde and Other Modernist Myths* (Cambridge, Mass.: MIT Press, 1985)

Krauss 1986 — Rosalind Krauss, *Richard Serra/Sculpture* (New York: The Museum of Modern Art, 1986)

Krauss 1990 — Rosalind Krauss, 'The Cultural Logic of the Late Capitalist Museum', *October* 54 (Fall 1990), pp. 3–17

Krauss 1991 — Rosalind Krauss, 'Overcoming the Limits of Matter: On Revising Minimalism', in John Elderfield, ed., *American Art of the 1960s: Studies in Modern Art* (New York: Museum of Modern Art and Abrams, 1991), pp. 122–41

Krauss 1994 — Rosalind Krauss, *The Optical Unconscious* (Cambridge, Mass.: MIT Press, 1994)

Kraynak 2002 — Janet Kraynak, '"Into the Light: The Projected Image in American Art, 1964–1977" at the Whitney, and 'Loop' at PS1', *Documents* XII (Fall 2002), pp. 60–65

Kwon 2002 — Miwon Kwon, *One Place After Another: Site-Specific Art and Locational Identity* (Cambridge, Mass.: MIT Press, 2002)

LaCapra 1994 — Dominick LaCapra, *Representing the Holocaust: History, Theory, Trauma* (Ithaca and London: Cornell University Press, 1994)

LaCapra 1998 — Dominick LaCapra, *History and Memory After Auschwitz* (Ithaca and London: Cornell University Press, 1998)

Landsberger 1946 — Franz Landsberger, *A History of Jewish Art* (Cincinnati: The Union of American Hebrew Congregations, 1946)

Legg 1978 — Alicia Legg, ed., *Sol LeWitt* (New York: The Museum of Modern Art, 1978)

Leider 1970 — Philip Leider, 'Literalism and Abstraction: Frank Stella's Retrospective at the Modern', *Artforum* VIII: viii (April 1970), pp. 44–51

Leider 1978 — Philip Leider, *Stella Since 1970* (Fort Worth: The Fort Worth Art Museum, 1978)

Leja 1993 — Michael Leja, *Reframing Abstract Expressionism: Subjectivity and Painting in the 1940s* (New Haven and London: Yale University Press, 1993)

Levi 1988 — Primo Levi, *The Drowned and the Saved*, trans. Raymond Rosenthal (London: Abacus, 1988)

Levi and Rothberg 2003 — Neil Levi and Michael Rothberg, The Holocaust: Theoretical Readings (Edinburgh: Edinburgh University Press, 2003)

Levinas 1990 — Emmanuel Levinas, 'Jewish Thought Today' in *Difficult Freedom: Essays on Judaism*, trans. Seán Hand (Baltimore: The Johns Hopkins University Press, 1990)

Levinas 1996 — Emmanuel Levinas, *Basic Philosophical Writings* (Bloomington and Indianapolis: Indiana University Press, 1996)

Levinas 1999 Emmanuel Levinas, *Ethics and Infinity*, trans. Richard A. Cohen (Pittsburgh: Duquesne University Press, 1999)

Levinas 2000 Emmanuel Levinas, *Totality and Infinity*, trans. Alphonso Lingis (Pittsburgh: Duquesne University Press, 2000)

Lewbin 1974 Hyman Lewbin, *Rebirth of Jewish Art: The Unfolding of Jewish Art in the Nineteenth Century* (New York: Shengold, 1974)

Lewis 1992 Jo Ann Lewis, 'Holocaust Museum to Acquire Art – Abstract Works Secretly Commissioned', *The Washington Post*, 14 November 1992, p. D1

LeWitt 1995 Sol LeWitt, *Critical Texts*, ed. Adachiara Zevi (Rome: Graffiti, 1995)

Linenthal 1995 Edward T. Linenthal, *Preserving Memory: The Struggle to Create America's Holocaust Museum* (New York: Viking, 1995)

Lingwood 2004 James Lingwood, ed., *Susan Hiller: Recall, Selected Works 1969–2004* (Gateshead: Baltic, 2004)

Lippard 1971 Lucy Lippard, *Changing: Essays in Art Criticism* (New York: E. P. Dutton and Co., 1971)

Lippard 1973 Lucy Lippard, *Six years: The Dematerialisation of the Art Object from 1966 to 1972* (New York: Praeger, 1973)

Lipstadt 1996 Deborah Lipstadt, 'America and the Memory of the Holocaust, 1950–1965', *Modern Judaism* XVI (1996), pp. 195–214

Liss 1998 Andrea Liss, *Trespassing Through Shadows: Memory, Photography & The Holocaust* (Minneapolis and London: University of Minnesota Press, 1998)

Losson 1999 Nicolas Losson, 'Notes on the Images of the Camps', *October* 90, Fall 1999, pp. 25–35

Loukomski 1947 George K. Loukomski, *Jewish Art in European Synagogues* (London and New York, Hutchinson and Co., 1947)

Lozowick 1947 Louis Lozowick, 'What, Then, Is Jewish Art?: Review of *A History of Jewish Art* by Franz Landsberger', *Menorah Journal* (Winter 1947), pp. 108–10

Lozowick 1948 Louis Lozowick, 'Synagogue Art: Review of *Jewish Art in European Synagogues* by George Loukomski' *Menorah Journal* (Autumn 1948), pp. 380–84

Lucier 1978 Mary Lucier, 'Video window dressing', *Theatre Crafts*, XII: iii, March/April 1978

Lyotard 1984 Jean-François Lyotard, 'The Sublime and the Avant-Garde', trans. Lisa Liebmann, *Artforum* XXII: viii (April 1984), pp. 36–43

Lyotard 1988 Jean-François Lyotard, *The Differend*, trans. Georges Van Den Abbeele (Minneapolis: University of Minnesota Press, 1988)

Lyotard 1990 Jean-François Lyotard, *Heidegger and 'the jews'*, trans. Andreas Michel and Mark S. Roberts (Minneapolis: University of Minnesota Press, 1990)

Lyotard 1991 Jean-François Lyotard, *The Inhuman* , trans. Geoffrey Bennington and Rachel Bowlby (Cambridge: Polity Press, 1991)

Marcuse 2001 Harold Marcuse, *Legacies of Dachau: The Uses and Abuses of a Concentration Camp 1933–2001* (Cambridge: Cambridge University Press, 2001)

Masheck 1970a Joseph Masheck, 'New York: Morris Louis', *Artforum* IX: i (September 1970) pp. 78–79

Masheck 1970b Joseph Masheck, 'Albert Stadler', *Artforum* IX: iv (December 1970), p. 78

Masheck 1971 Joseph Masheck, 'Letter to the editor', *Artforum* IX: ix (May 1971), p. 10

Masheck 1973 Joseph Masheck, 'Frank Stella, Castelli Gallery uptown', *Artforum* XI: viii (April 1973), pp. 80–81

Maybaum 1965 Ignaz Maybaum, *The Face of God After Auschwitz* (Amsterdam: Polak and Van Gennep Ltd, 1965)

McShine 1970 Kynaston McShine, *Information* (New York: The Museum of Modern Art, 1970)

Meier 1963 Richard Meier, *Recent American Synagogue Architecture* (New York: The Jewish Museum, 1963)

Mellencamp 1990 Patricia Mellencamp, ed., *Logics of Television: Essays in Cultural Criticism* (Bloomington and Indianapolis: Indiana University Press, 1990)

Melville 2001 Stephen Melville, Philip Armstrong and Laura Lisbon, *As Painting: Division and Displacement* (Columbus, Ohio: Wexner Center for the Arts and Cambridge, Mass.: MIT Press 2001)

Meyer 2000 James Meyer, *Minimalism* (London: Phaidon, 2000)

Meyer 2001 James Meyer, *Minimalism: Art and Polemics in the Sixties* (New Haven and London: Yale University Press, 2001)

Michaud 2004 Eric Michaud, *The Cult of Art in Nazi Germany*, trans. Janet Lloyd (Stanford: Stanford University Press, 2004)

Miller 1959 Dorothy Miller, *Sixteen Americans* (New York: The Museum of Modern Art, 1959)

Morgan 2001 Michael Morgan, *Beyond Auschwitz: Post-Holocaust Jewish Thought in America* (Oxford: Oxford University Press, 2001)

Morisse 2000 Karl August Morisse et. al., *Art Projects: Synagoge Stommeln* (Ostfildern-Ruit: Hatje Cantz, 2000)

Morse 1967 — Arthur D. Morse, *While Six Million Died: A Chronicle of American Apathy* (Woodstock: The Overlook Press, 1967)

Morris 1968 — Robert Morris, 'Anti Form', *Artforum* VI: viii (April 1968), pp.33–35

Motherwell 1992 — Robert Motherwell, *The Collected Writings of Robert Motherwell*, ed. Stephanie Terenzio (New York and Oxford: Oxford University Press, 1992)

Murphy 1993 — Jim Murphy, 'Memorial to Atrocity', *Progressive Architecture* (February 1993), pp. 60–79

Muschamp 1993 — Herbert Muschamp, 'Shaping a Monument to Memory', *The New York Times*, 11 April 1993, Section 2, pp. 1, 32

Namenyi 1957 — Ernest Namenyi, *The Essence of Jewish Art* (New York: Thomas Yoseloff, 1957)

New York Times 1970 — Anon, 'Met Museum Adds Hours in Evening', *The New York Times*, 22 May 1970, p.40

Newman Amy 2000 — Amy Newman, *Challenging Art: Artforum 1962–1974* (New York: Soho Press Inc., 2000)

Newman Annalee 1995 — Annalee Newman, 'Barnett Newman and the Kabbalah', *American Art* VIII: ii (Spring 1995), p. 117

Newman Barnett 1992 — Barnett Newman, *Selected Writings and Interviews*, ed. John P. O'Neill (Berkeley and Los Angeles: University of California Press, 1992)

Newman Michael 1995 — Michael Newman, *Avis Newman* (London: Camden Arts Centre, 1995)

Newsweek 1966 — Anon, 'Unanswerable Question', *Newsweek*, 9 May 1966, p. 100

Nochlin and Garb 1995 — Linda Nochlin and Tamar Garb, eds, *The Jew in the Text: Modernity and the Construction of Identity* (London: Thames and Hudson, 1995)

Nochlin 1997 — Linda Nochlin, 'Kelly: Making Abstraction Anew', *Art in America* LXXXV: iii (March 1997), pp. 68–79

Noever 2004 — Peter Noever, ed., *Peter Eisenman: Barefoot On White-Hot Walls* (Vienna and Ostfildern-Ruit: MAK and Hatje Cantz, 2004)

Nouvet 1991 — Claire Nouvet (ed.), *Literature and the Ethical Question* (Yale French Studies LXXIX, New Haven and London: Yale University Press, 1991)

Novick 1999 — Peter Novick, *The Holocaust in American Life* (Boston: Houghton Mifflin Company, 1999)

Noyes Platt 1989 — Susan Noyes Platt, 'Clement Greenberg in the 1930s: A New Perspective on His Criticism', *Art Criticism* V: iii (New York, 1989)

Orton 1994 — Fred Orton, *Figuring Jasper Johns* (Cambridge, Mass.: Harvard University Press, 1994)

Orton and Pollock 1996 — Fred Orton and Griselda Pollock, *Avant-Gardes and Partisans Reviewed* (Manchester: Manchester University Press, 1996)

Perec 1997 — Georges Perec, *Species of Spaces and Other Pieces*, trans. John Sturrock (Harmondsworth: Penguin, 1997)

Piechotka 1959 — Maria and Kazimierz Piechotka, *Wooden Synagogues* (Warsaw: Arkady, 1959)

Pincus-Witten 1977 — Robert Pincus-Witten, *Postminimalism* (New York: Out of London Press, 1977)

Politzer 1949 — Heinz Politzer, 'The Opportunity of The Jewish Museum', *Commentary* (June 1949), pp. 589–93

Portner 1953 — Leslie Judd Portner, 'Art in Washington: One a Newcomer, One a Veteran', *The Washington Post*, 12 April 1953. p. L3

Potts 2000 — Alex Potts, *The Sculptural Imagination* (London and New Haven: Yale University Press, 2000)

Progressive Architecture 1968 — Anon, 'Monuments to Ponder', *Progressive Architecture* (December 1968), p. 44

Pugliese 2002 — Stanislao G. Pugliese with photographs by Liana Miuccio, *Desperate Inscriptions: Graffiti from the Nazi Prison in Rome, 1943–1944* (Boca Raton, Florida: Bordighera Press, Florida Atlantic University, 2002)

Radical Software 1970–1974 — *Radical Software* journal, 1970–1974, now available at www.radicalsoftware.org

Ratcliff 1971 — Carter Ratcliff, 'New York Letter', *Art International*, XV: x (December 1971), pp. 59–60

Rauterberg 2005 — Hanno Rauterberg, *Holocaust Memorial Berlin – Eisenman Architects* (Berlin: Lars Müller Publishers, 2005)

Raynes 1969 — Alexander Raynes, 'Monument to 6,000,000' in Letters Page, *Jewish Currents* XXIII (April 1969), pp. 38–41

Reich 2002 — Steve Reich, *Writings on Music 1965–2000* (Oxford: Oxford University Press, 2002)

Richardson 1976a — Brenda Richardson, *Mel Bochner: Number and Shape* (Baltimore: The Baltimore Museum of Art, 1976)

Richardson 1976b — Brenda Richardson, *Frank Stella: The Black Paintings* (Baltimore: The Baltimore Museum of Art, 1976)

Richards 1993 — Paul Richards, 'Obscene Pleasure: Art Among the Corpses', *The Washington Post*, 18 April 1993, p. G1

Rorimer 2001 Anne Rorimer, *New Art in the 60s and 70s: Redefining Reality* (London: Thames and Hudson, 2001)

Rose 1971 Barbara Rose, 'Quality in Louis', *Artforum* x: ii (October 1971), pp. 62–65

Rose 1988 Barbara Rose, *Autocritique: Essays on Art and Anti-Art 1963–1987* (New York: Weidenfeld & Nicolson, 1988)

Rosenberg 1945 Harold Rosenberg, 'Chagall: Jewish Modernist Master', *Jewish Frontier* (April 1945), pp. 26–33

Rosenberg 1949 Harold Rosenberg, 'Does the Jew Exist?', *Commentary* (January 1949), pp. 8–18

Rosenberg 1961 Harold Rosenberg, 'The Trial and Eichmann', *Commentary* (November 1961), pp. 369–81

Rosenberg 1978 Harold Rosenberg, *Barnett Newman* (New York: Abrams, 1978)

Rosler 2004 Martha Rosler, *Decoys and Disruptions: Selected Writings, 1975–2001* (Cambridge, Mass.: MIT Press, 2004)

Roth 1961 Cecil Roth, *Jewish Art – An Illustrated History* (New York: McGraw Hill, 1961)

Rothberg 2000 Michael Rothberg, *Traumatic Realism: The Demands of Holocaust Representation* (Minneapolis and London: University of Minnesota Press, 2000)

Rothkopf 2002 Scott Rothkopf, *Mel Bochner: Photographs 1966–1969* (Cambridge, Mass.: Harvard University Art Museums and New Haven: Yale University Press, 2002)

Rowe 1995 Colin Rowe, *The Mathematics of the Ideal Villa and Other Essays* (Cambridge, Mass.: MIT Press, 1995)

Rubin Lawrence 1986 Lawrence Rubin, *Frank Stella: Paintings 1958–1965 – A Catalogue Raisonné* (New York: Stewart, Tabori & Chang, 1986)

Rubin William 1970 William Rubin, *Frank Stella* (New York: The Museum of Modern Art, 1970)

Rubin William 1987 William Rubin, *Frank Stella 1970–1987* (New York: The Museum of Modern Art, 1987)

Saidel 1996 Rochelle Saidel, *Never Too Late to Remember – The Politics Behind New York City's Holocaust Museum* (New York: Holmes & Meier Publishers, 1996)

Saltzman 1999 Lisa Saltzman, *Anselm Kiefer and Art After Auschwitz* (Cambridge: Cambridge University Press, 1999)

Sandler 1972 Irving Sandler, 'Stella at Rubin', *Art in America* LX: i, (January–February, 1972) p. 33

Sartre 1995 Jean-Paul Sartre, *Anti-Semite and Jew*, trans. George Becker (New York: Schocken Books, 1995)

Scheerbart 1972 Paul Scheerbart, *Glass Architecture* (New York: Praeger Publishers, 1972)

Schjeldahl 1973 Petter Schjeldahl, 'Frank Stella: The Best – And Last – of His Breed', *The New York Times*, 21 January 1973, sec. 2, p. 23

Schjeldahl 1993 Peter Schjeldahl, 'Joel Shapiro Now', in *Joel Shapiro – Sculpture and Drawings* (New York: Pace Gallery, 1993)

Schoenberner 1960 Gerhard Schoenberner, *Der Gelbe Stern* (Hamburg: Rütten & Loening Verlag, 1960)

Scholem 1949 Gershom Scholem, 'The Curious History of the Six Pointed Star', *Commentary* (September 1949), pp. 243–51

Scholem 1996 Gershom Scholem, *On the Kabbalah and its Symbolism* (New York: Schocken Books, 1996)

Schwabsky 1997 Barry Schwabsky, *The Widening Circle: Consequences of Modernism in Contemporary Art* (Cambridge: Cambridge University Press, 1997)

Scully 1962 Vincent Scully, *Louis Kahn* (New York: Braziller, 1962)

Scully 1993 Vincent Scully, 'Jehovah on Olympus – Louis Kahn and the End of Modernism' *A+V Monografias* XLIV (November–December 1993), pp. 97–100

Serra 1993 Richard Serra, *The Drowned and the Saved* (Stommeln: Synagogue Stommeln, 1993)

Serra 1994 Richard Serra, *Writings, Interviews* (Chicago: The University of Chicago Press, 1994)

Shuster 1943 Zachariah Shuster, 'The Passion of a People: Anno MCMXLII', *Contemporary Jewish Record* (February 1943), pp. 23–36

Shiff 2004 Richard Shiff, Carol C. Mancusi-Ungaro, Heidi Colsman-Freyberger, *Barnett Newman: A Catalogue Raisonné* (New Haven and London: Yale University Press and New York: The Barnett Newman Foundation, 2004)

Siegel 1973 Jeanne Siegel, 'Reviews and Previews', *ARTNews* LXXII: ii (February 1973), p. 78

Silverman 2002 Hugh J. Silverman, ed., *Lyotard – Philosophy, Politics, and the Sublime* (New York and London: Routledge, 2002)

Solomon 1997 Susan Solomon, *Secular and Spiritual Humanism: Louis I. Kahn's Work for the Jewish Community in the 1950s and 1960s* (PhD thesis, University of Pennsylvania, May 1997)

Soussloff 1999 Catherine Soussloff, ed., *Jewish Identity in Modern Art History* (Berkeley, Los Angeles, and London: University of California Press, 1999)

Steinberg 1957 — Leo Steinberg, *Artists of the New York School: Second Generation* (New York: The Jewish Museum, 1957)

Steinberg 1972 — Leo Steinberg, *Other Criteria: Confrontations with Twentieth-Century Art* (Oxford: Oxford University Press, 1972)

Steiner 1967 — George Steiner, 'A Kind of Survivor' in *Language and Silence: Essays 1958–1966* (London: Faber, 1967)

Stella 1986 — Frank Stella, *Working Space* (Cambridge, Mass. and London: Harvard University Press, 1986)

Steyn 1999 — Juliet Steyn, *The Jew: Assumptions of Identity* (London and New York: Cassell, 1999)

Stille 1993 — Alexander Stille, *Benevolence and Betrayal – Five Italian Jewish Families Under Fascism* (London: Vintage, 1993)

Strauss 1952 — Louis Strauss, *Persecution and the Art of Writing* (Chicago: University of Chicago Press, 1952)

Tafuri 1980 — Manfredo Tafuri, *Theories and History of Architecture* (London: Granada, 1980)

Tannous 1978 — David Tannous, 'Those Who Stay', *Art in America* LXVI: iv (July–August 1978), pp. 78–87

Teicher 1998 — Hendel Teicher, *Joel Shapiro: Sculpture and Drawings* (New York: Abrams, 1998)

Temkin 2002 — Ann Temkin, *Barnett Newman* (Philadelphia: Philadelphia Museum of Art, 2005)

Tennenbaum 1976 — Silvia Tennenbaum, 'Return to Germany', *Midstream* (December 1976), pp. 39–45

Time Magazine 1968 — Anon, 'Expressing the Unspeakable', *Time Magazine*, 25 October 1968, p. 46

Upright Headley 1979 — Diane Upright Headley, *The Drawings of Morris Louis* (Washington D.C.: National Collection of Fine Arts, Smithsonian Institution, 1979)

Upright 1985 — Diane Upright, *Morris Louis – The Complete Paintings* (New York: Abrams, 1985)

Van Alphen 1997 — Ernst Van Alphen, *Caught By History: Holocaust Effects in Contemporary Art, Literature, and Theory* (Stanford: Stanford University Press, 1997)

Varnedoe 1996 — Kirk Varnedoe, *Jasper Johns – A Retrospective* (New York: Museum of Modern Art, 1996)

Varnedoe and Karmel 1999 — Kirk Varnedoe and Pepe Karmel, eds, *Jackson Pollock – New Approaches* (New York: The Museum of Modern Art, 1999)

Vidler 1992 — Anthony Vidler, *The Architectural Uncanny* (Cambridge, Mass.: MIT Press, 1992)

Wagner 2000 — Anne Wagner, 'Performance, Video, and the Rhetoric of Presence', *October* 91 (Winter 2000), pp. 59–80

Waldman 1997 — Diane Waldman, *Ellsworth Kelly* (London and New York: Tate Gallery and Guggenheim Museum, 1997)

Welchman 1997 — John Welchman, *Invisible Colors: A Visual History of Titles* (New Haven and London: Yale University Press, 1997)

Weiner 1993 — Lawrence Weiner, STEEL PENNIES DON'T COME FROM OR GO TO HEAVEN (Halifax: Henry Moore Sculpture Trust, 1993)

Weiner 2004 — Lawrence Weiner, *Having Been Said: Writings and Interviews of Lawrence Weiner 1968–2003*, ed. Gerti Firzek and Gregor Stemmrich (Ostfildern Ruit: Hatje Cantz, 2004)

Werner 1951 — Alfred Werner, 'Return to Dachau', *Commentary* (December 1951), pp. 542–45

White 1999 — Hayden White, *Figural Realism* (Baltimore: The John Hopkins University Press, 1999)

Wiegand 1975 — Ingrid Wiegand, 'Multi-Monitors', *The Soho Weekly News*, Thursday March 20, 1975

Williams Goldhagen 2001 — Susan Williams Goldhagen, *Louis Kahn's Situated Modernism* (New Haven and London: Yale University Press, 2001)

Wischnitzer-Bernstein 1946 — Rachel Wischnitzer-Bernstein, 'Is there a Jewish Art?', *Commentary* (August 1946), pp. 194–96

Wong 1994 — Janay Jadine Wong, 'Synagogue Art of the 1950s, A New Context for Abstraction', *Art Journal* Vol.53, no. 4 (Winter 1994) pp. 37–43

Wright 1999 — Tamra Wright, *The Twilight of Jewish Philosophy: Emmanuel Levinas' Ethical Hermeneutics* (Amsterdam: Harwood Academic Press, 1999)

Yerushalmi 1989 — Yosef Hayim Yerushalmi, *Zachor – Jewish History and Jewish Memory* (New York: Schocken Books, 1989)

Young 1993 — James Young, *The Texture of Memory: Holocaust Memorials and Meaning* (New Haven and London: Yale University Press, 1993)

Young 1994 — James Young, ed., *The Art of Memory: Holocaust Memorials in History* (New York: The Jewish Museum, 1994)

Young 2000 — James Young, *At Memory's Edge: After-Images of the Holocaust in Contemporary Art and Architecture* (New Haven and London: Yale University Press, 2000)

Zĭzěk 2001 — Slavoj Zĭzěk, *Did Somebody Say Totalitarianism?* (London: Verso, 2001)

Zucker 1944 — Paul Zucker, ed., *New Architecture and City Planning – A Symposium* (New York: Philosophical Library, 1944)

Zweite 1999 — Armin Zweite, *Barnett Newman, Paintings, Sculptures, Works on Paper* (Ostfildern-Ruit: Hatje Cantz Publishers, 1999)

photograph credits

index

NOTE:
Page numbers in italics indicate an illustration on that page; page numbers followed by *n* indicate information is in a note.

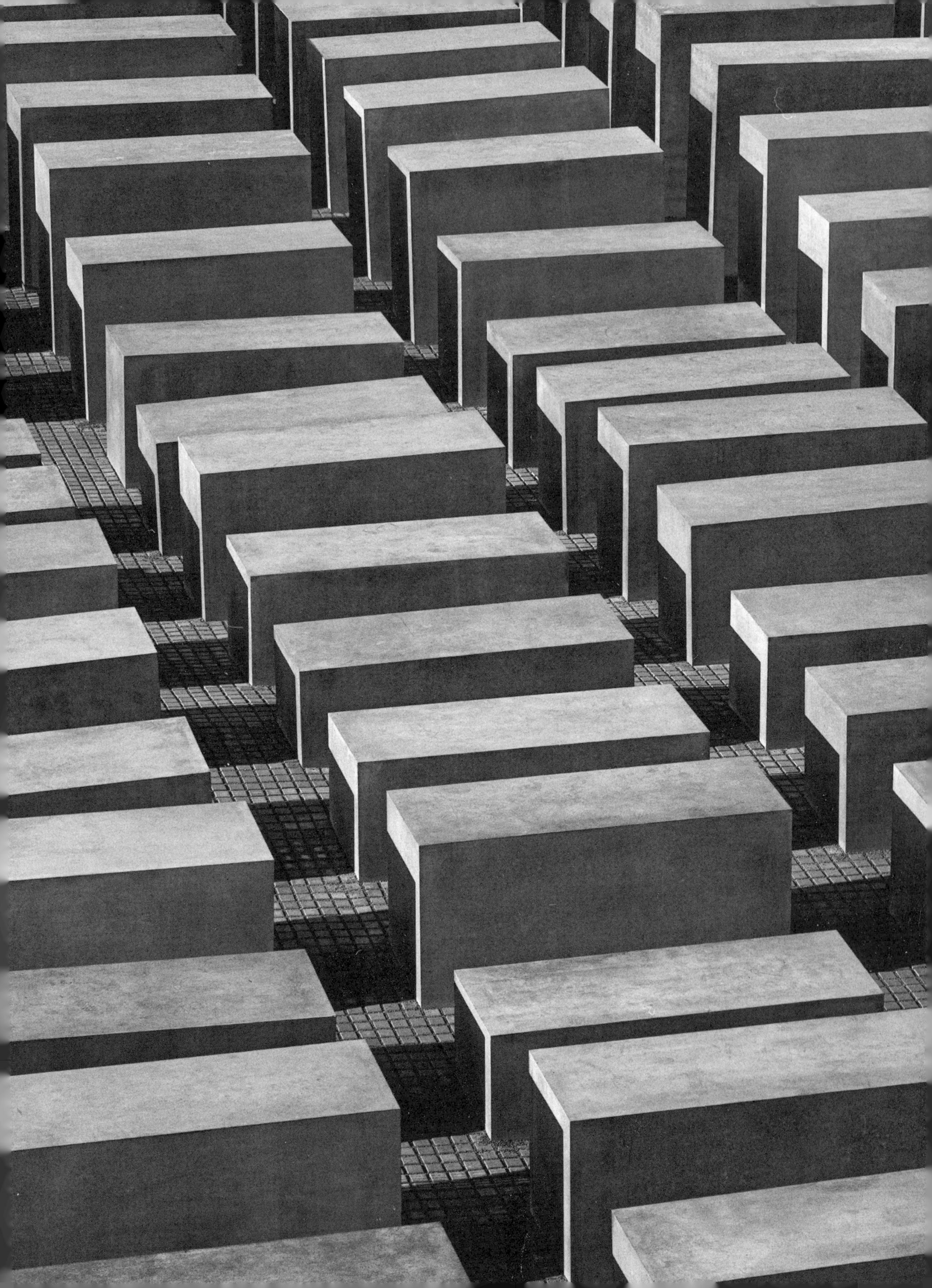